Betsy
AND THE
Emperor

ANNE WHITEHEAD is an author, historian and former TV producer-director with the ABC. She is the author of *Bluestocking in Patagonia* and her book *Paradise Mislaid* was winner of the NSW Premier's Award for Australian History.

'A fascinating exploration of the life journey of Betsy Balcombe Abell from St Helena to Sydney to London. This is a well-researched and readable history of the dramatic repercussions for an English family of its proximity to Napoleon in his final years on St Helena.'
—*Professor Ann Curthoys, University of Sydney*

'St Helena: an exiled emperor in the garden pavilion and in the house a pretty, flighty teenager. And therefrom spring some fascinating narratives, ending up, after a disastrous marriage to a stylish cad, in colonial New South Wales.'
—*Marion Halligan, award-winning author*

Napoleon Bonaparte

OTHER BOOKS BY ANNE WHITEHEAD

*Bluestocking in Patagonia: Mary Gilmore's quest for
love and utopia at the world's end*

Paradise Mislaid: In search of the Australian tribe of Paraguay

Betsy
AND THE
Emperor

THE TRUE STORY
of Napoleon, a pretty girl,
a Regency rake and an
Australian colonial misadventure

ANNE WHITEHEAD

ALLEN&UNWIN
SYDNEY·MELBOURNE·AUCKLAND·LONDON

First published in 2015

Copyright © Anne Whitehead 2015

All rights reserved. No part of this book may be reproduced or transmitted in any form or by any means, electronic or mechanical, including photocopying, recording or by any information storage and retrieval system, without prior permission in writing from the publisher. The Australian *Copyright Act 1968* (the Act) allows a maximum of one chapter or 10 per cent of this book, whichever is the greater, to be photocopied by any educational institution for its educational purposes provided that the educational institution (or body that administers it) has given a remuneration notice to the Copyright Agency (Australia) under the Act.

This book has been written with the generous assistance of a Writer's Fellowship from the Literature Board of the Australia Council

Allen & Unwin
83 Alexander Street
Crows Nest NSW 2065
Australia
Phone: (61 2) 8425 0100
Email: info@allenandunwin.com
Web: www.allenandunwin.com

Cataloguing-in-Publication details are available
from the National Library of Australia
www.trove.nla.gov.au

ISBN 978 1 76011 293 6

Internal design by Christabella Designs
Set in 11/15 pt Scala by Midland Typesetters, Australia
Printed and bound in Australia by Griffin Press

10 9 8 7 6 5 4 3 2 1

The paper in this book is FSC® certified. FSC® promotes environmentally responsible, socially beneficial and economically viable management of the world's forests.

*To Allan, with love
—who treated Napoleon with caution,
but accompanied me with Betsy and the
Balcombes every step of the way*

*And to Keith and Shirley Murley, with gratitude
—dedicated volunteer researchers at The Briars, Mt Martha, Victoria,
for their unstinting generosity*

CONTENTS

Preface		ix

PART ONE

1	The News	3
2	The Prisoner	12
3	Friends and Foes	20
4	The Briars	31
5	The Pavilion	42
6	Boney's Little Pages	51
7	The French Suite	63
8	The Admiral's Ball	70
9	Last Days at the Pavilion	81
10	Longwood House	90
11	The New Governor	106
12	Gold Lace and Nodding Plumes	115
13	This Accursed Place	126
14	The Thinning Ranks	138
15	The Sick Lion	146
16	Our Beautiful Island	157
17	The Company of a Green Parrot	165

| 18 | At the Mercy of the English | 175 |
| 19 | Farewell to the Island | 187 |

PART TWO

20	The Ties that Bind	201
21	The Embattled Surgeon	214
22	An Impending Tempest	223
23	The St Helena Plot	231
24	Official Disgrace	243
25	An Item of News	252
26	The One that Got Away	263
27	Marry in Haste . . .	270
28	'La Petite Angleterre'	286
29	The Clearing Fog	297

PART THREE

30	Sydney Town	309
31	'The Interesting Mrs Abell'	320
32	The Fashionables	335
33	A Fleeting Entente Cordiale	346
34	The Treasury Under the Bed	356
35	'Terrible Hollow'	371
36	A Fractured Family	383
37	Recollections of the Emperor Napoleon	394

Acknowledgements	407
Notes	409
Index	445

PREFACE

About ten years ago I was browsing along the shelves of an antiquarian bookshop, enjoying the sensual pleasure of the rich bindings, the gilded lettering, the mental travel to places called Abyssinia, Okavango, Patagonia, Smyrna, when I saw a little 1844 book, *Recollections of the Emperor Napoleon on the Island of St Helena* by Mrs Abell. Who was she, I wondered, and what brush with infamy had she inflated? I turned the fragile pages to discover that she had been a young girl called Betsy Balcombe when the exiled Bonaparte in 1815 was brought to the remote South Atlantic island of St Helena where she and her family lived. She had seen much of him over the course of three years. But how and why, I wondered, did this English family come to socialise with their nation's great enemy? And why did *he* bother with them? I bought the little book and found it a charming memoir. Mrs Abell, obviously a feisty person, wrote only about those three years on St Helena and revealed nothing of her later life except a hint of some tragedy. Who was she really?

I went back to work on other projects. However, Betsy's book lingered in my mind and years later I returned, to seek the larger story behind the memoir. My attempt to answer those questions has led me on a detective trail to the manuscripts collection of the British Library, sifting through the vast correspondence of Sir Hudson Lowe and Lord Bathurst's private papers; on a week's voyage on the last operational Royal Mail ship to the island of St Helena, to work in its archives and visit locations where Betsy and her family lived and Napoleon was imprisoned; to the English counties of Sussex, Kent and Devon, to their record offices, and up to bleak Dartmoor; to the highlands of Scotland; to Paris and the northern French town of Saint-Omer; to old Madras in India; and to state archives and libraries in Australia as well as the Balcombes' former homes in New South Wales and Victoria. The quest involved my reading several French journals by Napoleon's companions never translated into English and making surprising discoveries that have not been revealed before.

Since the Victorian era, authors have interested themselves in Betsy's story, sometimes as a children's book, sometimes confabulating it as Napoleon's last romance, rarely adding anything new to her *Recollections*. (A revised edition of Betsy's book, titled *To Befriend an Emperor*, was published in 2005, making this delightful story available to the general public.) A direct Balcombe descendant, the redoubtable Melbourne figure Dame Mabel Brookes, in 1960 published *St Helena Story*, her own account of her forebears. It was a brave attempt and told part of the story, but she lacked the research tools available to a biographer today and left many gaps. She could only say of Betsy's husband that he was reputedly 'a handsome man-about-town', whereas his family background and career are revealed here; she wrote that Mrs Betsy Abell lived in Sydney with her family 'for a brief period', when it was actually ten years.

Most books about Napoleon's captivity focus on the compelling prisoner, his anguish and his anger and his last great battle with the authoritarian British governor Sir Hudson Lowe. This book deals with that struggle, but from the perspective of the British family on the sidelines, who also incurred Lowe's wrath because of their friendship with his charge. Through their relationship with Napoleon they inevitably also became closely acquainted with his immediate companions on the island: his devoted chamberlain and biographer Count de Las Cases; the Count and Countess Bertrand; Count de Montholon and his wife; the temperamental General Gourgaud; the loyal valet Marchand; and Napoleon's physician and the Balcombes' good friend, the duplicitous Irishman Dr Barry O'Meara. As Bonaparte ruled over his little household, demanding imperial respect, settling their intrigues and disputes, we see the domestic Napoleon, 'father' of an unhappy, bickering family, still mentally refighting his old battles, deploying his armies of red and black pins across a billiard table, his prodigious brain fretting over trifles: the thickness of mattresses, the scrawniness of a roast chicken, the escape of a dairy cow.

We follow Betsy and the Balcombes as they leave St Helena under a cloud because of their dangerous friendship, only to confront larger and possibly life-threatening troubles in England; to another kind of exile in France; and then to the penal colony of New South Wales, at a time of transition to a new future in which they play significant parts. Although there are many references to Betsy, her father and the family in this new life, due to the shortage of source material in their own words, I have sometimes provided an imaginative interpretation of their possible feelings and responses to their changed circumstances.

Their transfer across the world reveals the rich network of connections between Britain and the colonies in the 1820s and 1830s, all controlled by the remarkable Lord Bathurst, Secretary of State for War and the Colonies, arbitrator and manager of the colonial governors, the prisoner Bonaparte, and the whole intricate skein of colonial connections.

This book argues that Napoleon, a master of strategy, had a particular reason for cultivating the Balcombes. It also answers how and why the lives of that English family on St Helena—the merchant William Balcombe, his wife who resembled the Empress Josephine, and their two pretty daughters, Betsy and Jane—came to be entangled with Bonaparte's; and the reason why he was anxious to entangle them. Finally, it shows how their involvement with him would change Betsy and her family for ever, and cast a very long shadow over the rest of their lives.

PART ONE

---

*A new Prometheus, I am attached to a rock
where a vulture is gnawing at me.
I had stolen the fire of heaven to endow France with it;
the fire has come back to its source, and here I am.*

NAPOLEON BONAPARTE

CHAPTER 1

THE NEWS

When HMS *Northumberland* anchored in James Bay, accompanied by four men-of-war and three troopships, it became known that the prisoner would not be brought ashore for another two days.[1] Word spread that it would be the most extraordinary event in living memory.

On the evening of 17 October 1815, people from all parts of the island made their way to the Jamestown waterfront, descending into the village, hemmed by mountains, by one of two steep roads. By dusk a great crowd had gathered at the narrow quay between the castle wall and the Atlantic Ocean.[2]

It did not take much persuasion for the merchant William Balcombe to agree that his wife and two daughters should witness the event. Betsy was thirteen and her sister Jane fifteen. Their little brothers Tom and Alexander, aged five and four, had to stay behind with their nurse, but their father knew that the girls would always remember the sight of the most powerful man in the world brought down to size. One of the Balcombes' slave boys opened The Briars' gates, guiding the horse cart with a lamp as they joined the Sidepath, the vertiginous road carved into the rocks by slave labour. The whole mountainside was aglow with dancing, glimmering lanterns as they joined the throng making the mile-long descent.

It was almost dark when they reached the marina. The whole population of St Helena, all 3500 of them, white, black, Asian and mulatto, bond and free, seemed to have gathered, their lanterns and torches bouncing and flaring. With apologies to this person and that, acknowledging familiar faces among the many strangers and soldiers, the Balcombes made their way through the crush. Betsy, just returned from school in England, could hardly believe that the island contained so many inhabitants. She found a position outside the castle wall near the drawbridge. Further along near the landing stage she made out the courtly figure of the governor wearing his plumed hat and full dress uniform. Beyond the row of sentries, the surf smashed and hissed on the rocks.

A hush descended on the watching crowd when the slap of oars was heard. As the tender approached from the looming dark hulk of the warship *Northumberland,* Betsy saw five huddled figures. They stepped onto the landing stage from the bobbing craft, and she heard someone say that the man in the middle was Bonaparte. He brushed past Governor Wilks, who had extended his hand in formal greeting, and walked up the lines between the British admiral and another important-looking man. Napoleon wore the familiar cocked hat but was enveloped in a greatcoat, and it was too dark to distinguish his features. The diamond star on his chest glinted within the coat's folds as he walked.

The crowd surged forward. Sentries with fixed bayonets moved to clear a path. Hundreds of eyes glared at that solitary figure but no word of welcome was uttered. As he went past, Betsy caught a glimpse of the famous aquiline face, tight with anger, his eyes downcast. He said later that he had been gawked at *'comme une bête féroce'*—like a savage beast.[3]

A mere four days earlier, Colonel Mark Wilks, the island's governor, had received the astounding message, brought by a fast sloop-of-war, that he and the motley inhabitants of their small remote island were about to play host to the most dangerous man on earth. The prisoner was on HMS *Northumberland,* accompanied by a flotilla of warships, and already sailing towards them.

News always came late to St Helena. It was an awesome distance to the rock marooned in the Atlantic between the African and South American continents, a dot on the charts known to seafarers, to British ships on the home route from the Far East, India and the Cape. It was said to be the most remote inhabited place on earth—1120 miles from the nearest land in Africa and over 2000 miles from the Brazilian coast.[4] For the past decade and a half of the Napoleonic Wars it had gained importance as a strategic base, but the St Helenians could still dream in the sun and proceed with their lives in their own relaxed, insular way. Mail took ten weeks to come from London to Jamestown, the island's capital and only town, so the locals were accustomed to receiving belated accounts of the goings-on in the world. At the same time they had their own important affairs and pursuits.

Governor Wilks was regular in sending his despatches to his masters in London, the directors of the Honourable East India Company in Leadenhall Street. His post was hardly taxing, a reward for services to the Company in India, where he had been Resident at Mysore. He took an interest in poultry-keeping and agricultural projects, the eradication of the introduced blackberry, the problem of the wild goats and sheep, while he worked on his memoirs and a book, *Historical Sketches of the South of India*. Described by an admirer as 'a tall, handsome, venerable-looking man with white curling locks and a courtier-like manner',[5] he was gracious with important visitors to the island, attended St Paul's church on Sundays, and hosted the odd fundraising levée and whist drive.[6] There was the usual Governor's Ball at the castle in Jamestown and an annual garden party at Plantation House, and those representing society on the island generally saw fit to attend. Many of these property owners were also employees of the East India Company as officers, administrators or merchants. Those islanders in private commerce depended upon the ships bringing news and trade goods.

In 1815, William Balcombe had his official duties as superintendent of public sales for the Company but also his separate interests as senior partner in the firm Balcombe, Cole and Company, supplying vessels calling at Jamestown. Saul Solomon, proprietor with his brothers Lewis and Joseph of the town's only emporium—'Ladies' Fashions, Fabrics, Lace, Jewellery and Rosewater'—studied the papers for trends, knowing that styles would be half a year out of date by the time their order arrived (allowing three months for the requisition and three for the despatch) but that this did not matter to the ladies of St Helena as long as they kept pace with one another. The officers of the St Helena Regiment did a little trading on the side with ships returning from the

East, while the regiment's 890 soldiers drilled, their garrison having been constantly on alert during the long war years. The 1200 or so black and mulatto slaves employed by the Company worked in the vegetable gardens and on the boats supplying fish to the local population, and the few hundred Chinese 'coolies' hewed wood and hauled water for passing vessels, with often up to fifty ships anchored off Jamestown.

While few people in the outside world bothered with St Helena, the islanders were eager enough for accounts of the world; for the bundles of newspapers and magazines, letters from relatives and friends, the items of gossip, delivered by passing ships. The newspapers that had arrived in April indicated that 1815 in Europe was shaping up as a very mixed year. They read that His Majesty King George III remained lamentably unwell; his son the Prince Regent had declined to attend the Congress of Vienna but still danced attendance on his mistresses; he continued to build his Oriental folly and reduce the national exchequer. Questions had been put in Parliament but waited for an answer. Lady Hamilton, the mistress of Admiral Nelson (who had died heroically ten years earlier), had died in January, lonely and overweight; Lord Byron had married Annabella Milbanke, but no one expected the match to last; the daring waltz was finally *in*, the visiting Czar having given a demonstration at Almack's Assembly Rooms; gaslights illuminated the London streets; and thin muslin dresses in the Parisian style were being worn by the girls in Vauxhall Gardens. In Africa, Shaka had become King of the Zulus; further afield, America had a new railroad charter, the first commercial cheese factory had opened in Switzerland, the Blue Mountains were finally crossed in the colony of New South Wales, and British missionaries packed Bibles for New Zealand to save the heathen Maori.

For years Napoleon Bonaparte was the leading story and a grim one, but for some nine months the English papers had been remarkably free of his outrages. The man who from the beginning of the century had dominated the news and the continent of Europe—with the notable exception of Russia—had from May 1814 languished in exile on Elba, an island off Italy in the Mediterranean Sea, where he survived very well. He was permitted the title 'Emperor and Sovereign of the Isle of Elba' and a new flag of his own design, featuring his beloved golden bees. He enjoyed the comforts of a modest palace, a large shabby villa high on the cliffs, and the presence of his mother, his favourite sister Pauline and a devoted group of courtiers. He had charmed the British commissioner, Colonel Sir Neil Campbell, and dined regularly with him. Some wondered if it was an oversight on his captors' part that he was allowed a private army of 1000 men, including 600 of his loyal Old Guard.

Even from the perspective of a remote island in the South Atlantic, Europe must have seemed unrealistically calm. But in May 1815 an East India Company ship brought the St Helenians the alarming information that in late February Bonaparte had escaped from Elba. He entered Paris in triumph on 20 March 1815 to the cheering of thousands of Parisians who lined the streets—those who did not applaud kept their feelings to themselves—and he was carried shoulder-high to the Tuileries Palace to cries of '*Vive l'Empereur!*'

Then on 15 September a ship arrived at Jamestown bringing splendid news. Bonaparte's new regime had lasted just 'One Hundred Days', as it came to be known. There had been an epic battle on the field of Waterloo in Flanders, conducted in an intermittent thunderstorm. The great warmonger had been defeated at last by a glorious British fighting force—there was grudging mention of Belgian and Dutch troops as well—led by the Commander-in-Chief, the Duke of Wellington. A Prussian force under General Blücher had arrived late to the battle. Bonaparte had escaped on horseback, weeping, it was claimed, into his saddle, but his days were numbered. France, after some silken diplomacy by the veteran courtier Talleyrand, was to be returned once again to the Bourbons.

Governor Wilks arranged for a royal salute to be fired in honour of the Waterloo triumph and approved celebrations at the garrison with an extra quota of wine for each soldier. He ordered that all prisoners, civil and military, be released, with the exception of a fellow awaiting trial for burglary. The island residents returned to their familiar routines.

But they were rudely awakened on 11 October. The news brought by Captain Devon of the *Icarus*, a sloop-of-war, was extraordinary, too much to take in all at once: Bonaparte, foiled in his plans to escape to America, had surrendered to a British ship at the French Atlantic port of Rochefort. The Allied powers, after convoluted negotiations (from which Prussia withdrew, preferring the firing-squad option), had reached agreement that while France, Austria and Russia would keep a watching brief, he was to be England's prisoner and England's problem.

But the most outrageous news was that the Monster of Europe, the Disturber of the World, the Corsican half-breed, the Villain Bonaparte, the Anti-Christ, the savage Butcher of Jaffa—no words were bad enough but all were used in the newspapers—was being brought into exile on their own peaceful island. His ship was on the seas behind the *Icarus*. He would be arriving in a few days' time.

And for five and a half turbulent years, St Helena would become one of the most talked about places on earth.

'Our little isle was suddenly frightened from its propriety,' Betsy Balcombe wrote later in her *Recollections*, 'by hearing that Napoleon Bonaparte was to be confined as a prisoner of state.' She felt 'excessive terror, and an undefined conviction that something awful would happen to us all, though of what nature I hardly knew'.[7]

The townsfolk had never been so rattled. It seemed unbelievable that the most evil man in the world, and not so long ago the most powerful, was within a few days' sail and coming to live among them. Apart from the St Helena Regiment—their own garrison, provided by the East India Company—there would be a huge body of soldiers and seamen arriving with him, just to keep him secure, all of them to be housed and fed, taking over the streets and taverns of the little town. The prisoner was travelling with the largest guard ever assembled in European history to watch over a single man. HMS *Northumberland*, with Bonaparte aboard, was accompanied by four warships with 116 guns between them and three troopships transporting the 2nd Battalion of the 53rd Regiment of Foot.

Rumours were rife and anxieties noisily expressed. Just where was the prisoner to be kept? And would the soldiers be able to prevent him escaping the island, just as he gave his guards the slip on Elba? What was to prevent a raiding party of Frenchmen—or Americans for that matter—coming to rescue him? And as Boney made his escape, what was to stop his henchmen cutting all their throats? There were frightful visions of blood on the cobbled streets of Jamestown.

The captain of the *Icarus* had brought Colonel Wilks a 'Secret letter' from the British government, advising him of the arrival of the prisoner; it emphasised that in all matters relating to 'General Napoleon Buonaparte' he was to defer to Rear-Admiral Sir George Cockburn, commander of the fleet.[8] Wilks was informed that the island would be removed from the jurisdiction of the East India Company, its traditional employer, and placed under British government administration. At the same time he received a confidential letter from the Company's directors acknowledging 'the high importance of effectually securing the person of a man whose conduct has proved so fatal to the happiness of the world'. Despite Wilks's great merits, His Majesty's Government had determined on appointing a new governor, a military man 'of the class of General officers who served in the scene of the late continental events'.[9] That officer was Major-General Hudson Lowe, most recently quartermaster-general to the Allied armies in the Netherlands and Belgium, who was then making his way from Europe to London. Lowe was to be promoted to the rank of lieutenant-general and created a Knight Commander of the Bath, befitting the gravity of his office as Bonaparte's custodian.[10]

The immediate issues were housing and catering. The official 'Secret letter' stated that any residence on the island could be allocated for Bonaparte, 'with the exception of the Governor's Plantation House'. Wilks learned from the captain of the *Icarus* that a retinue was coming with the prisoner, not only his officers and servants but also some aristocratic Frenchwomen. He thought that Longwood House, the lieutenant-governor's isolated summer residence, could be a possibility, but it was badly in need of repairs.

And what of Bonaparte's Austrian wife, the former empress Marie Louise—would she be expecting to join him, although she had declined to do so on Elba? Rumour had it that the Austrian foreign minister, Prince Metternich, had thoughtfully organised a handsome aide-de-camp for her, Count von Neipperg, who had lost no time in becoming her lover; he was reputed to be 'a perfect serpent in matters of seduction'.[11] But if the lady chose to make the voyage, she was authentic royalty, the daughter of the Austrian Emperor, and conditions must meet her satisfaction.

With the fleet imminently arriving under the command of the rear-admiral, there would also be another 2000 sailors and soldiers and the massive logistical exercise of feeding them all. Most of the island's food came from the Cape of Good Hope and shortages were chronic. It would be a challenge for the commissary-general and storekeeper, who allocated provisions brought by the twice-yearly storeship, and for Solomons Merchants and William Balcombe, the Company sales agent with a providore business on the side.

In fact, the merchants recognised splendid commercial opportunities in the new situation. Balcombe was pleased; as well as his providore business, he owned the Union brewery supplying beer to the garrison, and had an orchard and large vegetable garden at his home, The Briars. He would soon, like the Solomons, take advantage of the increase in the island's population by doubling his prices. But there were negative implications for the merchants as well: with the island removed from the jurisdiction of the East India Company and patrolled by the Royal Navy, ships of other flags would be unable to call for water, victualling and trading, thereby limiting business. However, Balcombe was a man who looked in every setback for an opportunity and usually succeeded in finding one.

Few people were more agitated by the news than Balcombe's younger daughter Betsy. Just five months earlier, she and her sister Jane had arrived back at the island with their mother from school in England.[12] Believing Bonaparte was still incarcerated on Elba it had at last seemed safe to make the voyage. At their Nottinghamshire boarding school the girls had heard of Bonaparte's outrages, the lands laid waste, the innocent souls massacred and, almost certainly, the whispered stories of unspeakable deeds perpetrated on young girls. The yellow cover of a contemporary English children's primer bore a picture of Bonaparte brandishing a cat-o'-nine-tails, and nannies warned disobedient children that he would come down the chimney to snatch them.[13] Betsy, a pretty adolescent with blonde curls, always a prankster and mischief-maker, was certain to have been chided by some grim teacher with a warning much in currency at the time, 'Be good or Boney will get you!', or by the more savage 'Limb from limb he'll tear you, just as pussy tears a mouse!'[14]

In 1812, her teachers had spoken gravely of his Russian campaign, how the buildings in Moscow were set on fire to repel him, and the devastating retreat of his great army in the snow. Hundreds of thousands of his soldiers died of starvation and frostbite, a horror that Betsy could not comprehend. What upset her most were the stories of the poor horses, not properly shod, slipping on ice and left to die or hacked at for food while still alive. And Bonaparte rode safely back to Paris in a carriage! She hated him! She knelt in church with the other girls and prayed for the successful progress of the war and a righteous victory for the great British Empire. But at night she tossed and turned in her narrow bed and the ogre with protruding teeth and one flaming red eye returned, his vast cape shadowed Europe and her own fevered thoughts; he circled like a vulture, swooping to leave battered, bleeding bodies and screaming horses in the snow. When she cried out, Jane would creep across the dormitory to hug her and smooth her hair.

And now here he was at her island home, walking right past her, the monster of her nightmares.

CHAPTER 2

THE PRISONER

From the deck in the dawn light, the island of St Helena appeared as a smudge on the grey horizon of the South Atlantic, a brooding apparition, something from Grimm. Another plunge and it was gone in a haze of sea mist and spume, a chimera. As we chugged closer, all that I'd read of its infamous, forbidding appearance could not prepare me for the starkness of those sheer basalt cliffs, their ridges shrouded in mist, plunging over 300 metres to murderous foaming rocks. All of us on deck were subdued.

'It consists of one vast rock,' wrote an 1815 visitor, 'perpendicular on every side, like a castle, in the middle of the Ocean, whose natural walls are too high to be attempted by scaling ladders; nor is there the smallest beach except at the Bay . . . which is fortified with a strong battery of large cannon, and further defended by the perpetual dashing of prodigious waves against the shore, which, without further resistance, makes the landing difficult.'[1]

I was on the island's own vessel, subsidised by the British government, RMS *St Helena*, the last operational Royal Mail ship in the world. There were 88 on board for this voyage, two-thirds of them St Helenians, or 'Saints' as they call themselves, descended from people stolen from the East Indies, Madagascar and Africa during two centuries of slave trading. It had taken five days to come from Cape Town, 3100 kilometres to the south-east, following the Benguela current, as did the great wandering albatrosses which occasionally and magically swooped in our wake.

We made a semi-circumnavigation north to the island's only town and shipping roadstead, and a pod of some two hundred dolphins leaped and plunged beside us, the essence of life and joy. But as I gazed at those barren brown escarpments it seemed hard to credit that humans lived somewhere beyond them, that trees and grass grew, that birds sang. The island seemed saurian, like an ancient, hulking giant tortoise.

'I almost feel sorry for Napoleon,' I said.

'He was a prisoner,' growled an Afrikaner passenger, 'he wasn't coming here for any damned holiday. They should have shot him.'

'The morning was pleasant, and the breeze steady,' wrote William Warden, HMS *Northumberland*'s surgeon. 'At dawn we were sufficiently near to behold the black peak of St Helena. Between eight and nine we were close under the Sugar-Loaf Hill. The whole of the French party had quitted their cabins, with the exception of Napoleon, and taken their respective stations. On the right stood Madame Montholon, with her arm entwined in that of the General her husband . . . On the poop-deck sat Madame Bertrand, and the Marshal stood behind her.'[2]

The flagship rounded a looming promontory behind the escort brigs and dropped anchor, heaving on the swell. Guns fired a salute from Munden's battery on the cliff above, answered from the gun emplacement high up the mountain across the bay. *Northumberland*'s guns responded.

Bonaparte stayed below deck. His French courtiers, their children and servants, and the British officers and men stared at the forbidding crags. Countess Françoise-Elisabeth Bertrand, born to an Irish military father—General Arthur Dillon—and a French mother from Martinique, was a woman of the world, equally at home in France, Britain, Italy and the Caribbean, but she was in despair contemplating this godforsaken rock. She said it was something the devil had shat on his way to hell.[3] Fanny, as her friends called her, was accustomed to the glittering life of the Tuileries palace where her husband had been Grand Marshal. It was feared that, in horror at what her husband's loyalty had committed them to, she might throw herself through a porthole again.

She had attempted this once before, off the British port of Torbay. This supremely elegant woman had been rescued when jammed halfway out, an undignified position.[4] 'Madame Bertrand really *did* attempt to throw herself into the Sea,' wrote an aristocratic English gossip, 'but there was stage effect in it, as assistance was so near at hand.'[5]

The Bertrands had shared Bonaparte's previous exile on the island of Elba, occupying a large comfortable villa with pleasant gardens. At the prospect of this new, infinitely harsher banishment, she had persuaded her husband they should endure twelve months at most. He risked a death sentence in France but she had highly placed relatives in England.

Bonaparte did not leave his cabin for a full hour after they had anchored. Closely watched by Dr Warden, who set down his impressions for posterity, the portly man in the green Chasseurs uniform then ascended to the poop deck 'and there stood, examining with his little glass the numerous cannon which bristled in his view. I observed him with the utmost attention . . . and could not discover, in his countenance, the least symptoms of strong or particular sensations.'[6]

The prisoner saw a compact settlement squeezed into a ravine between the steep sides of two mountains, their bare slopes devoid of vegetation and surmounted by gun emplacements. Behind a defensive wall at the waterfront were the whitewashed ramparts of the governor's castle with the Union Jack flapping above and the square tower of the Anglican church; beyond them, pastel-coloured houses straggled the length of the narrow valley.

The former emperor's dress was meticulous, presenting the image that had long become iconic: the cocked hat, the green cutaway coat with the scarlet cuffs, the Légion d'Honneur flashing on his waistcoat, the white breeches kept spotless by his 24-year-old valet Louis-Joseph Marchand. He was soon joined by his new personal physician—the appointment still a surprise to them both—Irishman Dr Barry O'Meara.

Admiral Sir George Cockburn, Knight Commander of the Bath, appeared in full dress uniform, ready to go ashore with Colonel Sir George Ridout Bingham, commander of the 2nd Battalion of the 53rd Regiment. During the voyage the admiral had formed a tolerable relationship with Bonaparte, walking with him on deck of an evening, allowing him to preside at mealtimes, and actually standing up in deference when he left the saloon. But such courtesies were about to end. He carried instructions from Lord Henry Bathurst, Secretary of State for War and the Colonies, conveying the wishes of the Prince Regent: 'His Royal Highness ... relies on Sir George Cockburn's known zeal and energy of character that he will not allow himself to be betrayed into any improvident relaxation of his duty.'[7] The prisoner, as far as British policy was concerned, was to be addressed as 'General Bonaparte'—or preferably 'General Buonaparte', the Corsican spelling offering further disparagement. There was to be no emperor arriving on the island.

Bonaparte retreated to his cabin to brood, telling General Gourgaud, a former ordnance officer: 'It is not an attractive place. I should have done better to remain in Egypt. By now, I would be Emperor of all the East.' Madame Bertrand turned to the attentive man behind her with her own decided opinion: 'Oh, Dr Warden, we are indeed too good for St Helena!'[8]

Taking in the whole scene was Count de Las Cases, the diminutive French aristocrat and the emperor's former chamberlain who was to become Napoleon's Boswell. When the anchor was put down in James Bay, he wrote: 'This was the first link of the chain that was to bind the modern Prometheus to his rock.'[9]

The mythologising had commenced.

After his defeat at Waterloo, Napoleon had fled back to Paris, conceding only that all was lost 'for the present!' He remained confident of raising another army—but found that the French people now craved only peace. The Allies refused to negotiate terms while he remained in power. In the end he had abdicated rather than be deposed, but only after his strict condition was granted, the proclamation of his four-year-old son as Napoleon II. But the little emperor's 'reign' was less than two weeks, because the Duke of Wellington had other ideas. Instead, he proclaimed the return of the Bourbons and invited Louis XVIII, the overweight successor to his executed brother Louis XVI, back to Versailles.

Meanwhile, Bonaparte stayed on at the Elysée palace. Here he met with his ex-wife Josephine's daughter, Hortense, who was both his stepdaughter and, through her marriage to his brother Louis, his sister-in-law. He sought Hortense's permission to come to the Château de la Malmaison where, in the days of the Consulate and before his marriage to Josephine soured, he had enjoyed family life with his wife and her children. When he had heard news of Josephine's death in May 1814 when he was in exile on Elba, it was said that he locked himself in his room for two days.

Hortense still liked to be addressed as the 'Queen of Holland'; Louis Bonaparte had been imposed on the Dutch throne by his imperial brother but had now been supplanted, and the couple had long since separated. It was an open secret in Paris that Hortense was involved in a passionate affair with General Auguste Charles, Comte de Flahaut, Napoleon's aide-de-camp in the Russian campaign and at Waterloo.[10] Four years earlier, in Switzerland, she had given birth to a son by Flahaut; it had been discreetly arranged for the child to be raised by a landowner in the West Indies.

Friends advised Hortense against taking Napoleon into her home but she did not heed them. Bonaparte's mother and brothers arrived at Malmaison with a group of supporters. Among them was Hortense's lover, Comte de Flahaut, who soon left on a hopeless mission to request more time from the provisional French government. However, he will appear again in an unexpected role in this story.

Instead of making his escape, Bonaparte lingered five days in some kind of emotional paralysis, reading novels and essays about America, where he planned to seek refuge. An adviser had suggested that from there 'you can continue to make your enemies tremble. If France falls back under the Bourbon yoke, your presence in a free country will sustain national opinion here.'[11] He thought often about Josephine and told her daughter: 'Poor Josephine, I cannot get used to living here without her. I always expect to see her emerging from a path gathering one of those flowers which she so loved . . . How beautiful La Malmaison is! Wouldn't it be pleasant, Hortense, if we could stay here?' 'I could not reply,' wrote Hortense, 'my voice would have betrayed all my emotion.'[12]

Guns rumbled in the distance. Blücher's Prussian army was advancing fast and Bonaparte's options for escape were closing. He decided at last to quit the country with his brother Joseph and sail to America—but he knew that the English anticipated this and their navy blocked the Channel. With Joseph and some faithful officers and servants he would aim instead for the port of Rochefort on the Bay of Biscay.

Finally, Bonaparte stood facing his strong-willed mother, Letizia, known throughout Europe as 'Madame Mère'. Hortense reported that they gazed silently at each other, then Letizia stretched out both her hands towards him and in a clear sonorous voice said: 'Farewell, my son!' He gathered her hands in his, looked long and affectionately in her face and, with a voice as firm as hers, exclaimed: 'Farewell, my mother!'[13]

Travelling in a series of carriages, spaced well apart, the fugitives reached Rochefort on 8 July. The valet Marchand rode in a carriage crammed with the accoutrements of gracious living that he had hurriedly packed—his master's campaign bed, table linen, a Sèvres porcelain dinner service, gold plates, silverware, an assortment of snuff boxes and almost six hundred books. At Rochefort the group boarded the frigate *La Saale*, but it could not weigh anchor for Boston. The harbour was emphatically blocked by the 74-gun British warship HMS *Bellerophon* and two naval frigates.

Bonaparte resolved to surrender, bargaining on the British sense of justice he claimed to admire. He told General Bertrand: 'It is better to risk confiding oneself to their honour than to be handed over to them as *de jure* prisoners.' He had in fact few alternatives: the naval blockade prevented his escape by sea, while General Blücher and the Bourbons wanted him shot. First though, on 13 July, he penned a grandiloquent letter to the Prince Regent, comparing the English royal to the King of the Persians who offered safe harbour to his enemy:

> Royal Highness—A victim to the factions which divide my country, and to the enmity of the greatest Powers of Europe, I have terminated my political career, and I come, like Themistocles, to place myself at the hearth of the British people. I place myself under the protection of their laws, which I claim of your Royal Highness as of the most powerful, the most constant and the most generous of my enemies.
> —Napoleon[14]

It is doubtful if the Regent saw the letter until much later, but when he did, despite his image as a wastrel and a rake, the reference from

Plutarch's *Lives* would not have been lost on him; he was said to be 'probably the only prince in Europe . . . competent to peruse the Greek as well as the Roman poets and historians in their own language'.¹⁵

Bonaparte sent Gourgaud and Las Cases under a flag of truce to deliver the letter to the *Bellerophon*. They were well received by Captain Frederick Maitland. Two days later, the former emperor and his companions stepped aboard the great warship, veteran of the battles of the Nile and Trafalgar, known affectionately by its crew as the 'Billy Ruffian'. As they came on deck the officers and seamen formed a parade of honour. A midshipman left an account: 'And now came the little great man himself, wrapped up in his grey great coat, buttoned to the chin, three-cocked hat and Hussar boots, without any sword, I suppose as emblematical of his changed condition. Maitland received him with every mark of respect . . .'¹⁶

'He is extremely curious,' wrote one of the officers. 'Nothing escapes his notice; his eyes are in every place and on every object . . . He immediately asks an explanation of the ropes, blocks, masts and yards, and all the machinery of the ship. He also stops and asks the officers questions relative to the time they have been in the service, what actions, &c, and he caused all of us to be introduced to him the first day he came on board . . . He inquired into the situation of the seamen, their pay, prize money, clothes, food, tobacco &c, and when told of their being supplied by a Purser or Commissary, asked if he was not a rogue!'¹⁷

Meanwhile, the devoted Marchand—a famous exception to the adage that 'No man is a hero to his valet'—had arranged that the 250,000 francs they had managed to hide from British investigation, their reserve against hard times, 'were in eight belts that we put around our bodies'.¹⁸ Walking in the stern gallery with Las Cases, Napoleon cautiously withdrew a weighty velvet band from under his waistcoat and gave it to his companion. The count wrote: 'The Emperor told me soon after that it contained a diamond necklace, worth two hundred thousand francs, which Queen Hortensia forced him to accept on his leaving Malmaison.'¹⁹

The men on board were bound to romanticise their brush with the most compelling figure in contemporary history, having actually found him human. One of them wrote: 'If the people of England knew him as well as we do, they would not hurt a hair of his head.'[20] Captain Maitland wrote in his book that although it might appear surprising that a British officer could be 'prejudiced in favour of one who had caused so many calamities to his country, to such an extent did he possess the power of pleasing, there are few people who could have sat at the same table with him for nearly a month, as I did, without feeling a sensation of pity, allied perhaps to regret, that a man possessed of so many fascinating qualities, and who had held so high a station in life, should be reduced to the situation in which I saw him'.[21]

But for all the graciousness and goodwill, when Bonaparte boarded the *Bellerophon* he had taken an irrevocable step: he was from that moment until the end of his life a prisoner of Great Britain.

CHAPTER 3

FRIENDS AND FOES

Friendly Saints extended helping hands as we stepped from the rocking launch onto the landing place. I could see that when a swell was running this could be tricky. (The island's governor, welcoming Prince Andrew in 1984, famously lost his footing and suffered a dunking, much replayed on UK television.)

RMS *St Helena* was moored out in the bay, its derricks already unloading vital cargo onto a barge, everything from frozen meat to roofing iron, refrigerators, cars, carrots, and cats and dogs. Our luggage, brought by an earlier barge, was stacked in the customs shed, where a copper-skinned policewoman—in her British bobby's uniform and chequerboard bowler—led a beagle on a sniffing inspection. Returning Saints hugged family and friends they had not seen for months, sometimes far longer. The isolation of the island and the poor local wages mean that many residents have become long-distance commuters, taking up jobs in the UK, the Falkland Islands, and at the British and American bases on Ascension Island, returning on the 'RMS' when they can. The economic necessity of such unwieldy commuting will change for many of them when the airport under construction is completed. Tourism is the great hope.

My companion and I were greeted by our new landlord, Edward Thorpe, a tall young man from one of the oldest English families on the island. Passengers were already signing up for excursions. Of the thirty or so tourists from the ship, mainly from South Africa, few had expressed much interest in the island's most famous exile. They were coming for the stark scenery, the Georgian buildings, the formidable hiking trails, and to visit the graves of some two hundred Boer War prisoners. However, most would devote a few hours of the nine-day stay—while the RMS made a circuit 1120 kilometres north-west to Ascension Island—to the 'Napoleonic tour' of Longwood House, 'the Tomb' and The Briars Pavilion.

'Well, Papa, have you seen him?' William Balcombe's children at The Briars rushed him on his return from visiting the *Northumberland*.

He had not, although he had paid his respects to General and Madame Bertrand, General and Madame de Montholon and General Baron Gourgaud. He had been in discussion with Admiral Sir George Cockburn and Governor Wilks, who had decided that the prisoner and a few of his companions could be temporarily accommodated at Henry Porteous's boarding house at the bottom of the main street next to the castle gardens, while the French servants would be billeted in nearby cottages. This was a concession on the admiral's part. Officially he was empowered to insist they all stay on board until a suitable house was ready. The choice of that house had still to be made.

During Balcombe's meeting with the admiral he was handed a sealed letter from the London mail brought by the flagship. It bore the House of Lords insignia and was from his patron, Sir Thomas Tyrwhitt, Gentleman Usher of the Black Rod in the House of Lords. This ceremonial position, established during the reign of Henry VIII, was by decree given to 'a gentleman famous in arms and blood'. He controlled entry of 'Strangers' to the House, made staff appointments and carried an ebony rod surmounted by a golden lion for all state occasions; he could arrest any lord guilty of breach of privilege or of disturbing the House's proceedings. During the opening of Parliament, 'Black Rod' carried the King's command to the House of Commons to attend him in the House of Lords.

But another factor altogether meant that Sir Thomas Tyrwhitt was close to the very centre of power in Britain. He had been an intimate friend and trusted confidant of George Augustus, the Prince Regent, for 26 years, ever since they met at Oxford and discovered they shared the same sense of humour and even the same birthday—12 August 1762. The then Prince of Wales invited his new friend to occupy an apartment at Carlton House, his sumptuous London mansion, and made him his unofficial secretary, confirmed a few years later. Tyrwhitt, a diminutive, bustling, rosy-cheeked man, rapidly became a favourite of both King George III and Queen Charlotte and of the royal princes and princesses, who described him with patronising affection as 'the Saint' or 'our little red dwarf'.[1] Nonetheless, he commanded great respect and for several years acted 'as sole mediator between the King and the prince during the time they spent apart in mutual dislike and disagreement'.[2] While the King was often impatient with his spendthrift son, he always had time for his 'old friend Tom Tyrwhitt'.[3]

In the nineteenth century, 'interest', the influence of a powerful person, was essential to advance in the professions. Horace Walpole pronounced that 'Merit is useless: it is interest alone that can push a man forward. By dint of interest one of my coach-horses might become poet laureate, and the other, physician to the Royal household.'[4] 'Interest' was virtually indispensable, and William Balcombe, said to be merely the son of a fisherman from the Sussex village of Rottingdean, obviously had access to it from a very high level. Those on St Helena who knew of the connection with Sir Thomas— and Balcombe had little hesitation in mentioning it—wondered how and why this influential man showed such concern for his young protégé:

5th August 1815

Dear Balcombe,
Napoleon is about to proceed to your island so quickly that there seems some doubt whether this dispatch will reach Plymouth in time to catch the *Northumberland*. Since yesterday Beatson has forwarded me a very strong letter indeed, recommending you to Sir George Cockburn as Naval Agent. This letter goes in this cover to him and I sincerely hope it will answer the purpose intended . . .

Sir George promptly approved the appointment, which would have gratified Balcombe, for, with the island now placed under government administration, his merchant's business was going to become severely restricted. The new position involved much the same service, supplying vessels, but the difference was that they would be exclusively of the British navy or East India Company, with few chances for private trade. But Sir Thomas had a further suggestion, a potentially lucrative one concerning the prisoner's possible accommodation: 'It appears that Ministers will not pledge themselves to purchase any particular spot, but that all is to be left to the choice of two commanders, as to what place is best adapted to confine Napoleon comfortably but severely. Beatson thinks that when this inspection has taken place, they will fix upon The Briars.'[5]

Major-General Alexander Beatson had been St Helena's energetic governor from 1808 to 1813. After his recall he was promoted, in recognition of his efficient administration of the island and especially for his suppression of a mutiny by soldiers at the garrison in 1811. He executed the ringleaders. In Beatson's despatch to the East India Company's Court of Directors concerning that episode, he had praised the assistance of William Balcombe among a handful of loyal residents. The merchant had returned the compliment by naming his youngest son, born in that year, Alexander Beatson Balcombe, which, according to convention, meant that the governor became godfather to the boy. Soon afterwards, Balcombe was granted a lucrative licence to operate a brewery supplying beer to the island garrison.[6]

Even though he and his family were greatly attached to their home, Balcombe had no objection to Sir Thomas's idea of renting it out, for there could be handsome compensation in making it available to the French, so that it would be well worth him leasing elsewhere.

Meanwhile, red-coated soldiers of the 53rd Regiment had come ashore from the transports and now patrolled the town. Every promontory was suddenly out of bounds, manned by armed sentries in sight of each other and able to communicate by a complex set of signals. Cannon were placed on ledges and in apertures in cliffs. Posters went up around the island, plastered on buildings and on rocks, formally announcing the detention of 'General N. Buonaparte' and serving notice that: 'This is to warn all inhabitants and other persons on this island from aiding and abetting hereafter in any way whatsoever the escape of the said General and that of any of the French persons with him, and to interdict most pointedly the holding of any communication or correspondence with them. Any person presuming to act in violation of this ordinance will be immediately sent off the island to be further punished as the circumstances appear to deserve.'7

Napoleon did not come ashore until the evening of 17 October and he refused to meet with the official party at the landing stage. There was time enough to encounter the governor of this savage little island. He found it hard to forgive the way he had been treated as a common exhibit, gaped at like a wild animal in Josephine's menagerie at Malmaison, a zebra or ridiculous *kangourou*!

Sir George Cockburn understood that the situation was difficult for the preservation of dignity. He ensured that an armed guard kept the jostling crowd at bay as he escorted Bonaparte and his French companions across the drawbridge, through the town gates, past the castle entrance and its gardens to the three-storey lodging house owned by Henry Porteous. Bonaparte detested the tall narrow building as soon as he saw it and complained of its very public situation and lack of a private courtyard. He was no happier when he inspected the arrangements inside.

As night set in, most of the crowd dispersed. Still holding lanterns and torches, people wended their way, mounted or on foot, up Ladder Hill or the Sidepath. But a few of the curious still loitered outside the Porteous house. Among them was Thomas Brooke, secretary of the governing council and the island's first historian; he hoped to see a legendary figure at the candlelit windows, 'everyone anxious to catch a glance whilst he walked up and down the room'. Brooke was astonished to be invited inside by the admiral and his credentials announced: 'I was accordingly ushered up to Buonaparte, who was standing, and introduced in regular form. His first words were "*Hah! L'auteur de l'*Histoire de St Hélène." He then said he had read it on the passage ... I observed that I trusted he would find the interior of the island more prepossessing in appearance than the first view of it might lead him to expect.'8

Three months earlier, at dawn on 24 July, Bonaparte had stood on the quarterdeck of HMS *Bellerophon* next to Captain Maitland and gazed through his field glass at the port of Torbay, the sea cliffs of Devon and green pastureland beyond. As the ship sailed on to Plymouth, he was astonished to find himself massively feted. They were surrounded by an immense clutter of small craft, filled with the curious, desperate to see the infamous enemy. Marchand tells us that 'accompanied by the grand marshal [General Bertrand], he went on deck and showed himself to the eager crowd . . . But a painful scene for us was that a few ships with our prisoners wounded at Waterloo sailed by, some distance from the *Bellerophon*.'[9] Within the month some 4000 French prisoners were marched 25 miles up to the grim granite prison on Dartmoor, established in 1809 by none other than Sir Thomas Tyrwhitt, who, as Member of Parliament for Plymouth before he was appointed Black Rod in 1812, had seen the opportunity.

The *Bellerophon* was at Plymouth for three weeks. During that time, Admiral Viscount Keith, Commander-in-Chief of the Channel Fleet, was responsible for the security of the prisoner and represented the voice of the British government.[10] *The Times* urged government ministers 'to do their duty and rid the world of a monster',[11] but it seemed 'the whole population of the country, without distinction of rank or sex', was descending on the port for a glimpse of him.[12] 'I am worried to death with idle folk coming, even from Glasgow, to see him,' Admiral Keith complained to his daughter. 'There is no nation so foolish as we are!'[13]

An officer reported that people had flocked from all parts of the country to see Bonaparte. His every appearance on deck was an event for thousands of citizens who came out in tour boats and waved their hats. Upwards of a thousand boats were from morning to night around the warship, and its seamen were willing to give an account of Napoleon's movements for the avid spectators. They wrote in chalk on a board, and exhibited a short account of his different occupations: 'At breakfast', 'In the cabin with Capt. Maitland', 'Writing with his officers', 'Going to dinner', 'Coming upon deck', et cetera.[14] One of the ship's officers reported that the 'great number of well-dressed females . . . never failed to attract his particular attention . . . He appeared greatly pleased with the beauty and elegance of our fair countrywomen, and was always wishing to know their names, families, and any circumstance that could be communicated to him concerning them.'[15]

The celebrity prisoner understood that he was awaiting the Prince Regent's decision. He hoped for a refuge in the English countryside and ruminated on the best place to retire as a county gentleman, perhaps to the Cotswolds under the name 'Colonel Muiron', after a fallen comrade-in-arms, so as not to cause a local fuss.[16] The ministers of the ailing George III did not trust Bonaparte's charm nor his ability to flatter the suggestible and vainglorious prince, whom the Duke of Wellington privately described as 'the most extraordinary compound of talent, wit, buffoonery, obstinacy and good feeling that I ever saw in any character in my life'.[17] They joined Admiral Lord Keith in the view that if the defeated emperor 'obtained an interview with His Royal Highness, in half an hour they would have been the best friends in England'.[18] The commotion about him at Plymouth demonstrated 'his genius for upheaval', his capacity for exciting a movement of sympathisers. The Prime Minister, Lord Liverpool, advised: 'We are all decidedly of opinion that it would not answer to confine him to this country . . . Very nice legal questions might arise upon the subject, which would be particularly embarrassing.' They obtained the agreement of the Allies in wishing him deported somewhere so remote that even he would find it impossible to abscond, and took up the Admiralty's suggestion, supported by Wellington, that the island of St Helena was 'the place in the world best calculated for the confinement of such a person'.[19]

Although Bonaparte had heard rumours, it still came like a physical blow when told he was destined for the remote Atlantic rock which had once been considered as an alternative exile to Elba. (Another, almost as bad, had been Botany Bay in New South Wales.) Bonaparte was instructed to select twelve servants and 'three principals' to accompany him. Of the fifteen officers who clamoured to join him—either through loyalty, misplaced ambition or calculated avarice, or to escape a death sentence in France—at last he chose generals Bertrand and de Montholon and Count de Las Cases. The British agreed to increase the number to 26 to include the generals' wives and children, the count's adolescent son Emmanuel, a physician, and more servants to personally attend them all. Some of these volunteers had been with Bonaparte on Elba.

General Baron Gaspard Gourgaud, a temperamental bachelor aged 31 was not initially chosen, for he was not a personal friend or a military officer of long standing, although he had taken part in the Russian disaster and was more of a campaign veteran than the effete Montholon. But he caused such a violent emotional scene, pleading to be with his emperor, that Napoleon reluctantly included him. To do so he was obliged to attach him as one of the principals and to designate the aristocratic Las Cases as merely his secretary, in effect a servant.

As it happened, Dr O'Meara, the Irish senior surgeon on the *Bellerophon*, had attended members of the French party—mainly for seasickness—during the voyage from Rochefort and had made a good impression on Napoleon.[20] The two enjoyed several conversations in Italian, a language in which O'Meara was fluent, and discussed Napoleon's conquest of Egypt, where the surgeon had been. Bonaparte proposed that O'Meara be seconded as his personal physician. The request went up to Admiral Lord Keith and was acceded to readily, because of the opportunity the position offered for close observation. O'Meara, in the self-justificatory introduction to the book he would publish after Bonaparte's death, stated that 'this was an employment which I could hold perfectly consistent with my honour, and with the duty I owed to my country and my sovereign'.[21]

O'Meara had already sent a lively description of Bonaparte and his French companions to his friend John Finlaison, a senior clerk at the Admiralty, where Lord Melville was First Sea Lord. At Plymouth he received a reply: 'My Dear Barry—Thanks for your kind letter which was so extremely interesting that I showed it to Lord Melville, who made some corrections in it and then expressly permitted and was well pleased that I should insert it in the *Sun* of tomorrow. This will do you no harm. You will on no account mention this to a soul, except your Captain if you find that necessary for your justification in having written. I cannot tell you now my reasons for printing it. When we meet you will find them good as they are partly political. It is the highest authority that did it.'[22] The following day an item appeared in the *Sun* and the *Plymouth Telegraph* reporting that a gentleman who saw Bonaparte regularly said that recent newspaper reports that Bonaparte was unhappy at the prospect of going to St Helena were incorrect: the Corsican seemed quite cheerful about going and frequently laughed.[23]

On 7 August, the French party was transferred to HMS *Northumberland* under Sir George Cockburn. The admiral permitted an English friend, Lord Lyttelton, to make a visit aboard. The aristocrat spoke good French and was introduced to Bonaparte. Afterwards, Lyttelton observed of the two wives in the French entourage that they were completely different in look and manner: 'Madame Bertrand, who had behaved with great violence in the *Bellerophon*, seemed rather exhausted than pacified, and had a look of great irritation and impatience. She is a tall, thin woman, with an aquiline nose, very like Lord Dillon, to whom she is, I believe, rather nearly related.[24] Madame Montholon, on the other hand, had all the quiet resignation that so well becomes her sex, and one could not help sympathising with her sufferings so meekly borne. She is a pretty woman, of a sweet and intelligent countenance.'[25]

Albine Hélène de Montholon was grieving. She and her third husband were travelling with their three-year-old son Tristan, but they had left behind in France her twelve-year-old boy from an earlier marriage and their own baby son, born the previous year, in the care of a wet nurse; Montholon had deemed him too young to travel. During this voyage to St Helena, as if in protest, Albine became pregnant again.

Napoleon was presented to the *Northumberland*'s flag captain, Charles Ross, who felt disappointed, as he had never seen a picture that showed Napoleon as he really was: 'He appears by no means that active man he is said to be. He is fat, rather what we call pot-bellied, and altho' his leg is well-shaped, it is rather clumsy and his walk appears rather affected, something between a waddle and a swagger ... He is very sallow and quite light grey eyes, rather thin greasy-looking brown hair, and is altogether a very nasty, priest-like looking fellow.'[26]

On 11 August, the *Northumberland*, with 1080 people on board, set sail. It was said that Bonaparte stood on deck for five hours, gazing at the receding coast of France; when it slipped from sight he was distraught.[27]

During the *Northumberland*'s 71 days at sea, twenty of them becalmed in the doldrums, Napoleon wondered aloud what to do with the dreary future stretching ahead. 'Sire,' answered Count de Las Cases, 'we will live in the past—there is surely enough there to satisfy us! Do we not enjoy the Lives of Caesar and Alexander? We will have a still better: you will, Sire, re-read yourself!' 'Yes,' Napoleon agreed, 'we must work. Work is also the scythe of time.'[28]

The dictation of the memoirs began, the count hunched in a corner of the cabin, creasing his old naval uniform, his quill scratching across parchment. Dr Warden was amused by his 'diminutive appearance'. Some Englishmen, he wrote, had 'expected Herculean figures to be employed in the service of a man who had lately bestrode so large a portion of Europe', whereas 'Count de Las Cases does not exceed five feet and an inch in height, and appears to be fifty years of age, of a meagre form, and with a wrinkled forehead'.[29]

Bonaparte and Admiral Cockburn occupied cabins either side of the saloon and were civil without going out of their way to be friendly. The admiral deplored the prisoner's habit of bolting his food—despatching his evening meal in fifteen minutes—and then abruptly leaving the table.[30] Sir George Bingham thought he was a secret drunk: 'he drinks regularly his bottle of wine at dinner; a bottle of claret is always carried into his cabin at breakfast, which never comes out again, but as his servants have no dislike to it, they possibly assist him'.[31] (Bonaparte was in fact abstemious and tended to see the British as drunks.)

When they briefly hove to at the island of Madeira, Bonaparte looked down at the assemblage of people on the shore and remarked to Dr Warden 'that he never beheld women with such beautiful bosoms'. Warden noted for his fiancée Miss Hutt: 'He is very anxious to know every particular respecting the females inhabiting the island of St Helena. Upon my word, I scarcely think Bonaparte can live without a wife.'[32]

The former emperor walked the deck with the admiral and played games with Tom Pipes, Cockburn's huge and amiable Newfoundland, throwing bones along the boards for the dog to retrieve, or he sat on a cannon and gazed at the flying fish. One day when a shark was caught, 'Bonaparte', wrote the admiral's secretary John Glover, 'with the eagerness of a schoolboy scrambled on the poop to see it'.[33]

He even took a few English lessons from Las Cases—who had spent years as an émigré teacher in Britain and promised he would have him reading an English newspaper in the course of a month. The lessons were soon cut short by Bonaparte's pronouncement: 'I well know that you think me a very clever fellow; but be that as it may, I cannot do everything; and among those things which I should find impracticable, is the making myself master of the English language in a few weeks.'[34]

Bonaparte's questing intelligence was forever alert, collecting facts that might be of value, classifying and storing them in his capacious brain. He gained an astute understanding from Cipriani Franceschi, his butler and a fellow Corsican, about whom it was worth talking to, and who might provide useful information to help him win freedom. Cipriani's espionage skills had made possible the escape from Elba and he would continue to be his master's eyes and ears on their new island of exile.

Dr O'Meara became Napoleon's companion for a regular game of whist and Italian conversation, so excluding others of the party. Barry O'Meara was 29 years old, a native of County Cork with an idiosyncratic past.[35] He had previously been in the British army, serving in Sicily, where he had gained his knowledge of the Italian language. But he had contravened military regulations by acting as second in a duel and was court-martialled and dismissed. He had then contrived to join the Royal Navy as a surgeon. He retained an abiding resentment of the British army, and showed sympathy towards the former emperor for his difficult situation.

General Gourgaud simmered with resentment to see his hero enjoying such friendly relations with the Irishman. From the beginning he had his suspicions that the man was a British spy, ingratiating himself for a purpose. He was not altogether wrong. O'Meara was preparing an account of the voyage for Finlaison, aware now that it was likely to be read by First Sea Lord Melville, and perhaps by 'the highest authority', the Prince Regent. While waspish about some of the French, his comments about the prisoner were benign, simply describing his daily routine, the hours he got up, walked about, dined and retired. 'He generally spoke a few words to every officer who could understand him; and according to his usual custom, was very inquisitive relative to various subjects.'[36] When the clerk Finlaison received the letter, he passed it on to his immediate superior, John Wilson Croker, the influential Secretary to the Admiralty and a regular at the Prince Regent's Carlton House dinners. A request came back from Croker to sight all further correspondence from O'Meara, in order to pass it up higher.

CHAPTER 4

THE BRIARS

I was quite prepared for the awefulness—and even the awefulness—of St Helena; what I had not expected was to fall in love with the island.

White fairy terns swooped against the harsh volcanic cliffs, and old cannon lay rusting along the waterfront marina. We passed over a moat—once there was a drawbridge—and through an archway in the town's massive stone wall. Inside was an almost perfectly preserved Georgian main street, like a film set for a Jane Austen or Thackeray adaptation—as long as one's eye did not stray to the grim cliffs looming on either side. The whitewashed castle—a seventeenth-century fort of the English East India Company—is still the centre of government administration. With brass cannon at its entrance and orange bougainvillea festooning the ramparts, it dominates the parade square and faces the old Company bond store and the eighteenth-century St James's Anglican church. Next to it is the prison with its cheerful blue balcony and accommodation for just twelve miscreants. Behind are the basalt slopes of Ladder Hill and an almost vertical staircase called Jacob's Ladder with 699 steps to the fort above. Brightly coloured Georgian houses, some with slave entrances to cellars, line the main street, along with a handful of shops, the post office and the Consulate Hotel, its wrought-iron balconies overhanging the footpath.

Accommodation for the ship's tourists had been booked beforehand—at the Consulate or other lodgings in Jamestown. My companion and I had an apartment in a classic Georgian building in Market Street above Thorpe & Sons' grocery store. There were comfortable couches, a Regency dining table, and a mahogany glass-fronted bookcase with volumes of Scott, Dickens and Charles Kingsley. Through tall windows we looked across at the brown cliffs and the fairy terns wheeling and shrieking.

For a long time St Helena has appeared an oddity, lost in a British imperial time warp. Overwhelmingly Anglican, its population varies now between 4500 and 5800, as transient workers for the building of the airport come and go, but they have His Lordship the Bishop presiding at St Paul's cathedral and His Lordship the Chief Justice at the Supreme Court; His Excellency the Governor is chauffeured from Plantation House to his office at the castle in a black Jaguar with a Union Jack pennant, and until a few years ago donned a white-plumed hat for ceremonial occasions. Painted in big white letters on the cliffs above is the greeting 'We Welcome You Prince Andrew', still there from the prince's 1984 visit as a member of the armed forces. Most shops display a fading portrait of the Queen.

Apart from the mostly local government employees coming in and out of the castle, tapping smartly over the cobblestones clutching files, it was evident that the people of working age had generally fled; most Saints in town appeared to be adolescent or younger, or older than fifty. But everyone I passed gave a friendly greeting in the soft singsong St Helenian accent, said to be a throwback to eighteenth-century English—part Dickensian Cockney, part West Country burr—blended with African cadences.

Admiral Cockburn elected to stay at the castle, where he had access to the warships in the bay, rather than be a guest at Plantation House, the governor's mansion out of town. It was determined that Bonaparte's permanent home would be Longwood House, up on the high plateau, remote enough to serve as a prison. It had recently been occupied by the lieutenant-governor and his family as a summer retreat from the humidity of Jamestown, but its earlier use was as a cattle house and barn, to which some rough additions had been made. It was dilapidated and at least two months' work would be needed before it could be acceptable accommodation.

Because of this decision, the Balcombe family did not have to vacate The Briars, although William probably regretted the compensation he would have been offered. He had first rented The Briars property in early 1806, not long after he and his family had settled on the island, and he bought it one year later when he was made superintendent of public sales for the East India Company. It was one of the most favoured locations on the island, a vale on the sheltered middle level, protected from the prevailing winds, with a waterfall tumbling over a horseshoe-shaped cliff into a deep gorge behind the homestead.

The house was in the style of a long Indian villa, with an upper section of three rooms; it had shuttered windows and a colonnaded verandah along the front onto which the ground floor rooms opened.[1] The kitchen was in a separate building, while the twenty slaves lived in huts at the rear. Balcombe had statutory ownership of seven men, four women, four boys and five girls.[2] Slavery was still legal on the island—the last outpost of empire where it was—despite the British government's legislation four years earlier against the transportation of human beings. Toby, the old Malay gardener, although a slave, was allowed his own hut in the orchard. He had made the garden of The Briars envied throughout the island for its beauty and productivity, while Balcombe enjoyed a profit of £600 a year selling the fruit and vegetables.

A leafy avenue of banyan trees and myrtles led from the front gates to the little paradise Toby had created. A creamy froth of pink and white roses, the sweetbriars that gave the place its name, mingled with geraniums and nasturtiums. Beyond was the orchard of oranges, guavas, mangoes and figs, with vegetable beds near the kitchen door. Pomegranate trees shaded a sloping path up to a little summer-house pavilion that Balcombe had constructed as a ballroom and occasional accommodation for guests and visiting officials of the East India Company.[3]

The eldest Balcombe boy, William, aged seven in 1815, had been left to continue his education in England under the guardianship of Sir Thomas Tyrwhitt. William's sisters had been 'finished' at Mrs Clarke's genteel Ladies' Boarding School in Mansfield, Nottinghamshire, where they had learned 'French, Music, Dancing, Drawing, Geography and the Use of Globes' with 'the greatest Care taken of the Morals and Conduct of the Pupils'.[4] The school was some 60 miles from South Cave in Yorkshire where the girls had spent holidays with their aunt, Mrs Balcombe's sister, and her stockbroker husband.

Once the Napoleonic Wars had seemed at an end and the perpetrator safely held on Elba, it had been possible for ordinary people to risk sea travel once more. Mrs Jane Balcombe had sailed to England at the beginning of 1815 to bring her daughters back home. Even without the threat of French warships, the voyage would have been a trial for this charming and attractive woman who suffered indifferent health. Although she was well liked in the island community, the isolation disagreed with her: she wrote to a relative that life on St Helena was 'worse than being transported to Botany Bay'.[5]

The girls were thrilled to return to the island. They found their father stouter than ever, more prone to gout, as volatile in temperament, but still for the most part cheerful and gregarious. Betsy was glad to abandon the strictures of school, to be petted and fussed over by their old black nurse Sarah Timms, to run barefoot in the garden, to lie on the grass by the fishpond and let the sun beat down on her face. She had grown up clambering up and down the island's rocky slopes and gorges. Up on the misty heights she had revelled in flocks of canaries twittering through the trees and huge spiderwebs shimmering between ancient tree ferns. Sometimes the sisters had followed the tortuous descent to a pool beneath the waterfall that cascaded behind their house, just deep enough to swim in after heavy rain.

But now they were young ladies of thirteen and fifteen and so had to forsake such escapades. Their duty henceforth was to acquire domestic skills and drawing-room graces to equip them for marriage to a gentleman of good prospects—or, if they were very fortunate or very pretty, as Betsy indeed was—perhaps to a gentleman of wealth and distinction. But this future held little attraction for Betsy Balcombe.

On Bonaparte's first full day on St Helena, the admiral planned a tour of the island, concluding with an inspection of Longwood. We know from General Gourgaud's journal that the outing started badly: the admiral and Governor Wilks arrived early on horseback at the Porteous house, accompanied by soldiers bringing two splendid horses for the former emperor and his marshal. But Napoleon was in no mood to be hurried. He had resented being subjected to the rude public gaze the previous night, he considered his room at the lodgings inferior, there was no private garden, and he was outraged to find a huddle of locals pointing at him and shouting as he passed a window. He took his time getting ready in his Chasseurs uniform; when he and General Bertrand emerged, they found the admiral already on his horse, irritable at being forced to wait.

As the party of riders ascended the Sidepath that morning, the horses found the gradient heavy going. Valet Marchand recalled in his memoirs that the emperor looked across the valley and 'saw a small house located in a site that seemed pleasant and picturesque. He was told it belonged to Mr Balcombe; he continued on his way but proposed to stop there on his return; he preferred in effect to stay in its little hut, if Longwood was not habitable, to the house in town where he could not move without being stared at by passers-by.'[6]

Napoleon knew about the governor's residence, Plantation House, a handsome Georgian mansion set in gardens and parkland. He indicated that *it* would be an acceptable home for himself and his retinue, but was told that a prisoner could not enjoy superior accommodation to the governor, and in any case the East India Company had specifically precluded it. Nor was the castle in Jamestown an option; it was the administrative centre, the admiral himself was staying there, and it opened directly onto the marina and the shipping roads. Great Britain was prepared to grant 'the General' certain comforts and freedoms, but not at any place with access to the sea.

The group rode beside bare rocky slopes studded with aloe, cactus and prickly pear. But as they climbed higher the air became cooler and the hillsides greener, the narrow track sheltered by cedars and cypresses, pines and firs. They circled a yawning crater known as the Devil's Punchbowl and came out onto a wind-blasted plateau. This was the location of the rickety collection of buildings Bonaparte and his retinue were to occupy.

Marchand observed drily that the emperor 'was not particularly enchanted with the house that enjoyed no shade or water, and was exposed to the southeast wind that prevailed there constantly and was quite strong at the present time'.[7] The house had gaping holes in the walls, rats' droppings on the floors and manure smells exuding from underneath. Bonaparte said that repairs would take months and that he doubted whether any projected improvements could ever make the place attractive. The only advantage he could see was the extensive plateau for horse riding.

They descended by the Sidepath and Bonaparte reminded the admiral of his wish to see The Briars. Marchand recorded that on their way there, 'the Emperor told him that if the good man of the house had no objection to his staying in the pavilion, which was twenty-five paces from the house, he preferred to stay there than return to the town'.[8] Napoleon's suggestion was surprisingly modest, but the admiral knew that the merchant was in fact willing to let the whole house and he no doubt recognised that this could provide a temporary solution.

The Balcombe children sighted the riders coming down the slope towards The Briars, and the man they most dreaded was with them. Betsy felt so anxious 'that I wished to run and hide myself until they were gone', but her mother bade her stay, for she spoke French better than anyone in the family, having excelled in it at school.

The party came through the gates and, as there was no carriage road right up to the house, Admiral Cockburn and General Bertrand politely dismounted. However, the imperious figure in the green Chasseurs uniform clearly felt no compunction about staying on his mount, 'his horse's feet cutting up the turf on our pretty lawn'.

The grown-up Betsy—Mrs Lucia Elizabeth Abell—wrote of that first meeting between her thirteen-year-old self and the most malignant figure of the age:

> How vividly I recollect my feelings of dread, mingled with admiration, as I now first looked upon him whom I had learned to fear so much. His appearance on horseback was noble and imposing. The animal he rode was a superb one; his colour jet black; and as he proudly stepped up the avenue, arching his neck and champing his bit, I thought he looked worthy to be the bearer of him who was once the ruler of nearly the whole European world.

Napoleon's position on horseback, by adding height to his figure, supplied all that was wanting to make me think him the most majestic person I had ever seen. His dress was green and covered with orders, and his saddle and housings were crimson velvet richly embroidered with gold. He alighted at our house and we all moved to the entrance to receive him.

On a nearer approach, Napoleon, contrasting, as his shorter figure did, with the noble height and aristocratic bearing of Sir George Cockburn, lost something of the dignity which had so much struck me on first seeing him. He was deadly pale, and I thought his features, though cold and immovable and somewhat stern, were exceedingly beautiful.[9]

The deposed ruler of half the world was gracious when introduced to Mrs Balcombe and the two girls. Balcombe himself was upstairs in bed with a bad attack of gout.

Betsy barely noticed the admiral, in his full dress uniform, nor General Comte de Henri-Gatien Bertrand, a slightly built but distinguished officer with heavy eyebrows, long side whiskers and a thin tonsure of hair. All her attention was focused on Napoleon. He stepped into the drawing room and seated himself in one of their little cottage chairs, his shrewd glance appraising the furnishings. He complimented Mrs Balcombe on the attractiveness of her home and engaged in small talk, probably with the admiral as interpreter. Betsy did not have to translate after all, and recalled that she shamelessly scrutinised Napoleon, observing his pallid complexion, his fine, silky hair, his neat dimpled hands and, most of all, the beauty of his clear blue-grey eyes. When he smiled at her, revealing teeth stained from eating licorice, she had to suppress a giggle.

But soon the point of the visit became clear, and Napoleon's proposal was put to William Balcombe upstairs. Marchand described the eager response: 'When they arrived at the house, the request was made to the owner, confined to his bed by gout, who agreed wholeheartedly; he even wanted to give over the whole of his house. The Emperor thanked him but refused to accept; he replied that he would with pleasure occupy the pavilion, which was detached from the main house, provided that the family's habits were not disturbed.'[10]

This was remarkably considerate of Bonaparte towards a family he had never met before, and in fact such fine concern was unnecessary, as we know from Balcombe's correspondence that he was more than willing to let the whole house for a handsome return and may have been disappointed not to do so. The Briars was well situated for security, a mile from the sea, bordered by a mountain on one side and a yawning gorge on the other, and the main building would have accommodated Napoleon and his principal companions, with the pavilion for a few of the servants. It was regarded as one of the most attractive residences on the island, in one of the most temperate situations. Perhaps only the governor's Plantation House was superior, and Napoleon had not hesitated to request the whole of that. Marchand makes clear in his memoir that his master wanted to occupy the pavilion even before he had seen it. With the Balcombes remaining in the main house, he would inevitably become closely acquainted with this English family. That may well have been his intention all along.

Only after the decision was made did he inspect the little building, walking along the path under the pomegranate trees and up a flight of steps. Betsy wrote that its position, on a grassy eminence with the waterfall splashing into the ravine behind it, pleased him greatly. The interior was a single room, some 20 feet by 15, empty, with a thick layer of dust on the floor. Its windows, one of them broken, lacked shutters and curtains, but looked out to the cascade and a distant view of Diana's Peak. Some narrow stairs, little better than a ladder, led up to a low loft space. As children, Betsy and Jane had watched from the loft when their parents hosted parties and dances there. Bonaparte announced that he wanted to stay that very night, that he did not care to see Jamestown ever again until the happy day he could leave the wretched island.

The admiral raised 'the cramped nature of this lodging'. Staying at The Briars' main house was feasible but the little pavilion was absurd. There were 26 in the French retinue. Where, in that little hut, would they all fit? General Bertrand and his wife, General de Montholon and his, all their various children, their maidservants, General Gourgaud, Count de Las Cases and his son, not to mention a butler, two valets, a footman, a cook, a steward, an usher, a coachman and a groom?! It was *impossible*! But Napoleon was not to be dissuaded. His people should remain in town at the Porteous lodgings. He had too many people around him altogether; he would welcome time alone. He advised Bertrand to return to Jamestown where his good wife was waiting for him, and Marchand should fetch his campaign bed. On the morrow, Las Cases should come to continue work on the memoirs. The rest of them were to live in town until the execrable Longwood House was ready. 'The admiral promptly acquiesced to his desire and the grand marshal returned to town alone.'[11]

Hurried arrangements were under way as Admiral Cockburn and Bertrand made their departure. A captain and two soldiers were appointed as sentries at the front gates. Mrs Balcombe gave instructions to the servants, who bustled between the house and pavilion with duster, broom and bucket.

Meanwhile, their new tenant made a leisurely and apparently favourable inspection of the garden. He noticed Betsy watching him from a wary distance and signalled for chairs to be brought onto the lawn. He sat in one and beckoned to her to seat herself opposite, which she did, she wrote later, with a thumping heart. He asked where she had learned to speak French. She told him they had once had a French servant in England and that it was her favourite subject at school. He wanted to know if she had studied history and geography, and startled her with a test:[12] 'What is the capital of France?'

'Paris, of course!'

'*D'accord!* And of Italy?'

'Rome.'

'Of Russia?'

She thought about it and answered: 'Petersburg now ... and Moscow formerly.'

'So what happened to Moscow?'

'It was burned to the ground.'

He fixed her with severe eyes and demanded: '*Qui l'a brûlé?* Who burned it?'

His expression was so intense she was out of her depth. She stammered: '*Monsieur, je ne sais pas.* I don't know.'

'*Oui, oui,*' he laughed. '*Vous savez très bien, c'est moi qui l'a brûlé!*'

She believed that was not right. He did not set fire to Moscow. She gained courage and said: 'I believe, sir, that the Russians burned it to get rid of the French.'[13]

In her account he laughed and slapped his knee at the bold answer. He was delighted with her. It was a long time since he had encountered such blunt honesty.

William Balcombe was well pleased with the extraordinary new arrangement. This amiable and hospitable man, known for the amplitude of his table, rose from his bed to host dinner for their new house guest.

Balcombe and his wife 'spoke French with difficulty', and Jane was less fluent than her sister, so the burden for the evening's conversation rested on Betsy's unworldly shoulders.[14] It is hard to imagine what was passing through the mind of the fallen emperor, sharing a repast for the first time in his life with ordinary English citizens, a people he had sought to conquer and rule. Mrs Balcombe was vivacious, relieved not to be losing her home. Napoleon found her very attractive: he later confided to Betsy that her mother bore a remarkable resemblance to the Empress Josephine.

Napoleon's approach with someone he found of potential use was to fire a salvo of questions: how long had they held a particular position, what had they done before, and had they seen military action? He would have been interested to hear that Balcombe had been a midshipman who saw action in the West Indies, for he always expressed admiration for the Royal Navy, while disparaging the British army. Balcombe had then gone to India as a ship's officer with the East India Company. Bonaparte was fascinated by the Indian subcontinent, which he had planned to conquer after Egypt. It is reasonable to speculate that he would have questioned his new host about his three long trading voyages to Madras and Bengal for the Company. After all, Napoleon made personal queries of most English people he met; how much more likely was he to do so with the man whose home he now occupied? And about whom he may already have heard certain rumours concerning his important connections?

They repaired to the parlour and sat appreciatively as Jane played the piano. Napoleon asked Betsy whether she liked music, adding: 'You are too young to play yourself, of course.' She wrote that she felt piqued by this and told him she could both play and sing. He requested an offering, so she sang, as well as she could, 'Ye Banks and Braes'. When she had finished he declared it was the prettiest English air he had ever heard.

'It's a Scottish ballad, Your Majesty.'

'Then that accounts for it. Of course it is too pretty to be English! Their music is vile—the worst in the world!'

He enquired if she knew any French songs; for instance, did she know Grétry's 'Vive Henri Quatre'? Betsy had never heard of it. He began to hum, left his seat and strutted about the room, tonelessly singing while pumping his arm in time.

Mrs Balcombe and Jane applauded politely. Very pleased with himself, Napoleon asked Betsy what she thought. She shook her head, reluctant to speak, favouring him with her smile instead. He encouraged her, beaming. He now knew that she was no court flatterer; her opinion could be worth hearing.

She said simply: 'I didn't like it at all!'

'Why ever not?'

'I couldn't make out any tune.'

'No tune?' He tweaked her ear. 'You are just saying that to provoke me.'

'No, sir, I'm just trying to tell the truth.'

No one had ever criticised his singing. Perhaps honesty was not always so delightful. Mrs Balcombe, who had missed most of the exchange, was surprised when their guest made an abrupt move to depart. Betsy observed: 'The emperor retired for the night shortly after my little attempt to amuse him, and this terminated his first day at the Briars.'[15]

At the Porteous lodgings in Jamestown, General Gourgaud finished a desultory meal as he listened to Bertrand's account of the day's events, the unsatisfactory tour of Longwood and the arrangement that had been made at The Briars. That evening he wrote in his journal: 'Bertrand remarks that there are two pretty young ladies at The Briars, and that I shall be able to marry.'[16]

CHAPTER 5

THE PAVILION

I walked past the Consulate Hotel down the steep main street, at the bottom of which the RMS *St Helena*, still at anchor, was framed in the town wall's archway. With some surprise I noted the sign 'Solomon & Company' on a substantial building—the largest island merchant during Napoleon's captivity and apparently still. At the colonnaded post office they were doing the brisk business only possible when a ship was in, selling St Helena's colourful stamps to tourists. In 1815, Joseph Cole was the postmaster in the same building. He shared the office space with William Balcombe, superintendent of public sales for the East India Company and senior partner in their private trading business, Balcombe, Cole & Company.

Although there is a Napoleon Street in Jamestown, it seems few locals waste time thinking about the exiled emperor, who was a disgruntled resident for less than six of the island's rich and varied history of more than five hundred years. A white-bearded Anglican priest with a country parish told me: 'Back in 1815 the Saints flocked to the waterfront. They saw this little man arrive and found him very uninteresting and they've remained uninterested ever since.'

But it is altogether a different matter for visitors to the island. One of the most popular excursions is a charabanc tour of the 'Napoleonic sites', the three French *'domaines'* looked after by the honorary French consul and Napoleonic scholar Michel Dancoisne-Martineau.

I booked for the Napoleonic tour: Longwood House; the empty Tomb where the emperor's corpse was interred for nineteen years before its return to France; and The Briars. I was pleased that the first stop would be the latter, William Balcombe's old property where Bonaparte stayed for two months in the summer-house pavilion.

It was all activity at The Briars, where a guardhouse had been established at the front gates. An oxcart was coming from town with 'the General's' baggage, while two of his followers walked up the steep Sidepath to settle their master into his new premises. The young valet Marchand enjoyed the physical exercise after the long sea voyage. A talented artist, he had purchased a set of paints during the Madeira stopover, and was now exhilarated by the dramatic scenery.[1] The diminutive Count de Las Cases, who lagged behind, was 49 years of age but looked older, with mournful but refined features, a sharp nose, and coarse grey hair tied at the back.

They were questioned by the British captain on duty at The Briars before proceeding to the pavilion. Marchand saw that the Balcombes were going out of their way to make Napoleon comfortable: 'The hostess and her two lovely daughters offered everything that could contribute to the furnishing of the room for the Emperor; I accepted a few chairs, an armchair and a table; what Noverraz was bringing from town would soon allow the Emperor to settle into his usual habits. At the Briars one had to consider oneself to be camping; the Emperor had around him the furnishings of a field tent.'[2] However, Napoleon was accustomed to field tents, having spent more time in them than in palaces.

Las Cases was delighted to see the solitary figure of Napoleon outside the pavilion, gazing at the view, and advanced to salute him.

'Ah,' said the emperor, 'here you are! Why have you not brought your son?'

'Sire,' replied Las Cases, 'the respect, the consideration I owe you prevented me.'

'Oh, you must learn to dispense with that,' said Napoleon. 'Bring your son to me.'[3]

The count's fourteen-year-old son Emmanuel had been removed from his *lycée* to accompany his father and the deposed emperor.

The boy's mother had remained in France, appalled by the prospect of America, let alone St Helena.

Las Cases had a rather grand lineage. A nobleman of the *ancien régime*, with the full title Marie Joseph Emmanuel Auguste Dieudonné, Comte de Las Cases, he was the elder son of a marquis.[4] During the Terror of 1793 he was an obvious candidate for the guillotine and escaped from France. With other desperate aristocrats he had thrown himself into an English coal ship and remembered being treated 'exactly like a cargo of negroes'. They landed on the banks of the Thames a great distance from London and he stumbled on foot to the city.[5]

The count's memoirs describe how he eked out an existence giving French lessons but was rescued from penury by Lady Clavering, a Frenchwoman living with her English baronet husband.[6] In 1802 (during the Peace of Amiens), Las Cases accompanied his employers to France as tutor to their children. Through old connections by then returned to favour, he met Bonaparte, and was soon in thrall to him, becoming convinced that he was 'the most extraordinary man who has appeared for centuries'.[7] He offered his life in service to his hero. In 1804, the Emperor Napoleon appointed him a chamberlain or Councillor of State at his court and made him a Baron of the Empire. Although Las Cases' devotion was unquestioned, many people found it astonishing that he volunteered for exile on St Helena. But there is little doubt that he had a shrewd idea of the value of becoming the deposed emperor's memorialist, and he applied himself seriously to the task, honoured to record the great man's account of how Europe had been won—and so inexplicably lost.

It was now agreed that the count and his son would live with Napoleon at the pavilion, sleeping in the tiny loft space and by day recording a description of his campaigns for the benefit of history. Napoleon himself took a sceptical view of the benefit of history and believed it would do 'what it usually does with those who have won a hundred battles but lost the final one. For what is history, but a fable agreed upon?' But he thought it worth telling some fables of his own.

The count spoke excellent English, a relief for the Balcombes to have an efficient interpreter.

※

William Balcombe and Admiral Cockburn had been busy trying to sort out the financial and logistical details. Balcombe informed his patron in England that he had become the first Englishman in history to entertain Napoleon Bonaparte as a house guest, which was braggadocio of the highest order: 'He is very affable and pleasant, plays at cards with us and speaks French with my Daughters, amuses himself about the garden and appears in very good spirits . . .'

In the rest of his letter of 20 October to Tyrwhitt he quickly got down to business. He explained that the admiral had recommended to the British government that he should have an adequate salary for supplying Bonaparte's wants: 'I assure you that I have enough to do to supply his Table and it is a very arduous task to do it at this place. Sir G. Cockburn has advised me to write to you to recommend to Government something handsome may be allowed me per Annum for my trouble. I should be satisfied if they were to give 7½ per cent upon what his expences amount to per Annum. The Admiral says he would fix a salary here but he is sure you will be able to get me more than he is authorised to give. I feel extremely grateful for your kindness and shall do everything in my power to deserve it.'[8]

Cockburn meanwhile was writing an official despatch to John Wilson Croker, Secretary to the Admiralty (unaware that Croker was privy to recent developments through Dr O'Meara's letters to the clerk Finlaison). He asked the Lords of the Admiralty to advise on 'the expenses to be incurred for the maintenance of General Bonaparte and his followers on this island'.

The admiral was in a quandary. His instructions, while exasperatingly vague, specified 'that, as far as it may prove practicable, such comforts and establishment as are usually enjoyed by officers bearing the rank of full General should be allowed to General Bonaparte, and a table of eight covers kept for him, with everything else in a similar ratio'. He was obliged to do this without a budget allocated by government. The French themselves, as far as he knew (they had managed to deceive him), had carried little apart from some silver plate, a handsome set of Sèvres porcelain and a negligible amount of money, the last since confiscated and transmitted to Treasury. In the circumstances, Cockburn proposed drawing such sums as were needed from the island's commissary. He explained that to enable him to do this at the cheapest rate and avoid being exploited, 'I have engaged a Mr Balcombe, a respectable inhabitant, strongly recommended to me by Colonel Beatson before I quitted England, and by the Governor since my arrival, as most conversant and efficient in such matters, to purvey for me, and generally to assist me in procuring the several things it becomes necessary for me to purchase upon the island'.[9]

Bonaparte had asked for a carriage, arguing that this offered the only exercise he could take (although his feet actually offered better exercise equipment). The admiral promised to enquire if Governor Wilks had a spare conveyance, and sent to the Cape for some horses.

Cockburn instituted the new shipping regulations decreed by the Admiralty. Foreign vessels were forbidden to anchor in the shipping roads; if they attempted it, they would be fired upon. All fishing boats, rowing boats and other small vessels owned by St Helena residents were to be ashore between six in the evening and six in the morning or risk all hands being shot. Two British frigates were permanently at anchor off the port and two brigs circled the island night and day. 'My cruisers,' Cockburn reported, 'are so well posted round the island that the devil himself could not get out of it.'[10]

The drawbridge in the town wall was raised at sunset, so cutting off access to the sea, and a general curfew instituted. Locals were forbidden to stir from their houses except in daylight hours. It caused little inconvenience at The Briars as they rarely went out at night; if they did, it was necessary to obtain the governor's permission, easily granted to any 'respectable inhabitant'.[11]

The fortifications were greatly extended, with cannon placed at regular intervals along the cliffs. An officer remarked: 'Sir George is at his old work of fortifying ... He is building a redoubt at Egg Island, about half a mile from St Helena, to defend the bay or beach ... Indeed there would be great difficulty landing anywhere on the island (but just at James's Town) from the tremendous surf. To the northward of the island it is always impossible; and to the westward, except James's and Lemon Valleys, you see nothing but an abrupt rock rising out of the water.'[12]

Captain James Mackay and the sentries guarding The Briars camped in a tent at the front gate and were relatively unobtrusive.

The French had few restrictions on their movements during daylight hours—with the exception of Bonaparte, who was to be accompanied on outings beyond the gates by an English officer at all times, and his visitors were subject to clearance. When General Gourgaud came up from Jamestown on 19 October, he was offended to be questioned before admission to the grounds.

Betsy wrote very little about Gourgaud in her *Recollections*. He wrote much more about her in his fascinating and scurrilous *Journal*, written in code and never intended for publication. Before actually meeting her he had been intrigued to hear of pretty Betsy Balcombe, an English rose. It seems that on encountering a mere cheeky schoolgirl, his fantasies turned to disdain.

Gaspard Gourgaud was born in 1783 to a court musician and a domestic at Louis XVI's palace. As a boy he saw the King carted off to the guillotine, a frightening experience which may have contributed to his emotional instability. After military college he gained a commission as an artillery officer; he was wounded at Austerlitz, fought bravely at Pultusk, and for his courage and loyalty was made a baron in the new Napoleonic peerage. Having been promoted to imperial ordnance officer, he joined the emperor's carriage when they left Moscow, so missing the worst of the Grande Armée's terrible retreat. On the voyage to St Helena it became evident that he worshipped his former commander with histrionic extravagance. Engravings portray him with a protruding upper lip, rendering the man an unfortunate sneering expression.

During Gourgaud's visit to The Briars, Napoleon suggested a walk. He wished to see something of the nearby countryside, although it angered him that this was only possible accompanied by an English guard. Betsy and Jane were invited to join the expedition and the four set off at a brisk pace, while Captain Mackay and the sergeant followed at a discreet distance. Napoleon chose to grandly ignore their presence.

They strolled into a meadow where cows belonging to The Briars' milking herd were grazing between the palm trees.[13] In Betsy's account, one of the beasts started behaving strangely, lowing and bellowing, swinging her head from side to side in a deranged fashion. 'Look at that poor brute,' said Napoleon. 'Going mad with the heat just as I am.'

The moment the cow saw the party, she put her head down, her tail up, bucked and advanced *au pas de charge* at the emperor. We are told he made a skilful and rapid retreat, despite his plumpness, leaping over a low stone wall. Gourgaud, to Betsy's astonishment, drew his sword—remarkably, these weapons had been returned to the French—and advanced towards the cow, exclaiming: 'This is the second time I have saved the emperor's life!'

Captain Mackay came running but the cow had lost interest. It turned away and resumed cropping grass. Napoleon joked to Betsy that the beast was a British agent: 'She wishes to save the English government the expense and trouble of keeping me.'[14]

The Balcombes came to inspect the pavilion and its new furnishings: an oriental rug, silver platters and tureens, the campaign bed with green silk curtains and floss mattress, and an elaborate silver washstand from the Élysée-Bourbon palace.[15]

Betsy was intrigued by two miniatures on the wall. One was a portrait of the emperor's son as a baby in his cradle, his tiny hand supporting a globe, the banner of France and helmet of Mars behind him. Napoleon told her this signified that his son would be a great warrior and one day rule the world. In the other, the boy was an angelic child with a nimbus of golden curls, a typical blond Habsburg in the arms of his mother, the plump Empress Marie Louise. Betsy said bluntly that she did not like that one as much as the other.

In her later account, Napoleon confided that the empress was an amiable creature and a very good wife; she would have followed him to St Helena, bringing their son with her, if only she had been allowed. However, by then he may have known—perhaps not, but it was an open secret in Europe—that Marie Louise was pregnant to the eye-patch-wearing courtly seducer Count von Neipperg, and his son was in the Viennese palace of Schönbrunn, effectively a prisoner of his grandfather, Francis I of Austria.[16] But it was important for Napoleon to emphasise his connection with the great royal house in order to argue the illegitimacy of his imprisonment and the dynastic prospects of his son, known in France as *'l'Aiglon'*— 'the Eaglet'.

Napoleon made a considerable effort to charm the Balcombes and in turn seemed charmed by them.[17] The company of children brought out the best in him, and the mountainous rocky locale must have stirred memories of his Corsican childhood, climbing granite slopes with a tribe of brothers and sisters among whom he soon won the position of leader.[18] He had been kind and affectionate with his stepchildren, Hortense and Eugene, adored his own son, and he could tolerate and laugh at the familiarities of Betsy, Jane and their two small brothers, for they posed no threat. With children he did not need to impose distance or insist on rank, although this was rigidly observed with adults. For Mrs Balcombe he felt both respect and attraction, given her uncanny resemblance to Josephine. But his friendship with William Balcombe would not have rested simply on that man's engaging and affable personality and his ability to furnish a good table.

One of the world's greatest strategists rarely wasted energy on being pleasant merely for the sake of civility, and certainly not at this nadir of his career. His principal motivation, just as it had been on the island of Elba, would have been to escape from the hellhole of imprisonment and resume the reins of power. He was always alert to the person or situation likely to offer him advantage. He perfectly understood the value of long campaigns and of building allies where it counted; the historian Philip Dwyer has observed: 'For Bonaparte, people were pawns in his political and military calculations, to be dispensed with if they could not be useful.'[19] The proprietor of The Briars was potentially extremely useful.

Bonaparte's best hope of release from the island to a less restricted situation (from where he could plan his resurgence) was the intervention of the Prince Regent. He would have recognised the importance of the patronage and affection Balcombe received from Sir Thomas Tyrwhitt, an intimate of the prince. The connection was well known on the island; Balcombe was inclined to boast of it himself. Tyrwhitt's name must have been known to Bonaparte, who had a remarkable memory. From his time as First Consul he would have remembered Tyrwhitt's diplomatic visit to Paris in 1801 as the secretary and emissary of the prince, bringing gifts of ornamental trees and shrubs for his wife Josephine's celebrated garden at Malmaison.[20] Without question he was aware of Tyrwhitt and his close relationship with the Regent. Once his exile on St Helena began, or even on shipboard before he arrived—for some of the officers and seamen had been to the island before—he would have learned that this man was the patron, protector and friend of the merchant William Balcombe.

This offers an explanation as to why Bonaparte expressed interest in occupying the little summer house of The Briars *before* he had even inspected it, and, when Balcombe offered him the whole property including the main house, the former emperor maintained a resolute preference for residing at the uncomfortable pavilion. What this allowed was the possibility of daily interaction with the Balcombes and whatever advantage might accrue from that.

CHAPTER 6

BONEY'S LITTLE PAGES

The charabanc tour of the Napoleonic sites was in a converted 1929 Chevrolet truck, rejuvenated in 1945 with a Bedford motor. The driver and guide was Colin Corker, a cheerful, entrepreneurial St Helenian, who had fitted out his eccentric vehicle with twelve seats and some plastic sheeting for when it rained. In the misty uplands beyond Longwood it usually rained.

Our first stop was The Briars, William Balcombe's old property, reached by the Sidepath, one of two steep roads out of town hacked from the rocky slopes by slaves. The Briars, a shelf of soft land perched above the fork of the Jamestown ravine, was now the name for a suburb of new houses; Balcombe's old Indian-style villa was gone, destroyed by termites.

The earliest mention of a house 'of some size' called the 'Bryers' on 59 acres of land was in 1768. Balcombe bought the property in 1807, changed the spelling and constructed the pavilion. After he left the island, the property fell into the hands of the East India Company; they planted mulberry bushes and attempted to establish a silkworm farm. Like other attempts to create a viable economic mainstay for St Helena—including lacemaking, coffee and flax—the silk industry failed.

In 1901, The Briars became the headquarters for the cable and wireless station. In 1914, in photographs taken by Graham Balfour, a cousin of Robert Louis Stevenson, it appeared to have been extended into a handsome two-storey villa with at least six upstairs rooms. In 1957, an Australian, William Balcombe's great-granddaughter, Dame Mabel Brookes from Melbourne, visited St Helena. By then the termites had done their worst: The Briars' main house had become a crumbling ruin, only the back quarters and cellar remaining.[1] Two years later it was demolished to build an ugly concrete-block house for the cable and wireless station manager.[2]

However, the Pavilion survived—now capitalised in honour of its important former occupant. Because of her family's connection with Napoleon, Brookes purchased The Briars Pavilion, and two years later, in a ceremony at Malmaison, outside Paris, she deeded it to the French nation. Since then it has been one of the three French domains of St Helena.

The prisoner's habits during the two months he stayed at The Briars proved to be simple and orderly in the extreme. His campaign bed was set up in the pavilion's one room, and Las Cases and his son would retire each night up the ladder to the two tiny garret spaces, where it was impossible to stand upright. Marchand slept on a mattress guarding the pavilion's doorway and wrote that his master's comfort was his chief concern: 'The table was placed in the middle of the room with a rug over it; it was used as a desk and a dining table, as the room itself was a bedroom, work room and dining room. It was impossible to be more restricted than the Emperor was, but he was free to move about so the rest could be overlooked. A dresser was offered to me with such insistence by Mr Balcombe that I accepted it. I spread out on it the Emperor's travel case, which, once opened, adorned the room. I sent to town for the silver washbasin from the Elysée-Bourbon palace.'[3]

The usual hour for rising was eight o'clock, and Napoleon seldom took anything but a cup of coffee before resuming the dictation of his memoirs. The garden of the pavilion with its view of the waterfall was a delightful place to work. He and Las Cases sat at an iron table in the coolness of a grape arbour while Napoleon relived his military campaigns, the details of his battles and his civil reforms. He aimed for a sequential order, beginning with the Siege of Toulouse, the Italian campaigns, the occupation of Egypt and then the history of the Consulate; however, he kept returning to the subject of Waterloo, which was a constant irritant, a scab he had to pick. He could not conceive how it had ended in defeat; his tactics should have worked! The little count covered reams of paper with his spidery calligraphy, confident that every page was money in his pocket. Back in the pavilion his son worked industriously, making fair copies of the work completed.

They broke for lunch at one and for dinner at nine. For the first week, meals were delivered by slaves from the boarding house in Jamestown, where, according to Dr O'Meara, there was now 'a suitable table in the French style provided by Mr Balcombe'.[4] However, the food always arrived cold. 'It was obvious that the Emperor would live very poorly as a result of this arrangement,' wrote Marchand. 'Count de Las Cases and his son had to do without table napkins the first day, as the table linen had not yet arrived.'[5] Not appreciating the difficulties in importing livestock and vegetables, the French grumbled constantly about the fare, none more stridently than Las Cases on behalf of his master: 'The bread and wine are not such as we have been accustomed to, and are so bad that we loathe to touch them. Water, coffee, butter, oil, and other articles, are either not to be procured, or are scarcely fit for use.'[6]

But Napoleon and Las Cases did not complain directly to Balcombe, thus preserving good relations. One evening Napoleon made a suggestion to Marchand: 'he said he had a butler and a pantry chef in town; one of the two could be with him and, without disturbing Mrs Balcombe, could take advantage of the room where the slaves cooked their food. In this way he could have a hot dinner.'[7] The Balcombes agreed to the arrangement, and two days later, Le Page, the chef, and Pierron, the pantry head, arrived. They were given the use of the slaves' kitchen and were accommodated in the servants' quarters. Cipriani the butler remained in town and cooperated with Balcombe to cater for the French people in rented accommodation, while sending up daily provisions for the pavilion.

At first Le Page failed to understand the limitations island living imposed, and startled the governor's council secretary, Thomas Brooke, with his extravagance: 'In a place where fresh beef was so precious as to have occasioned restrictions upon its consumption, it may well be conceived that sensations of no ordinary nature were excited at a demand from the *maître-d'hotel* of the Ex-Emperor, a few days after his arrival, for *four* bullocks, in order to make *a dish of brains!* ... Sir George Cockburn explained the objections to its being complied with, and the refusal is understood to have been received with perfect good humour.'[8]

'We understood that the time for self-denial had arrived,' lamented Marchand. He was relieved when the silver and table linen were brought, so 'the service for the Emperor's table took on a regularity it had lacked so far'.[9] Napoleon dined in the evening with the count and his son, and then, because space was at a premium, the man accustomed to the luxuries of the Tuileries obligingly vacated the little pavilion so Marchand and the cook could take their meal there.

Many in the 53rd Regiment were shocked by the deficiencies in their own food supplies, even more limited than before because of the new security arrangements. An officer wrote: 'This island supplies itself with nothing but vegetables, and depends entirely on imports for subsistence. Cutting off all trade prevents any supply to the inhabitants, but what they are allowed to purchase from the public stores (the same quantity as the ration to the troops), the fishing boats not being allowed to fish at night, which was the best time altogether.'[10] A soldier expressed the widely held view that the prisoner was to blame.[11]

But for Balcombe, catering for the prisoner was the opportunity of a lifetime. Napoleon's favourite dish—and therefore that of his retinue—was chicken. Balcombe owned a second property, Ross (or Rose) Cottage, with a few acres of land and soon established a poultry farm with 400 hens, some ducks, geese and guinea fowl. He was now in control, from production to market.

At The Briars, Napoleon began to relax, even to give the appearance of positively enjoying himself. He had been through the storm of war and the humiliation of defeat, always participating, action followed hard by reaction. Now he had time to analyse that bewildering defeat that had brought him to this, the most remote exile ever suffered by any head of state. He had no intention of adjusting to the situation; he would devise how best to escape from it—and the Balcombe family might just offer an avenue. Meanwhile, surprisingly, there was some pleasure to be had.

He may have believed he had the measure of his host—a bluff, hearty man alert for his own personal advancement—but Napoleon had not yet divined the full extent of Balcombe's mysterious influence in London, or the reason for it. The whole family were amiable and he joined them some evenings for games of whist or musical entertainments; the two daughters were attractive, and although Betsy was presumptuous, she made him laugh; the two small boys were lively and playful, clambering over him, fiddling with the toggles of his coat and the gleaming star of his Légion d'Honneur, and four-year-old Alexander reminded him of his own son in a way that was both painful and endearing. He asked Marchand to make a tiny cart for the boys; to their delight it was pulled across the floor by four scurrying mice.

In an article published in the *Quarterly Review* the following January, Napoleon was portrayed as not nearly so pleasant at these family card games: 'When Las Casses [sic] put down four gold Napoleons for markers, the youngest of the ladies, who had never seen any of that coin before, took up one, and asked what it was. Buonaparte instantly, with more haste than was consistent with politeness, snatched it out of her hand and exclaimed, with a tone half of vexation and half of triumph, "*Ne voyez-vous pas que c'est moi?*," ["Can't you see that it is me?"] pointing to the impression with his finger.'[12]

Betsy made no mention of this in her *Recollections*, although she did note another card game incident: 'One day Alexander took up a pack of cards, on which was the usual figure of the Great Mogul. The child held it up to Napoleon, saying, "See Bony, this is you."' In her account, Napoleon failed to understand what was meant by calling him 'Bony' and asked why the English gave him that name; he knew they called him many things, but why this one? Betsy explained that it was an abbreviation, short for Bonaparte. Las Cases offered a literal translation: 'It means a thin, bony person—*un homme osseux.*' Napoleon laughed and protested, '*Je ne suis pas osseux*' ('I am not bony'), which Betsy thought he certainly never could have been, even in his young days: 'His hand was the fattest and prettiest in the world; his knuckles dimpled like a baby's.'[13] So the Balcombe children were given permission to call him 'Bony' if they wished.

Napoleon's daily dictation in the grape arbour, involving the recall and justification of complex battle actions—and much creative fiction—was frequently interrupted by the younger girl's arrival. Her sister Jane rarely intruded except by invitation, but Betsy felt perfectly at liberty to turn up at any time. One day she was accompanied by the admiral's huge lolloping dog, Tom Pipes. She lured him into the goldfish pond, where he splashed about, plunging vainly after fish. When he scrambled out, he rushed to greet his old shipboard companion, vigorously shaking water all over him and his papers, just as Betsy had planned that he would.

Las Cases was appalled. What irritated him even more than Betsy's familiarity was the way that Napoleon, who always insisted on strict formal etiquette from his entourage and staff, seemed endlessly indulgent of her impertinences. On one occasion she deliberately jogged his elbow when he was making an impression of a rare coin and the hot wax spilled and burned his hand; another time she snatched his dictation papers from his desk and danced around the garden flourishing them, calling out: 'I shall keep these and then I shall find out all your secrets!'[14] The count warned the errant girl to have some respect: 'You need to understand you are talking to the man who governed the world. Once a mere decree from him sufficed to overthrow thrones and create kings. I remember the timidity and embarrassment with which he was approached by ministers and officials; the anxieties and fears of ambassadors, princes and even kings.'[15]

But Napoleon was charmed by this mischievous, irreverent sprite of a girl. There had been little laughter since he boarded the *Bellerophon*, but he laughed often now when she was about. Ever since he had risen to power, he had been surrounded by courtiers and by women who were, on the whole, docile, acquiescent and flattered his ego; he had known graceful adolescent girls such as Laure Permon (the later Madame Junot) and his stepdaughter Hortense—they were the kind of *jeune fille* of whom he approved. For her part, Josephine could be fiery—she was famous for her tantrums—but had never challenged his ultimate authority. 'You must submit to all my whims,' he had told her. 'I have the right to reply to all your complaints by an eternal *moi!* I am a being apart.' His second wife, Marie Louise, young and pliable, also accepted his dictum that 'I am not a man like other men and the laws of morality or custom cannot be applied to me'.[16] He was known to detest outspoken and intellectually brilliant women such as the author Germaine de Staël.

Betsy Balcombe 'represented a type which was new to the Emperor', wrote Lord Rosebery, prime minister of Great Britain for one short term and obsessed with Napoleon Bonaparte for far longer. She was 'a high-spirited hoyden, who said and did whatever occurred to her on the spur of the moment. The pranks that she played ... must certainly have been in the nature of a piquant novelty to Napoleon.'[17] The girl was honest, blunt in her opinions, a chatterer, loud, bold, giddy, dizzy, positively infuriating much of the time, but she was also enchantingly pretty and full of fun. She simply brightened Napoleon's day.

That summer of 1815, the Balcombes found themselves besieged by visitors. People called on the slightest of pretexts and lingered in the garden in the hope of catching a glimpse of the famous guest. A Scottish gentleman from a Company ship in port wrote to his father in Edinburgh that he had visited 'Mr Balcombe's country house' in the hope of seeing Napoleon: 'He is occupied during the day in writing the history of his life, and the evening is devoted to walking in the garden with his Generals and his society at Mr Balcombe's. The only chance strangers have of conversing with him, is by getting an introduction to Mr B. and stepping in, as if by chance in the evening. Our Captain and several of our passengers, by this means, have had long conversations with him; he talks upon every subject but those relating to politics, which he seems very desirous to avoid. He behaved with great politeness to the ladies, who have been echoing his praises ever since. We, for I had a companion with me, tied our horses to a tree, and slipt behind a bush, a little way from the walk where he was to pass; he passed several times within a few feet of us: we had a most distinct view of him.'[18]

Only on rare occasions—if the visitor was influential with the British government, a naval officer or a pretty female—did Bonaparte allow an actual introduction. But he warned Betsy that he had 'a peculiar horror of ugly women'.

Catherine Younghusband, the attractive 35-year-old wife of Captain Robert Younghusband of the 53rd Regiment, had recently arrived on the island. She was charming and accomplished, a competent portrait painter, fluent in Italian and French, and ambitious. She was determined to meet the great Bonaparte and was 'soon making social calls, with eight-year-old Emily, on the wife and daughters of the merchant William Balcombe ... a stratagem which shortly brought success. Napoleon, seeing an elegant lady in the garden with a young daughter, could not resist coming out demanding "*Qui est cette Dame?*"'[19] Catherine's account of the meeting was published in *Blackwood's Magazine*: 'The two young ladies, who were respectively about thirteen and fifteen years of age, and were quite familiar with the Ex-Emperor, ran playfully towards him, dragging me forward by the hand, and saying to him, "This lady is the mother of the little girl who pleased you the other day by singing Italian canzonets." Upon this he made me a bow, which I returned by a low and reverential curtsy, feeling, at the same time, a little confused at this sudden and unceremonious introduction.'

Catherine gave this description of the girls to her aunt, Lady Roche, in Ireland: 'These two unsophisticated young Ladies, who are quite schoolgirls recently arrived from England, are not in the least in awe of him, and call him "Boney" which amuses and astonishes him beyond measure, their behaviour being in curious contrast to the profound respect paid to him by the Generals and Ladies of his suite. He laughs at their fearless vivacity, corrects their bad French & plays at Cards in the evening with the whole Family at the Briars for Sugar Plums.'[20]

However, apart from a few favoured visitors, Napoleon found it infuriating to be one of the 'sights' of St Helena. One afternoon when he was relaxing in the grape arbour, he once again found himself the object of scrutiny by strangers and escaped in the only direction he could, by leaping into the prickly-pear hedge. He was rescued by Marchand; not only did he suffer the indignity of torn clothing and scratched legs, but Dr O'Meara needed to be called to extract dozens of sharp thorns from the ample imperial buttocks.

The Leggs, a neighbouring farming family, came to visit the Balcombes, and were entertained in the parlour. Their daughter, a few years younger than Betsy, confided that she was terrified of Boney the bogeyman and begged to be warned if he came near. 'Let's see,' said Betsy, and headed out the door and skipped over to the arbour. She intimated the little girl's fear to Napoleon and asked him to come to the house. He followed, surprisingly amenable, leaving Las Cases glaring. On the way, 'the former ruler of half the world' mussed his hair so it stood up in spikes. He pushed past Betsy into the parlour, contorting his features hideously, roaring like a savage beast (he later said it was his Cossack howl) as he rushed at the little girl. The child screamed so violently that Mrs Balcombe feared she was having a hysterical fit and shepherded her out of the room. Farmer Legg and his wife stared in shock. Napoleon stumbled back to the garden, choking with laughter. Between splutters, Betsy admitted that she used to be afraid of him as well. 'When I made this confession, he tried to frighten me as he had poor little Miss Legg, by brushing up his hair and distorting his features; but he looked more grotesque than horrible, and I only laughed at him.'[21]

Betsy's good looks, remarked upon in most memoirs produced from the exile (while they have little to say about her less advantaged sister Jane), no doubt allowed more tolerance of her wayward personality. In a plainer girl her behaviour would have been viewed as mere vulgarity—as it was by Las Cases, impervious to her appeal. Indeed, there may have been a sexual element to Napoleon's attraction. Her youth would not necessarily have forbidden such thoughts—his own mother had married at fourteen years of age.[22] But his relationship with Betsy remained chaste.

She was at that teetering stage of adolescence, her starched pinafore taut, her eyes bright with curiosity and impudence, not yet cautious from setbacks and disappointment, not too knowing from experience. There is just one likeness of her from that time, and it is barely a likeness at all, a French lithograph of her and her sister, almost certainly drawn by Marchand. The girls, in pale flowing dresses with long pantaloons underneath, offer flowers to Napoleon. The face of the shorter one is obscured by a large straw hat trailing ribbons.[23]

The portrait of Betsy that is commonly reproduced—and is displayed for tourists at The Briars Pavilion—is of a conventionally beautiful young woman with a heart-shaped face and large blue eyes, her golden hair elaborately arranged, ringlets brushing her shoulders. Her dark dress is daringly *décolleté*. It is not the portrait of an adolescent girl, and nor was it painted by Catherine Younghusband, as has been suggested.[24] It was adapted from a photograph of Betsy taken by G.W. Melliss in 1857, when she was Mrs Abell, a matron of 55.[25] In a sketch from the photograph, her pose, dress and coiffure are almost identical. The portrait may have been executed by the Victorian artist Alfred Tidey, who also painted *The Music Party* in the 1850s, portraying Mrs Abell and her daughter at the piano in their London house.[26]

Admiral Cockburn despatched two warships to take possession of the bare and unpopulated Ascension Island to foil any rescue attempt from there. He wrote to Croker at the Admiralty that he was impatient for the work at Longwood to be completed, as General Bonaparte had 'expressed himself more dissatisfied with the lot decreed him than he did before . . . nothing shall ever be wanting on my part to render the General's detention here as little afflictive and irksome to him as possible, so long as the paramount object of his personal security be not compromised'.[27]

A large tent or marquee was pitched on the lawn at The Briars' Pavilion to add more living space; it abutted against the permanent building as an extension of it and could be entered directly through one of the doors. It was a gift from Colonel Bingham, a veteran of the Peninsular War, Wellington's lieutenant and now commander of all the troops on the island. Bonaparte was pleased: 'One soldier understands another.'

Cipriani the butler moved up from Jamestown, and he and Marchand spent the morning rearranging furniture. The marquee was divided into two compartments as study and dining room. The pavilion was assigned as Napoleon's bedroom, containing the campaign bed and the silver washbasin on a stand opposite. The Las Cases father and son were now crammed together at night in one of the tiny loft spaces, and Cipriani was in the other.

Cipriani, a fellow Corsican, had a long connection with the Buonaparte family; his wife was currently in Rome with the matriarch, Madame Mère, while his son was in service to Madame's brother,

Cardinal Fesch. Cipriani had been in exile with Napoleon on Elba and had helped facilitate his escape. A man of few words, alert and watchful, he occupied a special position in the household and was generally believed to be his master's personal spy. He visited the shops and taverns and picked up information. Napoleon had complete confidence in him and showed it in a way that aroused jealousy among some of his courtiers.[28]

At last Napoleon was in a position to entertain. Betsy and Jane were to be the first dinner guests. The girls arrived at the marquee on the stroke of nine and found Las Cases and Emmanuel standing stiffly to attention. The emperor entered with a formality that astonished Betsy, the star of his Légion d'Honneur flashing in the candlelight.[29] Once seated, Napoleon began teasing the girls about their nation's fondness for roast beef and stodgy plum pudding. He opined that English people were gluttons and drank far too much. Betsy responded that his countrymen lived on frogs. With no thought for decorum she jumped up from the table, ran down to the main house and returned a few moments later, waving a caricature from a magazine. It was labelled 'A Frenchman's dinner' and showed a long, lean Frenchman, his mouth open and a frog on his tongue, ready to jump down his throat. Napoleon laughed and pinched her ear.

The disapproval of Las Cases and his son was palpable. But Napoleon saw an opportunity to repay Betsy in kind. He had joked before that she would make a suitable wife for Emmanuel, the fourteen-year-old '*le petit* Las Cases', and enjoyed her indignation: 'Nothing enraged me so much; I could not bear to be considered such a child, and particularly at that moment, for there was a ball in prospect, to which I had great hopes Papa would allow me to go, and I knew that his objection would be founded on my being too young.'[30] Napoleon insisted that young Emmanuel should kiss the girl and clasped her hands while the boy did as he was told. Betsy squirmed and, the moment her hands were free, boxed the ears of *le petit* Las Cases.

As was his habit, Napoleon ate his meal quickly and abruptly terminated it, pushing his chair away from the table. Protocol obliged them all to put down their cutlery and rise to their feet. It had been arranged that after dinner they would join the senior Balcombes at the house for a game of whist. The party descended to the main house for the card game, walking in single file down the steep, narrow steps at the side. Napoleon led the way, followed by Las Cases, then his son, with Betsy bringing up the rear behind her sister. She lingered about ten yards behind, then ran with all her force onto Jane, who fell with extended hands onto *le petit* Las Cases, who in turn was thrown upon his father. The count, to his dismay and embarrassment, was pushed against Napoleon, who stumbled and just managed to stay upright.

Betsy hooted with laughter at the confusion. But Las Cases was thunderstruck at the insult to his sovereign and his own loss of dignity. He seized the girl by the shoulders and pushed her violently onto the rocky bank. She burst into tears and cried: 'Oh! Sir, he is hurting me!'

'Never mind,' Napoleon replied, '*ne pleurs pas* [don't cry]—I will hold him while you punish him.' He held onto his distinguished chamberlain while Betsy boxed the man's ears until he begged for mercy. Napoleon released Las Cases, but only for more taunting, ordering him to run; if he could not run faster than the girl, he deserved to be beaten again. The little count skipped, breathless, around the lawn, frantic and humiliated, with Betsy after him, Napoleon laughing and clapping his hands. Of this episode Betsy concluded, unsurprisingly: 'Las Cases never liked me after this adventure, and used to call me a rude hoyden.'[31]

Perhaps Napoleon enjoyed these antics. But doubtless there was calculation on his part even amid the fun and silly games. He knew that accounts of them, received in London and even reported in *The Times*, made him seem sympathetic, humanised him: 'Mr Balcombe has two smart young daughters, who talk the French language fluently, and to whom he is very much attached; he styles them his little pages. There is a number of little stories of the innocent freedoms they take, and how highly he is diverted by it.'[32]

CHAPTER 7

THE FRENCH SUITE

I hung back behind the tour group and decided to take in the rest of the excursion on another day. At the side of the Pavilion I came down a flight of narrow stone steps leading to the garden—the same steep steps where Betsy had created havoc. The garden felt drowsy and peaceful, still dominated by two great yew trees and a date palm from the Balcombes' time, but there were no fish in the small dank pond where the dog Tom Pipes had splashed about. Where the villa with its long, colonnaded verandah had stood there was a graceless concrete-block building and beyond it some rusting scaffolding and old cable drums in the grass, the remains of the cable and wireless headquarters.

The canaries and Java sparrows Betsy described—brought by East India Company ships—had gone, but Indian mynahs flittered about in squabbling, fussy numbers. A former resident of The Briars was responsible for the preponderance of these drab little creatures all over the island: in 1868, Miss Phoebe Moss brought a cage of six mynahs from England and released them in The Briars' garden, imagining they might feast on the invasive white ants. The crumbling ruin that the house became testified to the fact that they did not.

Wandering across the grass, I picked up something that projected, shining, from a low rock wall—a curved shard of blue and white porcelain, a tiny piece of a cup, fragmented images of a teahouse and a fisherman in a boat, the willow pattern. It was probably part of a tea set brought from China on an East Indiaman. Perhaps Napoleon once drank from the cup. Or Madame Bertrand on one of her visits. I slipped it into my handbag.

On 21 October, a carriage arrived, bringing General Gourgaud, the Bertrands and the Montholons from the boarding house in town to see the emperor's accommodation at The Briars.

Lieutenant-General Henri Gatien, Comte de Bertrand, was, at the age of 42, a military man of vast experience, admired for his bravery and moral integrity. As the former grand marshal at the Tuileries palace, he was the most important person to have gone into exile with Napoleon, who said of him: 'Bertrand is henceforth identified with my fate, he has become historical.'[1] It was a sacrifice he volunteered for himself but imposed on his wife Fanny and their three small children.[2] However, he had no choice but to leave France: he had been proscribed from re-entering the country and knew that a death sentence would follow.[3] Marchand observed that Bertrand 'cared little about the judgement against him, but it was not the same for the Countess, who not only feared for her husband, but for the future of her children as well'.[4]

Betsy considered the Countess Bertrand the most distinguished woman she had ever seen, tall and upright in her bearing, her dress of the best Parisian quality but without ostentation. 'I always thought every one else sank into insignificance when she appeared; and yet her features were not regular, and she had no strict pretensions to beauty, but the expressions on her face were very intellectual, and her bearing queen-like and dignified.'[5] Mrs Balcombe found her gracious and was glad to converse in English, which Fanny spoke fluently, having been partly educated in England. The British side of her family claimed descent from the Plantagenets and Charles II.

Françoise-Elisabeth (Fanny) Dillon was born on 24 July 1785 at a French chateau close to the Belgian border, although the first few years of her life were spent in the West Indies.[6] Her grandfather Henry was an Irish peer who served in the military service of France's *ancien régime*, as did her late father, the Honourable General Arthur Dillon, who was made a count of the French nobility.[7] Most British Roman Catholics were prohibited from serving as officers in the

British army or Royal Navy by the Test Act of 1673. Fanny's father continued a century-long family tradition by committing to France as the commander of the Régiment de Dillon, part of the famous Irish Brigades founded in 1690 that fought with France in many wars in Europe, India and America. He served with distinction against the English during the American War of Independence and in the West Indies. Fanny's mother, Laure, was from a Martinique planter family and was a cousin of Josephine de Beauharnais, the future empress.[8]

A revolutionary tribunal condemned Arthur Dillon to death on 13 April 1794, and the following day he was sent to the guillotine together with seventeen other condemned persons, some of them distinguished by birth and others by crime. They were conveyed in common carts to the Place de la Révolution, where a crowd awaited them.[9] Fanny was nine years old at the time of her father's execution and was deeply traumatised by the horror; she grieved for him and remained a committed monarchist.

In 1795, Fanny's mother escaped with her to England. But with the advent of the Consulate, they felt confident they could return to France. Josephine, wife of First Consul Bonaparte, took an interest in Fanny, her attractive young relative who shared a Martinique background, and set about finding a good match for her.[10] Napoleon's loyal aide-de-camp, General Henri Gatien Bertrand, was smitten with the young woman. He has been described as 'a little man, bald and thin, not much of a personality, a good engineer, an indifferent general but not lacking in courage; of unquestionable honesty, of quick understanding, of unconquerable obstinacy and of the best moral character'.[11] Fanny was unimpressed and rebuffed his approaches. Bertrand, about to be made a divisional general and a Count of the Empire, was, according to another French historian, 'an eminently marriageable man, by his position, his military bravery and competence, and by his moral qualities. But he had been living as a celibate. For two years he sighed in vain after the beautiful Fanny Dillon.'[12] Napoleon, returning from Bayonne, ordered Fanny to settle for his aide-de-camp. She protested: 'What, Sire, Bertrand ... Bertrand! Imitator of the Pope by his mode of life!' 'That is enough, Fanny,' Napoleon told her bluntly as he left the room.[13]

In the end she had no option. Napoleon had often complained, 'Too many of my generals married when they were corporals,' resenting some of the vulgar officers' wives at his receptions. He was determined that Bertrand should have the refined woman he desired. The couple were married in 1808—Fanny was 23 and her husband twelve years older—with Napoleon sending directives from the Erfurt battlefield, for 'the great man had found time to rule on the most minute details of the wedding of his favourite aide-de-camp'.[14] The emperor was lavish with wedding presents: a grand home and surrounding park, and for the bride 'a dowry of 200,000 francs in shares in the Loing canal, diamonds to the value of 50,000 francs and trousseau costing 30,000 francs'.[15] Bertrand and Fanny became accustomed to grandeur.

It is small wonder that the Balcombes found the Countess Bertrand impressive. With memories of the luxuries of palace life behind her, Fanny and her husband now crowded into Napoleon's tiny pavilion with the other visitors. Fanny had brought a gift with her: a miniature of the Empress Josephine, her second cousin. As Napoleon held the cameo portrait of his dead ex-wife, Betsy watched on, touched by the expression on his face: 'He gazed at it with the greatest emotion for a considerable time without speaking. At last, he exclaimed it was the most perfect likeness he had ever seen of her, and told Madame Bertrand he would keep it, which he did, until his death.'[16]

General Charles Tristan de Montholon was a decade younger than Bertrand, handsome but effete, elegant and particular concerning his dress. Although from an aristocratic family, he was a comte rather than the 'marquis' he claimed for himself. His military career was as fraudulent. His family connections had enabled him to be promoted, astonishingly to the rank of general, but with rarely an experience of gunfire. He claimed a heroic role in numerous battle actions, but a biographer observes: 'None of these assertions can be corroborated either by official documents or even by a witness, while most of them are categorically denied.' In 1814, he did not accompany Napoleon to Elba, but sided with the Bourbons and was accused of misappropriating funds intended as wages for his regiment.[17] Count de Montholon has received some ferocious epithets from historians: 'coward', 'malingerer', 'bounder', 'inveterate gambler', 'spendthrift' and 'cuckold'. The puzzle most frequently posed is why he was allowed to join Napoleon in exile in the first place. The usual answer is that it had something to do with his wife.

Albine Hélène de Montholon was not in the first flush of youth: at the age of 35 she was three years older than her husband, but still attractive, with a heart-shaped face, dark eyes and fluttering lashes. However, she lacked the court manners and refinement of Madame Bertrand, and her décolletage may have been considered ill-advised for a morning visit in the country. The news had travelled around the island that Madame de Montholon had divorced two husbands already, and some speculated that—given the boredom of island life—she might sever from the third. She still grieved for her baby left in France, but was known to be pregnant again. Some whispered that Bonaparte was not averse to her charms and that she recognised advantage in encouraging him.

The visitors had to leave by mid-afternoon to be back in Jamestown for the curfew. But Napoleon walked around the garden with Gourgaud, who wrote later in his journal that 'we discussed women. He maintains that a young man should not run after them.'[18] After they had all gone, Napoleon, according to Betsy's *Recollections*, fell into a pensive mood, absorbed with the new miniature. He asked her to pass on his apologies to her mother: if Madame Balcombe ever found him staring at her, it was because she reminded him so much of Josephine.

Writing her memoir thirty years later, Betsy sometimes invested her younger self with a suspiciously mature understanding and word-perfect memory. While a biographer has noted that 'Napoleon, when deeply moved, always wished to confide his emotions to some patient female ear',[19] one cannot always credit the authenticity of conversations we are told he had with Betsy, such as the one concerning his former wife. 'Anything she wore,' he purportedly told her, 'seemed elegant, she was grace personified. She never acted inelegantly during the whole time we lived together. She was the very *best* of women.' As for the divorce, nothing would have induced him to do it, he said, except for political motives. He did it for the good of the French nation. No other reason could have persuaded him to separate from a wife whom he loved so tenderly. But he thanked God she had died in time to prevent her witnessing his last misfortune.[20]

He seemed lost in thought, then asked Betsy whom she regarded as the most beautiful woman on the island. 'I told him I thought Madame Bertrand superior, beyond all comparison to any one I had ever seen . . . Napoleon asked me if I did not consider Madame

Montholon pretty. I said "No". He then desired Marchand to bring down a snuff-box, on the lid of which was a miniature of Madame Montholon. It certainly was like her, and very beautiful. He told me it was what she had been, when young.'[21]

Betsy was a Miranda on Prospero's island, or even a sprightly Ariel, or else she was a court jester, a Shakespearean Fool, goading a tormented Lear across a blasted heath. She delighted in St Helena's savage grandeur, and when Napoleon railed at its ugliness, calling it a hideous bare rock, she put up a passionate defence: 'His natural prejudice against the island rendered him blind to the many beauties with which it abounded; he beheld all with a jaundiced eye.'[22] He asked how she dared to contradict his opinion, laughed at her impudence and pinched her ear (an annoying habit of his). But he was happy to take long walks at this time, despite being followed by the English guard. Betsy would often accompany him on these rambles, sometimes with Jane and always shadowed by Captain Mackay.

As they walked, Napoleon encouraged her to tell him stories about the island's history: how a top-heavy Portuguese carrack had almost foundered on its rocks in 1502, and its commander, João da Nova Castella, had claimed the uninhabited island for Portugal and named it Santa Helena in honour of the Emperor Constantine's mother. The sailors had come ashore and filled barrels from a stream, clubbed the tame seals, caught slow-moving birds, turned turtles on their backs, and gathered aromatic herbs and sweet-tasting plants. Then they left, dumping some goats and pigs, provisions for future visits. Over the years, Portuguese carracks called in for the sweet mountain water and easily slaughtered game. None of them stayed, until one man made the island his home.

Dom Fernando Lopez, a Portuguese officer and gentleman, was with the invading army that took Goa in 1512, overwhelming the defending Indian forces. But Lopez stood accused of leading a group of deserters. His garrison commander spared the men's lives but, according to the Portuguese historian Afonso D'Albuquerque, decreed 'that their right hands, and the thumbs of their left hands, and their ears and noses should be cut off'.[23] Most of them died from loss of blood, but Lopez survived. He scratched out a mendicant's existence, despised by his countrymen, shunned by the Indians.

Three years later, he stowed away on a ship bound for Portugal, dreaming of a reunion with his wife and child, of embracing them with his claw-like left hand and the stump of his right, trusting they would see past the hideous wound of his noseless face, the holes where his ears had been. The sailors may have cautioned him, for by the time the vessel put in for water at St Helena he had lost confidence in his dream. He bolted into the forest and hid. His shipboard companions searched for him in vain, and when they sailed they left behind a barrel of biscuits, hung beef, dried fish, salt, a fire, and some old clothes.[24]

One day, as another ship departed, a rooster fell overboard and was drowning when Lopez rescued it. The rooster followed him everywhere and slept in the cave with him at night. Lopez never dreamed of eating the bird. He had found love, of a sort. When Lopez finally died, in 1545, he had survived at his island refuge for thirty years.

Betsy described the colonisation of St Helena, how the Dutch followed the Portuguese, and then the British East India Company claimed and occupied the island in 1661. But it was the story of the disfigured hermit Dom Fernando Lopez and his lonely island exile that fascinated Napoleon; that was the story he always asked her to repeat.[25]

CHAPTER 8

THE ADMIRAL'S BALL

From the side balcony of The Briars' Pavilion one looks down towards Jamestown, the ocean in the distance, and across to the waterfall which spills over the lip of the horseshoe-shaped gorge into the rocky gloom far below. The sides of the gulch are barren except for aloes and prickly pear, an impenetrable clump of them in the foreground, descendants of those that once inflicted pain on some well-upholstered buttocks. But the cascade still sparkles just as Betsy described it, and those clear waters were the reason seafarers called at the island, that the poor hermit Lopez survived for so long, and that a settlement developed and supported the growth of a trading empire.[1]

Across the gorge and looming some 500 metres above the Pavilion is High Knoll Fort, St Helena's most spectacular military installation. Seen from below, with its martello tower, turreted stone walls and slit embrasures, it could be a medieval castle. It was actually built during the Victorian era as a redoubt against any possible invaders, its guns commanding James Bay while the whole island population could be herded into its keep. It has been described by a building archaeologist as one of the finest nineteenth-century forts in the world.[2] This citadel greatly extended an earlier fort on the same site, built in the 1790s. After Napoleon's arrival, soldiers kept a close watch on The Briars from up there; in the event of any suspicious activity involving the prisoner, they could signal to other watch-houses on high points right across the island.

Charles Darwin, visiting St Helena on HMS *Beagle* in July 1836, was astonished: 'It is quite extraordinary, the scrupulous degree to which the coast must formerly have been guarded. There are alarm houses, alarm guns and alarm stations on every peak.'[3]

At the end of October, Gourgaud made another visit to The Briars, on the way passing a slave auction at the crossroads in town. He had a familiar discussion with Napoleon: 'He cannot understand his defeat at Waterloo. "It isn't for me," he adds, "it is for poor France." His Majesty tells me again, that with twenty thousand men less, he ought to have won the battle. It is Fate which made him lose it.'

Gourgaud was annoyed to find the Balcombe girls joining them for dinner in the marquee. In fact, Betsy had been reluctant, as they had already dined. 'Then come and see me eat,' Napoleon had insisted.

Cipriani delivered his punctilious announcement: '*Le dîner de votre Majesté est servi.*' The girls sat beside their host at the table, opposite a sullen Gourgaud. A plate of elaborate sweets was placed in front of them, 'spun sugar confections, architectural delicacies', produced by Pierron, said to have been the most famous and accomplished confectioner in Paris. Betsy protested that she was not hungry but made herself eat half a cream. 'But although I was satisfied, Napoleon was not; and when I left off eating, he commenced feeding me like a baby, calling me his little *bambina*, and laughing violently at my woeful countenance.'[4]

The mornings always began with the dictation of the memoirs. 'The Emperor knew that the best way to counter boredom was work,' wrote Marchand, noting that Napoleon had tried to do the writing himself, but 'his hand could not follow his thoughts that were so highly-strung, concise and full of fire; his fingers could not keep up with the speed of his imagination'.[5] Gourgaud was bored and unemployed in town so was persuaded to help young Emmanuel de Las Cases transcribe fair copies, all the while protesting that he was not a clerk.

In Betsy's account, word of Gourgaud's complaints reached her brothers' elderly tutor, Mr Huff. The old man burst in on Napoleon and Las Cases during a dictation session and offered his services. When these were declined, he became distraught and was bustled out by Marchand. We are told that Mr Huff, who had lived on the island for more than fifty years, became obsessed with the former emperor, fantasising that he was personally 'destined to restore the fallen hero to his glory'. He so neglected his pupils that Balcombe felt compelled to dismiss him.[6]

The Reverend Mr Samuel Jones was engaged as the new tutor at The Briars and was able to stay at Ross Cottage, Balcombe's poultry farm, a comfortable walk some two miles away. Huff's former bedroom in the house was taken over by Captain James Mackay, who had been camping in a tent at the front gate. They had all become fond of this cheerful officer, whose main duty was to keep 'General Bonaparte' in his sights. Captain Mackay had become fond of young Jane Balcombe and kept her in his sights as well.

'It soon became evident,' Betsy heartlessly observed in her *Recollections*, 'that old Mr Huff was mad, and, though strictly watched, he found an opportunity one fatal morning to destroy himself.'[7] She did not describe the method of suicide, but 'the act was committed' where the road to The Briars joined the Sidepath, a favourite lookout point with its spectacular view over the cliff to Jamestown far below. No one seemed to grieve for Huff, least of all anyone at The Briars. A coronial inquest determined that he had died by his own hand. Custom and the church dictated that a suicide be buried with a stake through the heart. Mr Huff's corpse was refused a Christian churchyard burial so he was interred near where he had shuffled off his mortal coil, at the crossroads near The Briars, where his skeleton was discovered in 1957 during road mending on the island.[8]

Betsy did not care to think of the deranged old fellow lying in the ground nearby. She had 'a terror of ghosts'. She wrote that her weakness became known to Napoleon, and when she retired for the night, blowing out the candle, she could sometimes hear him prowling in the garden, calling softly: 'Miss Betsee, Ole Huff! Ole Huff!' One evening she and Jane were sitting with their mother on The Briars' verandah, enjoying the cool evening breeze, when 'suddenly we heard a noise, and turning around beheld a figure in white—how I screamed. We were then greeted with a low, gruff laugh, which my mother instantly knew to be the emperor's.'[9] Mrs Balcombe marched across the lawn to the flitting apparition. She lifted the edge of a white sheet to reveal the black face of Alley, the slave boy. The laughter from the shadows left no doubt who had organised the charade.

The Balcombe boys' new tutor Mr Jones had no proficiency in the French language. Nor had William Balcombe, but as he was catering for the French exiles he considered it imperative that his daughters' conversational skills uphold family honour. He ruled that Betsy and Jane should complete a translation a day. Bonaparte's own language lessons had not progressed far—he said he hated irregular English verbs—but he condescended to look over the girls' French assignments and correct mistakes. Betsy thought him overzealous in the role.[10]

One afternoon she took her work to the pavilion for correction; Count de Las Cases, receiving dictation, and General Gourgaud, labouring over a fair copy, did not welcome her intrusion. Betsy boiled with resentment as she watched Napoleon make decisive marks on her exercise. 'Look at your hand,' she said. 'It's like a baby's, so fat and pretty! I don't believe it was ever strong enough to hold a sword.'

The courtiers were predictably outraged. Gourgaud drew his sabre from its scabbard and prodded at stains on the blade. 'That is the blood of an Englishman!'

Napoleon ordered him to sheath it at once. 'It is bad taste to boast, Gourgaud, especially in front of ladies.' He told Betsy to judge for herself whether he could handle a weapon, and withdrew his own magnificent sword and scabbard from a richly embossed case of tortoiseshell studded with golden bees. The sword handle was of wrought gold.[11]

'May I hold it?' Betsy asked. Gratified to see her so impressed, Bonaparte placed it in her hands. 'I drew the blade out quickly from the scabbard, and began to flourish it over his head; making passes at him, the emperor retreating, until at last I fairly pinned him up in the corner. I kept telling him all the time that he had better say his prayers, for I was going to kill him.'

Her exultant cries brought Jane rushing from the house. 'Stop, stop! I shall tell Papa if you do not desist!' But the giddy girl laughed and continued to hold the great warrior at bay, until her arm dropped from the weight of the sword.

Napoleon's reaction was remarkably benign. When Betsy relinquished the weapon, he pinched her ear. This made her scream, for it had just been pierced for earrings, so he pulled her nose instead 'but quite in fun'. 'I never met with anyone who bore childish liberties so well as Napoleon,' she recalled later. 'He seemed to enter into every sort of mirth or fun with the glee of a child, and though I have often tried his patience severely, I never knew him to lose his temper or fall back upon his rank or age, to shield himself from the consequences of his own familiarity, or of his indulgence to me.'[12]

The story of Betsy and the sword swept across Europe. Bonaparte had been threatened by a young girl who seemed 'cracked in the head'.[13] Even the great Austrian statesman Prince Metternich was given a personal account of the incident.[14]

Mesdames Fanny Bertrand and Albine de Montholon had little to do each day but read, sew, watch their children play in the castle gardens, and find new ways of quarrelling with each other. During breaks in hostilities they visited Saul Solomon's store in the vague hope of finding something interesting to purchase. They were a popular sight from the doors of the taverns, wine houses and hostels, teetering on dainty Parisian heels up Jamestown's cobbled main street, holding lace-trimmed parasols aloft to protect their complexions. Their ensembles in satin and *mousseline de soie* (silk muslin) were the latest in Empire fashion, and Albine's hourglass shape belied her new pregnancy. Encased in whalebone corsets, the ladies found the summer heat unendurable.

Fanny, convent-educated and devout, grieved that there was no priest on the island. She still hoped to persuade her husband, despite his loyalty to the emperor, to depart after twelve months for England, where they could live in style with her relatives, influential figures in the English-Catholic aristocracy. In the meantime she had resolved that she and Albine must endure the place and, if possible, each other. However, she preferred the company of Mrs Jane Balcombe and the newly arrived Catherine Younghusband.

Catherine described Fanny Bertrand to her aunt in Ireland: 'She is an elegant woman, about 5 ft 7 inches in height, but pale & delicate, & miserable at being in this place. The Grand Maréchal, General

Bertrand, is a fine soldier-like & polite man . . . Their three children, Napoleon, Hortense and Henri, exceed in beauty any children I have ever seen. Madame Bertrand speaks English perfectly well. She is of Irish extraction & of the Dillon family. She seemed very much pleased to see us & took great notice of Emily. I think we are likely to have much pleasure in her society.'[15]

Tempers were becoming frayed among the members of the French suite. 'Cipriani annoys me continually with his questions and his visits to my room,' wrote Gourgaud at the Porteous house. 'There is a great quarrel between Madame Montholon and Madame Bertrand.'[16] A few days later, Gourgaud flew into a rage against Montholon and had to be restrained. Napoleon rebuked General Bertrand, who had failed to write a letter of formal complaint listing their various grievances. Bertrand replied that some of the grumbles about chamber servants and mattresses were unworthy of His Majesty.

A welcome distraction came with the news that Admiral Sir George Cockburn was to host a ball at the castle in late November. The local society people would attend, and also the military and ships' officers, one of whom wrote that if Sir George 'can find the ladies, of course we shall go there'.[17] The real excitement was that the French were to be invited, including their diabolical leader. Whom among the local ladies might he ask for a quadrille? Some felt faint at the thought. But those who had spoken to him on his rides had found him pleasant. And quite handsome really. At Solomons' store and along the promenade they talked of little else.

Gourgaud heard the rumours and was elated. He was already paying for sex with black and mulatto girls, but he craved the company of a genteel young woman. He fantasised about one in particular: Laura Wilks, the governor's daughter, whom he had seen just once. Napoleon's interest was piqued. He had not contemplated attending the ball and exhibiting himself for the titillation of the locals. There would be no one worthy to partner, he believed, except the two ladies of his own court. However, although a colonial governor's daughter was far beneath him, perhaps if she was very pretty . . . He asked Betsy to describe Miss Wilks, saying that 'Gourgaud spoke in raptures of her, and sketched her portrait from memory'. He produced the drawing and asked if it was a good likeness. Betsy replied that Miss Wilks 'was infinitely more lovely, and that it bore no trace of resemblance to her. I mentioned also that she was very clever and amiable. Napoleon said I was very enthusiastic in her favour, and had made him quite long to see her.'[18]

That opportunity presented itself at the admiral's ball. As the day drew closer, Betsy's own excitement could barely be contained. She had been in boarding school for years and had never attended such a grand occasion. She would need a new dress and chattered about fabrics and designs. However, her father ruled that she was too young; Jane could go, but Betsy must wait for at least a year before coming out into society. She resolved to change his mind.

Written invitations from the castle duly arrived for Napoleon and all his French companions except the domestics. But there was a major problem with the wording. On 14 November, which happened to be his birthday, Gourgaud made a glum entry in his journal: 'We receive invitations to the Admiral's Ball. There is one for "General Bonaparte".' Napoleon promptly refused it. He said he did not know of such a person on the island. 'Send this card to General Buonaparte,' he told Bertrand. 'The last news I heard of him was at the Battle of the Pyramids.'[19]

Betsy was still desperate to go, and pleaded with Napoleon to intercede with her father. He surprised her by arguing her case, and Balcombe relented. Soon she and Jane were paying a visit to Solomons' store with their mother to choose silks, muslins and ribbons and to pore over the London fashions in *The Lady's Magazine*. Betsy was entranced with the design for her dress, which was to be appliquéd with delicate paper roses.

One evening, as was their frequent habit, Napoleon and Las Cases came to The Briars' house after dinner for a game of whist, with sugar plums as stakes. The senior Balcombes were unaccountably absent—Mrs Balcombe, who suffered from recurrent hepatitis, may have retired early—but the little card table was set up in the parlour. Napoleon and Jane were to play together against the ill-matched partnership of Betsy and the count.

The cards were muddled and Las Cases was instructed to sort them into suits. While his former chamberlain was occupied with this fiddly task, Napoleon asked Betsy about her *robe de bal*. She was inordinately proud of the new gown, her first, and had him to thank that she would be wearing it to the castle. She ran upstairs and fetched it, showing off the fine needlework and appliquéd paper roses. 'Very pretty,' he said.

Las Cases returned to the table with the sorted deck, so Betsy placed the dress on the sofa and the game began. It was soon clear that Napoleon was not abiding by the rules. Betsy caught him 'peeping under his cards as they were dealt to him, he endeavoured whenever he got an important one to draw off my attention, and then slyly held it up for my sister to see. I soon discovered this and, calling him to order, told him he was cheating, and that if he continued to do so, I would not play.'

At the end of the hand, Napoleon claimed to be the winner; when Betsy disputed this, he laughed and declared that she was the cheat and should pay what she owed.[20]

'Never! You revoked! You cheated!'

At this Napoleon jumped up and, calling her wicked ('Ah, you are *méchante!*'), snatched up her ball dress from the sofa. He ran from the room with it and up to the pavilion. She gasped in astonishment. Then she set off up the path in pursuit. But he was too quick, darting through the marquee and locking himself in the inner room. Despite her remonstrances and tears, he called through the door that he was keeping the dress to teach her a lesson.

The ball was the following evening. There was no sign of Napoleon throughout the day. Betsy sent several begging messages to the pavilion but was told that the emperor was sleeping and could not be disturbed. Neither of her parents was willing to approach him. Because she was not yet of an age to 'come out' into society, they had not wanted her to go in the first place; nor would they have wished to engage their distinguished guest on such a frivolous matter—although they must have wondered why *he* bothered with it.

The day wore on and at last the hour arrived for their departure. The horses were brought around and the young slave boys loaded the tin cases holding the ladies' silks and satins—but not Betsy's beautiful gown. Her mother and sister would be able to change into their evening finery at the castle and she would still be wearing her plain little house dress. By the time they reached the gate she was inclined to return home, but then Napoleon came running across the grass with her gown over his arm. 'Here, Miss Betsee, I have brought it for you! I hope you are a good girl now and that you will enjoy the ball.' He walked beside their horses until they came to the end of the bridle track which joined the Sidepath. He asked idly about a farmhouse he noticed far below. As they waved goodbye he called out to Betsy: 'Make sure that you dance with Gourgaud!' The emperor was mocking her as usual. She detested Gourgaud.[21]

The whitewashed castle walls were lit by flaming torches, reflected in the waters of James Bay. Turbaned black pages in brilliant satin livery greeted the new arrivals in the forecourt, took charge of the horses and directed the ladies to the anteroom where they changed.

The Balcombes and the French party entered the ballroom together at nine o'clock. Madame Bertrand, in a Parisian gown of heavy brocade, and Madame de Montholon, in a low-cut dress, her breasts sparkling with diamonds and emeralds estimated to be worth £1000, were the sensations of the evening. (Admiral Cockburn was tolerant enough to overlook the fact that he had requested all precious jewellery to be surrendered when they boarded the *Northumberland*.) The locals had never seen such style and glamour.[22] A number of dashing officers, including Colonel Bingham, approached the French ladies, and soon their dance cards were filled. 'The dress of the French party is so magnificent,' observed Catherine Younghusband, 'as to throw all the English and St Helenians into the background.' However, in her view that was no great challenge: 'The English ladies born here are called Yam-stocks. They are, many of them, very pretty & blooming, but very ignorant.'[23]

A few midshipmen eyed off the local beauties, but were mindful of a lieutenant's warning that many of the girls viewed these occasions as a 'Ladder to Matrimony' and escape from the island: 'The Governor's ball gives them an opportunity of setting their caps to the best advantage, and many an unwary bachelor becomes inextricably enthralled by the sirens of St Helena.'[24]

Gourgaud was discomforted to be greeted by their host Admiral Cockburn, who requested—with a firmness that sounded like an order—that he should book the first quadrille with Mrs Balcombe, the second with Betsy Balcombe and the third with Miss Knipe, a farmer's daughter.[25] 'My intention was not to dance with the Balcombes but here I am caught,' Gourgaud complained to his journal. Betsy would have agreed with him. She failed to write about the ball herself and must have found it a disappointment after all her expectations. It was especially tedious to have to dance with Gourgaud. No doubt she looked delightful in her rose-trimmed gown and attracted some attention, but she was outshone by the French ladies. And by the governor's daughter.

Laura Wilks whirled past them in an officer's arms. It was only the second time Gourgaud had seen her—he was impressed enough the first time to rush home and sketch her—and now he was completely infatuated: 'She has a charming face; a mixture of sweetness, intelligence and distinction. She salutes me as she dances past. Ah! Why am I a prisoner?' Poor Gourgaud wanted to get married. He was tormented by erotic fantasies involving various women. He was not mollified when Napoleon told him, 'When you don't think about them you don't need them.' He *did* think about them, and his covert and hasty sexual encounters were not enough; he hoped to woo a young lady such as Laura Wilks for a wife. But alas, her dance card was filled and he was instructed by the admiral to escort Madame De Fountain, the dull wife of a councillor, to supper.

What was worse, he considered that he and his French compatriots were snubbed in the table seating, and the six quadrilles to which he was committed dragged on until five thirty in the morning. There were other annoyances: 'A rosy young lady made a terrible fart as she was dancing.'[26] In the November heat, the energetic, perspiring couples on the floor were observed by some to be 'not safe to approach . . . literally swimming through the dance'.[27]

The sun was rising as the Balcombes came down the castle steps to the courtyard to find a cart blocking the archway and only exit, with a group of carousing midshipmen on top, singing at the top of their voices 'Lord W's carriage stops the way'.[28]

While the dancing was still in progress that night, the admiral and Governor Wilks had received an alarming message. Bonaparte had slipped past the captain and duty sergeant at The Briars earlier that evening and clambered down the mountain track to Maldivia farmhouse in the valley below. His unexpected visit astounded its occupant, Major Charles Hodson of the St Helena regiment, who did his best to be hospitable, as he later recalled: 'I, of course, went out to meet him; he came into the house, looked about, and seemed very well pleased with it and the garden, which he walked over, paid Mrs Hodson a great many fine compliments, and took a great deal of notice of the children.'[29]

Napoleon joked that his tall and imposing host should be called 'Hercules', and was loaned an Arab pony for the ride home. He gave the servants who accompanied him some French coins. He was asleep at the pavilion, exhausted by the adventure, by the time the intelligence reached the castle.

No harm had been done. This time. But security would need to be stepped up at The Briars.

CHAPTER 9

LAST DAYS AT THE PAVILION

The main street of Jamestown leads up from the waterfront and the archway over the old drawbridge, past the castle and its gardens, the courthouse, church and gaol, the Georgian buildings now housing offices, hotels and stores, to the tourist office at the crossroads. Market Street leads off to the right and Napoleon Street to the left. At this central point, in front of the casement windows of the office, are two gnarled trees with bolts driven into their trunks. These were for the purpose of securing human beings in manacles.

At the time of Napoleon's arrival, St Helena was the last outpost of Britain's empire where slavery was still legal, although the importation of slaves was not. But on the island the practice continued. Every child born of a slave automatically became a slave also, the property of the owner, who could buy, sell and barter them at will. Slave auctions were held under the trees, centre stage for the town, as late as 1829. In the castle archives there are dozens of notices such as this:

TO BE SOLD & LET BY PUBLIC AUCTION

THE FOLLOWING SLAVES

Hannibal, about 30 Years old, an excellent House Servant

William, about 35 Years old, a Labourer

Nancy, an excellent House Servant and Nurse
Philip, an Excellent Fisherman
Clara, an Excellent Washerwoman
Fanny, about 14 Years old, House Servant[1]

※

Some horses had arrived from the Cape and Napoleon was given a handsome black stallion called Hope. He liked the name and said it was a good augury. He rode it around The Briars' front lawn, cutting up the turf. Soon he was enjoying a daily outing on horseback and frequently led Captain Mackay a merry chase, cantering on the ill-made roads and skirting perilously close to the edge of ravines. He was at his most imposing when mounted, as he was well aware, and people in the little cottages scattered among the hills looked forward to the sight of him in his high boots, green coat and cocked hat. They felt that to wave to him was to insert themselves into a small place in history. Sometimes he would rein in to talk to people on the road, startling a soldier, seaman, Chinese labourer or slave carrying building materials up to Longwood. As Dr O'Meara observed: 'Every day bodies of two or three hundred seamen were employed in carrying up from Jamestown, timber and other materials . . . so deficient was the island in the means of transport that almost everything, even the very stones for building, were carried up the steep Sidepath on the heads and shoulders of the seamen, occasionally assisted by fatigue parties of the 53rd Regiment.'[2]

Napoleon claimed to feel most compassion for the slaves, referring particularly to Toby, the old Malay at The Briars, and he criticised the British government for permitting the continuation of an evil it boasted elsewhere of having abolished. He was appalled when Gourgaud told him he had witnessed 'a woman slave sold publicly' in Jamestown.[3]

One day he stopped to chat with Mrs Balcombe on the road near The Briars' front gate and was introduced to her companion, Mrs Stuart, a pretty young Scotswoman from a ship calling in on its home voyage from Bombay.[4] He questioned her about the customs of India, Hindu saints and sadhus (holy men), and the difficulties of the sea voyage for women. As they conversed, Las Cases translating, Mrs Balcombe 'in rather an angry tone' indicated to a group of sweating slaves, laden with heavy timber beams, that they should detour around them. Napoleon interjected: 'Consider the burden, Madame,' and drew his horse aside to let them pass. Las Cases included an account in his *Mémorial*: 'Mrs Stuart, who had been taught to regard Napoleon as a monster, was inexpressibly amazed by this touching incident. In a low tone of voice she exclaimed to her friend, "What a countenance and what a character! How different from what I had been led to expect!"'[5]

Of course, Napoleon's own regime had been greatly enriched by the labour of slaves in the French possessions. Although the trade in human beings had been abolished in the colonies during the Revolution, he himself reinstated it.

A former slave, François-Dominique Toussaint L'Ouverture, had led the slave rebellion of 1791 in Saint-Domingue (present-day Haiti), the most valuable sugar colony in the West Indies. After the new French republic abolished slavery, L'Ouverture allied himself with it and established control over the whole island, repelling British attempts to invade (including the 1796 expedition in which Balcombe participated). But in June 1802, the slaves' revolution was savagely suppressed. Acting on First Consul Bonaparte's specific orders, French troops seized L'Ouverture and sent him to prison high in the Jura Mountains of France, where he died the following year.[6] Dictating his memoirs on St Helena, Napoleon was defiant about the decision: 'There was no longer room for deliberation; the honor as well as the interest of France called for the annihilation of the negro chiefs, who, in my eyes, were nothing more than ungrateful Africans and rebels, with whom it was impossible to establish any system.'[7]

However, on another occasion, keen to burnish his new image as a benefactor to slaves, he admitted that the French brutality on Saint-Domingue was an error: 'I have to reproach myself for the attempt at the Colony during the Consulate; it was a great mistake to have wanted to subdue it by force; I should have contented myself to govern it through the intermediary of Toussaint.'[8] During the 'Hundred Days' of his reign in 1815 after his return from Elba, he decreed the abolition of the French slave trade, although some historians suggest that he did so only to win over British public opinion, particularly that of the Whig liberals.[9] Once he was exiled to St Helena, French vessels were refitted as slave ships and the traffic from Africa resumed.

Since 1659, the British East India Company had used the slaves of St Helena for its vegetable gardens, plantations and stock, and for victualling and supplying water for its vessels returning from Asia to Europe. 'It has been observed,' wrote a visitor, Francis Duncan, 'that whites will seldom work in a warm climate when they can get slaves to labour for them.'[10] The slaves were primarily imported from Company possessions in the East Indies, the Indian subcontinent and the island of Madagascar, whose people, of mixed Malay, Arabic and East African descent, were prized. By 1676, the Company demanded that every English ship coming from Madagascar 'was obliged to leave on the island [of St Helena] one Negro, male or female, as the governor chose'.[11] As Company employees took up plantations on the island, more slaves were imported, some from West Africa. But whatever the slaves' racial background—and although most were olive- or copper-skinned—they were usually described as 'blacks' or 'negroes'.

In St Helena's early days, the slaves' treatment was some of the most horrific on record anywhere. In his *Isle of St Helena*, Oswell Blakeston wrote of the punishment of errant slaves: 'hot sealing wax was dropped on naked bodies, with ferocious floggings . . . with orders for all slaves to bring one faggot of wood each to a pyre so that a slave could be burnt alive, a screaming example to discourage others'.[12] A year after Napoleon's arrival, a census taken on St Helena indicated that there were 821 white civilian residents, 820 garrison troops and 618 Chinese labourers. These three groups combined were matched in numbers by slaves, a quarter of whom were 'free blacks', meaning that at different times, and for various reasons, they had been emancipated by their owners.[13] The slaves survived on a meagre diet of rice, yams grown on a Company farm, and whatever fish they caught themselves in their fraction of free time.

Sometimes when Napoleon had difficulty sleeping he wandered into the darkened garden and beyond to the orchard. Toby, the old Malay slave, was strict about entry to his domain, and according to Betsy none of the Balcombe family disputed his authority, but Toby had a soft spot for the occupant of the pavilion and always brought him the choicest fruit. 'Our old Malay was so fond of the man Bony, as he designated the emperor, that he always placed the garden key where Napoleon's fingers could reach it under the wicket. No one else was ever favoured in the like manner, but he had completely fascinated and won the old man's heart.'[14]

Count de Montholon wrote in his memoirs: 'The eldest daughter of Mr Balcombe one day seeing Toby carrying a heavy burden from the town, having learned the story of his misfortune and the bitter grief he felt at being separated from his children, conceived the idea of obtaining his liberty and sending him back to his home'. Balcombe said he would try to bring this about; he started slowly, by imposing no other labour on the old Malay than the care of the vegetable garden. Betsy applied pressure on Napoleon: 'The younger of the two, who was very pretty and even more mischievous than beautiful, felt that she could do anything and say anything with impunity, and had all the boldness of a spoiled child. She took advantage of a happy opportunity to ask the Emperor to buy the Malay, and, after her own fashion, related to him one evening the history of her protégé. "I won't love my father because he doesn't keep his promise, but I will love you well, if you restore Toby to his children: do you know that he has a girl just of my age, who is very like me?"'

At this, we are told, Bonaparte softened. 'He assured her that the next day he would give orders to purchase the slave, and request the admiral to send him back to the Indies by the first opportunity. But then the purchase was not in the power of the Emperor; it was not sufficient to pay the sum demanded by the master of the slave. In order to emancipate a slave, it was necessary to go through a long series of formalities, and our departure from Briars to Longwood surprised us before these formalities could be finished.'[15] (The 'ownership' of Toby was confusing: he had been 'purchased' by a Captain Wrangham who had left the island, so in a sense was 'on loan' to Balcombe. But as Wrangham had been gone for years, an executive decision *could* have been made by the governor to free Toby.)

The following year there was a new admiral and, more to the point, a new governor, Sir Hudson Lowe. Bonaparte put the request again, through O'Meara. The governor judged, probably correctly, that Bonaparte's strategy was to win favour as a compassionate figure with the Whigs back in England, in order to encourage their lobbying for a more amenable situation for him. Lowe advised the doctor to 'let him believe that I will submit his request to the council of the Company', but in reality he was emphatic that 'I would not do what you ask for anything in the world'.[16]

However, the episode achieved what was no doubt intended: the story spread, adding sentimental lustre to Napoleon's legend.

On 28 November 1815, Colonel Bingham hosted a farewell breakfast for Governor Wilks and his family, and those constituting society on the island were invited. Three large marquees were set up, one with a dance floor; there were tables for ninety guests and these were decorated with flowers. Bingham wrote to his wife Emma in England of these preparations: 'It appeared as if it were all enchantment to the natives of St Helena, who are so slow in their actions that it would have taken them one year to have accomplished what we did in six days.'[17]

For weeks Napoleon had observed the fatigue parties of the 53rd Regiment as they wound around the mountains to the beat of fifes and drums, building materials on their shoulders. Now they were no longer heaving stone blocks and timbers, but rather furniture, rugs and pictures. Longwood House would soon be ready for occupation.

According to Catherine Younghusband, Napoleon was 'not at all anxious to quit the Briars, or in a hurry to go to Longwood, which is being fitted up for him with all the little elegance St Helena can afford'. Nor did Madame Bertrand welcome the move. She 'dislikes the idea of leaving James Town and accompanying Buonaparte to what she calls his Country Castle. She prefers the town, wretched and hot as it is, because the French party there are much visited & they hear all the Gossip. The Admiral, however, says he cannot think of making the Government pay 55 guineas a week for Fancies.'[18]

Betsy's memoir describes how, as the time drew near for Napoleon's departure, 'he would come into the drawing-room oftener, and stay longer. He would, he said, have preferred altogether remaining at the Briars; because he beguiled the hours with us better than he ever thought it possible he could have done on such a horrible rock as St. Helena.'[19] He had suggested purchasing their property—apparently with Balcombe's approval, who would have done handsomely out of the deal—'but circumstances, probably political, prevented the negotiation from being carried out'.[20] However, according to Marchand, 'the Emperor was beginning to tire of his prolonged stay at the Briars; appearing in short britches and silk stockings for walks in the garden after sunset he had caught a cold and was coughing a lot'. Mrs Balcombe, kind and gracious, 'offered to make him an infusion of four flowers with honey from her own hives'. Napoleon thanked her and showed her a small candy box containing licorice, the only remedy he said he liked to use.[21]

Bertrand visited Longwood and reported that the house smelled badly of paint. Betsy would 'never forget the fury of the emperor. He walked up and down the lawn, gesticulating in the wildest manner. His rage was so great that it almost choked him. He declared that the smell of paint was so obnoxious to him that he would never inhabit a house where it existed.'

They were interrupted by extraordinary news. Montholon arrived, breathless from his climb up the hill, with a Paris *Gazette* just delivered. He said that the whole of France was in a state of revolution; that an army of 15,000 men had been organised and that everywhere they were shouting for the emperor. Admiral Cockburn had told him that such a state of affairs would be the ruin of England, as they would have to call up the militia. Gourgaud described Napoleon's distress at his inability to take advantage of the insurgency: 'The Emperor is so moved by this news of the 15,000 men that he strides along crying "It is now that it is cruel to be a prisoner here. Who will lead this movement? I see nobody capable of doing anything big. Eugene [his stepson by Josephine] has a good headpiece, judgment and good qualities, but not that genius, that resolute character that distinguishes great men . . . It is only I who could succeed!"'[22]

When Colonel Bingham came to escort his prisoner to Longwood, he found him in his dressing-gown; Napoleon 'excused himself from going on account of the smell of paint'. But he 'appeared to be in unusual good spirits, having on the table English papers to the 15th of September' detailing the political turmoil in France. He had read about the trial and execution of Marshal Ney, who had been one of his bravest commanders at Waterloo and yet was now deemed to be a traitor, and of the rise of the 'ultra-royalists', extreme conservatives who aimed to restore the *ancien régime* and purge the country of those who, in their view, had betrayed it. The papers reported 300 victims of their 'white terror' in the south of France, and in the August election the 'ultras' had been triumphant in the Chamber of Deputies; as a result, the country was divided and many feared the restored Bourbon monarchy would not survive. Bingham observed Napoleon's optimism: 'The greater confusion there is in France, the greater chance he thinks there is of his being allowed to return, as he thinks the English government will be obliged to recall him to compose the confusion that exists in that unhappy country.'[23] Catherine Younghusband had the same impression and wrote to her aunt: 'I am told that he is quite convinced that the French nation will recall him; indeed, he says, it cannot do without him; & he much fears it will not be safe for any English to travel in France through the exasperation of the French at his being kept at St Helena.'[24]

Las Cases went up to Longwood without Bonaparte and failed to notice a paint odour. Bertrand was chided for an exaggerated report. As dusk fell, Napoleon strolled in The Briars' garden with Gourgaud and confided his new idea—the English ought to raise an insurrection in Paris as a pretext for burning the city: 'It would be a great coup for England to destroy our capital. The English could probably sink our Fleet, overwhelm our ports, especially Cherbourg, Brest, Toulon. After this they would have nothing to fear from France for a long time.'[25]

But they would have much to fear from Napoleon Bonaparte. If he had the chance, the burning of Paris and destruction of the principal French ports and fleets were not too high a price to pay, if he could return to take control.

On the morning of 10 December, 'that good man Bony' went out to the orchard to farewell Toby and presented him with twenty Napoleon coins, a fortune for the old slave—but not enough to buy the freedom he craved. Bonaparte then joined his hosts at The Briars' house for a final luncheon. Marchand noted that although Balcombe would continue to have free access to the emperor in his role as providore, he 'was urged to come see him with his daughters and wife once we were settled at Longwood'.[26]

Admiral Cockburn arrived in a carriage with General Bertrand and an escort of guards to accompany the prisoner to his new home. Betsy could not be consoled at the departure of the man she had presumed to regard 'almost as a brother or companion of my own age'. He saw her weeping and came up to her: '"You must not cry, Mademoiselle Betsee; you must come and see me next week, and very often". I told him that depended on my father. He turned to him and said, "Balcombe, you must bring Missee Jane and Betsee to see me next week eh? When will you ride up to Longwood?" My father promised he would, and kept his word. He asked where mamma was, and I said she desired her kind regards to the emperor, and regretted not being able to see him before his departure, as she was ill in bed. "I will go and see her"; and up the stairs he darted before we had time to tell my mother of his approach. He seated himself on the bed, and expressed his regret at hearing she was unwell.' He thanked her for her kindness to him and presented her with a gold snuff box, asking that she give it to her husband as a mark of friendship. He gave the tearful Betsy a little good-luck charm she had often admired, joking that she should give it 'as a *gage d'amour* [a pledge of love] to *le petit* Las Cases'.

Marchand had gone ahead to Longwood: 'I wished to arrive there before the Emperor in order to receive him.'[27] Balcombe accompanied the main party on the three-mile ascent, arriving in the late afternoon. On his return his family wanted to know what Napoleon thought of his new residence and were told that 'he appeared out of spirits, and, retiring to his dressing-room, had shut himself up for the remainder of the day'.[28]

Napoleon may not have known it then, or perhaps he guessed, but his one period of gaiety—unexpected, incongruous, and principally due to Betsy Balcombe—on the island of St Helena was at an end.

CHAPTER 10

LONGWOOD HOUSE

During the two months that the exiled emperor stayed at The Briars he had gone out of his way to establish warm relations with the Balcombe family: with the irrepressible Betsy, of course; with sweet-natured Jane; with playful Thomas; and with young Alexander, who reminded him of his own son. He could not fail to like the attractive Mrs Balcombe, for she was liked by everyone. But he had made a particular effort to cultivate the gregarious, heavy-drinking and often boastful William Balcombe—hardly his type—and to flatter him that they were friends. It was tactical for him to flatter the protégé of Sir Thomas Tyrwhitt, who was close to the royal family and within their ambit of power.

Furthermore, an intriguing rumour was circulating about Balcombe. Montholon had heard it: 'It was said in the island that he was the natural son of the Prince of Wales.'[1] The story had been around for some years, for it was known to Balcombe's former business partner William Burchell.[2] The St Helena Archives holds a copy of Burchell's 'St Helena Journal'. On 6 July 1808 he had written: 'Balcombe dined with me; he mentioned that it had been said to Mr Tyrwhitt that it was reported that B. was a son of the Prince of Wales & that Mr T. desired B. to contradict such a report. By my letters I learn that he is the son of a poor fisherman of Brighton who was drowned & the Prince hearing of the distressed state of the widow desired Tyrwhitt to take care of the two children who were then very young. But it seems B. encouraged this report if not set it on foot.'³ Burchell clearly doubted the story of royal paternity and suspected his colleague of promoting it. He had reason to be sceptical.

Records show that William Balcombe was born at the seaside village of Rottingdean near Brighton on Christmas Day 1777.⁴ George Augustus Frederick, the Prince of Wales (later George IV), would not have turned fifteen when—or a very problematic *if*—he had sired William.⁵ It is an unlikely scenario, but not altogether impossible. The prince was flagrantly precocious, with at least three known sexual partners by the age of fifteen. His tutor at that time, Bishop Richard Hurd, predicted that he would be 'either the most polished gentleman or the most accomplished blackguard in Europe—possibly both'.⁶ The prince followed the pattern of his roistering uncles, the dukes of Gloucester and Cumberland: 'He was an ardent and unmitigated admirer of their sexual adventures and excesses. He eagerly followed their example, slipping out of the royal house for clandestine escapades when his parents thought he had retired to bed for the night. The King was aghast when he heard the open talk going round the household staff of the fifteen-year-old prince seducing one of the Queen's maids of honour, who clearly found it impossible to live up to the title of her job. More distressing was the news relayed to him that among his early conquests, George numbered the Duchess of Cumberland—his uncle's wife.'⁷

Balcombe's mother, Mary Vandyke, was from Lewes in Sussex; she was two months pregnant with William when she married Stephen Balcombe of Rottingdean on 27 May 1777. Was the baby his or was he accepting, knowingly or not, a royal 'by-blow'? But it is difficult to imagine how Mary and the prince could have met, let alone mated. George did not adopt Brighton and the Sussex coast as his playground until 1784.⁸

Burchell's journal entry indicates that the rumour of Balcombe as a royal bastard existed at least seven years before Napoleon came to the island to confer reflected celebrity on him. Balcombe did not dispute the story, and may indeed have encouraged it, and his indiscretion had annoyed Tyrwhitt, the prince's long-term secretary—knighted four years later for loyalty such as this—who requested he contradict it. (Of course, if William really *was* the biological son of the prince and not of the fisherman Balcombe, he may have compromised an agreed cover story and deserved Tyrwhitt's rebuke for bragging.)

The Sussex village of Rottingdean was notorious in the late eighteenth century for smuggling (brandy, wine, tobacco and French lace), the contraband brought across the Channel from France and Belgium in little boats. Rottingdean lacked shelter for larger vessels, so serious fishermen worked out of the Steine at Brighton, Stephen Balcombe perhaps among them.[9] There are three differing stories concerning his drowning.

William's great-granddaughter, Dame Mabel Brookes, while not absolutely denying 'the possibility of a royal father' for William, proposed in her *St Helena Story* that his father was 'captain of a frigate' who was 'reputedly ... lost at sea with his ship', and that 'the boys were educated by the King's Bounty' as a consequence.[10] But there is no Balcombe in Syrett's definitive lists of *Commissioned Sea Officers of the Royal Navy 1660–1815*.

A Rottingdean history has suggested that William's father was a privateer in the Channel during the wars with France and drowned at sea.[11] A fisherman with a substantial vessel could become a privateer by obtaining a government licence—a Letter of Marque—to attack enemy shipping and take prizes. If he was killed in action, his family might perhaps be given royal support. There are other examples of the prince's generosity to victims of misfortune.[12]

The most likely theory, however, because written to Lord Bathurst by Sir Hudson Lowe, who was about to become St Helena's next governor, had Balcombe's father drowned in a boating accident caused by a yacht belonging to the Prince of Wales.[13] After the prince moved to Brighton in 1784, advised by his physicians to take up sea bathing, it is known that 'aquatic excursions' became 'his favourite amusement in the summer months', his vessel negotiating its way through up to a hundred fishing smacks.[14] The contemporary Brighton newspapers make no mention of an accident causing a death, but nor were they likely to if it implicated the prince. Newspapers of the period were hamstrung, dependent upon whichever political party supported them. While many publications demonstrated their freedom to lampoon the prince's lubricious lifestyle, they were restricted in discussing more serious matters affecting the royal family or the state. The government 'used secret service funds—allotted to prevent "treasonable or other dangerous conspiracies against the state"—to ensure a favourable press'.[15]

What is certain is that Stephen Balcombe met an untimely death, between 1784, when his youngest son was born (who died in infancy), and December 1788, when Mary, the boys' mother, married again, to Charles Terry, a tailor.[16] The wedding, at St Margaret's Rottingdean, was held on William's eleventh birthday.[17]

A year later, young William went to sea as a 'captain's servant' in the Royal Navy and within two years was officially appointed a midshipman, a much-sought-after position only gained through patronage.[18] Whether he was sired by a precocious prince or was merely a beneficiary of his charity after his father's drowning (and one version does not necessarily exclude the other), it is undeniable that from an early age he enjoyed the protection and assistance of the royal go-between Sir Thomas Tyrwhitt.

Correspondence with the Royal Archives at Windsor Castle has produced acknowledgement of two illegitimate children born to George IV, but no record of a Balcombe in their files.[19] Nevertheless, it is intriguing to study images of the prince and the one known portrait of William Balcombe and to perceive a distinct likeness in the wide, genial countenance, tousled curly hair, the straight nose and determined chin, the high-boned meaty cheeks, large frame and tendency to overweight . . .

If the thought occurs that Sir Thomas himself was William's natural father, it should almost certainly be dismissed. Apart from the fact that there was not the slightest physical resemblance—Tyrwhitt was so florid and diminutive that he was known to the royal family as 'our little red dwarf'[20]—he was exactly the same age as the prince but, the son of a country parson, he was not known then or later to have sexual relations with the opposite sex.[21] Tyrwhitt never married and may not even have had the sexual orientation.

Balcombe's paternity cannot be confirmed now, and never was during the years of Napoleon's captivity. But the rumour persisted on St Helena. Baron von Stürmer, later the Austrian commissioner based on the island, mentioned it to Prince Metternich: 'Mr Balcombe, a trader, who is said to be the natural son of the Prince Regent . . .'[22] The fact that Balcombe certainly had the otherwise inexplicable patronage of the prince's friend and former private secretary meant there *could* be something to the story—so it could not be discounted by Napoleon and his retinue.

If the merchant was in fact the natural child of the prince, then no person on the island, not the governor nor the admiral, had more direct access to the centre of power in Britain. Napoleon believed that his best hope of removal from the hated rock, or at least of more lenient treatment, depended on the Prince Regent, or on the accession to the throne of his daughter Princess Charlotte. It was essential that the merchant's friendship be nurtured.

Bonaparte was known to always act in a measured way, calculating the odds best suited to achieve his objectives. As Germaine de Staël, the great female intellectual of the era, observed of him quite early in his career: 'I had the disturbing feeling that no emotion of the heart could ever reach him. He regards a human being like a fact or a thing, never as an equal person like himself. He neither hates nor loves . . . The force of his will resides in the imperturbable calculations of his egotism. He is a chess-master whose opponents happen to be the rest of humanity . . .'[23]

As rain closed in, our charabanc slewed along the narrow muddy lanes, rounding hairpin bends, climbing higher. The windswept plateau on which Longwood House is built, 520 metres above the sea, is open to the south-east trades blasting across the Atlantic. Trees are misshapen and bent from their impact.

The driver directed our attention to the looming mountain called the Barn; its jagged cliffs plunging to the sea are said to be shaped like Napoleon's profile, and indeed with a little imagination it was possible to discern an aquiline nose, chiselled lips and a severe brow.

The garden at Longwood, with agapanthus and iris in flower and the Tricolore flapping on the flagpole, is attractively wooded now, but was bare and unsheltered when the French were installed in December 1815. Napoleon was partly responsible for the improvement; in 1818, after three years of boredom, he began work, digging and planting out in the sun in loose trousers and a Chinese coolie hat, saying: 'One day, perhaps one hundred years from now, people will visit this area and admire the garden.'[24]

Napoleon was five and a half years at Longwood House, longer than he ever spent at any imperial residence, for he used his palaces only between campaigns. Our tour group was guided through the rooms, shrines to the former emperor: the billiard room where he rarely played billiards but spread his old campaign maps on the table; the circular holes in the shutters where he squinted at Governor Lowe and the British guards through a telescope; the huge globe of the world, sepia with age, where the island of St Helena does not appear in the Atlantic, allegedly rubbed out by a furious finger. There is the dimly lit dining room where meals were served with formal pomp, and the emperor's little bedchamber and sitting room, with his tricorne hat and a copy of the greatcoat he wore at the Battle of Marengo displayed on the pink chaise longue. We peered into the deep timber-clad copper bath in which he soaked for hours, reading and fretting away his life. 'Boredom,' wrote Gourgaud in his journal, 'boredom, boredom, sadness . . .' Most gloomy is the drawing room and the green-curtained campaign bed where Napoleon breathed his last on 5 May 1821.

Napoleon was unimpressed with the renovations to the sprawling and rackety farmhouse, still infested with rats. The only part he cared for was the new addition, an airy wooden reception hall with six windows and a small lattice-enclosed porch looking across to the Barn, dropping almost sheer to the ocean far below. His narrow bedroom on the ground floor adjoined a small study; an antechamber contained the one great improvement to his comfort: a deep lead-lined bath made for him by ship's carpenters from the *Northumberland* (later replaced by an imported copper one), and filled from buckets heated over a fire outside.

His male companions and their wives, children and servants arrived in a cavalcade of wagons loaded with baggage and were soon squabbling about the arrangements. Although the Bertrands had precedence when they were present, Gourgaud disputed Montholon for the position near the emperor at the dinner table.

Madame Bertrand showed her usual independence of spirit by refusing the rooms offered; her family was lodged instead in a small cottage at Hutt's Gate, about a mile distant. The Montholons were in two rooms opposite Bonaparte's apartment, Las Cases in a former pantry near the kitchen, and his son in a cockloft above. The roof space over the old part of the house had been floored as sleeping accommodation for Cipriani, the valets Louis-Étienne Saint-Denis (known as 'Ali') and Marchand, and the Montholons' maid Josephine; it was possible to stand upright only under the ridge beam and, in that intimate proximity, Josephine soon began an affair with Noverraz, the Swiss third footman. Rooms still had to be constructed for Dr O'Meara, General Gourgaud and the British orderly officer Captain Thomas Poppleton, who all had to make do with tents in the meantime and endure Longwood's frequent downpours for over three months.

Napoleon loathed the bare surrounds of Longwood. He was incensed to be told that he could walk and ride freely in an area only 12 miles in circumference, much of it cut by ravines and therefore unusable; beyond that limit he was to be accompanied by a British officer. A complex code of signals had been issued to every sentry post, tracking the prisoner's daily movements, whether inside the house, in the garden or within the 12-mile cordon: 'General Bonaparte is well; General Bonaparte is unwell; General Bonaparte is properly attended', with a blue flag to indicate the dire circumstance that 'General Bonaparte is missing'. O'Meara considered the restrictions extraordinarily rigorous, with a sentinel guarding every landing place on the island and every goat path leading to the sea.[25] After 9 pm 'the General' was not at liberty to leave the house at all. Sentries were posted around the garden.

Just before Christmas, the admiral received a terse letter, signed by Montholon, listing the emperor's objections and demanding they be rectified. Cockburn responded in the same tone: 'With regard to what is therein stated respecting an *Emperor Napoleon*, I have only to inform you that I have no cognizance of such a person. The very uncalled-for intemperance and indecency of the language which you have permitted yourself to use to me respecting my Government, I should not perhaps, Sir, condescend to notice, did I not think it right to inform you that I shall not in future consider it necessary to answer any letters which I may receive couched in a similar strain of unfounded invective.'[26]

Also in December, Lieutenant-General Sir Hudson Lowe was preparing to depart London for St Helena as Bonaparte's official custodian.

Although it has rarely been acknowledged, he was peculiarly well qualified for that role.

Lowe had been posted to Egypt early in his career. He had seen much action in Europe as attaché to Marshal Blücher; on the field at Bautzen in 1813 he had actually sighted Bonaparte. In the period before Waterloo he had been quartermaster-general to the Allied armies (British, Prussian, Belgian and Dutch) in the Low Countries, and was therefore in a position of considerable military influence in Europe—for commissariat, billeting and armaments—until the arrival of the Duke of Wellington. He had also commanded a regiment on Corsica that fought on Britain's side against the French.[27] When this latter qualification became known to Bonaparte, he expressed contempt for the commander of a bunch of mercenaries and turncoats.

Unfortunately, Sir Hudson Lowe had a stiff conversational manner and little sense of humour and, at the time of his appointment, he was unmarried. A wife was always an asset for a governor on an isolated station. This latter deficiency was repaired on 30 December when he married Susan Johnson, the pretty and lively widow of a colonel with two adolescent daughters. She was well connected and was said to be 'a very captivating woman' with 'a fine face, laughing eyes'.[28]

Once his appointment became known, Lowe was lionised by London society figures, particularly by those aristocratic Whigs, led by Lord and Lady Holland, who professed admiration for Napoleon; they hoped to persuade the new governor to treat his prisoner with dignity and compassion and to permit them to send books and newspapers. Lowe was invited to dine at Holland House on eight separate occasions, meeting other 'Napoleonists' there, including Lord Byron and his wife Annabella. Byron took an immediate dislike to Lowe: he asked him whether Napoleon's 'dispositions were those of a great General', and Lowe answered disparagingly that 'they were very *simple*'. 'I had always thought,' Byron wrote to a friend, 'that a degree of Simplicity was an element of Greatness.'

Other distinguished people sought other favours. On 8 December, while still in London, Lowe received a letter under the House of Lords seal with a pressing request from Sir Thomas Tyrwhitt, Gentleman Usher of the Black Rod:

My dear Sir

I believe Sir G. Cockburn has written home to advise the Government to make an agreement with Mr Balcombe (my young Friend at St Helena) for the supply of Napoleon's Table at a percentage. Will you be kind enough to ascertain this fact, and should it turn out there is such a recommendation, it may be brought to maturity before you leave us. In order that I may stand acquitted of any mistaken partiality for Mr Balcombe I enclose you a letter which I have lately received from Captain Browne [sic] of the *Ulysses* who brought home the last India Fleet, by which it will appear Mr B's charges will fully justify my solicitude for his welfare.[29]

Captain Samuel Brown, whom Tyrwhitt pointedly mentioned as endorsing the good opinion of his 'young Friend', was a greatly admired figure in the Royal Navy.[30] Lowe promptly approved the recommendation that Balcombe become providore to Napoleon and his court and be granted a handsome percentage from the allocated annual budget of £8000.

On New Year's Day 1816, Napoleon gathered his companions together for breakfast in the garden. 'A year ago,' he told them, 'I was at Elba.'[31] The thought saddened him and he said they must live together as a family: 'We are but a handful in one corner of the world, and all our consolation must be our regard for each other.'[32]

If the companions were a family, Tolstoy would have recognised them as unhappy in their own way: fractious, jostling and competing for their father's attention. They were suspicious of a new 'family' member who had arrived from England just three days earlier on the storeship *Cormorant*. Captain Charles Frédéric Piontkowski was a 30-year-old Polish officer who had been with Napoleon on Elba. After the defeat at Waterloo he had joined the devotees at Malmaison and on the flight to the port of Rochefort. He had sailed with them to England on HMS *Bellerophon*, but despite his pleas, he was not one of the designated companions chosen to join the *Northumberland*. Some of the group thought it suspicious that after three months the British had granted leave for Piontkowski, and only him, to join them.

Piontkowski was given a tent in the courtyard and was appointed horse-equerry under Gourgaud. He found him a hard taskmaster.

In order to oversee the catering, Balcombe was a regular visitor at Longwood. In mid-January, according to Gourgaud, he brought news: 'Balcombe informs me that Prince Joseph Bonaparte has arrived in America. The Emperor, overhearing these words, stops his reading, remains in thought for a moment, then expresses his satisfaction.'[33]

Soon afterwards, Balcombe brought his wife and daughters. They found Napoleon sitting on the steps of the green-latticed porch, chatting with young Tristan de Montholon. When he saw them he came forward: 'Running to my mother, he saluted her on each cheek. After which fashion he welcomed my sister; but, as usual with me, he seized me by the ear, and pinching it, exclaimed, *"Ah! Mademoiselle Betsee, êtes-vous sage, eh eh?"*—"Are you being good, eh?"'

He took them on a tour of his ironically dubbed 'palace', leading them first to his bedroom, which she found small and cheerless. The walls were covered in fluted nankeen fabric and the only decorations she observed were the different portraits of his son and the Empress Marie Louise which she had seen before. 'His bed was the little camp bedstead, with green silk hangings, on which he said he had slept when on the battlefields of Marengo and Austerlitz. The only thing approaching to magnificence in the furniture of this chamber, was a splendid silver wash-basin and ewer. The first object on which his eyes would rest on awaking, was a small bust of his son, which stood on the mantelpiece, facing his bed, and above which hung a portrait of Marie Louise. We then passed on, through an ante-room, to a small chamber, in which a bath had been put up for his use, and where he passed many hours of the day.'[34]

They proceeded to the stone-flagged kitchen, where Napoleon asked Pierron the confectioner to create creams and bonbons for the girls; he then led them into the garden. Betsy found the view dismal and forbidding: the overhanging cliffs and the great hulk of the Barn, the iron-coloured rocks scattered with prickly pear and aloes. Madame Bertrand had told Mrs Balcombe that the emperor stared for hours at the clouds rolling across it, wreathing into fantastic shapes.[35]

❇

Life for Napoleon and his court at Longwood settled into a pattern. He rose late and soaked in a hot bath, revelling in this pleasure. His offer to Las Cases to enjoy a plunge was declined with 'profound respect'. '*Mon cher,*' Napoleon chided him, 'in prison we must learn to help each other. After all I can't make use of this contraption all day long, and a bath will do you as much good as it does me.'[36] The count raised another subject: he wished to return Queen Hortense's diamond necklace that he still wore in a velvet band under his clothes. 'Napoleon asked, "Does it annoy you?" "No, Sire," was my answer. "Keep it then," said he.'[37]

Dictation of the memoirs continued during the day, broken by a three-course lunch and a more elaborate dinner. After the informality of The Briars, meals were now observed with great pomp and ceremony and a nightly tussle for precedence, the men in full dress uniform, the ladies resplendent in jewels and *décolleté* gowns. The liveried servants stood at attention throughout the meal. No one sat until invited by their emperor.

Fanny Bertrand sometimes found the dinners too tiresome. It demanded too great an effort to dress up, leave her children and walk or ride the mile to Longwood, particularly as Napoleon usually despatched his meal in twenty minutes, obliging his companions to stop eating when he did. However, he was annoyed when she and her husband absented themselves. 'They did the same thing at Elba,' he grumbled to Gourgaud. 'They think only of themselves, forgetting what they owe me. They take my house for a hotel. Let them dine here always or not at all.'[38]

After dinner there were games of chess and *reversi* [a strategy board game], or someone would read aloud from Racine, Molière or Voltaire. Madame de Montholon was often rebuked for nodding off. Intrigue, rivalry and jealousy simmered between members of the court, while their anger at the British often focused on the person of Sir George Cockburn, despite his efforts to make their lives more pleasant. As a New Year's offering, the admiral presented Napoleon with a German-built barouche—a four-wheeled carriage purchased from the departing governor.[39] He also returned the men's fowling pieces, but they responded that there was 'absolutely nothing to shoot upon the bleak rocks of Longwood'.[40]

After some prevarication, Napoleon was persuaded to join an excursion with the admiral and his secretary John Glover. They rode through undulating green fields and wooded hills; the lushness of the countryside was a surprise compared to the island's grim exterior. Their objective was Sandy Bay and one of the extraordinary sights of St Helena, the dramatic volcanic outcrop known as Lot, rising 1550 feet above the sea, with smaller jagged pinnacles—called Lot's Wife and Daughters—thrusting up from a barren ridge. But Napoleon would have been far more interested in the fact that Sandy Bay itself was one of the few places other than Jamestown where a boat could conceivably be landed, despite the roiling surf.

A few days afterwards, Napoleon entertained the admiral and several others to a formal dinner at Longwood. He managed to persuade Sir George that on walking and riding expeditions beyond the 12-mile boundary, Captain Poppleton, the English orderly officer, should follow on his horse 30 or 40 yards behind, instead of accompanying the party. Napoleon's ability to charm and ensnare a person was at work, for he later informed his followers 'that he could do what he liked with the Admiral'.[41]

The next day he rode off with Bertrand and Gourgaud to test the limits. Bertrand rebuked Poppleton: 'Captain, do you think that we are wanting to escape? You are almost on our backs! His Majesty desires that you should keep a greater distance.' The young officer deferred to him and, as they descended into a steep valley, kept his horse a hundred paces to the rear. At the bottom of the defile the French were out of Poppleton's sight. 'Let us gallop,' cried Napoleon. Suddenly he turned sharply to his left, and spurring his horse violently, urged him up the face of the precipice, making the large stones fly from under him and leaving the orderly officer aghast. The French took their mounts along a path observed during the Sandy Bay excursion, following the ridge above a valley which, a mile away, opened out to the sea and another possible, but still treacherous, landing place, Powell's Bay.

Captain Poppleton was in a state of panic, galloping wildly in every direction, but he baulked at the precipitous slope. In the end he gave up. At Deadwood Camp he ordered the flying of the blue flag, releasing the signal dreaded throughout the island: 'General Bonaparte is missing'. Poppleton had to personally inform Cockburn of the catastrophe. He found him at lunch with Colonel Bingham and the Balcombe family at The Briars, as Betsy described: 'He arrived breathless at our house, and, setting all ceremony aside, demanded to see Sir George, on business of the utmost importance. He was ushered at once into the dining room. The Admiral was in the act of discussing his soup, and listened with an imperturbable countenance to the agitated detail of the occurrence, with Captain Poppleton's startling exclamation of "Oh! Sir, I have lost the emperor!"'

Colonel Bingham was thrown into 'a state of anxiety', although the admiral said: 'There's no danger. Just a lesson for you.'[42] He advised Poppleton to return to Longwood where he would most probably find Bonaparte. 'This, as he prognosticated, was the case ... he found the emperor seated at dinner, and was unmercifully quizzed by him for the want of nerve he displayed in not daring to ride after him ... Napoleon often afterwards laughed at the consternation he had created.'[43] It had indeed been a lesson. Under the watch of Sir Hudson Lowe, Poppleton would have been court-martialled.

Henceforth the prisoner was obliged to have an officer in close attendance when outside the limits—with the result that he rejected the affront and would exercise only within the 12-mile boundary. For the next five years he stubbornly kept to this resolve. It was a decision that caused an inevitable decline in his health.

The bickering and backbiting continued, and stored resentments festered among members of the Longwood household. Gourgaud and Las Cases objected to someone of such lowly rank as Captain Piontkowski dining with them, and the Pole was relegated to the back dining room shared by Dr O'Meara and Poppleton, the British orderly officer. 'We still quarrelled,' wrote Las Cases, 'over the few remains of our life of luxury, and the relics of our ambitions.'[44]

Gourgaud was recovering from an attack of dysentery, and O'Meara, who attended him, thought he had never seen 'a man of the sword so excessively timorous'. Gourgaud's excessive devotion and endless carping were also wearying. Napoleon made a suggestion which was duly recorded: 'The Emperor orders me to buy a pretty slave for myself. I reply that I intend to do so.'[45]

Now that all the retinue lived within the Longwood boundary, Bonaparte's utterances, his grievances, his disputes with Admiral Cockburn and later his great battle with Governor Lowe were comprehensively documented by his followers, each with their own personal bias. Along with the daily reports of the two orderly officers, the place became a virtual literary colony—one of those benevolent residential retreats where catering is provided and writers work in seclusion but gather together to exchange ideas over meals.

There was of course the regular dictation of the emperor's vainglorious account of his military campaigns (which would become the massive and unreliable work *Mémorial de Sainte Hélène*, edited by Las Cases, who became known as the 'Boswell of St Helena'), but other French companions—General Bertrand, Count de Montholon and his wife Albine—were taking notes and storing up memories for future books to be published years later, as *Cahiers de Sainte Hélène*, *Récits de la Captivité* and *Souvenirs* respectively. Even the two valets, Marchand and Ali, recorded their exchanges with their master after leaving his presence, jotting down his confidences and *bons mots* for posterity.

On 24 February, the Balcombe sisters made another visit to Longwood. Betsy reminded Napoleon that when he was at The Briars he had promised to join in a game of Blindman's Buff but had not done so.[46] When he recalled what the game was (he knew it in France as *colin-maillard*), a foolish blundering about with a handkerchief tied over one's eyes, he tried to persuade her to choose something else, but then resigned himself to it.

Jane, young Tristan de Montholon and seven-year-old Napoleon Bertrand formed a circle in the reception room, with Marchand and Le Page the chef dragooned as well. They drew lots to see who would be blindfolded first. Betsy drew the paper with the words '*La Mort*' (death)—'whether accidentally or by Napoleon's contrivance', she wrote—and so was the first victim.

He tied a cambric handkerchief over her eyes. 'Can you see, Miss Betsee?'

'No,' she replied, although she could glimpse him through a corner. He waved his hat in front of her face and she flinched.

'Ah, leetle monkee,' he said in English. 'You can see pretty well!' He tied another handkerchief over the first, excluding all light.

She was led into the middle of the room, whirled about, and the game began.

Someone crept up and gave her nose a sharp tweak. She knew who that was and darted forward, almost succeeding in catching him, but he eluded her grasp. 'I then groped about, and, advancing again, he this time took hold of my ear and pulled it. I stretched out my hands instantly, and in the exultation of the moment screamed out, "I have got you! I have got you, now you shall be blindfolded!"'

He ducked out of the way and it was to her sister that she found herself clinging. Napoleon crowed that, as she had named the wrong person, she had to continue blindfolded.[47]

'Time,' declared Napoleon, 'is the only thing of which we have a superfluity.' He had been renowned for his economic handling of time and now that efficiency was useless. 'Our days,' wrote Las Cases, 'passed as may be imagined, in a great and stupid monotony. Ennui, memories, melancholy, were our dangerous enemies; work was our great, our only refuge. The Emperor followed with great regularity his occupations: English had become an important matter.'[48]

Since early in 1816, Napoleon had taken the study of English seriously, working at it for some hours every afternoon; he practised in the bath, but his lessons under Las Cases' tutelage never advanced far, as a scrap in his own handwriting testifies: 'Since sixt wek, y learn the english and y do not any progress. Sixt week do fourty and two day. If might have learn fivty word, for day I could know it two thousands and two hundred...'[49]

However, with the aid of a dictionary he was managing to read English newspapers. Every three or four weeks they received a large bundle of papers and journals from Europe, passed on to them by the admiral. Las Cases said that 'they were like a prod which aroused us and excited us very much for several days, when we discussed and appraised the news, and then we fell back once more, insensibly, into the morass'.[50] Everyone at Longwood was shocked in early February to learn of the death of Marshal Murat, Napoleon's brother-in-law and the former King of Naples. By order of the reinstalled monarch, Ferdinand IV, he had been executed by firing squad. They heard a rumour of a military revolt against Louis XVIII, but nothing came of it. They were startled and hopeful when unidentified ships in James Bay were fired upon by a cruiser and soldiers in the camp were called to arms. It turned out to be merely a failure of a visiting ship to respond to a signal.

A mysterious letter, delivered by clandestine means, assured Napoleon that his position would be much improved when Princess Charlotte, the twenty-year-old daughter of the Prince Regent, ascended the British throne.[51] Charlotte's mother, Caroline of Brunswick, was a cousin of Catherine of Württemberg, who had married Napoleon's youngest brother, Jerome, formerly King of Westphalia. Perhaps because of this family connection, Princess Caroline was said to have a 'fanatical admiration' for Bonaparte.[52]

Escape plans were whispered and stories circulated of rescue attempts being mounted by Joseph Bonaparte in America; after all, he had the ill-gotten crown jewels of Spain to finance a venture. They heard there was much enthusiasm for Napoleon in the United States and that a group of French émigrés were concocting schemes. The St Helena Archives holds correspondence relating to various ingenious plans foiled by the British, including one that involved a boat that 'will be in the shape of an old cask but so constructed that by pulling at both ends to be seaworthy and both boat and sails, which will be found inside, will be painted to correspond with the colour of the sea'.[53] Gourgaud wrote in his journal: 'In the morning, while out riding, we discuss our position. We should have been better off in the United States. I consider that the Prince Regent, yielding to public opinion, could get us brought back to England. We are also fortunate in that Princess Charlotte, on her accession to the throne, will wish to have us back.'[54]

It would not have been far from their minds that if the elusive rumours about William Balcombe were true, Princess Charlotte could possibly be his half-sister.

CHAPTER 11

THE NEW GOVERNOR

The charabanc tour of the Napoleonic sites ended in the grounds of Plantation House, an elegant Georgian mansion of 35 rooms, the official residence of St Helena's governors for over two hundred years. Napoleon never went there but always complained that it should have been made available for him and his suite.

Its front lawn extends as a level green field, a delightful location for garden parties, terminating in an abrupt shelf with a view of the vast grey Atlantic. We saw huddled in the grass five giant tortoises, celebrities for visitors. The most notable of them was the elderly Jonathan. Although it has been said that he is a living link with Bonaparte, that is not the case. He was a gift from the governor of the Seychelles and arrived in 1882 as a mature tortoise aged at least fifty, making him over 180 years old. *The Times* has claimed that he is the oldest animal in the world.[1] I tried to become acquainted with Jonathan but he regarded me blearily—he is blind in one eye and almost so in the other.

On 14 April 1816, the island's new governor, General Sir Hudson Lowe, Knight Commander of the Bath (KCB), arrived on the frigate HMS *Phaeton*. The 46-year-old veteran was accompanied by his wife of three and a half months, her two adolescent daughters, his aide-de-camp, a private secretary, a military secretary, other officials, and the 2nd Battalion of the 66th Regiment of Foot. Lowe had every reason to believe that this appointment as the guardian of England's greatest enemy would be a high point in his career, although not necessarily the highest; he had been assured that 'it should not stop there'.[2] He could not have imagined that his new position would ultimately cause him to be reviled by many of his own countrymen, including some in positions of power, for the rest of his days.

Napoleon was inclined to welcome the arrival of the new governor, who would supplant both Sir George Cockburn and Governor Wilks as his chief custodian. The admiral had proved upright, inflexible, difficult to charm—unlike the British commissioner on Elba, Sir Neil Campbell, who had been trusting enough to absent himself from the island, so facilitating Napoleon's escape. Campbell was an experienced military man, as was Lowe, and Napoleon claimed to understand soldiers. He heard that Lowe had seen action at Champaubert and Montmirail and remarked: 'We have then probably exchanged a few cannon-balls together, and that is always, in my eyes, a noble relation to stand in.'[3] It was hoped by the French party that the new governor was bringing instructions to 'extend the prison to the entire island' and so he was 'awaited with impatience'.[4]

The day after landing, Lowe was officially inaugurated as governor and then set about meeting his important charge, sending a message that he would call at Longwood at nine o'clock the following morning. Napoleon was not in the habit of receiving callers until the afternoon and simply ignored the message. He told O'Meara that it was a deliberate insult on Admiral Cockburn's part, an attempt to embroil him with the new governor, for 'he well knew that I never had received any persons, nor ever would, at that hour; he did it out of malice'.[5] The admiral, he grumbled, was a 'real shark'. But O'Meara had been in town and learned from someone on the governor's staff that Lowe brought instructions from the British government infinitely more severe than those the admiral had put into effect. As he left the room, the doctor whispered to Marchand: 'I wish the shark could remain with us; we will regret him, you can be sure.'[6]

When Governor Lowe, the admiral and some of their staff arrived in the pelting rain the following morning they were refused admission.

As the officially appointed custodian of the prisoner, Lowe naturally assumed that he could see him when he chose. He strode around the house, attempting to peer in. They were told that 'the emperor' was 'indisposed' but was prepared to offer an audience the next day at four o'clock.

When it took place in Longwood's drawing room on the afternoon of 17 April, the meeting was brief but pleasant enough. However, the admiral was summarily excluded, something he never forgave. 'He told me,' Lowe wrote in a despatch, 'that Bertrand had almost shut the door in his face as he was following me into the room; that a servant had put his arm across him.'[7] This slight to Cockburn had not been intended by Napoleon and was soon regretted by him.

The two men who faced each other in the room were born within a month of each other.[8] They were diametrically opposed physical types. Napoleon was short and increasingly rotund, with the famous Roman-coin profile, smooth olive skin and blue-grey eyes known from a thousand portraits and caricatures. His visitor was tall and wiry, with greying reddish hair, sandy tufted eyebrows and the mottled pink complexion of a sun-intolerant Celt who tended to blink through pale eyelashes. At Napoleon's request they spoke in Italian. He had heard that the new governor had commanded a regiment of Corsicans, although he may not have known that Lowe had requisitioned the Buonaparte house in Ajaccio.[9]

Napoleon asked how Lowe had found the Corsicans: 'They carry the stiletto; are they not a bad people?'

'They do not carry the stiletto, having abandoned that custom in our service,' the new governor replied. 'They have always conducted themselves with propriety. I was very well satisfied with them.'

The encounter passed off tolerably well and Lowe had clearly striven to be diplomatic. However, Napoleon had developed 'an instinctive antipathy' towards him.[10] He remarked to O'Meara: 'He is hideous. He has a most villainous countenance. But we must not decide too hastily. The man's disposition may, perhaps, make amends for the unfavourable impression which his face produces. This is not impossible.'[11] He was willing to wait and see.

Good relations were not advanced when Lowe—carrying out the specific instruction of Lord Bathurst—left a document with Montholon, requiring that all the French sign it. It stated that they were at liberty to leave St Helena and return to Europe; however, if they wished to remain on the island they must declare this in writing and submit to all restrictions imposed on them. Montholon showed a translation of the paper to Napoleon, who promptly tore it up and dictated new words: 'We, the undersigned, wishing to continue in the service of HM the Emperor Napoleon, consent, horrible as is the abode in St Helena, to remain here. We submit to the restrictions, though unjust and arbitrary, that are imposed upon HM and upon the persons in his service.'[12] This version was promptly rejected by the governor. All the French were eventually obliged to sign the original document.

Lowe had brought directions from Bathurst 'to supply Buonaparte's table in the most liberal manner' instead of just the eight dining places which the admiral, following instructions, had imposed.[13] This was good news for Balcombe, whose percentage increased accordingly. He now had 52 people to feed in the Longwood establishment: Napoleon's companions, their four children, 36 servants (many of them hired locally), the two orderly English officers and O'Meara.

British newspapers held that Bonaparte's appetite was voracious, that he drank a pot of port and two bottles of claret at breakfast. Napoleon, actually abstemious, read some of the reports and told O'Meara: 'Why, I do not know what the English will make of me in the end; they say that I drink so many bottles of wine daily, that I eat so much, that I will produce a famine on this detestable rock. I suppose that they will make me eat a *live bull* at a meal by-and-bye.'[14] Neither Lowe nor his prisoner nor anyone else on the island knew that the doctor's reports of their conversations were read at the highest level of the Admiralty. Bathurst had been made privy and chose not to tell the governor, so almost two years passed before Lowe learned of the conduit.[15] Meanwhile, he himself found O'Meara a useful channel for Longwood gossip.

Gourgaud and Bertrand visited Plantation House to farewell the retiring governor Colonel Sir Mark Wilks and his wife and daughter, departing in a few days for England. 'I pay my respects to Madame Wilks and say "Goodbye" to the adorable Laura,' Gourgaud lamented.[16]

But Bertrand had another agenda. He took Wilks aside to query if there would be 'any impropriety' in asking him 'to take charge of a communication from the Emperor to your Government, or would you consider such a charge to be troublesome?'

Wilks was appalled at the attempt to bypass his replacement, who had been on the island just five days. He chose to misunderstand Bertrand's meaning: 'Far from troublesome; I shall be very happy to take charge of any communication from General Bonaparte which may be committed to me for that purpose by Sir Hudson Lowe.'

Bertrand looked confused. 'And not otherwise?'

'Certainly not,' Wilks answered. 'I am sorry you should think it necessary to propose to any person a deviation from the prescribed channel of communication; and very sorry that you should think it proper to make such a proposition to me.'[17] Later in the day he informed Lowe of the exchange.

Nonetheless, Napoleon sent good wishes for Wilks's health and an agreeable voyage as the former governor took his leave.[18] On 23 April, the Balcombes were at the marina as the Wilks family embarked on the barge for the *Havannah*. As Betsy later recalled: 'Not a dry eye was to be seen amongst the crowd then collected; that leave-taking of our much loved and respected governor and his family resembled more a funeral than a *levée*, so sad and solemn was every face.'[19] Sir Hudson Lowe must have known that he would never inspire that kind of affection.

Lowe regarded Bonaparte's attempt to appeal to the Prince Regent behind his back as little less than a declaration of war. He instituted the new restrictions advised by Bathurst. No stranger was to meet with 'General Bonaparte' without the governor's permission. Certain officers of the 53rd Regiment who had been in the habit of making social calls on the Bertrands were told that their visits were not sanctioned. The number of sentries at Longwood was increased. Captain Poppleton was instructed to sight Bonaparte twice a day. Thomas Brooke, the governing council secretary, and Lowe's secretary Major Gorrequer visited the town's shopkeepers and instructed them to refuse credit to the French or risk severe punishment. 'The tradespeople were forbidden to sell anything to us directly,' wrote Montholon, 'and were threatened, in case of disobedience, with the seizure and confiscation of their goods. Everything was now to pass through the medium of the governor or his agents.'[20]

Lowe was alarmed when he received a report from Poppleton on 30 April that the prisoner had not been sighted the previous day. He hurried to Longwood and met Montholon at the door, who said that his master was indisposed and suffering. It was after four o'clock in the afternoon and Lowe was agreeably surprised when Napoleon indicated he would see him. The governor was ushered into the bedroom and found his charge reclining in his dressing-gown, breathing heavily.

It became clear that Napoleon had admitted him having heard that some commissioners were arriving soon, representing the French, Russian and Austrian Allies. He launched into a harangue. The Allies had made a convention declaring him their prisoner, but they had no authority to do so. 'I wish you to write to your Government and acquaint it I shall protest against it. I gave myself up to England and to no other Power . . . I misunderstood the character of the English people. I should have surrendered myself to the Emperor of Russia who was my friend, or to the Emperor of Austria who was my relation. There is courage in putting a man to death, but it is an act of cowardice to let him languish, and to poison him, in so horrid an island and in so detestable a climate.'

Lowe protested. St Helena had never been viewed in that light; except for necessary security precautions, it was the wish of the British government to render Napoleon's situation as comfortable as possible; in fact, the components of a new house and furniture were being shipped from England.

Napoleon listed his grievances: he hated the locality of Longwood, the sparseness of trees, his exclusion from free conversation with the local inhabitants, the fact that he was denied a greater range for exercise unless accompanied by an officer, and the outrage that the governor had presumed to interrogate his servants.[21]

This rancorous second meeting proved pivotal. After it, Napoleon characterised himself as 'a regular porcupine' on whom the governor 'does not know where to put his hand'.[22] He called for O'Meara to enter his bedroom. He wanted confirmation that he was not being spied upon and asked the doctor how he conceived his position, and whether he had 'orders to report every trifling occurrence or illness, or what I say to you, to the governor?'

O'Meara replied that his role was 'as your surgeon, and to attend upon you and your suite. I have received no other orders than to make an immediate report in case of your being taken seriously ill, in order to have promptly the advice and assistance of other physicians.' He denied that he was in any capacity a spy for the governor, omitting to mention, of course, that he *was* now in that capacity for the Admiralty and was playing a double game.

Napoleon accepted his assurance: 'I have never had the least occasion to find fault with you, and I have a friendship for you and an esteem for your character.'[23]

Napoleon took up riding again within the 12-mile limit with Las Cases and Gourgaud. They frequently visited a favourite glade in Geranium Valley where, at Napoleon's request, willow cuttings had been planted, reminding him of Josephine's garden and lake at Malmaison. Occasionally they would see two pretty farmers' daughters working in the fields and Napoleon would wave or stop and say a few words, although the girls' answers were always brief and nervous. He had invented names for them—the daughter of Farmer Knipe was 'Rosebud', and Miss Marianne Robinson, from a farm across the valley, was 'The Nymph'.

Returning from one of these outings on 5 May, the riders encountered William Balcombe, walking with James Urmston, the English manager of the Company factory in Canton, whose ship was in port. Napoleon invited both men to join him for lunch in Longwood's garden. In the course of the meal, the French voiced their bitter complaints about Governor Lowe. Gourgaud recorded: 'We don't have much to say in favour of the Governor! Balcombe, who was present at the interview, is confident that we shall soon be back again in France. That is the general opinion.'[24] According to Bertrand's journal of the same date, Balcombe said that the admiral was far superior to the governor in rank and 'played a straight bat'. He added that the governor knew nothing about administration.[25]

Balcombe's remarks would certainly have reached the governor's ears. It is on record that James Urmston 'saw a good deal' of

Lowe at Plantation House and maintained a correspondence with him, and that Lowe, 'who had a genius for systematizing his private intelligences ... gave Urmston a kind of roving commission as anti-Napoleonic informer for the Far East'.[26] This explains Lowe's early suspicion of Balcombe and his resentment of his intimacy with the people at Longwood. Although he was aware of Balcombe's influential connections in London and the fact that Admiral Cockburn seemed particularly friendly with him, he thought he should be closely watched. The agent he could rely upon was Lieutenant-Colonel Sir Thomas Reade, his deputy adjutant-general.

Reade had been his chief of staff at Genoa and afterwards had been 'employed in the intelligence department'. According to the historian Gilbert Martineau, the short, plump and baby-faced 31-year-old Reade was 'the most savage and the least scrupulous enemy the French possessed'.[27] About this time, Reade became a regular visitor at The Briars. People believed that he was paying court to young Betsy, but almost certainly those attentions provided a convenient cover.

If Napoleon was not reconciled to his situation, at least he was becoming realistic. He also seemed calmer, but this may have been because in mid-May he was working on an escape plan proposed by Las Cases. The plan is referred to in Montholon's papers, although without details.[28] Lowe's rigorous security procedures had fuelled Napoleon's determination to outwit him. If he could manage to escape he would destroy the governor's career.

Towards the end of May, the Balcombes came to lunch at Longwood, which would not have endeared them to the governor. Gourgaud had his usual objections to the girls, calling them 'silly geese': 'They refer to His Majesty as the "General", for which we twit them. They visit Mme Montholon and make grimaces behind her back.'[29] (The grimaces no doubt concerned Madame's advanced pregnancy—the baby was due the following month.)

Napoleon had a temporary distraction from his annoyance with the governor, a two-wheeled calash or jaunting car, for which he had paid £245.[30] Far speedier than Wilks's old four-wheeled barouche, it had just arrived from the Cape and he proposed taking Betsy and Jane for a ride. Archambault the groom lashed six skittish horses three abreast and they set off at a hard gallop. Napoleon took mischievous pleasure in calling for an increase in pace as they thundered around the yawning chasm known as the Devil's Punchbowl. He seemed gratified by the terror on Betsy's face. 'The party occupying the side nearest the declivity seemed almost hanging over the precipice,' she wrote, 'while the others were, apparently, crushed against the gigantic walls formed by the perpendicular rock . . . He added to my fright, by repeatedly assuring me the horses were running away, and that we should be all dashed to pieces.' She was relieved when they joined her mother at Hutt's Gate, to take tea with the Bertrands in their cramped cottage.[31]

A ship arrived on 29 May from England bringing general supplies, newspapers and mail. Napoleon asked O'Meara 'to procure the *Morning Chronicle*, the *Globe*, or any of the opposition or neutral papers'.[32] The doctor returned, bringing also the book-sized conservative *Quarterly Review*. With Las Cases assisting with translation, Napoleon began leafing through it. It contained eight lengthy articles on 'Buonaparte', including accounts of his humiliating 'unconditional surrender' on the *Bellerophon*, the voyage on the *Northumberland* and his stay at The Briars. Each article made him more infuriated than the last, especially a description of his 'series of weaknesses and petulances' at the Balcombes: his alleged bullying of the family at cards, of frightening young Alexander for asking if he was 'the Great Mogul', and of challenging Betsy over the question of the burning of Moscow.

When the mail was delivered, Napoleon received a letter from his mother, 65-year-old Madame Mère, who was living comfortably with his sister Pauline in Rome. Gourgaud watched him read. '"I am very old," she says in her letter to the Emperor, "to undertake a voyage of 2000 leagues. I shall probably die on the way, but what does it matter? I shall die near you." His Majesty tore the letter up.'[33]

CHAPTER 12

GOLD LACE AND NODDING PLUMES

In the late afternoon of 17 June 1816, the *Newcastle* frigate put in at James Bay, bearing the flag of Rear-Admiral Sir Pulteney Malcolm, KCB. He was to succeed Sir George Cockburn as commander of the South Atlantic naval station with its bases at St Helena and the Cape of Good Hope. Also on board were his wife, Lady Clementina, and the three foreign commissioners sent to monitor Bonaparte's detention, in accordance with the Allies' convention of August 1815. The Continental powers were determined that there should be no repetition of the escape from Elba. Count Balmain was the representative for Russia, Baron von Stürmer for Austria, accompanied by his wife, and the Marquis de Montchenu for France. Prussia had sent no commissioner, consistent with its position that Bonaparte should have been executed.

The following day (as it happened, the anniversary of the Battle of Waterloo), the dignitaries were welcomed ashore and Sir George Cockburn was farewelled with much ceremony, a military parade and salutes fired from the Ladder Hill battery.[1] Many of the leading citizens gathered for the occasion, including the Balcombes. They established an immediate rapport with the new admiral and his wife and invited them to stay at The Briars until a house was prepared for them.

Sir Pulteney Malcolm, in the prime of his career at 48, had entered the navy at the age of ten and seen action in the Caribbean, Mediterranean, North Sea, East Indies and China; he had served as third in command behind then Rear-Admiral Cockburn during the Anglo-American War of 1812–14. He was exceedingly well connected: three of his brothers were also knighted, one of them a vice-admiral; and his wife Clementina was the eldest daughter of the Honourable William Fullarton Elphinstone, a director of the East India Company. Significantly, she was also the niece of Admiral Lord Keith, who had informed Napoleon of his final destination.[2] Malcolm was on good terms with the Duke of Wellington, having commanded the squadron that co-operated with him during the Waterloo campaign.

At Longwood House, someone mentioned the Waterloo anniversary and 'a shade of anguish passed over the features of the emperor. In slow and solemn tones he said, "Incomprehensible day! Concurrence of unheard-of fatalities!"'[3]

Also on that day, Madame de Montholon gave birth to a daughter. Dr O'Meara, always spiteful about the Frenchwoman, sent a note to Major Gorrequer: 'I don't imagine there was half so much anxiety over the birth of the King of Rome. You would have thought it the case of a girl of fifteen, newly married, instead of the wrinkled, middle-aged woman who has three husbands, all living, and eight or nine children.'[4] Madame presented the baby to 'His Majesty', who permitted her to call the child 'Hélène Napoleone'.[5]

Keen to assess the new admiral, Napoleon agreed to the governor presenting him. Lowe was able to report to Lord Bathurst of the meeting on 20 June that Bonaparte's 'questions were of no significant import; but they indicated quite a different disposition to that with which he had received me on the occasion of my last conference with him, and had to Sir Pulteney Malcolm the appearance of a very marked overture'.[6] The charm was intended for the new admiral, whose person and rumoured connections had impressed Napoleon.

The presence of the commissioners disturbed Lowe. The British government had not welcomed their appointment or their purpose—to make clear that Bonaparte was 'a prisoner of Europe'. The *Newcastle* brought an official despatch from Bathurst and also his private letter to Lowe suggesting that the commissioners would 'have too little to do where they are going not to be tempted to do a little mischief', such as forming a 'cabal'—a conspiratorial group—with the French. He thought they should be encouraged 'to amuse themselves by going to the Cape by way of a change of scene,' and Lowe could engage to furnish them and their Court with a regular account of the state of the prisoner.[7] Napoleon actually agreed. 'What folly it is,' he exclaimed to O'Meara, 'to send those commissioners out here. Without charge or responsibility, they will have nothing to do but to walk about the streets and creep up the rocks. The Prussian government has displayed more judgment and saved its money.'[8]

Catherine Younghusband informed her aunt, Lady Roche in Ireland, that important personages seemed to be everywhere on the few streets: 'There is nothing now to be seen in St Helena but Generals, Admirals, Staff officers & Military & Naval heroes of all ages. You cannot walk through the streets of James Town without knocking against Knights or Knights Companions. My Eyes are dazzled by Gold Lace & Nodding Plumes & my Ears confused by the Sir Georges, Sir Thomases, etc.'[9]

Alexandre Antonovich, Comte de Balmain, capable, urbane, multilingual and literate, with a Scottish and Russian background, represented the Czar and was to send his reports through the Russian foreign minister, Count Nesselrode. Balmain was asked to make a daily record of what he observed and any conversations of interest. His astute despatches were soon eagerly anticipated and read with pleasure at the Russian court.[10]

The Austrian commissioner, Baron Barthelemy von Stürmer, an elegant young man of 29, came with instructions from Prince Metternich and a sense of self-importance. Another trained diplomat, he brought with him to St Helena a beautiful young French wife.[11] Betsy Balcombe left an account of how, soon after her arrival, Madame von Stürmer visited The Briars to see the pavilion formerly occupied by her hero, and burst into tears at its tiny size.[12]

The French commissioner came from an ancient and distinguished family. The Marquis Claude Marin Henri de Montchenu, aged 59, had escaped France early in the Revolution and been an émigré, living in Prussia, for over twenty years. A devout royalist, on the return of Louis XVIII he had pestered him for a position. It was

Talleyrand who suggested appointing him commissioner to St Helena: 'He will bore the prisoner to death.'[13] With his social ineptitude, portly build and old-fashioned pigtail tied with a ribbon, Montchenu was soon regarded on the island as a figure of fun, a buffoon.[14] Napoleon commented: 'When you have seen Montchenu you have seen all the old nobility of France before the revolution.'[15]

The commissioners were accommodated at the Porteous lodgings in town and took most of their evening meals with the governor and his wife at Plantation House. Montchenu spoke no English but performed excessive gallantries towards the attractive Lady Lowe, while his prodigious appetite soon earned him the nickname 'Old Munchenough'.

A parcel of books and journals, unloaded from the *Newcastle*, was delivered to Longwood. Napoleon was so eager he unpacked them himself. O'Meara found him in his bedchamber the next day, 'surrounded with heaps of books: his countenance was smiling and he was in perfect good humour. He had been occupied in reading nearly all the night.'[16]

Also included in the official despatch from Lord Bathurst to Lowe (which emphasised that the expense of Bonaparte's household should not exceed £8000 a year and hoped a number of the French would accept an offer to leave) was a confidential letter from Sir Henry Bunbury, Under-Secretary of State, giving Lowe cause to keep a close watch on all correspondence to and from Longwood: 'By an intercepted letter to Bonaparte which Sir George Cockburn sent home, it is clear that the ex-Emperor has large sums of money in different parts; and that his agents have lodged money on his account in the principal towns of America as well as in England, with the hope of his being able to get at some one or other of their deposits. We have been unable hitherto to obtain any clue to this matter: it is very desirable to discover both the treasure and the agents.'[17]

Napoleon looked forward to his next meeting with Sir Pulteney and Lady Malcolm. He was now aware that she was the niece of Admiral Lord Keith, Commander-in-Chief of the English Channel Fleet, whom he had met at Plymouth and through whom the decisions of the British government were conveyed. She was also friendly with the liberals Lord Holland and John Cam Hobhouse, who had protested in the press and Parliament against the severity of his incarceration. It was at this meeting that he was to learn from Lady Clementina Malcolm of an extraordinary, quite unprecedented circumstance concerning her first cousin, Admiral Keith's daughter.

The time came for the Malcolms' visit to Longwood on 25 June. Napoleon made a special effort to be hospitable. Lady Malcolm described for her cousin how he sent his four-wheeled 'German barouche drawn by six little Cape horses' for herself and Madame Bertrand while the admiral and grand marshal rode beside them. The visitors arrived and were ceremoniously shown into the drawing room, darkened with green venetian blinds. Lady Malcolm was invited to sit on the sofa beside the former emperor, a rare privilege.

When discussion turned to the East India Company, Napoleon hinted at a conflict between Lady Malcolm's father being a slave company's director and her own liberal sentiments. He expressed surprise, 'with a satirical expression of countenance, at finding slaves on an island so long in possession of the English, and belonging to so rich a Company'. She admitted that she could not reply, 'feeling it was a disgrace'.

It was from Lady Malcolm that Napoleon then heard a fascinating story. It was the talk of society circles in England. One of Napoleon's trusted aides-de-camp, Comte Auguste Charles de Flahaut, who had been with him during the Russian campaign and at Waterloo, had escaped to England after the final defeat. He was widely believed to be the natural son of the wily and brilliant Count Talleyrand, with whom his mother had lived openly for a decade. Talleyrand's care in furthering the boy's career virtually confirmed the assumption.[18]

In adulthood, as we have already seen, the dashing young Flahaut became the lover of Queen Hortense of Holland, stepdaughter of Napoleon and estranged wife of his brother Louis. After Waterloo, Hortense sent her lover anxious letters, beseeching him to join her in Switzerland. Instead, Flahaut stayed in England. In danger of arrest as a Bonaparte accomplice, he was given refuge at Holland House. At a Christmas dinner with the Hollands he met the attractive Margaret Mercer Elphinstone, the only child of Admiral Lord Keith.

Lord Byron was present and fancied her himself, but she and the Frenchman had eyes only for each other. Hortense was left to languish in Switzerland.[19]

Beneath the careful orchestration of Regency society courtship, with its balls, house parties, whist drives, assembly rooms and spas, was the ruthless marriage market depicted by Jane Austen, where high social status and wealth were the trading stocks, followed by beauty and youth. Margaret Mercer Elphinstone, possessing all four, was a grand prize. A graceful 28-year-old, the daughter of a viscount who was a much-respected admiral, she was independently wealthy, heiress to her mother's fortune. She was also the best friend and confidante of Princess Charlotte, the Prince Regent's daughter.

Margaret had declined numerous marriage proposals from rich and powerful men. Notably, she knocked back William Cavendish, the fifth Duke of Devonshire, owner of the magnificent Chatsworth in Derbyshire, Devonshire House in London and other great estates. Four months after the Holland House dinner, Byron sent her a message from Dover, 'that he would not have had to go into exile if he had married her'.[20] But she was smitten with the Count de Flahaut, former aide and personal friend of Britain's greatest enemy. On hearing of this, Admiral Lord Keith was apoplectic. He emphatically refused permission for his daughter to marry the Frenchman; when she persisted, he disinherited her. Margaret confided her distress to her cousin and close friend, Lady Malcolm.

London society was avid for details of the unlikely match (the wedding was to occur in June 1817, without Lord Keith's blessing). Gossip thrived in the newspapers. The story was naturally of riveting interest to the people at Longwood.

Lady Malcolm had actually arrived on the island with a letter from Flahaut for his good friend Fanny Bertrand; she had been asked by her cousin to deliver it secretly, but she replied from The Briars, where she and her husband were staying with the Balcombes, that she felt constrained from giving Fanny the letter from Flahaut. Governor Lowe had told her he objected to it being delivered as it had not come through the 'proper channels' and he was annoyed by the volume of mail that was reaching the Bertrands, 'sent in parcels and in various clandestine ways'.[21]

O'Meara reported that his patient was 'much pleased' with Sir Pulteney Malcolm and his wife.[22] Of course he was. Napoleon was bound to cultivate the Malcolms, given their connections. As fond as he was of his stepdaughter Hortense, now abandoned by her lover, he would have been delighted to hear of his former aide-de-camp moving in such influential circles in London, of his new romance and of Miss Margaret Elphinstone's close friendship with the Princess of Wales.[23]

Meanwhile, Hortense was residing at Baden Baden with her sons by her estranged husband: Napoleon Louis was aged twelve and Louis Napoleon four years younger. The latter, in subsequent years, was to become a friend of Betsy Balcombe and would entreat her to tell stories about his illustrious uncle. Later still he would proclaim himself Emperor Napoleon III.

Napoleon still considered that his best hope of release from St Helena, other than through the Regent himself, was by Princess Charlotte taking a personal interest in his case. He was delighted to learn that she had married Prince Leopold of Saxe-Coburg-Gotha at the beginning of May. He said that the prince, who had once applied to be his aide-de-camp, was one of the most handsome and pleasant young men he had ever met.[24] All the while, the tantalising rumour of William Balcombe's blood connection with the royal family persisted.

The purveyor visited the Bertrands at Hutt's Gate on 28 June and was particularly indiscreet about his house guests. According to Bertrand's 1816 journal, still with no published English translation, Balcombe reported that Lady Malcolm was very happy about her conversation with the emperor; that Napoleon had many supporters in England as well as many women admirers and that their numbers were increasing daily; and that Admiral Malcolm would be staying on the island for just one year, and for less time than that if the emperor himself departed, in which case he would accompany him.[25]

It may have been to impress the Malcolms that Napoleon reopened the issue of the slave Toby's freedom. O'Meara recorded: 'When Napoleon discovered some time after the departure of Sir George Cockburn that the poor man had not been emancipated, he directed

Mr Balcombe to purchase him from his master [a certain Captain Wrangham, who had left the island], set him at liberty and charge the amount to Count Bertrand's private account.' Both Balcombe and O'Meara had put this to the governor, who 'however, thought proper to prohibit this'.[26] Montholon's memoirs provide further details, including the alleged reason for Lowe's refusal: his fear of a great slave uprising such as that led by Toussaint L'Ouverture in the Caribbean.

On 2 July, Lowe visited Longwood and spoke to Montholon, the official manager of the household, about a reduction in expenses, particularly for food and wine. Balcombe's purveyorship was criticised too, not just for the excessive quantity of food provided, but for its inedible nature.

The governor refused Montchenu permission to visit Madame Bertrand, which drove her to distraction, as the marquis had seen her ailing mother in France before setting off for St Helena. Napoleon still declined to meet the commissioners, which suited Lowe. Count Bertrand had conveyed the message that 'if they wished to be introduced as private persons' they should apply to him, but 'The Emperor' would not receive them officially. He did not recognise the right of the Allied powers to arbitrate upon his fate. He was the prisoner of England 'in fact, but not in right', but not the prisoner of Europe.[27]

Lowe fretted about what the commissioners were doing, determined to prevent any undue association between them and the people at Longwood. They in turn, finding themselves watched and their freedom curtailed, complained about him to their home governments, so adding to Lowe's growing unfavourable reputation. Count Balmain's assessment went to the Czar: 'The responsibility with which he has been charged makes him tremble, and he becomes alarmed at the slightest incident, puzzles his brain for hours over nothing, and does with vast trouble what any one else would do in a minute.'[28] Balmain had no idea at the time that he was writing about his future father-in-law.

On 10 July, O'Meara sent a letter from Longwood to Sir Thomas Reade, officially the governor's deputy adjutant-general, effectively his espionage agent. In it the doctor sounded remarkably like a spy himself: 'I understand from Madame that they have it in contemplation here to forward a letter of complaint against Sir Hudson to England (by what channel I did not understand), containing, no doubt, divers untruths, and praying he may be recalled. You had better give Sir Hudson a hint about it, but let it be between you and him only; as, though I have some reason to think that some plot is hatching, I am not quite sure of it, and any premature disclosure of it would not be the thing.'[29]

He went on to protest again about the food supplies to Longwood, lodging the blame to Balcombe's partners rather than to the man he claimed as a friend. He said that Montholon was building up a file, finding out the price of every item of food and drink brought to the house. However, the purveyor had defenders in Sir Pulteney and Lady Malcolm, who were still at The Briars. Lady Malcolm wrote to her aunt, the wife of Admiral Lord Keith, that she sympathised with Balcombe for having to feed the ingrates at Longwood: 'They complained that the wine was bad, but how can it be otherwise, for if they get a week's supply at a time, the servants drink it all in three days.' Bonaparte had a great appetite and demanded a roast every day; after fourteen consecutive days of roast pork, he complained: '"*Encore cochon de lait*". It was the fault of his own people, who took the turkeys and geese, and continued to send the pigs to his table!'[30] But the cost of catering was enormous and Bonaparte himself had said that Balcombe 'costs more than he is worth'.

Meanwhile, the Colonial Office had sent out the components for a new prefabricated house to make the prisoner and his retinue more comfortable. Napoleon had refused to discuss it, saying he would not remain on the island long enough for it to be built. Lowe was trying to do his best and wanted to get workers started on the construction. He asked O'Meara where he thought General Bonaparte would like it erected. The doctor promptly answered: 'He would like the Briars.' The governor said that was out of the question—it was too close to town.[31]

'I hate this Longwood,' Napoleon fulminated. 'The sight of it makes me melancholy. Let him put me in some place where there is shade, verdure and water. Here it either blows a furious wind, loaded with rain and fog, or the sun beats on my head through the want of shade, when I go out. Let him put me on the Plantation House side of the island if he really wishes to do anything for me. But what is the use of coming up here proposing things, and doing nothing?'[32]

He was in a bad mood, having read an account in *The Times* which he recognised as being by Catherine Younghusband. In a private letter that her aunt had sent to the newspaper, she had boasted that after she and her daughter sang Bonaparte an Italian duet, 'I understood he talked of us for three days'. There was a description of the dinner to which she had been invited: 'The greatest state and etiquette is observed at the Court of Longwood; not a single word was uttered during dinner, excepting by Buonaparte himself. All the Marshals and Countesses sat mumchance; but I chattered away to his Majesty without any fear, which appeared to amaze them all. You cannot form an idea of the awe they all stand in of him, and he treats them, ladies and all, in the most cavalier manner.' The former emperor had offered her a plate of sweetmeats and 'I was told by his Secretary, Count Lascases [sic], that it was a favour Queens had never received from him'.[33]

There would be no further invitations for Mrs Younghusband. Las Cases defended her and said that her words had been misconstrued. He wrote later that she had 'declared openly that she had not written the ridiculous letter which had appeared under her name, and that either her friends in England had made alterations in that letter, or it had been read in company, imperfectly retained and incorrectly sent to the press'.[34] Nonetheless, Catherine's name never appeared again in the orderly's log of visitors to Longwood.[35]

The Times caused more trouble, reporting that Madame Bertrand was 'sick of the adventure, quarrels with her husband for being such a fool as to stay at St Helena and wishes to return home. All Buonaparte's French cooks and servants mutinied, and said they were prisoners of war as well as himself, and would not obey him.'[36]

The omens were not auspicious when on 16 July Lowe arrived at Longwood for his fourth interview with his prisoner, which he reported in detail to Bathurst. He was ushered into the presence to find Napoleon with his hat under his arm. The prisoner launched into a litany of complaints about the restrictions imposed on him and his suite, especially the opening of their mail before it was delivered to them. Lowe replied that he acted only in compliance with his instructions.

Napoleon observed that it was unnecessary to impose so many restraints—it was almost impossible to get away from the island: 'It would be impossible, unless with the connivance of the governor or of the admiral.' He was not interested in the building of a new house; it would take six years' construction 'and by then there will be a change in the Ministry in England, or a new government in France, and I shall no longer be here'. In the meantime he wished to move to a more pleasant location. Lowe answered, as he took his leave, that he was 'always happy to show attention to every request' which was not incompatible with the main object of his duty.[37]

CHAPTER 13

THIS ACCURSED PLACE

An American vessel, 'a very fast sailer', appeared off the island in July 1816 but eluded the British frigates that tried to intercept her. It returned day after day, as if reconnoitring landing places. It may have been the *True Blooded Yankee*; Bathurst had sent Lowe intelligence in May that this privateer had sailed from Bahia, Brazil, with the aim of liberating Bonaparte. Lowe supported Admiral Malcolm's request for another fast vessel to ward off such attempts: 'I really consider a small corvette well to windward as essential to prevent the approach of any suspicious vessel. There is hardly any obstacle otherwise to their coming in close to the shore during the night-time, sending in a boat, and disappearing before the morning.'[1]

Napoleon now found a use for the billiard table the governor had sent up to Longwood: to lay out his escape-plan maps. Montholon had received an offer from an English captain to help get Napoleon past the barrier of sentries, off the island and transport him to the United States, 'for a million, to be paid on landing'. Gourgaud took part in the discussion around the baize table: 'Napoleon said: "It could be assumed I was remaining in my room. The Governor is used to my remaining indoors for several days on end. We could send one of our ladies, or perhaps both of them, to call at Plantation House; O'Meara would go into town, and while Lady Lowe was making polite conversation about me in her drawing room, we should leave this accursed place.'" But he then rejected such tempting visions, shaking his head: 'It is a very seductive picture, but alas it would be madness. I must either die here or France must come and get me.'²

Soon after, Betsy and Jane Balcombe called. They found Napoleon firing at a mark with pistols and Betsy noted 'a gleam of the former playfulness' he had shown at The Briars. 'He put one into my hand, loaded, I believe, with powder, and, in great trepidation, I fired it off; he often called me afterwards *"La petite tirailleuse"* [*tirailleur* or skirmisher] and said he would form a corps of sharp-shooters, of which I should be the captain.' He invited them to inspect his new billiard table. 'I remember thinking it too childish for men, and very like marbles on a larger scale. The emperor condescended to teach me how to play, but I made very little progress.'³

On 24 July, O'Meara sent a secret report to Sir Thomas Reade, noting that Bonaparte had spent over two hours in the Montholon apartment the previous evening. 'This will make Madame Bertrand as jealous as the deuce, though I believe the real reason is that he has no other room to sit in until the chimney is finished or the library put to rights. Madame Montholon however exults much at the favour shown to her, and actually putteth on two extra gowns daily, in consequence thereof.' This was not the first of O'Meara's sly insinuations about Albine de Montholon, and it would not be the last.⁴

The following day, Admiral Malcolm came to Longwood and stayed for four hours, bringing French newspapers which had arrived on the HMS *Griffon*.⁵ An insurrection at Grenoble cheered Napoleon immensely. The Bourbons, he said, were seated on a volcano. The admiral and Bonaparte had taken the measure of each other and respected what they saw. Throughout their protracted discussion, they walked around the drawing room with their hats under their arms, for Sir Pulteney knew not to be seated while his host remained standing. He understood Bonaparte's need to salvage what vestiges he could of courtly dignity; he 'saw that he was determined to keep up as long as he could, within his own house, the state of an emperor'.⁶

On 6 August, William Balcombe made a visit not entered in the orderly's logbook and went for a ride in the carriage with Napoleon. He continued to raise hopes in a manner that, if the governor had known of his comments, would have caused him to be ejected from the island. Bertrand gave an account in his private journal, explicitly naming the purveyor: 'Mr Balcombe has gone to Longwood and promenaded for two hours in the carriage with the Emperor. He maintains that of all the officers who are here, there is not one who would not give something for Napoleon to return to his throne. All the officers of the 66th who crossed France declare that everyone, in the inns and cafes, mourns the Emperor, because, they say, he has been *chosen*, or because, say others, he gave to France much glory. In England the same, the party for Napoleon is growing; opinion is changing on his account.'[7]

On the same day, a lieutenant, two midshipmen and a party of seamen from the *Newcastle* arrived at Longwood to repair the garden marquee torn in recent rains. Napoleon strolled over and chatted with one of the midshipmen.[8] Betsy noted how impressed he was with the elegant youth: 'Napoleon was fond of sailors, and liked entering into conversation with the young midshipmen who conducted the fatigue parties at Longwood. On one occasion a remarkably handsome and high-born young reefer attracted his notice, from the activity he displayed in setting his men to work in erecting a commodious marquee out of studding-sail. He inquired his name, and when he heard it was the Honourable G C, he remarked that he was one of the very few instances in which he had observed high birth combined with so much amiability and intelligence.'[9]

Dame Mabel Brookes, in her *St Helena Story*, tells us that this midshipman was the Honourable George Carstairs, Betsy's first love interest.[10] It is clear that Betsy was intrigued by the youth, for the next time she saw Napoleon she said that she 'had the pleasure of being acquainted with the young middy he so much admired, and that he was the most popular of any of his young companions in the wardroom'. Her first sight of 'G C' had been after Admiral Cockburn's ball. He was drunkenly singing with other 'middies' (midshipmen) on top of a cart blocking the exit from the castle courtyard.[11]

On 10 August, Napoleon was breakfasting in the new marquee when the governor arrived to personally invite him to the Prince Regent's birthday celebrations. He hid from sight and Lowe went away disappointed.

Later that day, Sir Pulteney Malcolm and his wife had no trouble finding Napoleon, who invited them for what he called 'a drive round the Park' in his carriage. As they clattered between the gumwood trees and around the 'steep, black, dreary-looking hollow' of the Devil's Punchbowl, Lady Malcolm considered that 'going so fast, it did not seem quite safe; but the two Paris postilions were excellent'.[12]

Napoleon was interested to learn that the admiral had rowed around the island the previous day. It was useful information that a rowing boat could approach the cliffs.

The Prince Regent's birthday on 12 August was celebrated with a grand field day at Deadwood Camp. Salutes were fired from the batteries. Pacing about the Longwood garden, Napoleon watched the distant parade on the plain and the governor's review of the redcoats.

In the evening, a formal dinner for fifty was held at Plantation House, the women in their silks, satins and jewellery and the men's uniforms blazing with decorations, reflected from the great crystal chandelier above the table. Dinner was followed by a ball at Deadwood in a marquee lit by lanterns. The women came up from town crammed into carts pulled by horses or oxen, carrying their evening dresses in boxes. 'We got down from the carriage,' recalled one lady, 'into mud up to our knees in the damp darkness.'[13] Lady Lowe chose to stay in town; she was seven months pregnant and had told Major Gorrequer that she would never have married again 'if she had thought she would have got pickaninnies from a second husband'.[14] Furthermore, she complained, the local people showed no special attention to a governor's wife.

At the Deadwood ball, in the absence of his wife, Sir Hudson partnered Lady Malcolm for the first set. Betsy was invited up for the quadrille by the Honourable George Carstairs, 'the greatest beau that ever came to St Helena'. It would seem that if she had fancied him at first, her interest had since waned. She learned that he was 'such an exquisite' that before dressing for dinner or a dance he would sit for an hour with his feet propped above his head so he could squeeze them into elegant tight shoes. He wore huge showy epaulettes, his sword belt embroidered with golden oak leaves, and more embroidery around his silk stockings. He told her he was appalled that the provincial ladies of St Helena 'understood nothing but *kitchen* dances and reels', and he offered instruction in the mysteries of the quadrille. Even Mrs Balcombe joined his class, until she 'unceremoniously put her foot on his heel, because he stood bending before her' and the swallowtails of his coat nearly poked out her eye.[15] She retired, but the young people continued dancing until the dawn cannon fired.

Napoleon was amused when he heard Betsy's description, and urged her to obtain a pass for Carstairs to visit Longwood again. When one was procured, he told the young man, 'putting on a most comical look', that he 'had heard from Miss Betsee that he was a great *dandy*—which was anything but pleasing intelligence to the young hero, who began to think he was indebted for the honour of his interview with the great man to the circumstance of his being considered a sort of tom-fool'.[16] (Carstairs styled himself on Beau Brummell, unaware that the modish buck had recently left England because of gambling debts, having also angered the Prince Regent by describing him as a 'fat friend'.[17]) After the visit, Napoleon told Betsy that it was unrealistic for her to consider Carstairs as a romantic prospect: 'He is far too aristocratic for you, Betsee.' It was kindly advice, considering the possibility of social disgrace familiar to Jane Austen's readers (the fate of Lydia Bennet, for instance) which could befall a girl like Betsy: too pretty not to attempt to seduce, too poor or low in rank to marry. But according to Dame Mabel Brookes and Betsy's diary account, she answered 'You are jealous because he dances with me.' Napoleon pulled her ear and turned away towards the pavilion without answering.[18]

Three days after the Regent's fifty-fourth birthday, Napoleon's forty-seventh was observed with little fanfare. He breakfasted in the garden marquee with members of his court. Gourgaud annoyed him by making up a floral bouquet, saying it was from Napoleon's son, the King of Rome. 'Bah!' Napoleon exclaimed. 'The King of Rome does not think any more about me now.'[19] In the evening, according to O'Meara's sardonic account, 'the second class of domestics, including the English, had a grand supper and a dance afterwards. To the astonishment of the French, not an Englishman got drunk.'[20]

The following day, a birthday gift from Lady Holland was sent by the governor, an amazing machine for making ice using an air pump.²¹ Admiral Malcolm rode up to Longwood and discovered Napoleon and his companions in awe at a demonstration by the local upholsterer, 'who understood the process'.²² Napoleon was fascinated when a cup of water was frozen in his presence in fifteen minutes. He remarked what a gratification that would have been in Egypt.²³

Betsy and Jane came with their father to see the marvel. Napoleon was now the expert on the machine's workings. 'After making a cup of ice, he insisted upon my putting a large piece into my mouth, and laughed to see the contortions it induced from the excessive cold. It was the first ice that had ever been seen at St. Helena.'²⁴

The governor called at Longwood for a discussion 'principally about the necessity of reducing the expenses of the establishment'. He gave written instructions to Bertrand that the household budget be kept within £8000 a year. He offered to go through the items with him, but Bertrand replied: 'The less communication you and I have either verbally or in writing the better.' Lowe said the wish was reciprocal, and departed.²⁵

If relations between Bonaparte and Lowe were bad before, they were about to become a great deal worse. On Sunday 18 August, Admiral Malcolm met the governor at Hutt's Gate and, accompanied by Sir Thomas Reade and Major Gorrequer, they rode to Longwood together. They saw Bonaparte walking in the garden with Madame de Montholon and Count de Las Cases. The confrontation that followed was to sever all personal relations between the governor and his prisoner for the remainder of their lives. It was particularly painful for Lowe because he was insulted in front of the admiral and his own staff, with Dr O'Meara and Captain Poppleton listening in the background.

At first Napoleon exchanged pleasantries with the admiral, pointedly ignoring the governor's presence. Lowe interrupted, saying he was sorry to raise a disagreeable subject but that the rude and improper conduct of Count Bertrand made it necessary. His instructions were that the expenses at Longwood had to be resolved and he needed to know with whom he could communicate.

Napoleon was silent for several minutes, walking to and fro, then he addressed himself to the admiral: 'Count Bertrand is a man well known and esteemed in Europe; he has been distinguished and has commanded armies.' He nodded in the direction of the governor: 'He treats him like a corporal. Madame Bertrand is a lady well born, who has been accustomed to the first place in society; he does not treat her with the regard that is her due; he stops her letters and prevents her seeing those that wish to visit her, except under restrictions.'

Lowe interjected that he merely carried out his instructions; if his conduct was disapproved of by the government, he might readily be removed. 'Since your arrival we have experienced nothing but vexations,' Napoleon said, turning to him. 'Your instructions are the same as Sir George Cockburn's—he told me so—but you execute them with fifty times more rigour. He never vexed us with trifles . . . but there is no dealing with you—you are a most intractable man. You suspect everything and everybody. You are a Lieutenant-General but you perform your duty as if you were a sentinel; you never commanded any men but Corsican deserters. I know the name of every English general who has distinguished himself, but I have never heard of you except as a clerk to Blücher, or as a commandant of assassins. You do not know how to conduct yourself towards men of honour, your soul is too low. Why do you not treat us like prisoners of war? You treat us like Botany Bay convicts.'

Lowe spoke with cool deliberation: 'I have every desire to render your situation as agreeable as is in my power, but you prevent me . . . I am the subject of a free government. I hold every species of tyranny and despotism in execration, and I will repel every attack upon my character on this point.'

Bonaparte turned to the admiral again. 'There are two kinds of people employed by governments—those whom they honour, and those whom they dishonour; he is one of the latter; the situation they have given him is that of an executioner. I, who have been the Master of the World, know the type of man such positions are given to. It is only the dishonoured who accept them.'[26]

Soon an account of the meeting was circulating around the island. Sir Hudson Lowe had been spoken to with intolerable rudeness and Bonaparte knew it. 'I must not see that officer again,' he told Las Cases. 'He makes me lose my temper and forget myself. I said things to him that would have been inexcusable at the Tuileries. If they are excusable here it is because I am in his hands and in his power.'[27]

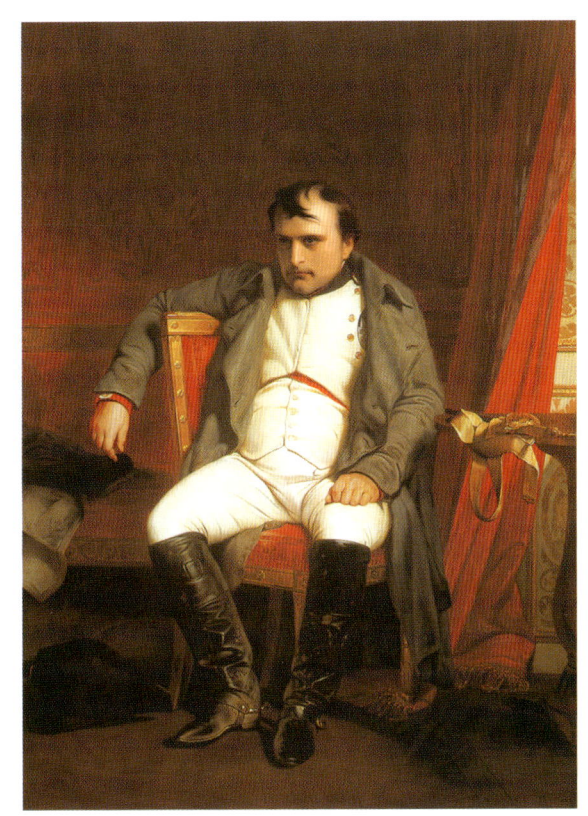

A dejected Napoleon, depicted after his abdication in April 1814, the year before he arrived at St Helena. *Napoleon at Fontainebleau*, by Paul Delaroche.

The Balcombe sisters with Napoleon at The Briars. The figure on the left may be William Balcombe. A lithograph, possibly based on a sketch by Louis-Joseph Marchand, Napoleon's valet.

The Balcombe's home on St Helena. *The Briars and Pavilion*, a watercolour attributed to Betsy Balcombe, possibly a copy of an earlier painting. (Courtesy of The Briars, Mt Martha, Victoria)

Napoleon's house on St Helena. *Longwood House, 1817*, a watercolour by Lieutenant Basil Jackson; the figures of Napoleon, Count Bertrand and General Gourgaud were added by Denzil Ibbetson, the purveyor to Longwood after Balcombe.

The main town on St Helena. *View of Jamestown from the Road Leading to The Briars*, lithograph after Vincent Brooks.

A portrait miniature, signed A. Mur, believed by Balcombe descendants to be of the young Countess Albine de Montholon and gifted to Betsy. (Private collection)

The steep hills and Georgian buildings of Jamestown. *Vue intérieure de la ville de Jamestown*, French lithograph, based on a drawing by H. Durand Brager.

Napoleon's obsession with his legacy was legendary. *Napoleon dictating his memoirs to Count de Las Cases, 1816,* by Sir William Quiller Orchardson.

Sir Thomas Tyrwhitt, the influential patron of the Balcombe family.

Mrs Jane Fraser, the Balcombe family friend from Saint-Omer, France. (Private collection)

Sydney around the time of Betsy's arrival. *View of Sydney Cove from Dawes Point*, attributed to Joseph Lycett, c.1817–18. (Mitchell Library, State Library of New South Wales)

Captain John Piper's home was the centre of Sydney society. *Henrietta Villa, Point Piper, Home of Captain John Piper, 1820*, by Richard Read.

A party at Henrietta Villa. *Dome Room, Point Piper*, by Frederick Garling.

Watercolour of an Australian rural scene by Betsy's brother Thomas Tyrwhitt Balcombe; he is now recognised as a minor colonial artist. (Private collection)

Thomas's wife, Lydia, on horseback, painted by Thomas Tyrwhitt Balcombe. (Private collection)

Elizabeth Jane (Bessie) Abell, daughter of Betsy Balcombe and Edward Abell, painted around the time her mother published *Recollections*. (Courtesy of The Briars, Mt Martha, Victoria)

After the death of her father and return to England, Betsy taught music in London. In this painting, Betsy is shown standing behind her daughter Bessie, who is playing the piano. *The Music Party*, by Alfred Tidey. (Worthing Museum and Art Gallery, UK)

The governor would never speak to Bonaparte again. For the next five years he saw him only occasionally and at a distance. His next close view was when he inspected the prisoner's corpse. For the present, he resented Admiral Malcolm's apparent friendship with Bonaparte—and with William Balcombe. He had heard that Balcombe had told Bonaparte that he, the governor, was gossiping about Madame Mère's letter and her offer to travel to the island to be with her son—something he categorically denied.[28] In his mind The Briars was shaping as a hostile camp. A hostile *naval* camp. He would ensure that Major Sir Thomas Reade kept the Balcombes under surveillance.

The next day Montholon delivered a long letter, signed by him, to the governor. It had been composed by Napoleon with input from his companions. It stated the rights he claimed as prisoner, listed all their grievances and demanded redress. A copy eventually found publication in Europe, where it became known as 'The Remonstrance' and caused a sensation. It concluded by explaining the impossibility of reducing household expenses: 'You demand from the Emperor £4000 sterling, your government allowing only £8000 for all expenses. I have already had the honour to tell you that the Emperor has no funds.'[29] Las Cases was confident that the document would 'set Europe on fire'. Malcolm asked Lowe for a copy and was offended to be refused. He noted that the governor 'was very desirous to have it kept secret . . . not so those at Longwood; they read it in French and English to everyone that called and offered copies, but none were taken'.[30]

Acting on his threat, Lowe further restricted the boundary of Longwood and commanded the 23 sentries to move close to the house at dusk, rather than at 9 pm, denying the prisoner his evening stroll in the garden, for he refused to go out under guard. Instead Bonaparte requested (not entirely seriously) that the servants dig ditches around the perimeter, eight or ten feet deep if necessary, so he could walk in privacy.[31] He then directed Montholon to write to the governor saying that if Count Bertrand could no longer grant passes to visitors, 'the Emperor desired the Governor would not give any, neither to officers, nor to the inhabitants, nor to passing strangers, for they rambled about the grounds and annoyed him'. Lowe sent this letter on to the admiral and asked that he refuse passes to naval officers as well. This had the effect of also inhibiting the Malcolms from visiting. Lady

Clementina's *Diary* noted: 'It is understood that Bonaparte wrote this letter under the influence of passion, and wished it recalled, but pride would not permit him to say so.'[32]

At the beginning of September, Captain Poppleton informed the governor that Captain Piontkowski had approached Lieutenant Nagle, who was shortly leaving for England. The Pole had asked if Nagle was going to France and whether he would be willing to deliver certain correspondence. Nagle refused and reported the matter to Poppleton.

At about the same time, the governor's secretary Gorrequer told Montholon that the reduction in annual household expenses was going into effect and he should arrange matters with Balcombe. Montholon protested mightily, but the truth was that pilfering and extravagance had been carried on at Longwood on a grand scale. Balcombe's prices were exorbitant. The chef, butler and valets, accustomed to the luxury of the Tuileries, had refused to lower their standards. While Napoleon was a moderate drinker, many in his retinue found alcohol a comfort during their windswept lonely exile. Each fortnight, 630 bottles of wine were sent to Longwood, where servants conducted a lucrative business at the kitchen door, selling wine to the soldiers of Deadwood Camp. Local residents, most of whom lived in straitened circumstances, heard about the high living and were appalled. It was said that they 'hated Bonaparte more for eating their sheep and running through all their poultry than for bringing England to her knees by his blockade'.[33]

Montholon advised Gorrequer that by discharging seven household servants, they could reduce yearly expenses to about £15,000, the bare minimum.[34] The blunt response from Plantation House was that this was not acceptable; if they exceeded the budget of £8000 they would have to send for further funds themselves.

Napoleon found it hard to credit that as a prisoner he was being asked to pay for his own detention. Two days before the deadline, according to O'Meara, he 'had a conversation with Mr Balcombe relative to the concerns of the establishment'.[35] He had devised a strategy that would create huge publicity for his situation, shame the governor and, incidentally, produce some income. 'Have my silver broken up with axes,' he ordered. Marchand collected a basketload of table silver (cutlery, salvers, covers, jugs and platters), erased the imperial eagles and coats of arms to avoid their becoming trophies, and then smashed the lot. He took 952 ounces of broken silver to Jamestown and, in the presence of Sir Thomas Reade, sold it to Solomons' store. Reade ordered that the resulting £240 should be held by Balcombe and drawn from in small sums as necessity required. O'Meara was amused that Reade asked him 'to try to get him some of Napoleon's plate *whole*, which, he observed, would *sell* better in that state than if it were broken up'.[36]

Two more sales of household silver followed. The ruse worked brilliantly. Locals came to believe that the French were reduced to this in order not to starve. Shortly afterwards, the governor, on his own initiative, revised Longwood's household allowance to £12,000 a year, the same as his own for Plantation House.

At the end of September, Lowe received a July despatch from Lord Bathurst. A London businessman named Menet based in Milan had written to say that there was a traitor among the English on the island: 'Your government is deceived. Napoleon has won over a person at St Helena. If you are a true Englishman, profit by this information which is given by a sincere countryman, and advise your Government to be upon its guard.' A second note from Menet read: 'Perfect confirmation. We cannot give the details, but the fact is positive. Keep your eyes well open; watch the slightest movement, and take away certain powerful means that always succeed in corrupting (gold). Burn this.'[37]

Even more alarming, his lordship sent on a warning from the British ambassador in Paris: 'The French Government have received intelligence that a person named Carpenter, who is a citizen of the United States of America, is equipping a fast sailing vessel in the Hudson River for the express purpose of facilitating the escape of Bonaparte from the Island of St Helena.'[38] In transmitting these enclosures, Bathurst stressed the need for further precautions. He believed that Bonaparte had hundreds of millions of francs held by supporters in Europe against the day when he would make his move. Any requests to visit Longwood should be refused, in order to prevent 'the clandestine communications sent over by Bonaparte's followers. It will be impossible to counteract this evil, but we must try to limit its extent.' In particular, he suspected O'Meara of being responsible for a recent letter which had appeared in a Portsmouth newspaper. Bathurst had decided that the time had come for the meddlesome doctor to leave the island, but told Lowe that 'in removing him you will so concert your measures, as to do it in the manner least likely to draw attention on the one hand and the one best calculated on the other to prevent his becoming the instrument of mischief on his arrival in Europe'.[39]

The governor was more than eager to dismiss the doctor, but as O'Meara was an Admiralty appointment, he had to take care how he did it. Meanwhile, he instituted Bathurst's other instructions. On 4 October, Bertrand was summoned to Plantation House to nominate the departure of four people to reduce expenses. Captain Piontkowski, for his misdemeanour, was 'particularly pointed out'.[40] Also to go were two household servants—Santini and Rousseau—and a groom, Joseph Archambault, the younger of two brothers. Those who stayed had to sign, stating their desire to remain 'and participate in the restrictions imposed upon Napoleon Bonaparte personally'. (Requests to insert the title 'Emperor' were rejected.) They were told that refusal to sign would mean instant deportation. Bathurst had urged Lowe that 'they cannot be too frequently reminded that their continuance in the island is an act of indulgence on the part of the British Government'. In the end they all signed the 'obnoxious paper'.

Bertrand's journal that day mentioned that Balcombe visited and informed Napoleon that the more the authorities tried to interrupt his communications, the more he should feel gratified, 'because it is proof that the urgency to keep you here increases, so your affairs are going well'. Two nights later, after returning home from Longwood, Bertrand wrote an enigmatic entry: 'At dinner, the Emperor speaks of letters inserted into newspapers and how one deals with St Helena intelligence.'[41]

He was not the only one busy with his quill pen by candlelight. In his room at Longwood, O'Meara composed a long letter to John Finlaison at the Admiralty. He described the events of recent weeks, including the epic verbal battle between his patient and the governor. He said that Bonaparte described Lowe as a weak man, 'a man of too weak intellect to be *cleverly* a wicked man', whereas 'the Admiral

[Malcolm], who is *really a man of talent,* has perceived the imbecility of that *coglione* [arsehole]'. O'Meara relayed more of Bonaparte's vituperation against the island and its governor, but he assured his exalted readers (he knew there were several) that 'I beg you *not* to imagine that I participate in Bonaparte's sentiments, because I record his words'.[42]

When the letter reached the Admiralty two months later, the Sea Lords decided that O'Meara's intimacy with Bonaparte made him a far too valuable resource. It was worth keeping him there, passing information to them, despite any attempt to remove him planned by the Secretary of State.

CHAPTER 14

THE THINNING RANKS

Island gossip continually swirled, as it always had. On 2 October 1816, Lady Lowe was delivered of a son and was rumoured to regret being a mother again. It was said that Count Balmain had proposed marriage to Miss Brooke, daughter of the secretary of the council, and she had refused him. Dr O'Meara's suit had been rejected by Farmer Breame's daughter. Montholon had kissed the hand of a sailor's wife, and the husband, unused to Continental gallantries, had taken offence.[1] The story that William Balcombe was a royal bastard was still around. Some locals in litigation with him, like Henry Porteous, considered that he was just an ordinary bastard.

The three departing French servants and Captain Piontkowski set sail on 19 October for the Cape, where they were to be held for two months before proceeding to England. All carried secret messages. Santini, the other faithful Corsican, had a copy of 'The Remonstrance' written on satin and sewn into his coat. For fear it would be discovered, Piontkowski had learned it by heart. Napoleon told them: 'If you reach London, get it printed. You will find a lot of good men in England; some of them do not at all approve of the way their government has treated me.'[2] Once there, Santini found Lord Holland, who paid for the printing. Joseph Archambault and Rousseau went on to America to join the household of Joseph Bonaparte. They carried a detailed map of St Helena. Their arrival activated the group of partisans—known as the Champ d'Asile—into a plan to rescue Napoleon.

On 20 October, the Bertrands were moved from Hutt's Gate to a custom-built wooden cottage across the road from Longwood, today known as Longwood Farmhouse. It consisted of four rooms on the ground floor and four above, with a kitchen and servants' quarters at the back.

At Longwood, Bonaparte huddled by the fire, suffering toothache and a cold. 'What a miserable thing is man!' he exclaimed. 'The smallest fibre in his body, assailed by disease, is sufficient to derange his whole system.' He marvelled that his body was a most 'curious machine . . . and perhaps I may be confined in it for thirty years longer'.[3]

O'Meara, who extracted the tooth, thought not. He informed the governor that in his view if Bonaparte continued to stay indoors and refused to take exercise he would become ill and 'in all probability his existence in St Helena would not be protracted for more than a year or two'. Lowe asked him to make a note of his opinion, cautioning the doctor that in writing it he 'must bear in mind that the life of one man was not to be put into competition with the mischief which he might cause were he to get loose'.[4]

Betsy Balcombe sneaked a visit to Longwood with her father. Napoleon said that he wished he could return to The Briars. Betsy found him less amiable than usual, his face swollen and inflamed. 'He told me that Mr O'Meara had just performed the operation of drawing a tooth, which caused him some pain. I exclaimed, "What! You complain of the pain so trifling an operation can give?"' She said he astonished her, he who had survived countless battles and bullets. 'I am ashamed of you. But nevertheless, give me the tooth and I will get it set by Mr Solomon as an ear-ring and wear it for your sake. The idea made him laugh heartily, in spite of his suffering, and caused him to remark that he thought I should *never* cut my wisdom teeth. He was always in good humour with himself whenever he was guilty of anything approaching to the nature of a witticism.'[5]

On 25 November, Sir Pulteney Malcolm called at Longwood and was received most amicably. Afterwards the admiral visited Madame

Bertrand at her new cottage across the road. As he came out he ran into a posse: Lowe striding purposefully, accompanied by Reade, Gorrequer, Captain Blakeney and a police commissioner (whose ship had called from the Cape) and some dragoons. The governor told the admiral that 'he was come to arrest Las Cases for having endeavoured to bribe a slave to convey letters to Europe'. He requested that Admiral Malcolm arrange for a ship to take the prisoner to the Cape.[6] At Longwood the diminutive count was seized, refused permission to farewell his beloved emperor and marched away. Napoleon remarked that the arresting soldiers looked like a party of South Sea cannibals.[7]

The charge was that Las Cases had attempted to smuggle two letters to Europe by means of James Scott, his sixteen-year-old mulatto servant, who belonged to the class of 'free blacks'. The letters were to Napoleon's brother Lucien Bonaparte and to Lady Clavering (Las Cases' former employer in England, said to have been his lover[8]); they had been written on white satin and sewn into the servant's waistcoat. James Scott had confessed the plot to his biological father, an Englishman who had sired him with a coloured woman. Scott senior went straight to the garrison with the story.

Once the governor had received the incriminating evidence, he ordered Las Cases' arrest. He said that the letters made false accusations against himself and his treatment of the French at Longwood and broke the strict rule that outward correspondence must pass through his office. Despite Las Cases' protests, all his writings, including his precious journal, were confiscated. He and his son were taken to Ross Cottage, Balcombe's poultry farm, and held there under house arrest until they could be deported.

Ten days earlier, James Scott, the young servant, had been caught taking a message from Las Cases to Madame von Stürmer, the Austrian commissioner's wife.[9] For this relatively minor transgression he had been removed from his position at Longwood and interrogated by Lowe, a terrifying ordeal. On St Helena slaves were flogged for far less.[10] The evidence suggests that the governor instructed the frightened boy to undertake a covert mission, effectively a sting operation.

As Las Cases was ruefully to recall, his former servant, taking advantage of the darkness 'and his knowledge of the localities of the island, had surmounted every obstacle, avoided sentinels and scaled precipices, to come and see me, in order to tell me that, having got a situation with a person who was going to set off for London in a very few days, he came to offer me his services without reserve ... Thus everything combined to urge me towards the precipice, down which I was about to fall.'[11] Las Cases accepted the boy's offer to carry correspondence and neglected to obtain Napoleon's approval: 'I should say that my servant had appeared to me honest, that I believed him to be faithful, and that I was still a stranger to any idea of instigating spies.'[12] Marchand observed that 'a trap was set for Count de Las Cases by the governor and the night visit of the servant had been facilitated'.[13]

If it was a trap, it actually suited Las Cases. He was separated from his wife; his son Emmanuel's health was failing, diagnosed as a weak heart; his own eyesight had been giving him trouble; he was often at odds with the other companions at Longwood; and the declaration he had signed, to remain at St Helena until the end, had panicked him. He wrote in his journal of being 'exiled, and probably for ever, to a deserted rock two thousand leagues from home'.[14] He was doubtless only too ready to leave the island, if he could do so with honour, taking his huge collection of notes, to complete what he believed would become the definitive memorial to his hero.

Napoleon told O'Meara: 'I am convinced there is nothing of consequence in the letter, as Las Cases is an honest man and too much attached to me to undertake anything of consequence without first acquainting me with the project.' If Las Cases had told him about it he would have stopped him—'not that I disapprove of his endeavouring to make our situation known, on the contrary; but I disapprove of the bungling manner in which he attempted it'.[15] O'Meara thought the count's 'bungling' had been deliberate, in order to achieve the desired deportation, and said as much in a letter to Finlaison.[16]

When the governor visited Las Cases at Ross Cottage, he brought with him an inventory of his papers. The count was appalled to learn that Lowe had been reading his private journal, thereby gaining an account, 'day by day, of all that happened amongst us at Longwood'. Lowe came almost every day, sometimes severe and threatening, at other times offering 'most marked attention', sending choice meals from Plantation House. Las Cases wrote him long, eloquent letters, ensuring that his demand that his papers be returned was on record, referring to the 'trap laid for me', and insisting that his papers proved there was 'no plot, no plan, not even a thought relating to Napoleon's escape. You could not find any, because none existed.'[17] (However, O'Meara informed Finlaison that in the papers it was revealed that correspondence *had* been carried on with 'some persons in London' by coded messages inserted in British newspapers.[18])

Finally, Lowe made a concession, bringing Las Cases a letter he had withheld for some days. It was from Napoleon, who had swallowed his pride by sending it unsealed to the governor; in it he professed such sorrow and affection at losing his intelligent companion that the count almost broke down in front of Lowe. He was not allowed to keep the original, but Emmanuel was permitted to make a copy:

> My dear Count Las Cases—My heart is deeply affected by what you now experience. Torn from me fifteen days ago, you have been since then imprisoned, in close confinement, without my being able to communicate with you . . . Your conduct at St Helena has been, like the whole of your life, honourable and irreproachable. I love to tell you this . . . Your papers, among which it was well known there were some belonging to me, were seized, without any formality, close to my apartment, and with expressions of ferocious joy . . . Your society was necessary to me. You alone could read, speak and understand English. How many nights have you watched over me during my illness! Nevertheless, I request you, and, in case of need, command you, to require the governor to send you to the Continent. He cannot refuse, because he has no power over you, except through the voluntary document which you signed . . .[19]

After the governor left, Las Cases and his son recopied the letter 'in many ways and in many places; we even learnt it by heart', so great was their fear that Lowe would still confiscate any copies.[20] The count was relieved that Napoleon had *commanded* him to quit the island: 'I can no longer, I thought, be of any great service to the Emperor here; but I may perhaps be useful to him elsewhere.'[21] However, he suddenly remembered the velvet band he wore secreting Queen Hortense's diamond necklace. He had become accustomed to it as if 'it were identified with my person'. He shrank from the idea of depriving Napoleon of such a valuable item, but 'how would it be possible now to make restitution? I was in the most rigorous confinement, surrounded by gaolers and sentinels, so that all communication was impracticable. I vainly endeavoured to contrive a plan; time pressed; only a few days were left, and nothing could be more depressing than thus to quit the island. In this predicament, I resolved to run all risks. An Englishman, to whom I had often spoken, came to the prison on a particular errand, and it was under the eyes of the Governor himself, or one of his most confidential agents whom he brought, that I ventured to communicate my wishes.'

This Englishman, clearly not an officer, could only have been William Balcombe, for even if his property was being used as a temporary prison, the governor could scarcely have denied him permission to oversee his poultry. Las Cases, in his account, no doubt disguised Balcombe's identity to protect him: '"I think you are a man of principle," said I, "and I am going to put it to the test—though with nothing injurious or contrary to your honour—merely a rich deposit to be restored to Napoleon. If you accept the charge, my son will put it into your pocket." He answered only by slackening his pace; my son, whom I had prepared for the scene, followed us, and the necklace was transferred into this man's possession, almost in sight of the military attendants.'[22]

Marchand noted in his *Mémoires* that ever since the count's arrest, Napoleon had remained in his quarters, seriously depressed. When the admiral called he was told that the emperor 'was ill and in bed. The host of the Briars, Mr Balcombe, was more fortunate—the Emperor received him in his dressing-gown; he was a man who had rendered services and was disposed to continue doing so; he said on leaving the Emperor that he was much changed; I said that given the conduct of the governor it could not be otherwise.'[23] The next day, 24 December, Bertrand recorded in his journal that in the Longwood billiard room Napoleon showed Madame Bertrand 'the diamond necklace of Queen Hortense, valued at 200,000 francs.'[24] Las Cases' own account confirmed the conclusion of this episode: 'Before quitting the island, I had the inexpressible satisfaction of knowing that the necklace had reached the hands of the Emperor.'[25]

The count and his son were transferred to the castle in Jamestown before their departure. The notes on Napoleon's military campaigns that Las Cases had transcribed were returned, but Lowe refused to give back his journal 'or any papers relating to General Bonaparte since he has been at St Helena'. These were sealed, awaiting the advice of the British government.[26] (They were not returned until after Napoleon's death.)

On 30 December, Count de Las Cases and his son, who was dangerously ill, boarded the sloop-of-war HMS *Griffon*, bound for the Cape. The two watched the island of St Helena fade into mist: 'We were rapidly sailing away from that dear and accursed spot, in the midst of the ocean and at an immense distance from both the old and the new world.'[27]

The dictation work at Longwood became more onerous. With Las Cases gone, the load shared among four was now divided between three, and young Emmanuel, who had transcribed fair copies, was sorely missed.

Marchand was concerned about his master: 'Since the new restrictions, the Emperor would not see any foreigners other than the admiral and Mr Balcombe; Dr O'Meara was the only man at Longwood who could inform him of what was happening on the island and give him recent news from Europe. O'Meara's importance increased for the Emperor and he was given access to his private apartment.'[28]

The doctor was anxious too, and wrote to Finlaison—knowing that his letter would be read at a much higher level—that his patient simply wanted to live quietly in England *under surveillance*, taking the name Colonel Muiron. Napoleon had told him he only insisted on 'Emperor' because he was exiled to such a miserable place: 'I have made noise enough in the world already—perhaps more than any other man will ever do—perhaps *too* much. I am getting old and only want retirement.'[29]

When Sir Pulteney Malcolm called at Longwood, he found Bonaparte thinner, his eyes sunken, but—considering that he had remained indoors for three months—thought him in better spirits than expected. Napoleon wanted to talk, for more than three hours as it turned out. Since the admiral's return from Cape Town, his relations with the governor had soured further. There had been a 'long and disagreeable correspondence', ostensibly a dispute about the deployment of transport ships between the island and the Cape, but the Malcolms' *Diary* concedes that the real reason was the admiral's social calls on Napoleon: whenever he went to Longwood 'his visit gave rise to unpleasant ideas in the Governor's mind'.[30]

On New Year's Day 1817, Betsy and Jane Balcombe visited Fanny Bertrand, who was in ungainly advanced pregnancy and exhausted by the summer heat. 'We always made a point of riding to Longwood every New Year's day,' Betsy recalled. They had become close to the countess, who helped with their French studies, and they were good with her three children, Napoleon, Hortense and Henri, playing with them and chattering in a mixture of English and French. Fanny probably told Betsy that she was now famous, for when Madame von Stürmer was in France she had heard 'much talk of Betsi Balcombe. If she was in France and they knew that the young person was she whom the Emperor treated well, everyone would run after her.'[31]

Betsy was admiring some of the elegant souvenirs the emperor had given the countess, 'when Napoleon himself waddled into Madame Bertrand's room, where my sister and I were seated ... In his hand were two beautiful Sèvres cups, exquisitely painted, one representing himself in Egypt, in the dress of a Mussulman; upon the other was delineated an Egyptian woman drawing water. "Here, Mesdemoiselles Betsee and Jane, are two cups for you, accept them as a mark of the friendship I entertain for you both, and for your kindness to Madame Bertrand."'[32] The girls were shocked to see his physical decline.

Within three months, the Longwood community had been reduced by six individuals. Napoleon remained in a sullen and moody state and said that he was 'in a tomb'.[33] He brooded about the malign intentions of the governor: 'He will send away all the French people about me by degrees. You see he has already commenced by taking away Las Cases and some of the servants, tomorrow or next day Montholon will go, by and by all the rest; and then, when a fit opportunity occurs, when I am surrounded by spies of his and fit instruments for him to work upon, he will despatch me, according to his instructions from Lord Bathurst.'[34]

CHAPTER 15

THE SICK LION

On 17 January 1817, an extremely nervous Fanny Bertrand, who had suffered four previous miscarriages, gave birth to a healthy boy weighing 12 pounds. Dr Matthew Livingstone, the island's medical superintendent, noted that it was a difficult labour and for some time afterwards the mother was 'in grave danger'.[1]

Napoleon had barely stirred from the house since the increased restrictions but walked over the road to inspect the new arrival, named Arthur in memory of Fanny's father, Sir Arthur Dillon, who was guillotined during the revolutionary Terror. She proudly showed off her baby. 'Sire,' she quipped, 'I have the honour to present to Your Majesty the first Frenchman who, since your arrival, has entered Longwood without Lord Bathurst's permission.'[2]

'There is not much news on the Island,' Lady Malcolm wrote to her aunt. 'Madame Bertrand and Mrs Wynyard have both got sons, and with their infants are doing well. Bonaparte still confines himself to the house, and all his exercise is sometimes playing at billiards. I am told he has invented a new game, which he plays with his suite; they have all the balls and push them about with their hands. I believe Pulteney is the last visitor who has seen him.' She said she hoped it was true that the admiral's successor had been appointed, as they were both tiring of the island.[3] They had long since tired of the governor.

At the end of the month, she and her husband visited Madame Bertrand. General Bertrand went over the road and informed Napoleon that the Malcolms were there, and returned with a request that they walk over. They enjoyed a lively chat in the Longwood drawing room: 'Bonaparte appeared to know every trifling occurrence.'[4] Since Las Cases' departure he had clearly felt deprived of stimulating conversation. 'Everyone lives in fear here,' Bertrand wrote in his journal after the Malcolms had gone. 'We cannot say what we think. This is something new for the English. The Admiral's wife says she cannot hide her thoughts, and who does not hesitate is in dread of Plantation House. It is said they open letters of all persons residing in the island.'[5]

The following day, Lowe called on the admiral, accompanied by Reade, and they had a terse discussion about supplies from the Cape brought by naval vessels. The Malcolms' *Diary* noted that as the governor took his leave he turned and, 'in an extraordinary manner', addressed Sir Pulteney: 'At your last interview with Bonaparte, did anything occur of which his Majesty's Government should be informed?' The admiral replied: 'Nothing.' He confided for his wife's diary that if Sir Hudson had expressed a desire to be informed of his conversation with Bonaparte, he would have had much pleasure in detailing it to him; 'but to be interrogated in that mode was repugnant'.[6]

Napoleon, isolated in the gloomy house on the windswept plateau, refused to take exercise and occupied his prodigious brain with trifles. There was the episode of the cow. He had complained that the milk was frequently sour, it being usually brought by bullock cart from Jamestown in the heat of the day. At his request, Balcombe had sent a cow and calf to Longwood and they were put in the stable. In the evening the cow broke loose from its tether and got away. After two days she was found, brought back and tethered again, and Montholon instructed the groom Achille Archambault that the cow should share the horses' feed. Whether by accident or because the grooms had no inclination to look after her, by evening the rope was broken again and the beast had gone. Gourgaud described the bother that followed: 'This morning, Montholon related the incident to the Emperor in such hectic colours, that the Emperor became very angry and sent for

Archambault. As he was long in coming, the Emperor then sent word by Noverraz and Ali, that if the cow was not brought back again to the stable, he would deduct the value of it from Archambault's wages. Also, he threatened that he would kill all the chickens, goats and kids that were in the yard!'

In the evening, Gourgaud found his master still fuming over the cow incident. 'At dinner, the Emperor asks Archambault: "Did you let the cow get away? If it is lost, you'll pay for it, you blackguard!" Archambault assures His Majesty that he caught the cow again at the other end of the park; that she twice broke her rope, and that she gives no milk. I hold my tongue throughout the meal. His Majesty, in a very bad humour, retires at 10.30, muttering: "Moscow! Half a million men!"'[7] Some days later, Gourgaud noted with irony: 'I am told that the cow has produced a bottle of milk, and that she may produce a second! Noverraz is going to make some butter.'[8]

William Balcombe noticed that Napoleon now 'did not disdain to interest himself in the merest trifles', and told Betsy it was because of his fight with Lowe: 'My father has often described him as appearing as much absorbed and occupied in the details of some petty squabble with the governor as if the fate of empires had been under discussion. He has often made us laugh with his account of the ridiculous way in which Napoleon spoke of Sir Hudson Lowe; but their disputes were generally on subjects so trivial, that I deem it my duty to draw a veil over these last infirmities of so noble a mind.'[9]

On 12 February, Mrs Balcombe and her two daughters came to visit their good friends the Bertrands and were invited to stay a few nights. Fanny was having difficulty breastfeeding her baby and feared she might lose this child too. She craved Mrs Balcombe's advice and congenial company, and the two girls were helpful with her other children.

Over at Longwood House, Napoleon attempted to break Gourgaud's bad mood, which had lasted for days: 'The Emperor sends for me in the reception room, treats me well, asks for champagne and gives me a glass to drink the health of my mistresses in France' ... After hearing that the Misses Balcombe were visiting Bertrand's cottage, 'he speaks a good deal about Betsy. "You should have one like her. She is very pretty."' Napoleon suggested Gourgaud should go across and invite the Balcombe ladies to dinner.[10]

In Betsy's *Recollections* she described how they arrived to find Napoleon in the billiard room, 'employed looking at some very large maps, and moving about a number of pins, some with red heads, others with black. I asked him what he was doing. He replied that he was fighting over again some of his battles, and that the red-headed pins were meant to represent the English, and the black to indicate the French. One of his chief amusements was going through the evolutions of a lost battle, to see if it were possible by any better manoeuvring to have won it.'[11]

In the careful notes he was keeping, O'Meara recorded: 'Mrs and Misses Balcombe arrive at Longwood. I dined with Napoleon in company with them. He was extremely lively and chatty, and displayed a fund of *causeries* [small talk] rarely to be met with. He instructed Miss Eliza [Betsy] how to play billiards.'[12] 'I had the honour of being initiated into its mysteries by him,' Betsy recalled, 'but when tired of my lesson, my amusement consisted in aiming the balls at his fingers, and I was never more pleased than when I succeeded in making him cry out.'[13] Napoleon was livelier than he had been for some time; Betsy lifted his spirits. She would be fifteen in October and was turning into a shapely young beauty. He knew from the island gossip that she had a number of admirers: the foppish midshipman George Carstairs; the surly Major Sir Thomas Reade, aged 32; and a more serious suitor in Major Oliver Fehrzen, acting commander of the 53rd Regiment, a year younger than Reade.

Fehrzen, born at the Cape of Scandinavian stock, was a well-respected officer who had acquitted himself bravely in the Peninsular Campaign under General Sir George Bingham's command.[14] He walked with a slight limp: a musket ball had lodged in his foot during the 1812 Battle of Salamanca. Captured by the French and surviving a botched attempt by one of their surgeons to extricate the ball, he managed to escape despite his wound, and rejoined Wellington's army.[15] Fehrzen was a good conversationalist and in more sociable days had dined several times at Longwood; it was said that Napoleon was always happy to receive him because of 'his fine presence and engaging manner'.[16] O'Meara mentioned that Fehrzen was 'very clever with his brush, and made many watercolour sketches of Napoleon'.

Gourgaud had just added himself to the list of Betsy's gallants; he played billiards with the girls and danced with them, with Madame de Montholon playing the out-of-tune piano: 'They cause us much enjoyment with their ingenuousness. They constantly style His Majesty as "Monsieur". His Majesty is more cheerful. We pass into the reception room. Betsy behaves amazingly.'[17]

The next day, Gourgaud was invited over to the Bertrands', which delighted him. But if he had expectations, what were they? To take this young girl as a mistress, which Napoleon had seemed to suggest—if so, an appalling betrayal of his friendship with the Balcombes—or as a wife? In any event, Gourgaud's hopes were soon dashed: 'I lunch at the Bertrands' with the Balcombes. Betsy is going to marry Mr Reade. I play with this young madcap, and at one o'clock return home to work. I give Napoleon Bertrand a lesson in riding. In the distance I see Mr Reade, arm in arm with his loved one, whom he had come to fetch. The Emperor visits the Bertrands. Betsy has everybody running after her.'[18]

Bertrand's journal confirmed that Reade was 'a known admirer of the young Balcombe lady and that there is some talk of marriage'. He seemed to connect this to Napoleon's sudden decline in spirits: 'This evening, while these ladies dance, play the piano and joke at billiards, the Emperor's demeanour is depressed.'[19] Gourgaud also reported that Napoleon was 'extremely sad and depressed' that evening. 'He wants to play chess but can't, because he is so taken up with his own thoughts ... The dinner is a sad one. The Emperor asks whether the Balcombes are coming. Montholon replies: "Your Majesty asked them to." We pass into the reception room and His Majesty asks Madame Montholon to invite the Balcombe girls to lunch tomorrow. But the young ladies refuse the invitation. The Emperor, with a serious air, chats for a moment with Betsy, and then passes into the salon with Bertrand.'[20]

The next day, Gourgaud called over the road and learned the girls had declined Napoleon's invitation because they were being hosted by the Bertrands. 'The Misses Balcombe lunch with the Grand Marshal. Later, their father and Fehrzen arrive. Betsy makes a thousand advances to Fehrzen. Poor Reade! Fehrzen is fond of me and invites me to shooting and picnic parties. He finds the Emperor very much changed. O'Meara boasts of having lunched with the Emperor. He escorts Madame Montholon to Lady Lowe's, while the Balcombe family return to the Briars. I go home, very sad at heart, and bored with all this stupid sort of life.'[21]

Gourgaud was not the only one cast down by Betsy's coquetry with the English officers. It is the one indication in sixteen months of friendship with the Balcombes that Napoleon's interest in Betsy seemed to have become less than platonic. If so, that interest was not acted upon; his declared philosophy was: 'it is only a question of knowing how to limit one's desires'.

(When I visited St Helena, the French consul and Napoleonic scholar Michel Dancoisne-Martineau confirmed to me an episode mentioned by Jean-Paul Kauffmann in *The Dark Room at Longwood*. In some unpublished notes by the valet Ali, a slave girl was brought to Napoleon. He ordered Ali to take her away, saying: 'She's too young!'[22] If that girl was too young, perhaps others were not. A few unacknowledged Bonaparte descendants may be walking the streets of Jamestown today.)

Escorted by the doctor, Mrs Balcombe rode with Albine de Montholon to Plantation House to see a baby that had arrived not only with Governor Lowe's permission but with his active participation. At the age of 35, Lady Lowe was, to her annoyance, breastfeeding four-month-old Hudson junior. She showed him off to the visitors, and while Albine, who spoke little English, dandled him on her knee, Lady Lowe confided to Mrs Balcombe her irritation with her husband's obsession with his prisoner. (Sir Hudson often irritated her—she frequently used to say that Sir Thomas Reade was the *real* governor.[23]) She said that Bonaparte 'could not so much as drink a glass of water without it being reported to the governor. She thought such spying ridiculous.'[24]

The next afternoon, Mrs Balcombe was back at the Bertrands' with her daughters and 'passed an hour in conversation with Napoleon after dinner'.[25] She described her indignation at her recent interrogation by Reade. Bertrand noted in his journal: 'When the Balcombes returned from Longwood, Sir Thomas Reade questioned them on what they had done there, saying it with such impertinence, that Mrs. Balcombe felt obliged to answer that she had not gone there to spy.'[26] O'Meara had the same story: 'I have heard reports that Balcombe had been questioned and scrutinized in every direction by the Governor and by Reade.'[27] The deputy adjutant-general was not exactly endearing himself as a prospective son-in-law—but again, it is probable that his 'courtship' of Betsy was a convenient cover to keep watch on the Balcombe family.[28]

A ship had brought a bundle of English books for Napoleon, who was still trying to master the language. He showed Betsy a copy of *Aesop's Fables*: 'In one of the fables the sick lion, after submitting with fortitude to the insults of the many animals who came to exult over his fallen greatness, at last received a kick in the face from the ass. "I could have borne every thing but this," the lion said. Napoleon showed me the wood-cut, and added, "It is me and your governor."'[29]

With her various suitors, Betsy was much talked about on St Helena, but it was not until some European newspapers were delivered that it emerged that she had been briefly the subject of international gossip.

An extract of a letter by the Marquis de Montchenu to a friend in France had appeared in a December 1816 issue of *The Times*:

> Buonaparte on his arrival here was long lodged at the house of an inhabitant of the name of Mr Balcomb [sic]. He has a daughter named Betsy who is celebrated for her independent spirit and her wild temper. She is rather handsome; he has appeared fond of her. Chatting with her the other day, I said, 'Miss, I am not surprised at your speaking French so well—Buonaparte was your teacher. I have been told that you knew how to tame him, and that he was amorous.'
>
> She replied 'Oh! You don't know him at all; he is not gallant enough for that.'
>
> 'Very well, what did this pretty hand do then?'
>
> 'I gave him a famous cuff, which put him in such a passion that he squeezed my nose, which continued red the whole day.'
>
> 'For my part, I should have embraced you'—and I kissed the pretty hand that had cuffed the great man.[30]

A more spiteful account of Napoleon's early sojourn at The Briars, again written by Montchenu, who got it as hearsay (not being on the island at the time himself), was published in the *Courrier de Mannheim* on 1 November 1816, and reproduced in French newspapers: 'Bonaparte, since he has been on St Helena, has formed a liaison with the daughter of a notary. This young person is so lively that one could almost believe she is cracked in the head. Bonaparte was alone one day in his room with this young girl (!); she, acting out a fantasy, picked up a sabre that was in the corner, took it out of its scabbard and assumed the posture of a master of arms, and she fell on Bonaparte, crying "Now, defend yourself!" Bonaparte, after having for a minute believed this was a joke, became fearful and hid behind an armchair; and the ex-master of the world cried out for his sentinels to come to his aid. Las Cases, his secretary, reproached the young girl for her conduct, but she answered that Bonaparte really liked it. "He loves me!" she said, laughing. "So let me go! He never really loved anyone, it is not in his nature."'[31]

The article, which also included an insinuating description of Napoleon and Betsy playing Blindman's Buff, noted that she was Napoleon's favourite and would tell him everything that passed through her flighty head. She asked him the most untoward questions but he answered them all without hesitation. Montchenu concluded that 'Miss Betsee' was the wildest little girl he had ever met and expressed the opinion that she was *folle*—a madwoman. His account was very damaging to a young lady's reputation and future prospects. Betsy observed in her *Recollections*: 'My father was much enraged at my name thus appearing, and wished to call the marquess to account for his ill nature.' However, her mother's intercession prevailed, a duel was averted and 'an ample apology' was obtained from the marquis.

When Napoleon heard of the affront that 'Miss Betsee' had received from the '*vieux imbécile*' (old fool[32]), he asked O'Meara to call at The Briars with a message for her on his way to Jamestown. He suggested how she might revenge herself: 'It so happened, that the marquess prided himself on the peculiar fashion of his wig, to which was attached a long cue. This embellishment on his head Napoleon desired me to burn off with caustic. I was always ready for mischief and in this instance had a double inducement, on the emperor's promise to reward me, on the receipt of the pigtail, with the prettiest fan Mr. Solomon's shop contained. Fortunately I was prevented indulging in this most hoydenish trick by the remonstrances of my mother.'

The next time she saw Napoleon, she made much of being too dutiful to disobey her mother, despite her inclination for revenge. 'He pinched my ear, in token of approval, and said, "*Ah, Miss Betsee, tu commences à être sage.*"—"You begin to be sensible." He then called Dr. O'Meara, and asked him if he had procured the fan? The doctor replied that there were none pretty enough. I believe I looked disappointed; on perceiving which, Napoleon, with his usual good nature, consoled me with the promise of something prettier—and he kept his word. In a few days I received a ring of brilliants, forming the letter N, surmounted by a small eagle.'[33]

It was almost three weeks before the Balcombe girls saw Napoleon again; their social life had become a flurry of picnics, parties and dances. On 17 February, they attended a ball on the deck of the *Newcastle*, hosted by Admiral Malcolm and his wife in honour of the third birthday of their son, who remained in England with a nanny. On this flagship the admiral was undeniably in charge and there is no mention of the governor's presence; perhaps the Lowes were invited but declined. Three days later, the Balcombes hosted a ball and supper at The Briars. The Malcolms of course were there, and General Sir George Bingham with his wife Emma, who had recently arrived on the island. Many officers attended, and the dancing continued until dawn because of the curfew. Betsy danced alternately with Major Reade and Major Fehrzen, and people puzzled their heads over which one she would marry.

Admiral Malcolm visited Napoleon on 7 March and found him in excellent spirits, reading the English newspapers that had come with the storeship. His comprehension of the language had greatly improved, although he refused to converse in it. They discussed events mentioned in the papers, including recent disturbances in Spanish America. Observing protocol, the admiral called afterwards at Plantation House to report the conversation, and the governor, somewhat mollified, asked him to transcribe it. Malcolm concluded his report by saying that he had never seen Bonaparte 'so moderate, and judging from his manner I think any indulgence that may be shown him will be acceptable'.[34]

It was O'Meara who broke the news at Longwood that Dr William Warden, the surgeon, had published *Letters written on board HMS Northumberland and at St Helena*, a book about his encounters with the former emperor. The storeship *Tortoise* had brought newspapers with extracts of the book, and many people on the island were already reading them. Above all things, Napoleon was particular about the cultivation of his legend. 'What is the nature of the work?' he demanded. 'Is it for or against me? Is it well written? What is the subject?'

O'Meara said it was in his favour, although it contained some curious statements, but also refutations of accusations formerly made against him. Napoleon began reading immediately, 'asked the explanation of a few passages, [and] said they were true'. O'Meara assisted with the translation and was asked to 'explain to him three times an article which stated that the Empress Marie Louise had fallen from her horse into the Po, and with difficulty had been saved from a watery grave. He appeared considerably affected by the perusal.'[35]

The governor sent up a bound copy of the Warden book for General Bonaparte. The next day, Betsy and her parents, who had been visiting Madame Bertrand, passed by Longwood. 'I had caught sight of the emperor in his favourite billiard-room, and not being able to resist having a game with him, I listened to no remonstrance, but bounded off, leaving my father in dismay at the consequences likely to ensue. Instead of my anticipated game of throwing about the balls, I was requested to read a book by Dr. Warden, the surgeon of the *Northumberland*, that had just come out. It was in English, and I had the task of wading through several chapters, and making it as intelligible as my ungrammatical French permitted. Napoleon was much pleased with Dr. Warden's book, and said, "his work was a very true one". I finished reading it to him whilst we remained with Madame Bertrand.'[36] (When Lowe was informed that the Balcombe ladies had been at Longwood, he said that 'they had no business to have spoken to General Bonaparte, as their pass had only specified Count Bertrand's family'.[37])

After finishing Warden's book, Napoleon concluded: 'The foundation of it is true, but he has badly understood what was said to him;

as in the work there are many mistakes, which must have arisen from bad explanation; Warden does not understand French. He has acted incorrectly in making me speak in the manner he has done. For, instead of having stated that it had been conveyed through an interpreter, he puts down almost everything as if I had been speaking to him all the time.'[38] Bertrand counselled: 'This book will be useful for you. It is of a new kind, since it sings your praises ... In some moments it shows you sad, or calm, imperturbable, good, sensitive, kind to all those around you, walking with Madame Bertrand and your pleasant manner with her, and your intelligence, which is superior to all. He represents you in a way so different from the way you have been painted, that it must have a good effect.'[39] Napoleon liked this argument and became a supporter of Warden's work.

Warden's *Letters* caused a stir for several days. Lady Malcolm remarked that in fifty years no work in England had enjoyed more vogue.[40] What particularly impressed and inspired O'Meara was that the book was already said to have earned the author 50,000 francs. 'That's possible—the British do not know me,' Napoleon said, 'anything relating to St Helena, published by an eyewitness and their countryman, piques their curiosity; they are hungry for details about me. Balcombe offered Marchand fifty guineas for the views of Longwood he had done; he would have made a good speculation in London if Marchand had agreed to his wish.'[41] The doctor decided to set about writing his own work. Bertrand noted: 'O'Meara, won over by the lure of 6000 pounds, would undertake to publish it if he had his independence.'[42]

CHAPTER 16

OUR BEAUTIFUL ISLAND

The storeship *Tortoise* arrived at Jamestown on 5 March 1817, bringing supplies and mail from England. Sir Hudson Lowe, who was still planning to move against O'Meara, was unaware that the doctor had just received a gratifying letter from his friend at the Admiralty: 'We thought you would have reached home now, as we did hear that the Governor had determined to send you home. Lord Melville however immediately applied to Lord Liverpool to interfere and prevent it. Of one thing, be certain your reports have given infinite satisfaction and you and them are highly esteemed in the highest quarters.'[1] That Viscount Melville, First Sea Lord, had personally applied to the prime minister to prevent his removal from the island and that he was esteemed by the Prince Regent himself gave O'Meara supreme confidence. He was safe as long as, like Scheherazade, he kept spinning stories that kept his audience spellbound.

On 25 March, the Malcolms came to Longwood with Captain Francis Stanfell, commander of the frigate HMS *Phaeton*, another of William Balcombe's naval friends. He was meeting Bonaparte for the first time and, having just been to the Cape, could tell him that he had visited Count de Las Cases at Newlands, the country house of Lord Somerset, the governor. Young Emmanuel de Las Cases had become a frequent visitor to Cape Town since his remarkable recovery after treatment by Dr James Barry, a skilled military surgeon. (Dr Barry was famously revealed after death to have been a woman.[2])

If the British visitors noticed the presence of numerous rats in the house, they were too tactful to mention it. On a recent occasion, when Napoleon took his hat off the sideboard a large rat had sprung from it and scuttled between his legs, 'to the surprise of those present'. Rats had killed 140 fowls in just three weeks, sucking out their brains as the birds slept.[3] With so much food thrown away after meals and with gaps in the floors and ceilings of the rickety building, the rodents had become a disgusting problem.

At the April races, Gourgaud was flattered to join most of the notables: Sir Hudson and Lady Lowe, Sir Pulteney and Lady Malcolm, Sir George and Lady Bingham and the three commissioners. He was paid particular attention by the commissioners, who aimed for access through him to Bonaparte. The Austrian commissioner, Baron von Stürmer, walked with Gourgaud as they left the ground, alerting Major Thomas Reade to watch them closely. '*En route,*' Gourgaud wrote that night, 'Sturmer assures me that things would be much more pleasant if we saw one another more often. I answer, that His Majesty's mind is made up—he will never receive the Commissioners.'[4]

Stürmer was seeking intelligence, but was unaware of the despatch Lowe had just received from Lord Bathurst. The British ambassador in Vienna had informed his lordship that the Austrian government had mastered the code employed in the Viennese *Antigallican* newspaper, sometimes delivered to Longwood. A deciphered message to Bonaparte said that news of the sale of his silverware had caused a sensation; funds had been sent to his brother Joseph; Hortense was well; the army would be increased to 500,000 men; and he should not sleep at night. Finally, 'If the British government make proposals to you, do not confide in Sturmer.' Bathurst advised Lowe that they needed to find evidence of the person in Vienna inserting these messages, and their objective. 'You will therefore permit the *Antigallican* newspapers to reach General Bonaparte in the usual manner.'[5]

The *Prince Regent* from Calcutta anchored in James Bay in late April, and a glimpse of Bonaparte was a memorable event for a five-year-old British child, William Makepeace Thackeray. He was on his way to boarding school in England with an Indian servant as escort. The servant took young William on an arduous walk up the Sidepath, over rocks and hills, until they could peer over a wall at 'a dumpy-looking man' prowling the pathways of an enclosed garden: '"That is he," said the black man: "that is Bonaparte! He eats three sheep every day, and all the little children he can lay hands on!"' Thackeray later commented: 'There were people in the British dominions besides that poor Calcutta serving-man, with an equal horror of the Corsican ogre.'[6]

Admiral Malcolm, who was soon to depart, was received again at Longwood on 3 May. He urged Napoleon to meet with the diplomat Lord Amherst, who would call on his way back from China and could mediate with the governor. Napoleon refused: 'They sent me, at my age, beyond the tropics into a terrible country and I was given into the custody of a man still more frightful than the country.' What he would like, he said, was for Lady Malcolm to visit him before her departure, 'as undoubtedly the Princess Charlotte will send for her after her arrival in England. I will undertake to tell her the shameful treatment that has been imposed on me.' The admiral was non-committal and Napoleon turned on him: 'You have influence. But I see it; when one is not English, there is nothing to expect from you. You don't feel obliged to do anything for those who are not English.'[7]

The mail brought to Longwood that month included much absorbing reading: there was an account of Lord Holland's speech in March to the House of Lords condemning the situation of the French exiles and moving that certain documents be tabled to make known the treatment of Bonaparte. He was referring to 'Remonstrance', which the Corsican servant Santini had smuggled out, sewn into his jacket, the printing paid for by Lord Holland. The motion was opposed by Lord Bathurst. The speeches were published in *The Times* and the *Morning Chronicle* and the 'Remonstrance' letter widely quoted in the press.

In an interview for *The Times*, Santini had deplored the conditions in which his master lived: the climate of Longwood was most unhealthy, with extremes of wind, humidity and heat. The house was a hovel and the roof leaked; it was 'infested by rats, who devour everything that they can reach. All the Emperor's linen, even that which was lately sent from England, has been gnawed and completely destroyed by them . . . When the Emperor is at dinner the rats run about the apartment and even creep beneath his feet.' However, his strongest criticism was reserved for the food sent by Balcombe the purveyor. The provisions were always too small in quantity and frequently of bad quality. Often there was no butcher's meat for the emperor's table, and Cipriani would send Santini to town to purchase a sheep for four guineas or some pork for making soup. 'I was even, from necessity, in the habit of repairing secretly to the English camp to purchase butter, eggs and bread, of the soldiers' wives, otherwise the Emperor would often have been without breakfast, and even without dinner.' Santini claimed that he sometimes rose at daybreak to shoot pigeons, or else the emperor would have nothing for breakfast, as 'the provisions did not reach Longwood until two or three o'clock in the afternoon'. He said that in publishing his account he was fulfilling a 'painful but sacred duty'.[8]

Santini had been a servant at Fontainebleau and at the small but gracious palace on Elba and he expected catering standards fit for an emperor. He failed to understand the paucity of provisions for most island residents then (and still today) and how shocked those residents would have been by a typical meal served at Longwood.

The editor of *The Times* fulminated: 'It is a fact, which will appear incredible, but which is not the less true, that *the Emperor is limited to a bottle of wine per day!* Marshal and Madame Bertrand, General Montholon and his Lady, General Gourgaud and Count de Las Cases have also each their bottle . . . We have ourselves always found fault with the expense which is imposed upon this nation by keeping this man which . . . amounts to £20,000 a year . . . and we think it hard that this nation is to be taxed to support such a creature as he is, in a state of dignity to which his original condition in life gave him no pretensions.'[9]

At about the same time as Santini's interview, the servants despatched with him, Joseph Archambault and Rousseau, arrived in America. Hyde de Neuville, the French ambassador based in Washington, informed his home government on 21 May: 'It seems that two members of Bonaparte's suite have just arrived from St Helena, by way of England. They are said to have met Bonaparte's zealous partisans, whose hopes have been greatly encouraged since this event.' He sent a more alarming report a few weeks later: 'The arrival of the two emissaries from St Helena is an established fact. Absurd rumours have been circulating ever since; they go so far as to announce Bonaparte's escape. The most probable explanation seems to be that these two individuals have been given a mission with this end in view, and have been sent to make arrangements with Joseph and the leaders of the party.'[10] Archambault and Rousseau had given Joseph Bonaparte a map of St Helena with information on landing spots, sentry posts and troop placements. Years later, Bertrand told Prince Metternich that 'their only hope ... had lain in an American plan to carry off the prisoner'.[11]

But Napoleon cautioned his companions against desperate escape measures. There was still a chance that the Whigs might come to power in Britain. 'If Lord Holland were to enter the Ministry,' he told Gourgaud, 'I would probably be recalled to England; and our greatest hopes lie in the death of the Prince Regent. In this event, little Princess Charlotte would ascend the throne. She would recall me.'[12]

Nothing cheered Gourgaud. He had taken dictation on Waterloo for the tenth time and Napoleon had exclaimed: 'I still cannot conceive how the battle was lost!'[13] The unwilling scribe complained to his journal: 'After dinner His Majesty declares that our stay at St Helena will make us all very learned, which remark provokes a unanimous "No!" Boredom. Bed at 10.'[14]

Life was not so dull for Marchand, who had a mistress, Esther Vesey, a mixed-race island girl who was a servant to Madame de Montholon.[15] At the beginning of June, Esther gave birth to a son. Napoleon said he did not want her staying at Longwood—the gossips would attribute the child to him. Before she had recovered from the birth, Esther and her baby were forced to move into town. The valet wanted to visit her there but was prevented. 'It is useless for him to go,' said Napoleon. 'I will not allow it. In a fortnight, Esther will be well again, and will be able to come and see Marchand. All this tenderness is ridiculous.'[16] Gourgaud agreed: 'Who can be certain that Esther's father will not thrash Marchand and make him sign a promise of marriage?'[17]

But in mid-June, Gourgaud made a curious journal entry about a conversation with Napoleon: 'He sends for Marchand, and lies down on his bed. He tells me that Marchand is supposed to be the father of Esther's son. This will be painful news to the Empress, when she hears of it.'[18] One wonders why Marchand was *supposed* to be the father, when earlier discussion had indicated that he was. And why would the news of a humble valet fathering an illegitimate child be painful news for Marie Louise, Napoleon's legal wife? The wording invites speculation that the child was in fact Napoleon's, that Esther Vesey had been *his* bed partner, or he had enjoyed her occasional sexual favours with the collusion of his devoted valet. British sentries patrolled Longwood's exterior but were not privy to what went on in the bedrooms.

Earlier in the month Gourgaud made a visit to town; escorted by Captain Poppleton and accompanied by the Montholons, they walked down the mountain. In Jamestown they visited the shops, despite the embargo the governor had placed on shopkeepers serving them, and Madame de Montholon bought 'numerous gowns' and Gourgaud some shirts; they were greeted by Major Fehrzen and called on Admiral Malcolm and his wife. When they arrived back at Longwood, Napoleon asked Gourgaud for news. 'The Montholons spoke of the welcome we received in town and the Emperor exclaims: "We are still notable people. In England, the Whigs speak of no one but me. We underestimate our own importance."'[19]

They read in the papers about factory workers in the north of England rioting against the installation of machines. Napoleon said they were crying out for him 'to lead them in defence of the rights of the people. They might seize several vessels and come and rescue us, after which they would go to France and expel the Bourbons.' He said that this was why Lowe had redoubled his vigilance.[20]

On 19 June, Admiral Malcolm rode up to Longwood on a final visit, accompanied by a ship's captain and a major of the marines who hoped to meet General Bonaparte. Lady Malcolm travelled in a little pony-drawn cart lent by Lady Lowe.[21]

Napoleon led the Malcolms into the drawing room to see the newly arrived bust of his six-year-old son, the King of Rome, whom he refused to call the Duke of Parma. (The marble bust was rumoured to have been sent by the former empress Marie Louise.) He said it was brought on one of the storeships and that Sir Thomas Reade had told the captain 'he ought to have thrown it overboard'. Napoleon turned to Lady Malcolm and asked if this was not barbarous. She replied that it was so barbarous she did not believe Sir Thomas capable of it.

Napoleon continued to rant about Lowe and his restrictions while the admiral defended the governor. Then Napoleon adopted a different approach, presenting Lady Malcolm with a coffee cup and saucer from his Sèvres set. 'This is a gift for my lady,' he said, adding that he would not make the admiral a gift, 'for he would not hear reason. Ladies had more compassionate hearts than men for an object in misfortune.'[22] Napoleon's strategy was still to win advantage from Lady Malcolm's family relationship with Admiral Lord Keith and friendship with Princess Charlotte. 'He hopes the gift of the cup will produce the desired effect,' Gourgaud noted.[23]

As it happened, on 20 June, the day after the Malcolms' visit, a wedding took place in Edinburgh, binding together in marriage Margaret Mercer Elphinstone and Auguste Charles Joseph, Comte de Flahaut de La Billarderie. The bride's father did not attend. The news rippled through society circles. One aristocratic English lady wrote to another of Admiral Lord Keith's fury at his daughter's marriage 'with the natural son of Talleyrand, the Aid de Camp of Bonaparte. Sure such a Fellow has a *Right to make Conquests*: though the Scotch People here tell me the Admiral is enraged to think of *his* Title ornamenting the eldest son of Monsieur Flahaut, for so it certainly will.'[24]

Lord Keith had spent his life fighting the French and had no intention of allowing his estates to be inherited by them. In July he wrote a deed of trust together with a revised will. The marriage of his daughter to Count Flahaut was, he wrote, 'most repugnant to my wishes and, I am convinced, to her true interest'. He was fully resolved that she should 'be excluded from all interest in or benefit from my Estates' and stipulated that his estates could only be inherited by persons 'educated as a Protestant in the United Kingdom, under no allegiance to any Foreign Power, nor holding any commission of service to any Foreign State'.[25] However, he could do nothing about the fact that Margaret was an heiress in her own right, the beneficiary of her mother's considerable wealth.

On 29 June, the flagship *Conqueror* appeared on the horizon, bringing Admiral Malcolm's replacement, Rear-Admiral Robert Plampin. Betsy Balcombe was visiting Longwood at the time and gaily bounded up to 'Ali' Saint-Denis, the second valet, asking where she could find the emperor. He told her that he was over at the Bertrand house, but was 'in no mood for badinage today, Mademoiselle'.

She found Napoleon standing on the sloping lawn, looking grim as he gazed out at the ocean that glistened like quicksilver far below. General Bertrand stood beside him. The *Conqueror*, a mighty 74-gun ship of the line, was beating up to windward. Betsy felt subdued by the intense melancholy of Napoleon's expression. After a long silence he said, 'The English are kings upon the sea,' and added: 'I wonder what they think of our beautiful island? They cannot be much elated by the sight of my gigantic prison walls.'[26]

CHAPTER 17

THE COMPANY OF A GREEN PARROT

Rear-Admiral Robert Plampin, aged 55, the new commander of the St Helena and Cape of Good Hope naval stations, made a ceremonial visit on 29 June to the governor at the castle. While he was no naval hero, he had served with modest distinction in the American Revolutionary War and in various naval campaigns against France. He had been a lieutenant at the 1793 Siege of Toulon when the artilleryman Captain Napoleon Buonaparte made his name. As a youth, Plampin had spent some years in France and acquired proficiency in the language; because of this, he had been Admiral Lord Hood's interpreter during the Toulon siege.[1]

On his second day on the island, Plampin called on Lady Lowe at Plantation House. People wondered why his presumed wife, who had sailed with him from England, did not accompany him. Dr John Stokoe, surgeon on the *Conqueror*, mentioned that the lady had not embarked at Portsmouth but had joined the ship from a boat which put out from the Isle of Wight, exciting 'suspicions unfavourable to the lady, for none of us supposed that the Admiralty would have denied a passage to the wife of the Admiral'.[2] The truth was not long in coming out. 'In this community where the death of a sheep was news,' noted Gilbert Martineau, 'the incredible fact was soon public knowledge: the Admiral and the person in question were not united by any of the contracts that bind man and woman in respectable society.'[3] Stokoe wrote that the outrage 'was most severe at Plantation House. The ladies who formed the court of the queen of the island were unanimous in the opinion that the Admiral's conduct was the grossest insult that could possibly be offered them, considering that he was the second rank in the island.'[4]

The *Caesar* from the East Indies arrived in James Bay, also in late June, bringing William Pitt, 1st Earl Amherst, the British ambassador to China, and members of his delegation after their failed trade mission.[5] Napoleon agreed to an audience; at the end of their meeting, Amherst offered to transmit any request by Napoleon to the Prince Regent, so inviting a catalogue of grievances. According to Bertrand, the diplomat was sympathetic, declaring 'that it was not the intention of the Chamber of Paris nor of the Parliament that he was thus treated, and they wanted a better situation for him'.[6]

Sir Pulteney and Lady Malcolm hosted a reception for Lord Amherst on the *Newcastle*; it was also their farewell to friends on the island, such as the Binghams and Balcombes, and they observed protocol by inviting Sir Hudson Lowe and his wife. Presumably Admiral Plampin was there too, but he would have found it wise not to bring his female companion. He had recently been preached at from the pulpit of St Paul's: the Reverend Mr Richard Boys, on a mission to root out evil where he found it, had begun to make 'thinly veiled allusions in his sermons to wickedness in high places'.[7]

At the reception, Betsy spent much of the time with Major Oliver Fehrzen, whose 53rd Regiment was about to depart; people wondered if they would become officially betrothed before he left. It may have been during the Malcolms' shipboard party that her sister Jane also acquired an admirer, the *Conqueror*'s surgeon, Dr John Stokoe. But Betsy disgraced herself that day, teasing a pretty young woman referred to as 'Miss P', who perhaps drew away some of the male attention Betsy regarded as her due. At the end of the party, as the other ladies were being lowered over the side of the ship to a barge, Betsy lured 'Miss P' into a cabin, slammed the door and locked it. It was not until the barge was near the shore that the absence was noted—infuriating Lady Lowe—and an officer had to row back to rescue the terrified girl.[8]

When Betsy next visited Longwood with her father, 'I was surprised and vexed to find that the emperor had heard an account of the party from other lips than mine, as I was anxious to forestall the narration of the exploits of a certain hoydenish young lady, namely, myself; but he had received a faithful detail of them from Dr. O'Meara. He pretended to scold and take me to task for being such a *petite folle*, and said he hoped the account were not true.' Balcombe assured Napoleon that Betsy would repent by doing more French lessons. She protested that she had been sufficiently punished and mentioned 'the scolding I had received from Lady Lowe, who kept desiring me to use my *reason*, and "not to be so childish"'. Napoleon said that 'he wondered at her ladyship's want of perception in giving me credit for what I never possessed'.[9]

Gourgaud remarked to Napoleon: 'It is fortunate for Fehrzen that he is to leave, otherwise he would have been foolish enough to marry Betsy Balcombe.' Napoleon ridiculed this: 'Betsy is a girl like any other. Moreover, life is short, and provided a woman produces children, what more does a man want?'[10]

On 4 July, the Malcolms sailed for England on the *Newcastle* frigate. Despite Admiral Malcolm's fractious encounters with Lowe, his time at St Helena was to add lustre to his already distinguished career. He was appointed vice-admiral in 1821 and for many years was commander-in-chief in the Mediterranean.

His successor in the South Atlantic, Admiral Plampin, moved into The Briars' pavilion with his mistress, creating a socially awkward situation for the Balcombes. While the rent must have suited William, his wife would not have appreciated the couple creating such an indelicate example for their daughters. We are told that thereafter The Briars 'was shunned by Lady Lowe and other dames who formed the high St Helena society'.[11]

The Reverend Mr Boys, in his zeal for the spiritual welfare of the community, became even more outspoken. From his pulpit he inveighed against moral lapses and 'did not hesitate to single out prominent examples of evil living ... The case of Rear-Admiral Plampin was one which excited his righteous anger to a considerable degree.'[12] This created a dilemma for Lowe, who appreciated Plampin's endorsement of his firm policy towards the French. His despatches to Bathurst indicated that while he had 'no sympathy with the moral obliquities of Plampin', he valued the admiral's unqualified support, unlike his naval predecessors. He also dreaded St Helena becoming a scandal in England because of 'the uncurbed tongue of Mr Boys'.[13] He therefore warned the senior chaplain that further personal attacks would jeopardise his position on the island. The provocative sermons ceased. Plampin was grateful and, for the duration of his command, proved to be Lowe's unswerving ally. The tacit understanding between the two men compromised any hope Napoleon may have had of greater freedom and made more perilous the position of those who sympathised with him.

Gourgaud was walking back to Longwood one July day when he met up with Marchand and his mistress Esther Vesey. 'I cannot see much of her baby, but Madame Bertrand, who has seen it, says that it has blue eyes and an enormous head. It does not resemble its father. The Emperor sends for me in the reception room. He is very cool and rather embarrassed.'[14] Gourgaud failed to explain the embarrassment—but Napoleon had just heard a description of Esther's baby, so his discomfort may well have related to his own blue-grey eyes and disproportionately large head. In the best-known portrait of Marchand, his dark brown eyes are his dominant feature, and as Esther was described as a 'mulatto', presumably her eyes were also brown.

The time had come to farewell the 2nd Battalion of the 53rd Regiment, departing for England. Napoleon received Major Fehrzen—soon to be promoted to lieutenant-colonel—and his officers. Although he resented the governor and the ever-increasing guard around Longwood, he felt sympathy for the 'poor devils' obliged to keep watch from dusk to dawn.

Napoleon was again contemplating the feasibility of escape. On 14 July, he discussed with his companions the few possible landing places along the island's coastline. Lowe was in a state of permanent suspicion. By now he knew that two of Bonaparte's servants deported from the island were in America and would have taken maps and information. They were in the employ of Joseph Bonaparte, who was fabulously rich and willing to finance a rescue attempt for his brother. Other transactions were in progress. Balcombe was given 7000 francs to distribute to the officers of the 53rd (it seemed principally to Fehrzen, who had agreed to a certain undertaking) and £300 for the gunner who had brought the bust of Napoleon's son—'a fortune for him', remarked Bertrand.[15]

O'Meara was called to Plantation House and engaged in a rancorous discussion with the governor lasting almost three hours. Lowe accused him of conveying clandestine messages. 'How can you think the French are not our enemies?' he demanded. Those at Longwood, he said, had become altogether too arrogant: 'It is the fault of Admiral Cockburn, who organised everything so badly here.'[16]

A ball was held at Deadwood Camp to farewell the departing regiment and welcome their replacement, the 1st Battalion of the 66th. It was followed by another party, at The Briars. That night, Major Fehrzen and Betsy announced their intention to marry. Fehrzen had also agreed to undertake a secret errand for Napoleon: with Balcombe as the intermediary, he was 'taking some of the Emperor's hair to Rome', to deliver to his mother, Madame Mère. She would give strands to her brother, Cardinal Fesch, and send some to Napoleon's wife, Marie Louise.[17] On the day of the 53rd Regiment's departure, Bertrand noted that 'Mr Balcombe, who accompanied Major Fehrzen to the sea, ensured that the Major undertakes to carry, perhaps to deliver personally, the Emperor's hair'.[18]

At this time, O'Meara was translating pamphlets for publication, protesting against the treatment of the French. But Napoleon had become wary of his physician, suspecting that he had revealed too much in conversations with the governor. He decided: 'If I see what the doctor says can become dangerous, I will distort confidences to him.'[19] Gourgaud was emphatic about the danger: 'O'Meara is completely compromised. We risk imprisonment, and he the rope. It seems he is out to make money by printing the pamphlets he has translated for the Emperor. His Majesty makes a mistake writing so many.'[20] But Napoleon objected: 'To be sure, the doctor does everything for our good. He listens to my complaints, but he would not betray his country. Even if we wanted to escape, O'Meara would not have a finger in it.'[21]

At that time, another despatch from Hyde de Neuville, the French ambassador in Washington, was on its way to Paris. It stated that the

French exiles surrounding Joseph Bonaparte had a plan afoot, acting on information brought by the two servants from St Helena: 'even if the exact nature of the danger is obscure, everything goes to prove that it exists. I do not yet know the situation of the fire but the heat proves there is one, and if it is not put out it will become a conflagration'.[22]

Bathurst warned Lowe that now more than ever he had to be on his mettle and wary of Bonaparte's 'peculiar talent for cajolery' which could 'seduce very intelligent men' from a strict line of conduct: 'The turbulent and seditious in this, as well as in every other country, look to the escape of General Bonaparte as that which would at once give life and activity to the Revolutionary spirit, which has been so long formidable to the best interests of Europe, and which they have all a common object in endeavouring to revive.'[23]

Among the French sympathisers in contact with Joseph Bonaparte was an ex-major in the imperial army called Persat; in his memoirs, he described various plans in 1817 to rescue Napoleon from St Helena. Joseph had declared that he was 'ready to give his life and fortune to deliver the Emperor, but that he had been obliged to give up this plan because of definite information from London about the barbarous orders issued by the British government. These were to put the Emperor to death, if any serious attack was made on the 4000 gaolers who kept watch on him.'[24]

Napoleon's forty-eighth birthday was celebrated quietly on 15 August. He sat down to lunch with his companions and their children. Gourgaud detested his hero's attentions to Albine de Montholon. Earlier he had complained: 'She is always scratching her neck and spitting her food into her plate. The woman has no manners. I never thought that Your Majesty would like her for—that! But she does her best to make people think you do.' Napoleon attempted to placate him: 'Don't imagine that I like her. I have been accustomed to living with too many charming women not to be aware of Madame de Montholon's ridiculous aspects and her bad manners. But after all, if one had nothing else, here one would have to find one's company in a green parrot. We have no choice . . . If the woman were prettier, I would take advantage of her for—that too.'[25]

If Napoleon felt weighed down by sorrows, his most recent was that his wife Marie Louise had given birth to another child by her lover General von Neipperg. Napoleon was determined that the Austrian court would hear no scandal concerning himself. He forbade Marchand's mistress Esther Vesey to come near the house with her baby in case he was accused of siring it.[26] He was morose, and a few days later told O'Meara: 'Had I died in Moscow, I should have left behind a reputation as a conqueror without a parallel in history.'[27]

In the third week of September, horse races were held at Deadwood once again and Betsy Balcombe became the centre of attention. As punishment for being lax with her French lessons, her father had refused to allow her to compete in the ladies' race. To ensure that she stayed at home, he lent her pony to a friend for the day. Betsy recalled: 'My vexation was very great at not knowing where to get a horse, and I happened to mention my difficulty to Dr. O'Meara, who told Napoleon; and my delight may be conceived when, a short time after all our party had left the Briars for Deadwood, I perceived the doctor winding down the mountain path which led to our house, followed by a slave leading a superb grey horse called "Mameluke" with a lady's side-saddle and housings of crimson velvet embroidered with gold.'

When Napoleon had heard of her disappointment, he had requested that the quietest horse in his stable be prepared for her use. He then witnessed the races from Longwood's latticed porch with his 'battlefield spyglass'. According to Marchand, 'the Emperor eyed Baroness Stürmer, whom he found attractive and well seated on her horse'.[28] But he was delighted when Betsy, galloping side saddle on the richly caparisoned Mameluke, was first past the winning post in the ladies' race.

While the event was still in progress, O'Meara was interrogated by the governor: 'Sir Hudson Lowe sent for me and asked if "some of General Bonaparte's horses were not on the race-ground." I replied in the affirmative. His Excellency asked how they came there? I replied that I had borrowed the horses from General Gourgaud, one of which I had lent to Miss Eliza Balcombe, and the other to the surgeon of the *Conqueror*. Sir Hudson immediately broke out into not the most moderate expressions, and his gestures attracted many of the spectators. He characterised my having dared to lend any of General Bonaparte's horses without his (the Governor's) permission as the greatest piece of presumption he had ever witnessed. I observed that I had come to St Helena to learn that it was a crime to borrow a horse for the use of a young lady.'[29] After O'Meara left him, Lowe remarked to his secretary Gorrequer: 'I'll lay that fellow sprawling yet before I have done with him.'[30]

Betsy's triumph was short-lived. Her father was rebuked by Lowe for having 'committed a breach of discipline in permitting one of his family to ride a horse belonging to the Longwood establishment'.[31] But the commissioners had been distracted from the races by watching the portly figure at Longwood 'standing at a veranda outside his door'.

Fanny Bertrand invited the Balcombe women to stay for the night of the races ball. They could dine with the emperor and show off their gowns before riding in his carriage to Deadwood Camp. Madame de Montholon sent her maid Josephine to arrange Betsy's hair, and she piled it up high in the current French fashion. 'She combed and strained it off my face,' Betsy recalled, 'making me look Chinese. It was the first time I had seen such a coiffure, and I thought I had never beheld anything so hideous in my life, and would gladly have pulled it down, but there was no time, and I was obliged to make my appearance before Napoleon, whose laugh I dreaded, with my eyes literally starting from my head.' To her surprise he liked her hair and said it was the only time he had seen it neat. While her new coiffure made her seem elegant from the neck up, her childish frock did not pass muster: 'he declared it was frightful, from its extreme shortness, and desired me to have it lengthened'. Betsy protested, but Napoleon twitched the skirt about, and the obliging Josephine managed to lengthen it by letting out three tucks.

After dinner, Napoleon accompanied the women and Gourgaud to the carriage; Achille Archambault the groom cracked his whip and they took off, the spirited Cape horses galloping on one side of the track, then the other, until they crashed into a gumwood tree. The members of the party were obliged to scramble out and plod nearly a mile through mud, Madame Bertrand carrying her squalling infant, who would not be pacified by the nurse. They had to scrape mud from their shoes when they arrived. In spite of the setbacks, Betsy remembered it as 'a very merry ball'; she was thrilled to be compared to the prettiest woman on the island, Baroness von Stürmer, the wife of the Austrian commissioner. The party did not end until long after the booming guns from the forts announced the break of day.[32]

Four days later, on 25 September, the normally calm and temperate General Bertrand rushed to Longwood, crying: 'Great news!' He had heard that the royalists had been massacred at Guadeloupe and Martinique. He waited for everyone's attention before announcing something more momentous: 'In France, everybody wants the Emperor back again. Montholon has learned all this from Balcombe, who was requested by the Governor to deliver the news to the Emperor tomorrow, and after that, to go and dine at Plantation House.'

Gourgaud was sceptical: 'I discredit this—but we shall see!'

Bertrand's exuberance would not be dampened. 'Let's go and pack our bags.'[33]

Balcombe and O'Meara were the main channels for news. In their absence, those at Longwood received garbled accounts from Jamestown brought by servants and soldiers. It is curious that on this occasion they believed that the governor had entrusted Balcombe, of all people, as his emissary. But the next day Napoleon was swept up in the excitement; from the billiard room he trained his field glass on the guardhouse. 'You've heard the news?' he exclaimed to Gourgaud. 'It must be very good news for the Governor to send Balcombe to us.' He thought the stir could mean that there had been a regime change in France and the Bonapartist forces had triumphed and were demanding his release.

At two o'clock, Napoleon saw the purveyor enter Bertrand's house. The delay tormented him. An hour passed. They must be discussing something of great moment, he thought. It could even be possible that his six-year-old son had been placed on the French throne. At last Bertrand came across the road, very downcast. Gourgaud recorded: 'It appears that Balcombe has no news! He merely has a paper, reporting the riots at Martinique. His Majesty's countenance changes. He rages. He asks to see Balcombe.'[34]

When the purveyor arrived, Napoleon confronted him in a fury: 'My legs are swollen, I have the beginning of scurvy in the mouth.

My appearance shocks everyone. My doctor whose duty is to tell the truth, does not dare. I am abused, without having the law to defend me. I hope one day to be avenged by the people of London who will seize the governor or throw stones at him passing in the street! I don't have enough wood to warm myself or the food I like, pasta, because there is none in this country. I charge you to tell the governor all of this—but do you dare?'

'I will say,' said Balcombe, 'you have swollen legs and you are being killed by the restrictions.'

That was clearly not enough. What Napoleon said next amounted to an order: 'You will also write to the secretary of the Prince Regent.' Bertrand noted: 'The Emperor was extremely worked up, Mr Balcombe very pale and agitated.'[35] In his extremity of disappointment Napoleon was at last attempting to gain advantage from Balcombe's close connection with Sir Thomas Tyrwhitt.[36] Bertrand considered he had 'never seen the Emperor as angry as he was today. Balcombe was completely disconcerted by it. None of the news was true—not a single word of it!'[37]

At dinner, Napoleon needed to consume a whole bottle of wine to calm himself. The thwarting of his hopes made him bitter. He told Gourgaud: 'The English have no exalted feelings. They can all be bought. I would have done well to buy Poppleton—he would have let me go riding alone. Do you imagine that O'Meara is sympathetic towards us? He hopes to receive some recompense. He considers that he is worth £3000 sterling a year.'[38] That O'Meara accepted a bribe soon afterwards is clear from Gourgaud's journal entry of 4 October: 'His Majesty is sure of O'Meara and of his devotion ... The Emperor again remarks that, with money, one can buy any Englishman. "The doctor has only been good to me since I gave him money."'[39] William Balcombe was clearly also included in Bonaparte's cynical view of Englishmen.

Meanwhile, the governor had just received an urgent despatch from Lord Bathurst: 'I transmit to you herewith the copy of a paper containing intelligence of an expedition stated to have lately sailed from Baltimore, the real object of which is represented to be to furnish the means of General Bonaparte's escape from St Helena. I have directed a copy of this paper to be transmitted to the Admiralty in order that it may be communicated to Rear Admiral Sir Pulteney Malcolm. I have the honour etc, Bathurst.'[40]

CHAPTER 18

AT THE MERCY OF THE ENGLISH

Everlasting daisies—*immortelles*—are scattered across the plateau at Longwood. Lady Holland sent the seedlings to remind Napoleon of his native Corsica, and now the *immortelles* have become the wildflowers of St Helena, extending as far as Hutt's Gate and the entrance to the Tomb.

With permission from honorary consul Michel Dancoisne-Martineau—for the Tomb is strictly part of the French domains—I squelched down a path past grazing donkeys to a woodland clearing in Sane Valley, or 'Geranium Valley' as it used to be called. On his walks Napoleon often came to this glade, and he requested the planting of weeping willows to remind him of those bordering the lake at Malmaison. Now the willows have gone and a sentry in a pillbox guards a grave surrounded by an iron railing. The most singular thing about the Tomb is that it is empty. Napoleon's remarkably preserved corpse was exhumed in 1840 after nineteen years and taken back to Paris to lie in splendour at Les Invalides (formerly a military veterans' hospital) by the Seine. I gazed at the bare slab inside the iron fence—no name ever appeared on it, because Governor Lowe would not approve the simple and elegant 'Napoléon' and the French rejected the addition of 'Bonaparte'.

After Napoleon's death, this place became a pilgrimage site for the passengers of every ship that called. Charles Darwin, who stayed six days on the island during his epoch-making voyage on HMS *Beagle* in 1836, had more important things to do with his time—studying the island's geology, vegetation, birdlife and marine species—and found all the fuss irritating: 'After the volumes of eloquence which have poured forth on this subject, it is dangerous even to mention the tomb. A modern traveller, in twelve lines, burdens the poor little island with the following titles—it is a grave, tomb, pyramid, cemetery, sepulchre, catacomb, sarcophagus, minaret, and mausoleum!'[1]

The willows that once shaded the grave no longer exist, destroyed by visitors over the years who broke off sprigs or whole branches. Some of those people were on their way to Australia and planted their souvenirs when they arrived. So it could be said that Napoleon made a posthumous invasion of the great southern land with the willows that still border its inland creeks and rivers.

Betsy's fifteenth birthday, on 4 October 1817, was celebrated with a lavish party at Ross Cottage, Balcombe's poultry farm. The main reason it was not held at The Briars was no doubt because of the embarrassment of Admiral Plampin and his mistress living in the pavilion there. However, another reason was the hope that Napoleon would join the festivities, as the cottage was within the permitted 12-mile boundary, beyond which he had to be accompanied by a guard. Betsy wrote: 'There was so very little to vary the monotony of Napoleon's life, that he took an interest in the most trifling attempts at gaiety on the island, and he generally consented to our entreaties to be present at some of the many entertainments which my father delighted in promoting.' (Here Betsy was surely being imaginative as there is no record of Napoleon attending *any* of her father's earlier entertainments! However as Ross Cottage was within his boundary, this account of a party he had no intention of attending may be true.)

Gathered around the generously laden tables were most of the island's eligible young women, also O'Meara, the Bertrands and their children, and a group of military and naval officers, including Dr John Stokoe and Ensign George Heathcote from the *Conqueror*. The party was in full swing when Betsy saw a lone figure on horseback on the hill above. She beckoned to Napoleon but he shook his head. 'I did not consider this was fulfilling his promise of coming to the party.' So she scampered up the hill and begged him to join them, saying he could not refuse on her birthday. He said he could not face all those people staring at him. She insisted he taste her birthday cake and ran back down. The cake, sent by a friend in England unaware of the governor's strict rules, was decorated with a confectionery eagle. The governor had rebuked Balcombe for it. Betsy returned with a large slice for Napoleon, saying: 'It is the least you can do for getting us into such disgrace.' He pinched her ear, called her a saucy simpleton, and rode off humming 'Vive Henri Quatre'.[2]

Dr Stokoe had become a welcome visitor at The Briars; some believed he was paying court to Jane Balcombe, who had recently been ill but had recovered. Stokoe hailed from Durham, Northumbria, and was a man of refined sensibilities, a lover of chamber music 'from Corelli through the eighteenth century to Beethoven and Kreutzer'.[3] O'Meara liked him and promised an introduction to Bonaparte; the emperor's state of health was worrying and O'Meara valued his colleague's opinion.

A few days after the party, O'Meara and Stokoe walked about in the garden at Longwood, contriving to attract the emperor's attention, and the doctor was permitted to present his friend. When O'Meara explained that Stokoe spoke fluent Italian, Napoleon asked him where he had seen action and learned that he had served almost three years in Sicily.

When Napoleon asked, 'Are you married?', it produced an awkward response from Stokoe: 'To this question I stupidly replied, *non ancora* [not yet], when I observed a smile on Madame Montholon's face, and I thought there was a faint reflection of it on Napoleon's countenance, which I was puzzled to account for. O'Meara explained it afterwards by telling me that I only confirmed the common report on the island that I was paying my addresses to the eldest Miss Balcombe. This report arose from my having attended the young lady soon after our arrival during a serious illness. On her recovery we were often seen together on the public walk. The people of St Helena, accustomed to see marriages take place after a very short courtship, soon made up their minds that we were to make a match of it. As it did not take place so soon as they expected, they chose to account for its failure in their own way, ie. by saying that I could not obtain the consent of the father by reason of my age.'4 Jane was seventeen and Stokoe forty-two.

According to Stokoe's memoir, a few days after this interview Napoleon confronted Balcombe and asked: 'Why have you refused your daughter to the surgeon of the flag-ship? *C'est un brave homme*. [He's a good man.]' Balcombe replied: 'But I have not refused. The doctor has never asked me for my daughter.'5 Perhaps Stokoe protested too much. His memoir was written years later, after he had wed late in life, and it is not surprising that he denied a prior marriage proposal. In fact, Lowe noted in a despatch to Bathurst that the surgeon *had* formally requested Jane Balcombe's hand and been refused by her father.6

Attempting to follow correct procedure, Stokoe reported his interview with Napoleon to Admiral Plampin, but received a severe reprimand for having spoken to General Bonaparte without permission. At Plantation House the surgeon was marked as a man to watch.

On 9 October, the same day as Stokoe's meeting with Napoleon, the East India Company's *Woodford* anchored in James Bay. It had come from India by way of Île de France (present-day Mauritius) with a number of Company civil servants and officers on board, returning home to England. One of them, Edward Abell Esquire from Madras, would, five years into the future, become Betsy Balcombe's husband and give her a daughter and nothing else but misfortune.

The *Woodford* was in port for five days. No record has been located in the St Helena Archives of a meeting between Edward Abell and the Balcombes, but nor would there be such a record unless something eventful occurred. However, as the Longwood purveyor and one of the island's leading traders, Balcombe went aboard every Company ship calling at the island and, due to his hospitable nature, anyone personable usually received an invitation to The Briars.

A plan had been developed at Longwood, apparently with the connivance of O'Meara, to emphasise Napoleon's ill health—which was wretched enough—to justify his removal from the island on medical grounds. Gourgaud noted: 'I inform Bertrand that I have warned my mother not to be distressed if I mention Napoleon's liver trouble in my letters, as a pretext for getting away from here.'⁷ The plan was to rebound on them.

In the middle of the month, the Balcombe family moved to a rented house at Arnos Vale, a narrow valley three miles across the mountain from The Briars. The move was to an inferior dwelling but resolved the socially compromising situation of Admiral Plampin and his paramour living at the pavilion; it also had economic benefits, with the admiral renting the whole Briars property. Lowe, who rarely had anything good to say about Balcombe, conceded to Bathurst that the purveyor was generous in giving up his house 'at great personal inconvenience for him and his family'.

Napoleon was in much physical pain that October and fractious because of it. It did not help his temper when O'Meara issued a health bulletin referring to him as 'General Bonaparte'. However, most of all it would seem he was angry with the Balcombes. This may have been because the purveyor had failed to write to Tyrwhitt; but Betsy was also the object of considerable wrath. Gourgaud recorded: 'The Emperor remarks that the Balcombes are a family of scoundrels [*canaille*]. "They belong to the lowest people," he says "and dare not invite me to dinner. Betsy will not marry the Major—he has too much intelligence to lose caste in this way!"' Gourgaud added his own comment: 'I always thought that Fehrzen never intended to marry—all this is His Majesty's invention!'⁸ It is difficult to fathom the reason for this righteous indignation about Major Fehrzen, who had already left for England with the 53rd Regiment in July and was then on his way to India. Could it be that Betsy had been seen dallying with another man—perhaps with Edward Abell Esquire, passenger from Madras, whose ship had left for England just two days earlier?

She had acquired a new admirer—who fancied Jane as well—in Ensign George Heathcote. He had been ill and was convalescing in a nearby house at Arnos Vale. Young Tom and Alexander Balcombe visited to read to him, but it was the sisters who interested Heathcote and he simply could not decide between them. He would wait for their visits; as he recovered, they played games on the lawn. Jane observed the rules, but Betsy was always rough, knocking the invalid down on the grass and delighting in his feebleness compared to her own strength. Years later he wrote to the girls' mother, admitting that his heart 'was held so completely divided that I thought I loved neither because I loved both. Besides, I had no fortune, and all these things kept back those strong feelings which future circumstances have brought to light.'[9]

Napoleon was ill and depressed. The English papers brought news that the Allied powers had determined that his son would never succeed to the Duchy of Parma. 'His Majesty is tired and unable to walk,' wrote Gourgaud. 'He says he would have lived until he was eighty, if he had not come to St Helena. Here, he will never make old bones.'[10] They read in the papers about the marriage of Charles de Flahaut and the heiress Margaret Mercer Elphinstone. 'I tell you,' Napoleon assured Gourgaud, 'that I will find you a bride, with three or four thousand pounds a year. That should justify your staying here with me. When we are in England, all the women will want you. Look at Flahaut.'[11]

Romance was in the air, but not for Gourgaud. Ali the valet announced that he was in love with Josephine, the Montholons' maid. Napoleon disapproved of 'such an ill-assorted marriage. I do not believe in sympathy, the love that exists in novels. This is not nature . . . The best marriages are of convenience.'[12]

A few days later, the Balcombe sisters came to stay overnight with the Bertrands.[13] Something clandestine was occurring. The next morning, Gourgaud was invited to the Bertrand house to breakfast with the girls, 'but when we get there, they are still in bed. It seems that Hudson Lowe suspects something, for, last night, he increased the number of sentries. It is probably because of a rumour that an American schooner is cruising in the neighbourhood. Later in the morning, when the Emperor sends for me, he is quite gay, and sends me to lunch with the Balcombes.'[14]

Meanwhile, O'Meara was having a difficult time determining how to describe his patient in his reports to satisfy both Bonaparte and the governor. 'If you send any more bulletins without showing them to me,' Napoleon said, 'you will be acting the part of a spy, which is what the gaoler of St Helena wishes.' He refused to discuss his complaints and would see the doctor only as a friend. Lowe relented and agreed that Napoleon could sight future bulletins.

In early November, Gourgaud recorded in his journal: 'For several days past Bertrand has been holding conferences with Balcombe.'[15] He gave no hint of the nature of these discussions. But some intelligence gleaned from the English newspapers cheered them all. 'Great news!' Napoleon announced. 'I hear there is to be a change of Ministry in England. We shall see Wellesley [the Duke of Wellington], Holland and Grenville in power. The Little Princess will punish the Ministers for ill-treating her mother ... The Bourbons are to be cleared out. Austria and Russia are going to withdraw their troops [from France]. The English will be asked to recall theirs, and, then, the Bourbons will be expelled. There is to be a complete change. Wellesley is for me. He says they were wrong in driving me out of France in 1815. Lowe is being abused in the Gazettes.'[16]

O'Meara knew the editor of the *Morning Chronicle* and offered to arrange publication of whatever Napoleon wished to write. He said, according to Bertrand, that English opinion about the emperor had changed; 'as for the threat of libel, we laugh and know what to expect'.[17] His overweening confidence of being in favour with the Admiralty meant he did not fear the governor's threats.

When Napoleon heard that a French translation of *Letters from St Helena* by William Warden was on sale in Brussels, he sat down to write a pseudonymous refutation of the exaggerations in the book, pretending to be a Bonapartist supporter in Cape Town. He asked Fanny Bertrand to translate it into English, and it was eventually published as *Letters from the Cape of Good Hope in reply to Mr Warden*.

The relationship between the governor and O'Meara deteriorated further. On 18 December, they had another argument in the library at Plantation House about the nature of his conversations with his patient. 'I am caught between the anvil and the hammer,' O'Meara told Marchand.[18] A few days later, when his cantankerous patient was still arguing about the wording of the health bulletins, O'Meara collapsed. Napoleon shouted to his valet, who was in the adjoining room. Recalled Marchand: 'I came hurriedly and found him busy undoing the doctor's necktie which seemed to interfere with him; I grabbed a bottle of cologne and poured a large quantity onto a handkerchief which the Emperor applied to his temples, while I put smelling salts under his nose. O'Meara slowly came to his senses. "I feared," said the Emperor, "that it was a stroke, your face became that of a dead man: I thought your soul had left you."'[19]

This show of concern touched O'Meara. The stress of working for two masters (or actually for three), of being between the anvil and the hammer, had become too great. The episode was the turning point. He crossed to the Bonapartist side.

On 20 December, the Bertrands came to dinner at Longwood, leaving their children and going to the trouble of dressing formally, as demanded. But Napoleon was displeased with Fanny's effort. 'That hat doesn't suit you!' he exclaimed. 'And your dress—it comes from China. I don't like it!' Earlier he had remarked to Gourgaud: 'Madame Bertrand dresses badly, and when she *is* dressed up, she looks like a country wench all decked out in her Sunday clothes.'[20]

They endured a dull Christmas. On New Year's Eve the Balcombe sisters stayed with the Bertrands once again and went to a ball at Deadwood Camp in torrential rain, Gourgaud accompanying them. Madame de Montholon, once more in advanced pregnancy, stayed at home. (Napoleon complained about her habitually 'protruding belly'.[21] Some wondered if he was responsible for it.) During the quadrilles and supper, Gourgaud watched Madame Bertrand and then O'Meara enjoy a lengthy discussion with the Russian commissioner.[22] Count Balmain gleaned sufficient information to send a grim report on Napoleon's health to St Petersburg: 'Bonaparte's liver is seriously affected, and his health is visibly deteriorating. The devouring air of the tropics, his excessive leisure, are altering his blood and his temperament. At night he does not sleep. In the daytime he is torpid. His complexion is livid, his eyes sunken. His condition excites pity. Dr O'Meara told me confidentially that he did not give him more than two years of life. Only exercise can bring him back.'[23]

On New Year's Day, Napoleon sent sweetmeats on Sèvres porcelain plates to the Bertrand house for Betsy and Jane. There was news that a ship had arrived directly from England. O'Meara hurried to town to gain information. 'It is a boat specially sent,' Napoleon speculated. 'The Governor is recalled!' They waited anxiously for the doctor's return. He dismounted amid great excitement. Gourgaud reported: 'His Majesty receives him in the reception room, while we stay in the billiard room. The Emperor returns to us with the news. It is a boat from Brazil, which has brought two despatches from another boat from England. One is for the Governor and the other for the Admiral, both countersigned by Lord Bathurst. Their contents are as yet unknown. Balcombe has been dining with the Admiral, attempting to find out something.'[24] They soon learned, apparently from Balcombe, the gist of Bathurst's communication to Lowe: letters to Longwood with the word 'Emperor' would not be delivered; a new house was to be built for General Bonaparte; and a chambermaid would be provided for Madame Bertrand, paid for by her English aunt, Lady Jerningham.

Another despatch arrived for Lowe, enclosing a letter from the British ambassador at Rio de Janeiro outlining what could have been a very serious rescue attempt. An American schooner had landed four Frenchmen at Pernambuco in north-east Brazil. 'They soon attracted the notice of the Governor and they were arrested.' Their leader, Colonel Paul de Latapie, 'had been a Lieutenant Colonel in the French Army under Bonaparte, in all whose campaigns he had served'. He was offered his liberty and a free passage to America if he made a full disclosure of their plans: 'These were nothing less than the liberation of General Buonaparte from St Helena, which he said all Frenchmen who had served under him that were gone to America, are determined to attempt—that being chiefly indebted to him for all they possess, they will never cease to regard him as their Sovereign, and that not only he, Latapie, but many thousand others are ready to sacrifice the last drop of their blood for his sake.'

The rebel Frenchmen had intended to fit out a number of fast sailing vessels, 'sufficiently capacious to contain several small steamboats'. The larger ships would keep at a safe distance from St Helena while the steamboats were to be sent at night to various landing places, indicated to Napoleon in clandestine messages. The French chargé d'affaires at Rio had decided that Colonel Latapie was 'too dangerous a man to be allowed scope for making other attempts', and the whole scheme was quashed at the outset.[25]

Longwood was more than ever an unhappy place, swept by rumours, the atmosphere suffused with resentment and mistrust. Gourgaud's jealousy of the Montholons dominated his thoughts. He grumbled to Bertrand: 'I shared the dangers of the battlefield with His Majesty when he didn't know what Montholon looked like.' Bertrand advised him to be calm, not to suffer torments just because the emperor preferred the Montholons above them all.

On 26 January 1818, Albine de Montholon gave birth to another daughter. Gourgaud wrote: 'The child is born with a caul. She wanted a boy—probably in order to have a Napoleon in the family!' The namesake remarked: 'And I too was born with a caul,' referring to a membrane sometimes found covering a newborn's head. It was thought to be a good omen, signifying that the child would be special. Gourgaud and Fanny Bertrand whispered their belief that Napoleon had sired the child, who was christened Napoleone Josephine.[26] 'The Emperor refrains from visiting Madame Montholon,' Gourgaud wrote in his journal, 'for such visits provoke scandal in the eyes of the English.'[27]

Count Balmain met Gourgaud and confided to him details of the elaborate attempt to liberate Napoleon by the French partisans in Brazil. 'They were planning to attempt the Emperor's rescue in a steamboat.'[28] The apparent sophistication of this plot had greatly alarmed Lowe. He was determined that no future attempt would succeed. In February 1818, he extended the fortifications, ordered new semaphore signal posts and batteries for various places and doubled the guard at Longwood. Balmain noted: 'The Bonapartist plots at Pernambuco have greatly excited the Governor ... I see him always on horseback, surrounded by engineers, and galloping in all directions.'[29]

Gourgaud finally announced his intention to leave St Helena. 'What do you want then?' Napoleon demanded. 'To take precedence over Montholon? To see me twice a day? Am I to dine with you every day?' He warned Gourgaud that he was likely to be detained as a prisoner at the Cape: 'The Governor will think you have been sent on a mission.' He advised that the best excuse was to say he was unwell: 'I will instruct O'Meara to give you a certificate of illness. But listen to my advice. You must not complain to anyone. You must not talk about me, and once in France, you will soon see the chess-board on which you are to play.'[30]

The following day, 3 February, the storeship *Cambridge* anchored at Jamestown, bringing news of Princess Charlotte's death in childbirth three months earlier, her baby lost as well.[31] The Prince Regent was said to be inconsolable to have lost his only legitimate child and heir. O'Meara informed Napoleon, who was shocked to hear of the princess 'cut off in the prime of youth and beauty'. He was even more cast down by the collapse of his own expectations of her future lenience towards him. He blamed the midwives for incompetence or worse, 'and expressed his surprise that the populace had not stoned them to death. He thought the business had a strange appearance, and that precautions appeared to have been taken to deprive the princess of every thing necessary to support and console her in a first accouchement. It was unpardonable in the old Queen [Charlotte's grandmother, wife of George III], not to have been on the spot.'[32] Gourgaud described Napoleon's disappointment to Baron von Stürmer, who sent a report to Prince Metternich: 'He regards it as one more misfortune. Every one knows that [Caroline] the Princess of Wales has an almost fanatical admiration for him. He hoped that when her daughter came to the throne, she would try to have him transferred to England. "Once there," he said, "I am saved."'[33]

Gourgaud packed his bags and his papers, including some that were not his. Napoleon was waiting for him in the reception room. 'Well,' he said, 'you're leaving then?'

'Tomorrow, Sire.'

'First of all, go to the Cape, then to England. You will be well received there. They are creating a national army in France—I can imagine you commanding the artillery against the English. Tell them in France that I still detest those rogues and scoundrels—the English. Everybody will give you a welcome, now that Louis XVIII has turned nationalist ... We shall meet again in another world. Come now, goodbye. Embrace me.'

Gourgaud wrote that he wept as he embraced the man he claimed to love. Bertrand farewelled him, expressing sorrow that he was leaving; his wife would be lonely without him. He confided that the emperor had assigned a yearly income of 12,000 francs for him and so his future was assured.[34] Perverse to the end, Gourgaud refused to accept the money.

When he had gone, Napoleon exclaimed to Bertrand: 'Speak to me no more of that man; he is mad. He was jealous, in love with me. *Que diable*, I am not his wife and can't sleep with him! I know he will write these things against me, but I don't care. If he is received in France, he will be shut up, hung, or shot.'[35]

※

A fine dinner was waiting for Gourgaud at Plantation House and he was gratified that the governor was so obliging towards him. Secretary Gorrequer retained Gourgaud's papers, to study his dictation notes on Waterloo and other campaigns. These Gourgaud had surrendered willingly—'My bags are open'[36]—while managing to hide his coded journal among his clothing. Bertrand wrote: 'We know that at Plantation House, everyone is busy copying.'[37]

Gourgaud paid little heed to the news that Cipriani, the Corsican butler, was desperately ill, stricken with agonising pains in the abdomen, nausea and vomiting, and had fallen to the floor in convulsions. Gourgaud felt too slighted by those at Longwood to care, resentful that he had not received £20 owed to him by Bertrand and concerned that his funds were diminishing. But his sense of self-importance grew by the day and the governor believed he would soon be primed to impart information.

Gourgaud told Balmain of Napoleon's offer of 12,000 francs (then equalling £500 sterling) and why he had refused it: 'Those five hundred pounds are too little for my needs, and not enough for my honour. The Emperor gave as much to his groom and to the servants who returned to France. Las Cases got two hundred thousand francs. You might remind Bertrand that I am in a position to play the Emperor a scurvy trick, if I were so inclined; that I could reveal a good many secrets. My Longwood diary would be worth fifteen thousand pounds in London, and he had better not go too far.'[38]

Over another delightful dinner at Plantation House, Lowe told Gourgaud that there was no need for him to go to the Cape: 'I have never spoken to you about your departure, but I hope that a boat will be available soon to take you to Europe. Whatever you do will be all right. No one will hear from me any complaint or objection concerning you.'[39]

During the night, Cipriani died. O'Meara and the military physicians Baxter and Walter Henry diagnosed 'inflammation of the bowels', but no autopsy was performed. Gourgaud heard the news from the Marquis de Montchenu, who called in, drenched from the rain. 'I rather think,' Gourgaud mused, 'that His Majesty will miss Cipriani more than any of us.'

Cipriani was interred that morning in St Paul's churchyard, close by Plantation House.

CHAPTER 19

FAREWELL TO THE ISLAND

The inexplicable suddenness of Cipriani's death was a huge shock to Napoleon. He felt a blood tie with the Corsican, for their two families had been friends back in Ajaccio. Cipriani's espionage work had facilitated the escape from Elba; on St Helena he had frequented the town shops, mixed with seamen in the taverns, and been tireless in collecting intelligence. An elaborate headstone was ordered (but apparently never completed), and Bertrand paid Saul Solomon his hefty fee of 1400 gold francs for the burial arrangements.[1]

Poison was suspected and Napoleon feared assassination himself. He became especially vigilant about his food, which was Balcombe's department, supervised in his absence by his partner Joseph Cole. The purveyor had not been to Longwood for some time, a violent attack of gout preventing his daily ride up the mountain. Meanwhile, Lowe learned from Gourgaud about the Sèvres plates given to the Balcombe girls on New Year's Day; he said they had been accepted without his consent and that Balcombe must hand them over. Lowe told Gorrequer: 'How we'll do him when we come to that!'[2]

Gourgaud was relishing his new life. He dined out most evenings, at Plantation House, where Sir Hudson and Lady Lowe treated him with respect, or at Rosemary Hall with Baron von Stürmer and his wife and Balmain. He had regular interviews with Stürmer, who sent verbatim accounts to Prince Metternich and made copies available to Balmain. The reports were read avidly in Vienna and St Petersburg. Much of the information was passed on to Lowe, who then shared the intelligence extracted from the Frenchman by his agents Reade and Gorrequer.

Balmain, generally astute in his judgements, considered the Frenchman a vain braggart, 'jealous of Napoleon as of a mistress'. Although he had heard a rumour that Gourgaud was play-acting, while really on a secret mission for Bonaparte, he doubted the man was clever enough for that.[3] Indeed, much of the information Gourgaud imparted, far from helping those at Longwood, was treacherous to them. He informed Gorrequer that correspondence, pamphlets and money could be transmitted with ease, thanks to the help of visiting Englishmen and captains of merchant ships, mostly for payment, but sometimes offered freely. He said that Napoleon had no trouble gaining access to large sums of money through his stepson Prince Eugene, who had arranged an account he could draw upon with Andrews, Street & Parker of London. Most damaging of all for Napoleon, he said that his apparent illness was feigned and that O'Meara was taken in by him. 'He will bury us all; he has a constitution of iron. His swelling of the legs dates from Moscow. As for his insomnia, since I have known him he has never slept several hours in succession.'[4]

One of Gourgaud's most spiteful revelations was that Captain Poppleton, the well-liked former British orderly officer at Longwood, had received a gold snuff box as a parting gift from Napoleon. He mentioned this knowing that Poppleton, who had done many favours for the French, including some for Gourgaud himself, could be 'demoted or worse for having accepted the gift'. As it turned out, Lowe attempted (without success) to obstruct the officer's career.[5]

Naturally, the garrulous Frenchman was probed about sexual relationships at Longwood. The commissioners knew that any gossip of Napoleon having a lover would greatly enliven reports to their superiors; it would also tarnish the annoying legend growing up about him in the liberal press. The jealous and resentful Gourgaud, not mentioning his own seedy liaisons with slave girls and prostitutes, was only too happy to suggest that Napoleon had flirted with Betsy Balcombe, and also with a pretty neighbour, Miss Robinson, whom he called the 'Nymph of the Valley', another one he called 'Rosebud' (Miss Knipe), and even with Madame Bertrand. But in particular he implicated his two prime enemies, Madame de Montholon and her allegedly compliant husband.

Baron Stürmer repeated the salacious stories for Prince Metternich's titillation: 'After having flattered for a long time the whims of the former Emperor, fulfilling the role of royal procurer, Madame de Montholon has been able to triumph over her rivals and managed to get to the imperial bed herself. Her husband, it is said, is quite proud.'[6] The amount of epistolary chatter concerning a carnal relationship between Napoleon and Albine de Montholon with the acquiescence of her husband suggests it very likely existed.

Certainly Napoleon became heavily dependent on Montholon. The dictation work on the memoirs had originally been divided between Napoleon's four principal companions, the 'four apostles', but Las Cases and Gourgaud had departed. Marchand noted that of the two who remained, General Bertrand went to his home at nine o'clock each night. The overwhelming majority of the work fell to Montholon, as did the management of the household. The valet made a generous observation of his ascendancy: 'Count de Montholon—without the grand marshal losing any of the Emperor's esteem and his old friendship for him—became the man sharing his everyday habits and his affection, until the day of his death. Count de Montholon became entirely the Emperor's man after the Countess was forced to return to Europe.'[7]

In mid-February, O'Meara was called to Plantation House. The governor enquired after Bonaparte's health, but—according to the surgeon's account, which must be treated with caution—the interview soon deteriorated. Sir Hudson rose and, looking at O'Meara 'in a menacing manner', accused him of communicating with Napoleon and other members of his household on matters that were not medical.[8]

Secretary Gorrequer, observed the entire encounter. He wrote in his coded diary: 'After the confab with Dr O'Meara was over, he desired me not to take any notes on it.' Lowe remarked to him that the doctor 'had conducted himself very properly till the arrival of Sir Pulteney Malcolm. It was that fellow who was the cause of it all.'[9]

O'Meara returned to Longwood and found Napoleon in better spirits. The doctor related his clash with Lowe and the ban placed on his discussing any but medical matters. Napoleon warned him to watch out for Gorrequer, who would perjure himself at the governor's bidding. 'You are in a very dangerous situation,' he said. 'He has a witness, who is his creature and who will sign everything that he dictates, and have no other conscience or will than his. You have only your own word to plead; and this man's conduct, in endeavouring to make a spy of you, by ill treatment and abuse, is so extraordinary that people unacquainted with him will with difficulty believe it. I see no other mode for you to act than to maintain an absolute silence.'[10]

Apart from more positive days such as this, Napoleon's health continued to decline. O'Meara believed that the location of his problem was the liver, and diagnosed hepatitis.[11]

Lord Bathurst had profound suspicions about William Balcombe. One French Bonapartist escape plan had mentioned possible assistance from a 'Colonel Bouher living at the Briars', perhaps a code name.[12] Balcombe's excessive invoices could be used to pin him down for a start. In a stern letter to Lowe, Bathurst urged that he set up an enquiry into the purveyor's charges, for 'there must be some foundation for aspersions so confidently made, and that therefore it is to be presumed that the Purveyor imposes upon the Government and does not supply Longwood as he ought, and the blame which in this supposition attaches on you is that you may not have taken proper measures to provide against such imposition'.[13]

Sir Thomas Tyrwhitt must have heard that his protégé was in official disfavour, for he sent him an urgent communication, warning that it would be politic to take a break from the island for a few months, and come to England with his family.[14]

On 16 February, Lowe himself received a letter from Sir Thomas, who had returned to London from France on hearing of Princess Charlotte's death:

Parliament Place, Dec 8th 1817

My Dear Sir

It is impossible for me to allow the first conveyance to St Helena since my arrival in England to pass unnoticed without thanking you very sincerely for the protection and kindness you have been pleased to shew Mr Balcombe at my recommendation. I do trust and believe he will not prove unworthy of it—Upon the event that has lately not only plunged this Country but the Continent also into such deep affliction, I was at Marseilles and as you may suppose lost not a moment in repairing hither to be of what service I could to my Royal friend. Thank God he bears up against his loss with Resignation though at moments his grief is dangerous to his health. I think however his general looks are more pleasant than when I left him in August. He takes more exercise than he did but I wish I could say he was less in size.

In thanking Lowe for the 'protection and kindness' he had shown to Balcombe, there was clear encouragement for this to continue. Sir Thomas managed at the same time to refer to his own intimacy with the Prince Regent and to flatter Lowe by including him in royal gossip—'Rumour gives wives both to the Duke of Kent and Clarence but I do not believe anything is yet determined upon'—and by sending a special memento for Lowe's wife: 'There are Portraits and Drawings without end which have appeared of the lamented Princess, but that which I take the liberty of sending to Lady L is thought to be the most striking resemblance of her.' Sir Thomas concluded with an assurance that he personally had no patience with those who were soft on Bonaparte: 'Lord Holland is in a week or two to give us a Display upon Napoleon's Calamities; but as long as you keep him close, nobody cares for speeches.'[15]

Tyrwhitt's letter created a difficulty for Lowe. For two years he had suspected Balcombe of transmitting messages for the French, perhaps aided by his family, and had planned to move against him. He wrote to Bathurst that an examination of Gourgaud's papers confirmed that the persons at Longwood had 'no difficulty in sending any letters they pleased'. Gourgaud had provided an even more critical piece of information: 'that of an equal facility of obtaining money here. He does not state any Individuals, but the number of persons who have free access to Longwood is so few, that suspicion must too naturally fall on some of them. Those I refer to are Mr Balcombe the Purveyor (his wife & daughters who occasionally visit Madame Bertrand on my passes), and Mr Cole, his Partner, who is also Postmaster. It is by Messrs Balcombe & Cole that the whole pecuniary business of the Persons at Longwood is managed.'[16] Lowe wrote that what made his suspicion 'fall the more strongly on these persons is the particular Intimacy subsisting between them and Mr O'Meara, which long since made me caution Mr Balcombe against adopting him as a medium of interpretation with the persons at Longwood', but instead 'his intimacy has since been increased rather than abated'.[17]

Balcombe's merchant business meant that he had regular dealings with Indiamen and naval ships calling at the island and he offered hospitality to many captains and officers. Nor did he always abide by the strict letter of the law as the governor defined it; Lowe believed that Balcombe's form in the past demonstrated his wobbly ethics. The governor had learned that sixteen years earlier, when Balcombe was second mate on an East India Company ship on the Bengal run, he had disobeyed his captain's orders at sea, neglected his duty and shown 'mutinous conduct'.[18] He was arrested and confined to his cabin until a court-martial was held in Calcutta before the governor general, Sir Richard Wellesley.[19] The charges warranted imprisonment or transportation to Botany Bay, yet Balcombe seemed to incur no penalty and was freed to make his own way back to England. Soon afterwards, the East India Company granted him permission to take up a position at St Helena. Then, just before his departure in 1805, Balcombe was arrested by bailiffs at the Isle of Wight for debt, but it was settled by a friend.[20] It all seemed unfathomable, unless there was powerful intervention on Balcombe's behalf. A few years later, while holding the position of Company sales agent on the island, the man had been rebuked by Governor Beatson for carrying on a contraband trade with Cape Town in his schooner the *Bonetta* and had been forced to sell the vessel.[21] And yet the merchant had inveigled the governor into being godfather to his newborn son and all was forgiven.

For a long time Lowe had intended to remove the purveyor from his post, but he had to finesse how he did it. There was that rumour that never quite died, whispered at the castle and the barracks and by guests at Plantation House, that Balcombe was the natural son of the Prince Regent. Lowe could find no evidence for this—beyond a slight physical resemblance and a tendency to excess—but there was that baffling connection with Tyrwhitt, the prince's former secretary and still his close confidant, as the recent letter from him had confirmed. The governor knew of few patrons who kept such a close and affectionate watch on a protégé, even supervising the education of Balcombe's eldest boy in England. Sir Thomas, universally respected, had personally met with Lowe in London to secure for his favourite the position of supplying Bonaparte's table, and had followed up his request with a written reminder.[22] Without definite proof of Balcombe's complicity with clandestine correspondence, money transfers or worse, it would not do to offend his influential protector.

Lowe was aware—for his intelligence agents Reade and Gorrequer had informed him—that Balcombe had recently received a letter from Sir Thomas with the House of Lords insignia. While he sighted all letters intended for Longwood, Lowe would not presume to break the seal on Balcombe's mail. In a private letter written on 24 February, he informed Bathurst that he understood that Tyrwhitt had advised Balcombe to absent himself for a few months and return to England with his family.[23] Therefore it was no surprise when the purveyor applied to the governor and council for six months' leave of absence, citing his wife's ill health as the reason; it was true that she suffered from chronic hepatitis and her recent convalescence had been slow.

The actual letter from Sir Thomas does not seem to have survived, although there are references to its content. Another reason for Balcombe requesting leave could have been that he had heard that his stepfather at Winchelsea was in failing health, in which case his mother would welcome his support. Six months in England, away from the intrigue, bickering and suspicion, would do the whole family good. In the interim, Admiral Plampin's rental of The Briars could continue, and Balcombe's partners Joseph Cole and William Fowler could manage his trading business and the brewery, and supply Longwood's table.

With the governor's approval, Gourgaud sent a letter to Bertrand, requesting the return of his loan of £20, 'for I am without a sou. What can I do when I arrive in England?' Lowe had assured him that he would not be placed under house arrest at the Cape like Las Cases, but would sail directly to England on the *Marquis of Camden*, due to depart on 14 March. Lowe could not have been more obliging to Gourgaud. He said that if Bertrand failed to send the money, he would take it upon himself to provide him with the wherewithal for the voyage home, 'and he gives me five or six letters of introduction to his friends in London'.[24]

Lowe was by this stage aware that romance was developing under his own roof between his sixteen-year-old stepdaughter Charlotte Johnson and the 40-year-old Russian commissioner Count Balmain, who despised his prospective father-in-law. Lowe returned the dislike and disapproved of the disparity in the couple's ages. His wife, who actively sought to marry off her daughters, welcomed the possibility of visiting St Petersburg and perhaps waltzing with the handsome Czar.

Lieutenant Basil Jackson accompanied Gourgaud to Longwood; Jackson advised him to wait at the boundary and accosted Bertrand at his house, demanding the £20 owing to Gourgaud. This provoked the normally placid Bertrand: he said that the money was already deposited with Balcombe, who intended paying it. But what really angered him—he pushed Jackson against a window as he made his point—was that Gourgaud had three times refused the 12,000 francs the emperor had offered him; therefore His Majesty had made out the same amount as a pension to Gourgaud's mother.[25] In an ironic twist, Gourgaud's damaging disclosure of the method by which Napoleon arranged transfers of funds to and from Europe probably meant that the pension for his mother was never paid.

The volatile Frenchman's final day on St Helena was 14 March. The Stürmers and Balmain came to town for a farewell breakfast with Gourgaud. They were joined by the Marquis de Montchenu, who flourished a letter of introduction to the French ambassador in London. Finally, Lieutenant Jackson arrived, bringing Balcombe's payment of £20, settling Bertrand's debt.[26]

In her *Recollections*, Betsy neglected to mention that her father was out of official favour and instead offered a conventional excuse for their leaving the island: 'In consequence of my mother's health declining, from the enfeebling effects of the too warm climate of St. Helena, she was ordered by her medical adviser to try a voyage to England, as the only means of restoring her shattered constitution.'[27]

The governor viewed Balcombe's departure as convenient and had no wish to see him back. On 16 March, two days before the Balcombe family sailed, he covertly appointed Denzil Ibbetson, the assistant commissary of the military stores, as the new purveyor to Longwood.[28] At the same time, he granted permission for Balcombe and his daughters to visit General Bonaparte to make their farewells.

During Napoleon's first two years on St Helena he had received British visitors more than a hundred times, on average at least once a week. After the imposition of Lowe's restrictions in 1817, he had refused all socialising with the outside world, except for the calls of his purveyor, occasionally accompanied by his daughters. That final visit by William Balcombe with Betsy and Jane in March 1818 was the last audience permitted by Napoleon until his death in May 1821, with the single exception of a relative of Prime Minister Lord Liverpool, whom he met in April 1819 in the hope of improving his conditions.[29] That meeting was clearly for political reasons. His affections were rarely stirred, but perhaps he really cared for the Balcombes, especially for Betsy. However, there was still strategy in maintaining his connection with them: he knew that the family would soon be reunited with Sir Thomas Tyrwhitt in England.

They found Napoleon in the billiard room, unpacking a consignment of books. He seemed greatly depressed that they were leaving and asked after Mrs Balcombe's health, for she had been too unwell to accompany them to Longwood. Betsy and Jane, who had not seen him for months, were appalled by the deterioration in his appearance.

His face was the colour of yellow wax, his cheeks fell in pouches and his ankles were so swollen that the flesh hung over his shoes. He needed to lean on a table to support himself when he stood. He saw their shock and made light of it, saying that the good O'Meara would soon have him cured.[30] He insisted they stay and dine with him.

The two adolescent girls may have been too naive—or in Betsy's case too self-absorbed—to comprehend certain financial transactions that then took place. According to Montholon, co-executor of the emperor's will, Napoleon gave Balcombe a bill, drawn upon Lafitte's Bank in Paris, for 75,000 francs, and in addition authorised a pension for him of 12,000 francs a year. Balcombe, for his part, agreed to undertake certain commissions. He would contact Napoleon's mother, Madame Letizia, and Prince Eugene, his stepson, and give them a full account of the affairs at Longwood. Furthermore, he agreed to agitate in London, using whatever influence he had, for the removal of Lowe, ideally to be replaced as governor by either Sir Pulteney Malcolm or Sir George Cockburn.[31]

Marchand was co-executor and his memoirs note: 'The Emperor was kind and gracious to his guests, and concerned to show his thanks for the kind hospitality he had received from them at The Briars. In giving his requests to the head of that family, he added a gift and a draft for 72,000 francs a year, begging him to please take care of his affairs in Europe. (So Balcombe was being offered the approximate equivalent of £3000 sterling.) The Emperor asked him to see his family and to tell them of the shameful way he was being treated. Mr Balcombe, without failing in his duty to his government, was able to satisfy the Emperor's wishes.'[32]

Their business affairs concluded, Napoleon limped as he led the family out into the garden; they stood gazing past the looming hulk of the Barn to the vast grey ocean below, merging at the horizon into a limitless grey sky. Napoleon said: 'Soon you will be sailing away towards England, leaving me to die on this miserable rock. Look at those dreadful mountains—they are my prison walls. You will soon hear that the Emperor Napoleon is dead.'

Betsy began to weep uncontrollably, rubbing her wet cheeks until Napoleon produced a handkerchief and told her to keep it. At last it was time to say goodbye. He embraced both girls, saying that he would always remember their friendship and kindness. He asked Betsy what she would like as a remembrance and she requested a lock of his hair. He sent for Marchand and the valet snipped four silky brown strands, 'for my father and mother, my sister and myself... I still possess that lock of hair', she later wrote, 'it is all that is left me of the many tokens of remembrance of the Great Emperor'. Napoleon then reached for her and pressed his lips on hers, not an avuncular but a frankly sexual kiss. Betsy cried out in shock, then submitted.

The three Balcombes mounted their horses and set off down the mountain. Betsy turned to take a last look at Longwood and waved at the portly figure standing alone on the trellised verandah.[33]

Betsy had brought out the best in Napoleon, that complex, brilliant, calculating and turbulent man, severely formal with others but always approachable for her. She had loved him and she would never recover from knowing him.

PART TWO

His fire, for want of fuel, consumed himself and those around him.

COUNTESS ALBINE DE MONTHOLON

CHAPTER 20

THE TIES THAT BIND

On the afternoon of 18 March 1818, the Balcombes boarded the *Winchelsea* storeship, on its way home from China. Sir Thomas Reade reported to Lowe that Balcombe 'has got the gout but is able to walk'.[1] According to a story related later by William's granddaughter Bessie, when the *Winchelsea* was about to sail, Balcombe produced a blank cheque given to him by Napoleon, which he had not liked to refuse, 'yet never intending to make any use whatever of it'. He showed it to his wife, who glanced at it, 'then without a moment's hesitation tore it into pieces and tossed the fragments into the sea'.[2] It sounds like a story from an affectionate granddaughter.

The Balcombe daughters had no sense of a final departure from St Helena. They believed that they would be in England for just six months. However, despite Betsy's protestations to the contrary in her *Recollections*, she must have had some understanding of the governor's displeasure with her father and that it related to his dealings with the French. Jane at eighteen was already a young woman. Betsy would turn sixteen in seven months' time. She must have known, as the island became a blur on the horizon, that a similar line had been ruled across her life. Her childhood was over.

❋

The loss of the Balcombes' company was greatly regretted by Fanny Bertrand; it made her sense of isolation almost insupportable; other local residents were forbidden to socialise with her and she had just received news of the death of her mother in Paris.[3] The St Helena Archives holds a letter she wrote the day the Balcombes sailed. It was clearly not vetted by the governor and was probably smuggled out on an Indiaman.[4] 'Mr Balcombe and his family have left St. Helena this day ... He has been our accredited purveyor to Longwood House for almost 3 years and has been most helpful and considerate to me. I understand that Mr. Balcombe was required to sign a certificate before his departure saying that he was not carrying any letters or messages from Longwood. At first *l'Empereur* was very friendly with the Balcombe family; he often played with young Betsy, but of late he has tired of their company complaining they are miserable. His Majesty wearied of Betsy who became very jealous when he entertained either *The Nymph* (Miss Marianne Robinson) or *The Rosebud* (Miss Knipe)'.[5]

The last comment is curious given that Napoleon had received no visitors except the Balcombes since the imposition of Lowe's restrictions in 1817; if he had hosted the pretty daughters of neighbouring farmers, it would have been in early 1816, his convivial entertaining days, before the arrival of Sir Hudson Lowe.

Napoleon may have complained about the Balcombes near the end—particularly after the purveyor declined to intercede with Sir Thomas Tyrwhitt—but undoubtedly he regretted the loss of Balcombe's usefulness (relaying news, gossip, correspondence and even a diamond necklace). Most of all, he would never again have someone like Betsy in his life, with her prettiness and pranks, her artless chatter and laughter.

On 22 March, Lowe was outraged to hear from Baron von Stürmer that Gourgaud had let slip that he was leaving the island carrying a journal, written in code, 'of everything that had passed or been said remarkable during the last three years'. Gourgaud was by then a week's sail away on the Atlantic. The governor, who had praised the man to Lord Bathurst, insisting that he could be trusted with a direct passage to England, now had to explain to his lordship that 'General Gourgaud said he had got all his conversations with Napoleon Bonaparte for the last three years, in Cypher, of which he alone had the key'. Nothing like a journal had been found among Gourgaud's papers, but his clothing had not been examined.

As the despatch would follow too late for Gourgaud to be searched on his arrival in England, Lowe advised that he should be questioned 'to draw forth a full explanation from him on the subject'. However, although 'some Trick or Artifice' must have been resorted to in order to smuggle the journal, 'still I do not ascribe this to any design of serving the views of Napoleon Bonaparte, as it may be accounted for so much more readily on personal interest alone & on this ground I presume his justification will be attempted'.[6] Lowe still wanted to believe in his prize defector.

On 10 May, after a voyage of 54 days, the shores of England were sighted through mist. The *Winchelsea* entered the Solent River and sailed up a tributary to anchor in the late afternoon at the ancient port of Lymington. There were important despatches for London and a fast chaise-and-four could reach the capital far more speedily than the ship could negotiate the English Channel. Several passengers took advantage of the opportunity, including Mrs Jane Balcombe.[7] In alighting at Lymington it seems that she seized the chance to collect their eldest son, William, from school. Her husband was apparently too unwell to disembark, and so with his daughters and the two younger boys, in the care of Sarah Timms, stayed on the *Winchelsea* as it made its way up the Channel to Hastings.

Gossip preceded them. 'There are various reports in circulation respecting a fracas at St Helena,' noted *The Times*. 'Mr Balcomb [sic] and his family with whom Buonaparte was so intimate on his first landing, is certainly arrived in England; and it is generally rumoured that he was not allowed to spend much time in packing up.'[8] However, before Balcombe had even landed at Hastings, some 'undoubted authority' put the editor of *The Times* smartly in his place, requesting a retraction. It could only have been Tyrwhitt, having heard Mrs Balcombe's account of events: 'We are desired by a Correspondent to state, as from undoubted authority, that no other cause existed for Mr Balcombe's quitting his situation at St Helena, than the dangerous state of Mrs Balcombe's health at the time of her embarkation.

The writer suggests that if there had been any improper conduct on the part of Mr Balcombe, Sir Hudson Lowe would scarcely have been so indulgent as to appoint Mr Cole, the partner of Mr Balcombe, to act for him as purveyor to Buonaparte during the period of his absence in England.'[9] The Balcombes and Sir Thomas were not yet aware that even before the family's departure the position of purveyor *had* been taken away.

By the time the *Winchelsea* put in at Hastings on 19 May, Balcombe's gout had become so excruciating that it was considered news. But, at the time, everything about the family was of interest because of their notorious connection: 'Mr Balcomb, who landed at Hastings on Tuesday morning, from St Helena, was taken so extremely ill, immediately on his going on shore, that three physicians were instantly called in, and were almost in constant attendance the whole day. Mrs Balcomb who had previously arrived in this country with her son, left town yesterday to attend her husband.'[10] All the family gathered at Balcombe's bedside. His wife had already made contact with their distinguished friends from former days on St Helena—Sir George Cockburn and Sir Pulteney and Lady Malcolm—and also with a naval shipping agent, William Holmes of Lyons Inn, London. O'Meara had engaged Holmes to send books and journals to the French at Longwood, not intending them to arrive at the island through official channels.

The one letter by Mrs Jane Balcombe that has survived in archives was written to O'Meara on 27 May from her husband's bedside:

> My Dear O'Meara
> Poor Balcombe has been confined to his bed almost ever since he left your dear Island he is now getting better of this long and melancholy fit of Gout and we hope in the course of another fortnight that he will be able to proceed to London. Thank God I am much better notwithstanding all the *nursing* anxiety &c—Mr B has written to your agent [Holmes] and he sent him a Book and wished to know if it had reached St Helena yet and also his opinion of it—which B appears much pleased with. All our friends Sir T Tyrwhitt, Sir George C and Lady Malcolm &c have been very solicitous and kind writing continually to inquire after poor Balcombe—whom they

are very anxious to see in London—I am very anxious to be there also. You must excuse my not writing you a long letter—as the Sick room affords nothing that can amuse you. My kind remembrance to Madame Bertrand and all her family—I will write you again the first opportunity. The Girls unite with me their kindest regards to you.

—Remaining very Sincerely Yours, Jane W. Balcombe[11]

Once Balcombe was sufficiently recovered, he hastened to Winchelsea in East Sussex, where his mother and her second husband, Charles Terry, had settled after leaving Rottingdean. He arrived to be confronted by a family tragedy. When he left St Helena in March the news had not reached him that his stepfather had died in mid-January at the age of 70. Now he had to absorb a greater shock, that his mother, Mary Terry, had passed away on 1 May, almost three weeks before he landed in England. There had been no chance to be with her at the end. This must have been devastating for William, who had not seen his mother for thirteen years.

General Gaspard Gourgaud had arrived in London on the *Marquis of Camden* on 8 May and his belongings were not searched before disembarking. Two days later, he was intensively questioned at the Colonial Office by Henry Goulburn, under-secretary to Lord Bathurst. Gourgaud gave him much the same information as that which had startled Lowe and the commissioners on St Helena: that the French at Longwood had no difficulty enjoying 'a free and uninterrupted communication' with Britain and the Continent for correspondence, pamphlets, money and any items they wanted. They were enabled to do this by means of visiting Englishmen, attendants and servants. The captains of visiting merchant ships were 'peculiarly open to the seduction of General Bonaparte's talents', so that it was 'a matter of small difficulty to procure a Passage on board one or other of the ships for General Bonaparte if escape at any time should be his Object'. Escape for General Bonaparte was apparently easy; he could without difficulty elude the sentries posted around the house, and this had been discussed. But Gourgaud said that Bonaparte was waiting for a change of government in England, or for the refusal of the English to continue the expense of detaining him. In particular, he 'has always looked to the period of the removal of the Allied Armies from France as that most favourable for his return'.

Goulburn noted in his report that Gourgaud had revealed that General Bonaparte had received a considerable sum in Spanish dollars, equivalent to £10,000, at the very time that he disposed of his silver plate. 'He assured me however in answer to my inquiries, that neither Mr. Balcombe nor Mr. O'Meara were in any degree privy to the above transaction; and that the former, although recently much dissatisfied with his situation, had never, in any money transaction, betrayed the trust reposed in him. He declined however most distinctly, giving me the same assurance with respect to their not being, either or both, privy to the transmission of a clandestine correspondence.'

In discussing Bonaparte's health, Gourgaud was at his most malicious. He said that the British 'were much imposed upon'. He could confidently assert that Napoleon's physical health had changed very little and that it was 'not at all worse than it had been for some time previous to his arrival at St Helena'. O'Meara was certainly 'the dupe of that influence which General Buonaparte always exercises over those with whom he has frequent intercourse'.[12] This confirmed for Bathurst that his recent instruction to Lowe to dismiss the Irish doctor from the island was the correct one. The Admiralty had at last been persuaded that the man was too much trouble. It left Bonaparte without a physician acceptable to him, but it seemed he did not need one.

Gourgaud, after this treachery, was permitted to remain in England, a free man. When he met with the French ambassador, the Marquis d'Osmond, he told him how easy it would be for Napoleon to escape. The ambassador answered: 'Easily said.' 'No,' replied Gourgaud, 'easily done and in all kinds of ways; supposing, for instance, that Napoleon was placed in one of the barrels that are sent to Longwood full of provisions and returned to Jamestown every day without being inspected. Do you believe it impossible to find a captain of a craft who for a bribe of one million francs would undertake to carry the barrel on board a vessel ready to sail?'[13] The marquis passed this information on to the Colonial Office. It was noted that any barrel of provisions fell within the business of the purveyor.

Gourgaud's information had confirmed their suspicions that Balcombe was the conveyor of clandestine correspondence, although not yet of anything more heinous. For the present, there was no necessity to move against him—partly because of his important connections, but possibly also because of his earlier confidential services for the Colonial Office, as much later events would suggest. But he had shown that he could not be trusted and should be watched.

Balcombe had given Lowe his forwarding address in London as 26 Cornhill, in the heart of the City financial district, opposite the Royal Exchange.[14] This was the head office of Hornsby & Co., Stockbrokers and Lottery Office Keepers; the director, Thomas Hornsby, was married to Mrs Balcombe's elder sister, Lucia Elizabeth, after whom Betsy was named.[15] The couple, who had a country house at South Cave in Yorkshire, had been guardians to the girls when they were at school in Nottinghamshire. Now the Balcombe family were welcomed into their London home, but there was no time to celebrate a happy reunion.

William's brother Stephen, younger by three years, was dying at his Pentonville house. He had never married, so Mrs Balcombe, her daughters and the servant Sarah Timms immediately took over his care. There is no record of his illness, but soldiers returning from the Napoleonic wars had brought various pestilences with them: tuberculosis, influenza and measles were rife, and dysentery was an epidemic in London in 1818, causing an estimated 45,000 deaths.[16] Another scourge was typhus fever, a major epidemic in Ireland in 1818, with 65,000 deaths, and it had reached London as well.[17] Any of these diseases could have struck Stephen, and he may have passed the infection to his mother. Stephen Balcombe, a businessman and 'Gentleman of Pentonville', had made out his will in April, naming his mother Mary Terry as a joint executor, which indicates that her death in May was sudden. He died in June or July, for his will was proved on 7 September, leaving his estate of approximately £500 to be shared equally between the children of his brother William, to be accessed when they turned 21.[18]

Within three months, William had lost his only immediate family in England. But he still had his protective patron. It is curious to note that if there was validity in Lowe's hearsay that the Balcombe boys were cared for by Tyrwhitt after their father's drowning in an accident involving the prince's yacht, one would expect Sir Thomas to have acted in the same nurturing way towards Stephen. But there is not the slightest evidence that he did.

After their arrival in London, the Balcombes paid several visits to Sir Thomas at the tiny grace-and-favour home he had occupied for the past six years. From 1785, he had occupied a suite of rooms at the prince's Carlton House, but since being knighted in 1812 and appointed Gentleman Usher of the Black Rod, he moved into the snug Gothic-style cottage that went with his new position. It nestled on the north bank of the Thames, adjoining the medieval complex that was the old Palace of Westminster. Known as 'Black Rod Lodge', its address was simply 'Parliament Place'.

Betsy and Jane remembered Sir Thomas as the kind man who had been helpful to their mother three years earlier when she had come from the island to collect them from school. Young Thomas and Alexander, born on St Helena in 1810 and 1811 respectively, were meeting their father's friend for the first time, but Thomas understood his middle name was Tyrwhitt because this man was his godfather.

Tyrwhitt would have been much taken with the two attractive young women and they with him. They were bound to have been fascinated by his aura of glamour, knowing that he knew the Prince Regent so well and all the princes and princesses. They heard that he had also been friends with the old King, who was now said to wander about at Windsor Castle in a white nightdress, and slip in the mud with the pigs at his little 'farm'. (It is usually now suggested that the mental illness of George III was caused by the blood disease porphyria, although J.B. Priestley argued it was brought on by distress over the death of his favourite child Amelia, in 1810.[19])

For Balcombe, this reunion with Tyrwhitt, the tiny man with the ruddy complexion and curly powdered wig, was meeting up again with someone who had been like a father to him since childhood, and more recently a guardian to his eldest son. But there was one particular piece of business that the two men needed to address. Balcombe had now discovered that his purveyorship to the French at Longwood had been removed from Balcombe, Cole & Company by Governor Lowe. He was furious that this had been done with no warning or explanation, the position annexed under his nose while he was still on the island, and he hoped that the decision could be reversed. He knew that his patron saw Lord Bathurst frequently in Parliament and he may have asked if an interview could be arranged. But it is more likely that the Secretary of State initiated the request (or summons), because three meetings between Bathurst and Balcombe were to follow in rapid succession.

Sir Thomas Tyrwhitt and Earl Bathurst knew each other well. In the oligarchy that ran the British government—men who had been to Eton or another of the great public schools and thence to Oxford or Cambridge—there were always connections. Bathurst and Tyrwhitt were both born in 1762 (like the Prince Regent), and both went to Eton and then on to Christ Church, Oxford, 'the college most favoured by the peerage', although they probably did not mix there. Bathurst (then Lord Apsley, not yet having succeeded to the earldom) joined, as his biographer observed, 'other sprigs of aristocracy, conspicuous in gold-trimmed silk gowns and with gold tassels in their caps', who 'had their own table in hall and could dine with the dons at high table'. Tyrwhitt was on a 'canon's fellowship' and worked hard, awarded a Bachelor of Arts degree in 1784 and a Master of Arts three years later, whereas 'like most aristocrats, Apsley did not trouble to take his degree at Oxford', embarking on a tour of France and Germany instead.[20] In 1794, Bathurst succeeded to the earldom, and in 1812 he was made Secretary of State for War and the Colonies, the same year that Tyrwhitt became Black Rod. Thereafter the two men saw each other in the House of Lords whenever it was in session.

Balcombe went to meet Bathurst at the Colonial Office, a house at the end of Downing Street, situated where steps now lead down to St James's Park. This was the first time they had met in person, and he was surely overawed. Tyrwhitt would have counselled him that this was a chance to make his mark and that, despite his recent difficulties, he had the experience to qualify for a new colonial appointment. Bathurst, the brilliant administrator, then aged 56, must have seemed almost legendary to Balcombe, ruling as he did through the governor on almost every aspect of life on St Helena. Yet the island and its prisoner, in theory at least, formed a very small part of his administrative remit. Until 1815 and the victory at Waterloo, the pursuit of the war against France was his main concern. After peace was restored, trade resumed, and the consolidation of Britain's far-flung empire became of prime importance: the administration, through colonial governors, of Upper and Lower Canada, Newfoundland, Malta and Gibraltar, the Cape Colony, Sierra Leone, the Gambia and the Gold Coast, Ceylon, New South Wales, Van Diemen's Land, New Zealand, Mauritius and the Seychelles, an assortment of islands in the Caribbean, and in the South Atlantic, tiny Ascension, St Helena and Tristan da Cunha. Bathurst was a friend to both George III and the Prince Regent, and was so trusted by the Tory prime minister Lord Liverpool and his foreign secretary Castlereagh that, according to his biographer, 'he quickly became a member of a triumvirate that for all practical purposes decided the country's foreign, military and imperial policy for the next decade'.[21]

Balcombe's three personal meetings in June with Bathurst can be seen as a watershed in his life: if he was viewed with disfavour, any prospect of a return to St Helena was dashed. Notwithstanding his patron's influence because of the affections of the royal family, Bathurst possessed far greater political power, if compelled to exercise it, a fact that Tyrwhitt would have understood. Certainly Sir Thomas would have prepared his protégé for this august audience. He would have warned him to moderate how he expressed his dislike of Lowe and his annoyance at the loss of the purveyorship. He would have made clear to Balcombe that he should not interpret Bathurst's ability to be exceedingly amiable and even humorous as an indication of a less than totally serious and resolute mind, able to see through any dissembling or bravado; but he may also have made the point that Balcombe need not fear facing some austere, remote official, ready to condemn all fallibilities.

Therefore Balcombe was truly on notice that he would be judged on Bathurst's assessment of his merits and weaknesses. Clearly the immensely powerful and busy Bathurst considered him sufficiently interesting to grant him a personal audience three times rather than have one of his under-secretaries or clerks 'debrief' him, although Under-Secretary Goulburn was almost certainly present, taking notes. For Bathurst, listening to Balcombe was gaining first-hand knowledge of his great foe. No other Englishman had been so close for so long to Britain's prisoner and his entourage.

Balcombe would certainly have mentioned his unhappiness at the loss of the purveyorship, and a later letter suggests that he also defended his friend O'Meara and confirmed that Bonaparte's poor state of health required a trusted physician.[22] If Balcombe attempted to learn what information Gourgaud had passed on to the Colonial Office, Bathurst kept his own counsel, evidently preferring to listen to Balcombe and study him. However, a discussion of Balcombe's position and Bonaparte's health would have been worth one meeting at most for the Secretary of State; instead there were three within a month. This was a large commitment for a man with many responsibilities, but nothing compared to the cost if Bonaparte escaped.

Receipt of every piece of information about Longwood was important to Bathurst, given that he was facing constant Whig criticism in Parliament over allegations of arbitrary harsh treatment of the exile. Here was a man who had enjoyed unique access, both to Bonaparte and the members of his entourage and, in London, to a trusted Parliamentary official who was a friend of the royal family. It would have seemed almost negligent on Bathurst's part if he had *not* from the beginning requested Tyrwhitt to engage Balcombe in some intelligence role. Any correspondence from Balcombe to his patron avoided Lowe's scrutiny and was guaranteed secure transmission to London and thence to Whitehall. Moreover, in certain respects Balcombe's personality would have made him less suspect at Longwood as an agent than almost anyone else on St Helena. He was an authentic rough-and-ready extrovert, something of a buccaneer in business dealings; he gave every appearance of genuinely disliking Lowe; while his wife and daughters had become close friends with the Bertrands and their company obviously gave much pleasure to Bonaparte himself. And Balcombe gained prestige from the persistent rumour that he was the natural son of the Prince Regent.

That three meetings were held suggests that Bathurst, after the first encounter, asked Balcombe to prepare a detailed account of his points made orally, to be followed up by further discussions and questions. But if a record was kept of what was said, those minutes have not been located.[23] They may have been filed as classified documents, or destroyed—*if* Balcombe had been acting as a secret government agent for Bathurst on St Helena. Later, there was possible substantiation that for a time he did operate in this way.

When Bathurst considered St Helena (which Lowe's correspondence ensured that he did far more frequently than he wished), there were matters of immediate concern. Another member of the ruling class, Admiral Lord Cochrane, heir to the earldom of Dundonald, had gone rogue. A hero of the Royal Navy for his leadership, courage and brilliant tactics (he was later a model for Patrick O'Brian's Jack Aubrey books), he had been forced out of the navy and Britain, risking gaol because of his monumental gambling debts. He had become a privateer, and was appointed commander-in-chief of the Chilean navy, assisting their liberation struggle against Spain. *The Times* reported that he had called Bonaparte an 'illustrious prisoner' and was said to be willing to mount an expedition to rescue him.[24]

The newspapers published an alarming story in early June: a British sailor at St Helena, one of the original crew of the *Northumberland*, the ship that took Napoleon into exile, had swum around the island at night from an Indiaman at anchor, scaled the sheer cliffs below Longwood and slipped past the sentries unseen. The next evening he did it again, taking a comrade, and they strolled into the Longwood garden and actually spoke with Bonaparte. Apparently the sailors intended it as a prank and meant no harm but were found out when they boasted about their escapade, and were 'put in irons and sent home'.[25] But if they could do it, so could the French or Americans. Or Lord Cochrane. Lowe sent a brief account of the incident and built more fortifications.

It concerned Bathurst that, as Gourgaud had revealed, Bonaparte looked forward to the period when the Allied armies were withdrawn from France as that most favourable for his return. Despite the Duke of Wellington's demands for more men, Bathurst had experienced difficulties finding 30,000 soldiers to remain as an occupation force in France. The Whig opposition complained of the unnecessary expense.[26] But Earl Stanhope had given Parliament a grim warning earlier that year. Addressing the Prince Regent and the combined Houses, he had deplored the size of the Allied troops' withdrawal. He argued that the Bourbons could only be kept in power by the presence of foreign bayonets. Many in France were still working for

Bonaparte's return and there was the active possibility that he could escape from St Helena. There was always the danger of being plunged into another war.[27]

William Balcombe was becoming increasingly anxious about money, as few remittances were coming through from his trading business and brewery to Wm Burnie & Co., his London agents; Admiral Plampin, occupying The Briars, continued to be recalcitrant about paying rent. If Balcombe still had the generous bill of exchange we are told Napoleon had given him (and hadn't ripped it up as his granddaughter claimed), it could only be drawn at Lafitte's Bank in Paris. Aware that his movements might be watched, he would not have dared to make the journey.

On 24 June, he called, not for the first time, on O'Meara's naval agent William Holmes at 3 Lyons Inn, the Strand. From there he penned a letter to the doctor on St Helena which would later form the basis for a major scandal—indeed a national scandal.

CHAPTER 21

THE EMBATTLED SURGEON

After the long years of war with France, the lives of the poor were desperate. Grain crops failed, returned soldiers and the thousands thrown out of work by the new factory machines were unemployed; they listened to speakers urging rebellion. But the Regency period of 1811–20—when the prince assumed the powers of the monarch in the place of his mentally ill father—was defined by elegance and fashion for the privileged classes. The Prince Regent saw himself as setting the style. His Royal Pavilion at Brighton was the most extravagant display of all, an oriental fantasy, derided by the press as 'a pot-bellied mad-house', 'a minaret mushroom'.

Betsy and Jane Balcombe, with the encouragement of their family, set out to enjoy London's delights, possible for those with means and suitable connections. The social 'Season', which ran from April to August and coincided with the sitting of Parliament, was in full swing. The aristocratic and gentry families came down from their country houses to socialise, engage in politics, and launch their children of marriageable age into society at debutante balls, dinner parties and charity events. It was essentially the courting season, and the two attractive Balcombe sisters, like eligible young women in a Jane Austen novel, were staying at the comfortable London home of a kind and wealthy aunt. They had entrée, through their friends the Malcolms, the Cockburns and Sir Thomas Tyrwhitt, to upper levels of society. They had maintained a correspondence with Lady Malcolm from St Helena, and now, in London, she was no doubt happy to introduce them to her friends, including her cousin Margaret, now the Countess de Flahaut.[1] Margaret's husband, Napoleon's former aide, would have been eager to hear all they could tell him about his former emperor and friend.

The two sisters possibly took for granted the trouble older women relatives and friends went to for them, dressing up and going out of an evening to act as chaperones: it was the expected thing, *noblesse oblige*, to see them make a good match; whereas it was the duty of Jane and Betsy to appear demure, charming and graceful in order to attract those gentlemen who might become reliable husbands, able to support them well.

But the young women—and their relatives and friends—would have realised their serious handicap. Despite their aristocratic connections, they were not high-born themselves and nor did they have money. The possibility of either of them being considered by an aristocrat was out of the question, and in any case there was too much competition. A British officer of the period described how the rich Duke of Devonshire 'was hunted down by mothers and daughters with an activity, zeal and perseverance—and, I am sorry to say, a vulgarity—which those only can conceive who have beheld the British huntress in full cry after a duke'.[2]

The £100 each that Betsy and Jane expected from their late uncle's will was a great deal of money—constituting up to four years' wages for some labourers—but they could not access it until it was probated and they came of age.[3] Perhaps they borrowed against it from their uncle Thomas Hornsby, as there were many expenses involved in joining society. There was the purchase of gowns, corsets, petticoats, dancing slippers, bonnets and ribbons, feathers and jewellery, and the hire of carriages, in order to show themselves at their best. It was an investment in their future. But their father was already fretting about his financial difficulties and was in no position to make a marriage settlement on them, should that happy possibility arise.

The diversions of the London season were various and delightful, some cultured, most frivolous: concerts and breakfast parties in mansions, garden parties, picnics at Vauxhall Gardens, horse riding in Rotten Row and strolls in Hyde Park, still a semi-rural place where cows and deer grazed. Almack's Assembly Rooms was one of the most select venues, its entrance vetted by 'ladies of distinction', such as the ladies Castlereagh, Jersey and Cowper, Princess Esterhazy and the Countess Lieven. Even the Duke of Wellington, before he became the hero of Waterloo, had been rejected for wearing trousers rather than the approved knee breeches.[4]

With the Balcombe sisters' connections they would have been acceptable to the ladies 'who controlled the *entrée* to Almack's and the balls and routs of high society'. A typical party was 'a concourse of nodding feathers and stars under chandeliers ... seldom any room to sit, no conversation, cards or music, nothing but glittering clothes and jewels and lights, shouting, elbowing, turning and winding from room to room, vacant, famous, smiling or evasive faces, and, at the end of an interval, a slow descent to the hall where the departing guests, waiting in their orders and diamonds for their carriages, spent more time among the footmen than they had spent above with their hosts'.[5] It was all about 'cutting a dash' and showing style. It was said that Lady Londonderry went to a ball 'so covered with jewels that she could not stand and had to be followed round with a chair'.[6] People who could afford it rebuilt and improved their houses, added porticoes, loggias and circular driveways, hired landscapers to create vistas of sweeping grasslands, terraces, ponds and fountains, prospects of artificial lakes, marble temples and follies.

Perhaps during that London season Betsy hoped to encounter Edward Abell, the dashing former Indian army officer whom she had almost certainly met on St Helena the previous year when his ship had been in port for a week. But as it happened, Abell, a resident of St Gregory's parish when he was in London, had the previous month, on 22 May, sailed for India. He had just been appointed the civil agent of the Government of Ceylon to the East India Company Presidency of Madras.[7] It would have been as well for Betsy if he had stayed in India.

The Balcombes were able to learn much of what was happening on St Helena from the newspapers, especially from the Whig-leaning

Morning Chronicle. Napoleon was still a subject of great interest and there was no shortage of information. They read that 'General Bonaparte' still remained closeted.[8] Six of his servants had left, including Le Page, his valued chef. It was reported that a paper in Antwerp had published a stock of anecdotes by Count de Las Cases from his forthcoming memoir of the Emperor Napoleon; an English edition was anticipated.[9]

Back on St Helena, Dr O'Meara still believed he had special protection and that, if he left the island, it would be when he chose. He wrote to his friend Finlaison that if the governor made life too difficult, it worried him to abandon Napoleon without a physician; he had raised with his patient 'in as delicate a manner' as he could the idea that other medical men should be consulted, and proposed Baxter or Stokoe. The former had been a military surgeon with Lowe on Corsica and Napoleon said he had repugnance for him, 'but after some time he consented to see Mr Stokoe (the surgeon of the *Conqueror*), to whom I wrote directly and sent the letter through the channel of the Governor'.

But Stokoe 'did not like to take any responsibility upon himself or to run any risk of getting himself into a scrape with such a vindictive character' as Lowe, so he feared attending Napoleon, 'unless Mr. Baxter or someone else chosen by the Governor was present and begged leave to decline seeing him'.[10] In a letter to Admiral Plampin, Stokoe explained that he was unwilling to visit 'the General' alone as it 'would place me in an extremely delicate situation . . . but that I should be happy to share it with any other medical man'.[11] Events would prove Stokoe's caution well founded.

Some time before, the Reverend Mr Boys was preparing to leave the island, his departure encouraged by Lowe, who had had enough of his thunderous sermons.[12] Napoleon asked O'Meara to give the parson a silver snuff box in appreciation of the respectful funeral service he had conducted for Cipriani. O'Meara handed the gift to Boys, who returned it on his departure day, nervous that people would hear of it; severe penalties applied for accepting anything from Bonaparte. Soon enough, Lowe learned of the transaction. On 10 April 1818, he issued an order that O'Meara should be confined to Longwood, unless given permission otherwise by himself or Admiral Plampin. O'Meara immediately fired off a letter of resignation, requesting to return to England. He also wrote to Bertrand, explaining his reasons: 'it is impossible for me to sacrifice my character and my rights as a British Subject'.[13] Lowe accepted his resignation, but advised that he was restricted to Longwood until instructions were received from London and another physician found.

O'Meara's response went to Plantation House on 19 April. He arranged for copies to be smuggled onto ships and delivered to the three principal London newspapers. He would not accept Lowe's treatment quietly. It was now a matter of preparing his defence. In an open cover note to the editors he stated that publication of his letter was 'essential' to demonstrate that no 'improper or dishonourable conduct on my part' had caused his departure from a situation 'to which history affords no parallel'.[14]

The *Morning Chronicle* published his letter to Lowe on 18 July. It was reprinted two days later in both *The Times* and the *Morning Post*: 'For some months your Excellency has several times manifested to me instructions to subject me to the same restrictions as the French prisoners, to which I have always refused to consent . . . I will never agree to it, as it would be signing the dishonour of the Naval uniform.' He reminded the governor that Admiral Lord Keith, then commander of the Channel Fleet, had authorised his attachment to Napoleon as surgeon, assuring him that the government would be obliged, for 'it is a situation which may, with propriety and honour, be held by an Englishman'. O'Meara could but follow the advice of such a distinguished officer, who had stipulated that he was at liberty to resign if he wished, and that he would remain on the navy list in his rank as surgeon, 'with my time going on', paid as a British officer and 'not subject to any restrictions inflicted upon French prisoners'. When he had received instructions from Lowe 'contrary to my natural rights, the stipulations I had made, and the protestations which I frequently made to yourself . . . I immediately comprehended that it was merely a way of *obliging me to quit Longwood* . . . For some months I have been made to lead a most wretched life by your Excellency's obliging me to proceed to your house twice a week, reviling me, turning me out of doors in a most ignominious manner, once, indeed, having experienced everything except personal violence, menaced by words and looks, because I did not choose to comply with *verbal* instructions.'[15] The published letter gained O'Meara enormous sympathy, even among the conservative readers of *The Times*. It added to Sir Hudson Lowe's poor reputation, which had been deteriorating for years.

Meanwhile, mail ships to and from the island crossed in the Atlantic. The embattled surgeon was surprised to receive an encouraging letter from his friend at the Admiralty office:

> My dear O'Meara
>
> Your last letters up to the 14th November have all come safe and I am specially commanded by my Lord Melville to express his Lordship's approbation of your correspondence, especially of the minute attention you have paid to details, and to add his wish that you continue to be equally full, candid and explicit in the future.
>
> Sir Pulteney Malcolm who is now beside me, begs I should express to you his particular wish that in every future discussion or report, you will as much as possible avoid bringing up his name, as he is of opinion it can do no good. He sends his compliments and wishes you well through your arduous employment, which he thinks no one could ever be found to fill so well.
>
> Believe me, my dear O'Meara, yours always
> John Finlaison.[16]

The good wishes of the respected Admiral Malcolm must have greatly buoyed O'Meara's confidence, suggesting hopeful prospects for his future naval career.

In the interim, however, Gourgaud's 'revelations' that Napoleon's health was excellent had caused Bathurst to change his mind about the doctor, and he had convinced the prime minister and First Sea Lord Melville. He wrote to Lowe on 18 May that although he had formerly withheld his consent to the proposition that O'Meara should be removed, the information provided by Gourgaud had altered the case: 'I have now no longer any difficulty in giving you the instruction to withdraw him from a situation for which he has shown himself to be unfit.'[17] Admiral Plampin received a similar message from the Admiralty. No one there was prepared to save O'Meara a second time.

As usual, the despatches still took up to three months to arrive. Meanwhile, the surgeon continued his attack on Lowe. He sent the *Morning Chronicle* and *Morning Post* the sharp note he had received from Sir Thomas Reade which said that his resignation was accepted, 'without prejudice' to the law's decision regarding 'any breach of law or regulation committed by you'. The governor had advised that if Bonaparte was willing to receive any other medical person on the island, O'Meara could quit Longwood immediately. Otherwise he must remain in his present restricted situation until instructions were received from England and another doctor took over his duties.[18] Napoleon refused to accept O'Meara's medical attendance under such conditions. What made Reade's letter particularly interesting for the British newspapers was that their nation's prisoner had inserted margin comments, which O'Meara assured were authentic: 'This fresh outrage only dishonours this coxcomb. This crafty proceeding has one object—to prevent your exposing the criminal plot they have been contriving against my life for these two years past . . . Desire this note to be sent to Lord Liverpool and also your letter of yesterday, with those of the 13th and 24th April, that the Prince Regent may know who my _____ is and be able to publicly punish him.'[19] The word 'murderer' was deleted in the newspapers—but understood by most readers.

The *Morning Chronicle* and other papers published Napoleon's margin notes with an article under the heading 'SEVERE TREATMENT OF BONAPARTE': 'Serious differences still exist at St Helena between Bonaparte's establishment and the chief authority of the island . . . Altho' it may be considered requisite for the peace of Europe that the person of the Ex-Emperor should be detained, we shall be extremely sorry to find the boasted magnanimity of this country tarnished by the exercise of unnecessary rigour towards a fallen foe.'[20]

Bathurst lost no time in sending an alarmed despatch to Lowe: 'You will see that General Bonaparte's Notes and Mr O'Meara's letter to you of the 19th April in which he refers to his letter to General Bertrand, are published in the *Morning Chronicle*.' The articles themselves were of no great concern, he wrote, but the clandestine means by which O'Meara sent them were, and 'as communications of a more serious nature, tending to further General Bonaparte's escape (attempt at which there is reason to believe are in contemplation) may be carried on by the same channel, it is on that ground necessary to call your attention to this publication.' He asked Lowe to remain extra vigilant and circumscribe the liberty of 'General Bonaparte's' followers. However, 'the situation of General Bonaparte is different' and the strict regulations applying to his followers 'need not be extended to him', especially concerning his exercise.[21]

In his remaining time on the island, O'Meara prepared for his dismissal by escalating his publicity campaign. By his secret means he sent off a barrage of correspondence to the newspapers, principally the *Morning Post* and *The Times*, syndicated to other publications, documenting a history of outrage with copies of Lowe's and Reade's letters to him and his own righteous, indignant replies. The heading 'St Helena: Further Correspondence' became a familiar one. The St Helena dispute had become a *cause célèbre*, its details reprinted in provincial papers. The Balcombes were certain to be avid readers, knowing intimately the various characters involved. More than that, William knew he himself was a figure in the mosaic, and must have feared to see his name mentioned.

O'Meara's crusade had become a subject of wide discussion, and opinion was running against Lowe, as reflected in an article in the conservative *Morning Post*: 'While Bonaparte was the despot of Europe, certainly none were more hostile to him than ourselves, but from the moment he became a captive, we were sincerely anxious that he should be treated with the humanity which a vanquished enemy has a right to expect from a generous conqueror. Whenever it shall be made out that he is subjected to unnecessary hardships, we shall be ready to lift our voices on his behalf, and to demand some mitigation of the rigour of his fate. At present nothing of the kind has been proved, and our consideration must incline us to pity him, for the awkward advocate and injudicious friend he has found in Mr O'Meara . . .'[22]

On 25 July, Lowe had his military secretary Wynyard take a letter to the doctor, ordering 'by an instruction received from Earl Bathurst' that he was to withdraw his attendance upon Bonaparte, without holding any further communication whatsoever with the persons residing at Longwood.

On receiving this order, O'Meara went to Napoleon and was said to have remained with him for a considerable time. In his 1822 book he gives an account of a touching and mournful farewell: '"Well doctor," Napoleon said, "you are going to quit us. Will the world conceive that they have been base enough to make attempts upon my physician?

Since you are no more than a simple lieutenant subjected to arbitrary power and to military discipline, you have no longer the independence necessary to render your services useful to me. I thank you for your care. Quit as soon as you can this abode of darkness and of crimes. I shall expire upon that pallet, consumed by disease and without any assistance. But your country will be eternally dishonoured by my death." He then bade me adieu.'[23] But according to William Forsyth, who made an extensive study of the Lowe papers, and the 1915 historian Norland Young, both hostile to O'Meara, the meeting was a far more commercial transaction: 'Besides the bribe of October 1817, and the order for £4000 given in April, Napoleon gave him a letter to his [Napoleon's] mother, which ultimately produced a pension of £320 a year. He gave him also two gold snuff-boxes and a bronze statuette.'[24]

O'Meara was informed he would be sailing on HMS sloop *Griffon*, and a cart was sent to Longwood for his baggage, to be taken to Hutt's Gate and the following day would be brought to town. When O'Meara's luggage was delivered to the ship, he claimed that many papers were missing, also snuff boxes Napoleon had given him and almost all his jewellery, 'except a cornelian necklace which the thieves probably thought too common for them to trouble themselves with'.[25] If the theft was genuine (a judicial enquiry under Sir George Bingham decided otherwise), at least the doctor had kept his precious journal and copies of many letters, which he would later use to great effect.

The *Griffon* sailed on 2 August. Two days afterwards, in a British general election, the Tory government under Lord Liverpool won another term.

O'Meara had lost his position, but he would step ashore in England a famous figure, the magnanimous physician to a former great foe, both men mistreated by petty bureaucrats who failed to understand the spirit of humanity with which Britain treated its vanquished enemies. Anything the doctor cared to say would be published in the newspapers, for he had become a household name. And there was much that he wanted to say. He knew that he had all the material he needed for a book, and in it he would have the satisfaction of further punishing the governor.

Sir Hudson Lowe had lost a great deal. The tide of public opinion had turned against him.

CHAPTER 22

AN IMPENDING TEMPEST

The manuscripts department of the British Library has a dim, hushed, almost religious calm, scholars, illuminated by individual lamps, transcribing from documents or weighty tomes onto notepads or laptops, all under the watchful eyes of the librarians at the long desk at the front, like priests at the altar presiding over their congregation.

I was at the foremost desk, directly under the gaze of the head priest. She had just placed a large volume in front of me, the first of my requests from the 3rd Earl Bathurst's Private Papers, to be allocated strictly one at a time.

It had been a complicated effort over some days to obtain them, but it was all worth it. I opened the volume and carefully turned the pages of copperplate correspondence, mostly distinguished from the official despatches by the salutation 'My Dear Lord—Private' instead of 'My Lord' or 'Sir', and kept by Bathurst at his home. Among these I found Lowe's letter dated 29 September 1818, which described an important discovery. A box had been brought ashore at St Helena containing correspondence. The governor was exultant to find his suspicions confirmed.

> Your Lordship will peruse with feelings of no ordinary disgust, the details of the accompanying Report, disclosing such mean and

unworthy tricks and artifices to elude the Regulations in force on this Island, to establish a secret correspondence with Europe for pecuniary and other concerns, and to raise a cabal at this same time on the Island itself, in favor of Napoleon Bonaparte . . . Whatever may have been said by General Gourgaud with respect to other persons that have been employed in clandestine communications, I could never fix a direct suspicion on any others than Mr. O'Meara or Mr. Balcombe (however assistance may have been afforded by others as the instruments or bearers), for they were the only persons who by their official situations had free access to the persons at Longwood, and if they were unprincipled enough whilst receiving the public money for their services there, to become the tools for any indirect purpose whatever, it was next to impossible to prevent it.[1]

William Balcombe was unaware of the impending tempest soon to break over him.

The Balcombe family were no longer living in London but staying at Hythe, near Southampton, with Mrs Balcombe's niece, another Lucia, and her husband Luke Dodds, a former East India Company captain who had retired, having made a fortune doing several voyages on the China run. The Balcombes had in a sense been instrumental in bringing the couple together. Ten years earlier, Lucia had come out to St Helena on the Indiaman *Walmer Castle* to marry her fiancé William Burchell, Balcombe's then business partner. On the voyage, she and the ship's commander, Captain Luke Dodds, fell in love. The jilted Burchell left the island soon afterwards, and never recovered from the shock. Future fame as a naturalist awaited him in southern Africa, but he avoided women for the rest of his long life.[2]

Lucia and Luke had now been happily married for a decade, with a son and a daughter. They had a large, comfortable house at Hythe and welcomed the Balcombes into their home. It was a fortunate arrangement for William; being not far from Portsmouth, he was able to keep in touch with old friends from St Helena: Captain Ross, formerly of the *Northumberland*, as well as Admiral Sir George Cockburn and his secretary John Glover. Sir George had been appointed a Junior Lord of the Admiralty in April, and in the recent general election of 4 August he had won the seat of Portsmouth for the Conservative Party. Balcombe had helped his campaign, coming down from London to assist.³

On 21 August, Balcombe wrote from Hythe to his business associate William Fowler on St Helena: 'I send some newspapers for Barry O'Meara—if he should not be there endeavour to give them to General Bertrand. I have this moment heard from Town that Sir H.L. is recalled—Keep this to yourself & Cole. I have been with Cabinet Ministers. Of course I told the truth—whoever comes out as Governor you will have strong letters of recommendation to from different quarters. I find Mr Holmes, Barry O'Meara's friend is an excellent fellow. He is coming down to stay with us—Sir G.C. has been very kind.'⁴

Wherever Balcombe had obtained the inaccurate story that Lowe was soon to be recalled, it was a shock to the governor. When he read the letter, his secretary Gorrequer heard him in his office muttering: 'They had better not remove me or I'll raise such a clatter about their heads that will astonish them!'⁵

Balcombe's friends on St Helena, Fowler and Stokoe, were worried about receiving mail that could embroil them in trouble. Stokoe was sent two notes and some newspapers by the naval agent Holmes, whom he had never met, asking him to deliver the enclosed letters 'in private' to Count Bertrand. 'I have also sent you a late publication of Las Cases, which when you have perused it, give to those friends you think it will amuse.'⁶ Stokoe himself was not amused and took the letters straight to Admiral Plampin, who presented them to the governor. Lowe noted that the newspapers were recent issues of the *Morning Chronicle*, *Statesman* and *Examiner* containing O'Meara's 'gross slanders', and the letter to Bertrand listed 'pecuniary transactions of considerable amounts'. His case against his enemies was growing.

In the meantime, however, Lowe had assumed a leading and generally overlooked role in making St Helena a more humane place than it had been for the 160 years of its East India Company administration. Since the law passed by the British Parliament in 1807, enacted four years later, the island remained perhaps the only Company possession where slavery still continued. What wealth it had accrued—from its plantations, stock, and trade with passing ships—had all been built on slaves' sweat.

To his credit, Lowe had frequently questioned the continuation of the practice at the island council, but with little result. (The issue of the slave Toby's freedom was an exception; he claimed he had refused that request only because Bonaparte aimed to make it a political issue, to incite all the slaves to rise up.) But in August 1818 an event occurred which demanded action. Sir George Bingham, commander of troops on the island, came out of the courthouse to see 'a poor slave girl, about 14 years old, limping down the road with blood dripping from fresh wounds on her arm and back which had been produced by a whip'. Profoundly shocked, he asked the girl who had assaulted her. She told him it was her 'owner', Charles De Fountain. Bingham called De Fountain to the magistrates' court and ordered he pay the statutory fine of two pounds. He said he wished he could make it twenty times greater and force him to have 'the same treatment he had meted out to the poor slave'. When De Fountain complained to the governing council about being spoken to in that manner, Bingham refused to withdraw his words.[7]

This gave Lowe the opportunity to raise the whole issue of slavery. On 13 August, he convened a meeting at the castle of the principal slave proprietors and delivered an eloquent speech, urging them to agree to a new law declaring all children born of slave parents free after a stipulated date. At a meeting four days later, the slave owners unanimously gave their approval. Lowe delivered a proclamation that after 25 December 1818, all children born to slaves would be considered free.

The East India Company Court of Directors (which included Lady Malcolm's father) wrote praising Lowe for his 'wise, humane and liberal measures . . . for preventing the perpetual continuance of slavery in the island'.[8] But there were few mentions in British newspapers of Lowe's role. The *Morning Post* was typical in congratulating 'the honour of the inhabitants of this island', omitting to state who it was that had raised 'this laudable proposition'.[9] Lowe was by now widely unpopular because of his alleged treatment of Bonaparte and thus failed to receive the acknowledgement he deserved.

A few newspapers ran advertisements for the English translation of the *Memoirs of Count de Las Cases*, 'the Companion of Napoleon.

Communicated by himself'.[10] Of far greater interest to the public was the arrival at Portsmouth on 10 September of the HMS *Griffon* with Dr Barry O'Meara, 'late surgeon to Buonaparte', aboard. *The Times* reported: 'She brought despatches from Sir H. Lowe. The cause of the dispute between Mr. O'Meara and Sir H. Lowe is before the public, and his return home has arisen out of that circumstance. He left Buonaparte in a very dangerous state of health. His complaint is a confirmed disease of the liver, which his dull inactive life most powerfully contributes to increase ... The medical care of him has been confided to Mr. Stokoe, surgeon of the *Conqueror* ... who had consented to undertake the office with great reluctance.'[11]

Balcombe, living close to Portsmouth, was certain to have greeted his old companion O'Meara on his arrival and to have asked after their friends and the latest events on the island. But he would have been alarmed to learn that O'Meara had not received the letter Balcombe had sent him from Holmes's office on 24 June, carefully secreted within three envelopes.

Portsmouth could not hold O'Meara for long. He was now a celebrity, and newspapers and journals vied to publish his personal account of living with his patient, the fallen emperor, what confidences he had received, and details of how they were both treated by the governor. The *Edinburgh Review* won special access and published a long and sympathetic article that vilified Lowe: 'A very general belief prevails, both in England and on the Continent, that the treatment of the prisoner is unnecessarily harsh ... we confine ourselves at present to the consideration of the documents recently given to the publick by Mr. O'Meara, the respectability of whose character is beyond all question—the facts stated by whom have been wholly uncontradicted.'[12]

When Lowe eventually saw the article, he said with some justice that it was a virtual eulogy 'on the conduct of Mr O'Meara'.[13] He wrote a despatch to Bathurst concerning a letter Admiral Plampin learned that Stokoe had received from Balcombe. Plampin had not seen it himself but heard that in speaking of 'leaving no stone unturned to serve "our friend Barry"', Balcombe had added that 'he had got Sir George Cockburn and Sir Pult— M— on "our side" or words to such effect'. It seemed to Lowe, who was now dangerously paranoid, that his suspicions of a former naval 'cabal' or conspiracy on the island were all but confirmed. However, a British Library margin note indicated that his draft despatch was 'never sent in entirety'. No doubt Lowe wisely deleted his remarks about the admirals Cockburn and Malcolm. As targets of his wrath, they were too powerful—but Dr John Stokoe was not.

On 19 September, seven weeks after O'Meara's departure from St Helena, a box was brought ashore by Captain Brash of the *Lusitania* storeship. It had been sent down to the port of Deal by the naval agent William Holmes. The captain had been asked to deliver it, along with a parcel and a letter, to William Fowler of Balcombe, Cole & Company. When Fowler received the items, he opened the envelope to find another inside addressed to 'James Forbes Esq'. Not knowing such a person on the island, he gave everything to Sir Thomas Reade, who promptly took it all to the governor. It turned out to be just what Lowe had been waiting for.

The hapless Fowler was brought before the governing council and formally interrogated. He said that he did not know of any James Forbes, nor of a William Holmes either. Lowe instructed that the box be opened in the presence of himself and of Sir George Bingham and Thomas Brooke, two members of his council. The box was found to contain French books, histories and a copy of a recent *Morning Chronicle*. The books were clearly destined for Longwood, and although they were mostly scholarly works, the clandestine mode of their arrival excited Lowe's suspicions. Both Bingham and Brooke agreed that it would be perfectly proper to open the letter addressed to the mysterious 'James Forbes'. Inside was a letter to 'Dear O'Meara' from Holmes, clear evidence of secret and illicit communications being carried on with London:

> I have persuaded Brash to take the French books, and they follow him to Deal tonight to be shipped; and he has instructions to give them to Fowler. The English books are sent to Stokoe. I intend starting for Paris next week to see Lafitte, and perhaps will see Las Cases, but fear my journey will be useless from the insufficiency of the documents I hold. Balcombe much regrets that he did not bring me full authority to act; he does not wish to appear active himself; he nevertheless acts in concert with me on all occasions.

I am seriously concerned to hear of Napoleon being so ill; do advise him to take exercise; for, if he shortens his life by refusing to do so, he will only the more gratify the savage malignity of his foes: he ought not to despair, for, rest assured, a change for the better will, sooner or later, take place, and his great mind should not at this juncture forsake him . . . Street and Parker [banking house] refused to pay Gourgaud's bill for £500, but they have since heard from Las Cases, and it is settled. I understand the old General [Bertrand] does not mean to publish, but, should he, Perry of the Chronicle has promised his assistance. I understand you are to draw for £1800: you shall hear the issue of my visit to Lafitte; and, if your remittances are paid, trade of that kind can be carried on to any extent.[14]

Admiral Plampin was called, and agreed that the tenor of the letter and the duplicity of its delivery warranted opening all the items brought by Brash. The parcel was found to contain English books intended for O'Meara and two more letters for him. One was the already quoted letter from Mrs Balcombe, written on 27 May when her husband was on his sickbed at Hastings. The second envelope was opened and found to contain a further envelope addressed to Mr Stokoe.

The surgeon was summoned; he denied knowing any Mr Holmes and was willing to have the letter opened in the presence of Lowe and the admiral. It contained a *third* envelope, addressed: 'For our friend Barry O'Meara, St Helena'. Three envelopes—to O'Meara, Stokoe and O'Meara again—tucked inside each other, like a set of Russian dolls, a complicated but clumsy subterfuge. When that final envelope was opened, it revealed what Lowe reported to Bathurst as 'Mr Balcombe's singular and extraordinary letter', written to O'Meara from Holmes's office on 24 June:

My dear Barry,
Everything has been done that can be done; all your books were sent on board *Lucytania* [sic], but the captain has just called at our friend Holmes' office, where I am writing this, to say he can't take them (I mean the French books). Holmes is indefatigable in his exertions in *your cause*, and all my friends, among the rest Sir George and Sir P—, are of the same opinion with us. All communications whatever

must be sent to Holmes, as I mean to leave off any agency business in England except through him. *He is more acquainted, and has a very extensive knowledge of what ought to be done for you*; rest perfectly easy that no stone will be left unturned to serve our friends on the island. I have been hard at work for you, and what has been said has been listened to. I am just going to the Secretary of State's office, where I have been twice before on your business. The election is going on rapidly; the opposition members are all coming in, the ministerial going out; a change in the administration is expected. The *Leveret*, Sir George C— has told me, will sail for your island in the course of ten days, when you will receive the French books from Holmes. I have delivered all up to Holmes, who is making the best use of them. Pray burn all my scrawls, as they are not fit to read—written so bad. With best regards to all our friends,

 I remain, &c

 James Balcombe'[15]

As a pseudonym, 'James' Balcombe seemed such a thin disguise it was hardly worth the effort! Lowe had no doubt whom Balcombe meant when he wrote of 'all our friends' on the island—they lived at Longwood. We know from his correspondence that he was disturbed by Balcombe's continuing relationship with Sir George Cockburn, now a junior Sea Lord, and Sir Pulteney Malcolm—never friends to himself. Furthermore, Balcombe had mentioned two meetings with Bathurst and that he was to have a third; in his lordship's frequent despatches to Lowe there had been no indication of these encounters. (But Lowe would have noted with some satisfaction that Balcombe's predictions of a change of government in Britain had proved incorrect, and that his comments would have displeased his kind patron, the Tory Sir Thomas Tyrwhitt.)

Despite the irregularity of the books' arrival, Lowe arranged for all 44 of them to be sent to Longwood—works such as *Brougham's Speech on the Education of the Poor*, two volumes of *The Last Reign of Napoleon*, three volumes on *Histoire des Croisades* and four on *Campagnes en Russie*. He then retired to his office to compose voluminous reports to Bathurst—private letters and a long official despatch—on the outrage of the discovery.

CHAPTER 23

THE ST HELENA PLOT

The Balcombes had moved again, to a lodging house in Hastings, probably not wishing to outstay their welcome at Hythe. William would still have been reading with avidity and anxiety all the newspaper accounts concerning St Helena. Most of them, except for *The Times*, condemned the governor's harsh treatment of England's prisoner and his attempt to make a spy of an honourable doctor.

O'Meara was staying at lodgings next to Holmes's house at 28 Chester Place, Kennington, in London. On 28 October, he wrote a long, defensive memorandum to John Wilson Croker, Secretary at the Admiralty, justifying his behaviour as Bonaparte's physician and setting out the history of his difficulties with the governor; his aim was to forestall any of Lowe's charges against him. He expected that his memorandum would be read by the Sea Lords, including Admiral Cockburn, and still hoped that some advantageous position might result from the confidential information he had supplied to the Admiralty for three years. (At the time of writing he did not know that Lowe had intercepted the correspondence that had arrived from Balcombe after he left the island.) But in his memorandum O'Meara went too far. He wrote that before his relationship with Lowe broke down, the governor had overwhelmed him with civilities, and invited him to dinner, as if seeking something from him. 'On some of these occasions, he made to me observations upon the benefit which would result to Europe from the death of Napoleon Bonaparte of which event he spoke in a manner which, considering his situation and mine, was peculiarly distressing to me.'[1]

The response from the Admiralty was swift and brutal. Croker wrote that 'their Lordships ... find in your own admission ample grounds for marking your proceedings with their severest displeasure'. Concerning the governor's alleged comment on the benefit of Napoleon's death, 'It is impossible to doubt the meaning which this passage was intended to convey, and My Lords can have as little doubt that the insinuation is a calumnious falsehood; but, if it were true, and if so horrible a suggestion were made to you, directly or indirectly, it was your bounden duty not to have lost a moment in communicating it to the Admiral on the spot, or to the Secretary of State, or to their Lordships'.[2]

O'Meara was summarily removed from the list of naval surgeons and dismissed from the navy, so depriving him of his pension.

On 6 November, the sloop-of-war HMS *Mosquito* anchored at Portsmouth, having come from St Helena. It caused a flurry of excitement when a temporary shore ban prohibited anyone on board communicating with the land, and 'wild surmises' began. One story was 'that Buonaparte was dead, and that his body was on board'. Rumours multiplied when the *Mosquito*'s Captain Brine 'took post-chaise-and-four' to London and a council was immediately summoned at the Admiralty. But *The Times* believed that the real reason for the meeting was that there were suspicions about correspondence that implicated Balcombe in plans for the release of Napoleon.[3]

Brine was carrying an urgent official despatch from Lowe. Contained in it were Holmes's letter referring to his planned visit to the bank in Paris and the incriminating letter by 'James Balcombe', both written to O'Meara and sent on the *Lusitania* with the box of books; also an earlier one for O'Meara left ashore by Balcombe at Ascension Island on his voyage back to England.

There was said to be 'a bustle at the Colonial Office'.[4] A message was sent to Balcombe, who happened to be with Holmes at Chester Place, Kennington, probably having gone there to confer on what might have been discovered. He was summoned to attend the Colonial Office the following day.

On Sunday 8 November, Balcombe must have entered the Downing Street building with great trepidation. He would have been even more alarmed when ushered into a spacious room to see four men waiting for him. It was an ambush. He was to be interviewed not by an under-secretary as he had expected but by three of the most powerful men in Britain: Earl Bathurst; Viscount Melville, First Sea Lord of the Admiralty; and Viscount Sidmouth, the stern Secretary of State for the Home Office. These were heavy hitters indeed, and hardly less so was John Wilson Croker, Secretary to the Admiralty, who took the minutes. They are worth reproducing verbatim, given the grave nature of the interrogation:

> Lord Bathurst informed Mr Balcombe that he had to acquaint him that a correspondence of a very serious nature had been seized in which he was sorry to state that Mr Balcombe was concerned, but it gave him pleasure to find that Mr Balcombe had shewn more unwillingness to take an active part than others who were engaged in it, and that he now gave Mr Balcombe an opportunity of making some amends for what he had done by giving such information as he was able to afford.
>
> Mr Balcombe said that he had not been concerned in any correspondence of which he was ashamed, and that he could give no information.
>
> Lord Bathurst acquainted Mr Balcombe that there was a letter of his in that correspondence.
>
> Mr Balcombe asked to whom.
>
> Lord B said to Mr O'Meara.
>
> Mr Balcombe declared that he had not written a letter to Mr O'Meara, and he then added that he did not remember having written one. He said he had avoided all French people—that he had been at Hastings on account of his health.
>
> Lord B asked him if he had been charged with any Commission on quitting St Helena.
>
> He said none.
>
> Lord B said—'Not to Paris?'
>
> Mr Balcombe said 'No'—He had not been at Longwood for a fortnight before he left that Island.

He was then asked whether he had not left a letter at Ascension to be forwarded.

He said he had—that it contained Bills of Exchange and nothing else.

He was asked if he had been commissioned at St Helena to act here [in London] for anybody.

He said he had not—that he had indeed been desired to send some Books to St Helena, but that he believed that somebody else had sent them, and he did not know what they were.

The letter referred to in the beginning of the conversation having been again mentioned by Lord B, Mr Balcombe said that he might have written a letter to Mr O'Meara but that he did not recollect it, and rather thought that he had not.

Lord Bathurst then said that he would detain Mr Balcombe no longer.

The above Minute was taken by Mr Croker from the dictation of Lords Bathurst and Sidmouth immediately after Mr Balcombe had retired and it contains to the best of our recollection a correct statement of what passed.[5]

Afterwards, deeply shaken, Balcombe walked down the road and around the corner to confer with Sir Thomas Tyrwhitt at his little cottage. He was in desperate trouble. Sir Thomas helped him compose a letter, addressed from 'Parliament Place', to be delivered to Bathurst the following day:

My Lord
With reference to the Conversation which took place at the interview with which your Lordship honored me yesterday, I take the liberty most respectfully to advert to two points to which your attention was directed, and upon which I feel it to be my duty more fully to inform your Lordship . . .

He gave a detailed list of the bills of exchange he had left at Ascension Island on his voyage to England. They were triplicate bills for his mercantile business, and were left at the island in case of an accident befalling his own ship; two were to ships' captains, one to a naval lieutenant and the fourth 'a Bill drawn by Dr O'Meara on his Agent for the amount of a debt owing to me'.

> Secondly—As to any correspondence of mine with Paris, I beg leave most confidently to state to your Lordship that I never have, nor has any individual of my Family as far as my knowledge and belief go, had any correspondence with that City or with any other part of the Continent, directly or indirectly in any manner whatever.
>
> With regard to my general conduct during a residence of 14 years on the Island of St Helena and since my return to Europe, I should feel truly happy were it submitted to the most rigid examination, confident that in no act of my life have I intentionally done anything in contravention of the regulations to which I have been subject, and equally confident that the results of such an enquiry could not fail to place my character above the reach of suspicion.[6]

No doubt still following Sir Thomas's advice, Balcombe then called at South Sea House, the office of his agents, William and James Burnie, to ascertain if there was mail from St Helena that might illuminate what had been discovered. He found a letter waiting from William Fowler with a message about 'a most mysterious affair which has taken place and in which I am sorry to say your name is made use of'. Fowler was even more unhappy that his own name had been used; he recounted how the box of books had been opened in the presence of the governor and letters discovered. He and Cole had fortunately been exonerated from blame. 'You however have incurred strong suspicions whether from the use made of your name by the writer of the letter or anything contained in its inclusions I know not, but I confidently look forward to your honorably exculpating yourself, which you will see the necessity of doing immediately, and I have therefore sent you the earliest intelligence. Without a line from you at all, both Cole and myself feel very uneasy at any such accusations going abroad, as to your conniving or assisting in any thing being forwarded to the Longwood Establishment except through the regular channel, however unfounded they may be and we shall wait most anxiously to hear the result which we beg you will acquaint us with without delay.' He sent 'best wishes to Mrs Balcombe & the young Ladies'.[7]

This was devastating for Balcombe. During the interview at the Colonial Office, his inquisitors had known of the letters included with the box of books and had been waiting for him to admit to them. He had been caught lying. Again with Sir Thomas's help, he sent a second letter to Bathurst:

> My Lord
> Since I had the Honor of addressing your Lordship yesterday I have received a letter from Mr Fowler, one of the partners in my Establishment at St Helena, by which it appears that a letter had been received by him from Mr Holmes, Navy Agent of Lyons Inn with an inclosure addressed to Mr Jas. [James] Forbes, and referring to a Box of French Books, in charge of Captain Brash of the *Lusitania*; that the letter so addressed to Mr Jas Forbes was in point of fact written to Dr O'Meara and that the Books were also destined for that individual.
>
> Understanding with feelings of great regret that suspicions are entertained of my being privy to this transaction, I take the liberty with a view of submitting to your Lordship all the information which I have received upon this subject, to inclose a copy of W. Fowler's letter, and I beg leave most solemnly to apprise your Lordship that until the receipt of that letter I was totally ignorant of any such consignment having been made to my House [Balcombe, Cole & Co.] and least of all of the transmissions of any letter or package to my partner under a fictitious name.

He claimed that before his departure from St Helena, O'Meara had requested that he send some French books and pamphlets, but when he arrived in England and found in the newspapers 'imputations injurious to my character', he had declined to execute the commission. He later learned that O'Meara had made the same request to his agent, Mr Holmes, and some books had been forwarded. 'Deeply affected by these imputations as attached to myself individually and to the Credit & Character of my Establishment at St Helena, I have considered it to be my duty to make this representation to your Lordship, and I beg permission to add that I shall at all times be most ready and anxious to obey your Lordship's commands in any way, to impart any information in my power upon this or any other subject connected with my own conduct as well as with my House, conscious that I have in no instance compromised my loyalty or deserved the aspersions which have been cast upon my character.'[8]

'PLOT UNCOVERED TO HELP NAPOLEON ESCAPE!!' shouted the *Morning Post*.[9] The press was onto what was sensed as a big story. Rumours had been spreading ever since the arrival of the *Mosquito*. *The Times* took a more measured approach: 'The curiosity which was excited by the arrival of the *Musquito* [sic] from St Helena at Portsmouth, and the summoning of a Council as soon as possible after her Captain reached London, may be esteemed as subsiding . . . the real truth we suspect to be the detection of some correspondence, having for its object, if it should ever come to a conclusion, the release of the prisoner . . . There are some sagacious Statesmen in this country who think that BUONAPARTE, driven from every other country, and at enmity with us, had still a right to put himself into our hands, and prescribe to us how he would be treated; but as this is not the general notion of that person and his deserts, we hope we shall keep him as long as we think proper, and certainly not let him escape, or others take him from us without our consent.'[10] And so the story of the 'St Helena plot'—of collusion, clandestine letters, cyphers, transfers of money, all to help Bonaparte escape—was rolling off the presses.

In the middle of this drama, Balcombe did a most unusual thing: he took a trip to the country. Tyrwhitt would have made clear that his situation was immensely serious, that he could be facing a gaol term or an even direr fate. Balcombe urgently needed to sever any association with O'Meara and Holmes. He could perhaps avoid gaol by going to live quite close to one, at Sir Thomas's large house, Tor Royal, at Princetown on Dartmoor. The living would be more economical in Devon, and besides, Sir Thomas believed that there could soon be gainful employment for Balcombe. With the last French and American inmates repatriated, the great war prison now stood empty, but Tyrwhitt hoped that it would shortly have a new use, for he had various schemes for more inmates. In addition, his plans for a horse-drawn railway between Plymouth and Princetown had been listened to with interest by the Plymouth Chamber of Commerce.[11]

Six days after his Colonial Office interview, Balcombe wrote to a cousin, Miss Cheal, who agreed to accompany him on a visit of inspection to Tor Royal so as to check the house's suitability for his family. After that, he told her, he had 'very urgent business' at Southampton,[12] which was possibly a chance to consult with Admiral Cockburn on how he should proceed in the current crisis.

Agents of the government, employed by Lord Sidmouth's Home Office, had been watching Holmes's house at Kennington and his office at Lyons Inn, in order to identify his associates. One of them proved to be none other than General Gaspard Gourgaud. Now that Lowe's strict custodianship seemed somewhat vindicated and Napoleon appeared less of a wronged martyr in the newspapers, the emperor's supporters were in a delicate situation. It proved the wrong time for Gourgaud to have come out claiming to be a Bonaparte supporter after all.

Gourgaud had started to fear that he might have gone too far in betraying those at Longwood. If his treacherous confessions were ever revealed, Bonapartist partisans would prevent his return to France—or else assassinate him. In an attempt to rehabilitate his image, he had written letters to Bonaparte's family—to Madame Mère in Rome and Prince Eugene—as well as to the Emperor of Austria and even the Russian Czar, deploring Napoleon's 'pitiful circumstances' on St Helena and his harsh treatment by Lowe. The letters were promptly published in European newspapers. Gourgaud had sent the first of these letters in August 1818 to the former empress Marie Louise, now the Duchess of Parma. He described her husband as 'dying the cruellest death, a prisoner on a rock in the middle of the ocean, separated by two thousand leagues from his loved ones, alone, without friend or relative, without news of his wife or his son, and bereft of every consolation. Since my departure from this fatal rock, I hoped to be able to come and tell you of his sufferings, convinced as I was of all that your generous soul was capable of doing.'[13]

The British government resolved to help him on his way. Two officers were sent to his lodging house at 7 Compton Street, Brunswick Square. On 25 November, the *Courier*'s headline read: 'ARREST OF GENERAL GOURGAUD'. He was taken with his papers to the Lord Privy Seal's office at Whitehall and interrogated. He was then conveyed to Romford, where a scuffle ensued. It was market day, and while the horses were being changed he shouted in the inn yard: 'Thieves! Murder! I am General

Gourgaud. They are going to rob and murder me!' He was bundled back into the coach, then onto a ship and out of the country. The *Courier* noted: 'His papers, which are of considerable importance, as pointing out the chief agents of the St Helena plot, and unravelling the clue to the secret machinations by which hopes were entertained of achieving the release of Napoleon, are all secured and will, it is understood, lead to discoveries of the highest interest. They are said to implicate several persons of no mean consideration in this country.'[14]

But the authorities did not obtain Gourgaud's St Helena journal, written in cypher, which he had somehow managed to keep with him. Surprisingly, he did not attempt to cash in on it—probably because it was too explicit about his own failings. It was not published until many years later.

Henry Goulburn, under-secretary at the Colonial Office, wrote to tell Lowe that his favourite defector was a disappointment.[15] It was now believed at the Colonial Office that Gourgaud had been an agent of Bonaparte's all along. Goulburn added that Balcombe was another disappointment, having declined to give satisfactory answers: 'Lord Bathurst thought that it might be possible to induce Mr Balcombe, under an apprehension of the consequences of the discovery of the correspondence to give some information with respect to the other persons concerned in it and therefore sent for him immediately. Mr Balcombe was evidently alarmed but as you will observe from the enclosed Minute of what passed, declined giving any satisfactory reply to the questions put to him. He has subsequently addressed two letters to Lord Bathurst, of which I now enclose you copies. You will not fail to observe in them many inconsistencies and, I think, a great anxiety to know the extent of information which we possess. A letter from Mr Holmes of which I also enclose a copy betrays a similar feeling. To these of course no reply has been given, Lord Bathurst considering that our best chance of making further discoveries rests in concealing the extent of those we have made. I will take care and let you know whenever any thing occurs to throw light upon the nature of the commissions with which Mr Balcombe and Mr Holmes have been charged. All that now appears is that the latter did go to Paris in the course of the autumn.'

Lowe was asked to send more information concerning an American ship that had made a suspicious call at St Helena for water and was since seen hovering off the island, although repeatedly chased away by the warships. 'If these facts are true it would give some reason to suppose that they were connected with some attempt at escape.' Goulburn required more details, 'as the tone which will be taken by the friends of General Bonaparte is that escape is quite out of his contemplation and that all alarm on that score is therefore imaginary'.[16]

The Colonial Office was building a substantial case. Bathurst wrote to congratulate Lowe on the interception of the letters carried by the *Lusitania*, establishing 'beyond contradiction the clandestine correspondence carried on by Mr. O'Meara. The contents of the letters, and the manner in which Mr. Balcombe endeavours to conceal the part which he has taken in this transaction, clearly show that the commissions transmitted by Mr. O'Meara were not of the innocent nature ascribed to them, and that they were something more than orders for books for his own, or even for the amusement of Longwood. Although no judicial proceedings can be held against any of the parties yet, the papers, even should nothing more be discovered, will be satisfactory documents in the event of any parliamentary discussions.' He still thought the books sent by Holmes were suspicious and that their bindings should be opened in case they concealed something.

Bathurst was willing to believe that neither Stokoe nor Fowler were parties in the transaction, 'and that those who have taken a part on the side of Mr. O'Meara have been duped by him, and are sincere in the regret which they express'. (He seemed to be referring to Balcombe as one of the dupes.) He advised Lowe 'to show no ill-humour' and to conceal his suspicions. 'It will be a trial of your temper to read Mr. O'Meara's charges against you. The answer which the Lords of the Admiralty gave to it must be satisfactory to you, more especially when you know that Sir George Cockburn was the first person who, on reading the charges, declared that Mr. O'Meara ought to be instantly dismissed from the service . . . You will observe that Mr. O'Meara's great object is to involve as many persons as possible in the attack against you; and he has therefore introduced the names of many individuals.'[17]

A legal action against O'Meara, Holmes and Balcombe was in serious contemplation. One charge being considered was of assisting Bonaparte in an escape attempt—a hanging offence, 'without benefit of clergy' [last rites], so condemning a prisoner straight to hell. Goulburn wrote to Lowe asking him to prepare documents in such a form that they could be presented in court if legal proceedings were to go ahead.

The newspapers were so full of these developments that little space was given to the death of Queen Charlotte, the consort of the sadly ailing George III, who was beyond comprehending her passing.[18] In some newspapers the emphasis was changing concerning the nature of the 'plot' and who had contrived it. The *Morning Chronicle* asked if there was a coincidence in the timing of the arrival of the despatches from St Helena, the arrest of Gourgaud and the discussion of 'the Ex-Emperor's case' at the current Congress of European heads of state at Aix-la-Chapelle. It speculated that 'such a *stir* as was created' as if 'planned to exculpate or to screen Sir Hudson Lowe from the charges laid against him of inhuman treatment towards the fallen foe'. The *Chronicle* confirmed that O'Meara had been removed from the list of naval surgeons, 'and the pretext alleged is that some passages of a very serious nature' were contained in his letter to the Admiralty concerning Lowe. The newspaper was authorised 'to contradict the statement that Mr O'Meara had asserted that Sir H. Lowe had made a proposal to him to poison Bonaparte. No such accusation has been made; but Mr O'Meara stated that suggestions against his conscience were made to him.'[19]

Bathurst had no doubt of the existence of a plot. He had 'laid out all the despatches concerning the case' and discussed it with the Prince Regent, who did not attend the European Congress, having sent Lord Castlereagh and the Duke of Wellington instead. Bathurst wrote to inform Lowe that although it was clear that O'Meara and Balcombe were channels of illicit communication, there was not yet sufficient legal evidence 'to authorize the Adoption of any legal Measures against the parties concerned'. Lowe had received 'the full Approbation of His Royal Highness'. It was a matter of waiting until the plotters revealed themselves.[20]

'The great business of the Congress at Aix-la-Chapelle is now finished,' announced the *Morning Post* on 25 November. 'Happiness is expressed by all at the ascertained fact that BONAPARTE remains in perfect security at St Helena . . . with nothing likely to occur to cause an alteration in the situation . . . He, it is a lamentable fact, has still many adherents in France.'[21] But the Congress had concluded with an agreement by the Allied powers that all occupation troops would be removed from that country.

The ex-empress of France, 'Maria Louisa', had prevailed on her father, the Emperor of Austria, to support the proposal made at the Congress 'to remove Napoleon to a climate more congenial to his health'. The motion did not succeed, but Gourgaud's letters had clearly had some effect, for there was also lobbying from Rome: 'It is rumoured that the Pope has requested leave to send a priest to comfort Napoleon in his confinement, supposed to be at the instigation of his family resident at Rome.'[22]

James Perry, editor of the *Morning Chronicle*, still demanded Lowe's recall: 'We wish that we could doubt of the reality of the persecution; however, all who arrive from St Helena unite in bearing testimony to it. But a fallen enemy, who threw himself on the generosity of the nation, is the last who ought to experience inhumanity from us. We may have no regard for the prisoner, but we ought to have some regard for the national character.'[23] The *Morning Post* stated that there was no intention of recalling Lowe, 'for certainly no man could possibly fill his arduous office more faithfully or effectively than he does ... In all this, it is quite forgotten that BONAPARTE is a Prisoner and that his escape might be followed by fresh convulsions and wars, in which thousands would again probably perish.'[24]

At Plantation House, Lowe still fretted that Balcombe seemed to be on such easy terms with the admirals Cockburn and Malcolm and felt so free to speak against him.[25] He sent a despatch to Bathurst, requesting that Sir Thomas Tyrwhitt be informed of the behaviour of his protégé.[26] Lowe still felt besieged by the continuing accusations made against him. A far wider public than just those of a Whig persuasion believed that he had diminished their country's honour and had cruelly treated not just Napoleon and his French retinue but also O'Meara, causing him to lose his career in the navy and his pension, simply because he had stood up for what he believed was right. Indeed, O'Meara was to achieve enduring recognition for such steadfastness when Lord Byron devoted a couplet to him in *The Age of Bronze*:

> ... the stiff surgeon, who maintained his cause,
> Hath lost his place, and gained the world's applause.[27]

CHAPTER 24

OFFICIAL DISGRACE

Driving on Dartmoor, along an unfenced road over green hills and dales broken by granite outcrops and tors, I occasionally had to stop the vehicle to let cattle cross. Grazing on the slopes were small, spry Dartmoor ponies and horses, and black-faced sheep so heavy with wool they looked like wheelbarrows. At last, at dusk, Princetown appeared on the horizon, at 1400 feet (430 metres) above sea level the highest town in England. From a distance the vast granite prison dominated, dramatic, grey and forbidding. As I drove closer it loomed, even more massive than I had expected: five huge four-storey buildings with tall square chimneys, radiating out from a central core and encircled by a high perimeter double wall.

This great penitentiary, still in operation, the small town that serviced it and the inn where I had booked a room were all the creations of Sir Thomas Tyrwhitt. This was the other side of the amiable little courtier dubbed 'our little red dwarf' by the royal family: this was Tyrwhitt the visionary, the builder, the ambitious entrepreneur.

Sir Thomas realised that his protégé was in critical danger of arrest and imprisonment. If it was deemed that he had assisted Bonaparte in an escape attempt, he could face a charge of treason, for which the penalty was death. Tyrwhitt could not save him if it came to that. He thought it wise for Balcombe to lay low, away from London, and remove himself from his associates, O'Meara and Holmes.

The Balcombes, with their two servants, settled in to Tyrwhitt's country house, Tor Royal, outside the village of Princetown. Although not grand, it was a very large country house for Dartmoor, with a two-storey bedroom wing each side of the living quarters. It was on land of little use for farming other than grazing, although Sir Thomas, after valiant attempts, had cultivated nine acres of flax.[1] It was nestled under the South Hessary Tor and, on rare days when mist or rain did not impede, had a view across the valley.[2] Today it is still the finest house on Dartmoor and is a successful B&B.

Nearby was the grim war prison Sir Thomas had ordered built over three years, completing it in 1809, when it began housing some 5000 French prisoners of war who were marched up from Plymouth.[3] Dartmoor had not been the only prison for French and American prisoners, but it was the largest—with eventually some 8000 inmates—and conditions were regarded as the worst in Britain.[4] (The Americans were there as a result of Britain's 1812–14 war with America.) After 1815, however, with peace declared and Napoleon exiled to St Helena, the prisoners were discharged in batches. By February of the following year, the great prison was empty. Sir Thomas needed to find another use for it. In his view it could take the 2000 convicts who were being transported each year to New South Wales and Van Diemen's Land.[5]

The village of Princetown had almost emptied, all the prison staff gone, but Tyrwhitt believed it still had a future. The surrounding area was rich in natural resources, mainly minerals, but its prosperity was limited by the lack of a transport connection to the coast. So he would bring industry to the moor by building a link to the sea. His new idea was a horse-drawn railway to transport granite down to Plymouth and to bring goods back, supplies for the new prison inmates.

Perhaps the big granite buildings might be occupied, he thought, if not by prisoners, by the paupers of London, who could be trained as domestic servants—it could be a School of Industry! Balcombe could manage the catering: he had gained experience on St Helena, purveying for 52 people, obtaining food supplies in a place with difficult access; now he could do that on a much larger scale. The job would keep him out of London, give him an income, shield him from trouble and make him forget his connection with Bonaparte. But Balcombe and his family were not going to forget, not for the rest of their lives.

Sir Thomas commissioned a survey of the 23-mile route for his proposed horse-drawn railway, climbing more than 1000 feet and contouring around peat bogs and granite tors. He submitted his plan to the Plymouth Chamber of Commerce on 3 November 1818, pitching the enormous benefits for the two towns it would link. The railway would transport granite, iron, copper and tin from the quarries of Dartmoor (his quarry being the largest) to the port of Plymouth, as well as flax and peat. In return, timber, coal, food supplies and fertiliser could be brought from the coast, enabling new industries for Princetown. He predicted that shareholders could expect an 18 per cent return on their investment. The Chamber of Commerce naturally agreed.[6]

Tyrwhitt's enthusiasm inspired others, and nearly £28,000 was raised, although he himself was the main contributor. The initial sum was enough to finance the first section of the line, while much fundraising was still needed for tunnelling and bridges.[7] A charter was drawn up for the Plymouth and Dartmoor Railway Company and announced in the county's newspapers. The 26 founding subscribers bought £25 shares. The largest purchaser was a rich local politician, Sir Masseh Lopes, with 50 shares, followed by Tyrwhitt with 40 and Sir William Elford with 20; William Balcombe was listed next, with four shares totalling just £100.[8] But nothing was happening with the Dartmoor prison; no new inmates arrived, despite Sir Thomas's proposals to bring, if not convicts, if not paupers, perhaps the orphan children of London.

It was a harsh winter at Dartmoor and the Balcombes' African servant Sarah Timms suffered in the abominable weather. (A former prison physician had noted that 'it was not unusual in the months of December and January for the thermometer to stand at 33 to 35 degrees below freezing, indicating cold almost too intense to support animal life'.[9]) Sarah had been nanny to the girls since their early childhood and was now the household maid. She had been given her freedom to accompany the family to England, where slavery was illegal, but had been told the stay would be for only six months. Now nine months had passed and snow was thick on the ground. Balcombe promised they would all soon be returning to St Helena.

The family, accustomed to a tropical climate, hated the rain, rolling fogs and snow and yearned for their island home and friends. Balcombe missed the trade opportunities and his many investments there. The small 'dame school' was not satisfactory for the boys, and Princetown was far too isolated for the young women. There was no society life whatsoever. The Balcombes moved to lodgings down in Plymouth, much to the disappointment of Sir Thomas. He assured William that there would be plenty of work for him when the prison had new occupants and the railway project was completed. Then Princetown would flourish!

In early February 1819, Balcombe wrote to the Court of Directors of the East India Company, requesting permission to return to St Helena in order to resume his position as superintendent of public sales. The issue was discussed on 24 February, but the court moved at a majestic pace in such matters, especially with someone so recently controversial in the news.

Balcombe was told that his request was being considered.[10] Meanwhile, he needed to put his commercial affairs on the island back in order. He wrote from Plymouth to his business partner Joseph Cole clearly disassociating himself from O'Meara. His old friend the doctor was by then down on his luck. He had rented rooms on Edgware Road in London and set up shop as a dentist. In the window he displayed a wisdom tooth with a notice that it had been extracted from the jaw of Napoleon Bonaparte. The dentistry practice did not flourish.[11] In 1819, he published a bound booklet, *An Exposition of some of the Transactions at St Helena since the Appointment of Sir Hudson Lowe*, 'Price 8 shillings', which earned a little more for him.[12] It was a precursor to a major work that would follow three years later.

Even without the provocation of this new publication, which had not yet reached him, Lowe was still fulminating over O'Meara's earlier attacks, portraying him in the British press as a tyrant. He was considering legal action.

The Balcombes read in *The Times* that their surgeon friend Dr John Stokoe, once a disappointed suitor for Jane, was abruptly leaving St Helena for England on the *Trincomalee*. He had lately been 'the medical attendant on the person of Buonaparte'. The paper reported that his 'sudden return' was explained in a letter from a St Helena officer: 'Mr Stokoe, the surgeon of the flag-ship, whom Buonaparte accepted as his medical attendant, after the return home of Mr O'Meara, has incurred the displeasure of the Governor and returns to England in the *Trincomalee*.'

According to the paper, Stokoe had tried to make it conditional with the governor of accepting the situation with Bonaparte, that he should not be required to detail any personal conversations into which he might be drawn, 'or any circumstances which he might overhear, at Longwood; but pledging himself as a British officer that if any thing should come to his knowledge in which his allegiance to his King and country would be compromised by his secrecy, he would then instantly give information to the Governor. This has passed on until a few days since, when Buonaparte was suddenly seized with a serious illness in the middle of the night. Mr Stokoe, as soon as the necessary forms were gone through, visited him and found that he had a slight apoplectic fit. After a few hours he appeared free from the attack, but it had left a considerable degree of indisposition. Mr Stokoe made official reports of the circumstances to Sir Hudson Lowe and the Admiral Plampin, and gave copies of them to Buonaparte. Whether it was this latter circumstance, or whether Mr S. had represented Buonaparte as being in a worse state of health than suited the predisposed notions of Sir Hudson, is not known; but he was instantly forbidden to go to Longwood—was threatened to be tried by a court-martial—or, as an act of mitigation of his offence, he was told he might invalid home. Of course he preferred the latter, as the least incommodious to him, and he sails tomorrow in the *Trincomalee*. The reports were drawn up, of course, with conscientious accuracy, and were such as the case demanded. I understand Buonaparte is really in a serious state of health. His dwelling is sealed against all visitors.'[13]

Three days after this article, *The Times* reported that Stokoe had already arrived and been interviewed at the Admiralty and was returning to St Helena immediately: 'This gentleman, we understand, was on Tuesday examined by ministers, and the result has been that he is immediately to resume his functions at St Helena. The inference from this is, that his conduct has been fully approved of.'[14]

The Balcombes were longing to depart for the island themselves, but could not do so until official permission was received from the East India Company, although it seems they heard encouraging rumours. However, Sarah Timms could endure England no longer. Balcombe travelled up to London with her and arranged her passage on the ship *Larkin* and her travel bond with the Company.

While in London, Balcombe called in to see Holmes the naval agent and booked into lodgings next door to his Kennington house—something that would count against him. He wrote letters from there to Cole and Fowler, which Holmes arranged that a ship's officer would deliver to St Helena, bypassing the official mail. Yet another foolish mistake.

Lowe was alarmed to hear that Balcombe still had every intention of returning to the island, and that although the purveyorship to the French had gone, he planned to resume his other business interests if permitted to do so by the East India Company. In a private letter to Bathurst, the governor noted that two more letters had recently arrived from Balcombe, brought by a ship's officer for Cole and Fowler. Cole had shown Lowe his letter and there was not a great deal in it. Balcombe had said that 'he had been recommended by Sir T. T. to go to Plymouth for Economy'. The officer delivering the letter admitted that he had picked it up from Balcombe at Kennington, 'the place where Mr O'Meara & Mr Holmes met'.

The governor then informed Cole 'that the partnership of Balcombe, Holmes & O'Meara in England could not be long found compatible with that of Balcombe, Cole & Fowler at St Helena'. Cole replied that he understood that. Lowe wrote to Bathurst: 'I was inclined to make this remark as Mr Balcombe enjoys the benefit of the Naval contract in this Island for the supply of Beer & Vegetables, delivering perhaps to him & his house here not less than £2000 a year. He still retains also the Situation of Superintendent of Public Sales, for which, however, if he does not return here, one of the Company's Civil

Servants, tho not at my suggestion, has applied. If Mr B thinks such matters worth pursuing, the only way I conceive he has to proceed is to make a full compleat disclosure of everything that has passed & to recant. He will probably avoid this, so long as he can play a desirable game & secure an interest in both quarters. The Person whom I conceded would have been able to obtain everything from him was Sir Thomas Tyrwhitt, but if all these arguments from him have failed, I presume those of his Interests may still succeed.'[15]

Sarah Timms arrived back on the island in late June and reported to Lowe, who thoroughly questioned her. He wrote to Goulburn: 'She mentioned that Captain Wallis had gone down to Plymouth to see Mr Balcombe & his family & was with them two or three days. Mr Balcombe, she said, took lodgings next door for some time to Mr Holmes at Kennington. She knows nothing of their connection, nor is not likely to have brought out anything from them.'[16]

On the same day, 29 June, Albine de Montholon, claiming ill health, announced that she was departing St Helena, leaving her husband to keep Napoleon company. She had had enough of the island's loneliness, the bickering and Fanny Bertrand's hostility. She may have had enough of occasionally warming Napoleon's bed. Although his declining health probably meant that he was incapable of much sexual activity, she was a comfort to him. It was rumoured that Albine was heading to England to warm the bed of Lieutenant Basil Jackson, something hinted at in her own later *Journal Secret d'Albine de Montholon, maîtresse de Napoléon à Sainte-Hélène*, in which her relationship as 'mistress' to Napoleon was explicit in the title. The journal lay unpublished for almost two centuries.[17] She left the island, with her children, on the *Lady Campbell* on 2 July. Napoleon was said to be devastated by her departure.[18]

Bathurst wrote to Lowe, counselling him against directing 'any prosecutions against the *Morning Chronicle* or Mr. O'Meara's publications', not because he felt indifference on the subject, 'but because London juries are very uncertain in their verdicts, and one ill-disposed juryman would be able to acquit the parties, which would give occasion for triumph and appear to justify the complaints which have been made against you'. Knowing that Lowe was likely to be disappointed by this advice, he offered some good news: 'With respect to Mr. Balcombe, you will let it be known that, in the event of his arriving at St Helena, you have orders to send him away. His partners must not be allowed to continue their contract if his name is in it. I imagine he cannot be dismissed from his office of Surveyor of Sales but by order of the Court of Directors; and I am not sure what may be the result of the representation which I shall probably make to them on the subject. I say probably, for I do not much like making representations of that description unless there is a good chance of their being attended to.'[19]

However, there was another member of the suspected 'naval cabal' whom Lowe had no wish to see return to the island. He wrote to Bathurst that a Portsmouth newspaper indicated that Stokoe was a passenger on board the *Abundance* and was returning to St Helena to resume his duties as a naval surgeon. The news had given rise to 'an extraordinary declaration' from Count Balmain, that in his view 'Mr Stokoe was not in any respect to blame'. Lowe still refused to acknowledge that Balmain was courting his stepdaughter Charlotte, and he found the man's comment outrageous.[20]

The first Plymouth and Dartmoor Railway Act successfully passed through Parliament in July 1819 as a result of Tyrwhitt's exertions. In a ceremony on 12 August, Sir Thomas laid the first iron rails on granite sleepers.[21]

There was a small setback for the project when the largest original investor, Sir Masseh Lopes, a wealthy Devon landowner, local magistrate and (even by the standards of the time) notoriously corrupt politician, was convicted of electoral bribery at the County Assizes in 1819 and gaoled for two years. Born a Portuguese Jew (who had later converted to Protestantism), he was probably a convenient scapegoat for token parliamentary reform.[22]

In August, Napoleon's fiftieth birthday passed with little fuss on St Helena.

The following day, 16 August 1819, would long be remembered as a day of shame in England. In Manchester some 60,000 men, women and children, wearing their Sunday best, walked peaceably, carrying no arms, to St Peter's Field to listen to the famous radical orator Henry Hunt. He called for 'quietness and order' and the crowd complied.[23] But the Manchester magistrates had a warrant for Hunt's arrest. England still possessed no police force, but out of sight, in case of trouble, was an enormous force of soldiers; at the front was the local yeomanry, shopkeepers and 'newly enriched manufacturers', armed and on horseback.[24] It was this local militia that made a bungling charge to arrest the speaker and attacked the crowd, which tried to prevent Hunt's removal. The troops followed, sabres drawn, charging into the melée and killing up to fifteen people and wounding more than 400. It was a massacre of the defenceless, leaving a field strewed with 'caps, bonnets, hats, shawls and shoes . . . trampled, torn and bloody'.[25]

The reverberations of 'Peterloo', as it came to be called, on the British middle class led eventually to parliamentary reform.

CHAPTER 25

AN ITEM OF NEWS

News from St Helena was always welcome to the Balcombes, still living at Plymouth. In mid-August 1819, the *Morning Post* had two stories which would have delighted them. It noted that General Sir George and Lady Bingham were departing the island for England: 'Report says that he will soon return as its Governor.' That was bound to please many islanders too, for the article mentioned that the locals knew 'nothing of what passes in Europe, as all the newspapers that arrive are obliged to be forwarded to Sir Hudson Lowe, who destroys them after perusal'.

What was particularly delicious was the story of Sir Thomas Reade, the deputy-adjutant-general, who had been 'desirous of gratifying Lady Lowe with the representation of a naval night action'. He had therefore given directions to the captain of the visiting naval warship HMS *Eurydice*. 'Accordingly at ten o'clock at night, the *Eurydice*, after a brilliant discharge of rockets, blue lights &c commenced a vigorous cannonade, which was answered by a brig, and kept up with great spirit on both sides, to the great admiration of such ladies as were in the secret, and to the consternation of the inhabitants, amongst others, of Admiral Plampin.' It was astonishing that Plampin, the admiral of the South Atlantic naval station, had not been informed; 'imagining that the Yankees were endeavouring to land in order to carry off Bonaparte, he sent his Secretary and the signal midshipman galloping down the steep sidepath from the Briars at the risk of their necks, to ascertain what was the matter. Nothing could exceed the confusion amongst the natives, the greatest part of whom flocked to the alarm-posts, where they remained until daylight.' The article concluded: 'Nothing further is known about Bonaparte, than that he is on the island.'[1]

Betsy and Jane and their parents would have wondered about Napoleon's actual state of health, with rumours that an Italian doctor had now arrived to look after him. That mention of The Briars, still occupied by Plampin, must have caused more than a twinge of heartache and determination to return to the island, especially if the good General Bingham was to be governor there.

The Times of 3 November provided an account of the tribulations of their friend John Stokoe: 'Our readers will learn with surprise and no doubt with indignation, the disingenuous manner in which Mr Stokoe, Naval Surgeon on board the Admiral's flag-ship at St Helena, has been treated.' Stokoe, 'this most respectable naval surgeon', had 'like his predecessor incurred the displeasure of Sir Hudson Lowe' because of the bulletins he wrote on the ex-emperor's state of health. He had been allowed to return to England on half-pay, and 'was received in the most gracious manner at the Admiralty', then given an order to return to the island and his station on the flagship. 'No sooner, however, had he arrived at St Helena,' the report continued, 'than he was told that a court-martial was to be assembled to try him on several charges, preferred against him by the Lords Commissioners of the Admiralty, relative to his conduct during his attendance on General Buonaparte! They are such as would, in any other case and situation, be considered frivolous and vexatious; but coming from so high an authority, and supported by the local influence of his enemy, he can have very little hope of relief.' Because Stokoe had returned with expectations of taking up his old position as flagship surgeon, he had left behind in England 'the original documents of official correspondence' which would have supported his case, as well as 'testimonials of character, which after twenty years of approved service, he had received from every commander under whom he had sailed. The system of terror so powerfully operates in St Helena, that a military officer declined giving Surgeon Stokoe his countenance and assistance, during the trial, on the plea of ill-health.'

The ten charges were extraordinarily petty, even in the view of *The Times*: 'The first charge, we understand, was for having held communications with Buonaparte otherwise than in his professional capacity and the last, for having in his official documents designated or described Buonaparte as "Napoleon" and the "Patient" and not as "General Buonaparte".'[2]

The outcome was inevitable and merciless. Stokoe was found guilty of all charges and stripped of his naval career. The court-martial judges, 'in consideration of his former faithful services and his excellent character, recommended him to the Lords of the Admiralty to be placed on the half-pay list'.[3] All Stokoe's fears of angering the governor and Admiral Plampin if he offered Napoleon any medical attention had come to pass. The emperor's shadow had fallen on him, but looming behind it was the bitter, punitive spectre of Sir Hudson Lowe.

Balcombe was still awaiting the decision of the East India Company regarding his application of February to return to his beloved island. The St Helena Archives still holds the court book with the decisions of the Court of Directors on various applications.[4] On 8 December, the directors gave the answer he had hoped for: 'Resolved. That adverting to the Court's Resolution of the 24th February last, Mr William Balcombe be permitted to return to St Helena for the purpose of resuming his former situation of Superintendent of Public Sales at that Island.' Despite his gout, Balcombe might have danced a jig if he had known of that result. Unfortunately, he never did. One week later, before it was communicated to him, the decision was reversed. It was noted in the court book that Lord Bathurst had 'declined to comply' with the court's request for 'the proposed return of Mr W. Balcombe to St Helena' and 'would not consider himself justified in departing from that decision'. The application was refused.[5] Whatever friends Balcombe might have had influencing the Court of Directors, Bathurst—who in this instance was going to oblige Lowe—was more powerful.

It was a heavy blow for the whole Balcombe family, particularly for William and his wife. She had first thought of St Helena as 'worse than Botany Bay', but had come to love their 'dear island', the friends they had there, such as the Bertrands, and most of all their beautiful home, The Briars. Balcombe's worries were predominantly financial. He had a great deal of money tied up in the Briars property and the brewery; the naval contract alone, for supplying beer and vegetables, was worth £2000 a year to his company.[6] Admiral Plampin was still neglecting to pay rent, having apparently seen the fracas surrounding the 'clandestine letters' as a justification for not doing so, and only a trickle was coming from Cole and Fowler for the business, through Wm Burnie & Co. in London.

Tyrwhitt was not in a position to help Balcombe financially, having directed all his funds towards his passion, the Plymouth and Dartmoor Railroad, and had taken out a heavy mortgage on it as well. At the same time, he was much occupied in discussions and actual arguments with the Prince Regent. Old King George III was totally delusional, in ever failing health and expected to die at any time. As J.B. Priestley wrote: 'The idea of the mad old King haunted the Regency like an accusing ghost.'[7] The Regent insisted that when he acceded to the throne, he would not have his legal wife, Princess Caroline of Brunswick, as his queen. Tyrwhitt advised that he could not do otherwise, but the Regent said that he had a legal right to annul the marriage if she had proved to be unfaithful. Princess Caroline was living in Italy and there was a rumour that she had a lover. Tyrwhitt may have been asked to go on a mission to ascertain this fact, but if so, he refused. Prince George wanted to marry again. With the death of his daughter Charlotte, he now had no legal heir to the throne. His younger brother Edward, the Duke of Kent, the fourth son of George III, had just that year produced a daughter, the Princess Victoria.[8] His other brothers had plenty of illegitimate offspring but no legitimate children, and now a few of them were scrambling among the European princesses to find a wife who would deliver a male heir. The Regent was determined to outwit them.

The Duke of Wellington had no time for any of the King's seven surviving sons, lumping them all together as 'the damndest millstones about the neck of any government that can be imagined'.[9] One of those millstones sank soon after: Edward, Duke of Kent, died suddenly on 23 January 1820.

His death was followed six days later by the more expected passing of his father, George III. There was an outbreak of mourning among the English for the late King; they had developed a real affection for their 'Farmer George'. They feared what would happen to the nation under the rule of his spendthrift, disreputable, roistering eldest son.

George IV acceded to the throne at Windsor Castle, and plans were made, with the help of Tyrwhitt, for his coronation.

Lowe wrote promising news for Bathurst about the new gardener at Longwood: 'Nothing can exceed the bustle & activity which has been recently displayed by General Bonaparte in giving directions about his Flower Garden & superintending the servants employed in it. He is hemming it in, all round with as bushy trees and shrubs as he can get transported & with rock walls so as to screen himself as far as possible from external observation.'[10] For Lowe, it confirmed his belief that there was nothing wrong with the general—he had been malingering all along. Napoleon, who had always been so particular in his dress, was now sometimes seen in the garden in loose blowsy trousers and a Chinese coolie hat. The orderly officer had even sighted him in a dressing-gown![11]

As Balcombe was permanently blocked from returning to St Helena and needed to settle various debts, he at last made the decision and mortgaged The Briars, including the Union brewery for £9000, to his agents, William and James Burnie. Balcombe was now in possession of a considerable amount of money, but it had to last for an unforeseeable length of time. He had lost his career and his businesses and was out of official favour. Tyrwhitt, as always, wanted to help him, but was unable to use his influence with government. Bathurst had turned decisively against Balcombe, who was fortunate so far to have escaped legal action and possible imprisonment.

Many people in Balcombe's situation would have fallen into a state of depression, but his natural ebullience must have helped him through this difficult period. His prospects had collapsed, his affluent life had disappeared, his good name had gone. All he could look forward to was a job obtaining food supplies, with immense logistical difficulty, for a prison in the bleakest place in England. Tyrwhitt still had great hopes that a use would be found for his Dartmoor prison, and a position for Balcombe, now that the railroad was laboriously snaking, one granite sleeper after another, towards Sutton Pool. But most of the time Tyrwhitt was with the new King, trying to dissuade him from his plan to put the Queen Consort on public trial for adultery.

However, at the end of February 1820, Sir Thomas was in a state of shock, as were all members of Parliament. On the twenty-third, a plot was exposed, just before it was enacted, to murder Prime Minister Lord Liverpool, Lord Bathurst, Lord Sidmouth and all the Cabinet ministers. The conspirators, a revolutionary group spurred to action by the Peterloo massacre and the old King's death, held their meetings at Cato Street, off Edgware Road (near Dr O'Meara's dental practice, although he of course had nothing to do with it). The conspirators were infiltrated by a government spy, who exposed their plan to use pistols and grenades to kill all the Cabinet members while they were at a dinner, seize key government buildings, and invite all workers, war veterans, farm labourers and the unemployed to join them in revolution. Five members of the 'Cato Street conspiracy' were hanged and five others transported to Australia.[12]

Princess Caroline, the King's wife returned from her expatriate life in Italy, landing at Dover on 5 June to enjoy her time of glory as the Queen Consort of the United Kingdom of Great Britain, Ireland and Hanover. Although few regarded her as saintly, she was seen as being a great deal more so than her rakish, libidinous, grossly overweight husband. The rumour had spread, even among the common people, that George IV had taken some strands of pubic hair from every woman with whom he had had sexual congress and there was said to be enough to stuff a mattress.[13]

Caroline's route to London was greeted by welcoming crowds. With public opinion so much on her side, the King's ministers and Tyrwhitt advised that his insistence on a marriage annulment would rebound. George opposed them and demanded that the House of Lords introduce a 'Bill of Pains and Penalties'; if passed, it would deprive Caroline of her royal title and her privileges, and if proved that she had been unfaithful, the marriage would be annulled.[14] The King postponed his coronation until the case was resolved.[15]

The preamble to 'the Trial' began on 5 July. The evening before it commenced, Tyrwhitt was deputed to present the Queen with the House of Lords Bill. Several newspapers reported what followed: 'Her Majesty received the Bill with great calmness. The words which she used were not distinctly understood. They were in substance or sound like the following: "I am sorry that it comes so late, as 25 years ago it might have been of some use to His Majesty." What followed was more audible: "But as we shall not meet in this world, I hope we shall in the next," (pointing her hand towards Heaven, and then adding with great emphasis) "where justice will be rendered me". She requested Sir Thomas Tyrwhitt, if he had an opportunity, to convey these sentiments to His Majesty. Sir Thomas Tyrwhitt is said to have been much affected on delivering the message to the Queen. He had not seen Her Majesty since she was living in the King's house.'[16]

Sir Thomas was obliged to vacate his cottage and other officers of the House of Lords their apartments to make 'safe houses' for the foreign witnesses, some of whom had already been threatened by angry mobs after landing in England. 'On Friday evening,' it was reported, 'eleven foreigners were landed out of a boat at Parliament-stairs, and immediately conducted into the apartments. They appeared to be young men, and some of them had a military air. Most of the windows which overlooked the yard are fastened down and the apartments to which they belong kept locked.'[17] Some of the men would have been very anxious; by the Act of Edward III, it was 'high treason to violate the wife of the King of England, even with her own consent, provided the offence be committed either within the territories of the King or by one of his liege subjects'.[18]

The trial began in mid-August. Within the House of Lords, Tyrwhitt was responsible for all the arrangements. Lady Granville wrote to a friend: 'The Queen said to Sir Tommy as he led her into the House, "I am sure you would have much greater pleasure in leading me to my coronation."'[19] Caroline attended the trial every day, but sometimes stayed in an adjacent room, playing backgammon, especially when prurient statements from her Italian butler and valets regarding bed stains and alleged intimate relations with her chamberlain Pergami were too demeaning to suffer. The evidence of the prosecution witnesses was damaging for her, but later not one of them was credible under cross-examination by the Queen's counsel, the Whig politicians Henry Brougham and Thomas Denman.[20]

The action brought by the dissolute, extravagant, widely hated King against his wife became a focal point for cartoons, broadsides, gross caricatures, petitions, radical demonstrations, and demands for parliamentary reform and even for women's rights. Petitions with close to a million signatures were sent in from around the country. *The Times*, which had chosen to support the Queen, doubled its circulation.[21] The stability of the throne and indeed of the government seemed threatened; the 'Cato Street conspiracy' had been foiled only six months earlier.[22]

The trial in the House of Lords continued until November, the greatest show in the country, exhibiting the grubby royal linen to the eager press. (As Tyrwhitt controlled who entered as spectators, it is quite possible that he found places for some of the Balcombe family.) There were daily revelations and scandals, but the general public remained steadfastly devoted to Caroline and hostile to the King. In the end the Bill passed in the House of Lords by the narrow margin of just nine votes, which meant it was certain of defeat in the House of Commons. The government withdrew the Bill. The Queen was effectively acquitted: 'The government, if not the King himself, was throwing in the towel.' The King reacted with petulance and spite and threatened to 'retire' to his Kingdom of Hanover.[23]

The crowds went wild. Cannon and muskets were fired, bells rang, fireworks exploded and London was illuminated for three days.[24] At the height of the celebrations, the poet Coleridge 'said to a friend he met on the street, "I hope you are a Queenite". "No," replied the friend, "only an anti-Kingite." "Aye," replied Coleridge, "that's all I mean".'[25]

Patrick O'Reilly, the purser on the *Northumberland*, was in England in July 1820 and followed up on a bill for £50 made out to him from the firm Balcombe, Cole & Fowler. He wrote to Denzil Ibbetson, the purveyor for Longwood, that he found Balcombe 'living at Plymouth with his family at an expense which I hope his revenue is adequate to' and the bill was settled. He had then visited the naval agent Holmes on another matter and asked after Dr O'Meara, as he had heard that he was working on a new translation of Bonaparte's memoirs. 'All I could learn was that the latter is at present with Bony's mother, I believe at Rome, and affects to get from her either a pension or a sum of money. It is very easy to conjecture on what grounds he makes the application—he being out of England is I believe not generally known, at least I should suppose so from the manner in which it was told me.' Ibbetson passed this information to Lowe, who sent it to Bathurst.[26] O'Meara was indeed working on a memoir of Napoleon's exile on the island of St Helena and his persecution by the governor. No doubt Madame Mère was happy to provide funding for it.

There were rumours about Balcombe travelling abroad. His great-granddaughter Dame Mabel Brookes claimed to have found 'considerable correspondence' in the Lowe papers 'in reference to his actual whereabouts' at this time: 'Had he gone to France? It was feared he carried messages to the Bonaparte family on the Continent.'[27] However, without evidence, this must remain conjecture.

Many pamphlets and broadsides had circulated in England during the Queen's trial. One declared that Bonaparte had escaped from St Helena in a hot-air balloon.[28] Many people actually believed it. Bathurst knew it was satire, but feared that more practical attempts might be under way. He wrote to Lowe on 30 September: 'The reports which you have recently made of the conduct of General Buonaparte and of his followers make me suspect that he is beginning to entertain serious thoughts of escaping from St Helena, and the accounts which he will have since received of what is passing in Europe will not fail to encourage him in this project . . . You will therefore exert all your attention in watching his proceedings, and call upon the Admiral to use his utmost vigilance.'[29]

Bathurst need not have feared. In fact, Napoleon had abandoned all thoughts of escape, and explained why in a secret letter he dictated to Montholon on 1 November: 'I would not survive six months in America before being assassinated by the comte d'Artois's contract killers. In America I would be either assassinated or forgotten. I'm better off in St Helena.'[30] Napoleon had lost his energy, the old fighting spirit had gone. Nearly all his companions had left, one way or another—Las Cases, Cipriani, Madame de Montholon, O'Meara, the Balcombes, Le Page the chef and Santini. Apart from a few servants, only his faithful remained: Marchand, Montholon and General and Madame Bertrand.

He had made his last visit outside the boundary of Longwood, his last anywhere. Sir William Doveton, a member of the governing council, had extended an invitation and made it known to Lowe that General Bonaparte was welcome to call at his home, 'Mt Pleasant' at Sandy Bay, if he wished.[31] On 4 October, Napoleon paid a surprise visit with Bertrand and Montholon, suffering to be followed by British officers. They brought a picnic with them and proposed having it on the lawn, with its spectacular view of the ridge and the volcanic pinnacles of Lot, his Wife and Daughters. Sir William and his daughter-in-law joined them for cold pie, potted meat, cold turkey, curried fowl, ham, 'coffee, dates, almonds, oranges and a very fine salad'. They drank champagne and Doveton's homemade liqueur, orange shrub. Napoleon asked his host if he ever got drunk and seemed disappointed with the response that he occasionally liked 'a glass of wine'.

Reporting on the meeting to the governor, Sir William said that he thought General Bonaparte seemed in good health and 'looked as fat and as round as a China pig'.[32] Napoleon was in fact in appalling health, with constant and acute pains in the stomach and frequent vomiting. He found some relief by taking saltwater baths, and his Italian physician, Dr Antommarchi, was in attendance.[33] In late November, Lowe had an unexpected sighting of 'General Bonaparte', who was riding in his phaeton with Count de Montholon, and reported to Bathurst: 'He appeared much paler than when I had last seen him, but not fallen away.'[34]

His lordship admitted to some concern: 'As the General obstinately persists in refusing the admittance of an English physician, it is very difficult to form a right judgment of the reports which you receive, since they come almost exclusively from persons whom you know to have every disposition to deceive you ... Still, however, there are many circumstances which now tend to confirm the reports which you have transmitted—not to the extent of apprehending immediate danger, but to the belief of his health really beginning to decline.' He requested that Bonaparte be told that 'we are concerned at accounts of his declining health—they have not been received with indifference'.[35]

On 1 April 1821, the new Italian physician, Dr Antommarchi, asked the English Dr Arnott to see his patient. Arnott reported: 'I went with him & was walked into a dark room, where General Bonaparte was abed. The room was so dark that I could not see him, but I *felt* him, or *someone there*. I examined his pulse & state of skin. I perceived there was considerable debility, but nothing that indicated immediate danger ...'[36] Lowe wrote to Bathurst that he tended to agree with Arnott that much of the prisoner's illness seemed to be play-acting:

'Notwithstanding all that Dr Arnott has said to me respecting General Bonaparte's state being Hypochondria, I have thus refrained from asking anything in the form of a regular Bulletin from him . . .'[37]

This report was sent just a fortnight before Napoleon's death.

The patient himself was in the process of dictating his lengthy last will and testament to Count de Montholon. He left 97 legacies, and even remembered the men who had laboured with him in Longwood's garden: 'see that those poor Chinese get something'. He especially asked that 10,000 francs should go to Subaltern Officer Cantillon, who had been convicted of attempting to assassinate the Duke of Wellington: 'Cantillon had as much right to assassinate that oligarch as the latter had to send me to perish upon the rock of St Helena.'

He wrote 'I have always had reason to be pleased with my dearest wife, Maria Louisa. I retain for her, to my last moment, the most tender sentiments—I beseech her to watch, in order to preserve, my son from the snares which yet environ his infancy.'

His most personal possessions and fondest messages were for his son: 'I recommend to my son never to forget that he was born a French prince, and never to allow himself to become an instrument in the hands of the triumvirs who oppress the nations of Europe: he ought never to fight against France, or to injure her in any manner; he ought to adopt my motto: "Everything for the French people".'[38]

On 5 May, Napoleon breathed his last, surrounded by his remaining loyal companions. Madame Bertrand, for so long the most reluctant of the little company, had sat through long nights with him and was with him at the end. The following day, Lowe wrote to Bathurst: 'It falls to my duty to inform your Lordship that Napoleon Bonaparte expired at about ten minutes before six o'clock in the evening of the 5th May 1821 . . .'[39]

When, some weeks later, reports of the death reached an influential gathering in Paris, one of those present exclaimed: 'Napoleon dead! What an event!'

'It is not an event anymore,' murmured the cynical diplomat Talleyrand. 'It is only *an item of news.*'[40]

At about the same time, a courtier brought the information to King George IV: 'It is my duty to inform your Majesty that your greatest enemy is dead.'

'Is she, by God!' exclaimed the King.[41]

CHAPTER 26

THE ONE THAT GOT AWAY

Count Talleyrand might have pretended that Napoleon's death was *only an item of news*, but it was of enormous symbolic significance for two generations. As general and emperor, Napoleon had stalked through the nightmares of children, inspired young men to lug cannon to the Caribbean and Egypt and Moscow, rattled thrones, excited the hopes of revolutionaries, and become the muse—until disillusionment set in—for poets, painters and composers.

The Napoleonic legend in France had been building for years and now it gained added lustre. It was said that a comet had been seen above Ajaccio in Corsica at the time of Napoleon's birth; now it was claimed that a few days after his death, a comet crossed high in the heavens over the island of St Helena.[1] It all confirmed the story of 'a man of Destiny'. In Britain, as all over Europe, the obituaries, whether for or against, were vehement and passionate. Each aimed to capture the man for posterity. It was, after all, a History War.

A published letter from St Helena informed that 'Buonaparte was buried beneath the willow trees, in the spot he had pointed out, about a mile and a half from Longwood House. A procession of the military staff and all the naval officers followed the corpse, which was laid on a black car, in a plain mahogany coffin (laid wood and tin within), and was received, on emerging from the grounds, by a line of 2000 troops, including artillery and a party of marines, with four bands drawn up by the roadside.'²

Although Lowe had acquiesced to Napoleon's request to be buried in his favourite little valley under the willows, and the funeral service was conducted with all due ceremony, on another matter he was characteristically difficult. He and the French could not agree on the wording for a plaque on the coffin. Knowing that no mention of an 'Emperor' would be permitted, the French had asked for the simple inscription: *Napoleon—né à Ajaccio 15 Août 1769—Mort à St Helena 5 Mai 1821*. Lowe had refused, unless the surname 'Bonaparte' was added. Montholon and Bertrand rejected this. It detracted from the elegance and dignity.³ The coffin remained bare, no inscription at all.

At his club in London, the Duke of Wellington publicly expressed his great admiration for Napoleon. He privately told his friend Mrs Arbuthnot: 'Now I think I may say I am the most successful General alive.'⁴ He slept in a bed that had belonged to Bonaparte, and although his admiration was somewhat tempered on learning that the Frenchman who had tried to assassinate him was rewarded in Bonaparte's will, it was not erased. He had recently acquired a statue, an unwanted item sent by Louis XVIII to the British government and presented to the victor of Waterloo. Wellington erected it on a plinth outside his London mansion, Apsley House on Hyde Park Corner. Sculpted by Canova, it was a towering figure 12 feet high (the little Corsican would have been happy with half of that), presenting the young Napoleon quite nude but for 'a Republican fig leaf'.⁵

Napoleon's death would have been devastating for eighteen-year-old Betsy. Apart from her immediate family, he had been the most important figure in her young life. The newspaper accounts, offering such grandiloquent descriptions of his rise to power and historic achievements, must have astonished her and placed in an almost unrecognisable perspective the man she had known. It would have made her marvel that this heroic or ruthless man, this designer of a just system of laws or else a savage murderer, had been her friend, often her playmate, and had tolerated her impudence.

At about this time the Balcombe family moved from Plymouth to the Devon village of Chudleigh. It is not clear why they moved, except that house rentals were bound to be much cheaper in the village, and it was still only 23 rugged miles from Princetown; if the Dartmoor School of Industry became a reality, Balcombe's family could remain in Chudleigh while he rode to work at the prison.

Lowe's concern to monitor the Balcombes' activities diminished after Napoleon's death and his useful documentation of them became only occasional. With the uproar over the 'St Helena plot' subsiding, they were rarely mentioned in the newspapers, so in an era twenty years before the first official census, only major life events such as births, deaths and marriages could help trace such a family. Only one of those events was to occur and be recorded within the next few years.

Three weeks after Napoleon's death, his faithful companions—the Count and Countess Bertrand and their children, Count de Montholon, the valets Marchand and Saint-Denis, Dr Antommarchi, the newly arrived priest Abbé Vignali—and the few remaining French servants of the Longwood establishment all made their departure from St Helena on the storeship *Camel*.[6] None of them had ever loved the island; some of them had loved its prisoner. As the great rock receded, none would have felt regret—except surely Marchand, abandoning his mistress and the child he had (perhaps) sired. A blue-eyed boy with a very large head . . . Even Count de Las Cases' precious papers were leaving the island at last. Lowe had written to Bathurst that it occurred to him that Las Cases 'will probably be claiming them, on hearing of the event that has happened here'. He was sending the documents to Bathurst, with safety copies on a second ship.[7]

Lowe had made an embarrassing admission to his lordship. After all his complaints about the Russian commissioner, he had been obliged to accept him as his son-in-law. Count Balmain's offers to his stepdaughter Charlotte were 'of the most flattering & advantageous nature' and Lady Lowe was in favour. The couple had been married on 26 April 1820, followed by a celebration at Plantation House. Lowe now described Balmain as 'honourable, gentlemanlike & agreeable'.[8] The secretary Gorrequer made a sarcastic comment in his thinly coded diary on how much Lowe 'had changed his tone after Bear's proposal'.[9]

It was another two months before Lowe could leave the island. He was having a difficult time, in dispute with the East India Company over various issues.[10] A 'Secret and Confidential' letter from the directors, written three days before Napoleon's death, was on its way to him. It was a scorching rebuke, listing all the areas in which his administration was viewed as wanting. 'We cannot suffer Ourselves to be thus dictated to as to the manner in which we may chuse to seek for Information relative to our affairs at St Helena ...' They rejected Lowe's remarks that they were influenced 'by the ex-parte opinions or advice of any Person whatever'. They trusted that he had not 'intentionally shewn Disrespect' and that he would 'on mature reflection be convinced' that he had 'been led into Error or Misconception' and that 'this unpleasant Correspondence will here terminate'.[11]

It was apparent that Lowe could never hope for a future appointment from the East India Company. But before he quitted the island he had the gratification of receiving an address from the British residents, gratefully acknowledging 'the consideration, justice, impartiality and moderation which have distinguished your government'. They particularly praised him for abolishing slavery in a colony where the practice had existed for so long, 'proof of our entire confidence in your concern for our welfare'.[12]

The Third Plymouth and Dartmoor Railway Act of Parliament received royal assent at the beginning of July 1821, making financial provision for the building of a 620-yard tunnel. Sir Thomas Tyrwhitt hosted a festive 'breakfast' for as many people as cared to attend at the planned station of Roborough Down on Dartmoor, where horses would be changed and stabled.[13] The Balcombes as shareholders were bound to have been present to show their enthusiasm and to meet new people.

Village life at Chudleigh may have seemed limiting for the young Balcombe women, particularly for someone as bright, spirited, attractive and sociable as Betsy. However, there are indications that the family was not isolated from society, for she somehow made the acquaintance of one of Devon's more interesting residents, Thomas Leversidge Fish, who spent a few months of each year at his extraordinary home, 'Knowle Cottage', in neighbouring Sidmouth.[14]

Fish was 36 years old in 1821, personable, immensely wealthy and a bachelor. Betsy may have met him at one of Sir Thomas's levées, which a few society people attended, but, more than likely, curiosity led her to visit Knowle Cottage with her mother and sister, just like scores of other tourists. Fish opened it to the public, free of any entry charge, on the first Monday of every month during the season when he was in residence, July to October.[15]

Sidmouth, with its dramatic red sandstone cliffs sheltering the beach, had become a fashionable watering place for the upper and middle classes during the Napoleonic Wars, when they were prevented from going to the Continent, and especially so since the King's brother the late Duke of Kent—with his wife and their little daughter Princess Victoria—had adopted it as a favoured holiday spot.[16] In 1810, it had been a quiet fishing village with a population of 1252, but by 1821 this had more than doubled.[17] The rich arrived and built fashionable houses, calling them 'marine villas' or 'cottages'.

The grandest, most eccentric, most beautiful, most famous and least 'cottagey' was Fish's Knowle Cottage, also known as 'The Knowle'. This very rich and very eligible bachelor had purchased it that year, 1821, as a neglected deceased estate. Even then it was a grand property of some 14 acres, described in the auction listing as 'an elegant marine residence ... situated on a beautiful eminence commanding extensive prospects of the surrounding country, and boundless views of the ocean'.[18] Fish then set about restoring the house and grounds; hired gardeners, craftsmen and artists; and began expending his fortune on fine furniture, statues, vases, chandeliers and stained glass. He raided Europe, an extravagant and tasteful collector, the William Randolph Hearst of his day. In the gardens, Fish created ponds, fountains, Gothic arches, conservatories, a huge aviary and a large private zoo, importing rare plants, birds and animals from all over the world. The Knowle became his obsession, and he was happy to share its wonders with the breathless public free of charge, once a month, weather permitting, when he was in residence.

Soon Fish had a nickname—denoting both his wealth and his generosity—'the Golden Fish of Knowle Cottage'. Mothers of marriageable daughters all over the county were alert to his arrival in their midst. Jane Austen's opening to *Pride and Prejudice*—'It is a truth universally acknowledged, that a single man in possession of a good fortune, must be in want of a wife'—was still a truism in 1821. Fish was rumoured to earn some £20,000 a year, although no one was quite sure what he did when he was away from Sidmouth.

The Balcombe women, and even William, would not have been able to resist a visit. Like all the sightseers, they would have been astonished. The local guidebooks described the road to the house as 'overshadowed by exuberantly rich foliage' and leading to an entrance park with the most exotic collection of animals: 'Alpacos [sic], Gazelles, Indian buffaloes, Cape sheep, Georgian axis and other deer; antelopes, Cashmere goats, Marmoset monkeys and kangaroos'. A domed aviary with tropical plants and palm trees within was said to provide 'a sumptuous place of confinement' for rare foreign birds: 'emeus [sic] from New Holland, seven feet high; pelicans of the wilderness, parrots, gold and silver pheasants, Peruvian cockatoos, paroquets, demoiselle birds, crown birds from Brazil, macaws, American, French and English partridges, a stork of Egypt, Virginian and cardinal nightingales, and fire birds from Africa'.[19] Peacocks strutted uncaged about the lawns and flaunted their fans.

The Balcombes had 30 rooms of the 'cottage' to explore, starting with the main suite, 'one hundred feet in length, with two elegantly painted glass bay windows, which give light to the splendid apartments'. There were chandeliers, lamps, paintings, marble busts and bronzes. A dazzling collection was laid out on 70 tables, a glorious clutter of Parisian and Geneva clocks, Dresden china, oriental vases, carved ivory, Florentine boxes, 'everything necessary to ease and enjoyment'. The guidebook rhapsodised: 'It is impossible not to be struck with the contemplation of the wealth that has been expended and the taste which has been displayed.' The Balcombes would have been struck by that too. They would have seen 'an elegant basin ewer of opal, which cost 300 guineas, manufactured at Dresden for the Empress Catherine of Russia', and then the item which may well have brought them to the attention of the owner, 'an exquisite specimen of carved ivory, late the property of Josephine Buonaparte, which occupied a place in the chapel at the Palace of St Cloud'.[20]

Betsy, or another of the family, might have exclaimed about this and soon their particular connection with Bonaparte would have come to the attention of Fish. Or else, as an aesthete, a cultured man with an obvious interest in history, he heard about their Bonaparte connection, their friendship with Sir Thomas Tyrwhitt, and even their rumoured royal bloodline, and sought them out himself. In some such way the friendship with Betsy must have begun. But it continued. She and her family and Tyrwhitt would have been guests at the 'splendid dinner' he occasionally hosted for 'the nobility and gentry of Sidmouth and its vicinity'.[21]

Betsy must have seen Fish on many occasions, for in an 1834 *Guide to Illustrations and Views of Knowle Cottage* is this passage, amusing in its bizarre historical inaccuracy: 'On one of the tables there is a magnificent piece of topaz, which once belonged to Bonaparte; it was given by him to Miss Balcombe, the daughter of the Governor who preceded Sir Hudson Lowe, at St Helena, and presented by her to Mr. Fish, when on a visit to him. The exiled Emperor was living at the Governor's house whilst Longwood was in a state of preparation, and the young lady having the honor of beating him at a game of chess, he rewarded her with this splendid specimen in return.'[22]

For Betsy to present Fish with a 'magnificent topaz' that Napoleon had given her was more than generous. News of her former friend's distressing death had only recently reached her, so to part with the gem was a precious gift. But perhaps she could already see herself as mistress of The Knowle, with its peacocks, collections of treasures, luxuriant gardens and vistas to the sea. To become Mrs Thomas Fish would raise her in rank to a level to which she felt entitled, and it would solve all her parents' financial problems. Perhaps her gift of the topaz was not a sprat to catch a mackerel, but a mackerel to catch a Golden Fish. If so, this Fish was one that got away. The relationship did not progress. Betsy must have felt hurt and rejected, and vulnerable to the next man who might more readily seem to appreciate her charms.

It may not have been personal. The thought would never have occurred to her that Thomas Leversidge Fish Esquire was perhaps not inclined towards the female sex, except for platonic friendship. His aesthetic sensibilities and contentment to live alone among his vast collections, adding to them each year, refining and redesigning his gardens, acquiring new exotic animals and birds for his menagerie, might suggest this.[23]

He continued to open his house for viewings for the next 40 years. He never married. An obituary after his death in 1861 remarked on his solitary life and noted that his wealth had come from owning 400 public houses or 'pubs'.[24]

CHAPTER 27

MARRY IN HASTE . . .

The official coronation of George IV, postponed from the previous year because of the Queen's trial, took place on 19 July 1821 with as much pomp and fanfare as his courtiers, including Sir Thomas, could contrive. After the King's disastrous attempt to divorce his wife, he hoped to erase the embarrassment and improve his public image, as historian Steven Parissien has observed, 'by casting himself as the embodiment and inspiration of a newly-confident and militarily-successful nation'. He had always had a reluctant admiration for and sense of rivalry with his old foe Bonaparte, 'and intended to outshine Napoleon's imperial coronation of 1804'.[1] A tailor was even sent to Paris to measure the former emperor's robes, to ensure that George's were longer and more splendid.

On the great day, Westminster Abbey was decked out with all the trappings of Tudor pageantry. But the grandeur of the occasion was somewhat marred by Queen Caroline's attempt to gatecrash it. (Caroline actually had a ticket of entry, 'sent to her by the Duke of Wellington, who seems to have been struck with sympathy for her predicament'.[2]) A public riot had been anticipated if she was not crowned as well, so guards had been placed at each door of the Abbey to bar her entrance. However, it was said that 'the sight of her on foot, jostled by the rabble, frantically but vainly rushing from door to door, evoked nothing but catcalls from the spectators'.[3] Blocked at every entrance, by the Lord High Chamberlain's orders, she left in her carriage, admitting defeat. Queen Caroline was said to be 'destroyed' by her public humiliation. Her former counsel at her trial, Henry Brougham, thought she had 'lost incalculably' for 'getting out of her carriage and tramping about'.[4] Her health deteriorated from that time.

After the five-hour ceremony, the 312 invited guests proceeded to Westminster Hall for a sumptuous banquet. Continuing the Tudor theme, trumpets announced a young man on horseback in Elizabethan armour. He rode his horse between the tables, but unfortunately the horse 'defecated dramatically'.[5] The Duke of Wellington was naturally more stylish; his friend Mrs Arbuthnot noted how he 'performed to perfection his duty as High Constable, riding a white Arabian horse up to the King's table and backing out again. Lord Anglesey said he was "the only man in England who can back his horse down Westminster Hall".'[6]

The King had been crowned at last, with enormous pageantry and expense, never to be attempted by succeeding monarchs. After the banquet, even the gold plate and silver cutlery were plundered by drunken guests.

Since the brutal Battle of the Boyne of William of Orange in 1690, no British monarch had dared visit his dominion of Ireland. But George IV had always professed himself to be 'Irish at heart' and wished to attempt a conciliation of the fractious religious and political differences. On 6 August, just over a fortnight after the coronation, he boarded the royal yacht at Portsmouth for his state visit to Ireland.[7]

Given that the King was a covert admirer of Napoleon, it was a strange coincidence that his yacht passed the storeship *Camel*, bringing Bonaparte's closest companions to England after their long sojourn on St Helena. *John Bull* magazine reported: 'When the Royal yacht passed through Spithead, immediately on coming abreast of the *Camel* store-ship (on board of which were the suite of the late Ex-Emperor Napoleon) His Majesty, with the usual urbanity that ever marks his noble character, condescendingly sent Sir William Keppel, and others of his suite, on board, to inquire after the health of Madame Bertrand and her family, as also the health of others, the attendants of Napoleon. They fully appreciated the high honor done them.'[8]

The royal yacht put in at Holyhead in north Wales, where a messenger brought the King news of the Queen's sudden death. Caroline had not fulfilled her threat to 'live some years to plague him' and George did not pretend dismay. But he took the advice of the Home Secretary and interrupted his journey, staying a few days at Lord Anglesey's house as a token of bereavement. He wrote to Sir William Knighton—with whom he had become confidential, still cool with Tyrwhitt over the issue of the Queen's trial—that 'the Hand of God had bestowed a blessing' upon him.[9]

Napoleon's former companions were obliged to disembark at the naval base at Portsmouth, but were greeted by onlookers with enthusiasm and interest. According to Marchand, 'the population was curious to see men who had remained faithful in misfortune'. The customs officials were respectful in examining Napoleon's relics, his 'silver, legacies and uniforms'.[10]

The Bertrands and Montholon went to London, taking rooms in Brunet's Hotel, Leicester Square. They were overwhelmed by visitors wishing to show their support and learn of Napoleon's last days. No doubt the Balcombes were anxious to see their old friends, but travel was expensive, they were financially distressed, and they must have feared official ire. There would have been little time anyway, for within the fortnight the French were provided with passports by their embassy in London and on 16 August sailed for their homeland at last.

Three weeks earlier, on 25 July, Sir Hudson Lowe and his suite had left St Helena on the *Dunira*. Lowe took with him a great deal of furniture, including many pieces from Longwood 'bought for a derisory sum', and a vast hoard of documents. He wrote to Henry Goulburn before sailing, requesting special treatment by customs on his arrival, to avoid his boxes 'being broken open & examined'.[11]

On 14 November, Lowe had the gratification of being presented to King George IV. As he bent low to kiss His Majesty's hand, 'the King took hold of his and shook it heartily, saying, "I congratulate you most sincerely upon your return, after a trial the most arduous and exemplary that perhaps any man ever had. I have felt for your situation."'[12]

'But evil days were now before him,' according to Lowe's apologist, William Forsyth. 'The partisans of Bonaparte could not forgive the man who had had the guardianship of his person, and for six long years discharged the duties of his trust with such firmness and fidelity. The floodgates of abuse were opened against him, and he had to endure insinuations and attacks the most painful to an honourable mind.'[13] Lowe was having a bad time of it. He also had difficulty obtaining the remuneration he considered owing from the East India Company. He complained to Bathurst that 'no Pay or Allowance whatsoever was granted to me by the East India Company, until the day of my landing, though my Commission as their Governor & Commander in Chief had been signed & delivered *Seven Months* preceding'.[14]

Bathurst no doubt took solace from the thought that Lowe's regular reams of correspondence were coming to an end with his governorship (but if so, he would find himself mistaken). The Secretary of State had many other pressing colonial concerns. Securing Upper and Lower Canada was an enormous worry, and so was the expense occurring in New South Wales. In that colony, John Thomas Bigge, the Trinidad chief justice he had commissioned, was concluding his exhaustive enquiry into 'all the laws, regulations and usage of the settlements'. Bathurst had already appointed Sir Thomas Brisbane, another Scottish military man, as the new governor of New South Wales, to succeed Lachlan Macquarie, whose expenditure on public buildings seemed to be out of control.

It was at the end of 1821 that Betsy Balcombe made the acquaintance of the dashing former Indian army officer Edward Abell, whom she had almost certainly met, albeit briefly, four years earlier when his ship had called at St Helena on its homeward voyage from Madras in October 1817. No record survives as to how they encountered each other in Devon, but it is not difficult to imagine a scenario, as Abell's family home was in the village of Alphington, just over eight miles from Chudleigh. At the time, Edward was actually living in St Gregory's parish in London, but must have come home to visit his ageing parents. He may have met Betsy at one of Sir Thomas Tyrwhitt's celebrations for the Plymouth and Dartmoor Railroad or through mutual friends.

Dame Mabel Brookes wrote that Edward Abell was 'a relative of the Nevill family, and reputed to be an extremely handsome man-about-town', and this she had 'learned from the late Lord William Nevill'.[15] The Nevills, the Earls of Abergavenny, were members of the aristocracy in an unbroken line back to early medieval times, with their family seat at Eridge Castle in Kent. Tyrwhitt would have known the 2nd Earl through Parliament.[16]

Edward Abell was some eleven years older than Betsy, probably born in 1791.[17] Other than the reputed connection with the Nevills, he came from a modest and respectable family settled at Alphington. His father, Francis Abell, was a tanner who had done well and expanded his business, enabling him to give his sons a good education and for himself to retire and add the gentlemanly 'Esquire' to his name. His first wife, mother of three children, had died; his second wife died without issue; and Edward was the youngest of three surviving sons by the third wife, Mary Stock.[18]

Edward's eldest full brother, William, owned a sugar plantation in Jamaica, worked by slaves, and had married an English girl the previous year. (He had sent a young mixed-race girl 'reputed' to be his daughter to be raised by his elderly parents at Alphington.) The other brother, Charles, an officer in His Majesty's 83rd Regiment of Foot, was stationed in Ceylon and leased a tea plantation in Colombo.[19] Edward himself was more footloose, but had profited in India from his proficiency at gambling and from various other exploits. He was adventurous, dangerous, unreliable and alert for his own advantage. He was exactly the sort of man Betsy should have avoided—but just the sort whom Napoleon would have predicted was likely to attract her. The appearance of a stylish cad is almost mandatory in any story about the Regency or Georgian era, and Betsy Balcombe had found hers.

In 1810, when Edward Abell would have been aged nineteen, he sought to join the service of the East India Company as a cadet. The application papers show that he was nominated by an East India Company director, Robert Thornton, and was recommended by his half-brother Frank Abell of Colchester, his father's eldest son by his first wife.[20] Edward wrote in a firm hand that his education was 'principally at Exeter, Classical and Mathematical', and that the profession of his father was 'A private gentleman'. He was accepted for the coveted position of cadet in the military service of the Company, and on 2 March 1811 sailed for Madras on the *Princess Amelia*, along with other cadets and the usual collection of soldiers, civil servants and their wives. They went in convoy as protection against French attacks. On the *Marchioness of Exeter*, sailing in tandem with them, was the Reverend Richard Boys, bound for St Helena, so the whole convoy must have called at the island. Young Abell may even have glimpsed a tomboyish child called Betsy scrambling about the rocks.

The armies of the three 'presidencies' of the East India Company (Madras, Calcutta and Bombay) had been formed for no other reason than to protect the Company's trade interests. India was divided into a number of kingdoms or states ruled by local princes or warlords. Some had already become vassals of the Company and received privileges in return, but if other rulers presumed to resist the foreigners taking riches from their state, the Company's military units attacked them. Some wars continued for years with much bloodshed on both sides.

At Fort St George, the Madras headquarters, Abell was given the junior rank of ensign and appointed to the 7th Regiment of the Madras Native Infantry.[21] As was standard, all the soldiers were Indian, commanded by Indian officers but with British officers above them in the hierarchy. Abell would have been attached to a lieutenant or captain to learn how to wage war and gain territory and riches for the East India Company and win some plunder for himself.

He was soon thrown into battle, in skirmishes against the Pindaris from central India, among the forces of the powerful Hindu Maratha Empire, but their artillery was outdated and the British had been victorious in the previous war against them. Abell was soon hardened by the deaths of enemy warriors and his own comrades, and inured to the squabbling over spoils that followed a battle. Looting after a victory was an approved Company activity—an incentive for the soldiers, a larger benefit for the officers—but the Company was widely hated for the practice.

Between campaigns, Abell learned he could accumulate further wealth through trading on the side and through gambling. Nor would it have taken him long to discover, as did most officers, that many Indian women were beautiful and sensuous, and they could be taken as mistresses, or sometimes as wives. His particular cronies, especially for card nights, gambling with other officers, were James Patterson, a military surgeon in the Company's service, and an older officer, Colonel Francis Torrens, who had been in India for over forty years and had surrendered to its available vices; he had no doubt risen in rank to colonel through the assistance of his distinguished younger brother, Major-General Henry Torrens, who between 1812 and 1814 was aide-de-camp to the Prince Regent.[22] However, it is remarkable that the junior officer Edward Abell was hobnobbing at this level and suggests that he had connections and social skills.

The final, decisive conflict with the Marathas—giving the East India Company control of most of the subcontinent—did not take place until the Third Anglo-Maratha War of 1817–18. But long before that, in the autumn of 1814, Abell and the 1st Battalion of the 7th Native Infantry, along with the 1st Battalion of the 6th, had joined other Company forces to undertake a massive invasion of Nepal.

There was no provocation for the invasion, only the pretext that British irregular forces which had already entered the country needed the support of the Company army. But this was a ploy. In the ruthless view of the East India Company, its commerce had to be protected at all costs. The Gurkhas of Nepal (or 'Nypaul' as the British then spelled it) had encroached on the Company's own potential trade routes to China and Tibet through the northern provinces.

Rather than an initial explicit invasion with its own army, the Company gave tacit permission to two irregular fighting forces to enter Nepal. The first were the warriors of William Fraser, a wild Scot from Inverness, whose official position was with the Company army, as political agent to Major-General Sir Rollo Gillespie. But Fraser was a law unto himself; he had been in India since 1802 as assistant to the Resident in Delhi, spoke several languages and had built up his own band of warriors for mercenary expeditions. His men were joined by an irregular army, called Skinner's Horse, led by Fraser's comrade-in-arms James Skinner, son of a Scottish officer and a Rajput princess, to lead the foray against the Gurkhas. Because of his Indian heritage, Skinner had been excluded from becoming an officer of the Company army and had for years fought instead with its enemy, the Marathas. Skinner had raised his own private cavalry, a distinctive band with their yellow tunics, black shields and scarlet turbans.[23]

But the flamboyant William Fraser had arrived in India twelve years earlier for a particular reason. Like his four brothers, who followed him to the subcontinent, his intention was to restore the Fraser family fortune. The Frasers, like most late-eighteenth-century landowners in the Scottish highlands, had suffered from the economic depression that continued for decades after the 1746 Battle of Culloden. Few tenants could afford to pay rents and the Frasers were hard pressed to pay workers to tend their land and stock. The boys' father, Edward Satchwell Fraser, had bought into a cotton plantation in Guyana, along with a neighbour, seeing it as an investment for his sons. But with cheap imported cotton from India, prices collapsed, and Edward Fraser needed to mortgage the family estate against it. They were badly in debt, their estate at risk.

But between William's good intentions and the reality a shadow had fallen: the seductive lure of India. An impressive bearded character, he pruned his moustaches like a Rajput prince and acquired a 'harem of Indian wives' by whom he fathered several children. While he held various administrative positions with the East India Company, he had soon, unlike his British colleagues, learned to read ancient Sanskrit texts and developed a love of Persian poetry. However, his main passions were for hunting, riding and fighting with his own private band of warriors. (He was said to have killed some eighty tigers, hunting them on foot, and a number of lions, which helps explain the absence of lions in India today.)[24] According to the author William Dalrymple, fascinated by this man to whom he had a family connection, Fraser remains 'a strange enigmatic figure—misanthropic, antisocial and difficult to fathom—part severe Highland warrior, part Brahminized philosopher, part Conradian madman'.[25]

The East India Company found unofficial and irregular fighting forces such as Fraser's and Skinner's most useful. As Gillespie's political agent, Fraser's challenging brief was to recruit sturdy Nepalese Gurkhas to harass the supply lines of their own people. That he succeeded in recruiting a large number is testament to his language skills and powers of persuasion.[26] The intrepid Fraser became legendary among the Company troops and somehow, at this time, Edward Abell met him.

Abell was a minor player in the war as a second lieutenant in the 1st Battalion of the 7th Native Infantry, part of Gillespie's forces.

One of four British columns, their task was to strike mid-west Nepal at Dehra Dun, attempting to divide the kingdom. In one of the first battles of the Anglo-Nepalese War, some 3000 British troops laid siege to Kalanga Fort. Gillespie led a rash assault against the strongly fortified position while his men held back; he was killed, along with nine officers and 62 men, followed in the second assault by twenty officers and 649 men.[27] The 600 Nepalese within the garrison held out for over a month. The war ended with the Treaty of Sugauli on 4 March 1816. A British colonial administrator, Sir Charles Metcalfe, remarked of the conflict: 'In this war, dreadful to say, we have had numbers on our side, and skill and bravery on the side of the enemy.'[28] As part of the treaty, two Gurkha regiments were formed and taken into the permanent British army service.[29]

Towards the end of the war, William Fraser's elder brother, James Baillie Fraser, arrived in Nepal. The two brothers took off together, officially to report on conditions in the Himalayan states, exhilarated to be together on the arduous trek. William needed to return to Delhi, but James continued on, riding and walking to the sources of the Jumna and Ganges rivers, sketching the dramatic landscape he passed through, for 'the Devil of Drawing' had taken hold of him. Later, in Scotland, he reworked the sketches into a series of superb aquatints, 'Views of the Himalas', and published a book about his travels.[30]

On 23 December 1816, Abell unexpectedly resigned from the Company army, still at the rank of second lieutenant. This was an unusual decision for an officer in good standing, for it meant he would have to finance his own accommodation and ship's passage back to England, an expense of hundreds of pounds. It usually only occurred when an officer had chosen to become a merchant or found another activity profitable enough, or attractions sufficient, to make worthwhile his staying on independently. From December 1816 to May 1817, Abell's activities are unaccounted for. One can only speculate that he may have taken up private trading or professional gambling, or that he had an Indian wife or mistress—or several. It is also not impossible that his resignation from the East India Company meant that he had become an officer in Fraser and Skinner's now merged private army based at Delhi. If so, his timing was poor, with the Nepal war just having ended, but he may have engaged in some of their mercenary expeditions.

But some event changed his mind about staying on, for Abell departed from India as a private gentleman in May 1817, his ship the *Woodford* calling at St Helena on the way home.[31] However, India drew him back; there must have been some great attraction. By late 1818 he was resident again in Madras, having been appointed civil agent for the British colony of Ceylon to the Madras Presidency, an apparently honorary position obtained with the help of his brother Charles in Colombo. The position was endorsed by Colonial Under-Secretary Henry Goulburn and the East India Company, although his travel and accommodation were at his own expense and the Company stipulated: 'it being understood that Mr Abell will quit Madras whenever he shall cease to hold the said office'.[32] The work could not have been onerous as he was listed in the Madras Year Book for the next two years as a British resident, with 'Occupation: None'.[33]

On 5 August 1820, his gambling friend Francis Torrens died in Madras at the age of 72, perhaps of cholera, which was rife. He had enjoyed an unbroken residence in India of 51 years and had only recently been promoted (surely on retirement) to the rank of lieutenant-general in the 18th Native Infantry.[34]

That particular misfortune was followed a year later by the abrupt removal of another of Abell's regular companions. In October 1821, the military surgeon James Patterson was charged with the crime of forgery. He was tried in Madras before two judges and a jury and found guilty. Using chemicals, he had expunged the signature of a deceased officer and substituted his own on a promissory note for a considerable sum. The sentencing judge particularly rebuked the 'bad example and influence' of Patterson's crime, 'committed by a British subject and by a person of your understanding, education and profession ... upon the low and uninformed classes of the Natives'. It was an additional aggravation 'that this crime was committed by some chemical process by a person in the medical line, whose profession furnishes (to one viciously inclined) such easy modes and materials for doing mischief'. He said that Patterson was fortunate, because if found guilty of the crime of forgery in the United Kingdom, he would have forfeited his life. 'The sentence of the Court is that, you

James Patterson, for the crime aforesaid, be transported to New South Wales during the term of fourteen years.'[35]

Patterson delayed his departure by brazenly launching his own legal action, claiming that the late Lieutenant-General Francis Torrens had died owing him a large sum of money. As the executors of his will, Torrens's younger brothers were greatly perturbed. They suspected that their brother's promissory note to Patterson had also been forged. Colonel Robert Torrens wrote a 53-page letter from India to General Sir Henry Torrens, by then adjutant-general to the British Forces at the Horse Guards in London (the army equivalent of the Admiralty), explaining the circumstances as he understood them: 'You may depend upon it he will lose no opportunity of tormenting the expectations of this Estate by keeping the business in a state of agitation if it is *merely to make believe his innocence*. He is now about 45 years of age, so that if he is not pardoned, for which God forbid, he will be at the expiration of his term of 14 years, sixty. I trust however before that age he may have made his peace and gone to heaven . . . This very day however I believe he embarks for Calcutta on his way to Botany Bay, and I hope we have now done with this Chemical Hero!'[36]

It was after these events that Edward Abell came home to England and to Devon to visit his parents. There he met the pretty Betsy Balcombe.

The romance between Betsy and Abell developed rapidly, no doubt far too rapidly for the senior Balcombes to feel comfortable. Balcombe may have been taken in at first by Abell's apparent charm and reputed connection with the Nevills; but he himself had spent much time in India as a youth, both at Calcutta and Madras, and had observed the wild lifestyles of some of the East India Company army officers—gambling, hookah, *nautch* girls and prostitutes. There must have been something in Abell's manner that made Balcombe begin to think he was of that kind. He and his wife Jane were bound to take the view that this adventurer, with no distinction and an unreliable access to money, was not the sort of husband they had imagined for their beautiful younger daughter. After all, Betsy had been admired by every officer on St Helena, she could have wed Major Oliver Fehrzen, a military hero, and for years she had been the favourite of Napoleon

Bonaparte, former ruler of half the world! It is probable that they tried to talk her out of continuing to see Abell; they may even have forbidden the couple to continue to meet.

Then came the news: Betsy was expecting a child.

No record survives of how her parents reacted, but much as they may have disliked Abell, everything had now changed. They would have determined that he had to wed their daughter, otherwise her life was ruined. She would never be able to show her face in society again. Did Balcombe confront Abell—as right-thinking fathers did in Jane Austen's novels—and tell him that unless he did the honourable thing, he would expose him for the scoundrel that he was?

Probably there was no argument. At the time, young men in society who lacked inheritances were willing to go to extremes to secure their position. Such a man would marry a very plain or much older woman as long as she had wealth or useful connections; some would actively seek out such women, often planning to leave them soon after the wedding, knowing that the law entitled them to take the wife's assets. (The parliamentarian Henry Fox (later an earlier Lord Holland), in debating Lord Hardwicke's 1753 Marriage Bill had agreed that 'something needed to be done to halt the fraudulent seduction of heirs and heiresses'. His hope was that the Marriage Act would stop this, but even after it was passed, the practice continued.[37])

It would have been a bonus for Abell that Betsy was attractive. There are indications that he was a more than willing bridegroom, that he had actively courted her, and may have aimed to get her pregnant, having heard stories that her father was the natural son of George IV—stories that may have come from Balcombe's own bragging when in his cups. Abell must have had expectations of future riches and influence from marriage to the granddaughter of the King of England. He would have observed what seemed clear evidence of a connection to the palace in the family's protection by Sir Thomas Tyrwhitt, known to be close to the King.

Once the news of Betsy's situation was confided to Sir Thomas, he would have made his own enquiries concerning Abell's background, and naturally turned to General Sir Henry Torrens, whom he knew well from the latter's period as aide-de-camp to the Prince Regent. He must have been disturbed by what he heard, and would have felt no confidence that this footloose former officer without prospects could be a reliable husband. What concerned him even more was that Balcombe, at the age of 44, had a family to support and no foreseeable future. He would do what he could for the family that he loved.

On 29 March 1822, Sir Thomas paid a surprise visit to Sir Hudson Lowe at his lodgings at 1 Edgware Road. Lowe had always had respect for the diminutive courtier, who clearly still had influence with George IV. He would have made him welcome. Sir Thomas told him that he was distressed to see William Balcombe and his family living in near-penury; it was making Mrs Balcombe ill with anxiety. He could not help them financially himself, having had to underwrite the float for the Plymouth and Dartmoor Railroad when too few subscribers were found. He believed it might be a year or so before any financial return could be expected. However, he had reason to believe that Lord Bathurst was willing to offer Balcombe a position in the colonies, but not if that offended Sir Hudson himself, who had been such a loyal servant of the government. These comments flattered Lowe, but he remained truculent. He said he did not see how he could assist Balcombe to any position of responsibility when he had shown no remorse, nor willingness to change his ways.

Sir Thomas then asked Balcombe to come up to London. Once they were together, this experienced strategist explained the politics of the situation to him: William should realise that Lowe's hatred of O'Meara had come to embrace him as well. He saw them as part of a conspiracy against him, even though William had tried to disassociate himself. Tyrwhitt would have indicated that he believed it almost certain that Bathurst did not particularly care for Lowe—not least because of his time-wasting correspondence—but the governor had after all been a loyal public servant in following Bathurst's instructions, even if he had interpreted them rather too rigorously. Therefore his lordship would not permit Balcombe to return to St Helena nor assist him to any government or colonial position if that offended Lowe. So William should realise that the barrier to his future was Sir Hudson Lowe. A profound apology was necessary.

On 4 April, Balcombe posted a letter from the London office of his wife's brother-in-law Thomas Hornsby. He must have gritted his teeth writing every word of it:

Sir

Having just learned from Sir Thomas Tyrwhitt that you are pleased to lay aside all feeling of displeasure which my conduct towards you had so justly excited, I take the liberty of returning to you my sincere and grateful acknowledgement and to assure you that no person can more deeply feel Penitent for past indiscretions than myself.

I beg also to express to you my sincere thanks for your extreme kindness in your intention, in pity towards my family, of furthering my hopes of some Provision from the Colonial Office.

I have the honour to remain, Sir

Your faithful and obedient servant,

(Signed) W. Balcombe[38]

It must have given Lowe tremendous satisfaction to enclose Balcombe's letter with his own, dated 7 April, to Wilmot Horton, the colonial under-secretary who had replaced Goulburn:

Dear Sir,

I beg leave to acquaint you that I was visited upon Friday last by Sir Thomas Tyrwhitt, who spoke to me at some length respecting Mr Balcombe, whom with his family, he represented to be in the greatest distress on account of the loss of the offices he had held at St Helena. He told me he had grounds to believe Lord Bathurst was not indisposed to some act of consideration towards him, if it was understood no objections prevailed on my part. I acquainted Sir Thomas Tyrwhitt that although Mr. Balcombe's conduct had been in the highest degree improper, both as regarding the public services and his personal relations with me, yet I had always considered him more as the Dupe & Instrument of others than as having acted originally from his own impulses, and knowing the distress he had brought upon his family, I would certainly not think on *their* account of opposing anything that might be done for him.

Sir Thomas Tyrwhitt wished me to make this much known either to Lord Bathurst, or to you, which I accordingly take the present means of doing. I afterwards received a letter from Mr Balcombe which I beg leave to inclose. In reference to the concluding passage of it, I should say, nothing of any actual interference in Mr Balcombe's favour was assured by me, but simply that I would not oppose any steps Sir Thomas Tyrwhitt might take regarding him. In other respects the contrition his letter manifests will furnish the best argument in his favor.[39]

※

The wedding of Lucia Elizabeth Balcombe and Edward Abell was booked to take place not at Chudleigh but at St Martin's Church, Exminster, and not by the traditional 'thrice-called banns', which involved waiting three Sundays in a row while a notice of the intended marriage was posted on the church door, but by the swifter process of a licence, the document to be purchased from a bishop or one of his surrogates. While marriage by licence in the nineteenth century often signified that the bride was with child, that was by no means always the case; because a licence wedding was private and cost at least four guineas (a workingman's weekly wage), it became the preference of the 'patrician class'.[40] However, in the case of the wedding of Betsy and Edward there is no doubt that the bride was four or five months pregnant.

It is curious that Exminster, eight miles away, was chosen for the ceremony instead of Chudleigh, noted for its beautiful thirteenth-century church. The Marriage Act required that 'at least one party had to be resident for at least three weeks in the parish where the marriage was to be celebrated'.[41] One can only assume that Betsy's pregnancy was so obvious that the family wished to avoid gossip among neighbours and had briefly become residents of Exminster. Otherwise, as John R. Gillis notes in *For Better, For Worse*, sometimes families rented a room in the parish where the wedding would be held just long enough to fulfil the Act requirement without actually living there.[42]

Sir Thomas almost certainly gave Balcombe some further advice: that while the outcome of his apology to Lowe was awaited, it might be advisable to move with his family—including the young married couple—to France. There they would be away from prying eyes and gossip about Betsy's advanced pregnancy, and the actual birth date would not be on English church records. In addition, the living was far more economical in France. Sir Thomas, who visited the country regularly, recommended Saint-Omer, inland from Calais, where there was a large British community.

Betsy's marriage to Abell was solemnised on 28 May 1822 at Exminster. The ceremony conformed with all the requirements of the Marriage Act. The certificate stated: 'Edward Abell Esquire, Bachelor of the Parish of Saint Gregory, London, And Lucia Elizabeth Balcombe, Spinster of this Parish, Were married in this Church by Licence with Consent of Parents this twenty-eighth day of May in the Year One thousand eight hundred and twenty two By me H. J. Burlton.' The other signatures followed: 'This marriage was solemnized between us—Edward Abell, Lucia Elizabeth Balcombe, In the presence of Wm Balcombe, Thos Tyrwhitt, Francis Stanfell RN, Jane Sophia Turner, Henry Brown.'[43] Sir Thomas Tyrwhitt had come to be a witness at the wedding, supporting the family as always, and also Captain Stanfell, their old friend from St Helena.

It was clearly a desire to obscure the circumstances of the marriage that caused Dame Mabel Brookes to inform enquiring historians that it had taken place exactly one year earlier, 28 May 1821; as she was a Balcombe descendant, this date has been followed in most subsequent biographical listings and was accepted until pesky biographers began digging.[44] The marriage certificate exists and the wedding was noted in the *Trewman's Exeter Flying Post or Plymouth and Cornish Advertiser* of 29 May 1822: 'Yesterday at Exminster, by the Rev. H.J. Burlton, Edward Abell Esq, to Lucia Elizabeth, daughter of W. Balcombe, Esq, of this place.'

Betsy had done just what Napoleon had forecast on the last day they met at St Helena. Afterwards, her father had informed Lowe of his prediction, which was immediately reported to Bathurst: Napoleon 'told her she would be married immediately on her arrival in England & then railed her on her immediate Pregnancy'.[45]

CHAPTER 28

'*LA PETITE ANGLETERRE*'

I was in a large house in the Scottish highlands. It was an unlikely place for me to be researching the Balcombes' time in France—so far a frustratingly blank canvas—but that was the reason I was there.

Next door to my room was a library, with floor-to-ceiling books on mahogany shelving, some in Persian, others in Urdu, books of nineteenth-century travel, some of them written by former occupants of the house. An old leopard-skin was slung over a chair, an Oriental rug on the floor, trophies of the East. In other parts of the house old prints of India and the Himalayas graced the walls, cheerful fires warmed the rooms.

I was in the home of the five Fraser brothers who had gone to India to save the family estate—and in the end had succeeded. The eldest son, James Baillie Fraser, a Persian scholar, writer and talented artist, had returned home, riding or walking all the way overland through India, Afghanistan, Persia and the Ottoman Levant. He later added a Palladian portico to the house in expectation of the visit of a Persian prince who never turned up.

The property was saved, but at enormous human cost, heartbreaking for the parents, Edward Satchwell Fraser and his wife Jane. Four of their sons never came back; three of them succumbed to the fevers and infections of India, which, in an era before modern vaccines, killed tens of thousands of the British (and hundreds of thousands of Indians).[1] William, the most famous, swashbuckling brother, spent 33 adventurous years in India and has been written about extensively by William Dalrymple, who described his 1835 murder in Delhi, after offending 'a raffish Mughal nobleman'.[2]

The first of the Fraser boys to die was Edward, who had gone to India in 1813 at the age of 27 with his younger brother Alexander (Aleck). Soon after his arrival he became so ill that Aleck believed he could not survive unless taken to a more temperate climate. The two brothers joined a vessel bound for St Helena. Aleck was able to rent a cottage from a certain William Balcombe, whom he described as 'an open-hearted liberal Englishman'.[3] Aleck nursed his brother at the cottage, with the Balcombes kindly offering whatever assistance they could, until Edward passed away two months later.

Malcolm Fraser, my host, is a direct descendant of Edward Satchwell and Jane Fraser. Malcolm's wife Kathy is completing a book about those five sons and the parents who prayed and waited for their return. Her source material is a remarkable collection of family letters and the mother's diary, hidden in an old trunk in the cellar with a label noting it contained papers 'of great interest'; they were first researched in 1979.

Edward Satchwell Fraser was highland gentry, a laird, but until his sons returned from India with the riches they hoped were possible, he and Jane were in financial difficulties. It had been a disastrous decision to buy into the cotton plantation in Guyana and then mortgage the family estate against it. With their only surviving daughter, Jane Anne, having made a good marriage to a cousin, the big house felt empty. Mr Fraser (as his wife always called him, even in her private diary) made the decision at the age of 70 that the most practical thing to do was to rent it out—almost certainly to wealthy English people who would play at being lairds—and he and his wife Jane would make a temporary move to Saint-Omer in France. Her sister Catherine was already there, married to Gregoire, a Frenchman, and she had convinced them that living costs were much cheaper.

Since 1593 there had been a particular connection across the Channel with Saint-Omer. After the Protestant Reformation, many

British Roman-Catholic families, finding their sons barred from a Catholic education at home, sent them across the Channel as boarders to St Omer College, founded by English Jesuits. In 1762 the school moved to Bruges, and later to Liège. But with the building of the Catholic college of Stonyhurst in Lancashire in 1794, the need for the annual migration of British Catholic boys ceased.

After the Napoleonic Wars, another large British community formed at Saint-Omer, so much so that in local parlance the town became La Petite Angleterre (Little England). It began with the army of occupation: many British soldiers, finding life in northern France pleasant and economical during their posting, returned with their families after demobilisation. Jane Fraser's sister had assured her that there were also a number of British gentlefolk living in the town, a congenial social group.[4]

William Balcombe delayed the planned move to France, in the hope that the outcome of his apology to Lowe might result in Bathurst making an early decision to offer him a colonial posting. He knew that Sir Thomas was working for him behind the scenes. It is likely that Betsy, in advanced pregnancy, had gone to live with Edward Abell at his home in St Gregory's parish, near St Paul's in London; only her close family and friends knew how short a time the couple had been married, but a decision had to be made about where she would give birth. Balcombe was bound to be unhappy about the reliability of Abell as the protector of his daughter and expected grandchild and would have been reluctant to leave the country without them.

Meanwhile, Lowe was hoping for a colonial or government position himself. On 6 June 1822, he wrote to Bathurst with the news that he had received a letter from His Royal Highness the Duke of York, 'acquainting me His Majesty has been graciously pleased to appoint me to the command of the 93rd Regiment'. He said that he was flattered by His Majesty's favour. But the appointment was a long way short of a governorship.[5]

That same month, Dr Barry O'Meara launched his massive two-volume work, *Napoleon in Exile or A Voice from St Helena*, not on an unsuspecting world but on a fully expectant one. There had been four years of previews in newspapers around the country of the correspondence between O'Meara and Lowe. The public had not lost its appetite for more. The Irish doctor was still seen as something of a hero, and Napoleon's death had confirmed his forecasts about his critical state of health.

Napoleon in Exile was composed from the detailed notes O'Meara had taken almost every night at St Helena, plus a great deal of imagination and personal vitriol. It was an instant bestseller. The publishers rushed out a second edition, then a third.[6] Readers, whether on the side of O'Meara or infuriated by him, devoured his accounts of his conversations with Napoleon, his quarrels with Lowe, and the governor's relentless persecution of his prisoner. Gilbert Martineau, former honorary French consul at St Helena (father of the present consul), has observed: 'Napoleon emerged from the book ennobled, even purified by his end, but the gaoler of St Helena, Sir Hudson Lowe, was branded for ever as infamous by one of his own staff, and his portrait hung in the rogues' gallery of history.'[7] The book enraged Lowe, who engaged a prominent lawyer and planned a defamation suit.

O'Meara had become rich, with a fourth edition of his book soon printed to meet the demand. It was banned in France, but young Emmanuel de Las Cases obtained a copy. Reading it reignited his fury at the mistreatment of his father and he planned revenge. He would go to London and challenge Lowe to a duel. But in order to find him he had to contact O'Meara.

Before he did so, the Balcombe family, along with Edward and Betsy, crossed the Channel to France in the regular packet boat. At Calais their luggage was cleared by customs and they took a coach for the 22-mile journey to Saint-Omer, passing through flat fertile pastureland, the road lined with elms on either side. When they were still a long distance away they sighted the towers of the town's great medieval cathedral and the Gothic Abbaye Saint-Bertin.[8]

I arrived at Saint-Omer by train from Paris with a change at Lille. In my bag I had my notes from the collection of Fraser papers in Scotland. The station building was an imposing *belle époque* ruin, propped up with scaffolding. There was not a person in sight. I crossed the bridge of the River Aa, walked two deserted blocks to the Hôtel Le Bretagne, and left my bag in my room.

Several blocks uphill I found the spacious market square, Place Foch, with its handsome Hôtel de Ville. It seemed the whole of the town was at Sunday lunch in the buzzing restaurants. The British had left evidence of their patronage in a nineteenth-century Queen Victoria Bar-Pub and Le Dickens Brasserie.

Later, as I returned to my hotel, a dense mist swirled in from the surrounding wetlands. *Le brouillard.*

In a family portrait Jane Fraser is a pretty woman with a heart-shaped face, warm brown eyes and auburn curls under a lacy bonnet. On 28 August 1822, her husband brought startling news from the centre of town: he had briefly met a Mr Balcombe from St Helena who had come to Saint-Omer with his family with the intention to remain some time. 'How many sensations does his very name call up to me & the memory of those that are gone,' Jane wrote in her diary. The grief never left her: the loss of her sons Edward, who died in 1813 at Balcombe's cottage, and Aleck, who tried to save him, and three years later in India succumbed to fever himself.[9]

Mr Fraser said that the Balcombes had a son-in-law with them—a man called Abell 'who had known William in Nypaul'.[10] This was to Jane a remarkable coincidence: not just one connection between the Balcombe family and theirs through her sons Edward and Aleck, but also a second connection through the Balcombes' son-in-law having known William. She was most anxious to meet this Mr Abell, to hear his description of William, to learn anything at all about her second son who had set off for India twenty years earlier and who rarely wrote home. She and her husband fretted about him and wished he could find a good Scottish wife.

She immediately wrote a letter to William in Delhi: 'We have lately had a very interesting acquaintance come to St Omer in the family of a Mr Balcombe formerly of St Helena & in whose house your Beloved Brothers lived when it pleased God to spare them & received much kindness & attention. Their very name was sacred and interesting to us & yr Father waited on Mr B as soon as we heard of their arrival—he & his Lady remembered our Dear Boys with the fondest affection—indeed to know must have been to love them—they have been in England some years & have lately married their youngest Daughter (a favourite of Buonaparte as a girl on his first arrival) to an Indian [army man] of the name of "Abel" who knew you in Nypaul! Mrs B is in bad health & they seem to have changed climate on her account. Their acquaintance is extremely interesting to us & you may believe we shall endeavour to show them every attention in our Power.'[11]

Jane Fraser's letter to William was more informative than her diary. If Balcombe had said that his daughter Betsy was with their family at Saint-Omer, Jane's letter does not mention it, only that Abell was. Her diary entries are brief and circumspect. However, without my fortunate access to them, I would have no information at all about the Balcombes' time in France, nor about what was happening concerning Betsy and her husband. Jane Fraser's diary entries, as well as being concise, seem to be incredibly discreet, as if she did not trust even her journal with gossip. So I must read the entries as faint clues along a mystery trail; a code written in onion juice, which, brought to the light, reveals more than was at first apparent.

What does emerge clearly is that Betsy and Edward Abell had arrived in France *with* her parents; otherwise there would be absolutely no reason for Abell to be there without her, especially as it is probable that her parents actively disliked him. But where *was* Betsy?

The explanation could be that while the Balcombes might always have planned that Betsy and Abell would come with them to France for her to give birth there, both enabling her mother to be with her and avoiding English gossip, she may have gone into labour just at the time of their arrival. It took another seven days for Balcombe to respond to Mr Fraser's invitation to visit, despite their remarkable St Helena connection. They were being offered entrée to British society in the town but did not immediately take it up.

On the eighth day, a curious Mr Fraser called at their lodgings himself, but he found the household unprepared and the son-in-law and both daughters absent. A newborn baby in the house would have been worthy of note but was not noted. He told his wife that Mrs Balcombe had seemed 'very interesting but extremely "scatty"' (which I take to mean 'distracted').¹² That certainly seems unlike the calm, hospitable woman of St Helena who, with no prior warning, received without fuss the just-exiled former emperor of the French at whose command thousands of British soldiers had been slaughtered.

It is likely that Betsy's baby girl, Elizabeth Jane (Bessie), was delivered at a 'lying-in' hospital or convent at Saint-Omer and that her sister Jane, with whom she had always been close, was with her for much of the time. Betsy must have given birth in 1822, for the daughter was 'a little girl', not a newborn, when they sailed for Australia the following year. (Furthermore, in 1832, a friend described Bessie as being aged 'about ten'.) Betsy was unlikely to have given birth without her mother present, and this first fortnight at Saint-Omer is when Mrs Balcombe tended to be absent, either physically or else distracted, 'scatty'. Unless the baby was premature, a September birth places her conception at the end of December 1821, soon after Betsy met the 'man-about-town', and would mean she was five months pregnant at the wedding.¹³

If Jane Fraser was aware during this period of Betsy and the birth of a baby, she did not mention it. The startling thing is that she did not even note the *existence* of Betsy anywhere in her Saint-Omer diary, although she referred to her in her letter to William. But Betsy *does* appear in Jane's diary a year later, after the Frasers had left France.

Despite the charm of the little town with its medieval precinct and the beauty of the surrounding marshlands with their rich birdlife, the Balcombes' year-long sojourn in Saint-Omer was miserable, relieved only by their friendship with the Frasers.

When Jane Fraser at last met Mrs Balcombe on 7 September, she found her 'a mild & interesting woman but in very indifferent health'. She thought the elder daughter 'a good looking girl about 20' and promptly invited Jane and her brothers to come to visit in the afternoon.¹⁴ (This does suggest that she may have been giving Mrs Balcombe time with her younger daughter.) Around 8 and 9 September, Jane Fraser seemed to be minding the three Balcombe boys—William, fourteen, Thomas, twelve, and Alexander, eleven—at her house for much of the time. This could well have been the period when Betsy was still 'lying in' (recovering from the birth) and wanted the company of her mother and sister.

The two families became extremely friendly, despite the difference in age between the parents: William Balcombe was 44 in 1822 and his wife 49, whereas Edward Satchwell Fraser was 71 and Jane in her mid-sixties. The Frasers were of course predisposed to like the Balcombes from the beginning, and introduced them to their circle of friends. The days continued, when health allowed, in a series of house calls on each other and walks along the ramparts, the remaining medieval walls of the town.

Balcombe had explained his wife's need for a change of climate as the reason they had come to Saint-Omer, although the damp atmosphere and recurring fogs could hardly have been helpful for her persistent hepatitis condition. While the two couples frequently called on each other for an hour or so, there were numerous days when Jane Fraser noted in her diary 'Mrs Balcombe is unwell', and others when she observed that 'Mrs Balcombe is in a very distressed state'.[15] Jane Balcombe must have experienced great anxiety about the relationship between Betsy and Abell and about the wellbeing of her new little granddaughter, who was no longer in France. The 'son-in-law' never appears again in Mrs Fraser's Saint-Omer diary and Betsy never, so the young couple must have returned to Abell's home in London. The Balcombes' elder daughter was often mentioned (adding to the surfeit of 'Janes' in this story) and Jane Fraser became very fond of the three boys, although they must have reminded her painfully of her own lost sons.

As the Frasers waited for mail from their son James on his perilous journey overland, William Balcombe hoped for word from Lord Bathurst, or inside information from Sir Thomas Tyrwhitt concerning a colonial preferment. Sometime during their stay the Balcombes tried to get in touch with their old French friends from St Helena. General Bertrand's military rank had been restored to him and he and Fanny had retired to their estate in the Berri, making only occasional visits to Paris to stay at their splendid house in the Rue Chantereine, purchased with Napoleon's bequest. Montholon, according to Gilbert Martineau, 'went off to his chateau at Frémigny, where he lived in lavish style, making frequent excursions to the capital'.[16] Contact was clearly made with the Montholons, who sent a wedding gift for Betsy, a beautiful sewing and writing box made of tortoiseshell veneer with silver inlay and blue silk lining.[17] Given her hasty wedding in Devon, it must have been sent to Saint-Omer.

The Balcombes were dissatisfied with their lodgings, and on 13 September William, on horseback, called by the Frasers at Rue de Dunkerque to tell them that he had found a better house. Although the two younger boys were enrolled at the local *école*, Balcombe worried about his son William's education. He consulted the Frasers, who recommended an English boarding school in Boulogne. He took William to enrol there and was absent for three days while Thomas and Alexander stayed with the Frasers, as their mother continued to be ill.[18] While Balcombe was at Boulogne, he may have just missed seeing a young friend from St Helena, Emmanuel, son of Count de Las Cases. It was at about this time that 22-year-old Emmanuel boarded a packet boat for England, to confront an old enemy.

When Balcombe returned to Saint-Omer he called at the *bureau de poste*, always hoping for news of an appointment. He was surprised to find that he had a letter from Sir Hudson Lowe, seeking his support. Lowe was outraged at the huge popularity of O'Meara's book and at its portrayal of him as a vicious persecutor of a stoic prisoner and his caring physician. He was collecting evidence from former St Helena residents for his defamation case, 'to refute the calumnies contained in the book' and to win recompense for the insults to himself. (He did not mention that Bathurst had counselled against this action.[19]) There was no mistaking the obligation. Balcombe had sought a favour from Lowe and was now being asked for one in return. It concerned Bonaparte's application to free the slave Toby, as O'Meara had stated that the governor had rejected it out of spite. Balcombe replied, confirming that the final decision against Toby's purchase had been made by the sitting magistrate. His response was about as muted a show of support as was possible.[20]

In London on 22 October, Lowe received a much more direct affront resulting from O'Meara's book. Emmanuel de Las Cases had arrived in the city and booked into Dog Tavern, near the doctor's lodgings. He laid in wait outside Lowe's new address at 21 Paddington Green.

Lowe had ordered a hackney coach and, unsuspecting, was walking towards it, when the young man dashed across the street and charged into him, challenging him to a duel. Lowe staggered back, not recognising his attacker. He described what happened next in a letter sent the following day to Bathurst: 'I turned round to him to express my surprise at his behaviour, when he accosted me with a foreign accent by the following expression: "What do you mean Sir by insulting me!" or "Do you mean Sir to insult me?" "Insult you!" I replied, "Why it was you who ran up against me!" He persisted however in repeating that I had insulted him, and spoke in such a strange manner that it really struck me he must be insane, and finding it of no use to argue with him, I was getting into the carriage when he struck at me with a small whip, and then immediately drew away. Having an umbrella in my hand, and feeling myself thus provoked, I desisted from entering the carriage and followed him with the intention of giving him a blow with the end of the umbrella, when a person, apparently an Englishman who had been coming up behind him, instantly interfered and forcibly prevented me from striking him. Finding myself thus situated, and still under an impression the *rencontre* had been one of mere accident, I got into the carriage and was driving off when the young person who had first ran against me, came up with an impudent air to offer me his card, and finding I took no notice of him, he threw it into the carriage, and I threw it immediately out again, without even looking at it.'[21] According to passers-by, the youth had shouted: 'This man insulted my father!' When Lowe returned home later that day he found that the maid had picked up two cards from the road, with the inscription 'Baron E. de Las Cases, Dog Tavern, Holywell-street'. Lowe insisted that he had not recognised him: 'the young man had left St Helena, a mere boy, between five and six years before' and he 'could not conceive him to be a gentleman'.[22]

The newspapers loved the story. 'SIR HUDSON LOWE HORSEWHIPPED!' reported *The Examiner*. The episode was soon news around the country. The *Morning Chronicle* published Baron de Las Cases' own account and reported that the young Frenchman with 'great manliness' avowed 'that "the sole object of his visit to England was to compel

Sir H. Lowe to afford satisfaction for his wrongs". The Baron concludes, by remarking, "that a son who vindicates the cause of an aged, sick and honoured father, only fulfils a most sacred duty imposed upon him, and in so acting pursues the path of honour and of rectitude". And who will not agree with him?'[23]

A few days later, Lowe wrote to Bathurst from Tunbridge Wells that the young Las Cases, 'having braved the Government and Laws of this country, has fled to his own, where he has dared to make a public boast of the Insult he offered to me'. He requested 'Your Lordship's consideration and that of His Majesty's Government, as to the means of my obtaining due redress'.[24] The letter was marked 'Never sent', so Lowe had thought better of it, but a week later he posted another protest, this time about a new French translation of O'Meara's book, and asked if an injunction could not be taken out against it.[25] His Majesty's Government remained obdurately silent.

CHAPTER 29

THE CLEARING FOG

Winter was closing in at Saint-Omer. A network of waterways and marshland around the town regularly produced a fog, *le brouillard*, which usually cleared by midday; fires were lit each morning and evening. In late October, Jane Fraser made almost daily visits to assist her friend Mrs Harrison who was in much pain in advanced pregnancy. Jane sat with her for three nights and was devastated when she died on 2 November. Jane's distress continued and she could rarely sleep without laudanum. She noted in her diary that on some afternoons Miss Balcombe came and sat with her.[1]

For the last week of November and the first two weeks of December, William Balcombe appeared to absent himself from Saint-Omer, and Mrs Balcombe's brother from London stayed with her for some of the time at least.[2] Jane's diary, discreet as always, does not mention why Balcombe was away or where he was, although it is most probable that he had gone to London and in his absence Mrs Balcombe's brother had arrived as a protector for the family. It must be conjecture as to what matter caused Balcombe's absence, but it could have been trouble between Betsy and Abell, or else a meeting at the Colonial Office to discuss the possibility of a position. In either case, there was apparently no immediate outcome. Balcombe was away for almost three weeks. It cannot be proved that he came back by way of Paris, his one opportunity to make a withdrawal at Lafitte's Bank—the final gift to him from Napoleon—but, without bank records, it cannot be disproved either.

He returned to Saint-Omer on 12 December to find that his wife was critically ill. Jane Fraser was very concerned for her. Mrs Balcombe was to remain unwell right up until the beginning of January 1823, a period of almost three weeks. Again it sounds like a bout of depression, as if whatever matter had caused her husband's absence had impacted badly on her.

Meanwhile, Edward Satchwell Fraser had found an absorbing distraction. He had been lent O'Meara's *Napoleon in Exile* and could not wait to get into it. He devoured the first volume of the enormous work—with its numerous mentions of the Balcombes—in three afternoons, then started on the second.

And so the two families endured a hard winter at Saint-Omer, while Mrs Balcombe remained unwell, and nothing at all was mentioned in Jane Fraser's diary or her correspondence about Betsy and her husband. William junior came home on vacation from school in Boulogne, and the boys were around at the Frasers' for much of the time; Balcombe joined them there for celebrations on New Year's Eve. They were all glad to see the end of 1822. 'The last morning of this tedious year that we have been entirely in Saint-Omer,' Jane wrote. 'God grant our residence here may be soon over . . .'

Her wish was answered. On the bright morning of 19 January they received a long letter from James; the doughty traveller had arrived in Paris. She read with 'sorrow & surprise' that he had not calculated on their accompanying him to Scotland but saw them as 'remaining quietly at St Omer till he returned from the North'. She knew that before he left for India he had been courting a cousin, Jeanie Tytler, and apparently was now anxious, after a reunion with them, to head to Scotland to see her. But if he imagined that his parents would languish in Saint-Omer while he played the gallant, he had not bargained on his mother. Jane persuaded Mr Fraser that they could wait for James in England, visiting friends in Bath and Tunbridge Wells. She started packing and was so elated that she made few diary notes from that time.

Just after dawn on Saturday 25 January, James arrived at their door in the Rue de Dunkerque. There was much jubilation, so much to discuss, so many questions about his epic journey, his future plans, that they did not stop for breakfast until three hours later. After this there were bills to pay, passports to arrange, and dear friends to farewell. Mr Fraser visited the Balcombes to introduce James.

On the Frasers' last morning in Saint-Omer, 28 January, Jane 'made a hurried call at the Balcombes . . . saw both Mr & Mrs B. Mrs B gave me a little Golden Locket as a remembrance.' Just after 1 pm the coach came for the Frasers. The Balcombes had lost their good friends and the chronicler of their days in Saint-Omer, but they would stay on there for another ten months.

William Balcombe and his family lingered in France because he had not yet received word of any appointment. But nor had Lowe. Despite Bathurst's advice against doing so, Lowe was proceeding with his attempt to prosecute O'Meara; he was paying an expensive barrister and had a conference with him and the Solicitor General.[3] However, because Lowe had delayed so long with his defamation application, and his legal counsel, Mr Tindal, procrastinated, the Trinity legal term passed by, and with it the prescribed period for an application expired.

Count de Las Cases' *Le Mémorial de Sainte-Hélène* (written after Lord Holland negotiated the return of his papers) had caused a sensation on the Continent. When the eight-volume translation (inevitably critical of Lowe) was published in England in late 1823, it resulted in yet another stir. It was hailed in France 'as the greatest literary success of the century'.

At last Balcombe received some good news. Bathurst offered him a newly created position, the first Colonial Treasurer of the distant colony of New South Wales. Sir Thomas Tyrwhitt's intercessions on his protégé's behalf had paid off. Balcombe's granddaughter Bessie later suggested that Sir George Cockburn and even (but surely less likely) George IV had had some influence as well.[4]

New South Wales would not have been Balcombe's own first choice, which may have been a Caribbean posting. Formerly it would have been St Helena, but after Napoleon's death, conditions on the island had dramatically deteriorated. The departure of Napoleon's entourage, of Lowe and his establishment, and particularly the

2000 military and naval forces had led to a major collapse in economic life from which the island never recovered. Imports from the Cape, which had been the mainstay of Balcombe's income from his naval victualling business, had virtually ceased.

The colony of New South Wales was very far from home, and—founded as it was to take Britain's criminal class—conditions were bound to be rough; Balcombe must have thought there would be little opportunity to enjoy a society life. But he was now in his sixth year without a paid position and would hardly have needed Sir Thomas's counsel to know that he must be grateful to accept the one offered.

He would certainly have gone to London to see Sir Thomas and to take advice at the Colonial Office. He learned that his new post had been created following recommendations by Commissioner J.T. Bigge. The colonial treasurer position was proposed to amalgamate revenue previously collected by other departments. Balcombe was told that he was likely to sail in November along with other newly appointed government officials.[5] He must learn what he could to equip himself for the position, and he and his family should prepare themselves for the voyage and a new life in Australia.

But Balcombe could not fully rejoice, because he had found his daughter Betsy in a desperate state. She was living south of the Thames in the poor area of Blackfriars. Edward Abell had recently deserted her and their baby girl. As he would later admit, he had never loved her and had only married her 'under the hope of gaining something good' through her father 'and his exalted interests'. Instead he had found that the family lived in near-penury. As a final insult, he took all of Betsy's jewellery as he fled.[6] Under the law, it was not theft but his legal right as a husband to claim all of his wife's property.[7]

Balcombe would certainly have urged his daughter to leave the wretched lodgings and return with him to Saint-Omer, where a loving family awaited her and where her mother would care for her and the infant Bessie. He would have explained that they would not be leaving for New South Wales until November; it made sense for them to remain in France until then, with William at school in Boulogne, but when they sailed, she and the baby must accompany them. Betsy apparently agreed, but had her reasons for not wanting to leave Blackfriars immediately. While there was a remote chance that

Abell might return she would wait, because she wanted something from him. Unable to persuade his daughter, Balcombe sailed for Saint-Omer to give his wife the very mixed news. Before he left, he apparently contacted the Frasers—who were visiting friends in Bath and Kent while they waited for James to finish courting in Scotland—and asked them, when next in London, to call on his daughter.

In August 1823, the star attraction at the Waterloo Rooms in London was the horse Marengo, Napoleon's famous white charger, which had survived many battles with his master, although not quite as many as were claimed for him. (Napoleon *had* gone into battle on several other horses as well.[8]) Edward Satchwell and Jane Fraser did not join the crowds queuing to see Marengo tossing his mane, 'Admittance one shilling'. They had other business, as Jane noted in her diary of 22 August: 'This day by previous appointment we were to go to Great Surry St Blackfriars to visit Mrs Abell, the Daughter of Mr Balcombe of St Helena—unfortunately married—and deserted by her Husband with an infant Child.'[9]

I peered at maps of Blackfriars, unable to find Great Surry Street, until a helpful librarian at the British Library searched an old map of 1820s London and was able to tell me that Blackfriars Road, the high street today, was then called Great Surrey Street.[10] A further search revealed that in 1823, Great Surrey Street Blackfriars was a district of working-class folk and small merchants. It was definitely not one of London's more salubrious areas, and Betsy must have considered it humiliating, far beneath her expectations for herself.

Jane Fraser may not have looked forward to the outing south of the Thames. It is apparent from her account that she was meeting Betsy for the first time: 'Mrs A is a tall handsome elegant looking young woman with an amiable & pleasing countenance & very like her Father—She ... with much cordiality & grace entered into her sad story of which she gave us the particulars & expressed herself much gratified with our visit & our attention to her mother & sister while at Saint-Omer. She brought her little infant, a lovely little girl, to show us & after sitting an hour with her we took leave ... cast down with her unfortunate situation & agreeable manners. Still—there was such a lightness of manner, of almost levity or want of feeling—in her being able to recount & dwell on the circumstances of her Husband's conduct & deserting her, as took somewhat from the deep feeling it would otherwise have inspired—but she is very young not much being over 20 & seems burdened to have been of a light, volatile character, tho' very interesting.'[11] Jane's perceptive description of Betsy suggests that something of the wild, flighty girl of St Helena days, some almost manic quality in her personality, still remained, despite her recent personal hardship.

The Frasers continued on their way and were never to see their friends the Balcombes again.

Betsy had agreed to join her parents in Saint-Omer and seemed to have given up whatever expectation had detained her at Blackfriars, most likely a hope that her husband would return. If she had hope it would not have been fuelled by love (she must by then surely have hated him) but because she wanted something he could grant. She would have known of marriages where the couple frankly disliked each other but the woman found that preferable to lacking a protector; 'Better a bad husband than no husband at all,' the saying went.[12] Abell, however, had proved to be very bad indeed and Betsy probably could not have endured the thought of living with him again. Yet she also knew that as a deserted wife she would barely have a position in society. She would be like one of the old maids who sat on the margins at balls. Unless she could marry again she would always be lonely, a burden to her parents, and without a protector she and her adored child could only look forward to impoverished lives. If she did earn a little money, her husband would always be entitled by law to come and take it. That was one advantage of going to the remote convict colony—it was very far away.

It is reasonable conjecture that Betsy, above all, wanted to be a free woman again. She would have investigated how this could be achieved and discovered that it was almost impossible. A full legal divorce required an Act of Parliament and the costs ran into thousands of pounds—only a few very rich men had ever attempted it, and no woman ever had.[13] An annulment was possible on the grounds of incest, lunacy or impotence (hardly to be argued when Abell had sired their daughter); however, another ground that was frequently used, and which may have interested her, was bigamy. She may always have had suspicions that Abell had left a woman behind in India; if he had actually married the woman and would admit to it, that would be the basis for an annulment—but as the penalty for bigamy was transportation for seven years, she must have known he would not acknowledge any such marriage.[14] There was still *one* realistic possibility, the avenue most often used by 'the middling and better sort'. If Abell returned, perhaps she hoped to persuade him to agree to a 'private separation', which would allow her a degree of economic independence. It would even enable them both to marry again without being charged with bigamy, even though any new marriage would never be approved under strict ecclesiastical law.[15]

Abell, however, did not come back. Betsy must have believed that he had left the country and returned to India—beyond the reach of her suspicions of an Indian wife or mistress and perhaps of children in Madras. What made Abell's return to south Asia more likely is that his elder brother Charles, a former lieutenant in the Indian army, had died the previous year at his tea plantation in Colombo. The news may recently have reached Edward, initiating his flight. Charles had left behind a wife and a daughter, but Edward, always alert for advantage, may have had some expectations from his will.[16] However, it seems that in his haste to depart from his wife and child, Abell had forgotten something: a promissory note for £120, allegedly owed to him by a Lieutenant-General Francis Torrens of Madras. Betsy hoped that she might retrieve that sum for herself.

She packed up her few possessions, and with little Bessie, by then around eleven months old, crossed the Channel to France.

General Sir Henry Torrens at the Horse Guards in London, by then commander-in-chief of the British army under the Duke of York, could scarcely have been pleased when a letter arrived from France from a Mrs Lucia Elizabeth Abell, asking if he would kindly honour the promissory note made out in India by his late brother Lieutenant-General Francis Torrens to Edward Abell Esquire. She would have explained that Mr Abell had proved to be a scoundrel, deserting her and leaving her almost penniless, and that she was about to embark with her family for New South Wales. General Torrens probably doubted the authenticity of the note, almost certainly aware that Abell had been a crony of James Patterson, the forger (since transported to Sydney) who had dared to contest his late brother's will. However, General Torrens was both an officer and a gentleman. On 8 October he replied:

> My dear Madame—I have great pleasure in accommodating you . . . I therefore send you a Draft for £120—and I shall certainly procure the sum, which Mr Abell advanced for the late General Torrens. I received your letter from France with its mysterious Enclosures, & no doubt the Writer is the misguided Man with whom you are, unfortunately, connected. I beg to wish you all happiness & success in your intended voyage, and I remain, Dear Madam,
> Your most faithful Servant,
> H. Torrens[17]

There is no record of the remaining period of the family's time at Saint-Omer, but if William was wise he would have been reading the three weighty reports by Commissioner Bigge with their advice, in meticulous detail, on transforming New South Wales from a penitentiary to a functioning British colony.[18] The reports had by then been approved and published in the British Parliament, and Sir Thomas Tyrwhitt could have obtained copies for him. Time existed on the voyage to study them in depth.

In mid-October, the Balcombes and Betsy with her baby left Saint-Omer for London to prepare for their voyage. One significant date *is* on record: this Anglican family would never have countenanced the christening of Betsy's daughter in a Catholic church in France. She was baptised in London on 23 October 1823 as Elizabeth Jane Balcombe Abell. The record would probably also have been required in order to register her for the voyage to Australia.[19]

William and his family made their farewells to Sir Thomas Tyrwhitt, no doubt with anguish on both sides, wondering if they would ever see each other again. The Balcombes were sorry they would be missing the grand celebrations for the official opening in November of the Plymouth and Dartmoor Railroad, Tyrwhitt's great passion.[20] (It would never be the successful business enterprise he had hoped and would end up bankrupting him.)

It may well have been Sir Thomas who proposed to Lord Bathurst that a young gentleman, James Stirling Harrison, should accompany the family to Sydney as a tutor for the boys. Harrison was certainly well qualified—he spoke five languages—and Balcombe knew not to question the wisdom of his patron's suggestions. Tyrwhitt was aware that Balcombe was inexperienced bureaucratically (at St Helena the office side of the business was handled by Fowler and Cole, while Balcombe excelled at trading, negotiating, and building personal contacts). As it happened, young Harrison was well conversant with bureaucratic and financial matters. His father was the former principal accountant at the Transport Office in London, and a possible relative was Sir George Harrison, the highly regarded under-secretary at the Treasury in Whitehall. It is likely that the designation 'tutor' for the young man was a ruse, avoiding any accusation of recruiting office staff before the approval of the New South Wales governor. If this was another contrivance of Tyrwhitt's, Lord Bathurst, not unknown as a wily operator himself, might have been content to look the other way.

Before leaving London, Balcombe met again at the Colonial Office with Wilmot Horton, Under-Secretary for the Colonies, and had a useful briefing. No doubt he expressed gratitude: he had been lifted from penury and appointed to an important official position with many responsibilities. But it was typical of his confidence and insouciance that his last question to Horton was a request for a personal loan of £50, to tide him over for the voyage.[21] He was virtually asking: 'Can you lend me fifty quid, mate?' Horton obliged and may have thought wryly to himself that the new treasurer was going to fit in well at the colony of New South Wales.

At Plymouth the family, with all their luggage, boarded the small 430-ton transport ship *Hibernia*, commanded by Captain Robert Gillies. They made a sizable group: William, his wife, their elder daughter Jane, the three boys, and Betsy, a 21-year-old single mother, with her baby daughter. They were accompanied by the boys' new tutor, James Stirling Harrison, and two unnamed domestics.

On board they met the other significant passengers who would be joining the Balcombes for meals at the captain's table: the new chief justice for Van Diemen's Land, John Lewes Pedder, with his wife and that colony's new attorney-general, Joseph Tice Gellibrand, all three to disembark at Hobart; the barrister Saxe Bannister, soon to become Balcombe's colleague as the new attorney-general for New South Wales, was travelling with his two sisters. Captain Edward Macarthur, the eldest son of the colony's leading landed family, would also have an honoured place at the table; a 34-year-old bachelor, he had served in the British army fighting Napoleon's forces at Corunna and Sicily and in the Peninsular War, and had been with the army of occupation in France.[22]

On 8 November 1823, the *Hibernia* weighed anchor at Plymouth and raised her sails; with the Balcombes on deck to watch the cliffs of England recede into the mists, they set off on their uncomfortable five-month voyage halfway around the world.

PART THREE

You tell yourself: I'll be gone
To some other land, some other sea,
To a city lovelier far than this
Could ever have been or hoped to be . . .

There's no new land, my friend,
No new sea;
For the city will follow you,
In the same streets you'll wander endlessly.

C.P. CAVAFY

Napoleon facing The Briars. A lithograph from late 1815 by Major Stewart of the 24th Regiment of Foot.

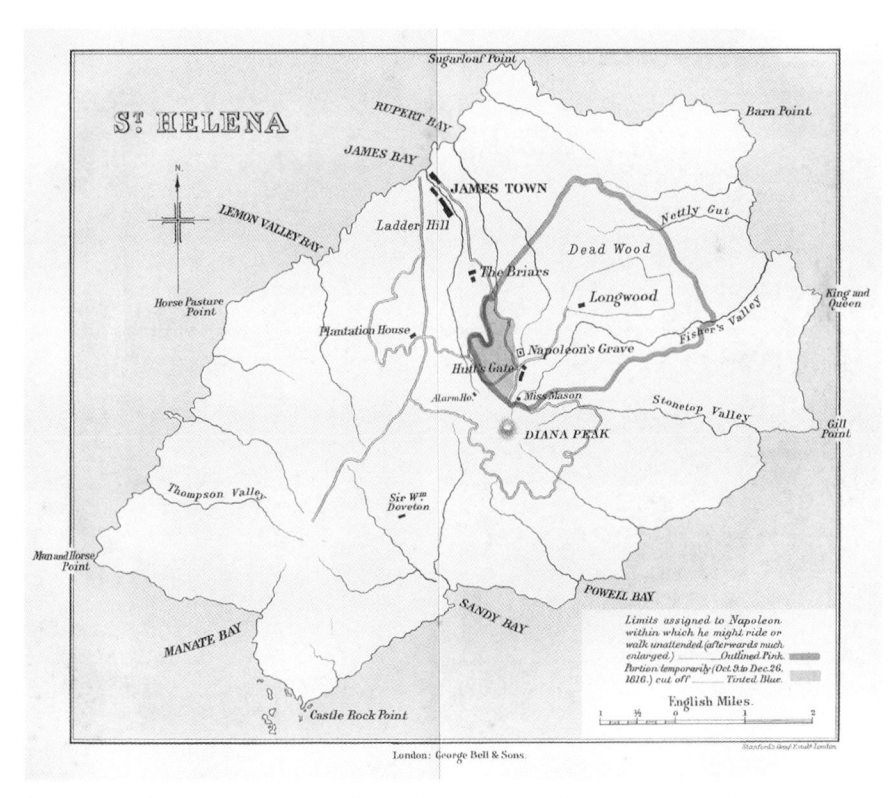

A map of St Helena, showing the boundary within which Napoleon could move unescorted.

The Porteous lodging house next to the castle gardens in Jamestown. Napoleon stayed here on his first night ashore.

Plantation House, the governor's residence on St Helena. Based on a sketch by Lieutenant F.R. Stack c.1845–46.

Jane Balcombe

William Balcombe (Courtesy of The Briars, Mt Martha, Victoria)

A sketch of the Balcombe family with Napoleon and Count de Las Cases that appeared in one of the many books about Napoleon's final days.

Countess Albine de Montholon

Count Charles Tristan de Montholon

Louis-Joseph Marchand

Major Gideon Gorrequer

Count de Las Cases

Dr John Stokoe

Sir Hudson Lowe

Lord Henry Bathurst

Count Henri-Gatien Bertrand

Countess Françoise-Elisabeth Bertrand

Dr Barry O'Meara

Laura Wilks

Napoleon dictating his memoirs to General Gaspard Gourgaud, 1818. (Getty)

Napoleon perched on the island of St Helena. Caricature by George Cruikshank, 1815.

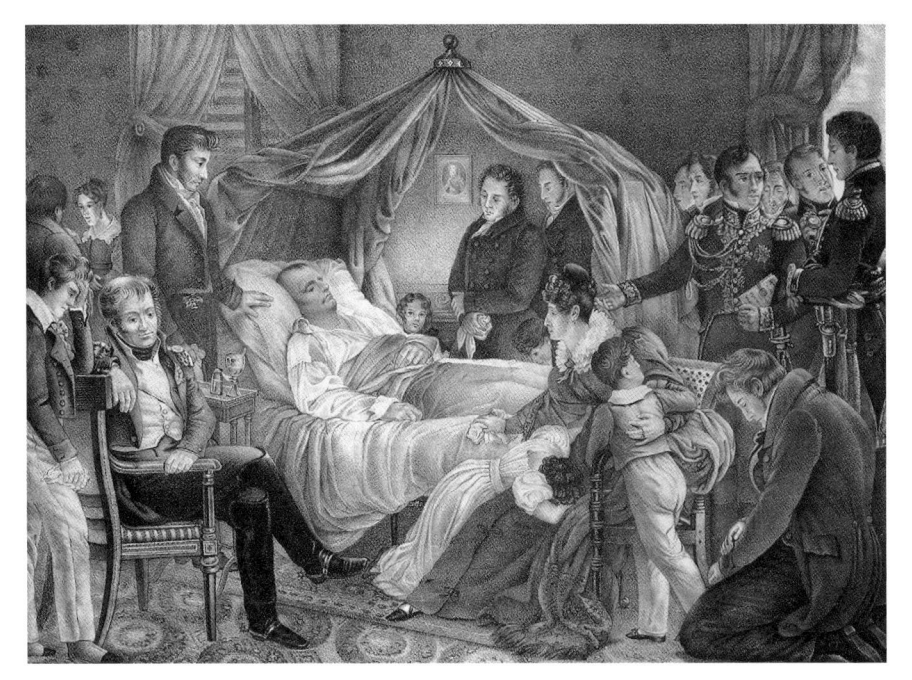

Napoleon on his deathbed surrounded by the faithful, 5 May 1821.

Betsy in her early forties.

Betsy in her mid-fifties. A sketch adapted from a photograph taken by G.W. Melliss in 1857.

A colonial kangaroo hunt. A pen and ink wash by Thomas Tyrwhitt Balcombe.
(Private collection)

Sydney harbour and foreshore. A pen and ink wash by Thomas Tyrwhitt Balcombe.
(Private collection)

CHAPTER 30

SYDNEY TOWN

It is difficult today to imagine the modest settlement around Sydney Cove where the *Hibernia* put down its anchor on 5 April 1824. It joined seventeen vessels in line for position at the two long wooden wharves beside a row of warehouses and a jumble of jetties and slipways.

The Balcombes stood on deck, trying to get a sense of their new home: across the waters to their left (where the Opera House now stands) was Fort Macquarie guarding the cove, cannon on its low battlements and crenellated tower. Beyond it, the roofline of the rambling Government House could be glimpsed among the bushes and Norfolk pine on the rise.[1] At the head of the cove a noxious stream, fenced against wandering cattle, disgorged its sludge onto the mudflats. To their right, through the forest of masts and rigging and the cargo being winched down, the bellowing cattle off-loaded in netted cradles, beyond the warehouses were huddled shops, cottages and taverns squeezed against high sandstone cliffs, punctuated by a gun battery on the point. They were told that this area was The Rocks, where many convicts lived, a place not to venture, especially at night.[2] Little could be seen of the streets of Sydney but for some fine civic buildings; a squat, blunt church tower; a graceful steeple in the distance; and, further still on higher ground, the sails of windmills turning.

The labourers on the wharves were convicts, some wearing shirts and trousers of coarse yellow cloth, groups of them straining to pull heavy carts.³ Watching the activity was a group of dark-skinned Aboriginal people in ragged clothes. The scene would not have been entirely unfamiliar to the Balcombes: Sydney was clearly a far bigger settlement than Jamestown and it lacked the dramatic mountain backdrop, but a few of the Georgian buildings looked similar, the sunshine was as bright, the sea as blue, and they were accustomed to the presence of people of many different races.

During the voyage there had been a grim tragedy for the Balcombe family. On the long haul between the Cape and Hobart Town they had lost Jane, the beloved elder daughter and Betsy's sister and confidante. The cause of Jane's death is not known and the captain's log has not survived. She had never been in robust health and at St Helena had suffered a long illness, perhaps tuberculosis.⁴ She had been buried at sea, as was the practice, a Union Jack over the coffin during the funeral service and then her body released into the depths. It would take her parents and Betsy a very long time to recover from her loss. For her mother in particular, after her prolonged illness at Saint-Omer and Abell's desertion of Betsy, the tragic death of her firstborn must have been almost impossible to bear.

The voyage had offered very few consolations. It had taken five months, bypassing the usual port of call of Rio de Janeiro, so not stocking up with water and fresh food supplies, although it was a smooth enough passage to the Cape of Good Hope. But then they had lost Jane on the way to Hobart Town.⁵ The family had endured the cramped cabin space (and their two domestic servants suffered far worse between decks), the sweltering heat of the long crossing of the Indian Ocean, the stink, neighing, bellowing, grunting and screeching of the cooped farm animals, then the terror of howling gales in the Southern Ocean, lashing rain, heavy seas, and the massive rolling waves of the Roaring Forties that tossed their little vessel like a leaf. But that was all nothing, compared with the loss of Jane.

Until then, the long voyage had been endurable for the Balcombes because of some interesting companions. They naturally sat at Captain Gillies' table in the saloon for meals, along with seven others. The new attorney-general, Saxe Bannister, travelling with his two adult sisters, had an awkward, slightly haughty manner, which would not have endeared him to Balcombe.⁶ Captain Edward Macarthur was sometimes willing to discuss early days in the colony. His father was the well-known John Macarthur, a former officer of the New South Wales Corps; later to be revered as 'the father of the Australian wool industry', but in the 1820s he was a controversial figure. Edward was a baby when his parents settled at Elizabeth Farm, Parramatta. He was nineteen in 1808 when he joined his father and other officers in ousting Governor William Bligh, who had experienced a major rebellion before, having survived the *Bounty* mutiny of 1789. Young Edward was sent to London to give the officers' version of the coup, accompanied by the first bale of merino wool exported from the colony. He had subsequently obtained a commission and joined the British army; after honourable service, he was returning to Sydney and his family for the first time in fifteen years.

He was now acting as the agent for the wealthy British politician and landowner Thomas Potter Macqueen. He carried a despatch, approved by Lord Bathurst, directing the governor to grant Macqueen an extensive run of 10,000 acres, to be chosen by Edward, with the possibility that once it was in production an equivalent grant might follow. Macqueen had read the Bigge report with its recommendation to expand the colony from a penitentiary and encourage independent agriculture and commerce. He would remain an absentee landlord but proposed, instead of convict workers, to send out 'British subjects' where possible, even 'Parish Paupers', so contributing to a more 'honest and wholesome Population' in New South Wales.[7] Balcombe listened and was inspired by the possibilities if he owned land.

When the *Hibernia* arrived at Sydney Cove, Sir Thomas Brisbane, the governor of New South Wales, was 15 miles away at his official country residence in Parramatta. However, the colonial secretary Major Frederick Goulburn (who also acted as the governor's private secretary and had assumed many of the governor's responsibilities) would have been at the wharf to welcome the new officials. An earlier ship, the *Guildford*, bringing the chief justice, would have conveyed the news that the new attorney-general and the colonial treasurer with his family of six plus servants were not far behind. Acting on that information, Governor Brisbane had arranged for the Balcombes to occupy a recently vacant house on the corner of O'Connell and Bent streets in the centre of town. Goulburn probably led them to see the property, a short walking distance from the quay. He was another beneficiary of patronage, a younger brother to Bathurst's former under-secretary, whom Balcombe had met (not always in auspicious circumstances).[8] Balcombe must have wondered what information concerning himself might have passed between the brothers.

The substantial two-storey brick house with shuttered windows, behind a stone boundary wall, was better than the family could have hoped. It even had an established English oak tree shading the garden, planted at the time the colony was first settled, probably next to an original bark hut.[9] This new house had been built for William Cox, a military officer and engineer still appreciated in the colony for supervising the construction of the first road over the Blue Mountains just ten years earlier. As a reward, Governor Macquarie had granted him good grazing land at Bathurst on the western plains and Cox had moved there to take up the life of a country gentleman and magistrate. Balcombe was not to know that Cox had previously agreed to rent his house to another man, an arrangement overruled by the governor.

Small societies are habitually plagued by factionalism, enmities and intrigue, and Sydney was no exception. Balcombe had already made one enemy without being aware of it. George Boyes had arrived in the colony in January, appointed deputy assistant-commissary-general, while he awaited the expected arrival of William Lithgow, the head of the accounts branch of the Commissariat. Boyes was an intelligent man and a talented artist, but he was perpetually embittered that too few people seemed to recognise this. Within a month he reported to his wife in England that he had dined at Government House and had come to know 'everyone in the colony worth knowing', but that he disliked them all, preferring 'my own fireside and a book'.

Boyes had expectations of sitting by the fireside in Cox's house and gave his wife a detailed description of the property: 'There are some good houses in this place—that I have taken is one of the best, 3 rooms on the ground floor, one of which is about 36 feet by 28 and 18 high; over these are six tolerably sized rooms which I propose for Lithgow and myself—there are fine cellars, dairy etc, a pump (the greatest of all luxuries in a place so badly supplied with water as this), coach house—stables for 4 or 6 horses and a green on one side of the house—fit for drying clothes—a verandah running two sides of it—rent £125 per annum.'¹⁰ It had all been settled with Cox, and Boyes had just been waiting for Lithgow in order to take possession, when the governor had learned of the Balcombes' imminent arrival and took the prize away from him! He would not forgive Brisbane nor the usurping newcomers: 'Mr & Mrs Balcomb & family—he comes out Colonial Treasurer—tis the man who was at St Helena, whose daughter teased Buonaparte so abominably'.¹¹

The house was ideal for the Balcombes. Two rooms on the ground floor were suitable for the treasurer's office and an assistant's, while the huge room with its lofty ceiling would be appropriately gracious for both dining and entertaining. The six upstairs rooms could accommodate the whole family, as well as young James Harrison and the two servants. They stayed on the ship for a few days until basic furnishings were organised and their luggage delivered, and then settled in.

However, the day after their arrival, 6 April, Governor Brisbane came into town along the dusty road from Parramatta in a carriage drawn by four horses. At midday he was to preside at the High Court of Appeal to be held at Government House.¹² In the morning he had time to welcome the new officials and their families. For Balcombe it was a short walk from the wharf to Government House. Brisbane, aged in his early fifties with long patrician features, had a relaxed and pleasant manner, unruffled by the many conflicting issues that were the daily challenge of his administration. He had behind him a distinguished military career, serving in Flanders and the West Indies, and had been a brigadier-general under the Duke of Wellington in the Peninsular War. After Waterloo he was again with his patron Wellington, commanding a division of the occupation force in France.

The arrival of Balcombe and the other new officials was most welcome to him. The colony had expanded in size and population in recent years and he had long complained that he had too few men for the work of government; in fact, his relations with one significant official, Frederick Goulburn, his colonial secretary, had become fraught.

The new officials gave the governor their letters of introduction from the Colonial Office. Bathurst's communication of 2 October 1823 regarding Balcombe and his new position was remarkable for its brevity. He wrote that in order to establish the New South Wales government 'upon a system of more immediate efficiency, I have appointed Mr W. Balcombe to proceed to New S. Wales as Colonial Treasurer. I have thought it preferable however not to assign any particular Salary to Mr. Balcombe, but to leave it to you to submit a proposition to me', based upon Balcombe's duties 'and the degree of pecuniary responsibility which will necessarily be imposed upon him'. In the meantime, his lordship asked Brisbane to issue 'such a moderate salary' as seemed reasonable and to advise on the securities Balcombe should pledge in a bond as protection against 'all monies which may come into his hands. His personal bond may be taken in the Colony, and that of his Securities will be entered into hereafter with the Board of Treasury.'[13]

That was the extent of the information. However, it would be surprising if no private letter for the governor from Bathurst or Wilmot Horton had come on the *Hibernia*, no explanation of the scandal from which Balcombe had been extricated, no mention of his influential protector, Sir Thomas Tyrwhitt, and, in particular, nothing concerning his experience at St Helena and his too close connection with Napoleon Bonaparte.

Brisbane must have learned some background from Goulburn's correspondence with his elder brother who was formerly at the Colonial Office, and local gossip was not long in coming. Mail from Hobart had arrived on the *Hibernia*. Robert Lathrop Murray, a former soldier in the Napoleonic Wars, transported to Van Diemen's Land for bigamy, was a journalist for the *Hobart Town Gazette* and the following year would become its editor. On 27 March 1824, he had dashed off a letter to his good friend D'Arcy Wentworth, Superintendent of Police in Sydney, who until then was mainly responsible for managing the government funds. Murray ensured that the family would not make a quiet arrival in New South Wales: 'This ship the *Hibernia* takes up a number of Newcomers to relieve the old Hands,' he wrote, 'amongst them Mr Balcomb, your successor as Colonial Treasurer. This is the gentleman who was sent by Sir Hudson Lowe from St Helena for being too intimate with Napoleon. His daughter, now Mrs Abell, is also on board. She was Napoleon's great favorite and married a Mr Abell in England who has deserted her, leaving her unprotected with a child. So here she is, a very beautiful young woman, bewitching . . .'[14]

That was obviously a story worth several retellings. The word spread. Many gentlemen were soon interested to make the acquaintance of the beautiful, bewitching Mrs Abell, tantalising because almost available to court and yet, in genteel society, not so. Meanwhile, Boyes, whose position as deputy assistant-commissary-general was much lower in rank than Balcombe's, bitterly complained in a letter to his wife about the loss of the house he had planned to occupy.

Brisbane had settled on a tentative figure of £1200 per annum as Balcombe's salary and agreed that the New South Wales government should pay the hefty rent demanded by Cox.[15] Balcombe considered that reasonable given that his home was expected to double as the Treasury building, which was why the governor had thought it suitable, being of 'unusual solid brick' with barred windows. However, there was no vault or safe, so Balcombe soon decided that the safest place to keep government monies was in his bedroom and 'armed himself with a brass-barrelled blunderbuss and two pistols beside the bed'.[16]

Nothing the family had heard before their arrival about the crime rate in the colony made them feel comfortable. In 1819, William Wilberforce, best known for his crusade to end slavery, had made an alarming speech in the House of Commons about the practice of transportation. He denounced it as inhuman and wanted it ended, warning that they were creating in New South Wales 'a nest of vipers' which could 'form a nucleus of contagion in that part of the world'. He quoted figures showing that the crime rate in 'Botany Bay' was sixteen times greater than in the English county of Warwickshire. British government ministers thought that only to be expected, as criminals were sent there.[17]

Balcombe and his family had come to a young colony that was at a stage of awkward but assertive adolescence, still gawky and uncertain, between its origins as a gaol for unwanted felons and its new future as a productive colony of the British Empire with its own democratic institutions. Sydney town and its surrounding districts had grown into a bustling, lively centre of trade, with numerous commercial connections with India and with the islands of the Pacific for sealing and whaling. It was inevitably still a society with distinct divisions of social class, but the divisions were more flexible of entry and exit than those in the old country from which it had sprung.

Sydney society was a composite of free-settling landholders, government employees, emancipated convicts, convicts still serving their sentences, and the children of convicts or emancipated convicts. Former convicts who had served their term or gained their 'ticket of leave'—the 'emancipists'—were free to take up farming or fishing or to find ways to cater for needs not yet met in the various communities. So much was needed in this new society in the process of inventing itself, so many openings were available for the enterprising, that some former convicts had already exploited them with such resourcefulness and daring—or unscrupulousness—that they had grown wealthy. A few were even fabulously rich, such as Samuel Terry, 'the Botany Bay Rothschild', who had arrived in Sydney in 1801 at the King's pleasure after stealing 400 pairs of stockings. Having served his term, he opened a public house in Pitt Street that soon became notorious. He would encourage drunken customers to sign away their properties, their jewellery or literally the shirts off their back at his pawn shop next door. Historian Michael Cannon has noted: 'By 1820 he held about one-fifth of all mortgages in the colony—more than the Bank of New South Wales itself.'[18] Terry had been no friend of Governor Macquarie's, but some emancipists were: Dr William Redfern, Simeon Lord and Mary Reibey had dined occasionally at Government House, blurring social boundaries in ways not approved of by the pastoral elite, dubbed the 'exclusives', who wielded great influence.

At the time of the Balcombes' arrival, the fluidity of this new society was beginning to congeal into an approximation of the old social patterns of the mother country. There was now an influx of free settlers, eager for land grants. Some earlier settlers and former officers had become so wealthy and established that they saw themselves as the aristocracy of the new society. The Macarthurs led these 'exclusives'. John Macarthur, aged 57 in 1824 and 'incorrigibly haughty', had long been a successful and entrepreneurial pastoralist, with government assistance for his breeding flock of merino sheep. Having connived to oust one governor, Bligh, he and his younger sons William and James and nephew Hannibal exercised a vigorous and informed voice in colony matters. Along with their pastoral colleagues—the brothers John and Gregory Blaxland and the formidable parson the Reverend Samuel Marsden—this group, dubbed the 'Parramatta party', rather thought they determined the rules. They were a constant irritant to the governor.[19]

Balcombe formally took up his appointment as colonial treasurer on 28 April, although he and Harrison began setting up his office from the second day ashore. As recommended by Commissioner Bigge, the new role was designed to consolidate the administration of the finances of the colony, taking over responsibilities previously divided between a number of officials. The colonial revenue was raised by import duties; royalties on timber and coal; wharf taxes; fees on shipping; tolls on public roads and bridges; dues on markets, fairs and auctions; and fees for slaughtering cattle and sheep at the public slaughterhouse. Monies derived from these sources had been collected principally by D'Arcy Wentworth, treasurer of the police fund, and by Captain John Piper, the naval officer.[20] The revenue was then expended on public works; the maintenance of gaols, the police force and the orphan institution; grants in aid of official salaries; and rewards for services rendered.

The Colonial Office, according to one historian, 'showed typical empiricism in the manner in which the new system was to be inaugurated, although "indifference" would be a better term. Balcombe was given no instructions about his responsibilities or the nature of his duties.'[21]

The new treasurer was expected to shape his role as he went along, but essentially he was to be a collector and custodian, not a policy-maker on financial matters. In some ways Balcombe was peculiarly suited to the post, given the colony's former guise as a penitentiary: he had provided for prisoners on St Helena, another remote outpost; he was an experienced businessman; and he understood dealings with a commissariat and the intricacies of negotiating a variety of coinage and monetary bills. (Because of a shortage of sterling, Spanish dollars were still widely in use.) But in response to the Bigge report, the colony could no longer be regarded merely as a gaol: it was in the process of transition to a more complex future, and Balcombe, if running the Treasury by himself, lacked the managerial and office skills to cope.

However, he immediately had enormous support from young James Stirling Harrison. Born in the same year as Betsy, Harrison was 22 and more than equipped with the skills required. In recommending

James, his father had written that 'he has had a most liberal Education, speaks five Languages, was four years in a Dutch Counting House, two at Smyrna and Constantinople for improvement; he is a complete man of Business'.[22] As it was the governor's prerogative to appoint clerical staff in the colony, the title 'tutor' had obviously been used so as not to offend him—and Harrison would have been an excellent tutor for the boys during the five-month voyage. But Sir Thomas Brisbane, at his first meeting with Balcombe on 6 April, approved Harrison's appointment as principal clerk at the Colonial Treasury.[23] It was the beginning of a productive professional relationship between Balcombe and Harrison and a personal friendship also.

Betsy must surely have delighted in exploring the town. It was more extensive than she might have imagined, with some fine buildings, although many of them coexisted with less desirable neighbours, such as rackety shanties and grog houses. One eccentric shop, built of slabs, was mounted on large wheels, so that when business proved slack in one place, the owner could try his luck in another.[24] Horse-drawn carts and carriages jostled in the unpaved streets. Mud spattered pedestrians as they passed. This could never be mistaken for an English town: people walked along to the sound of trilling, squawking and screeching, for many shops had parrots and cockatoos in birdcages at their doorways.[25] 'Talkative birds' were offered for a guinea each and there were many stories about their cleverness.[26] 'George Street was brilliant with jewellers' shops,' a colonist recalled, for Sydney had become a useful place to dispose of stolen goods.[27]

Everywhere Betsy would have seen convicts at work, shackled at the ankles in chain gangs. Roger Therry, a lawyer who arrived in the colony a few years later, was appalled: 'Early in the morning, the gates of the convict prison were thrown open, and several hundred convicts were marched in regimental file and distributed amongst the several public works in and about the town ... one met bands of them in detachments of twenty yoked to wagons laden with gravel and stone, which they wheeled through the streets; in this, and in other respects, they performed the functions of labour usually discharged by beasts of burden at home.'[28]

Perhaps Betsy accepted the treatment of these men as the natural order of things. She had grown up in a slave society; as she has left no personal observations on the life of the convicts we do not know. But as Helen Heney observed in *Australia's Founding Mothers*, Georgian women 'lived in a time of harsh reality'.[29]

I imagine Betsy escaping to a favourite place with her little daughter Bessie in her arms. She might have followed a path behind Government House that wound through the exotic trees, palms and ferns of the Botanical Gardens, established with the encouragement of Sir Joseph Banks, and emerged onto the sloping lawns that extended to the promontory of land on the far side of Farm Cove. At its tip a ledge in the sandstone offered a comfortable seat. It would have pleased her to learn that this had been a favourite resting place for Elizabeth, the wife of the previous governor, who had come there so often that the rock shelf was still called 'Mrs Macquarie's Chair'.

Sitting there, Betsy could take in the activity across the bay at Fort Macquarie and at the wharves beyond it, ships coming into port and others unfurling their canvas sheets as they sailed down the harbour and out through the headlands to the open sea. Occasionally she would see other craft on the harbour: the local Eora people fishing from bark canoes. She could not have known—for few Europeans knew or cared—how restricted the diet of the Eora had become since the arrival of white men, how the strangers' wharves and ships and rubbish had fouled the clear waters of the bay and destroyed their oyster and mussel beds.

CHAPTER 31

'THE INTERESTING MRS ABELL'

The Balcombes began to make new friends. Given William's *bon vivant* personality and the gentle, hospitable nature of his wife, they rarely had trouble doing so, except with those of a highly rigid, conservative nature. Mrs Abell was of interest to many in Sydney Town who had heard of her friendship with Napoleon or could remember the newspaper stories about the cheeky Betsy Balcombe. The family soon found some congenial companions. The new chief justice Francis Forbes and his wife Amelia had arrived a month earlier and were settled in a house in Macquarie Place, just around the corner.

Mrs Forbes was well pleased with her 'commodious dwelling' with its broad verandah shaded by trees. Beyond the garden wall was a stone obelisk, established during Governor Macquarie's term, 'which marked the distance from that spot to the settled towns, up country'. A military band played once a week in a little rotunda near the obelisk, 'and, as we could hear it, quite distinctly from our verandah, we generally made the band day the occasion for a pleasant gathering of friends at our house. Sydney was not very extensive at that time, nor were the inhabitants of the best class, but we soon made some agreeable acquaintances.'

Justice Forbes was a man of learning and broad liberal sympathies. His previous appointments, accompanied by his young wife, had been as attorney-general in Bermuda and chief justice of the Supreme Court of Newfoundland. He was generally considered to have acquitted himself with humanity, integrity and wisdom in both positions, and—with the exception of a few enemies—came to be so well regarded for his role in New South Wales that a knighthood was conferred in 1837.

Among the regular visitors for the 'band evenings' were John Campbell, Sydney's wealthiest merchant and owner of a number of warehouses down at the wharves, who had a fine house and garden nearby. As well, there were the commanders of the two regiments stationed in the colony, and government officials with their families, including the governor's aide-de-camp Major John Ovens, the colonial secretary Major Frederick Goulburn, John Oxley the surveyor-general, and the new attorney-general Saxe Bannister with his two sisters.[1]

Not long after their arrival, the Balcombes and their daughter Betsy Abell were invited to one of these evenings on the verandah. Amelia Forbes later recounted that as the wine flowed, William Balcombe was willing to open up on a subject of great fascination to everyone present and 'had some very interesting stories to tell about Napoleon Buonaparte'. At The Briars summer-house 'the great man who had once kept the world in awe took up his residence, and became very intimate with Mr Balcombe's family'.[2]

'We enjoyed, of course,' wrote Amelia Forbes, 'the usual interchange of dinners, dances, and receptions, and all went happily in this new sphere of life in Australia.'[3] Through these connections, the Balcombes were introduced into the most lively stratum of Sydney colonial society. In the absence of a true aristocracy, those of the 'Parramatta party' considered themselves the colonial version, but they kept to themselves and were rarely in town. The people the Balcombes met through the Forbes tended to be liberal in attitude, with progressive ideas for the future of the colony. They were called 'the fashionables', and the most fashionable among them was Captain John Piper, the naval officer.

Piper had previously been an officer of the New South Wales Corps, but his attachment to a convict's daughter twenty years his junior, Mary Ann Shears, obliged him to leave his regiment. Governor Macquarie rescued him by appointing him naval officer in Sydney, a position which involved the control of lighthouses and the collection of harbour dues, customs duties and excise on spirits. It was extremely remunerative, involving a percentage on all monies collected, so that Piper's income was on average just over £2000 a year, which 'still put him among the highest paid public servants in the colony'.[4] He had been granted 190 acres of land on a promontory four miles across the harbour from Sydney Cove (today called Point Piper); at a cost of £10,000, he had constructed a dazzling white mansion, Henrietta Villa, which had a domed ballroom.

Piper enjoyed sharing his wealth with his friends and was well loved for his generosity. When he hosted a party at his villa, which he did almost every evening, the lights glimmered and bounced across the harbour waters with the strains of music from his personal band. His musicians doubled as his boatmen, ferrying the guests there and home. Captain John Piper seemed a colonial version of F. Scott Fitzgerald's Jay Gatsby in almost every sense, except one: he had a wife, to whom he was devoted. He had married Mary Ann and they produced many children. Once introduced to the Pipers, the Balcombes were soon welcome guests, particularly the glamorous and mysterious Mrs Abell.

On Monday 17 May 1824, the Charter of Justice, establishing the new Supreme Court, was formally promulgated by Chief Justice Forbes in a ceremony at Government House attended by Governor Brisbane and all the leading civil officials, naturally including Balcombe, as well as the magistrates, clergy and senior military officers. After the Oath of Judicial Office was administered, the governor congratulated the chief justice and thanked the Mother Country for the privileges bestowed upon 'her distant and rising Colonies in the Southern World'. The battery at Dawes' Point fired a royal salute.

The first Supreme Court of New South Wales was ready to function that afternoon and Criminal Court sessions began. That evening, Brisbane entertained the chief justice, the retiring judge advocate John Wylde and all the heads of the various public departments to dinner at Government House, Sydney.[5] He no doubt attempted to convey an atmosphere of peace and goodwill, but he had just sent a letter to Lord Bathurst complaining of Frederick Goulburn's 'arrogance and insubordination'. (John Macarthur, no stranger to arrogance himself, agreed with the governor on this point, expressing the view that Goulburn was a worthy successor to Bligh in 'despotic behaviour'.⁶) It would not have taken long for Balcombe to realise that he and Goulburn could never be natural friends, unlike himself and Brisbane, but he soon became adept at navigating his way around departmental enmities. His everyday life and future success in the colony depended on obtaining the goodwill of both men.

Ten days later, William Wemyss, the deputy commissary-general, gave 'a grand dinner party' for the same key government officials, in order to discuss what was effectively the creation of a new society.⁷ Almost all of them were the first to occupy their positions.

The Balcombes had made a new friend among 'the fashionables', Sir John Jamison, one of the colony's largest landholders. He was formerly a physician in the Royal Navy, serving in many parts of the world. In 1809, he had been on a hospital ship with the Baltic Fleet and helped curb a serious outbreak of scurvy among Swedish seamen. For this he had received a knighthood from King Charles XIII of Sweden, later confirmed by the Prince Regent. On the death of Jamison's father, he inherited several grazing properties in New South Wales, and in 1814 had arrived in Sydney to look after his interests. By the 1820s he had acquired more land by grant and purchase and was immensely rich, influential and assertive.⁸

On 20 May, Jamison hosted a large ball and supper at Regentville, his grand mansion beside the Nepean River, 34 miles from Sydney at the base of the Blue Mountains. The Balcombes and Mrs Abell attended, as did almost anyone who mattered in the colony. Even Boyes was there, who reported: 'I think we sat down about a hundred and forty. He has a famous large house and one room contained the whole party. About a dozen private carriages conveyed us all to the house by nine o'clock—and the doors were not open till eight.' What Boyes found most remarkable about the evening was that there was only one theft: 'Somehow or other the Constables at the doors permitted a great number of people looking like servants to fill the lobbies and though they were all convicted felons, I heard but of one Robbery—D'Arcy Wentworth, the chief of Police lost a diamond brooch of considerable value. The whole thing with that exception was conducted in the most orderly way and might be quoted as an example to the most fashionable routs in the English Metropolis. The women danced tolerably well—but all preserved their good humour. I returned pretty well sick of it at three in the morning but a large proportion kept it up till daylight.'[9] The dyspeptic Boyes was fed up with most things and told his wife: 'Generally speaking I dislike the people here beyond anything I have ever experienced and except our own little circle I do not mean to visit or receive.'[10]

The Balcombes, however, had been swept up in a social whirl. On 24 June, they were at another of Sir John's sumptuous parties, this time at his Sydney home. Under the heading 'THE FASHIONABLE WORLD', the *Sydney Gazette* gushed: 'The Ball and Supper, given by Sir JOHN JAMISON on the evening of Thursday last, was of the most fascinating and splendid description. The ballroom was fancifully fitted up for the occasion. The Company flocked in from 8 to 9: the carriages were rolling rapidly down our streets between those hours. Captain PIPER, with his usual zeal in these cases, had his own Band in attendance upon the noble Host.' The most distinguished of the 170-odd guests were listed: Chief Justice Forbes and his wife, the Wyldes, Pipers, Blaxlands, Coxes and Oxleys, Saxe Bannister, the Balcombes 'and the interesting Mrs Abell', the latter being the only one singled out for a special description 'among the happy group of Fashionables that were invited from all parts of the country to this elegant banquet'.[11] A hostess was conspicuously absent from the list, as always. The 'invisible woman' who shared Sir John's bed never appeared.[12] She was like Charlotte Brontë's madwoman in the attic in the Rochester household, for the 'convict stain', like madness, was a disgrace to polite society.

'Dancing, consisting of country dances, quadrilles, and Spanish waltzes,' the *Gazette*'s report continued, 'presently commenced, and was maintained with the utmost animation till midnight, when the guests were ushered in to the supper-room . . . All the rare and choice delicacies that Australia possesses, whether natural or imported, decorated the festive board: upwards of 170 sat down to supper. The rooms were elegantly festooned, and exhibited one refulgent blaze.' The 'concentration of beauty, rank, and fashion' returned to dancing until dawn, when carriages took them home, presumably to collapse, although it was a weekday.[13]

The wealthy 47-year-old emancipist businesswoman Mary Reibey did not attend any of these events and was not considered one of the 'fashionables'. Having made a visit to England three years earlier, she gave an ironic account of the Sydney social scene to her cousin in Lancashire: 'You wish to know what Public ammusements we have in Sydney—You will be surprised when I tell you we have not one not even so much as a Public Ball or Assembly—I assure you my dear Cousin our ears are not assailed by any of the Wanton or corrupting airs of the opera no nor the majestic and ennobling melody of the Oratorio but they are frequently assailed with the noise of intoxicated People and the disgusting language of the Aborigine—The Winter generally passes away with but one or two Balls and when sweltering summer arrives there are very frequently 4 and 5 in succession sometimes the "Sheriff" entertains a numerous assemblage of fashionables when the "Interesting Mrs Abel" makes her appearance—sometimes our gay Naval Officer entertains his friends . . . as to the Eligibility of it I think I should not presume to offer an opinion as I never enter into Society except a few friends who we sometimes dine with or spend the Evening.'[14]

Reibey's gently mocking use of the *Gazette*'s expression 'the Interesting Mrs Abell' suggests that Betsy had become somewhat famous in the colony—for her beauty, her style, her obvious lack of a Mr Abell, and most of all, for the rumour that she had been 'the favourite' of Bonaparte. While this would have made her an object of fascination for some, it would not have endeared her to others. Many men in the colony had been soldiers or naval men and spent years of their early adult lives fighting Bonaparte's forces. They may have been wounded themselves or lost fathers, brothers and comrades.[15] Few would have cared to know about what old newspapers described as a silly girl who got up to high jinks with the villain. Indeed, numerous Napoleonic War veterans held important positions in society, not least the governor, Sir Thomas Brisbane, who at the Duke of Wellington's request had been promoted to brigadier-general and commanded a brigade heavily engaged in battles from Vittoria to Toulouse.[16] Major Ovens, his aide-de-camp, had been by his side in those conflicts. Major Frederick Goulburn had spent much of his life in active service, in the Peninsular War, in France and at Waterloo. It would be unsurprising if Goulburn felt resentment towards people said to have admired Napoleon, and that may be the reason he never liked Balcombe.

Betsy and her parents kept quiet about their former connection, except with friends, but even her father's storytelling on the Forbes' verandah may have embarrassed her. It is frustrating to have no account in her own voice—in a journal or letters to friends abroad—of their early years in Sydney. But she was soon to write a letter that *has* survived, albeit on a very different and most urgent matter.

Young Thomas and Alexander Balcombe, aged fourteen and thirteen, had been enrolled in April at the Sydney secondary school. By June they were successful in their half-yearly public examination, having 'read, and explained Seleciæ and Profanix, and applied the Rules of Syntax, with much promptitude and accuracy'.[17]

The following month their father joined the scramble for land, submitting a request to the governor for grants for himself and his sons. He had no doubt enjoyed many useful discussions with Edward Macarthur during the five-month voyage, and although Edward was away prospecting for the huge Macqueen grant of 10,000 acres, goodwill between them remained. Balcombe was only too aware of the importance of owning land: in Britain it entitled you to vote, it gave status, made you a gentleman; if your domain was extensive enough you might become a Member of Parliament and even acquire a title. In New South Wales he saw how obtaining land by government grant and purchase had made men rich, and he intended to secure a future for his family.

Betsy also knew that owning land would provide a measure of independence for herself and her daughter, and chafed at the ruling that single women—which included deserted wives—could not apply. She had spoken to Governor Brisbane, who said that only a very influential patron could persuade the Colonial Office to make an exception.

Balcombe's application to the governor was successful and he was granted 2000 acres in the county of Argyle at Bungonia, 20 miles south-east of the then smaller settlement of Goulburn. The land had frontage to the north side of Yarralaw Creek and he was able to purchase land on the southern side, making his total property 2560 acres. He resolved to call it 'The Briars' after his beloved home on St Helena. William, the eldest at sixteen, intended to take up farming immediately, so made an application in his own right, and Brisbane granted him an additional 800 acres at Bungonia. But it seems young William did not take up the grant, because of the obligations and expense involved, managing his father's land instead.

Once a land grant was obtained, regulations demanded that the new owner invest a quarter of the land value in improvements within seven years—in fencing, dams, stockyards, and residential and farm buildings—and assign convicts to work the land and look after the livestock. No sale of the land was permissible until at least seven years after acquisition, sometimes longer, and if the owner did not intend to live on the property, he had to employ a resident manager. After 1825, annual payments to the government called 'quit rents' were also mandatory, usually 10 per cent of the land valuation.[18]

The Balcombes made a wearisome journey of five days and four nights, stopping at roadside inns, to visit their land at Bungonia; William and his eldest son rode, and Betsy drove her mother in their new two-horse gig. At their land grant, they found green grassland after the winter rains, verdant along the banks of the watercourse, and copses of wattle and eucalypts. A recently established farm, 'Inverary Park', adjoined theirs, and Balcombe introduced himself and his family to their new neighbour, Dr David Reid. He was a former naval surgeon from Aberdeen, Scotland, who had served at Trafalgar on the *Bellerophon*. Balcombe had always enjoyed the companionship of naval men, and a friendship was quickly established and hospitality offered by Reid and his wife Agnes. The Balcombes learned that Reid had been a surgeon-superintendent on convict ships, had decided to settle in New South Wales in 1822, and that it was only a few months earlier that he and his wife and children had moved to the new farmhouse they had built on their property. They already had some land under cultivation, worked by convicts assigned to them. It was the beginning of a warm and lifelong friendship between the two families, which would be bonded in the next generation by marriage.

Dr Reid would have warned the Balcombes to watch out on their return journey for bushrangers—escaped convicts who adopted the practice of highwaymen.[19] He may also have mentioned that the Aboriginal people of the district were disaffected, but he probably did not comprehend how much their traditional hunting grounds were being displaced by the new farms. Sheep and cattle were taking over the grasslands formerly cropped by kangaroos.

On 18 June, Brisbane had sent a despatch to Lord Bathurst, informing him that seven stock-keepers in the Bathurst region had been murdered by Aboriginals 'in the most cruel and barbarous manner'. He therefore sought his lordship's permission 'to raise a Troop of Colonial Cavalry' to keep in check the Aboriginals, 'against whom Infantry have no chance of success', nor the police.[20] This resulted two months later in a declaration of martial law in regions west of the highest point of the Blue Mountains. Beyond that boundary, soldiers, settlers and even convicts could legally take up arms against the Aboriginal people.[21]

On 15 July, the ship *Alfred* arrived in Sydney from London, having called on the way at Madeira and Hobart Town. Among the passengers were some who intended to cause ructions and would change the way of life in New South Wales forever.

Foremost among them were two barristers at law, Robert Wardell and William Charles Wentworth. The editor of the *Sydney Gazette*, Robert Howe, made the dry observation: 'We have no occasion to announce the latter Gentleman to be, by birth, an Australian—such being old news.'[22] These two men would soon give the government-supported *Gazette* some competition in the newspaper business and put Governor Brisbane on his mettle, attempting to reform the way the colony was governed. That was the avowed aim of the Sydney-born Wentworth, a tall rangy man with a shock of red hair, already famous in the colony for having pioneered the crossing of the Blue Mountains when he was just 23 with his friends William Lawson and Gregory Blaxland, a few servants, horses and dogs. (The Aboriginal people had known how to cross for generations but had not been consulted.)

Six years later, Wentworth had published a book *A Statistical, Historical and Political Description of the Colony of New South Wales*, outlining his views on how the colony of New South Wales should be run. These opinions were vehemently opposed by John Macarthur: 'Anything in the shape of a Legislative Assembly in the present condition of our society... would seal the destruction of every respectable person here.'[23]

Before his departure for England to qualify to practise as a barrister, Wentworth, son of police superintendent D'Arcy Wentworth by a convict woman, Catherine Crowley, had pressed for the institution of representative government—as had been conceded to the British colony of Canada in 1791—and trial by a civil jury, as advised in the Bigge report. However, these issues had not been advanced.

Now, the audacious Wentworth had returned. With a good legal degree behind him, an understanding of the British Constitution, and praise from Cambridge dons for his poem 'Australasia' (prophesying 'A new Britannia in another world'), he saw himself as 'the instrument of procuring a free constitution for my country'.[24] But the loss of freedom for the indigenous inhabitants was never his concern.

Wentworth's colleague Robert Wardell, an Englishman, had met him at Cambridge and been inspired by his vision of an independent future for New South Wales. He had qualified at the London Bar two years earlier than his friend and applied for the new office of attorney-general in the colony, but lost out to Bannister. He had now arrived with his mother with the intention of practising law with Wentworth. As it turned out, their first case was to be a suit against the owner of the ship *Alfred* for subjecting them to 'a wet and comfortless cabin' and denying 'sufficient nourishment and refreshments' on the voyage. They would be successful, awarded damages and costs.[25]

Other significant passengers arriving on the *Alfred* were John Mackaness, a 54-year-old barrister with some radical liberal views, appointed the new sheriff for the colony, and Dr William Redfern, a former naval surgeon, who had earlier been convicted of encouraging a seamen's mutiny at the Nore (a naval anchorage in the Thames estuary), and in 1801 had been transported to New South Wales. There his medical skills were recognised and he received a conditional pardon and became a friend and family doctor to Governor Macquarie. He rose to be surgeon and acting supervisor at the new Sydney hospital, the first teacher of Australian medical students, and he instituted important reforms for the health of convicts on transport ships that saved many lives. Redfern was returning from London to his Sydney home.

These were remarkable personalities to have found themselves on the same vessel; all being of a liberal or radical persuasion, they must have enjoyed lively political discussions over meals, mapping plans for their own futures and that of the colony during the long, comfortless voyage.

However, it would not have been any of their names that caught the attention of Betsy and her parents in the *Sydney Gazette*, but that of another arriving passenger: 'E. Abell, Esq.' They must have thought it was a mistake or coincidence, that it could not possibly be Betsy's scoundrel of a husband. They would have known by then that there was an Abell family in Van Diemen's Land of convict origin, but those people were by definition excluded from the gentlemanly label 'Esquire'.

It was indeed Betsy's husband, an officer and no gentleman, but with sufficient connections to pass as one. He had come to Sydney to seek her out. We have only Betsy's account of his visit. On 10 August, she wrote an impassioned, pleading letter once again to the distinguished Major-General Sir Henry Torrens, Commander-in-Chief of the British army, based at the Horse Guards:

Dear and most honoured Sir,

Since I had the pleasure of addressing a letter to you I have been shocked and annoyed by Mr Abell's appearance in this colony. He arrived here in a ship named the *Alfred* intending to proceed against my Father for keeping his Wife from him but very fortunately his intentions were frustrated by a Bond being produced of his for £4000 belonging to a notorious swindler by the name of Patterson who died here about a year and half ago he was transported to this place for forging Notes and it was strongly suspected poisoning his patients. The persons who administrated to his Will found among other papers this Bond of Mr Abell's. It happened most fortunately for Abell that the very vessel which brought Patterson to this place was underweigh for Van Diemen's Land and he without further delay got on Board. Before he embarked he called on my Father's Attorney and made a most extraordinary confession of villainies which he had practised since the age of 15 till now. The only crime he would not accuse himself of (unfortunately for me) was a prior marriage. That he strictly denied but said he was quite as anxious to get it annuled as I could possibly be. He had a confession to make which when he arrived at the Derwent [in Van Diemen's Land] he should wish to do to any confidential friend of my Father's which would chill the blood of those who heard it with horror. I am anxiously expecting to hear this communication. No tongue can tell the atrocities he has practised and the shocking character he bears. He owned having robbed Papa & said he took my jewels merely that they might be in a place of safety.

I think he is the most dreadful character of low measure heard of. He said he never had any affection for me that he merely married under the hope of gaining something good thru my Father and his exalted interests.

I fear that I am intruding too much on your patience but indeed it is such a gratification and delight to be writing to you who have been so *very very* kind to me when friendless and deserted by my Husband that I can never think of your benevolence without the acutest emotions of gratitude. I have taken the liberty to send two of the Pheasants of this country and as they are esteemed as curious I trust Lady Torrens will do further favour to accept them. I should feel much honoured indeed. My Father and Brother beg to offer their respectful compliments to Lady Torrens & yourself and I trust you will believe me to be,

Most Gratefully & Truly obliged,

L.E. Abell

P.S. Would it be presuming too far on your friendship was I to beg of you to intercede for a Grant of Land for myself and child as it would be a certain independence for her when she becomes of age. The Governor told me if in his power he would give it immediately but it was not customary to grant land to Females or Children but if I had any Friend in England who would ask Sir Wilmot Horton it should be done immediately upon my getting the order. Will you be that kind Friend to me respected Sir. I humbly request this favor as it would be a certain independence for my dear little Girl. As for me I have nothing to hope for deserted as I am by my Husband and thereby out of favor for any future prospect of bettering my condition.

My Father's health is very precarious caused by the violent attacks he has of Gout. He has promised if I succeed in Getting Land to stock it for me. I entreat you and your wife forgive me for beseeching this but if I have erred I implore forgiveness for my presumption and trusting Heaven will shower down its blessings on yourself and Family, I beg to succeed by your assistance.

Your Gratefully Obliged and humble servant,

L.E. Abell[26]

Edward Abell had obviously learned of Balcombe's new position as colonial treasurer and imagined it was a lucrative one. The posting was announced in British newspapers and much colonial news was relayed in Madras papers. He would have thought that Betsy was likely now to have money also; if she had acquired a land grant, he was legally entitled to it as her husband. He must have expected sufficient advantage in coming to Sydney to more than pay for his ship's passage.

Lawrence Stone in *Road to Divorce: England 1530–1987* outlines the appalling position for a deserted wife in the early nineteenth century, totally at the mercy of her husband: 'He retained the right to all his wife's earnings during her life, "every farthing she makes by her labour being his, because she is his wife, though separated."' He noted that there were 'many cases on record of an estranged husband swooping down, sometimes years or decades after the separation, seizing or selling all his wife's goods and chattels, taking all her savings, and disappearing again. And he was legally within his rights to do so.'[27]

Betsy's letter is too disjointed and emotional to make much sense of what happened when Abell arrived, but there are enough clues to suggest one scenario. It seems he may have confronted Balcombe and demanded to see Betsy and to claim whatever assets she had as his legal entitlement. This would naturally have enraged Balcombe, but he must have controlled his temper sufficiently to make a suggestion very much in his daughter's interests. He would have indicated that Abell was mistaken if he thought that Betsy owned land; there was a ruling against single women and deserted wives doing so. And instead of a stick, Balcombe may have offered a carrot—that he would be willing to pay Abell a certain amount of money if he would agree to liberate his daughter from the marriage. As mentioned, divorce, because of its high cost and requirement of an Act of Parliament, was out of the question.[28] But if Abell would admit that he had a previous marriage—perhaps in India—an annulment would be possible. It is clear from Betsy's letter that Abell hotly denied 'a prior marriage' (as he would, knowing that bigamy incurred a seven-year sentence) but said that he was as anxious to have the marriage annulled as she was.

So Balcombe may have suggested the only realistic alternative, a private separation, which required a deed of agreement to be signed by both parties in front of an attorney or conveyancer. It would give both of them independence and enable each to marry again in a way that would be broadly acceptable to society.[29] That something very like this was proposed is evidenced by the fact that Abell *did* have a meeting with Balcombe's attorney, and there is no other reasonable explanation as to why he would do so. But the meeting clearly did not go well. If Balcombe offered a sum as an inducement to sign the deed, perhaps that sum was not sufficient. Or the attorney may have pushed too far—often with a deed of private separation an attorney or conveyancer asked for a maintenance allowance for the wife and any children; Stone notes that 'in the nineteenth century this usually came to about a third of the husband's net income'.[30] If this ambit claim was made, perhaps without Balcombe's knowledge, Abell might well have exploded into an angry rant, in the course of which he confessed to various villainies which would 'chill the blood'.

During this unpleasantness, the name of James Patterson apparently came up, Abell's old crony in Madras, the forger and swindler convicted and transported to Sydney, who had died eighteen months earlier.[31] Somehow the attorney knew of the late, unregretted Patterson and of a forged bond among his papers in the name of Edward Abell. That seemed to be effective in frightening off Betsy's blackguard husband, but it left her in the same unhappy position of a deserted wife.

If correspondence or a journal by Balcombe's attorney was still available in archives today, that could have clarified the confused situation described by Betsy. But if that possibility offered hope to a biographer, it has been extinguished. Assuming that Balcombe's solicitor in 1824 was Messrs Moore of George Street, the same he retained in later years, unfortunately no such record survives.

Betsy's sad and rather desperate letter to Sir Henry Torrens in London was apparently accompanied by the unlikely gift of 'two Pheasants of this country' for his wife. Pheasants are not native to Australia; an 1819 watercolour, pen and ink drawing entitled 'The Mountain Pheasant', by the convict artist Richard Browne, is actually of a lyrebird displaying its plumage.[32] Betsy could surely not have afforded the expense or persuaded a ship's captain to convey two live lyrebirds. (Although live birds *were* sent—cockatoos and even emus and Western Australian black swans—it was at great expense, as crew had to be specially deputed to feed them and keep them away from the ship's dogs.) For Betsy to have the lyrebirds stuffed by a taxidermist, as well as boxed and shipped, would still have been costly, but a small investment weighed against the possibility of obtaining a land grant.

However, there is no evidence that Torrens made an effort to press her case for a grant. At the time he had other concerns, with reports from India that far too many soldiers, including his own nephew, were dying of 'fever and bowel disease'.[33] He may have been less than impressed when Betsy had written to him the previous year asking that he honour his late brother's promissory note to Edward Abell. Although he had probably suspected that the note was a forgery, as a gentleman he had complied.

Betsy believed that Abell had 'jumped ship' for Van Diemen's Land after the meeting with her father's attorney—but shipping lists show that he did not leave Sydney immediately. In fact, he was still around when she wrote her letter to Torrens. He was to remain in the colony for two months, melding into the shadowy world of convicts, gamblers and ne'er-do-wells. Perhaps from The Rocks or the Botanical Gardens he watched her as she walked around the cove with their daughter in her arms. His name does not appear again in the newspapers until 'Shipping News' reveals his departure on 20 September on the *Prince Regent*, and another list picks him up in Hobart Town for two weeks, before he sailed on the same vessel, 'passenger for India'. After Mauritius the *Prince Regent* continued via the Cape to England, but Abell would have changed to another vessel bound for Madras.[34]

In India his trail is lost.

CHAPTER 32

THE FASHIONABLES

The Balcombes and Betsy were delighted when asked to dine at Parramatta as guests of the governor and his Scottish wife, Anna Maria. They enjoyed what Amelia Forbes described as the 'Beneficent Rule of Sir Thomas Brisbane'.[1]

Old Government House at Parramatta, just over 15 miles from Sydney, is of the same vintage as St Helena's Plantation House. Although considerably smaller, its elegant Georgian architecture is similar: two-storeyed, slate-roofed, with tall shuttered windows flanking a front portico. Its construction was more sound than the earlier official residence in Sydney, which was blighted by the haphazard additions of various governors. Government House Parramatta was a more substantial building, graciously situated with lawns sloping to the Parramatta River, where there was a wharf for boats from Sydney. The bucolic vista of parkland with the placid river winding through it was reminiscent of gentler parts of Scotland and had more appeal for the Brisbanes than the view of Sydney harbour. They preferred living at a distance from the rough and tumble of commercial life, the raucous noise of convicts and the interruptions and complaints of difficult departmental officials. The price was that some of those officials, such as Frederick Goulburn and Commissary-General William Wemyss, took on not only more responsibility but also more personal power and made life difficult for the governor. But of more importance to Sir Thomas was that the distance from the sea allowed a clearer observation of the southern skies.

Three hundred feet from the house was his favourite haunt, his observatory, called 'the Greenwich of the Southern Hemisphere', built at his own expense in 1822. All that currently remains are two monolithic sandstone blocks, the anchors for his transit instruments, two telescopes aimed through domes, their shutters allowing movement on a north–south axis, measuring longitude and the exact position of the stars. Brisbane's passion resulted in a major contribution to astronomical science—but that was not why he had been appointed. When the Duke of Wellington had recommended him for the post, Bathurst had protested: 'I need a man who will govern not the heavens, but the earth in New South Wales.'[2] Wellington's clout had prevailed. But Brisbane's preference to reside at Parramatta continued to draw criticism from many quarters, despite the fact that he was generally well liked.

Bathurst had ruled that the colonial treasurer should guarantee a personal bond, as was customary for public servants handling government monies. On 21 September 1824, Brisbane requested from Balcombe a bond of 50,000 Spanish dollars in response to Lord Bathurst's demand. This bond, however, was not sent to London; Brisbane must have decided that the amount would be considered insufficient. Instead a new bond of £30,000 sterling was prepared and ultimately sent to Bathurst on 8 February 1825.[3]

At this time Balcombe was embarking on some lavish expenditures, fencing his land at Bungonia, stocking it with sheep and cattle, and a dwelling house and huts for his convict workers were being built, in accordance with the provisions set down for government land grants. At The Briars on St Helena he had enjoyed running a small farm, because there were slaves to tend the dairy cattle, poultry, vegetable gardens and orchard. On this far more extensive spread of the same name, he had convicts as workers. But unless he had been very fortunate in the choice of those assigned to him, they would not have been as obedient as the slaves or as skilled at farming. Most convicts came from the urban conglomerates of Britain.

Balcombe's son William had also begun farming land his father had purchased on the Molonglo Plains (near present-day Canberra), and he was the first in the family to fall victim to bushrangers. A brass-nailed 'leathern trunk' containing his wearing apparel was stolen from a cart on the road west of Sydney, beyond Parramatta, 'by two men, supposed to be Bushrangers'. Balcombe offered a reward of twenty Spanish dollars for its recovery.[4]

The *Australian*, the colony's first independent newspaper, with an avowed aim of making the colonists aware of their legislative rights, was launched on 14 October by its joint editors, the barristers William Charles Wentworth and Robert Wardell; it was as robust and political as they were. Balcombe characteristically made a point of befriending them. At this time, ambitious to succeed, he was making his presence felt in colonial society: he subscribed to the Catholic chapel, although he was not a Roman Catholic; signed a petition (a 'memorial') for a Scots church although not a Presbyterian; and subscribed to the Wesleyan Missionary Society although not a Methodist.[5] An Anglican, Balcombe was determined to be recognised as a good citizen.

He succeeded. In October, he joined the new Agricultural Society and was soon asked to be an office-bearer. But the Society made a poor show at the Parramatta Fair, with only a few head of horned cattle, some sixty sheep and lambs and a dozen sale horses exhibited. It determined to do better next time and concluded with an excellent dinner at Walker's Hotel, attended by the governor. Shared interest in the Society brought together people who were not natural companions—the Reverend Samuel Marsden and the brothers John and Gregory Blaxland with Wentworth and Wardell, for example. John Macarthur had not deigned to join them, however. 'After the cloth was removed', many toasts were drunk, a few songs were sung and 'good humour prevailed till past nine o'clock, when the Governor retired'.[6] It was a long time, if at all, before such a group sat down to a meal together again.

Whatever Balcombe privately felt about the 'emancipist faction' of Wentworth and Wardell as opposed to the 'exclusives' led by Macarthur, over issues such as trial by jury, representative government and freedom of the press, he was careful not to become identified with either.

An initial battle seemed to go Wentworth's way when the first civil jury of twelve was empanelled in November; Justice Forbes had ruled that the case should proceed 'in like manner as Courts of Session proceed in England'.[7] But emancipists were still excluded from the juries, radically reducing the number of men qualified for jury duty: 'In Sydney, only 180 men out of almost 1500 free or colonial born adult male residents qualified as jurors. They were predominantly merchants, householders or settlers, tradesmen, officials, publicans and shopkeepers. Very few were colonial born.' Brisbane was willing to consider 'limited participation by former convicts' but not before he had consulted with the British government.[8]

Balcombe was gaining an understanding of the need for civil reforms but, having been less than a year in the colony, he was unfamiliar with the intricacies and nuances of such a stratified society. (Britain had been far more stratified of course but he had never been in a position there to affect the way society operated.) However, he now understood the social position he and his family might best occupy and, despite his brief friendship with Edward Macarthur (who returned to England in January 1825), it would not be with the exclusives. Balcombe's rumoured friendship with Bonaparte put him beyond the pale for many old soldiers, such as John Macarthur.

There were often reminders of Napoleon in the press. Large extracts from his last will and testament were published in the *Gazette* on 13 January 1825. It must have had a powerful emotional impact on the Balcombes to read their former friend's last request—'It is my wish that my ashes may repose on the banks of the Seine, in the midst of the French people, whom I have loved so well'—and to see the names of all their old companions and to study the share allocated to each. They would have been shocked that the loyal Bertrand received a meagre 500,000 francs, while Count de Montholon was left over two million, a fortune. They would have wondered if it had something to do with the favours offered by his wife, although she had departed in 1819 and Montholon *had* shown fidelity by staying to the end, as had the Bertrands. Napoleon had also asked that his Austrian wife, Marie Louise, for whom he retained 'the most tender sentiments', preserve their son 'from the snares which yet environ his infancy'. His son should never forget that he was born a French prince. He left to him his swords and daggers, his two pairs of pistols, his plate, field bed, saddles, spurs, books and the linen he had worn. Counts de Montholon and Bertrand and the valet Marchand were appointed the executors of his will. The companions with him at Longwood were all remembered and a sum distributed to some favourite officers who had fought with him in different campaigns. His bequest of 10,000 francs to Cantillon, the subaltern who had attempted to kill the Duke of Wellington, could be seen as a final glint of humour.[9]

When Napoleon was mentioned in the *Sydney Gazette* and the *Australian*, the tone had changed: nostalgia had crept in and attitudes were softer. Most anecdotes showed the conqueror of much of Europe in a favourable light, not as a 'usurper' or a ruthless despot. One went as far as calling him 'the greatest man of the age'.[10]

Also in January, Justice Forbes appointed Balcombe a Justice of the Peace and honorary magistrate, one of eight in Sydney. Balcombe's duties as colonial treasurer were clearly not regarded as sufficiently onerous to prevent him taking on the magistrate role; but this new responsibility—which generally involved hearing and adjudicating upon crimes committed by convicts—was in fact enormous, as magistrates could consign people to multiple floggings, the treadmill or to the harsh penitentiaries of Norfolk Island and Moreton Bay. The lawyer Roger Therry thought that magistrates colluded too much and had excessive power: 'A facility for the abuse of it was afforded by a prevalent practice of entertaining the complaints of masters against their assigned servants in the private residences of magistrates, where they were exempt from public criticism.'[11]

On 6 February, Lord Bathurst sent a sharp rebuke to Governor Brisbane for fixing Balcombe's salary at £1200 a year, although he himself had asked the governor to determine what was appropriate. 'As I was unacquainted with the full extent of the Duties and responsibility which would devolve upon the Treasurer, when I appointed Mr Balcombe to that office I deemed it adviseable to defer fixing the amount of his Salary until I had heard from you on the subject, when I should be better enabled to form an opinion as to what would be a proper remuneration.' Bathurst regretted that 'Mr Balcombe's Emoluments' had been set 'at an amount which the circumstances of the case do not appear to authorize'. He had approved the government paying for Balcombe's house rent, 'not conceiving for one moment that you would have fixed his Salary at a rate so much above my intentions. I consider that a salary of one thousand pounds per annum, without any other advantages, will be a remuneration fully adequate to the Rank and Station of that officer.' His lordship stated that from the time of the receipt of his despatch, Balcombe should go onto the reduced salary and pay his own house rental. Balcombe's role in the 'St Helena plot' clearly still rankled with the Secretary of State. He mentioned once again that 'the amount of the Securities which Mr Balcombe was to enter into with the Board of Treasury' had not yet arrived.[12]

When Brisbane received the despatch some five months later, he could have been forgiven for thinking that if his lordship had such firm ideas on the subject of Balcombe's salary, he might have determined it himself instead of asking him to nominate what he thought appropriate.

Bathurst was angry with the governor that neither his requests for a description of Balcombe's duties nor the bond had reached him.

Despatches crossed on their long voyages. The bond was in fact on its way to Bathurst. It stated that Balcombe would 'faithfully and diligently execute and perform the duties of the Office of Treasurer of New South Wales', and should he fail in that execution, 'I bind myself, my heirs, Executors and Administrators' to the 'Penalty of Thirty Thousand Pounds Sterling'. It was witnessed by Balcombe's invaluable principal clerk, James Stirling Harrison and his relative, Robert Stirling, Lieutenant in the 3rd Regiment.[13]

In early March, the *Australian* announced the 'Sydney Races': 'The lovers of the turf were on Monday last gratified with a taste of this their favorite sport.' A piece of ground 'tolerably well adapted for the purpose' had been chosen just south of the turnpike gate near Liverpool and a large marquee erected for the spectators. The military officers were there in force and 'most of the respectable inhabitants of Sydney', ladies as well as gentlemen, and many 'fashionables'. The course was a mile long and because of recent rains the ground was heavy. Balcombe had taken to the sport with gusto with his friends Captain Piper and Sir John Jamison. Because gout had often disabled him on St Helena, he had not actively participated in its race meetings, where the residents and officers rode their own horses. But in Sydney he could be a stylish racehorse owner and hire a former convict as his jockey. He had bought a large colt with the unpromising name 'Unwilling'. Captain Piper's horse lived up to its name, 'Everlasting', and won the first race with ease. In the second race, 'Mr Balcombe's horse took the lead and kept it till within a short distance of the winning post', when Piper's horse won again. 'There were two other races, but the horses were so unequally matched,' reported the *Gazette*, 'that they afforded no sport. Besides, one of them bolted and took to the swamp, where he stuck.' Afterwards, Jamison entertained a large party at dinner, concluding with a 'merry dance' with the ladies, including Betsy Abell and Mrs Jane Balcombe.[14] In Sydney, the semi-invalid woman of Saint-Omer had sparkled back into life.

The enthusiasm for the race meeting and festivities resulted, a fortnight later, in the inauguration of the Sydney Turf Club. Governor Brisbane agreed to be the club's patron and Chief Justice Forbes became an honorary member. Sir John Jamison was elected president and Balcombe and George Mills, the registrar of the Supreme Court, accepted the positions of honorary treasurer and honorary secretary. Captain Piper, William Wentworth and the sheriff, John Mackaness, completed the committee. They agreed—no doubt over several libations—that they would hold two race meetings a year and that a ball would be held after the spring meeting, much along the lines of the races held on St Helena.

The gregarious Balcombe, a man's man, had found his social niche among the fashionables, the group who shared his new passion for horse racing and for the wining and dining, laughter and conviviality that went with it. It was an outlet for his good spirits and energy, and he won popularity for his willingness to serve as an officer-bearer for the Turf Club and Agricultural Society, adding to the official demands of his public roles.

The Balcombes were given an especial mark of favour on 31 March 1825 when Sir Thomas Brisbane dined at their home in O'Connell Street. There is no mention of Lady Brisbane accompanying him— she was said to rarely leave Parramatta.[15] Although Balcombe and the intellectual Brisbane may not have seemed easy companions, the conversation could have been lively. Apart from the governor's passions for astronomy and the natural sciences, he had a great love of France, its culture and its people, having lived three years there as part of the army of occupation. He was bound to be interested in Balcombe's relationship with Bonaparte on St Helena and the matters they might have discussed: particularly the former emperor's encouragement of the sciences, his famous expedition to Egypt with a shipload of '*savants*'—artists, historians and scientists.

Furthermore, the embattled governor might already have considered Balcombe an ally. But they were not to know that they were both under attack at that very time in the 19 March issue of the London *Morning Chronicle*, by a pseudonymous Sydney resident calling himself 'Austral-Asiaticus'. The writer, most probably George Boyes, complained of 'an almost incredible deterioration' in the economy and circumstances of the colony under the present regime. The price of wheat had plummeted. Farmers and graziers were in debt. Merchants, extending credit, were 'saddled with a heavy premium for Treasury Bills'. He made clear that he attached no particular blame 'to his Excellency personally, who I am convinced is a well-meaning, an amiable and benevolent man; but, to that system of injudicious economy and retrenchment, which he was *directed* to introduce into his various departments by the Ministry at home'. As an example of bureaucratic excess, the writer quoted the role of the colonial treasurer, formerly carried out by the 'Treasurer of the Police Fund, whose integrity in that office was unimpeached, and unimpeachable, and who received for the performance of its duties one hundred pounds sterling per annum'. But he had been displaced, 'to make way for a Mr. BALCOMBE, of St Helena notoriety, with a salary of £1200 per annum—an allowance of £150 for a Clerk—and £150 for a house! Illustrious specimen of financial economy!!'[16]

Given the snide mention of Balcombe by 'Austral-Asiaticus', it is interesting to speculate on who knew, or thought they knew, something about the Balcombes as a result of English newspapers and personal letters from the 'home country'. Ships regularly delivered newspapers, albeit five or six months out of date. Balcombe had been much in the news in 1818—but, more than six years later, who remembered his involvement in the alleged 'St Helena plot'?

Barry O'Meara's best-selling book, *Napoleon in Exile*, condemning the former emperor's treatment by Sir Hudson Lowe, published in

1822 but regularly reprinted, contained many favourable mentions of Balcombe and his family. It certainly reached the colony. Indeed, a copy was put up for auction in 1825.[17] There was still huge interest in Napoleon. On 7 April 1825, the *Sydney Gazette* published a 'Biography' of 'Barry Edward O'Meara Esq', a virtual panegyric, not just of the doctor but of Bonaparte also. O'Meara, according to the article, 'merited distinction and respect by the generous feelings with which he was inspired towards the greatest man of the age'. The *Gazette*'s editor, Robert Howe, a devout Wesleyan, seemed an unapologetic admirer. He knew and liked Balcombe, and was well aware of his Bonaparte connection from gossip and O'Meara's book. But no revelations from Balcombe about the exiled emperor ever appeared in the *Gazette*'s pages. There would have been a very mixed reaction.

The King's Birthday celebrations were held on Saturday 23 April.[18] The sixty-third year of George IV was marked in fine style in his colonial outpost of New South Wales with a holiday observed throughout the territory. Perhaps even the convict treadmills ceased operation. At sunrise the Royal Standard and the Union Jack were raised; the governor came into town for the ceremony, and at midday a royal salute was fired from Dawes' Battery, responded to by the sloop-of-war HMS *Slaney*. In the evening, a party of 63 gentlemen 'partook of a sumptuous dinner at Hill's Tavern in Hyde Park'. Sheriff Mackaness presided at one end of the long, boisterous table, and Balcombe occupied the chair at the opposite end. Inevitably, some at the table would have heard the whispered rumour (whether it followed Balcombe to Australia or he brought it with him) and believed that they were looking at the natural son of the King, whose birthday they were celebrating with 'loyal and appropriate toasts'.[19]

At this dinner, Boyes decided to drop his frosty attitude towards the popular and exuberant Balcombe, as he wrote to his wife:

> I have told you already that I was very much offended with Balcomb in his mode of treating for a house—from that time I refused all intercourse with him—until last 23rd April when we all—I mean *Des Gens comme il faut* [the proper sort of

people]—dined together—the Sheriff had requested me to take the bottom of the table—but I was not in very good spirits that day and declined. Balcomb overheard what passed and thinking it a fair opportunity for stopping a breach—offered his services and took the seat. I got as far off as I could. As soon as the soup was removed I heard him roaring out in the midst of sixty people at least:

'Boyes, Boyes, will you allow me the pleasure of drinking wine with you?'

He drank his bumper and I pledged him. So there was an end of our difference. I met him at Government House the other day where we were assembled to be introduced to the new Archdeacon Scott and we shook hands.[20]

At the same time, Governor Brisbane received a letter from the Colonial Office, recalling him to England. He understood he was to be replaced by another military officer, General Ralph Darling. It was not entirely unexpected but it was privately hurtful and infuriating. He believed it had come about through unkind gossip and misrepresentations in the press.

Many of the citizens of Sydney rallied around the governor, expressing regret that he was leaving. He was surprised to find he had so many friends. The *Sydney Gazette* reprinted an item from the *Hobart Town Gazette* deploring the replacement of Brisbane: 'The appointment of General Darling, in succession to our beloved Governor in Chief, Sir Thomas Brisbane KCB, was noticed in most of the London papers.'[21]

The Balcombes entertained Sir Thomas to dinner a second time on the evening of 19 May. Chief Justice Forbes and his wife may have joined them. The Forbes couple had bonded 'like one family' with the Brisbanes during the fortnight they had stayed with them at Parramatta when they first arrived, and Amelia Forbes also regarded the Balcombes as their 'firm friends'.[22]

The governor needed the advice of the magistrates who now included, as well as Balcombe, the new police chief Francis Rossi (a Corsican, who had been in charge of Indian convicts on the island of Mauritius). Brisbane requested the magistrates' opinion of trial by jury and its effects—how far they viewed it 'as proper to admit the Emancipist class of Colonists to a participation of the privilege of sitting in Juries'.[23]

Brisbane would take with him to the British government the response of the eight magistrates: 'We beg leave to state, that it is our unanimous opinion that the Juries have conducted themselves with great propriety, and that the establishment of the Trial by Jury, even upon its present limited scale, has given a general feeling of security in the enjoyment of our civil rights; and we beg leave to further respectfully submit to your Excellency, that we consider this Colony is now in a state to allow of the Trial by Jury being extended with public advantage to the Supreme Court.'[24]

William Wentworth wrote an editorial in the *Australian* of 6 October heartily endorsing the magistrates' verdict: 'When so respectable and weighty a body as the Justices of the Peace thus step forward and pledge their opinions so liberally and so publicly, it would be madness for any party here to resist the introduction of Trial by Jury; it would be frivolous trifling, and serious injustice.'

CHAPTER 33

A FLEETING ENTENTE CORDIALE

The present-day suburb of La Perouse in Sydney occupies the protective northern arm of Botany Bay, a wide, relatively shallow body of water 'discovered' as an anchorage by Captain James Cook in 1770, its shores long occupied by the Eora people who fished its abundant waters. Eighteen years later, an extraordinary encounter occurred there.

On 18 January 1788, Captain Arthur Phillip, in charge of the First Fleet of eleven ships and over a thousand people—convicts, marines and officers—arrived to found the penal settlement of New South Wales. Returning from investigating a large waterway further north, Phillip was astonished to discover two French vessels, *La Boussole* and *L'Astrolabe*, in the bay. They were under the command of Captain Jean-François de Galaup, Comte de La Pérouse, renowned as a great explorer of the Pacific. He was seeking sanctuary after some of his two hundred crew had been attacked by Samoans. Captain Phillip treated the French with civility but great caution, uncertain of relations between their two countries on the far side of the world. He sailed nine miles north with his fleet and entered the magnificent waterway of Port Jackson, having chosen Sydney Cove as the preferred site of settlement.[1]

La Pérouse anchored in Botany Bay and set up camp on the northern promontory so that his wounded men could receive medical attention.

A scientist on his expedition, Father Receveur, died in February and was buried at the site. A First Fleet surgeon, Philip Gidley King, came to visit in February and enjoyed an amicable dinner with the French.[2] After six weeks, La Pérouse with his vessels sailed on into the vast Pacific and disappeared. Nothing was heard of them for decades, a mystery and source of grief for the French people.[3]

Today the Sydney suburb of La Perouse has the name and three reminders of that lost expedition. On the tip of the peninsula is the grave of Father Receveur and a large monument, erected in 1825, honouring Captain La Pérouse and his men. A small museum nearby gives visitors an account of the history. There is mention that before the great navigator set off from France, a young trainee French army officer had applied to switch to the French navy to join his expedition to the Pacific. Napoleon Bonaparte's application was rejected because of his lack of seafaring experience. Otherwise the course of modern history would have been very different.

Two large and handsome vessels came through Sydney Heads on 29 June 1825 and dropped anchor. They were flying the French flag. The pilot boarded them, and the following day Captain Piper, as naval officer, went out to investigate. The large frigate *La Thétis*, he was delighted to discover, was under the command of Commodore Baron Hyacinthe Yves de Bougainville, a 43-year-old French naval officer and the son of the famous navigator of the South Seas, Louis Antoine, Comte de Bougainville.

This was Hyacinthe's second visit to Sydney, where he had been as a young man more than twenty years earlier with the Nicolas Baudin expedition. He was in overall command of this one, with the corvette *L'Espérance* under Captain Paul-Anne de Nourquer Du Camper. It was explained to Piper that theirs was a scientific voyage through the southern seas, to conduct hydrographic research, discover trade possibilities and hopefully to learn the fate of the La Pérouse expedition after it left Sydney in 1788, a mystery still haunting their nation.

Piper, who viewed diplomacy as being part of his duties as naval officer, welcomed the two commanders and invited them to make his home their own while in Sydney. 'Although we were always shown a great deal of kindness by the local inhabitants,' wrote Bougainville in his private journal, 'this fine fellow outdid all others by his efforts to please us and his extremely obliging behaviour towards us.'[4] Nothing was too much trouble for Piper. He had found the previous French visitors from the 1824 Duperrey expedition stimulating company and was sure that these men would be also.

On the evening of 5 July, Piper hosted a party in their honour at his home, Henrietta Villa. Bougainville and Du Camper brought three of their officers. Governor Brisbane and Lieutenant-Governor Stewart arrived at 6 pm, and almost everybody who was anybody in the colony made an appearance: the chief justice, the archdeacon, the attorney-general and the colonial treasurer, with their families. The Macarthurs, however, had declined.

At dinner, the bachelor Bougainville found himself next to 'a certain Mrs Abel, the daughter of the colonial treasurer', which seemed well-judged seating on the hosts' part, placing him next to an attractive young woman who spoke fluent French (although his English was excellent). He was astonished and intrigued to learn that she had lived on St Helena when Napoleon was exiled there. He wrote that night in his journal: 'She is reportedly famous and goes by the name of Betsy Balcombe who was "a great favourite of Napoleon's". He gave her the nickname of Rosebud of St Helena. She told me all this in good French and thought Napoleon a very amiable gentleman.'[5]

Betsy was perhaps trying too hard. She may not have reported that she was famous, but clearly she had claimed to have been 'a great favourite of Napoleon's', which was of course true (Bougainville seemed to have doubts). Furthermore, Betsy's former relationship with Napoleon was interesting enough without inventions; it is odd that she told him that Napoleon gave her the nickname 'Rosebud', when it was actually his name for the pretty daughter of a neighbouring farmer on St Helena. His admiration for 'Rosebud' had annoyed Betsy—perhaps it still rankled sufficiently for her to wish to annex the name for herself.

After dinner, which probably involved many toasts in the English fashion and which Hyacinthe thought 'took far too long', he danced with Betsy Abel to the music of Captain Piper's band. He was dancing with 'a great favourite' of the fallen conqueror who had died just four years earlier. The historian Colin Dyer has suggested that 'here in Sydney, as Bougainville danced with her, he held in his arms an almost personal link with the Emperor who had dominated Europe for so many years'.[6] At 10 pm, Governor Brisbane 'took his leave', wrote Hyacinthe, 'and was hailed by salvos from Captain Piper's artillery'. When he himself and his compatriots left near midnight, they 'were saluted with three hurrahs'.[7]

As Betsy and her parents returned home, probably in Balcombe's new purchase, a handsome barouche pulled by two grey horses, one wonders if her emotions were in turmoil. Her life in Sydney was giddy, but unreal and essentially lonely. So many parties, so many balls, dancing close to gentlemen, especially in the waltz, their arms around her, bodies pressed together, reminding her of her physicality, her sexuality. She was 22 years old, blonde, beautiful and vivacious; she had always been a flirt. Was she to be alone for the rest of her life? In a colony where the ratio of the sexes was radically unequal, three men or more to one woman, it is certain that any number of men were interested in her, even without knowing of the added piquancy of her former connection with Bonaparte.[8]

Perhaps she cared for none of the men she had met so far in New South Wales; perhaps none of them attracted her, amused her, compelled her interest. But if her interest *was* ignited, she was still in an impossible situation, as she had explained in her letter to Sir Henry Torrens. She was a deserted wife, not a widow, so she could not marry again without breaking the law by committing bigamy. There was no legal ruling preventing her from cohabiting with a man, but polite society had its own strict rules that would brand her as an outcast. Genteel women would no longer call on or receive her. Betsy had only to remember how Admiral Plampin's mistress had been shunned on St Helena; that was a future she could not possibly contemplate for herself.

She was in a worse position than any 'old maid' depicted in a Jane Austen novel. An old maid was in a wretched situation, dependent on her family or humiliated as a governess or lady's companion. But at least an old maid could hope that a rescuer might appear, perhaps a suitor from her past, as Captain Wentworth did for Anne Elliot in Austen's *Persuasion*. The only hope that Betsy could have to be courted again respectably was a 'private separation', which required Edward

Abell's signature on a deed; there may have been such an attempt but it had failed. Otherwise she could hope for his death. She must have devoutly prayed for that.

So far in her life in Sydney it did not appear that she had met anyone who made the matter an issue. Despite all the dinners, parties, race meetings and balls she attended, there is no indication in the newspapers or in others' private correspondence that she evinced the slightest interest in any particular man. But perhaps Hyacinthe de Bougainville, who happened to be a bachelor, was different . . .

She would have been horrified by Hyacinthe's further description of herself in his journal that night: 'She is twenty-five or thirty years old, perhaps even younger, but is worn out because of ill-health. However, she still has a certain charm and must have been quite a beauty in her day. We talked about Napoleon but it seemed to me that she had fonder memories of M. de Monelon [Montholon]. She stressed several times that she preferred Frenchmen to Englishmen and French customs to English ones. Except for this example of sound judgement, I do not believe that she is very bright.'[9]

Betsy may have seen Bougainville again two nights later at another 'splendid Ball and Supper in honour of our distinguished French Visitors' at Tavern Hill, financed by subscription of the gentlemen of the colony. If so, he did not single her out for comment.[10]

The next week was a tragic one for Captain Piper. His second son, Hugh, was killed in a riding accident. The French commanders paid a visit to express their condolences to their first and most generous host. 'The whole family was in mourning.'[11]

The Frenchmen's social calendar rapidly filled as other leading families in the colony played host to them. They dined with attorney-general Saxe Bannister, who, the following day, 29 July, took Hyacinthe to see the treadmills in the Sydney penitentiary, which police chief Rossi had boasted were restoring law and order. Hyacinthe found it 'a sickening spectacle'.[12]

Two days afterwards, taking what he described as his 'customary walk from 4 pm to 5.30 pm' in the Botanical Gardens, Bougainville 'met the Rosebud of St Helena (Mrs Abel)', but he said no more about their encounter. At the same time three afternoons later, again in the Gardens, he was in discussion with the colonial botanist Charles Frazer, who promised him some Norfolk pine and casuarina seeds, when again he met up with 'Mrs Abel', perhaps not by accident. She apparently told him 'it is [sic] her sister and not she who was Napoleon's favourite'.[13] This was odd, even bizarre, as Betsy was of course the indisputable favourite. Perhaps she sensed that she had been too boastful on the first night she met Bougainville and was now attempting an ungainly retreat. She was hardly being cool and mysterious.

For almost six weeks Betsy did not see the Frenchmen. Bougainville and Du Camper were entertained out of town, many of their activities reported in the newspapers. They visited the governor at Parramatta and had a more enjoyable time during a week with Sir John Jamison at Regentville, from where they visited other established settlers around the area. They learned the correct procedure on their return from an outing: 'We fired three shots to warn the lady of the manor of our arrival (the invisible lady who lives with Sir John in a de facto relationship).'[14]

After all the hospitality they had received, the Frenchmen knew it was their turn. 'We made preparations on board,' Hyacinthe wrote in his journal of 24 August, 'for the official dinner which we are obliged to give.' On the deck of La Thétis, a long table was set with 25 places. It was an all-male event. The main office-bearers of the colony were all invited, as well as several officers of the garrison and all the French naval officers. Betsy would have heard an account of the dinner from her father.

Bougainville and Du Camper went touring again, this time welcomed at the homes of some of the colony's most distinguished and self-regarding settlers: John Oxley, John Macarthur (his sons James and William took the Frenchmen on a kangaroo hunt), Archdeacon Scott and the Reverend Samuel Marsden. On his way back to Sydney, Hyacinthe sailed down the Parramatta River 'alone in a yawl' to revisit 'the attractive Blaxland family'.[15]

Three nights later, on Saturday 10 September, the indomitable Captain Piper, who would long grieve over the death of his son, re-entered the social scene, hosting a ball at Henrietta Villa. Betsy danced again with Bougainville, as did Mrs Harriott Ritchie, one of John Blaxland's daughters. (Her French mother gave Harriott her unusual first name.) 'There was a charming small ball,' Bougainville wrote in his journal, 'where I danced like a young beau.' He added that 'Mrs Ritchie is a beautiful woman with a jealous husband'. His comment about his other dancing partner was unkind: 'Mrs Abel, formerly Betsy Balcombe, the Rosebud of St Helena, today looks like a large spring-loaded doll.'[16]

There are two ways of interpreting Bougainville's response to Betsy. She had always had a fey, giddy element to her behaviour as an adolescent girl on St Helena, in her pranks and laughter, her boisterousness. Perhaps that quality remained in her reaction to a man she found appealing, and her attraction to Bougainville is evident in her flirtatious declaration that she 'preferred Frenchmen to Englishmen', in her possibly contrived meetings with him in the Botanical Gardens, and in the invitation she was about to extend. On the other hand, it could simply be that Betsy's sparkling vivacity, fascinating and even 'bewitching' to some men, did not appeal to Bougainville—and she was tall; he may have preferred a petite, more demure, docile type of woman, such as Mrs Ritchie. Betsy must have noticed his interest in Harriott, but may have convinced herself that her rival was at least six years older,[17] and above all was a married woman with a protector, a wealthy husband who had sat glowering all evening.

Betsy took the initiative and invited Bougainville and the French officers, who were planning to sail the following Wednesday, to 'a small ball' in farewell on the Tuesday night at the Balcombe house in O'Connell Street. She must have invited them that very evening, along with the Pipers, the Ritchies and the Blaxlands, for even a 'small ball' took three days' planning: having the dance floor cleared and waxed, and arranging for a supper and musicians, although the kind Captain Piper would have loaned his band.

Hyacinthe said little in his journal about the 'small ball' at the Balcombes', but wrote: 'I found that I was more and more attracted to Mrs Ritchie, perhaps a little too much . . . How I miss her!' He made the decision that night to delay the departure of his expedition, a frustrating matter for his few hundred seamen, who were refused shore leave unless accompanied by an officer.

Bougainville and Du Camper spent the next few days making social calls to thank their many hosts. On Friday 16 September, their closest friends were invited back to *La Thétis* for a lunch. Hyacinthe personally escorted Mrs Rossi and Harriott Ritchie, whose husband was not mentioned. The other guests were already on board—the Pipers, the Balcombes and Betsy Abell. Afterwards they all proceeded to Henrietta Villa where, Hyacinthe noted, 'everyone offered his arm to his lady and went for a stroll in the garden'. They were joined for dinner by Francis Rossi and some of the French officers and midshipmen, and afterwards there was dancing. 'I wooed the lady in question most assiduously,' Hyacinthe wrote, 'despite the jealous husband made rapid progress and fixed a rendez-vous for the next day. How unfortunate it is that we are on the eve of our departure!'[18]

Doubtless disappointed herself, Betsy by then must have been fully aware of Bougainville's attentions towards Harriott Ritchie. She would have thought her foolish in seeming to accept those attentions, a married woman from one of the families of the first rank of society. But she could not have known quite how foolish Harriott was.

The following evening, Hyacinthe dined with the Corsican Rossi family, but afterwards went on to the Balcombes', who had generously organised another small farewell gathering. But in the Frenchman's account only one guest mattered: 'finished off the evening at Mr Balcombe's, where Mrs Ritchie had pledged she would be'. The layout of Balcombe's house allowed for only one large room for entertaining, so Hyacinthe and Harriott must have slipped out into the garden, under the oak tree. That was indiscreet; but what they arranged was potentially disastrous for her: 'We enjoyed a romantic tête-à-tête and promised to meet the next day at midnight on board.'[19]

The following day, common sense prevailed. A message was delivered to Bougainville on shipboard: 'Received a letter from Mrs R. who has been obliged to go to Newington due to a prior engagement.'[20] Harriott had thought better of it. Sydney was a very small town. A married woman from one of the leading families going aboard a French ship at midnight would be observed and recognised by someone, no matter how well she tried to disguise herself, and the word would spread. Her marriage would be over, her life ruined. If Bougainville had spoken of taking her with him, that was impossible. *La Thétis* was a French naval vessel; another French officer who took his wife on an earlier voyage through the Pacific had narrowly avoided a court-martial.[21] Harriott would have been in a more contemptible situation, merely a mistress.

It is hard to sympathise with Bougainville as he wrote: 'I suffered from deep melancholy. I struck off a reply and felt indisposed.' That evening he called on Mrs Rossi and later 'dined at Mr Balcombe's', where he 'spent a very dull evening... Mrs R. haunts my thoughts... What a pity I became acquainted with her so late in the day! Beloved Harriott!'[22]

On the morning of departure, Wednesday 21 September, Bougainville ensured that all the live Australian fauna he had collected were 'penned on the quarter-deck so that they might be better looked after': two or three kangaroos, at least one surviving emu (the other had died and been stuffed), a black swan and various other caged birds. They left little room for the captain and officers on the deck.

He recorded that 'a large number of people came to bid us a last adieu. As may be expected the good Captain Piper was not the least eager to do so.' As *La Thétis* and *L'Espérance* made their way under sail they gave a 21-gun salute which was returned from Dawes' Battery. Piper's Henrietta Villa came into view and 'we were saluted with his own fanfare and small artillery as we sailed past. I responded with a salvo from the frigate. This was followed by three hurrahs from both the shore and our ships.'[23]

Hyacinthe de Bougainville continued to be known as a ladies' man and never married. He had clearly not recognised Betsy Abell's much-vaunted charms, although other men would. Harriott Ritchie died as Lady Dowling in England in 1881, 'unaware that she occupied such a special place in private diaries that were to remain unread for over two hundred years'.[24]

But Bougainville and his officers had made many generous friends, including the governor. Those friends would not have been happy that Bougainville was carrying the *Most Secret Instructions of the Minister for the Navy*, issued in Paris on 17 February 1824: 'Europe is at present enjoying a period of peace... However, in the event of war breaking out we must plan ahead... If England were to become our enemy, the French navy may, as a result of our forward planning, enjoy considerable success... But for this to happen we must have at our disposal precise information regarding the fortifications of the targeted positions. You must therefore attempt to gather such information, while at the same time taking every precaution to avoid acting in any way which may arouse the suspicion of others as to our secret plans.'[25]

The clandestine mission had been fulfilled by Bougainville. He reported that Port Jackson was 'far from invincible, and its defences are so negligible that one might be tempted to dismiss them as insignificant. Three batteries are the sum total of its defences.' He described the siting of the batteries and the number of guns in each. 'So much for the town's fortifications. As for the defence personnel, only some 700 of the 1325 men belonging to the third, fortieth and forty-eighth regiments are posted in the Sydney and Parramatta barracks. The rest are scattered in various settlements in New South Wales and Van Diemen's Land.' It seemed, he said, that the British government despatched to New South Wales the minimum number of armed forces to keep order. They relied 'on the colony's remoteness from any powerful nations that might launch an offensive, as well as on the speed with which its colonies in India would be able to send relief'. The greatest danger, he speculated, 'would probably come from its own inhabitants. Of the 34,000 Europeans living in Australia, barely 7000 would have anything to gain [from] defending the territory ... But who would wish to form an alliance with such auxiliaries? Who would dare risk the infamy of such an action, and the disastrous consequences of the sudden emancipation of such a large number of criminals?'

His conclusion for his superiors in the French navy was that 'New South Wales is a master-piece of the spirit of colonisation, and all civilised peoples should strive to imitate rather than to destroy such a beautiful establishment'.[26]

CHAPTER 34

THE TREASURY UNDER THE BED

The Balcombes and Betsy had settled into New South Wales society, in the perfectly respectable if rather racy second tier where the 'fashionables' disported themselves. But the lines between their group and those of the 'first rank' were not strictly defined and were occasionally quite fluid. Sir John Jamison, with a mansion and an extensive property on the Nepean, was colonial 'landed gentry', but as the convivial sort, a lover of parties and horse racing, he at first moved easily enough between the two social groups. Francis Forbes and his wife Amelia were happy to attend some of Captain Piper's entertainments and dinners, and were initially welcomed by the 'Parramatta party' too, although they later fell out with the latter over what were viewed as the chief justice's too liberal judgements. The wealthy and often remote Blaxlands of Newington had enjoyed Piper's hospitality, and had also been entertained by the Balcombes' during the recent visit by Commodore Bougainville.

Despite greatly increased revenue from various sources, the Treasury office continued to operate well enough, but with an enormous workload for James Harrison, who, according to his proud father, 'managed the NSW Treasury'.[1] Balcombe had obtained a stout brass-bound padlocked box for the public revenue and, still lacking a vault or more secure storage, stashed it under his bed, his blunderbuss and pistols beside it.

Meanwhile, he was extending his landholdings with further grants and purchases. He had leased a small property at Petersham on the edge of Sydney, probably a temporary holding for his stock before sale, and had paid the down payment on a cottage on a Church estate, 'Glebe Farm'.[2] The family visited The Briars at Bungonia when they could, and their friendship with the Reids, their neighbours at Inverary Park, deepened.

Life was good and Balcombe had more prestige in the community than he had ever had at St Helena. He was gratified to be asked to become a governor or trustee of the Sydney Public Free Grammar School (today the Sydney Grammar School), promoted by John Macarthur and opened in early October 1825; trustees were expected to subscribe at least 50 guineas. Among the trustees of the new college were 'several Macarthurs and both judges of the Supreme Court but also five leading ex-convicts'.[3]

Balcombe also became a member of the local Masonic Lodge, transferring his membership from the St Helena branch.[4] (The Free Masons' movement in France was known for its large number of pro-Bonapartists.[5]) By then the Balcombes were acquainted with the small number of French expatriates in Sydney. There was the police chief Francis Rossi, a Corsican (who hated his infamous former compatriot), and Nicholas Bochsa, who had actually been Napoleon's harpist at the Tuileries. The merchant Prosper de Mestre, son of a French officer who had fled France during the Revolution, was on the board of the Bank of New South Wales, so Balcombe came to know him well.

Balcombe was making many visits to the Bank, where his friend Captain Piper was chairman of directors, and had taken to depositing Treasury funds there.

If William Balcombe was riding a wave of success, Sir Hudson Lowe's career was drifting in the shallows on an ebb tide. While remaining commander of the 93rd Regiment, a position he clearly felt beneath him, he had applied for the governorship of Ceylon but was overlooked. Unpopularity followed him wherever he went. When his name came up in articles about Bonaparte, it was suggested that he, as the prisoner's torturer, had brought shame on Britain.

Lowe became even more embittered when he discovered—coming upon the news rather late in the piece—how well Bonaparte's former providore was doing in a senior government position in New South Wales. He expressed his resentment from Paris in a letter of 26 October 1825 to the Colonial Office, brooding on Balcombe's suspected former dealings: 'It is a fact known to all the followers of Bonaparte and I believe to the Foreign Commissioners that the person spoken of received clandestinely (upon whatever ground this may have been done) the sum of £3000 from Bonaparte in direct violation of the trust reposed in him by his office & of the regulations established for Bonaparte's safe custody & afterwards became one of the most active agents (as recorded under his own hand) of that conspiracy which was formed against me.' (If Lowe's estimate of £3000 was correct, and we follow the calculations of the editor of *Regency Recollections* and multiply by a factor of fifty for a rough modern equivalent, Balcombe had received something like £150,000.[6]) Lowe's letter appears to have been intended for Wilmot Horton, but may have been a draft not sent, for the addressee is not named.

A small paragraph appeared in the *Sydney Gazette* in early December that must have caught Balcombe's notice: 'Sir Hudson Lowe, late Governor of St Helena, has been appointed second in command at Ceylon.'[7] Balcombe was not one to bear grudges and probably wished him well, while realising that 'second in command' was not what Lowe would have wanted.

The Colonial Treasury was in need of additional resources, and James Harrison was overworked: revenue in the colony in 1821 had been a little over £32,000; with the tremendous growth in trade, agriculture, capital transfers and settler population, by 1825 it had increased, mainly from land fees and import duties, to almost £72,000 and was still growing rapidly.[8] Balcombe convinced Governor Brisbane that he needed a second clerk to support Harrison. He had composed a request to Lord Bathurst, which Brisbane promised to personally deliver. For Balcombe to appeal directly to the Secretary of State for the Colonies was another example of his insouciance (he had, incidentally, repaid Henry Goulburn the £50 loan). That Brisbane was willing to act as messenger and advocate indicates his liking for Balcombe;

he must have realised that his support for a new government appointment at the end of his own tenure would annoy his successor, but that his lordship would probably not wish to deny it and further anger him over his abrupt recall. (Brisbane still had strong supporters such as the Duke of Wellington.) One of Brisbane's last acts as governor was to grant provisional approval for a 'confidential clerk' at the Treasury. John Wallace soon proved very capable.[9] (Despite Bathurst's caution over colonial staff increases, he did not prevaricate on this occasion, and accepted the appointment.[10])

Governor Brisbane's departure was preceded by a flurry of farewell dinners and addresses of appreciation which became heavily political. The 'Parramatta party' of pastoralists had invited the governor to a dinner at Walker's Hotel in Parramatta. When Wentworth discovered that this was to be 'exclusive', he made much of that in the *Australian*. A separate dinner was organised by another group, principally emancipists. When Brisbane asked the Parramatta group to invite at least the organisers of the other function to theirs, the original invitation to Walker's was withdrawn, snubbing the governor. When this became known, the governor was overwhelmed with further invitations.

On the first day of December 1825, Sir Thomas Brisbane, his wife, sister-in-law and new aide-de-camp Robert Stirling, departed from New South Wales on the *Mary Hope*, bound for Europe.

Just over two weeks later, on a wet windy Saturday, 17 December, the ship *Catherine Stewart Forbes* dropped anchor in Sydney harbour, bringing the new governor, His Excellency Lieutenant-General Ralph Darling, as well as his family and staff. As the rain was pelting down—which some later saw as an augury—the decision was made that they should stay on board and be formally welcomed to the colony when the weather improved.

The new governor had brought with him his wife Eliza, her two brothers, captains Henry and William Dumaresq, and Lieutenant Stoddart, the governor's aide-de-camp. Darling established his difference from his predecessor by settling them all into the uncomfortable and rambling Sydney Government House. Three days after his arrival, he got down to business, calling a meeting of the first executive council to be set up in New South Wales. Chief Justice Forbes was taken aback when the new governor appointed his brother-in-law Henry Dumaresq as clerk to the executive council. Four days later, the other brother-in-law, William, was placed in temporary charge of the Civil Engineers Department.[11]

Lieutenant-General Darling, aged 53, had been a military officer all of his adult life—in the West Indies, at Corunna in Spain, and during the disastrous Walcheren expedition. At the Horse Guards in London, Darling had been commander-in-chief under the Duke of York, a position later occupied by General Sir Henry Torrens. He was appointed acting governor at Mauritius from August 1818 to July 1820, and was afterwards military commandant there. The colonists—*colons*—were mainly French, the island having been wrested from their nation eight years earlier. Its economy was based on sugar plantations worked by 70,000 African and Malagasy slaves. Darling was determined to end the traffic in slaves, who were mainly smuggled from the island of Madagascar. The French *colons* hated him for that.[12]

One biographer has said that 'Darling's brief dictatorship over an alien population in Mauritius was an unfortunate preparation for his heavier and much more complex responsibilities in New South Wales. His concept of government was one of military simplicity: strict adherence to regulations, and the unquestioning personal allegiance of his subordinates.'[13] After the relaxed style of Sir Thomas Brisbane, many government officials were astonished by the new governor's abrupt commands. Balcombe would not have been—he had seen that style before.

Not long after the arrival of Darling, an 'event' occurred that caused Balcombe to resign from the Agricultural Society on Christmas Day 1825. It appears to have been some personal and deeply wounding insult. It can only be speculation that it may have been related to his former connection with Bonaparte. Robert Howe, editor of the *Sydney Gazette*, described the 'event' as most regrettable and Balcombe as blameless. He made his resignation a big story:

> The Agricultural Society: From undoubted authority we have just ascertained that that highly respected and much valued Public

Officer, *Mr Balcombe*, has forwarded his resignation to Mr Berry, the Secretary of this institution. The only reason that *Mr Balcombe* assigns for depriving the Society of his powerful influence is a 'recent event'. That this 'event' must be extremely painful to beget so decided a step, we are constrained to admit, and from what the numerous members of the Agricultural Society know of *Mr Balcombe* and his amiable and interesting family, we are certain that they will fully sympathise with him in the cause which has led to so disagreeable an 'event'; since we feel assured, that the whole body of the Colonists, from certain reports which have been flitting about, will feel profound regret that *Mr Balcombe* should be obliged to forego further connexion, with one of the most respectable and weighty Bodies in New South Wales. If *Mr Balcombe* were only a private individual in our Society, he might be indifferent to our regard, but we esteem him as one of the Members of the Colonial Government, of high rank, and unsullied honour, and it is the knowledge of such facts that renders it imperative on us, as we stand connected with the Society, and also with the Public, to notice a resignation which, at least, we fervently hope, will be enquired into; it being our opinion, that so efficient a Member should not be lost to the Agricultural Society, unless upon good grounds.[14]

Almost as much fuss was being made about Balcombe's departure from the Society as had been made over Governor Brisbane's from the colony. In the light of later developments, this glowing endorsement of Balcombe can be looked back upon as the apex of his colonial career.

If the new governor startled with his stern efficiency, his wife Eliza won praise for her active concern to help the young women of the colony, daughters of convicts or native-born 'currency lasses'. In January 1826, a month after her arrival, she became involved with the Female Orphan School. Established by Governor Philip Gidley King, the school was free for girls who had lost one or both parents and was government-supported.[15]

Eliza made it her business to get to know the gentlewomen of the colony and to encourage them to join her in other philanthropic projects. She set up a ladies' committee to organise sewing classes at the Female Factory at Parramatta (a gaol for convict women, where they were employed manufacturing cloth), a Benevolent Society to care for women in childbirth, and a Female Friendly Society which operated like a savings bank for poor and convict women. At his wife's insistence, the governor agreed to set up the Sydney Dispensary, offering medical advice to the poor, dependent upon voluntary expertise.[16]

Having organised a group of ladies as helpers, Eliza Darling expanded her philanthropy projects. In March, she set up the Female School for Servants (soon renamed the Female School of Industry), a voluntary organisation to help the daughters of the poor, training them for domestic service and aiming to save them from poverty or prostitution. It took in girls aged between five and eighteen, fed and accommodated them, and provided 'an education to imbue them with religious ideals and equip them as domestic servants'. The school depended upon donations and the cooperation of willing helpers. Mrs Jane Balcombe and Betsy Abell were readily persuaded to become involved as founding subscribers, along with their good friend Amelia Forbes. They were joined by their new acquaintances Elizabeth Macleay and her daughter Frances (known as Fanny), wife and daughter of the new colonial secretary, Alexander Macleay, who had recently arrived to take up his appointment, replacing Frederick Goulburn.

The admirable Elizabeth Macarthur was another founding subscriber, coming in from Parramatta, sometimes with her young daughter Emmeline, to join the group. Elizabeth was the mainstay of the difficult man described as 'the father of the Australian wool industry'; in fact, it was she who had managed his pastoral and agricultural estates, supervised the breeding and tending of the flocks by assigned convicts and managed her husband's business affairs during his eight-year absence in England from 1809 to September 1817 (involved in legal wrangles as part of the defence team for the rebellion against Bligh). Betsy and her mother were doubtless acquainted with Elizabeth already, after their five-month voyage with her eldest son Edward, but now a friendship developed between the women.

The huge Australian Agricultural Company, with a one-million-acre grant in the Hunter Valley, north of Sydney, had been envisaged and passed through the British Parliament because of the energy of John Macarthur. His son in London, John junior, was on the court of directors. Robert Dawson, the Australian manager, later wrote that 'entire power' was vested in the Macarthurs, with four family members on the local Australian board of five.[17] It may have been because of the Balcombes' new connections with the Macarthurs that their middle son, Thomas Tyrwhitt Balcombe, aged sixteen in 1826, was given a position.

Thomas went to Port Stephens in the Hunter River region to take up his job with the company. He was a 'superintendent', which was not as grand as its title—he was almost certainly appointed to watch over a group of convict labourers or shepherds.[18] He had developed a talent as an artist. His supervisory job must have given him much free time and he may have used it to make sketches, of the landscape, convict labourers and groups of Aboriginal people crossing the land. (Later he was to make many portraits of tribal groups 'up country'.)

But the local Wonnarua people soon discovered that they were prevented from crossing their traditional lands. In 1826, Governor Darling began employing 'colonial cavalry'—the newly formed mounted police—to 'disperse' the Wonnarua people of the Hunter by brutal means to make way for the Australian Agricultural Company's flocks and herds.[19]

In Sydney Town the respectable citizens prepared for the King's Birthday Ball at Government House on 26 April, happily ignoring the fact, as they had every year since his coronation, that he was actually born on 12 August. Governor Darling had invited an assembly of two hundred of the colony's 'worth and respectability', to dance gracefully in the room that Brisbane had used merely for meetings of the Legislative Assembly. William Balcombe, his wife and daughter were among the gathering dancing the quadrille and supping into the small hours, and no doubt they shared the sense of fellowship borne from the two good years just passed.[20]

But if Sydney's 'first two-hundred' happily danced and dined the night away, it was done against an unease soon to emerge that all was not well with the economy. From the time of Balcombe's arrival two years earlier, all *had* been well, with increasing imports of capital and trade goods and ever-expanding levels of investment in Sydney and the countryside. More and more land was surveyed and settled. Sales of wool and timber to Britain were booming. Large-scale land developments triggered a mania for the possession of flocks and herds, causing a scramble to purchase stock and seed, inevitably escalating prices, without proper regard for the ability to repay borrowings. A building boom in Sydney, well underway by the end of 1825, added to the relentless demand for materials and finance, tempting the Bank of New South Wales and other lending agencies to take undue risks, most notably for pastoral development. Few of the new pastoralists understood the unpredictable nature of Australian weather, with its cycles of floods and drought.

Balcombe was a participant in the troubled events both officially and as a private investor, having rushed to stock his 2560 acres at Bungonia; he had also recently paid a 10 per cent deposit on 4000 acres on the Molonglo Plains, and was already transporting sheep and cattle to the land.[21] As a consequence, he was soon to fall victim to the first season of drought that he encountered in 1827, the resultant slide in wool yields and income, and pressure on his mortgages. The economy slumped, leaving many settlers stranded.

In this volatile economic situation, Balcombe once again made a serious error of judgement. He believed that he could quietly join his rich new friends by acting as a lender—of Treasury funds—to those Sydney merchants clamouring for cash. He had become aware that his shareholding friends at the Bank of New South Wales, including Captain Piper, chairman of directors, were reaping extraordinary dividends from the practice of discounting bills of exchange. They were paying cash to merchants who were happy to forfeit 10 per cent on money owed to them (i.e. discounted) but not due for weeks or months, so that they could obtain cash immediately. Those at the Bank would wait until the bill was due and then make a healthy 10 per cent profit.

But Balcombe could not know that his 'banking' activities would be exposed, as a result of an investigation following a cash crisis, ironically unconnected with him, which confronted the Bank in May 1826. Because of complications arising from the changeover from a mixed sterling and Spanish dollar monetary system and a scarcity of sterling, merchants had exhausted almost entirely the Bank's holdings of dollars, which they needed to send overseas to pay for imports. On 3 April 1826, the Bank held $122,933, but by 10 May that had been reduced to only $4739.[22] Unfortunately, on 13 May the *Sydney Gazette* went public with an account of the 'scare': 'Tremendous was the stir that was created in the afternoon of Wednesday and the morning of Thursday last by certain evil rumours being indiscriminately circulated that the Bank had stopped payment. It soon spread but the evil was as speedily counteracted.' But the prompt correction (an injection of government funds) was not sufficient for the resumption of business as usual.[23]

To avoid risking further public panic, the Bank had sought a loan of £20,000 sterling from the government. As part of an agreement to help the Bank's directors, Governor Darling ordered an enquiry into the Bank's affairs to rectify any poor management issues. In minutely investigating the Bank's deposits and payments, particular attention was given to the deposit account for the Colonial Treasury.

For Balcombe, the investigation was massively prejudicial. On the very eve of the governor's enquiry, Balcombe had paid into the account $76,743 in Spanish dollars, making a total balance for the Treasury account of $99,465, a third of it in cheques from four major Sydney merchant companies and five individual businessmen.[24] He had made the deposits of public revenue on a day when the Bank's liquidity was seriously in doubt.[25]

At a meeting four days later, Darling's executive council directed the Bank to arrange with the colonial treasurer to avoid drawing on the deposit of almost $100,000, except for the immediate needs of the public service, and he was strictly ordered not to withdraw cash. Clearly, any sizeable withdrawal would render the £20,000 sterling cash injection 'ineffectual', as Darling put it.[26] The governor wasted no time in writing to Bathurst and laying before him all that the enquiry had revealed about Balcombe's machinations.[27]

Balcombe sought to defend himself by arguing that he had never received instructions 'as to the mode in which I should keep the Public Money', and that the procedure he had adopted had been practised before when government funds were managed by individual departments. He said that he had deposited the funds in the Bank because there was no secure place to keep government revenue; the alternative had been to keep it under his bed. Further, he had no reason to 'doubt the stability' of the Bank, 'many of the proprietors of which are people of the most extensive property in the Colony'. He added that because he had given 'such ample security' before taking up his duties, he considered that he was at liberty to manage the safety of the funds as he saw fit, 'believing that all that was necessary on my part was the production at a moment's notice of the money when required for the public service'.[28]

His response to the charge of lending Treasury money to private citizens and of gaining interest himself from discounted bills was lame. He had obviously hoped that these practices would never be discovered, but tried to defend himself: 'The circumstances of my having deposited some money for security in the custody of one or two of the principal Merchants arose from the alarm occasioned by the breaking open of the Commissariat Stores and the robbery of a large sum of money . . . and as the money in question could at any time be drawn at the shortest notice, I considered it safer under their custody there than it would have been at my own house in which there is no money vaults to secure it.'[29]

Balcombe's defence failed to impress Darling, who advised him, through Colonial Secretary Alexander Macleay, of his 'decided disapprobation of you having deposited the Public Money either in the Bank or in the hands of private individuals'. He made clear that his belief was that keeping the funds in the Treasury—that is, Balcombe's house, where an armed sentry was continually posted—would have been equally safe. Balcombe was informed that the matter would be reported to Lord Bathurst.[30]

On 22 May, Darling sent another despatch to his lordship: 'It is impossible to account for his having placed this Money in an Establishment apparently on the very verge of Bankruptcy, otherwise than by supposing as it was not forthcoming when the Inspection of the Treasury took place, that his intention was to conceal the fact of his having been in the habit of Discounting the Bills of Private Individuals; hoping, as may be presumed, that the Money appearing to be in the Bank at the time of the examination of that Establishment, that his previous transactions would not be enquired into or discovered . . . Had the Bank failed, Mr Balcombe, no doubt, would have been liable; But he possesses no property and the recovery of the money would, I have no doubt, been found totally impracticable.[31] It is my intention, though not authorized by my Instructions, to order the Inspection of the Treasury at uncertain times, and to forbid Mr Balcombe's lodging the Public Money in the Bank, or making use of it, as he appears most improperly to have done, for his private purposes.'[32]

Upon learning that the whole matter was to be placed before the Secretary of State, Balcombe's usual confidence must have deserted him. He would have feared that Darling's account would be strongly worded, but he would have been shocked to learn how scorching it actually was. He was aware that he would have to wait for at least eight months, in a state of anxiety—while a ship took the despatch to London and brought a response back—to learn if he was to be dismissed from his position and lose his good life. His health began to decline from that time.

The surprise raids on Balcombe's office, ordered by the governor and executed by Macleay, happened soon enough. In late May, there was a virtual ambush, startling the clerks, Harrison and Wallace.

Once again, Balcombe had managed to fall foul of an authoritarian military governor, and once again it was through his own indiscretions. As on previous occasions, it would be surprising if he had not sent off a hurried letter to Sir Thomas Tyrwhitt, hoping that his protector could intercede with Bathurst to save him from dismissal, if that was contemplated. At the same time, Balcombe must have had misgivings about Tyrwhitt's reserves of patience, having been pressed into service so many times over the years.

Whatever was said privately in London, in mitigation or otherwise, Bathurst's reply, received by Darling nine months later, in February 1827, endorsed the governor's proposals to tighten control over Balcombe's management of the Treasury. Bathurst went on to state: 'But I cannot close this despatch without marking, with His Majesty's strongest displeasure, the conduct of Mr Balcombe in risking the loss to the Publick of so large a Sum, as that which he deposited in the Bank; and I am sorry that I must further observe that, notwithstanding Mr Balcombe alleges in his excuse that he had no other object in this transaction than the desire of placing the money, entrusted to his charge, in a more secure situation, than was afforded by the unprotected state of his own residence, it is but too evident, from your report of the case, that he was actuated by other far less unobjectionable motives.'[33]

Once Balcombe learned from the governor of the King's 'strongest displeasure', he would have known that he could no longer expect

Tyrwhitt to protect him from his own mistakes.[34] He had been repeating the pattern, which had emerged on St Helena, of excessive spending on high living and an over-eagerness to be liked and accepted, and he was displaying the same flawed judgement that had made him vulnerable to the manipulations of Napoleon. In the process he had sullied the good reputation he had established in Sydney.

Meanwhile, another scandal was unfolding that would fully occupy the attention of Darling, distress Balcombe, and set all Sydney society upon its ears.

Since his arrival at the end of 1825, Governor Darling had been quietly observing Captain John Piper, no doubt keeping in mind Bigge's recommendations for a wholesale change in various positions, including transferring the collection of customs and port revenues from the 'Naval Officer' to a 'Collector of the Customs'. At the beginning, Darling had not been immune to Piper's generous and engaging personality, but he increasingly wondered how he juggled his many roles without detriment to their effective management. Piper was not only naval officer, with its manifold tasks, but also a magistrate, the chairman of the board of directors of the Bank of New South Wales, and involved in Scots Church affairs; further, he had extensive pastoral and business interests. On top of all this, he was a perennial party-giver, hosting the grandest dinners and balls at his splendid mansion, an extravagant way of life that must have caused the governor concern.

Piper's role as chairman of the board during the period of inadequate management at the Bank of New South Wales, and his obvious intimacy with Balcombe, would have raised Darling's apprehensions. He must have wondered whether Piper was complicit in Balcombe's revenue deposits in the Bank at the time of the crisis. Piper had stepped down from the board shortly afterwards.

At the beginning of 1826, Bathurst had written to Darling directing that Bigge's recommendation should be implemented and the naval officer advised of his new commission as collector of customs. On 21 October, Darling informed Bathurst that before installing Piper he would carry out an inspection of Piper's management of his office to judge whether he deserved the appointment. Thus Piper, like Balcombe, became the subject of a government raid on his office. The economic historian S.J. Butlin has written: 'John Piper was also found by Darling's board of enquiry into the Bank of NSW, to have been operating a similar discounting system, although on a smaller scale than his friend Balcombe. In addition, D'Arcy Wentworth, when Treasurer of the Police Fund was rumoured to have engaged in the practice as well as the proprietors of the Bank, using loans which they then privately employed, undercutting their own Bank's interest rates!'[35]

Piper was aware that an even more detailed inspection of his books was about to take place in April 1827. He knew that the officers would discover an appalling deficit of some £12,000 in the naval officer's accounts, and that his disastrous financial situation would become public. His biographer, Marjorie Barnard, described how he decided to resolve the situation: 'He took no one into his confidence, going about as usual, but he made his will and on the eve of the dreaded day invited a number of his closest friends to dinner. After dinner he made an excuse to leave them on official business, pressing them in his usual hospitable way to continue the party without him. He ordered the barge and told the crew, which was also his band, to take their instruments with them. When he had been rowed outside the Heads and the crew had hoisted sail to catch the fresh breeze, he ordered them to play. Under cover of the music he threw himself overboard. One of the crew dived to his rescue but with the lively sea and the strong wind it was some time before his men could get him aboard. He was unconscious when they did, more than half drowned. His return in this state to his friends, who were still keeping up the party, caused a profound sensation. The experience purged the Captain of all desire for suicide and nothing remained for him but to tear up the valedictory letters that he had left for his friends.'[36]

Barnard noted: 'The news of the fall of the most popular man in the colony came as a bombshell to the city. There was a loud hubbub in the newspapers.' His assets all had to be put up for sale at a time when the market was unfavourable; the city properties, the farms, 100 acres at harbourside Vaucluse and Piper's beautiful Henrietta Villa, 'its contents, furniture, wine, carriages, horses, boats and guns', were all sold at auction on 4 June. They went for a fraction of their worth, mainly to 'the Merchants and shopkeepers of Sydney, the greatest portion of whom are Emancipists'.[37]

Historian S.J. Butlin has offered a defence of both Balcombe and Piper, on the grounds that they had merely continued practices common enough in individual departments since early times in the colony, after the raffish practices of the founding days were brought into some kind of departmental order: 'In extenuation, it may be pointed out that officials were still expected to provide their own place of safekeeping, and that the principle that officials holding public moneys were entitled to the perquisite of private investment of the funds held had, within living memory, been officially proper.'[38] But as the colony advanced far beyond being merely a gaol, it was clearly time that such buccaneer practices ceased, and that had been one good reason why a Colonial Treasury had been instituted. As for Balcombe's misdemeanour, according to Butlin, while 'the episode was itself trivial, it led to significant changes in the colonial Treasury's potential impact on money supply, by virtue of it now having to hold the "major part" of its revenue holdings in hard cash, which in turn meant it could influence economic activity'.[39]

However, the personal impact of this event on Balcombe's health and the future wellbeing of his family was enormous.

CHAPTER 35

'TERRIBLE HOLLOW'

Not even ruins remain of what was once the Balcombes' farmhouse 'The Briars' at Bungonia, but the homestead of their neighbours, the Reid family of Inverary Park, still stands. It is a handsome old bungalow with a chimney at each end of its deep roof and a long, wide front verandah. The house is surrounded by ancient trees and set back from the road at the end of a long straight drive.

The countryside around it and the old Briars property is gentle, wooded and undulating. But less than two kilometres away there is a yawning cleft in the earth's crust: Bungonia Gorge, the deepest canyon in the whole continent of Australia. One comes upon it suddenly after walking through sclerophyll forest, and in the past it would have been abrupt and alarming. Today the approach is signposted and the lookout fenced, as part of a national park. The canyon is only 76 metres wide but the view down is of a terrifying sheer drop of 300 metres to the Shoalhaven River far below. Experienced bushmen know where to find tracks down into the gorge and there are said to be many caves in the cliffs.

As early as 1798, Governor Hunter sent an ex-convict, John Wilson, to explore the area and discover where escaped convicts, heading south-west, found seclusion. Wilson did not succeed.[1] Bungonia Gorge may have been one lair from which bushrangers emerged to pillage local farms and stores and return with their plunder. In his 1888 novel

Robbery Under Arms, the Victorian author Rolf Boldrewood called such a bushranger hideout 'Terrible Hollow'.

Balcombe's final years as colonial treasurer have a visual metaphor in his own farmland at Bungonia—fertile, prosperous and green, then descending abruptly into a sudden abyss.

Balcombe had partially recovered from the Treasury scandal. His arguments that the same procedure of discounting bills had been practised before and that he had deposited government revenue in the bank because there was no secure place for it other than the box under his bed appeared to have been accepted by his superiors, if not approved. After a further enquiry, more efficient practices were set up for the Treasury. Some very large padlocked boxes, too heavy for any burglar to carry off, were requisitioned. Balcombe had escaped with a warning, although his probity and competence would long remain in question.

However, he must have felt badly about his friend John Piper, the colony's former 'favourite son', now somewhat neglected by old acquaintances and only occasionally mentioned. He had sold all his remaining assets and retired to a small farm near Bathurst. On the one hand Piper's practice of discounting bills may have led Balcombe astray, on the other, Balcombe was responsible for the receipt of revenues collected by Piper, and should have been more thorough in checking his friend's accounts. That had been the trouble: he and Piper were too similar in their enjoyment of exuberant revelries and in their casual attitude to reaping a few perquisites from their merchant friends. Piper had been a particular hero of Betsy's, and Sydney gossips thought he had been rather too fond of her.

During the horror month of May 1826 for Balcombe with the governor and the Treasury crisis—he received a message from his friend and Bungonia neighbour Dr David Reid, who had been appointed magistrate for the area. There were 'troubles' with the Aboriginal people of the district. Two stock-keepers, assigned convicts, had been murdered. Other convict workers and farm labourers had formed a party planning revenge on 'the blacks'. In defence against them, 'an assembly of upwards of a thousand natives' had gathered 'within four miles' of Inverary Park. Reid sent an official account of the developments to the governor, through the colonial secretary in Sydney. It must have been Reid who gave an explanation for the fury of the local Aboriginal people which had ended in the killing of the two white men: 'Stock keepers had been stealing the natives' women, committing violence against them.'[2]

Governor Darling ordered that 'preventive measures' be taken to avoid what would inevitably be multiple deaths on both sides. A force of thirty men, led by a captain and a subaltern, was despatched to Bungonia. They were instructed to 'try to protect natives from injury and insult' and attempt 'to conciliate'. The officers were asked to 'endeavour to communicate with Chiefs of tribes and assure them of the Government's good intentions'.[3] The swift action taken by Darling on that occasion avoided further bloodshed on both sides.

On 1 July 1826, the beginning of the new financial year, the Australia Bank opened its doors for business, setting up in direct competition to the Bank of New South Wales. It was backed by some of the wealthiest and most prestigious people in the colony, who preferred not to rub shoulders with former convicts when they made their deposits and withdrawals.[4]

Balcombe, with all his stock and land commitments, found it difficult on his reduced salary to pay the steep rent of the O'Connell Street house. As two rooms were used for the Treasury offices, he put in a request to Darling for an allowance for them. Instead of making his own decision, as Governor Brisbane surely would have done, the inflexible Darling sent the request in a despatch to Bathurst. That meant a seven or eight months' wait for a reply.[5] It must have given Balcombe an unpleasant reminder of that other military governor who played everything by the book and followed his lordship's instructions with overanxious zealotry.

Reminders of Bonaparte and St Helena continued to appear in the local newspapers. The *Gazette* had a story about Kleber, a tall French officer brought before General Bonaparte in Egypt for insubordination. He looked truculently down at the general from his commanding height. '"Which of us," said Bonaparte, "is above the other here? You are higher than I am only by a head—one act of disobedience more, and that difference will disappear." Kleber obeyed.'[6] The *Australian* reported that an old soldier now resided near Napoleon's grave with its weeping willows 'in consequence of some French officers who had been there, having taken off several branches from the willows as a memento of their former sovereign'.[7]

Betsy must often have thought of those days on St Helena, when she had delighted in provoking the former great conqueror and nothing she did seemed to annoy him too much; when she had been a happy careless flirt, admired by so many officers. They would have seemed in memory such golden halcyon days.

Darling was very much distracted in November 1826 and for long afterwards by an episode which became notorious as the 'Sudds and Thompson affair'. Many military officers and soldiers were resentful of wealthy ex-convicts who seemed to gain many privileges from the government. Two soldiers, Joseph Sudds and Patrick Thompson, were frustrated under their strict military regime. In contrast, they felt, assigned convicts were given easy jobs, such as stock-keepers, carriage drivers or shop assistants, while those who had served their terms or gained tickets of leave had received land grants and set themselves up as small farmers. The two soldiers decided to join them. In front of witnesses, they stole a bundle of calico from a Sydney shop, in the confident belief that they would be dismissed from their regiment, serve a short gaol term and then be free to set up as civilians themselves.

But this small crime turned out very badly for them. It also occupied a great deal of time for Darling. The case of Sudds and Thompson was a key factor in abbreviating his career in New South Wales.

The men were stripped of their uniforms and drummed out of the regiment to 'The Rogue's March'. They were convicted by a Court of Quarter Sessions of theft and sentenced to seven years in a penal settlement such as Norfolk Island or Moreton Bay. At the time of his sentencing, Sudds pleaded that he was ill, but that was dismissed as a ruse. Darling 'commuted' their sentences to work in a road gang, to make a spectacle of their punishment. They were shackled in a particularly punitive, heavy set of irons, intended only for the most desperate of convicts, with spiked iron collars around their necks—personally designed by Darling—attached by short chains to their ankle fetters. This prevented them from standing upright. If they attempted to lie down, the spiked collars stabbed their necks. Five days into the sentence, on 27 November, Sudds died.

The press exploded. Wardell, in the *Australian*, questioned the legal validity of the proceedings. Wentworth lashed out at the governor, accusing him of torture and murder. Edward Smith Hall for the *Monitor* produced a pamphlet, widely distributed, with a sketch of Sudds in his shackles, dying in agony, watched by a helpless Thompson.[8]

Governor Darling was portrayed as a repressive military despot, suitable to run a penitentiary but not an enterprising civilian colony. Hall made a direct comparison for punitive measures between Darling and a certain other governor: 'there are two ways of fulfilling painful instructions. When *Sir Hudson Lowe* received very imperious orders respecting the safe custody of Napoleon, the world will never believe that such men as Bathurst and Liverpool intended *Sir Hudson* to put them in force in the manner in which he did.'[9]

Chief Justice Forbes advised Darling that his severe punishment of the two soldiers was 'contrary to law' and had been conducted at the 'sole fiat of the Governor'.[10] Amelia Forbes recalled 'the cruel punishment of Sudds and Thompson' in her memoirs and said—as she may have told her friends the Balcombes—that she 'could never feel comfortable in General Darling's presence again'.[11]

In late November, farmers in New South Wales experienced a 'long dry spell'. They waited for the rains to come, and most were sure that they would. They had stocked their land and planted crops as if the green years would go on for ever, with no understanding that drought was a cyclical pattern in Australia. Many small settlers were bound to the Bank of New South Wales by debt, having borrowed to fence and stock their land and build dams and farmhouses, planning to repay when their crops yielded and their sheep were shorn. Balcombe was one of the optimistic ones: wherever he had lived—Rottingdean at the edge of the Sussex Downs, monsoonal India, St Helena, Devon and Saint-Omer—he had always been able to count on the heavens opening and drenching the earth. It was a preordained blessing to mankind and to animals and plants. But this country was different. The life-bringing rain did not arrive. It did not come for months. He never dreamed it would be years. Three years. The old Australian hands knew about it. Drought.

By early 1827, Balcombe had enormous worries pressing down on him. He had overextended himself financially by purchasing the additional 4000 acres at Molonglo. Although he had paid only a 10 per cent deposit on the dry and scratchy land, he had to pay interest on the loan; he had also been required to fence the land, and had bought a large number of sheep and cattle to stock it and incurred costs for their transport. If no rains came and the markets for his wool and grain continued to worsen, his heavy investment in his farming properties could end in ruin.

For the present he was managing. His sheep, heavy in wool from the previous good season, were shorn, producing seven bales to send to the London market.[12] But he had another setback when Darling informed him that a despatch had arrived from Bathurst in response to his enquiry of seven months earlier. His lordship refused any additional allowance for Balcombe's house rent, even though the Treasury was based at his home.[13]

Balcombe's recurrent gout returned. He had to drop some of his commitments and relinquished his position as magistrate, deciding that he had stretched himself too far, although he would later be persuaded to resume the role.[14]

The long drought continued. The grasses dried up, and their roots were eaten out by the sheep and cattle. Yarralaw Creek on the Bungonia property receded from its banks to a thin trickle. Trying to reach the water, cattle became bogged in the mud and died. The circling crows flew down to feast.

Alexander, the Balcombes' youngest son, was now out in the world, with employment as a clerk in the government Commissariat—where a report later judged him to be 'negligent'. The eldest, William, with assigned convict workers, was managing his father's Molonglo land and 'The Briars' at Bungonia. Thomas was still working at Port Stephens with the Australian Agricultural Company—possibly thanks to the Macarthur connection.

Elizabeth Macarthur was staying in town with her married daughter. She wrote to her son Edward in London: 'We have just had a visit from Mrs Abell. She generally comes in about once a week and chats with us. I told her I was writing to you. She desired to be remembered. Her father has been confined by gout to the house for some weeks.' Betsy told Elizabeth she had been to some parties and found them 'a strange mixture of finery, ostentation and vulgarity'.[15]

Captain Piper had recovered his spirits and occasionally returned to the social scene in Sydney, just as the Balcombes and their daughter Betsy seemed to be withdrawing from it. A Captain Chestakoff wrote to Piper saying he was forming a party including Sir John Jamison, Mr Mackaness, Mr Stirling, Mr Bannister and Miss Bannister and Captain Mitchell, but he was 'kind of thunderstruck by the refusal of Mrs Abelles [sic]'.[16]

In July, the new attorney-general, Alexander Macduff Baxter, arrived. A Scottish barrister from Perthshire, aged 29, he had married after his appointment and brought his new wife, Maria del Rosaria Anna Uthair, an attractive Spanish heiress. From the beginning, Baxter set out to 'cut a great dash' in colonial society, taking over Apsley House, one of Sydney's few splendid mansions, and furnishing it in lavish style. But Darling had his doubts about him. Within two months he reported to the Colonial Office that '"Dandy" Baxter appeared to have little legal experience and was helpless in court against Robert Wardell and William Charles Wentworth'.[17]

The trial of the convict Thomas Sweetman was held in the Criminal Court on 10 August. He was charged with breaking and entering the dwelling of William Balcombe, and of larceny, of stealing two hats that were the property 'of the said William Balcombe'. Various witnesses were called: a neighbour who lived opposite witnessed the burglary, raised the alarm and with the assistance of others prevented the prisoner's escape. Thomas Balcombe was called as a witness. He had been residing with his father that Saturday evening, was alarmed by a noise and found a stranger in the hall who made off with two hats. The prisoner pleaded intoxication 'in excuse for his being found in the way described' but denied the charge of robbery. The judge summed up the evidence for the burglary then delivered the verdict: 'guilty. Remanded for sentence.'[18]

The fact that the convict Sweetman had got past the sentry, and may have planned to steal Treasury funds, not just two hats, gives some vindication to Balcombe's claim that he had deposited funds in the Bank, fearing the house was insecure.

Three weeks later, the chief justice and the assistant judge took their seats in the court. The prisoners, including Sweetman, 'who had been previously tried, convicted and remanded to gaol, were brought up for sentence'. Judgement of death was recorded against all of them.[19] It was usually mandatory for reoffending convicts. Amelia Forbes noted in her memoirs that it gave the chief justice much anguish to deliver death sentences for relatively minor crimes.

In September, Attorney-General Baxter hosted a ball and supper at his grand new home in York Street. The Governor and Mrs Darling did not attend, but otherwise all the usual suspects were there, including Mrs Balcombe and Mrs Abell. 'The entire of the party did not retire till an early hour on Saturday morning.'[20] William Balcombe may not have been well enough to be present, but that evening Betsy made a new friend, Baxter's attractive Spanish wife. Before long they were visiting each other and walking in the Botanical Gardens together.

Balcombe had been ill for some time with gout, and probably depression occasioned by the distressing state of his landholdings and financial affairs. But he managed to go to the annual Turf Club dinner on 9 November at Cummings Hotel. It was a strictly all-male affair. About forty members sat down, with William Charles Wentworth acting as chairman and Sheriff John Mackaness as vice-chairman. The band of the 57th Regiment was there to entertain. Darling, officially the club patron, was invited but declined, instead spending the weekend at Government House in Parramatta. As the wine flowed, the evening became boisterous. Wentworth proposed a toast to their first patron, Sir Thomas Brisbane, extolling his virtues as a 'political friend'. A perfunctory toast was made to Governor Darling as the band played 'Over the Hills and Far Away'. An article in the *Monitor* stated that the tune expressed 'the feelings of the company and the colony'.[21]

On reading the *Monitor*, Darling withdrew his patronage from the club. He sent a stiffly phrased letter to Sheriff Mackaness, informing him that he was sending a copy of it to Lord Viscount Goderich, the British prime minister (Liverpool had resigned in April). He said he knew that Mackaness had not just presided at the 'most calumnious and indecent' event, but 'you had given your countenance to the proceedings'. Given his 'association and intercourse with certain factious Individuals, who in the most open and wanton manner have endeavoured to degrade the Government in the eyes of the Public, and to create discord between it and the People', Darling would not be reappointing him sheriff at the close of the current year. Mackaness wrote a humble reply, claiming that in no way had he 'endeavoured to degrade the Government in the eyes of the public or to create discord'. But it did no good. His job was finished.[22]

At that, 29 Turf Club members took fright at the degree of the governor's hostility and decided to withdraw their membership. Balcombe was among them, emotionally weakened by the previous year's Treasury scandal and his impending financial ruin.

In January 1828, the *Sydney Gazette* published an article of huge interest not just to the Balcombes but to the numerous readers of Sir Walter Scott. The best-selling British novelist of the age, author of *Ivanhoe*, *Rob Roy* and the *Waverley* novels, had recently published a new book in a number of volumes, *The Life of Napoleon Bonaparte*. For his research, Lord Bathurst had allowed Sir Walter, a prominent member of the Tory establishment in Scotland and a figure of international renown, access to his St Helena papers and (no doubt wishing him joy) to Sir Hudson Lowe's voluminous correspondence.

Several journals in France had since translated and published passages from Scott's work, including the minutes of General Gourgaud's treacherous 'confessions' at the Colonial Office in which he had asserted how easy it would be for Napoleon to escape and claimed that the former emperor was not ill at all. Gourgaud had responded with an open letter to the editor of the *Courrier Français*, refuting 'the odious imputations directed against me', in an attempt to save his skin. There was such a groundswell of affection in France for Bonaparte and the glory days that Gourgaud's life was in actual danger if Bonapartists believed Scott's claims. And the Colonial Office minutes of his interview made very credible reading. 'I have read with indignation the passages in which an attempt is made to stigmatise my character,' Gourgaud wrote. 'If I reply to them it is because silent contempt is not always enough to oppose calumny.' His protests continued at length. He said he was considering making his way to Edinburgh to challenge Scott to a duel.[23]

When the old literary baronet, nearing sixty, heard of this, he wrote with relish to an Edinburgh friend, William Clerk, on 27 August 1827, requesting 'an especial service': to be his second in a duel with Gourgaud, if the latter acted on his threat. 'Why, *I will not baulk him, Jackie!*'[24]

In 1828 a census was conducted in New South Wales. It listed Balcombe as a man of considerable property, with 6560 acres (which included both the Bungonia and Molonglo land), 1100 acres cleared and 74 cultivated. He had 900 sheep, 500 cattle and ten horses. He had clearly overstocked his properties, and his sheep and cattle were close to starving. There were 28 servants on his landholdings, all of them convicts except two who 'Came Free'. There were more staff at his rented property in Petersham—three labourers and a male servant. The Glebe plot was not mentioned so may have been sold. At the O'Connell Street house in town there were six staff: a coachman, an overseer, a footman (a particular affectation!) and three domestic servants.

Balcombe—financially overextended as the drought continued, and with his convict farm labourers cutting down tree branches to try to feed the desperately foraging stock—was hard pressed on his reduced salary. The price of grain had risen enormously, much of it now imported from Van Diemen's Land, and, like other settlers, he had not just his family but also servants to feed. With a glimmer of his old jauntiness he had a horse running at the race meeting in April. It did not win.

Captain Piper now often visited town and, almost back in form, was always up for a party or a ball. Betsy wrote him an apologetic note: 'My father begs me to say he is too unwell to accept your kind invitation for today' and she herself had a cold, although she hoped to 'be well enough to dance the first Quadrille with you on Tuesday next'.[25]

Balcombe's illness continued, and on 13 January 1829 he took sick leave from the Treasury. The governor's brother-in-law Henry Dumaresq took over his responsibilities, but James Harrison and John Wallace were well experienced at running the office.

On 19 March, William Balcombe died at his O'Connell Street home of dysentery, his constitution ravaged by that illness, and by gout and over two years of stress. He had left his financial affairs in great disorder.

Ralph Mansfield, the new editor of the *Sydney Gazette*, gave him a fine tribute:

> The funeral of this respected gentleman took place on the evening of Monday last, and was attended by His Excellency the Governor, the Hon. The Colonial Secretary, the Judges of the Supreme Court, the Civil Officers resident in Sydney, several of the military officers of the Garrison, and a number of private friends of the deceased. Mr Balcombe had seen a considerable deal of public life. He resided at St Helena during the period of Napoleon Bonaparte's exile to that island, and his family circle at 'The Briars', as his residence was designated, was a frequent resort of the Emperor, and beguiled him of many of those restless moments by which he was afflicted in his captivity. It is also stated, upon good authority, that Mr Balcombe was once indighted by Bonaparte to aid him in a projected escape from St Helena. The character of Mr Balcombe in this Colony was sufficiently known. Perhaps no gentleman, holding a public situation, has ever kept clearer of parties and politics (in the acceptation of the term in this Colony), and there are few, we feel assured, whose memory will be more generally respected.[26]

The burial ceremony was performed four days later at St Philip's Anglican Church, Sydney, by the Venerable Archdeacon Scott, with many of Balcombe's friends there to see him off. He had few adversaries. He had somehow managed to maintain good relations with seemingly everyone in senior official positions. While he had earlier been a gregarious member of Sydney's high-flying 'fashionables', this had later been balanced by his need to avoid factional influence, in order not to compromise his impartiality as both a magistrate and a senior government official.

The lynchpin in the family had gone; after almost three years of illness, it was the attack of dysentery that felled Balcombe at the age of 51.[27]

But Betsy must have been confident that they would manage. Her brothers were all young men carving out lives for themselves in the colony. She would have to be the one to look after her mother and six-year-old Bessie. There would surely be enough money for them when all her father's financial affairs were sorted out. There would be some debts to pay off, but they would still have the properties, and her mother was certain to be given a pension by the government. They would probably need to rent a smaller villa in town, but she felt sure that Governor Darling would not dream of hurrying them out of the O'Connell Street house, he would give them time to grieve. And they would still be able to enjoy their trips to the country to stay at The Briars. Her father had loved going to the property; he used to say that he 'found so much benefit from the change of climate, he would give up half his salary to breathe that pure air of the interior!'[28]

Darling had already sent a despatch to the new Secretary of State, Sir George Murray:

> Sir, I have the painful duty to report the death of Mr Balcombe the Treasurer which took place last night. Mr Balcombe had long been subject to severe attacks of Gout, which occasionally confined him for several weeks at a time to his bed. His constitution at length became much impaired, and for the last three years he had been a complete invalid. About 4 months since, he was attacked with dysentery, a disease which his exhausted Constitution was unequal to resist, and he continued to decline gradually until last night, the period of his dissolution.
>
> I regret to add that Mr Balcombe has left a large family in very distressed circumstances. His widow and daughter will suffer severely, as they are without any means of support; for although Mr Balcombe possessed some land, he has died, I fear much in debt, and his land and stock are not in a state at present to make any return. There are also three sons, young men, who must provide for themselves, and, with industry and the assistance of their friends, can find little difficulty in doing so.[29]

A few creditors took some near-starving livestock immediately, sending them straight to the slaughterhouse. Young William and his assigned workers continued to look after the others as best they could, and rain began to fall. The worst of the drought was over.

CHAPTER 36

A FRACTURED FAMILY

Balcombe's death was a catastrophe in every imaginable way for his family. He had died bankrupt, owing many creditors. Three weeks after his death, a huge auction was held at his O'Connell Street house, attended by a crowd of sightseers as well as bidders. Part of the drawcard was Napoleon Bonaparte: buyers thought there was a chance to own a chair upon which the great warmonger might have sat (although the Balcombes had in fact brought no furniture from St Helena) or put their lips to a cup from which he had drunk.

At the auction's conclusion, the accoutrements of the Balcombes' comfortable, elegant lives had been dismantled. But that was not all. Even the remaining lease of their house was up for sale. Then it was over and the waiting horse-drawn carts took away the family's worldly possessions. Jane, Betsy and her daughter were left to stare at each other in a daze in empty rooms that were no longer theirs to occupy.

As the eldest son and heir (to a lot of debt), William took charge of the family's affairs. Having just turned 21, he was able to undertake legal responsibilities, and would have been closely involved with his father's solicitor in meeting obligations to redeem debts now threatening the family's future. He might well have possessed the necessary business skills. Today it seems astonishing that from the age of sixteen he had been in the bush by himself, managing two large farms, overseeing the work and welfare of a dozen or so convict labourers. However, it was simply the case that in the nineteenth century the adult world began much earlier: a boy of twelve could be transported or hanged for theft.

His brother Thomas had gained some farming experience from his job as a superintendent with the Australian Agricultural Company at Port Stephens. Drought had impacted on the massive pastoral company, which could explain why Thomas was released and in 1829 began work in Sydney as a clerk at the Commissariat. The previous year, the youngest brother, Alexander, had been dismissed from there for 'negligence',[1] but he was now working as a clerk in the Office of the Chief Justice, probably out of Forbes's kindness. All the children except William had been living in the O'Connell Street house, and all would now have to move. It is understandable that after their father's death and given the penury of their womenfolk, the sons were emotionally disturbed at this time.

It certainly appears that Balcombe had intended to set up his sons as pastoral landholders. His initial request to the governor in 1824 for a 2000-acre grant was meant for himself, Thomas and Alexander. Because William junior was sixteen in 1824, he had commenced management of his father's Bungonia property after tenure was granted. Balcombe's purchase in 1825 of 4000 acres at Molonglo was undoubtedly made with Thomas and Alexander in mind as well, once they were old enough to join William in learning to farm the estates. Balcombe's additional purchase of 560 acres at Bungonia was another useful increment of the better quality land across Yarralaw Creek from his own holding. In his own small way, Balcombe can be credited as one of the early pioneer pastoralists of New South Wales. His endeavours in managing the 6500 acres under his control could have led to great prosperity for the family, but for the terrible drought years of 1827 to 1829.

Balcombe's Bungonia and Molonglo properties were advertised for auction on 13 June, to be sold 'for the benefit of those who have claims on the estates'. However, insufficient money resulted from the land and stock auction to pay off all the creditors. So Mrs Balcombe petitioned the governor for a pension. On 28 July, the executive council considered her petition and agreed to write to London 'in consideration of the state of utter destitution of herself and family, that she be allowed a quarterly allowance of thirty pounds'.

Jane Balcombe, Betsy and her daughter then moved out of town. They possibly went to young William's land in Bungonia, where he had a simple dwelling, or else to the home of their kind neighbours the Reids, who may have insisted they stay with them.

However, good news was on its way. Some months before her father's final illness, Betsy had written to Admiral Sir George Cockburn, by then First Naval Lord in the Wellington ministry, hoping that he could help with a land grant. She wrote: 'I have had stock left me by a friend who died lately, and, not having any land of my own, my father at present takes care of my stock for me; if I was fortunate enough to procure a grant of land I should wish it to be near my father's in the County of Argyll.'² (The 'friend' may have been her father, giving her stock before his creditors closed in.) When Cockburn received Betsy's request he promptly wrote to Viscount Goderich, then Secretary of State, saying that it would be a special favour to him to accede to the request. The response came from the new minister, Sir George Murray, urging approval to Darling, who subsequently informed Betsy that he was able to grant her 1280 acres in the Argyle district near Bungonia.³ Betsy was delighted, but anxious not to have the land registered in her own name, for fear that Edward Abell might return to the colony to make a legal claim on it. It was agreed that it would be registered in the name of a trustee, Attorney-General Alexander Baxter.

But good news was followed by yet another blow. In February 1830, Jane Balcombe was sent news that her petition for a pension had been rejected in London.

In the Argyle district that year, bushrangers were menacing farms and travellers on the road. It may have been for this reason that Betsy, her mother and daughter moved closer to town. They settled into one of the church cottages at Glebe Farm, about three miles out of town on the main road to Liverpool. Soon after they were there, they experienced the robbery they had feared in the country. In late March 1830, according to reports, three 'ruffians' made an attack 'on the dwelling of Mrs. Balcombe': 'They did not ill-use Mrs. Balcombe. Mrs. Abell was absent.'[4]

In Sydney, the middle Balcombe son, Thomas, had applied to become a draftsman in the surveyor general's department. With his artistic talent, the appointment turned out to be a boon for him. Work as a draftsman was akin to attending an art school, with the demands on his nascent drawing abilities to provide sketches and maps of topographical features, under the tutelage of competent draftsmen who were often also artists. Robert Hoddle, with whom Thomas worked on surveying trips beyond the colony's boundaries, was one such accomplished mentor.

Alexander was not doing so well. In early 1831, he left the chief justice's office, deciding that he did not care for clerical work. He went to live with his brother William at Molonglo Plains.

William had obviously learned some lessons about astute dealing from his father. Not only had he secured a grant for himself of 1280 acres at Molonglo, but somehow the 4000-acre property that had been his father's and some of Balcombe's stock became his also. Exactly how this was accomplished is unclear—but it may simply have been part of William's inheritance once his father's equity in it was paid to the government, leaving the heavily mortgaged farm to himself. He sent a few of his assigned convicts to mind his sister's sheep and cattle, given to her by her mysterious 'friend', on her grant of 1280 acres in Bungonia.

Betsy was uncomfortable with the fact that Attorney-General Baxter was the trustee for her land, for she disliked him and gathered that the feeling was reciprocal. Now that she was living in Sydney again, she sometimes saw his wife Maria, who had been beautiful at first, but had become drawn and haggard. One day when they met, Maria tried to hide her face with a veil. Betsy was shocked when her friend confessed, weeping, that her husband had knocked out her teeth. He was often drunk and angry, and would then become violent. Betsy insisted that she make an official report. The two women went to the office of the lawyer Roger Therry, a big-hearted man and a social reformer. There Maria made a formal deposition about the brutality of her husband, and went to stay with Betsy and her mother. Therry presented the deposition to Chief Justice Forbes, who requested that police chief Rossi lay charges against the attorney-general.

Baxter went berserk. He raged that his wife was a liar, and wrote in a letter to the Colonial Office that Maria 'had the assistance of a number of *demi-monde* Ladies—among the most remarkable of whom for everything connected with vice and blackguardism is the Daughter of the late Colonial Treasurer, Mrs Abell, formerly of St Helena celebrity'.[5] Betsy had become his bitter enemy and he would stir up scandal about her if he could.

Fortunately, Darling considered Baxter incompetent and a drunk, and wrote an official despatch stating that Mr Baxter's 'disreputable habits' had become 'notorious . . . his Conduct has been disgraceful in the extreme, having been almost constantly in a state of inebriety'.[6] Baxter was asked to resign and Colonial Secretary Macleay spelled out some of the reasons: 'His Excellency laments that your treatment of your Wife, as stated in a deposition of which the enclosed is a copy made by her before two Magistrates on the 17th of last month, and the general notoriety of your irregular and disreputable habits more especially of late, together with the fact of your having been declared Insolvent' rendered it highly inappropriate that Baxter should continue in his important office.[7]

Betsy decided that if she and her mother were not to live as paupers, they must travel to England, to ask influential friends to help plead their case. It was a rather desperate and expensive journey. The *Nancy* departed Sydney on 13 February 1831. The women were returning to a Europe they had not seen for more than seven years and that would be all new to eight-year-old Bessie.

In July of the previous year there had been a revolution in Paris against Charles X. It had been brutally crushed, and a new king, Louis Philippe, from the house of Orléans, had been installed on the French throne. However, the seemingly indestructible Letizia Buonaparte, aged 80, never flagged in her ambitions for her family. She was convinced her grandson in Vienna would inevitably become Emperor Napoleon II.

Meanwhile, reports of Darling's unpopularity continued to reach London, and the Whigs warned that there would be more 'serious disturbances' in the colony 'if the tyranny of General Darling is allowed any longer to continue'. Secretary of State Goderich wrote a despatch in March 1831 which reached Sydney in July. Darling was shattered by the totally 'unexpected communication' that his appointment at the colony of New South Wales was terminated.[8]

On 9 December there was a large headline in the *Australian*: 'REPORTED LOSS OF THE *NANCY*'. A French ship had found the vessel stricken off the West African coast, 'waterlogged and deserted'. The *Gazette* also had the report.[9]

This must have been the most terrifying time in the lives of Jane Balcombe, Betsy and her daughter. They would have been far from shore, for ships to England never hugged the African coast, and in grave danger of drowning. The passengers had abandoned the ship in lifeboats and, after what must have been days in the baking sun, perhaps with little food and water, had all come to shore somewhere on the barren south-western coast of Africa (today's Namibia). It seems they waited for up to two weeks for the *Nancy* to be towed and repaired, while accepting the hospitality of the local people.

When the ship's captain was confident of taking the *Nancy* to sea again they set sail, only to make an unexpected call at St Helena, presumably for resupplies of food and water and to ascertain that the repairs were holding. The emotions of Betsy and her mother must have been in turmoil to see their beloved home The Briars. The upper floor now extended right across the building with at least six bedrooms. The house was surrounded by mulberry trees, ripe with red berries. They learned that the East India Company had purchased the property for £6000 from the merchant Solomon in August 1827, to establish a mulberry plantation for feeding silkworms.[10] The production of silk was to be St Helena's new industry, and like most other ventures it was doomed to failure.

They must have visited Napoleon's tomb, the willows shading it almost denuded by tourists breaking off souvenirs. But what would have come as the greatest shock was to ascend the mountain (perhaps even taken by the governor in his carriage) to see Longwood. It was a wreck, having reverted to being a barn and granary. There was a threshing machine in the drawing room where Napoleon had died, his billiard room was filled with potatoes and straw and his bathroom was a stable.[11]

Bessie, aged eight, had heard stories about St Helena and Napoleon as long as she could remember and now vivid images were engraved on her mind. Later, as a young woman, she would complete a few sketches for her mother's *Recollections*. In the appendix to the third edition, published after her mother's death, she wrote: 'I will only remember that my family ever loved the Buonaparte dynasty, that the first Napoleon loved us, and that we loved and love his nephew.'[12]

Jane, Betsy and her daughter arrived in London towards the end of August 1831, two or three weeks later than the *Nancy* had been due. The women had to find influential support for Jane's petition for a pension. Their main hope was Balcombe's old patron and the family's loyal friend, Sir Thomas Tyrwhitt. But they were devastated to discover that he had resigned on 7 August as Black Rod in the House of Lords, because of his poor health and huge debts: the failed Plymouth and Dartmoor Railroad had bankrupted him. They learned that he had already left the country; he had retired to a small town in northern France—to Saint-Omer, no less. The women had no family to accommodate them in London, so they booked into a hotel in St James to keep up appearances. A petition was sent to the Colonial Office in Jane Balcombe's name. Because of her mother's ill health after the appalling voyage, it is likely that Betsy assisted with the poignant document: 'The humble Petition of Jane Balcombe, Widow of the late William Balcombe, Colonial Treasurer of New South Wales', which concluded that she and her family were 'in a state of absolute destitution and your said Petitioner being far advanced in life and in infirm health, she therefore must humbly pray ... that your Lordship will take her case into your consideration'.[13]

Betsy made a personal visit to the Colonial Office and was politely rebuffed by Under-Secretary Hay. She then wrote to an MP, Lord Marcus Hill (whom she had perhaps met through Tyrwhitt), 'imploring Your Lordship's favourable consideration to my poor Mother's petition. Indeed did your Lordship only know how utterly destitute my Father's death has left my Mother you would I am sure take her case into your benevolent interest ... Earnestly my Lord I entreat and supplicate you not to decide unfavourably upon her petition for her case is one of utter destitution.'[14]

The women waited for a reply; they had no option other than to wait, lacking funds to return to Sydney. They probably barely had funds to survive, for it took almost a year for the wheels of the great bureaucracy to turn and issue a result.

Meanwhile, Betsy was saddened to read in the newspapers of the sudden death, on 22 July 1832, of Napoleon's only child, the handsome young Duke of Reichstadt, at the age of 26. He had 'caught a chill', which became pneumonia.

By coincidence, two days before his death, a certain 'Comte de Survilliers' sailed from Philadelphia in the United States, bound for London. He was Joseph Bonaparte, elder brother of the former emperor. Joseph had lived for many years in America as the rich Comte de Survilliers. But his cover was not very successful: the authorities there and in Britain, and the newspapers too, knew perfectly well who he was—the former puppet king of Spain during his brother's empire, who had stolen the Spanish crown jewels as he fled. In London he learned of the death of his nephew, whose rights he had come to defend.

Joseph was still banished from France by order of King Louis Philippe and so he decided to stay in London for a time. His new plan, now that Napoleon's son was dead, was to summon his three remaining brothers and his nephew Louis Napoleon to London, 'for a conference to determine the future course of the Bonaparte dynasty'.[15] Joseph's presence in London was mentioned in the newspapers and Betsy managed to contact him, probably expressing her condolences for the death of his nephew. Once Joseph saw the name 'Betsy Balcombe' he knew exactly who she was.

Bessie (writing later as Mrs Jane Elizabeth Johnstone) recalled: 'How well I remember going with her to see Joseph Buonaparte, then in England after a sojourn in America.' She enjoyed hearing him praise her mother's 'really exquisite and remarkable beauty'. He sat Bessie on his knee and she was overwhelmed to be in the lap of royalty, as the former king of Spain continued to question Betsy about his late brother's life on St Helena. As they bade Joseph farewell, he took a cameo ring from his finger and gave it to Betsy; it was of a robed woman leaning against an urn. It looked classical Grecian, but he said it had been found by a soldier in a pyramid during the Egyptian campaign and had once been worn by Napoleon. He was happy to give it to her, 'whose family possessed so strong a claim upon the Buonaparte family'.[16]

A decision had been made at the Colonial Office. On 1 May 1833, Viscount Goderich sent a despatch to the new governor of New South Wales, Richard Bourke: 'Having lately had under my consideration the peculiar circumstances connected with the late Mr. Balcombe, whose appointment to the situation of Colonial Treasurer at New South Wales resulted from claims which he had upon this Department in consequence of certain transactions which occurred at St Helena during the period of Napoleon Buonaparte's detention there.'

The mysterious and perhaps deliberately obfuscating wording could refer to confidential information that Balcombe may have offered Lord Bathurst, via Tyrwhitt, at least during the early period of Napoleon's captivity. Goderich advised that a gratuity of £250 should be granted by Treasury, 'to enable her to return with her family to New South Wales, where two of her sons appear to be at present residing, and with whom she is desirous of passing the remainder of her days'. An attached Memorandum from Under-Secretary Hay suggested a clerk position might be found for her son Alexander: 'If the above can be done for Mrs Balcombe, she will quit England with her Daughter Mrs Abel for ever, not only perfectly satisfied but full of gratitude to Lord Goderich and the Government.'[17]

That was unlikely to be the case. There was no mention of a land grant or a pension for the widow. So that was that. The women had come halfway around the world and endured a near-drowning to gain little more than the 'privilege' of having their passages reimbursed.

Betsy, her mother and ten-year-old Bessie boarded the small 352-ton *Ellen*, which sailed on 13 October 1832.[18]

Edward John Eyre, a young gentleman aged seventeen, was on board, coming to Sydney as an unassisted immigrant. He would later become famous for his explorations across vast tracts of the Australian continent. He was soon enchanted with the 30-year-old Mrs Abell. Eyre's *Autobiographical Narrative* was edited and annotated by Jill Waterhouse, who noted: 'On the voyage he seems to have cherished a youthful ardour for Mrs Lucia Elizabeth Abell, if the space he devotes to her in comparison with that given to any other lady is to be taken as proof.'[19]

Eyre described Betsy as being 'in the prime of life, regular and pretty in features, commanding in person, a good figure, stylish in her dress and having a strange mixture of high polish and dash in her manner which was very captivating. She had beautiful hair—a rich nut-brown, shot with gold, in unusual profusion and of an extraordinary length. She had travelled a good deal, seen much of the world, was a linguist and sang ballad music with great sweetness and pathos. In her teens I can well imagine she must have been a lovely girl, for she was still most attractive and had a singular power of fascinating all those who came within her influence. Altogether she was likely to prove a lively, cheerful and pleasant *compagnon du voyage*—if she did not set us all by the ears in our rivalry to obtain her notice and patronage, for she was full of fun and very fond of mischief.'[20]

Eyre encouraged Betsy to tell him her memories of Napoleon, and offered to write them down as her 'amanuensis'. He was astonished by the lines of poetry she could quote, and very rarely misquoted, 'from Byron, Milton, Cowper and Shakespeare, chosen by Mrs Abell to embellish her chapters'. It would seem that she started composing her *Recollections* during that five-month voyage, although it took her ten more years to complete them. The *Ellen* put into port at Hobart on 20 March 1833. Eyre noted that 'Mrs Abell, who seemed to know everybody ... was made much of during her stay'—so much so, indeed, that she was dancing at a ball on the evening the ship was ready to depart and 'was very nearly losing her passage, having only returned on board just before we got under weigh'.[21] The *Ellen* arrived in Sydney Cove on 28 March, and it would seem young Edward Eyre was sorry to be losing Betsy Abell's company.

For a time after their return, Jane, Betsy and Bessie lived with William at his property on the Molonglo Plains. Alexander was still staying with William; he had taken to country life and become adept at farming, supervising some twenty men working on the property.[22] But the remote Molonglo Plains district, with its harsh winters, was not Alexander's kind of country and he suspected that he would do better one day, perhaps when he was married. On his trips into Sydney he always called by Bungonia to visit Inverary Park. He was forming a special friendship with Dr Reid's daughter Emma.

At the end of May, Betsy drove their two-horse gig in to Sydney with her mother. They missed the society of their friends. It was a mad, almost impossible journey of at least seven days, stopping at friendly farms or inns. Near Liverpool, their way was blocked by two men who had 'a brace of pistols' pointed straight at them. They wore black masks entirely covering their faces except for holes for their eyes. One man held their horses while the other took their purses, containing seven pounds in cash, and the rings on their fingers.[23] While according to newspaper reports Mrs Balcombe and Mrs Abell were uninjured, the terror of this encounter was just about the end for them in New South Wales.

In late July, the mail brought distressing news from England. Sir Thomas Tyrwhitt had died earlier that year, on 24 February. Jane grieved for the man who had been so very good to them. William grieved too. He had grown up in an English boarding school at Plymouth, under the care of Sir Thomas, virtually his grandfather. William had had a different experience of the world to the rest of the family. He had been born on St Helena and remembered with vague affection his early childhood at The Briars, but that was in the past. The rest of the family talked endlessly about Napoleon Bonaparte, but he had never met him.

William was a loner who never married. He emerges from the relatively few records as a classic bushman, possessing all the toughness and endurance that characterised early Australian settlers. He was a genuine pioneer, not only on the frontier world of the Molonglo Plains, but also later in the even more remote and wild country of Krawarree, south of the town of Braidwood.

A hard basic life seemed to suit William, but it did not remotely appeal to his mother and sister. It has been observed of the colonial period in Australia: 'The English women came and stayed because they had to. Their children were here and stayed because they wanted to.'[24]

With no means of survival, except as dependants, life was humiliating for Mrs Balcombe and Betsy. In the patriarchal society that was colonial New South Wales, there was no place for gentlewomen without a protector. To stay in the colony was to drop out of the society of the people they knew, for they had lost their status with Balcombe's bankruptcy and death. Young Bessie would grow up unschooled and would never meet a presentable suitor. It was an unthinkable future for them.

CHAPTER 37

RECOLLECTIONS OF THE EMPEROR NAPOLEON

Mrs Balcombe, Betsy and Bessie occupied one of the better cabins on the East India Company barque *Sir Joseph Banks*, determined to maintain standards. No doubt the only anguish, as they departed Sydney on 20 March 1834, was farewelling the three boys. Unlike their nightmare voyage to England on the *Nancy*, this one went smoothly. On 1 September, news came from Portsmouth that the *Sir Joseph Banks* from Sydney 'passed by this morning for the river'. The passengers first listed were 'Mrs Balcombe, Mrs Abell and Miss Abell'.[1]

It is not known where the women stayed in the few months after landing. It is possible they went to stay with relatives; in 1835, Jane was definitely at the fashionable spa town of Tunbridge Wells, where she had friends and may have had family (having been born in Kent). Betsy, soon after arrival, almost certainly settled in London, where she hoped to make a life for herself and her daughter. Since her childhood there had always been a piano in their home and she had a modicum of talent and a good singing voice, so she set herself up as a music teacher. Perhaps at first she hired a piano and put up notices in the local area. In twos and threes the students came. Word spread that

Mrs Abell had talent and a sympathetic manner, and she would sometimes be invited to instruct a girl in the drawing room of a grand London home. Soon she and Bessie could move to a better class of accommodation and she purchased a piano.

But at Tunbridge Wells, Jane Balcombe had become very ill, probably collapsing with a heart attack. She died suddenly at the age of 63 in early February 1835, perhaps so unexpectedly that Betsy and Bessie were not able to be with her at the end. Betsy arranged for her funeral and her burial at Kensal Green cemetery in London.[2]

Betsy probably never knew it, but in the same month, Edward Abell's mother Mary died at the age of 86. She left an estate of some size, bequeathing her 'Dear son Edward' over £300 in stock and annuities. Edward's spinster aunt, Martha Stock, had died two years earlier and her will had been probated. The majority of her considerable estate, with investments worth £4550, was to go to Edward. A shipping record shows the departure of a Mr Abell in June 1835 from Calcutta for Liverpool on the *Prefect*. Edward had come to collect the money. Thanks to his aunt Martha, he was now rich.[3]

In London, Betsy continued to prosper as a music teacher. She was surprised and delighted that her own daughter had developed a beautiful singing voice, a pure soprano. Bessie intended to aim high, a career in opera if she could achieve it; she dreamed of Milan, Paris, Rome.

At some stage in 1836, Betsy would have heard with sadness of the death of her old friend Fanny Bertrand at Châteauroux in France. Her connections with Napoleon's world, so important to her, were slipping away.

Two years went by, during which Betsy and her daughter continued to make a tenuous living from their music, their survival made more challenging by Betsy's steely determination to maintain their position in society by employing a minimum of two household staff. Her land grant in New South Wales had disappeared with the man who had held it in trust for her—the disgraced former attorney-general Alexander Baxter; he had died in England in 1836 after his release from the Marshalsea debtors' prison.

At the age of 71, King William IV died in June 1837 and, to the great excitement of Britons, was succeeded by the eighteen-year-old

Princess Victoria. Much later, Queen Victoria would form an unlikely friendship with Emperor Napoleon III.[4]

The erratic Louis Napoleon Bonaparte arrived in London in October 1838, just evading arrest after the fiasco of his attempt to provoke a rebellion against the French monarchy at Strasbourg in eastern France. Left a fortune by his late mother Queen Hortense, he rented a grand London house with a staff of 27 and was joined by a group of friends and partisans. He was now planning another coup that should surely succeed.[5] He told his supporters, who included Count de Montholon: 'I believe that from time to time men are created whom I call volunteers of providence, in whose hands are placed the destinies of their countries. I believe I am one of those men.' He saw himself as 'the principal embodiment of the Napoleonic heritage'.[6]

His uncle Joseph had told him about Betsy Balcombe and he wanted to acquaint himself with this Englishwoman who had known his illustrious uncle in exile, an uncle whose aims and ideals he was determined to perpetuate. He was also told that Mrs Abell was an attractive woman, and he was always willing to add to his conquests. Somehow through his contacts, perhaps through Montholon, he located her.

Betsy was surprised when a calling card was left, followed shortly afterwards by the caller. He was a tall man of thirty, according to one biographer, with a prominent nose, slightly bulging eyes and thinning hair; his long torso was out of proportion to his legs.[7] At the end of the third edition of her mother's *Recollections,* Betsy's daughter gave a description of the encounter. Disappointingly, their visitor did not resemble Napoleon, whereas Betsy had been startled by Joseph Bonaparte's likeness to his brother, despite being older and of a more solid build. Betsy was now 36 and Bessie an attractive sixteen-year-old. Louis, an inveterate womaniser, probably took an immediate interest in the daughter.

It was to be the first of a number of visits in late 1838. 'In one topic,' Bessie wrote, 'Prince Louis was engrossed even more than in the repetition of the tiniest and most trivial incidents which marked the sojourn at St Helena. This was the personal appearance of his great illustrious uncle. Did he resemble him in any point? Was not his general style the same—if not his features, at least the mould of them?' Betsy's responses were not satisfactory. Her daughter observed: 'All who knew my mother will remember that she spoke out resolutely what she thought honestly, never sparing herself, and only grieved when compelled to disappoint others.' The prince was unhappy that Betsy was 'telling him plainly that in no respect did he resemble his illustrious uncle. He always seemed to be disappointed, yet always recurred to the subject after a short time.' At last she found something encouraging to say, even if it was not strictly true. 'Your hair is very like his,' she said. That pleased him.[8]

Louis Napoleon escorted Betsy to at least one evening hosted by Lady Blessington at Gore House in Kensington. Lady Blessington, an Irishwoman, was clever, witty and beautiful, but not considered quite acceptable in society herself, being the author of *Conversations with Lord Byron* (widely considered a most scandalous man), and most of all for openly cohabiting with the Count d'Orsay, who was the former husband of her stepdaughter. But at Gore House she ran a virtual salon, where leading intellectuals of the day, writers, politicians, artists and scientists, were always welcome and generously hosted. Betsy enjoyed a chat with an ambitious politician, the future prime minister Benjamin Disraeli.

All the while, Louis Napoleon was taking long walks in Hyde Park, turning over his ideas. He and his supporters were plotting another coup to win government in France. His old friend Montholon was helping him to hatch the plans.

Alexander Balcombe had been living and working with his brother William at the Molonglo Plains property, but in 1838 he joined a neighbour in an expedition of several months, taking livestock overland down to Port Phillip (the area surrounding present-day Melbourne), then just opening up for exploration and development. Alexander immediately liked the fertile green country, so different from William's arid land. He resolved to return to Bungonia to propose to the young woman he wished to join him in this new life.[9]

In 1841, when Alexander was 30, he married Emma Juanna (Joanna) Reid, the seventeen-year-old daughter of the respected Reid family of Inverary Park, firm friends of the Balcombes. Dr David Reid had been a military surgeon during the long Peninsular War (which perhaps explains why his daughter was given a Spanish middle name). He had tended the wounded and dying attacked by Bonaparte's forces. In the early days he must have wondered about his new Bungonia neighbours who seemed to have such fond memories of Napoleon, but those days were long past. He would have considered Alexander a worthy son-in-law, who had waited patiently for Emma to be old enough to marry. Alexander and Emma became notable pioneering figures on the Mornington Peninsula near Melbourne and had a large family; later there were many distinguished descendants, including Dame Mabel Brookes.

The story of Alexander's brother Thomas Tyrwhitt Balcombe, older by a year and also born on St Helena, was by no means as happy. He had been courting a young woman, Lydia Stuckey, who had accepted his marriage proposal. But returning to Sydney in late March 1840 from a visit to William, his two-horse gig overturned and Thomas pitched out onto his head. The *Sydney Herald* reported that it was 'an accident which was very near being attended with loss of life'.[10] Thomas recovered sufficiently to marry Lydia three months later, and they settled into a house in the Sydney suburb of Paddington that he named 'Napoleon Cottage'. A year or two afterwards, a baby girl was born, named Jane Elizabeth after her two aunts. She remained her father's favourite when two other children followed.

Thomas pursued his interest in art while working as a field surveyor with Robert Hoddle. The earliest examples of his artworks are landscape sketches and images of an Aboriginal man, made in field notebooks during survey trips to the Hunter and Goulburn river valleys in 1834 and 1835. Over the ensuing years he became noted for his paintings of horses and horse races, genre studies of town and country life, sympathetic representations of Aboriginal tribal life (although his caricatures of town Aborigines sold better) and lively portraits, suggestive of a decidedly playful imagination. Commissions began to be a profitable source of earnings. Thomas Tyrwhitt Balcombe remains an important but underrated figure in Australian art history; he left a vivid and singular collection of paintings, sketches and sculptures. But Thomas seemed unable to enjoy companionable family life; the brain damage from his accident was perhaps responsible for his increasingly disturbing mood swings.

In May 1840, the French King, Louis Philippe, bowed to overwhelming public sentiment and agreed that Napoleon's remains could come back to Paris, to fulfil the emperor's final wish that he could rest 'on the banks of the Seine, in the midst of the French people whom I have loved so well'. After the British government gave its formal permission, a special law was passed that Napoleon's body should be returned from St Helena and taken to Les Invalides, a former military veterans' hospital by the Seine. The expedition would be led by the King's son, the Prince de Joinville. There was a squabble over who should accompany the body on its homecoming, but preference was given to Napoleon's former companions in exile.

The old grand marshal, Count Bertrand, now a widower, requested to take his son Arthur, born on St Helena. Count de Las Cases was blind and ill, with only two more years to live, but his son Emmanuel, former scribe to Napoleon and famed for horsewhipping Sir Hudson Lowe, was proud to take his place. General Gaspard Gourgaud, stout, bewhiskered and rich (somehow having escaped reprisals for his 'confessions'), insisted on going, and claimed to be the first to have demanded Napoleon's return. Dr O'Meara, who had married a wealthy old widow, was dead or he would have been invited; the faithful valets, Louis Marchand and 'Ali' (Saint-Denis), elected to go; and the confectioner Pierron, footman Noverraz and Archambault were there 'to represent the imperial household'.

While the French people waited for the return of their former hero, Louis Napoleon chose this time to launch himself as the successor. On 5 August, he and his supporters arrived at Boulogne in a chartered pleasure boat, a tame vulture tethered at the prow (not having located an eagle). They planned to capture the Boulogne garrison, but the colonel had been forewarned and was expecting them. The bold conquerors were captured instead. Louis Napoleon and Count de Montholon were thrown into the fortress of Ham in Picardy, imprisoned for over five years for their trouble.

On 15 December, the frigate *La Belle Poule*, bedecked with flags for the occasion, arrived with the immense casket at Cherbourg in drenching rain. As the great sarcophagus was borne by a funeral carriage with gilded wheels drawn by sixteen caparisoned horses along the way to Les Invalides, there were huge crowds of spectators. People clung to rooftops. The Emperor Napoleon had come home.

The 1841 census, the first to be taken in England and Wales, listed Mrs Abell as 'Independent' and living with her daughter 'Elizabeth' at a good London address, Dukes Street, near Grosvenor Square, Westminster, St James. It also indicated that she had a boarder, Joseph Green, aged 45, on army half-pay; as Betsy's mother's maiden name was Green, he was probably a cousin.[11]

Betsy wished to launch nineteen-year-old Bessie into society during the winter Season. She would accompany her as chaperone. Outfitting the two of them was costly, but it would be a worthwhile investment if Bessie were to meet a gentleman who would become the steady protector that she had never had.

Brighton was no longer the dizzy sparkling place it was during the Prince Regent's time, but it now had more social cachet, especially when Queen Victoria and her husband Prince Albert were in residence at the Royal Pavilion. On 19 January 1842, Betsy and her daughter attended a fancy dress ball at the Old Ship Hotel at Brighton. They were both mentioned in a London paper, the *Morning Post*, and the 'beautiful Miss Abell, in a rich Persian costume' was the only one of the assembly singled out for her own beauty, not that of her dress.[12]

The two women were still in Brighton a month later, obviously at considerable expense, but the next occasion took them to the height of society. The *Morning Post* of 22 February published an article headed 'FASHIONABLE WORLD, HER MAJESTY & BRIGHTON'. Queen Victoria and Prince Albert were staying at 'the Palace'—the fanciful Royal Pavilion built at vast national expense by the Prince Regent. In the morning they set out for an airing, 'but in consequence of wet weather Her Majesty did not leave the Palace'. Others of the royal family were staying with them and in the evening there was a grand dinner party, which a few dignitaries attended. But during the day, Her Majesty and His Royal Highness received calls at the Palace from 'Sir Thomas, Lady and

Miss de Trafford, Mrs Colonel H. Streatfield, Lieut. R. Colegrave, Captain Green, Mrs and Miss Abell ...'[13] It is likely that the Captain Green mentioned was the same officer, probably a relative, listed as living with them in the previous year's census.

While the month of mixing in society at Brighton had been a delight, there was usually an ulterior motive for mothers of daughters of marriageable age, and that particular aim had not borne fruit. Bessie had danced with any number of charming gentlemen, but then Betsy would hear from friends that certain gentlemen had made discreet enquiries as to the financial position of Bessie's family, and those charming gentlemen would drift away.

Betsy was desperate to find a way to improve their circumstances. And then the thought would have occurred. Napoleon! Everyone was curious about him; whenever she mentioned that she had lived on St Helena, people's questions were always about Bonaparte. Well, she would tell them; she would write a book. And with so many people interested in him, even more so since his body's return to France with such pageantry, the book should make money. She had one half-written already, all the stories she had told to Edward John Eyre ten years before, and he had written them down and given her the notes. So many more memories had come back to her since, with the questions of Joseph Bonaparte and Louis Napoleon. She began work on it immediately, fired with enthusiasm and optimism.

When she had a few stories together but not yet a book, she found she could earn money in the meantime. She sent some chapters to the *New Monthly Magazine*.[14] The editor was delighted, published them immediately and asked for more.

Occasionally ideas came to her that could have, might have, should have happened, they were such good stories, she would have thought, why not put them in? So she dreamed up a story about how she got up to some mischief, committed some prank or other that provoked Napoleon, and her father had locked her up *all night* in the old slave cellar (as if he would!) and the rats came at her and wanted to gnaw her feet, so she threw her father's best bottles of wine at them to keep them away. She came up with another tale about how one evening her mother and father, her sister Jane and herself were visiting the Bertrands at their place over the road from Longwood House and forgot the nine o'clock curfew. The governor had ordered them to be locked in the sentry box for the whole night!

A gentleman from the publishing house of John Murray came to visit her and offered an advance for her book. She was overwhelmed— John Murray published Jane Austen, Sir Walter Scott and Lord Byron. The gentleman said that she could build up her sales if she had friends who would take out a subscription to buy the book. So she wrote to Lady Blessington requesting 'that you will permit me the honor of adding your name to my list of friends who have promised to take copies'. Lady Blessington proved most obliging, and Betsy was very busy herself, for over five hundred subscriptions came in for the book. They were from members of the aristocracy, from bishops and admirals, and even from the writers Robert Southey and Captain Marryat.[15]

In January 1844, Sir Hudson Lowe, who was 'poor, ill and forsaken', died at the age of 74. He had died with his life in ruins, just as Betsy, the girl who had so often annoyed him, was becoming a celebrity. In the same year that Joseph Bonaparte died in Italy, *Recollections of the Emperor Napoleon* was launched by John Murray, and Mrs Abell was suddenly famous. The Victorian artist Alfred Tidey asked to paint her. In *The Music Party* he portrayed Betsy, tall and slim with long blonde hair, leaning over Bessie at the piano, while a harpist and another student look on.

Betsy had written the book to improve their financial situation and in the hope that it would also help Bessie's prospects. Her royalties would never make her a fortune, but what the book did achieve was to raise them to a higher rank in society, and that fulfilled her aim. It was through the publication of *Recollections* that Bessie met her future husband. On the list of subscribers was the name Charles Johnstone Esquire. He was just seventeen, the eldest son of George Johnstone Esquire of 53 Tavistock Square in London and of Broncroft Castle in Shropshire, and he came from a distinguished line of baronets. Maybe young Charles Johnstone met Bessie at a celebration for the launching of the book, perhaps hosted by Lady Blessington. At that gathering, the author's 22-year-old daughter, a budding operatic soprano, would have been invited to sing. Young Charles Johnstone must have been smitten with her.

So why, one wonders, did they not marry for another four years, until 1848? The answer becomes obvious. In four years' time, Charles, the heir to Broncroft Castle and considerable estates, would turn 21 and could marry without his parents' permission. They clearly did not approve of Bessie: she was five years older than their son, she had no money, and she was a singer, almost an actress and therefore fast. But worst of all, her family had been friends of Bonaparte's! So Charles and Bessie had to bide their time, while his parents hoped that he would lose interest and find a more suitable partner.

After the revolution of September 1848 in France, the monarchy was overthrown and the Second Republic established. In an amazing turn of events, Louis Napoleon was elected by the French as their new president. The mass of the people had voted overwhelmingly for him because they recognised his name—the greatest name in France— and they knew nothing else about him.[16]

In England, the *Trewman's Exeter Flying Post* announced that a wedding had taken place on 23 November 1848 at Stoke Damerel church of 'Charles Edward, eldest son of George Johnstone Esq of Tavistock Square London and Broncroft Castle, Shropshire, to Jane Elizabeth Balcombe, only child of Edward Abell Esq and granddaughter of William Balcombe Esq., late Colonial Treasurer of New South Wales'.[17] Charles had turned 21 and was free to marry the bride of his choice. There was no mention of the groom's parents attending. Bessie now had a good protector.

And so did Betsy. She moved in with the young couple at a lodging house at 7 Upper Spring Street in Marylebone parish, London. She still had a desire to maintain a connection with the Bonaparte family, especially now that Louis Napoleon was President of France, so she wrote to him in 1849 and was overly effusive in her gratitude when he sent 'several most interesting autograph notes, not the usual signature, but charming little comments upon men and things'.[18] Betsy also wrote to her brothers to inform them of the happy development of Bessie's marriage to the eldest son of a notable family. She heard back from Alexander in 1851.

After his marriage to Emma Reid, Alexander had bought livestock and settled at Merri Creek, north of Melbourne. Then in 1843, he moved to Schnapper Point on the Mornington Peninsula, where he took over the lease of the 1000-acre run that his brother-in-law Captain Reid had established three years earlier. Alexander named it 'The Briars', in memory of his childhood home. He built a comfortable homestead and held the property under pastoral licence until 1854, when he bought the land.

In 1843, his eldest brother, William, had started selling his land on the Molonglo Plains; within a year he had moved to Krawarree, further inland, and bought two substantial properties there. But after two years he sold the farms and lived in the town of Braidwood. He was restless and found it difficult to settle into town life.

Alexander wrote to Betsy that William had gone with Thomas to the goldfields near Bathurst on the Turon River (today called Hill End). A new gold rush was on there and they hoped to make their fortunes. The goldfields adventure ended in tragedy. In January 1852, William became ill. He died on 29 January, the local paper reported, 'of dysentery'. Thomas buried his brother, then made a poignant sketch of his grave and that of two other men, just cairns of stones under a tree. He asked for a copy to be sent to his sister Mrs Abell at 43 Park Street, Grosvenor Square, London.

William's death shattered Thomas, who began exhibiting more frequent episodes of rage, affecting Lydia and the family. Neighbours in Paddington reported hearing shouting and what sounded like violence and a woman's cries from within the house.[19] Worse was to come. On Boxing Day 1858, Thomas's first and favourite child, eighteen-year-old Jane, died of typhus. This almost completely unhinged him.

In the mid-1850s, even Alexander had briefly joined the search for gold (in the Bendigo area, with Emma's brother David), without success. He returned from the diggings disillusioned and settled down to pastoral pursuits and the life of a country squire. He was appointed a magistrate in 1855 and became a prominent citizen of Melbourne and of the Mornington area. He and his wife Emma kept in touch, by the occasional letter, with Betsy and Bessie in England, but never saw them again.

In New South Wales, Thomas was recognised as an artist of significance and praised for his paintings ever since the 1848 Aboriginal Exhibition, the first time paintings of the original inhabitants of the country were exhibited as serious studies. But after the death of his brother and beloved daughter, his mental and emotional stability had rapidly deteriorated; he was pressed by creditors and his marriage was in trouble—it was public knowledge that he had a mistress. On 13 October 1861, Thomas ended his life by putting a pistol to his head and pulling the trigger as he stood on the front path at Napoleon Cottage. Thomas's wife Lydia and his children were left in a state of poverty. But relief came from an unexpected quarter. The mistress died and in her will left all her estate to her lover's benighted family.[20]

Almost seven years later, Betsy was to write to her sister-in-law Emma Balcombe, about the shock of Charles Johnstone's death on 5 May 1868, aged just 41, 'from Haemorrhage and exhaustion'. She and Bessie were left in greatly reduced circumstances, and they received no assistance from Charles's family. There were no children from the marriage, probably a relief for the Johnstones. By the rule of primogeniture, Broncroft Castle and the estates went to the younger brother. Betsy informed Emma on 10 June: 'We are looking for a small house to suit our altered means. Poor Bessie is far from well.'[21]

Louis Napoleon's term of office as president had ended in 1851. When he failed to gain the support of the National Assembly for a second term in office, he demonstrated the ruthlessness of his uncle. He simply dissolved Parliament and engineered another coup. Several hundred insurgents and bystanders were shot. The following year he proclaimed himself Emperor Napoleon III.

Betsy, then aged 50, had not wished to burden her kind son-in-law with her financial support. Her daughter wrote in her appendix to the *Recollections*: 'though loved and cared for with the utmost generosity and affection by my husband, she would still have liked to possess some post of independence . . . She accordingly wrote to the emperor and requested in terms too vague (as my husband told her) to be worth anything, that he would remember her.' She received a reply, in French, from the Emperor's assistant secretary, dated 30 October 1852, which translated as: 'Madam—The emperor has received yours bearing date the 16th instant. On reading it, however, His Imperial

Majesty remarked that you had failed to state precisely what office you desire. I have therefore the honour to ask you to be good enough to state definitely in what way we may serve you, and remain, madam, Yours most respectfully . . .'[22]

Ultimately the imperial office came up with something. The assistant secretary wrote again to Mrs Abell with a proposal from His Majesty: they would be happy to offer her 'a thousand acres of the best of land' in Constantia, a province of Algeria, the new French colony. This was not, as it turned out, a derisory offer, especially if the land was located in the potentially lucrative Beni-Salah cork forest. But the land was not in fact the Emperor's to give. The rights of a large number of Algerian owners had been totally ignored and the forest was handed out in parcels to members of the Emperor's entourage and to cronies like Charles de Lesseps, brother of the builder of the Suez Canal.

Emperor Napoleon III is best remembered for his grand reconstruction of Paris by Baron Haussmann, for promoting the building of the Suez Canal and for increasing the French merchant marine to become the second largest in the world. He actually had much to be proud of. His weakness was his futile endeavour to emulate his uncle on the battlefield. In July 1870, he took France into the disastrous Franco-Prussian War, without allies and with an inferior military force. His men were crushed by Bismarck's army at Sedan, and in September he made what was widely considered to be a 'shameful surrender'. He himself was imprisoned in Prussia. In March 1871, he was deposed and went into exile in England. France had had quite enough of the Bonapartes.

But the Balcombe women had not, and remained devoted to the end. Mrs Lucia Elizabeth Abell was 68 when she died of a bladder disease at Belgravia in London on 29 June 1871. She never visited her vast acreage of Algerian land and there is no evidence that any benefit was ever derived from it. But until the very end, she always described herself as a 'fervent Bonapartist'. It was as if, in her early exposure to the once most powerful man in the world and to his magnetic, compelling personality, she had, like Icarus, flown too close to the sun and never recovered from the radiance.

ACKNOWLEDGEMENTS

The research for this book was made possible by the helpful staff of many archives and libraries: Archives of the Island St Helena; National Library of South Africa; University of Capetown Library; William Cullen Library of the University of Witwatersrand; Bibliothèque d'Agglomération de Saint-Omer; National Archives of Scotland; British Library Manuscripts Collection; Caird Library, National Maritime Museum, Greenwich; Devon Record Office; West Country Studies Library, Exeter; National Library of Australia; State Records of New South Wales; Richard Neville and the Mitchell Library, State Library of NSW; University of Sydney Library; and the Royal Australian Historical Society, Sydney, especially librarian Donna Newton.

Dr Terry Irving, Professor Emeritus Richard Waterhouse and Professor Emerita Desley Deacon all gave their support for this project, and my literary agent Rick Raftos took it on.

On St Helena I was given kind assistance by Garth Armstrong and Rachel Armstrong; Barbara and Basil George; and the French Honorary Consul Michel Dancoisne-Martineau.

For their help with the book in progress I must thank Dr Susan Adams; Margaret Barbalet; John and Fiona Blanche; Bob Connolly; Sylvia and Tony Francis, who offered a home for London research; Kathy and Malcolm Fraser in Scotland for their hospitality and revelations from their documents collection; Daniel Leunens in Saint-Omer; Dr Susan Lever, the 'godmother' for this book; Lisa Matthews; Tom Molomby SC for a rare reference and French translations; Pouya

Paymani for computer help; Sophie Raymond for author photographs; Stephen Scheding for research advice; Associate Professor Beverley Kingston; Associate Professor Zora Simic; former St Helena Governor, David Smallman; and Clinton Smith and Dr Diane Morgan for generous work on my website.

The research and writing has taken a number of years and during that time some who helped with it have passed away: Sarah Fried who read the manuscript in progress; on St Helena the archivist Ricky Fowler and the finance secretary Paul Blessington, and in England the St Helena historian, Trevor Hearl, who corresponded with me and whose papers are now in the Bodleian Library, Oxford.

I must thank Shirley and David Joy, Mornington shire local historians for their pioneering work on the Balcombes' story, and many Balcombe descendants and their families for research assistance: the late Richard a'Beckett, who made a gift of Alexander Balcombe's original farmhouse, The Briars at Mt Martha, as a museum and historic park, for family letters; his widow Sue and son Michael for continuing help; also Caroline Gaden, Dee Clements and especially Diana and Tony Bradhurst. The Briars staff Chris and Ilma Hackett have given tireless assistance, particularly with pictures from the wonderful collection, and thanks to Steve Yorke for permission for their use. The devoted volunteers for The Briars, Keith and Shirley Murley, supported this book from its inception to completion.

Gratitude to my publishers: Richard Walsh, who took it up when still an incomplete manuscript and always had faith in it; and to my wonderful team at Allen & Unwin, Australia—publisher Elizabeth Weiss, editorial manager Angela Handley, and copyeditor Clara Finlay—all of whose expertise saw it through to publication; many thanks also to Clare Drysdale at Allen & Unwin in the UK.

I have been fortunate to have readers of the manuscript who made detailed notes and gave encouragement from the beginning: Gil Brealey, Tony Bremner (and his friend Miss Picky), Janet Bell, who checked French translations, believed in the work, made insightful comments and bolstered my spirits when they flagged. Especial thanks to John Kerr, who has been a tower of strength in so many ways. I owe a great deal to Allan Deacon for his constant support throughout the research and writing. My thanks to all.

NOTES

CHAPTER 1

1. The 74-gun *Northumberland* was escorted by the brigs *Zephyr*, *Redpole*, *Ferret* and *Icarus* and troopships *Havannah*, *Bucephalus* and *Ceylon*.
2. Thomas Brooke, *A History of St Helena*, London, 1824, 387, noted: 'Napoleon landed and walked to the house prepared for his reception, accompanied by Sir George Cockburn and in the presence of perhaps the largest concourse of people that had ever assembled at St Helena on any former occasion.'
3. Mrs L.E. Abell (late Miss Elizabeth Balcombe), *Recollections of the Emperor Napoleon during the First Three Years of his Captivity on the Island of St Helena, including the time of his residence at her father's house, 'The Briars'*, [1844], 2nd edn, London, John Murray, 1845, 15.
4. Actually 1118 miles (1800 km) from the Angolan coast of Africa and 2025 miles (3260 km) from the Brazilian coast. (The South Atlantic island of Tristan da Cunha may have a stronger claim but it has a much smaller population.)
5. Mark Wilks, *Colonel Wilks and Napoleon: Two conversations*, London, John Murray, 1901 (first published in *The Monthly Magazine*, 1901), quoting Catherine Younghusband in the introduction by Julian S. Corbett, 5.
6. St Paul's, as the principal church of the island, was sometimes described as its cathedral.
7. Mrs Abell, *Recollections*, 10. The second edition of this book appeared in 1845, a third in 1853, and a fourth (incorrectly labelled 'third') in 1873 with a new appendix by Mrs Abell's daughter, Bessie (Mrs Charles Johnstone). Note that in Chapter 1 the author states that 'The news of his escape from Elba . . . had of course not reached us', but the news was brought to the island in May 1815.
8. Cockburn Papers COC/4, National Maritime Museum, Greenwich: 'Secret letter, Instructions to the Governor of St Helena, 1 August 1815'.
9. Letter from EIC Court of Directors to Governor Wilks, 1 August 1815, *Extracts from the St Helena Records*, compiled by Hudson Ralph Janisch, St Helena, 1885.
10. Desmond Gregory, *Napoleon's Jailer: Lt. Gen. Sir Hudson Lowe, A life*, London, Associated University Presses, 1996, 11–12.
11. M. Meneval, cited in *Eclectic* magazine, 1843.
12. Mrs Jane Balcombe and her girls returned in either May or June 1815. Eldest son William (aged seven) remained in England for schooling with Sir Thomas Tyrwhitt as guardian. To return with her family to the island—where they had been living since December 1805—it was necessary for Mrs Balcombe to apply to the East India Company for a bond. The amount needed as security was £1600. The guarantors were the merchants William Burnie & Co., Old South Sea House, London. Bond No. 236 was granted on 15 February 1815: 1815 Court Book, St Helena Archives.
13. Quoted in Arthur Bryant, *The Years of Victory, 1802–1812*, London, Collins, 1945, 62.
14. Quoted in Christopher Woodward, 'Napoleon's Last Journey', *History Today*, July 2005, 51.

CHAPTER 2

1. Anonymous broadside, *A Descriptive Sketch of The Island of St Helena*, London, J. & E. Wallis, 1815, 1. There were in fact other bays—Ruperts Bay, Sandy Bay, Powells Bay—but a landing was difficult at all of them.
2. William Warden, *Letters Written on Board His Majesty's Ship the Northumberland and at St Helena*, London, Ackermann, 1816, published in Clement Shorter (ed.), *Napoleon and His Fellow Travellers*, London, Cassell, 1908, 289.
3. Attributed to Madame Bertrand by Bernard Chevallier, Michel Dancoisne-Martineau, Thierry Lentz and Jacques-Olivier Boudon, *Sainte-Hélène, Île de memoire*, Paris, Fayard, 2005.
4. Lieutenant John Bowerbank, 'An Extract from a Journal Kept on Board HMS *Bellerophon*', in Shorter (ed.), *Napoleon and His Fellow Travellers*, 316.
5. Lady Charlotte Fitz Gerald, letter dated 11 August 1815 to 'dear Charles' (probably Sir Charles Imhoff, stepson of Warren Hastings), quoted in 'Napoleon and Richard III', *Notes and Queries*, January 1961, 5; Lady Jerningham to daughter Charlotte, 3 August 1815, *The Jerningham Letters, 1780–1843*, Egerton Castle (ed.), London, Richard Bentley & Son, 1896, Vol. II, 77.
6. Warden, *Letters*, in Shorter (ed.), *Napoleon and His Fellow Travellers*, 290.
7. Bathurst quoted in Gilbert Martineau, *Napoleon's St Helena*, translated from the French by Frances Partridge, London, John Murray, 1968, 3.
8. Warden, *Letters*, in Shorter (ed.), *Napoleon and His Fellow Travellers*, 290.
9. Emmanuel-Auguste-Dieudonné Comte de Las Cases, *Mémorial de Sainte-Hélène: Journal of the private life and conversation of the Emperor Napoleon at Saint Helena*, London, Henry Colburn, 1823, Vol. I, 241.
10. His surname is variously spelled 'Flahaut' and 'Flahault'; for consistency I have adopted the former.
11. Carnot, cited in Dominique de Villepin, *Les Cent-Jours*, Paris, Librairie Académique Perrin, 2001, 492; Steven Englund, *Napoleon: A political life*, New York, Scribner, 2004, 445.
12. Queen Hortense, *Memoirs of Queen Hortense, Mother of Napoleon III*, compiled by Sir Lascelles Wraxall and Robert Wehrhan, London, Hurst and Blackett, 1864, quoted in Dormer Creston, *In Search of Two Characters: Some intimate aspects of Napoleon and his son*, London, Readers Union & MacMillan, 1947, 236.
13. Queen Hortense, *Memoirs of Queen Hortense*, 320–4.
14. Louis Joseph Marchand, *Mémoires de Marchand*, Jean Bourguignon and Henry Lachouque (eds), Paris, Librairie Plon, 1955, Vol. I, 203–5.
15. Nathaniel Wraxall, Vol. III, 151, quoted in Saul David, *Prince of Pleasure: The Prince of Wales and the making of the Regency*, London, Abacus, 1999, 51.
16. George Home, 'Napoleon on Board the *Bellerophon*: Being a Chapter from *The Memoirs of an Aristocrat*, 1838', published in Shorter (ed.), *Napoleon and His Fellow Travellers*, 20.
17. Quoted in *Liverpool Mercury*, 4 August 1815; compiled in Anon., *Interesting Particulars of Napoleon's Deportation for Life to St Helena: His treatment and mode of living since his arrival and a description of Mr Balcombe's estate, The Briars, Napoleon's residence*, London, W. Hone, 1816, 5.
18. Marchand, *Mémoires*, Vol. II, 17.
19. Las Cases, *Mémorial*, Vol. I, 61n.
20. Captain F.L. Maitland, *Narrative of the Surrender of Buonaparte, and of His Residence on Board HMS Bellerophon*, London, Edinburgh, William Blackwood & Sons, 1826.
21. Maitland, *Narrative of the Surrender of Buonaparte*, vi–vii.

CHAPTER 3

1. Quoted in Christopher Hibbert, *George IV Prince of Wales 1762–1811*, Newton Abbot, Readers Union, 1973, 156n.
2. Trevor James, 'Sir Thomas Tyrwhitt: A brief appraisal', *Dartmoor Magazine*, No. 54, Spring 1999, 9.
3. J. Brooking-Rowe, *Sir Thomas Tyrwhitt and Princetown*, Plymouth, W. Brendon & Son, 1905, 9.
4. Horace Walpole, quoted in David, *Prince of Pleasure*, 8.
5. Sir Thomas Tyrwhitt to William Balcombe, 5 August 1815, Abell, *Recollections*, 3rd edn, 2. The letter from Tyrwhitt does not appear in the first edition of 1844, but was included in the 3rd edition of 1873 (which was actually the 4th edition).

NOTES

6 While the brewery was a reward to Balcombe for his loyalty, Governor Beatson's intention was that the supply of more beer to the garrison, rather than spirituous liquors and Cape wine, would reduce drunkenness.
7 Thomas G. Wheeler, *Who Lies Here? Napoleon's last days*, New York, G.P. Putnam's Sons, 1974, 30.
8 T.H. Brooke, appendix to Clement Shorter (ed.), *Napoleon in His Own Defence*, London, Cassell & Co., 1910, 262.
9 Marchand, *Mémoires*, Vol. II, 9.
10 Admiral Keith: George Keith Elphinstone (1746–1823).
11 Quoted in Shorter (ed.), *Napoleon and His Fellow Travellers*, 300.
12 Anon., *Interesting Particulars of Napoleon's Deportation*, 5.
13 Admiral Lord Keith to his daughter Margaret Mercer Elphinstone, 3 August 1815, 'The Journal and Letters of Admiral Viscount Keith', in the Earl of Kerry (ed.), *The First Napoleon: Some unpublished documents from the Bowood Papers*, Boston & New York, Houghton Mifflin Company, 1925, 167.
14 Anon., *Interesting Particulars of Napoleon's Deportation*, 5–6.
15 'Authentic Particulars of Bonaparte', *Morning Chronicle*, 18 October 1815.
16 Colonel Muiron was a comrade-in-arms of Napoleon who fell in the Battle of Arcola. In seeking settlement in England, Napoleon may have had in mind the experience of his younger brother Lucien, who from 1810 to 1814 lived as a British prisoner of war under comfortable house arrest at Dinham House, Ludlow, then at Thorngrove near Worcester: see Francis Abell, *Prisoners of War in Britain, 1756 to 1815*, London, Oxford University Press, 1914, 448.
17 David, *Prince of Pleasure*, 429–30.
18 Admiral Lord Keith, quoted in Vincent Cronin, *Napoleon*, London, HarperCollins Fontana, 1971, 414.
19 G.J. Marcus notes in *Heart of Oak: A survey of British sea power in the Georgian era*, London, Oxford University Press, 1975, 269–70: 'John Barrow, Second Secretary of the Admiralty, appears to have been chiefly responsible for the decision to send Napoleon to St Helena. "At such a distance and in such a place," he declared, "all intrigue would be impossible, and being withdrawn so far from the European world, he would very soon be forgotten."'
20 Maitland, *Narrative of the Surrender of Buonaparte*, 1826.
21 Barry O'Meara, *Napoleon in Exile or A Voice from St Helena*, London, Jones & Co., [1822], 1827, Vol. I, 5.
22 Finlaison to O'Meara, quoted in Norwood Young, *Napoleon in Exile: St Helena (1815–1821)*, London, Stanley Paul & Co., 1915, Vol. I, 77–8, citing Lowe Papers, BL Add. 20231 f.15; Add. 20232, f.245.
23 *Plymouth Telegraph*, reprinted in the London *Morning Post*, 8 August 1815.
24 Fanny Bertrand's cousin Henry Augustus (Dillon), 13th Viscount Dillon (1777–1832), succeeded to the peerage in 1813: Shorter (ed.), *Napoleon and His Fellow Travellers*, 83.
25 Hon. W.H. Lyttelton, 'Some Account of Napoleon Bonaparte's Coming on Board HMS the Northumberland, August 7 1815', in Shorter (ed.), *Napoleon and His Fellow Travellers*, 82.
26 Captain Charles Ross, 26 July 1816, to W.J. Hall of Kingston, Jamaica, in Shorter (ed.), *Napoleon and His Fellow Travellers*, 59.
27 George Home, in Shorter (ed.), *Napoleon and His Fellow Travellers*, 31.
28 Count de Las Cases, *Mémorial*, quoted in Creston, *In Search of Two Characters*, 247.
29 Warden, *Letters*, in Shorter (ed.), *Napoleon and His Fellow Travellers*, 139.
30 Anon., *Interesting Particulars of Napoleon's Deportation*, 11.
31 Sir George Bingham, 'Napoleon's Voyage to St Helena', in Gareth Glover (ed.), *Wellington's Lieutenant, Napoleon's Gaoler: The Peninsular letters & St Helena diaries of Sir George Ridout Bingham*, Barnsley, Pen & Sword Books, 2005, 257.
32 Warden, *Diary*, in Shorter (ed.), *Napoleon and His Fellow Travellers*, 194.
33 Glover, quoted in Young, *Napoleon in Exile*, Vol. I, 84.
34 Warden, *Letters*, in Shorter (ed.), *Napoleon and His Fellow Travellers*, 151–2. Clement Shorter notes: 'Napoleon did, however, acquire a sufficient knowledge of the English language in a year or so to read it by himself, although he never had any but the most elementary

command of the spoken tongue. Las Cases tells us that he had a very bad memory so far as the grammar was concerned ... The Emperor read much in the *Encyclopaedia Britannica* apparently without assistance. The article on the Nile in that work seems specially to have interested him.'

35 Albert Benhamou, *Inside Longwood: Barry O'Meara's clandestine letters*, London, Albert Benhamou Publishing, 2012, 11, gives O'Meara's correct age in 1815 as 29, concurring with the *Dictionary of National Biography*, which gives the year of his birth as 1786. Some other sources incorrectly state he was 33.

36 Dr Barry O'Meara, secret letter to Mr Finlaison at the Admiralty, 20 October 1815, quoted in William Forsyth, *History of the Captivity of Napoleon at St Helena, From the Letters and Journals of the Late Lieut.-Gen. Sir Hudson Lowe*, London, John Murray, 1853, Vol. I, 23–4.

CHAPTER 4

1 After the Balcombes' departure in 1818, the upper storey of The Briars was extended right across the ground floor, resulting in a handsome villa with at least six bedrooms.

2 St Helena Census, 30 September 1814, courtesy of the late Trevor Hearl, St Helena historian.

3 Trevor Hearl in letter to Anne Whitehead, 3 July 2006.

4 Betsy (Mrs Abell) did not name the school in her *Recollections*, but did so to a friend, Fanny Anne Burney, who reported it. See Fanny Anne Burney (Mrs Wood), *A Great-Niece's Journals from 1830 to 1842*, London, Constable & Company, 1926, 109. The curriculum at Mrs Clarke's is described in 'Mansfield in the News', *Nottingham Journal and Nottingham Review*, 1808, July 2 and 30.

5 Quoted in Dame Mabel Brookes, *St Helena Story*, London, Heinemann, 1960, 5.

6 Marchand, *Mémoires*, Vol. II, 30.

7 Marchand, *Mémoires*, Vol. II, 343.

8 Marchand, *Mémoires*, Vol. II, 34.

9 Abell, *Recollections*, 19–20.

10 Marchand, *Mémoires*, Vol. II, 34.

11 Marchand, *Mémoires*, Vol. II, 348.

12 Napoleon's interest in this pretty young girl's education was more solicitous than it had been for the young females of France when he designed a school system for girls, which, because of 'the weakness of women's brains, the mobility of their ideas, their destination in the social order', concentrated on religion to produce not 'pleasing women but virtuous women'. See Napoleon Bonaparte, *Note Sur L'Établissement D'Écouen*, quoted in Susan G. Bell and Karen M. Offen, *Women, the Family and Freedom: The debate in documents, Vol. I, 1750–1880*, Stanford University Press, 1983, 95.

13 Abell, *Recollections*, 23–4.

14 The Balcombes 'spoke French with difficulty, that language being then much less studied in England than it is at present': Abell, *Recollections*, 24–5.

15 Abell, *Recollections*, 25–7.

16 General Gaspard Gourgaud, *The St Helena Journal of General Baron Gourgaud, 1815–1818*, English edition, London, John Lane, The Bodley Head, 1932, 18 October 1815.

CHAPTER 5

1 Marchand, *Mémoires*, Vol. II, 34–5.

2 Marchand, *Mémoires*, Vol. II, 35–6.

3 Las Cases, *Mémorial*, Vol. I, 246.

4 Comte de Las Cases' aristocratic titles cited in Frédéric Masson, *Napoleon at St Helena 1815–1821*, translated by Louis B. Frewer, New York, Medill McBride Company, 1950, 80.

5 See *Memoirs of Count de Las Cases*, London, Henry Colburn, 1818, quoted in Shorter (ed.), *Napoleon in His Own Defence*, 7.

6 *Memoirs of Count de Las Cases*, quoted in Shorter (ed.), *Napoleon in His Own Defence*, 8.

7 Las Cases, quoted in Martineau, *Napoleon's St Helena*, 29–30.

8 William Balcombe to Sir Thomas Tyrwhitt, 20 October 1815, Yale-Beinecke Collection, Osborn Shelves FCIII-112/23.

9 Sir George Cockburn to J.W. Croker, Secretary to the Admiralty, 22 October 1815, in Forsyth, *History of the Captivity of Napoleon at St Helena*, Vol. I, 34.
10 Sir George Cockburn, quoted in Marcus, *Heart of Oak*, 270.
11 Colin Fox, *The Bennett Letters: A 19th century family in St Helena, England and the Cape*, Gloucester, Choir Press, 2006, 24.
12 Anon., *Interesting Particulars of Napoleon's Deportation*, 13.
13 According to the St Helena Census of 30 September 1814, the stock Balcombe owned consisted of one bull, six cows, five calves and eight swine: *Extracts from the St Helena Records*, compiled by Hudson Ralph Janisch, St Helena, 1885.
14 Abell, *Recollections*, 32–3.
15 'This piece of silver,' wrote Marchand, 'was very elegant, had cost 10,000 francs and was the focus of the Balcombe family's admiration': Marchand, *Mémoires*, Vol. II, 350.
16 Octave Aubry, *St Helena*, translated into English by Arthur Livingston, Philadelphia & London, J.B. Lippincott, 1936, 308.
17 The Bonapartist historian John Holland Rose has observed that this period at The Briars revealed 'the softer traits of his character, which the dictates of policy had stunted but not eradicated': John Holland Rose, *The Life of Napoleon I*, London, G. Bell & Sons, 1935, Vol. II, 499.
18 Las Cases, *Mémorial*, Vol. I, 114–15, refers to Napoleon's boyhood when he was 'turbulent, adroit, lively and agile in the extreme. He had gained, he used to say, the most complete ascendancy over his elder brother Joseph'; Philip Dwyer, *Napoleon: The path to power 1769–1799*, London, Bloomsbury, 2007, 11, quotes a letter by Napoleon in September 1786 in which he looked forward to returning to Corsica, 'seeing my compatriots and my relatives . . . Tender sensations that the memory of my childhood allows me to experience . . .'
19 Dwyer, *Napoleon*, 422.
20 'Ship News: Dover, September 29', *Morning Chronicle*, 1 October 1801.

CHAPTER 6

1 Brookes, *St Helena Story*, 291.
2 Information from the late Trevor Hearl in letter to Anne Whitehead, 3 July 2006.
3 Marchand, *Mémoires*, Vol. II, 36.
4 O'Meara, *Napoleon in Exile*, Vol. I, 13–14.
5 Marchand, *Mémoires*, Vol. II, 37.
6 Comte de Las Cases, from *Mémorial*, 24 October 1815, quoted in John S.C. Abbott, *The Life of Napoleon Bonaparte*, London, Ward, Lock & Co., 1850, 555.
7 Marchand, *Mémoires*, Vol. II, 37.
8 Brooke, *A History of St Helena*, 388.
9 Marchand, *Mémoires*, Vol. II, 37.
10 Anon., *Interesting Particulars of Napoleon's Deportation*, 12–13.
11 Quoted in Fox, *The Bennett Letters*, 24; *The Times*, 8 January 1816.
12 *Quarterly Review*, Vol. 14, No. 27, October 1815 and January 1816, 91; reprinted in *The Times*, 18 April 1816.
13 Abell, *Recollections*, 41.
14 Abell, *Recollections*, 56, 167.
15 Las Cases, quoted in Young, *Napoleon in Exile*, Vol. I, 115–16.
16 Napoleon quoted in Creston, *In Search of Two Characters*, 114.
17 Archibald Primrose, 5th Earl of Rosebery; British prime minister under Queen Victoria (March 1894 – June 1895). He described himself as an 'intelligent admirer of Napoleon' in his *Napoleon: The last phase*, London, Thomas Nelson & Sons, 1900, 133–4.
18 Anon., *Interesting Particulars of Napoleon's Deportation*, 14; reprinted in *The Times*, 17 January 1816.
19 Trevor W. Hearl, 'Puzzling Partners in Prestbury Churchyard II—Catherine's Encounters with Napoleon', *Prestbury Churchyard News*, March 2004.
20 Catherine Younghusband to her aunt, Lady Roche, 4 November 1815, 'Letters from St Helena', *Blackwood's Magazine*, Vol. 262, August 1947, 144–5.
21 Abell, *Recollections*, 31–2.

22 Felix Markham, *The Bonapartes*, NY, Taplinger Publishing, 1975, 14.
23 'Napoleon and the Balcombe sisters on St Helena, as visualised in a French lithograph of the period' is reproduced in Anthony Masters, *Napoleon*, Longman, Burnt Mill, Harlow, Essex, 1981, 64. (This is almost certainly by Marchand, as a sketch of Napoleon in the same style is signed 'Marchand'.)
24 The suggestion that Catherine Younghusband was the artist is proposed by Honorary Consul Michel Dancoisne-Martineau in his blog: <http://domainesdefranceasaintehelene.blogspot.com> under Biographies/The Family Skelton.
25 The G.W. Melliss photograph of Betsy (Mrs Abell) in 1857 is reproduced in Martineau, *Napoleon's St Helena*, 19.
26 Thanks to Keith and Shirley Murley, volunteers at The Briars museum, Mt Martha, Victoria, whose research found the Alfred Tidey painting *The Music Party*.
27 Admiral Cockburn to J.W. Croker at the Admiralty, 22 October 1815, quoted in Young, *Napoleon in Exile*, Vol. I, 120.
28 See Masson, *Napoleon at St Helena*, 91.
29 Abell, *Recollections*, 34–5.
30 Abell, *Recollections*, 36.
31 Abell, *Recollections*, 36–8.
32 Anon., *Interesting Particulars of Napoleon's Deportation*, 14; reprinted in *The Times*, 17 January 1816.

CHAPTER 7

1 Masson, *Napoleon at St Helena*, 49.
2 In 1815 Napoleon Bertrand was aged seven, Hortense five and Henri three.
3 Steven Laurence Delvaux, PhD Thesis, 'Witness to Glory: Lieutenant-Général Henri-Gatien Bertrand, 1791–1815', Department of History, Florida State University College of Arts and Sciences, 2005, 405; citing Maitland, *Narrative of the Surrender of Buonaparte*, 140.
4 Marchand, *Mémoires*, Vol. II, 132.
5 Abell, *Recollections*, 80.
6 B. De Gaissart, 'La naissance, le mariage et la mort de Fanny Dillon, Comtesse Bertrand', *Revue du Nord*, No. 193, April–June 1967, 333.
7 Henry, 11th Viscount Dillon (1705–1787); Honourable General Arthur Dillon, Henry's second son (1750–1794): H.C.G. Matthew and Brian Harrison (eds), *Oxford Dictionary of National Biography*, Oxford University Press, 2004.
8 De Gaissart, 'La naissance, le mariage et la mort de Fanny Dillon, Comtesse Bertrand', 334, notes that Laure was the 'widow of Francois Alexandre Le Vassor de la Touche Longpré', so she was known as Madame de Longpré; she was also a former mistress of Josephine's philandering husband Alexandre de Beauharnais.
9 Andrew O'Reilly, *Reminiscences of an Emigrant Milesian: The Irish abroad and at home*, 3 vols, London, Richard Bentley, 1853, Vol. II, 86–7.
10 Masson, *Napoleon at St Helena*, 50.
11 Masson, *Napoleon at St Helena*, 49.
12 De Gaissart, 'La naissance, le mariage et la mort de Fanny Dillon, Comtesse Bertrand', 335.
13 Masson, *Napoleon at St Helena*, 51.
14 De Gaissart, 'La naissance, le mariage et la mort de Fanny Dillon, Comtesse Bertrand', 336.
15 Masson, *Napoleon at St Helena*, 50.
16 Abell, *Recollections*, 82.
17 Masson, *Napoleon at St Helena*, 57–71.
18 Gourgaud, *Journal*, 21 October 1815.
19 Creston, *In Search of Two Characters*, 235.
20 Abell, *Recollections*, 83–4.
21 Abell, *Recollections*, 80–1.
22 Abell, *Recollections*, 89, 181.
23 *The Commentaries of the Great Afonso D'Albuquerque*, Hakluyt Society, quoted in Philip Gosse, *St Helena 1502–1938*, [London, Cassell, 1938], Oswestry, Anthony Nelson, 1990, 5.

24 Gaspar Corrêa, Portuguese historian c.1496–1563, Secretary to Afonso D'Albuquerque and author of *Lendas da India* (*Legends of India*). His account of Lopez, 'The Earliest Exile of St Helena', translated by Hugh Clifford, *Blackwood's Magazine*, Vol. 173, quoted in Gosse, *St Helena 1502–1938*, 5.
25 Abell, *Recollections*, 181–3.

CHAPTER 8

1 In 2006, the French honorary consul Michel Dancoisne-Martineau, who controlled the 'French domains', including the land of the 'heart-shaped waterfall' valley, donated it to the St Helena National Trust. An accessible path for tourists to the waterfall has been developed.
2 High Knoll fort, described by building archaeologist Ben Jeffs, a consultant to the St Helena National Trust, on St Helena government website: <www.sthelenatourism.com/pages/high_knoll_2.html>.
3 Gordon Chancellor and John van Wyhe (eds), *Charles Darwin's Notebooks from the Voyage of the Beagle*, Cambridge University Press, 2009, 13 July 1836.
4 Abell, *Recollections*, 77–8.
5 Marchand, *Mémoires*, Vol. II, 355.
6 Abell, *Recollections*, 199.
7 Abell, *Recollections*, 200.
8 Brookes, *St Helena Story*, 292.
9 Abell, *Recollections*, 201.
10 Abell, *Recollections*, 44.
11 Colonel Bingham inspected Napoleon's sword on the *Northumberland* and confirms this description: Glover (ed.), *Wellington's Lieutenant, Napoleon's Gaoler*, 257.
12 Abell, *Recollections*, 39.
13 *Courrier de Mannheim*, 1 November 1816, quoted in footnote to French edition of Mrs Abell's *Recollections—Napoléon à Sainte-Hélène: Souvenirs de Betzy Balcombe, Traduction annotée et précédée d'une Introduction par Aimé Le Gras*, Paris, Librairie Plon, 1898, 48–9. Reference thanks to Tom Molomby SC.
14 Baron von Stürmer, Despatch No. 10 to Prince Metternich, 4 July 1817, *Napoléon à Sainte-Hélène, Rapports Officiels du Baron Sturmer*, ed. Jacques St Cere et H. Schlitter, Paris, La Librairie Illustrée, 84.
15 Catherine Younghusband to her aunt, Lady Roche, 4 November 1815, 'Letters from St Helena' in, *Blackwood's Magazine*, Vol. 262, August 1947, 144.
16 Gourgaud, *Journal*, 3 November 1815.
17 Anon., *Interesting Particulars of Napoleon's Deportation*, 13.
18 Abell, *Recollections*, 28.
19 Quoted in 'Letters from the Cape', in Shorter (ed.), *Napoleon in His Own Defence*, 85.
20 Cronin, *Napoleon*, 233, noted that Napoleon 'invariably cheated at games'.
21 Abell, *Recollections*, 50–1.
22 Thomas Brooke, letter, 3 January 1816 in appendix to Shorter (ed.), *Napoleon in His Own Defence*, 264.
23 Catherine Younghusband to her aunt, Lady Roche, 8 December 1815, 'Letters from St Helena', *Blackwood's Magazine*, Vol. 262, August 1947, 147.
24 Lieutenant W. Innes Pocock RN, *Five Views of the Island of St Helena from Drawings taken on the Spot, to which is added A Concise Account of the Island*, London, S. & J. Fuller, 1815, 10.
25 Miss Knipe was a pretty farmer's daughter known by the French as *La Bouton de Rose* or 'Rosebud'.
26 Gourgaud, quoted in Martineau, *Napoleon's St Helena*, 129.
27 H.E. Busteed, *Echoes from Old Calcutta*, London, Calcutta and Simla, W. Thacker & Co, 1908, 144.
28 Abell, *Recollections*, 153.
29 Recollection of Major Hodson in appendix to Shorter (ed.), *Napoleon in His Own Defence*, 266.

CHAPTER 9

1. This is an abbreviated version of a poster for a slave auction held on St Helena as late as 18 May 1829. Slavery was to be eliminated under a graduated system introduced in 1818, but actually continued until 1838, when the condition of slavery was abolished throughout the British Empire.
2. O'Meara, cited in Fox, *The Bennet Letters*, 25.
3. Gourgaud, *Journal*, 30 October 1815.
4. Arnold Chaplin, *Napoleon's Captivity on St Helena 1815–1821*, [first published as *St Helena Who's Who*, 1919], London, Savannah Publications, 2002, 142, gives the date as 10 November 1815.
5. Las Cases, *Mémorial*, quoted in Abbott, *The Life of Napoleon Bonaparte*, 558.
6. On 20 May 1802 Napoleon reintroduced slavery into the French colonies, although it had been abolished during the French revolution. On 8 June 1802, French troops under order from Bonaparte seized the Haitian leader and revolutionary Toussaint L'Ouverture and sent him to prison at Fort de Joux. On 2 August 1802 Napoleon was confirmed as First Consul.
7. General Count Montholon, *Récits de la Captivité de l'Empereur Napoléon à Sainte-Hélène*, Paulin, Paris, 1847. English translation: *History of the Captivity of Napoleon at St Helena*, Philadelphia, Carey & Hart, 1847, Vol. I, 79.
8. Napoleon dictating his memoirs on St Helena, quoted by David Brion Davis, 'He changed the New World', *New York Review of Books*, Vol. 54, No. 9, 31 May 2007, 54–8.
9. See D.K. Basset, 'Great Britain in the Indian Ocean', *Historical Studies*, Vol. 14, No. 53, October 1969, 80–4.
10. Anon. (Francis Duncan), *A Description of the Island of St Helena*, London, Phillips, 1805, 8.
11. Gosse, *St Helena 1502–1938*, 81.
12. Oswell Blakeston (pseudonym of Henry Joseph Hasslacher, 1907–1985), *Isle of St Helena*, quoted by Tony Weaver in St Helena National Trust, *St Helena, 500 Years of History*, 2002, 6.
13. St Helena Census of 1817, St Helena Archives.
14. Abell, *Recollections*, 58, 166.
15. Montholon, *History of the Captivity of Napoleon at St Helena*, Vol. I, 68–9; see also Las Cases, *Mémorial*, 29 November 1815 and O'Meara, *Napoleon in Exile*, Vol. I, 18.
16. Montholon, *History of the Captivity of Napoleon at St Helena*, Vol. I, 78.
17. Bingham, letter to his wife Emma, 30 November 1815, Glover (ed.), *Wellington's Lieutenant, Napoleon's Gaoler*, 261–2.
18. Catherine Younghusband to her aunt, Lady Roche, 8 December 1815, 'Letters from St Helena', *Blackwood's Magazine*, Vol. 262, August 1947, 147.
19. Abell, *Recollections*, 89.
20. Abell, *Recollections*, 97.
21. Marchand, *Mémoires*, Vol. II, 40.
22. Gourgaud, *Journal*, 1 December 1815.
23. Bingham, letter to his wife Emma, 6 December 1815, Glover (ed.), *Wellington's Lieutenant, Napoleon's Gaoler*, 262–3.
24. Catherine Younghusband to her aunt, Lady Roche, 4 November 1815, 'Letters from St Helena', *Blackwood's Magazine*, Vol. 262, August 1947, 145.
25. Gourgaud, *Journal*, 2 December 1815.
26. Marchand, *Mémoires*, Vol. II, 50.
27. Marchand, *Mémoires*, Vol. II, 50.
28. Abell, *Recollections*, 93.

CHAPTER 10

1. Montholon, *History of the Captivity of Napoleon at St Helena*, Vol. III, 17.
2. William Burchell was later to earn fame as a pioneering naturalist for his great collecting expeditions in southern Africa and Brazil. His *Travels in the Interior of Southern Africa* was published to acclaim in 1822.

3 Noted by William John Burchell in his 'St Helena Journal', 6 July 1808, St Helena Archives (copy of original of 'St Helena Journal' in Hope Collection, Oxford University Museum of Natural History).
4 'William Tomset Balcombe: Born: 25 December 1777 Rottingdean, Sussex; Christened: 28 December 1777 Rottingdean, Sussex; Father: Stephen Balcombe, Mother: Mary née Vandyke': according to East India Company Navy 'Certificates of age & baptism' [L/MAR/C/699] No. 762 on reverse, 1020 on front, from naval researcher Stephen T.J. Wright, commissioned by Keith and Shirley Murley of The Briars, Mt Martha, Victoria. Christening details from International Genealogical Index (IGI). The 1777 birth date conforms with information on William Balcombe's death certificate that he was 51 years old when he died on 19 March 1829. St Margaret's Church records, Rottingdean, note the marriage of William's parents, Stephen Balcombe to Mary Vandyke on 27 May 1777, which would indicate that Mary was two months pregnant with William at the time of the wedding. They had three children—William, Stephen, and Thomas, who died in infancy in 1784. Mary Vandyke was born at Lewes in 1757.
5 George Augustus Frederick, the Prince of Wales, was born on 12 August 1762.
6 *Encyclopaedia Britannica*, Vol. 10, 188.
7 Harry Edgington, *Prince Regent: The scandalous private life of George IV*, Feltham, Middlesex, Hamlyn Paperbacks, 1979, 17; another sexual partner of the fifteen-year-old prince was said to be 'the robust wife of one of the Court grooms': Christopher Hibbert, *George IV, Prince of Wales 1762–1811*, Newton Abbot, Readers Union, 1973, 11–12, citing *Papendiek Journals*, Mrs Vernon (ed.), Delves Broughton, 1887, Vol. I, 91.
8 Brighthelmstone was not officially renamed Brighton until 1810. It is well documented that the prince did not meet Maria Fitzherbert, his long-term mistress, until 1784. (They married a year later in a ceremony that was not formally recognised because of her Roman Catholic faith.) Nor could William Balcombe's mother have been the prince's previous mistress, the actress Mary 'Perdita' Robinson, because she was not pursued by her royal beau until the London theatre season of 1779.
9 Andy Durr, 'The making of a fishing museum', *History Workshop Journal*, No. 40, 1995, 229–32; Anne Whitehead, correspondence with Brighton Fishing Museum and with historian Andy Durr, July 2009.
10 Brookes, *St Helena Story*, 5. There is a difficulty with Dame Mabel's suggestion that William had an elder brother, Robert, who became equerry to the Prince Regent, as his sole surviving brother was three years younger, and became a London businessman. IGI records show sons of Stephen Balcombe and Mary (née Vandyke) of Rottingdean as William, christened 28 December 1777, and Stephen, christened 21 May 1780. No Robert Balcombe could be located in army or court lists. A John Balcomb of the First King's Regiment of Dragoon Guards joined the army in about 1787. He was of sufficient rank in 1803 possibly to have been equerry to the prince, but he disappeared, at the rank of major, from army lists after 1805, perhaps indicating that he was killed in the French wars. He seemed too old to have been the stated brother of William. Despite the different spelling of the surname, perhaps this man was a cousin. Information from Keith and Shirley Murley of The Briars, Mt Martha.
11 Laurian d'Harcourt, *Rottingdean: The village*, Brighton, UK, DD Publishing, 2001.
12 The Prince of Wales was generous in compensating for accidents in which he had a part. Workers injured in an accident during the construction of the Brighton Pavilion were compensated: *Morning Herald*, Brighton, 3 July 1787. Even when he was in no way responsible, such as when a boxer called Earl dropped dead in the ring during a match at Brighton, the prince settled an annuity on Mrs Earl and family: John Ashton, *Florizel's Folly*, London, Chatto & Windus, 1899, 115.
13 The boating accident story is in Burchell, 'St Helena Journal', 6 July 1808; Sir Hudson Lowe to Lord Bathurst, 24 February 1818, Lowe Papers, BL Add. 20121 f.230; Brookes, *St Helena Story*, 5—Dame Mabel may have obtained the information from the Lowe Papers rather than family legend.
14 Percy Fitzgerald, *The Life of George the Fourth*, London, Tinsley Brothers, 1881, 641.
15 David, *Prince of Pleasure*, 113–14.
16 Information from Keith and Shirley Murley of The Briars, Mt Martha, and Jane Jones.

17 On 25 December 1788, Mary Balcombe *née* Vandyke married Charles Terry, a tailor. The family moved to a Tudor cottage in Rottingdean, next to the whipping post where wrongdoers were flogged.
18 India Office Records L/MAR/C/657 'Descriptions of Officers' Service 1798–1801', 140, lists William Balcombe, 22 years of age, having 'used the sea 8 years'. It is noted that he spent two years and six months as a Royal Navy midshipman, one ten-month voyage to the West Indies on the *Phoenix* as midshipman, and two voyages on the *Phoenix* to Bengal, one of one year and two months as fifth mate, and the other of one year and seven months as acting fourth mate. This rendered his service as six years and one month—but Balcombe 'used the sea 8 years'. The unaccounted period of one year and eleven months was spent in the navy as a 'Captain's servant', an officially unlisted position.
19 Correspondence from the Royal Archives to Caroline Gaden, wife of a Balcombe descendant (through the Thomas T. Balcombe line). Note that neither William Balcombe nor his brother Stephen make an appearance in the eight volumes of the prince's collected letters, nor in the three volumes of his correspondence as George IV: A. Aspinall (ed.), *The Correspondence of George, Prince of Wales 1770–1812*, 8 vols, London, Cassell, 1971; *The Letters of King George IV 1812–1830*, 3 vols, Cambridge University Press, 1938; David Hilliam, in *Kings, Queens, Bones and Bastards*, Phoenix Mill, Sutton Publishing, 1998, 229, observed: 'Unlike Charles II . . . George had very few bastards. Two illegitimate sons were privately acknowledged, and it is possible that he had four other children, but they were never given prominence or titles.' (Reference courtesy of Shirley Joy.)
20 Quoted in Hibbert, *George IV: Prince of Wales 1762–1811*, 156.
21 He was the son of the Reverend Edmund Tyrwhitt, rector of Wickham Bishops, Essex.
22 Baron Stürmer, Despatch No. 10 to Prince Metternich, 4 July 1817, *Napoléon à Sainte-Hélène, Rapports Officiels du Baron Stürmer*, 84; Queen Victoria's prime minister, Lord Rosebery, in his *Napoleon: The last phase*, 209, repeated it: 'the traditions of the island declared him to be a son of George IV'; the rumour is repeated in Aimé Le Gras's introduction to the 1898 French edition of Mrs Abell's *Recollections, Napoléon à Sainte-Hélène*, v, in which Balcombe is described as '*un honorable fonctionnaire de la Compagnie des Indes Orientales, que l'on disait fils naturel du Régent*'. Lord Rosebery had an incorrect theory about William Balcombe's parentage, *Napoleon: The last phase*, 180: 'Mr. Balcombe was a sort of general purveyor, sometimes called by courtesy a banker; and the traditions of the island declared him to be a son of George IV. As a matter of fact, his father was the landlord of the New Ship Inn at Brighton.' Not so.
23 Germaine de Staël, quoted in Paul Johnson, *Napoleon: A life*, London, Penguin Books, 2002, 119.
24 Count de Las Cases, *Mémorial*, Vol. IV, 80.
25 O'Meara, *Napoleon in Exile*, Vol. I, 19–22.
26 Sir George Cockburn to Comte de Montholon, 22 December 1815, quoted in Young, *Napoleon in Exile*, Vol. I, 183.
27 Desmond Gregory, *Napoleon's Jailer, Lt. Gen. Sir Hudson Lowe: A life*, London, Associated University Presses, 1996, 17–114, for pre-St Helena career, in particular p. 119.
28 Gregory, *Napoleon's Jailer*, 122, quoting Military Surgeon Walter Henry; see also Young, *Napoleon in Exile*, Vol. I, 219.
29 Sir Thomas Tyrwhitt to Sir Hudson Lowe, 8 December 1815, Yale University, Beinecke Collection, Osborn Shelves FCIII-112/24.
30 In 1816, Samuel Brown (1776–1852), who had retired from the navy, took out a patent for wrought-iron chain making and in 1817 the first chain-supported suspension bridge was built, followed by many constructions, including notably the Union Chain Bridge across the River Tweed and the Chain Pier at Brighton. In 1838 he was knighted by Queen Victoria.
31 Gourgaud, *Journal*, 1 January 1816.
32 Abbott, *The Life of Napoleon Bonaparte*, 561.
33 Gourgaud, *Journal*, 18 January 1816.
34 Abell, *Recollections*, 99.
35 Abell, *Recollections*, 102.
36 Napoleon to Las Cases, quoted in Creston, *In Search of Two Characters*, 254.
37 Count de Las Cases, *Mémorial*, Vol. I, 61n.

38 Gourgaud, *Journal*, 30 December 1815.
39 Lowe Papers, BL Add. MSS 20,114, f.253; see also G.L. de St M. Watson (ed.), *A Polish Exile with Napoleon*, London and New York, Harper & Brothers, 1912, 177n, for description of this carriage, which in May 1821 became Napoleon's funeral car.
40 Abbott, *The Life of Napoleon Bonaparte*, 561.
41 Young, *Napoleon in Exile*, Vol. I, 190.
42 Gourgaud, *Journal*, 6 January 1816.
43 Abell, *Recollections*, 62–3.
44 Las Cases, quoted in J.M. Thompson, *Napoleon Bonaparte*, Oxford, Basil Blackwell, [1952] 1988, 392.
45 Gourgaud, *Journal*, 28 January 1816.
46 Mrs Abell, writing 30 years later, placed the game at The Briars, but Gourgaud, writing at the time, placed it at Longwood on 24 February 1816.
47 Abell, *Recollections*, 72–5.
48 Las Cases, quoted in Young, *Napoleon in Exile*, Vol. I, 177, 194.
49 Napoleon in letter to Las Cases, 8 March 1816 in Las Cases, *Mémorial*, Vol. IV, 73.
50 Young, *Napoleon in Exile*, Vol. I, 194–5.
51 See Young, *Napoleon in Exile*, Vol. I, 198.
52 See Ralph Korngold, *The Last Years of Napoleon: His captivity on St Helena*, London, Victor Gollancz, 1960, 274: 'Gourgaud was to say to Sturmer: "Everybody knows that the Princess of Wales has for him an almost fanatical admiration. He hoped that when her daughter mounted the throne, she would take advantage of the influence she has over her to have him taken to England. 'Once there' said he 'I am saved.'"'
53 St Helena Archives and Lowe Papers, BL Add. 20115 ff.124–5.
54 Gourgaud, *Journal*, 19 February 1816.

CHAPTER 11

1 *The Times*, 4 December 2008.
2 R.C. Seaton (Robert Cooper), *Sir Hudson Lowe and Napoleon*, London, David Nutt, 1898, 215, quoting Prime Minister Lord Liverpool to Lowe at time of St Helena appointment.
3 Las Cases, *Mémorial*, Vol. IV, Part 8, 48, cited in Forsyth, *History of the Captivity of Napoleon at St Helena*, Vol. I, 132–3.
4 Marchand, *Mémoires*, Vol. II, 75.
5 O'Meara to Finlaison, cited in Forsyth, *History of the Captivity of Napoleon at St Helena*, Vol. I, 145.
6 Marchand, *Mémoires*, Vol. II, 76.
7 Lowe to Sir Henry Bunbury, Under-Secretary of State, quoted in Forsyth, *History of the Captivity of Napoleon at St Helena*, Vol. I, 142–3.
8 Napoleon was born on 15 August 1769, Sir Hudson Lowe just over a fortnight earlier, 28 July 1769. Lowe's father was a British army surgeon, his mother an Irishwoman from Galway: see Gregory, *Napoleon's Jailer*, 17–19.
9 Martineau, *Napoleon's St Helena*, 71.
10 Forsyth, *History of the Captivity of Napoleon at St Helena*, Vol. I, 135.
11 Napoleon, quoted in Abbott, *The Life of Napoleon Bonaparte*, 564.
12 O'Meara to Finlaison, including French translation, quoted in Forsyth, *History of the Captivity of Napoleon at St Helena*, Vol. I, 147.
13 O'Meara to Finlaison, quoted in Forsyth, *History of the Captivity of Napoleon at St Helena*, Vol. I, 149.
14 O'Meara to Finlaison, quoted in Forsyth, *History of the Captivity of Napoleon at St Helena*, Vol. I, 148.
15 It was not until 23 January 1818 that Bathurst informed Lowe that O'Meara's correspondence with Finlaison was sighted at the Admiralty: see Forsyth, *History of the Captivity of Napoleon at St Helena*, Vol. I, 540.
16 Gourgaud, *Journal*, 19 April 1816.
17 Wilks, *Colonel Wilks and Napoleon*, 26.

18 Wilks, *Colonel Wilks and Napoleon*, 28–35.
19 Abell, *Recollections*, 53.
20 Montholon, *History of the Captivity of Napoleon at St Helena*, Vol. I, 210.
21 Lowe, despatch to Secretary of State Lord Bathurst, 30 April 1816, quoted in Forsyth, *History of the Captivity of Napoleon at St Helena*, Vol. I, 158–62.
22 Quoted in Creston, *In Search of Two Characters*, 261.
23 O'Meara, *Napoleon in Exile*, Vol. I, 26–8.
24 Gourgaud, *Journal*, 5 May 1816.
25 Général Bertrand, *Cahiers de Sainte-Hélène, Journal 1816–1817*, Paul Fleuriot de Langle (ed.), Paris, Editions Sulliver, 5 May 1816.
26 Watson (ed.), *A Polish Exile with Napoleon*, 207n.
27 Martineau, *Napoleon's St Helena*, 81–2.
28 Martineau, *Napoleon's St Helena*, 197.
29 Gourgaud, *Journal*, 20 May 1816; Bertrand, *Cahiers 1816–1817*, 20 May 1816, 49n.
30 Colonial Office, 247.5; Young, *Napoleon in Exile*, Vol. I, 160; Watson (ed.), *A Polish Exile with Napoleon*, 177.
31 Abell, *Recollections*, 102–3.
32 O'Meara, *Napoleon in Exile*, Vol. I, 29 May 1816.
33 Gourgaud, *Journal*, 30 May 1816.

CHAPTER 12

1 *The Times*, 24 September 1816.
2 *Oxford Dictionary of National Biography*; Young, *Napoleon in Exile*, Vol. II, 259–60.
3 Abbott, *The Life of Napoleon Bonaparte*, Vol. II, 566.
4 O'Meara, letter to Gorrequer, 24 June 1816, quoted in Aubry, *St Helena*, 207.
5 Gourgaud, *Journal*, 18 June 1816. The little girl's formal name was soon abandoned for 'Lilli', just as her brother Tristan was usually called 'Charles'. Martineau, *Napoleon's St Helena*, 145, has noted that Lilli lived until 1907, 'the last of the "witnesses" of St Helena'.
6 Lowe to Bathurst, 21 June 1816, cited in Forsyth, *History of the Captivity of Napoleon at St Helena*, Vol. I, 195.
7 Bathurst to Lowe, 15 April 1816, cited in Forsyth, *History of the Captivity of Napoleon at St Helena*, Vol. I, 189–90.
8 O'Meara, *Napoleon in Exile*, Vol. I, 18 June 1816.
9 O'Meara, *Napoleon in Exile*, Vol. I, 18 June 1816.
10 O'Meara, *Napoleon in Exile*, Vol. I, 18 June 1816.
11 Young, *Napoleon in Exile*, Vol. II, 270; Julian Park (ed.), *Napoleon in Captivity: The reports of Count Balmain, Russian commissioner on the island of St Helena 1816–1820*, New York, The Century Co., 1927, xv.
12 Mrs Abell, *Recollections*, 238–9.
13 Martineau, *Napoleon's St Helena*, 100–4.
14 Park (ed.), *Napoleon in Captivity*, Introduction, xiii.
15 O'Meara, *Napoleon in Exile*, Vol. I, 31 March 1817, 476.
16 O'Meara, *Napoleon in Exile*, Vol. I, 23 June 1816, 67.
17 Bathurst to Lowe, 15 April 1816, with letter from Sir Henry Bunbury to Lowe, cited in Forsyth, *History of the Captivity of Napoleon at St Helena*, Vol. I, 189–92.
18 See J.F. Bernard, *Talleyrand: A biography*, London, Collins, 1973, 52. (Madame de Souza lived as Talleyrand's mistress from 1783 to 1792. Auguste Charles was born in 1785.)
19 E. Tangye Lean, *The Napoleonists: A study in political disaffection 1760–1960*, Oxford University Press, 1970, 176–7.
20 Tangye Lean, *The Napoleonists*, 176.
21 'Letters from Lady Malcolm During Napoleon's Captivity', in Earl of Kerry (ed.), *The First Napoleon*, 181–5.
22 O'Meara, *Napoleon in Exile*, Vol. I, 20 June 1816, 65.
23 Earl of Kerry (ed.), *The First Napoleon*, 156.
24 See Martineau, *Napoleon's St Helena*, 206.

25 Bertrand, *Cahiers 1816–1817*, 28 June 1816: 'M. Balcombe, venu à Hutt's Gate, dit que Lady Malcolm a été fort heureuse des réponses de l'Empereur; que l'Empereur a en Angleterre beaucoup de partisans, surtout parmi les femmes et que le nombre en augmente tous les jours; et que l'amiral restera ici plus d'un an, à moins que l'Empereur pareur ne parte et qu'alors il l'accompagnera.'
26 O'Meara, *Napoleon in Exile*, Vol. I, 19n.
27 Young, *Napoleon in Exile*, Vol. II, 271.
28 Park (ed.), *Napoleon in Captivity*, Report No. 6, 1 May 1817, 85–6.
29 O'Meara to Sir Thomas Reade, 10 July 1816, in Forsyth, *History of the Captivity of Napoleon at St Helena*, Vol. I, 237–8.
30 Lady Malcolm to Lady Keith from the Briars, 4 July 1816, in Earl of Kerry (ed.), *The First Napoleon*, 189.
31 O'Meara, *Napoleon in Exile*, Vol. I, 11 July 1816.
32 O'Meara, *Napoleon in Exile*, Vol. I, 11 July 1816.
33 *The Times*, 27 March 1816.
34 Las Cases, *Mémorial*, Vol. IV, 316.
35 See Chaplin, *Napoleon's Captivity on St Helena*, 'A Chronological List of Napoleon's Visitors in St Helena', 142–52.
36 *The Times*, 14 February 1816.
37 Lowe to Bathurst, 17 July 1816, despatch 27 July, cited in Forsyth, *History of the Captivity of Napoleon at St Helena*, Vol. I, 220–6. Note that Lowe dates this meeting as 17 July 1816, whereas other accounts place it on 16 July.

CHAPTER 13

1 Lowe to Sir Henry Bunbury, 29 July 1816, quoted in Forsyth, *History of the Captivity of Napoleon at St Helena*, Vol. I, 232.
2 Martineau, *Napoleon's St Helena*, 199.
3 Abell, *Recollections*, 94.
4 O'Meara to Sir Thomas Reade, 24 July 1816, cited in Forsyth, *History of the Captivity of Napoleon at St Helena*, Vol. I, 239–40.
5 HMS *Griffon* was a sixteen-gun brig-sloop, captured from the French in 1808. It was sold in 1819.
6 Clementina E. Malcolm, *A Diary of St Helena (1816, 1817): The journal of Lady Malcolm, containing the conversations of Napoleon with Sir Pulteney Malcolm*, London, A.D. Innes & Co, 1899, 25 July 1816, 35–43.
7 Bertrand, *Cahiers 1816–1817*, 6 August 1816.
8 O'Meara, *Napoleon in Exile*, Vol. I, 6 August 1816.
9 Abell, *Recollections*, 153.
10 Brookes, *St Helena Story*, 51–8. George Carstairs is not mentioned by name in Mrs Abell's *Recollections*, nor in St Helena records of the period such as Chaplin, who lists army and navy officers. Dame Mabel had access to family papers for her book and mentions a diary by the young Betsy as a source, although it is not included in her bibliography and seems no longer to exist. In her charming *The Emperor's Last Island*, London, Secker & Warburg, 1991, 62, Julia Blackburn claimed: 'The diary does exist and it has apparently made its way into a collection of papers and documents that lie in the archive department of an art gallery in Melbourne, Australia.' However, an extensive search by researchers at The Briars, Mt Martha, has not located a Betsy Diary in either The Briars' collection, the Mornington Regional Museum or the National Gallery of Victoria, nor is it held by any Balcombe family descendants they have contacted.
11 Abell, *Recollections*, 153.
12 Lady Malcolm to the Hon. Miss Mary Elphinstone, 26 January 1817, in Earl of Kerry (ed.), *The First Napoleon*, 197–9; Malcolm, *A Diary of St Helena*, 10 August 1816, 45–6.
13 Quoted in Martineau, *Napoleon's St Helena*, 128.
14 James Kemble (ed.), *St Helena During Napoleon's Exile: Gorrequer's diary*, London, William Heinemann, 1969, quoted in Martineau, *Napoleon's St Helena*, 145.

15 Abell, *Recollections*, 138–9.
16 Abell, *Recollections*, 139.
17 See J.B. Priestley, *The Prince of Pleasure and his Regency 1811-20*, London, Heinemann, 1969, 87.
18 Brookes, *St Helena Story*, 52.
19 Quoted in Creston, *In Search of Two Characters*, 301.
20 O'Meara, *Napoleon in Exile*, Vol. I, 15 August 1816.
21 The ice-making machine was the invention of Professor John Leslie in 1810.
22 Malcolm, *A Diary of St Helena*, 16 August 1816, 48–9.
23 O'Meara, *Napoleon in Exile*, Vol. I, 16 August 1816.
24 Abell, *Recollections*, 142–3.
25 Forsyth, *History of the Captivity of Napoleon at St Helena*, Vol. I, 243; Malcolm, *A Diary of St Helena*, 17–18 August 1816, 54–6.
26 Forsyth, *History of the Captivity of Napoleon at St Helena*, Vol. I, 246–56; Malcolm, *A Diary of St Helena*, 18 August 1816, 55–64; Gourgaud, *Journal*, 18 August 1816; O'Meara, *Napoleon in Exile*, Vol. I, 19 August 1816.
27 Martineau, *Napoleon's St Helena*, 57.
28 Gourgaud, *Journal*, 18 August 1816; O'Meara, *Napoleon in Exile*, Vol. I, 19 August 1816.
29 Martineau, *Napoleon's St Helena*, 57–8.
30 Malcolm, *A Diary of St Helena*, 23 August 1816, 66.
31 O'Meara, *Napoleon in Exile*, Vol. I, 26 August 1816.
32 Malcolm, *A Diary of St Helena*, 28 August 1816, 67.
33 Martineau, *Napoleon's St Helena*, 167.
34 O'Meara, *Napoleon in Exile*, Vol. I, 5 and 7 September 1816.
35 O'Meara, *Napoleon in Exile*, Vol. I, 13 September 1816.
36 O'Meara, *Napoleon in Exile*, Vol. I, 17 September 1816.
37 Bathurst to Lowe re warning from Milan-based Menet, Lowe Papers, BL Add. MS 20116, 310.
38 Charles Stuart, British ambassador to France, to Viscount Castlereagh, 8 July 1816, enclosed in Bathurst despatch to Lowe, 17 July 1816, Lowe Papers, BL Add. 20115 ff.190, 204.
39 Bathurst to Lowe, 12 and 17 July 1816, Lowe Papers, BL Add. 20115 ff.202, 210.
40 Bertrand, *Cahiers 1816–1817*, 5 October 1816.
41 Bertrand, *Cahiers 1816–1817*, 4 and 6 October 1816.
42 O'Meara to Finlaison, 10 October 1816, BL Lowe Papers, Add. 20146, 20116, 20117, quoted in Benhamou, *Inside Longwood*, 61–76.

CHAPTER 14

1 Aubry, *St Helena*, 286–7.
2 Martineau, *Napoleon's St Helena*, 200–1.
3 Quoted in Abbott, *The Life of Napoleon Bonaparte*, 571.
4 O'Meara, *Napoleon in Exile*, Vol. I, 5 November 1816.
5 Abell, *Recollections*, 134–5.
6 Malcolm, *A Diary of St Helena*, 25 November 1816, 76–7.
7 Young, *Napoleon in Exile*, Vol. II, 15.
8 See Park (ed.), *Napoleon in Captivity*, Report No. 20, 1 October 1817, III.
9 Montholon, *History of the Captivity of Napoleon at St Helena*, Vol. I, 279, claimed that it was an earlier letter Las Cases had attempted to send to Lady Clavering that was intercepted—but Montholon was often unreliable.
10 Martineau, *Napoleon's St Helena*, 178, noted that for stealing two glasses of wine from Sir Thomas Reade, 'a slave received two years hard labour; whoever cut down a tree without permission was threatened with two hundred lashes'.
11 Las Cases, *Mémorial*, Vol. IV, Part 7, 277–81.
12 Las Cases, *Mémorial*, Vol. IV, Part 7, 282.
13 Marchand, *Mémoires*, Vol. II, 135.
14 Las Cases' journal, quoted in Young, *Napoleon in Exile*, Vol. II, 12.
15 O'Meara, *Napoleon in Exile*, Vol. I, 25 November 1816.
16 O'Meara to Finlaison, 23 December 1816, quoted in Benhamou, *Inside Longwood*, 77–96.

17 Las Cases, *Mémorial*, Vol. IV, Part 7, 295.
18 O'Meara to Finlaison, 23 December 1816, quoted in Benhamou, *Inside Longwood*, 93.
19 Napoleon to Las Cases, 11 December 1816, quoted in Abbott, *The Life of Napoleon*, 573.
20 Las Cases, *Mémorial*, Vol. IV, Part 7, 319–20.
21 Las Cases, *Mémorial*, Vol. IV, Part 8, 3.
22 Las Cases, *Mémorial*, Vol. I, 61–2n. (O'Meara to Finlaison, 23 December 1816, quoted in Benhamou, *Inside Longwood*, confirmed the high security: 'They were kept *au secret* and placed in charge of an officer and sentinels properly placed about them . . . None but staff officers were afterwards permitted to see them.')
23 Marchand, *Mémoires*, Vol. II, 141.
24 Bertrand, *Cahiers 1816–1817*, 24 December 1816.
25 Las Cases, *Mémorial*, Vol. I, 62n.
26 Lowe, private letter to Bathurst, 3 December 1816, confirming procedure concerning Las Cases papers, quoted in Forsyth, *History of the Captivity of Napoleon at St Helena*, Vol. I, 385.
27 Las Cases, *Mémorial*, Vol. IV, Part 8, 40.
28 Marchand, *Mémoires*, II, 151.
29 O'Meara to Finlaison, 29 December 1816, quoted in Forsyth, *History of the Captivity of Napoleon at St Helena*, Vol. II, 62–78.
30 Malcolm, *A Diary of St Helena*, 11 January 1817, 81–97.
31 Bertrand, *Cahiers 1816–1817*, 17 November 1816.
32 Abell, *Recollections*, 148–9.
33 Bertrand, *Cahiers 1816–1817*, 31 December 1816.
34 O'Meara, to Sir Hudson Lowe, 16 December 1816, Bathurst Private Papers, BL 57/42 ff. 225–34.

CHAPTER 15

1   Gourgaud, *Journal*, 17 January 1817.
2   O'Meara, *Napoleon in Exile*, Vol. I, 26 January 1817.
3   Lady Malcolm to the Hon. Miss Mary Elphinstone, 26 January 1817, in Earl of Kerry (ed.), *The First Napoleon*, 197–9.
4   Lady Malcolm to her cousin Margaret, Madame de Flahaut, 3 September 1817, in Earl of Kerry (ed.), *The First Napoleon*, 199–205.
5   Bertrand, *Cahiers 1816–1817*, 17 November 1817.
6   Malcolm, *A Diary of St Helena*, 31 January 1817, 97–111.
7   Gourgaud, *Journal*, 4 February 1817.
8   Gourgaud, *Journal*, 8 February 1817.
9   Abell, *Recollections*, 242.
10 Gourgaud, *Journal*, 12 February 1817.
11 Abell, *Recollections*, 120.
12 O'Meara, *Napoleon in Exile*, Vol. I, 12 January 1817.
13 Abell, *Recollections*, 158.
14 Information from website 'The Journal of Ross Dix-Peek'—'Notes on Lieutenant-Colonel Olof Godlieb Fehrzen (1784–1820), 53rd Regiment of Foot; Bingham, who had been his commander in the Peninsular Campaign and was a personal friend, spelled the surname 'Fehrszen', perhaps the original spelling; however, the name was anglicised to Oliver George Fehrzen.
15 See Glover (ed.), *Wellington's Lieutenant, Napoleon's Gaoler*, 139–40.
16 Chaplin, *Napoleon's Captivity on St Helena*, 75–6.
17 Gourgaud, *Journal*, 12 February 1817.
18 Gourgaud, *Journal*, 13 February 1817.
19 Bertrand, *Cahiers 1816–1817*, 13 February 1817.
20 Gourgaud, *Journal*, 13 February 1817.
21 Gourgaud, *Journal*, 14 February 1817. In the interests of clarity I have corrected Gourgaud's spelling 'Ferzen' to Fehrzen.
22 Jean-Paul Kauffmann, *The Dark Room at Longwood*, translated from French by Patricia Clancy, London, Harvill Press, 1997, 118–19, citing unpublished notes by Louis-Étienne Saint-Denis in Fonds Jourquin-Jourquin collection.

23   See Chaplin, *Napoleon's Captivity on St Helena*, 97, citing Lady Russell, *Swallowfield and Its Owners*, London, 1901.
24   Quoted in Korngold, *The Last Years of Napoleon*, 242.
25   O'Meara, *Napoleon in Exile*, Vol. I, 16 February 1817.
26   Bertrand, *Cahiers 1816–1817*, 1 March 1817.
27   O'Meara, *Napoleon in Exile*, Vol. I, 8 & 11 March 1817, 415, 425–6.
28   O'Meara, quoted in Bertrand, *Cahiers 1816–1817*, 5 March 1817.
29   Abell, *Recollections*, 242–3.
30   *The Times*, 28 December 1816.
31   Footnote to French edition of Mrs Abell's *Recollections—Napoléon à Sainte-Hélène: Souvenirs de Betzy Balcombe, Traduction annotée et précédée d'une Introduction par Aimé Le Gras*, 48–9. Translation thanks to Janet Bell.
32   The expression should have been '*viel imbécile*'—so Mrs Abell's French left room for improvement.
33   Abell, *Recollections*, 106.
34   Malcolm, *A Diary of St Helena*, 7 March 1817, 111–21.
35   O'Meara, *Napoleon in Exile*, Vol. I, 5 March 1817, 410–11.
36   Abell, *Recollections*, 159.
37   O'Meara, *Napoleon in Exile*, Vol. I., 8 March 1817.
38   O'Meara, *Napoleon in Exile*, Vol. I., 8 March 1817.
39   Bertrand, *Cahiers 1816–1817*, 7 March 1817.
40   Bertrand, *Cahiers 1816–1817*, 5 March 1817.
41   Marchand, *Mémoires*, Vol. II, 157.
42   Bertrand, *Cahiers 1816–1817*, 11 March 1817.

CHAPTER 16

1   Finlaison to O'Meara, 25 February 1817, Lowe Papers, BL Add. 20121, quoted in Benhamou, *Inside Longwood*, 98.
2   Dr James Miranda Barry (born c. 1789–99, died 25 July 1865) was a military surgeon in the British army who served in India, Cape Town, Mauritius, and later on the island of St Helena. After dying in 1865, Dr Barry was revealed to have been a woman, born Margaret Ann Bulkley. See *Oxford Dictionary of National Biography*; Stephanie Pain, 'The "male" military surgeon who wasn't', *New Scientist*, 6 March 2008.
3   O'Meara to Sir Thomas Reade, 24 August 1816, arguing the need for a proper fowlhouse: B.L. Lowe Papers Add. 20115 and St Helena Archives Vol. 20115 f.304.
4   Gourgaud, *Journal*, 7 April 1817.
5   Bathurst to Lowe, 23 February 1817, St Helena Archives.
6   William Makepeace Thackeray, 'The Four Georges: Sketches of Manners, Morals, Court and Town Life', *The Cornhill Magazine*, London, Smith, Elder & Co, September 1860, 258; D.J. Taylor, *Thackeray*, London, Chatto & Windus, 1999, 24.
7   Conversation quoted in Bertrand, *Cahiers 1816–1817*, 3 May 1817.
8   'Buonaparte', *The Times*, 15 March 1817.
9   *The Times*, 14 and 18 March 1817.
10 Quoted in Martineau, *Napoleon's St Helena*, 201.
11 Martineau, *Napoleon's St Helena*, 202.
12 Gourgaud, *Journal*, 21 June 1817.
13 Montholon, *History of the Captivity of Napoleon at St Helena*, Vol. I, 20 May 1817.
14 Gourgaud, *Journal*, 15 May 1817.
15 Esther Vesey's mother was a mixed-race woman, possibly a slave, but her father was identified as 'a sergeant in the St Helena Corps' in a letter by Captain Thomas Poppleton to Lowe, 22 May 1816, listing the Longwood domestics: Lowe Papers, BL Add. 20115 f.110.
16 Gourgaud, *Journal*, 9 June 1817.
17 Gourgaud, *Journal*, 9 June 1817.
18 Gourgaud, *Journal*, 18 June 1817.
19 Gourgaud, *Journal*, 5 June 1817.

20 Gourgaud, *Journal*, 9 June 1817.
21 Lady Malcolm to her cousin Margaret, Madame de Flahaut, 3 September 1817, in Earl of Kerry (ed.), *The First Napoleon*, 199–205.
22 Malcolm, *A Diary of St Helena*, 19 June 1817, 146–66.
23 Gourgaud, *Journal*, 19 June 1817.
24 Hester Lynch Piozzi et al., *The Piozzi Letters 1817–1821*, University of Delaware Press, 1999, 100.
25 Piozzi et al., *The Piozzi Letters 1817–1821*, 100.
26 Abell, *Recollections*, 180–1.

CHAPTER 17

1 J. Ralfe on Admiral Plampin in *The Naval Biography of Great Britain*, London, Whitmore & Fenn, 1828, Vol. III, 372–86.
2 Paul Frémeaux, *With Napoleon at St Helena: Being the memoirs of Dr John Stokoe, naval surgeon*, translated from the French by Edith S. Stokoe, London, John Lane, The Bodley Head, 1902, 40.
3 Martineau, *Napoleon's St Helena*, 135–6.
4 Frémeaux, *With Napoleon at St Helena*, 41–2.
5 William Pitt, 1st Earl Amherst, 1773–1857. After his diplomatic mission to China he was appointed Governor General of India.
6 Bertrand, *Cahiers 1816–1817*, 18 July 1817.
7 Chaplin, *Napoleon's Captivity on St Helena*, 223.
8 Brookes, *St Helena Story*, 196. Dame Mabel Brookes claimed that Betsy's victim was Charlotte Johnson, Lady Lowe's elder daughter, which may well have been so, but the evidence must be in Betsy's untraceable diary.
9 Abell, *Recollections*, 41–2; Brookes, *St Helena Story*, 196.
10 Gourgaud, *Journal*, 8 July 1817.
11 Chaplin, *Napoleon's Captivity on St Helena*, 223; see also Martineau, *Napoleon's St Helena*, 135–6.
12 Chaplin, *Napoleon's Captivity on St Helena*, 222–3.
13 Chaplin, *Napoleon's Captivity on St Helena*, 222–4.
14 Gourgaud, *Journal*, 12 July 1817.
15 Bertrand, *Cahiers 1816–1817*, 18 July 1817.
16 Bertrand, *Cahiers 1816–1817*, 18 July 1817.
17 Gourgaud, *Journal*, 22 and 24 July 1817; Bertrand's *Cahiers 1816–1817*, on 22 July 1817, noted: 'The Emperor visits Mme Bertrand and returns when Mr Balcombe arrives. He gives his hair to Mr Balcombe for the Empress and the Cardinal Fesch; Major Fehrzen undertakes to carry them.'
18 Bertrand, *Cahiers 1816–1817*, 23 July 1817.
19 Bertrand, *Cahiers 1816–1817*, 23 and 25 July 1817.
20 Gourgaud, *Journal*, 27 July 1817.
21 Gourgaud, *Journal*, 28 July 1817.
22 Quoted in Martineau, *Napoleon's St Helena*, 201.
23 Bathurst to Lowe, 19 August 1817, St Helena Archives, Lowe Papers.
24 Quoted in Martineau, *Napoleon's St Helena*, 203–4.
25 Gourgaud, unpublished journal, 12 February 1817, translated and quoted in Aubry, *St Helena*, 209; Felix Markham, *Napoleon*, London, Penguin, 1995, 250.
26 Quoted in Martineau, *Napoleon's St Helena*, 145.
27 O'Meara, *Napoleon in Exile*, Vol. II, 22 August 1817, 156.
28 Marchand, *Mémoires*, Vol. II, 177.
29 Gourgaud, *Journal*, 8 September 1817, and O'Meara, *Napoleon in Exile*, Vol. II, 9 September 1817.
30 Kemble (ed.), *St Helena: Gorrequer's diary*, 19, entry for 9 September 1817.
31 Abell, *Recollections*, 112–13; St Helena historian Trevor Hearl noted in a letter to the author, 10 March 2006, that 'Mrs Abell herself did not attempt to embroider the occasion', but he considered some later writers overstated 'Betsy's equestrian performance at the races—such as it was!' One had her entering Napoleon's horse in a steeplechase, and Dame Mabel Brookes wrote that she was awarded a 'little silver trophy', presumably by the governor (Brookes,

St Helena Story, 151)—whereas, as Hearl observed, 'her father was later summoned before Sir Hudson and curtly warned that another display from his daughter like that, and he would be on the next ship back to Britain'. See Trevor Hearl, '"Derby Days" at Deadwood: Highlights of Horse-Racing at St Helena', Part I, article for *Wirebird: Journal of the Friends of St Helena*, Issue 29, Autumn 2004.
32 Abell, *Recollections*, 125–6.
33 Gourgaud, *Journal*, 25 September 1817.
34 Gourgaud, *Journal*, 26 September 1817.
35 Bertrand, *Cahiers 1816–1817*, 26 September 1817.
36 Sir Thomas had relinquished his formal position as the prince's secretary in 1812 when he became Black Rod in the House of Lords, while remaining a close friend of the prince. Balcombe, on the island since December 1805, may have been unaware that he no longer held the secretary position, or not have mentioned it, for he was known to boast of his connection through Tyrwhitt to the prince.
37 Gourgaud, *Journal*, 26 September 1817.
38 Gourgaud, *Journal*, 26 September 1817.
39 Gourgaud, *Journal*, 4 October 1817.
40 Bathurst to Lowe, 21 August 1816, St Helena Archives, Lowe Papers Vol. 20115 f.80.

CHAPTER 18

1 Charles Darwin, *The Voyage of the Beagle*, 1845, Heron Books, 1968, 486, entry for 9 May 1836.
2 Abell, *Recollections*, 114–16.
3 Information from A. Hyatt King, *Some British Collectors of Music c.1600–1960*, 2011, 51.
4 Frémeaux, *With Napoleon at St Helena*, 52–4.
5 Frémeaux, *With Napoleon at St Helena*, 54.
6 Lowe Papers, BL Add. MSS 20,140, f.53.
7 Gourgaud, *Journal*, 12 October 1817.
8 Gourgaud, *Journal*, 15 October 1817.
9 G.H. Heathcote in Edinburgh, letter to Mrs Jane and Betsy Balcombe in Sydney, 25 March 1826, Mitchell Library Folio ML MSS 848X.
10 Gourgaud, *Journal*, 15 October 1817.
11 Gourgaud, *Journal*, 16 October 1817.
12 Bertrand, *Cahiers 1816–1817*, 13 October 1817.
13 Bertrand, *Cahiers 1816–1817*, 18 October 1817.
14 Gourgaud, *Journal*, 18 and 19 October 1817.
15 Gourgaud, *Journal*, 6 November 1817.
16 Gourgaud, *Journal*, 18 November 1817.
17 Bertrand, *Cahiers 1816–1817*, 18 November 1817.
18 Marchand, *Mémoires*, Vol. II, 176.
19 Marchand, *Mémoires*, Vol. II, 181.
20 Gourgaud, *Journal*, 21 and 14 December 1817.
21 Martineau, *Napoleon's St Helena*, 145.
22 Gourgaud, *Journal*, 1 January 1818.
23 Park (ed.), *Napoleon in Captivity*, Report No. 27, 13 December 1817, 146.
24 Gourgaud, *Journal*, 1 January 1818.
25 H. Chamberlain, British ambassador to Brazil to Lowe, 3 December 1817, St Helena Archives, Lowe Papers.
26 Général Bertrand, *Cahiers de Sainte-Hélène, Journal 1818–1819*, Paris, Éditions Albin Michel, 1878, 19. Note that in this volume, precise dates are given only erratically, events grouped under months; therefore page numbers are indicated instead.
27 Gourgaud, *Journal*, 26 and 27 January 1818.
28 Gourgaud, *Journal*, 30 January 1818.
29 Park (ed.), *Napoleon in Captivity*, Report no. 3, 15 February 1818, 162.
30 Gourgaud, *Journal*, 2 February 1818.

31 Princess Charlotte died on 6 November 1817.
32 O'Meara, *Napoleon in Exile*, Vol. I, 3 February 1818.
33 Stürmer to Metternich, quoted in Park (ed.), *Napoleon in Captivity*, Balmain Report No. 3, 15 January 1818, 165.
34 Gourgaud, *Journal*, 6 and 11 February 1818.
35 Quoted in Park (ed.), *Napoleon in Captivity*, 164. Balmain (or editor Park) quoting Bonaparte to Bertrand, 'Speak to me no more of that man.'
36 Kemble (ed.), *St Helena: Gorrequer's diary*, 41, entry for 12 February 1818.
37 Bertrand, *Cahiers 1818–1819*, 71.
38 Gourgaud, as quoted in Park (ed.), *Napoleon in Captivity*, Report No. 3, 14 March 1818, 164.
39 Gourgaud, *Journal*, 27 February 1818.

CHAPTER 19

1 See Martineau, *Napoleon's St Helena*, 173.
2 Kemble (ed.), *St Helena: Gorrequer's diary*, 39, entry for 10 February 1818.
3 Park (ed.), *Napoleon in Captivity*, Balmain Report No. 3, 14 March 1818, 164.
4 Stürmer Reports, quoted in Park (ed), *Napoleon in Captivity*, Report No. 3, 15 January 1818, 165–7.
5 Sir Hudson Lowe to Major-General Sir Henry Torrens, 2 September 1818, BL Add. 20123 f.342: 'respecting a present reported to have been given by Napoleon Bonaparte to Major Poppleton ... I feel it a duty to address you officially on the subject'. Torrens was head of the Horse Guards, the army equivalent of the Admiralty and Poppleton's ultimate superior. Lowe wrote to him after he heard that Poppleton had been promoted to major; he obviously expected his information might cause Poppleton to be dismissed. He also wrote to Lord Bathurst on the same matter (Lowe to Bathurst, 4 September 1818, BL Add. 20123 f.351).
6 Jacques St-Cère and H. Schlitter (eds), *Napoléon a Sainte-Hélène, Rapports Officiels de Baron Stürmer*, Commissaire du Gouvernement Autrichien, Paris, a La Librairie Illustrée, n.d., Stürmer to Prince Metternich, Report No. 11, 31 March 1818, 174.
7 Marchand, *Mémoires*, Vol. II, 186.
8 O'Meara, *Napoleon in Exile*, Vol. II, 17 February 1818.
9 Kemble (ed.), *St Helena: Gorrequer's diary*, 43, entries for 11 and 17 February 1818.
10 O'Meara, *Napoleon in Exile*, Vol. II, 18 February 1818.
11 Forsyth, *History of the Captivity of Napoleon at St Helena*, Vol. II, 209: O'Meara reports to Lowe 'he apprehended his patient might be suffering under an attack of chronic hepatitis'.
12 Goulburn to Lowe, 18 September 1817, St Helena Archives, with enclosures from Charles Stuart, British ambassador in Paris, 4 September 1817.
13 Bathurst to Lowe, 1 January 1818, Lowe Papers, BL Add. 20121 f.3.
14 Although its content is referred to, the actual letter from Tyrwhitt has not been located. It may be that he asked for the letter to be destroyed, or that Balcombe did so on his own initiative.
15 Sir Thomas Tyrwhitt to Sir Hudson Lowe, 8 December 1817, Lowe Papers, BL Add. 20120.
16 Lowe to Bathurst, 24 February 1818, Bathurst Private Papers, 57/43 f.184; Lowe Papers, BL Add. 20121 f.230.
17 Lowe to Bathurst, 24 February 1818, Bathurst Private Papers, 57/43 f.184; Lowe Papers, BL Add. 20121 f.230.
18 Journal for 'Earl Spencer', 25 April 1803 to 16 April 1805, BL India Office Archives L/MAR/B/227D, naval researcher Stephen T.J. Wright via Keith and Shirley Murley of The Briars, Mt Martha,; census records, East India Company records and The National Archives, CO/201/229 under 'Balcombe'.
19 Journal for 'Earl Spencer', 25 April 1803 to 16 April 1805, BL India Office Archives L/MAR/B/227D.
20 Balcombe's debt was paid at Ryde on the Isle of Wight in 1805 by Matthew Burchell, father of William Burchell, Balcombe's new business partner, just before the departure of Burchell as well as Balcombe and his family for St Helena: Burchell, 'St Helena Journal', St Helena Archives.
21 Marcus Arkin, 'John Company at the Cape: A history of the Agency under Pringle 1794–1815', *Archives Year Book for South African History*, 1960, Vol. 2, Pretoria 1962, 257–8

(Arkin notes the following sources: re 'improper trade in East India goods', Pringle to Beatson, 17 May 1813, CGH, FR, XIX; re 'condemned by Customs', D. Denyssen (the Fiscal) to Pringle, 19 May 1813, CGH F.R. XII; re 'escorted out of Table Bay . . . no longer heard of', Pringle to Beatson, 19 May and 28 May 1813, CGH, FR, XIX).

22 Sir Thomas Tyrwhitt to Sir Hudson Lowe, 8 December 1815, Lowe Papers, BL Add. 20120; Yale University, Beinecke Collection, Osborn Shelves FCIII-112/24.
23 Lowe to Bathurst, 24 February 1818, Bathurst Private Papers, BL 57/43 f.184; Lowe Papers, BL Add. 20121 f.230; Brookes, *St Helena Story*, 211–12.
24 Gourgaud, *Journal*, 13 March 1818.
25 Gourgaud, *Journal*, 13 March 1818.
26 Gourgaud, *Journal*, 14 March 1818.
27 Abell, *Recollections*, 228.
28 Kemble (ed.), *St Helena: Gorrequer's diary*, entry for 16 March 1818.
29 See Young, *Napoleon in Exile*, Vol. I, 170.
30 Abell, *Recollections*, 189–90.
31 Montholon, *History of the Captivity of Napoleon at St Helena*, Vol. III, 17, and on 97 confirmed in Napoleon's will, dictated to Montholon, 26 April 1821.
32 Marchand, *Mémoires*, Vol. II, 187–8.
33 Abell, *Recollections*, 230–1.

CHAPTER 20

1 Sir Thomas Reade to Sir Hudson Lowe, March 1818, Lowe Papers, BL Add. 20121 f.473 & f.96.
2 Mrs Charles Johnstone, appendix to 3rd [4th] edition (1873) of her late mother Mrs Abell's *Recollections*, 311–12.
3 The death in Paris of the Countess Dillon was reported in the *Edinburgh Magazine and Literary Miscellany*, December 1817.
4 The Indiaman *Waterloo* sailed just after the *Winchelsea*, also the naval vessel HMS *Melville*. The name of the recipient of Fanny Bertrand's letter is obscured, but as the letter was written in English it was almost certainly to her aunt, Lady Jerningham in Norfolk.
5 The Countess Bertrand letter was supplied by Barbara George, found in the St Helena Archives by Lally Brown (aka Liz Sargeant) for her book *The Saint Helena Counterpoint: Napoleon's exile—The myth exploded*, Warwick, Sargeant Press, n.d., 90.
6 Lowe to Bathurst, 22 March 1818, Bathurst Private Papers, BL 57/43 f.190.
7 *The Times*, 12 May 1818, Ship News: Lymington, 10 May, half past 4 pm, 'Just landed here the Purser of the *Winchelsea* Indiaman'. Other passengers who disembarked were Major Gall of the Bengal Bodyguard with his wife and family and Mr Torin of the Bombay Establishment.
8 *The Times*, 8 May 1818.
9 *The Times*, 18 May 1818.
10 *The Times*, 23 May 1818.
11 BL Add. 20126, f.313.
12 Goulburn to Bathurst, 10 May 1818, BL Add. MSS 2021 f.119.
13 Clarence Edward Macartney and Gordon Dorrance, *The Bonapartes in America*, Philadelphia, Dorrance & Co., 1939, Ch XIV, 'American Plots to Rescue Napoleon'.
14 Lowe to Bathurst, 14 March 1818, Bathurst Private Papers, BL 57/43 f.186.
15 Information courtesy of Caroline Gaden.
16 'Irish typhus and dysentery epidemic', 1817–1818, George Childs Kohn (ed.), *Encyclopedia of Plague and Pestilence*, Facts on File Library of World History, 3rd edn, 2007; Keighley & District Family History Society, 'Major Epidemics and Disease Outbreaks Timeline', compiled in 2011 for the Australian Institute of Genealogical Studies.
17 In Ireland in 1818 one in six suffered from typhus out of a population of six million, and 65,000 died of it: 'Irish typhus and dysentery epidemic', 1817–1818, *Encyclopedia of Plague and Pestilence*, Keighly, Keighly and District Family History Society, 2011.
18 Will of Stephen Balcombe, proved September 1818, Public Record Office, UK National Archives.
19 Ida Macalpine and Richard Hunter, 'The "Insanity" of King George III: A classic case of Porphyria', *British Medical Journal*, 8 January 1966, 65–71; Priestley, *The Prince of Pleasure*, 14.

20 Neville Thompson, *Earl Bathurst and the British Empire, 1762–1834*, Barnsley, Leo Cooper, 1999, 9–10; J. Brooking-Rowe, *Sir Thomas Tyrwhitt and Princetown*, Plymouth, W. Brendon & Son, 1905, 9.
21 Thompson, *Earl Bathurst and the British Empire, 1762–1834*, 52.
22 In letter from 'James' [William] Balcombe to O'Meara on 24 June 1818 he noted 'I have been hard at work for you, and what has been said has been listened to. I am just going to the Secretary of State's office where I have been twice before on your business.' Enclosed in Lowe despatch to Bathurst, 29 September 1818, BL Add.20123 ff.399–406.
23 Lowe despatch to Bathurst, 29 September 1818, BL Add. 20123 ff.399–406, containing letter from 'James' [William] Balcombe to O'Meara, 24 June 1818.
24 *The Times*, 5 June 1818.
25 *The Times*, 10 and 13 June 1818.
26 Thompson, *Earl Bathurst and the British Empire*, 109–10.
27 *The Examiner*, 1 February 1818.

CHAPTER 21

1 Lowe to Bathurst, 24 February 1818, Bathurst Private Papers, BL 57/43 f.184; Lowe Papers, BL Add. 20121 f.230: 'The [Balcombe] daughters I believe correspond occasionally with Lady Malcolm, but of this I cannot speak with positive certainty.'
2 Christopher Summerville (ed.), *Regency Recollections: Captain Gronow's guide to life in London and Paris*, Welwyn Garden City, Ravenhall Books, 2006, 89.
3 Gronow, *Regency Recollections*, 131: Christopher Summerville (ed.) estimates that during the Regency the 'vast majority of British subjects, an impoverished working class [were] lucky to earn ten shillings a week', and that figures for the period should be 'multiplied by a factor of fifty for a rough modern equivalent'; by that calculation, the five Balcombe children had inherited £5000 each.
4 Gronow, *Regency Recollections*, 49.
5 Bryant, *The Years of Victory, 1802–1812*, London, Collins, 1945, 318.
6 Bryant, *The Years of Victory, 1802–1812*, 313–14.
7 EIC Court Book April 1818 to September 1818, 178, 22 May 1818, BL India Office 126-B/167. (Confirms appointment of Edward Abell Esquire as civil agent of the Government of Ceylon to the EIC Presidency of Madras. Travel at his own expense.)
8 *The Times*, 27 June 1818.
9 *The Times*, 13 January 1818.
10 O'Meara to John Finlaison, 12 July 1818, quoted in Benhamou, *Inside Longwood*, 161.
11 Dr John Stokoe to Admiral Plampin, 13 July 1818, quoted in Forsyth, *History of the Captivity of Napoleon at St Helena*, Vol. III, 404.
12 But Boys would return, to Lowe's disappointment—this was apparently only a holiday.
13 O'Meara, *Napoleon in Exile*, Vol. II, 235–6; letter published in *Morning Chronicle*, 21 August 1818.
14 *Morning Post*, 20 July 1818.
15 O'Meara to Sir Hudson Lowe, dated Longwood 19 April 1818; *Morning Chronicle*, 18 July 1818; duplicated in *The Times* and *Morning Post*, 20 July 1818.
16 Finlaison to O'Meara, 24 January 1818, BL Add. 20231, f.21.
17 Bathurst to Lowe, 18 May 1818, Despatch No. 132, quoted in Forsyth, *History of the Captivity of Napoleon at St Helena*, Vol. III, 400.
18 Sir Thomas Reade to Dr O'Meara, 19 April 1818, published in *Morning Chronicle*, 22 July 1817.
19 Napoleon's margin comments of 25 April 1818, published in *Morning Chronicle*, 22 July 1817.
20 *Morning Chronicle*, *Bury & Norwich Post*, 21 and 22 July 1818.
21 Bathurst to Lowe, 22 July 1818, BL Add. 20123 f.128.
22 *Morning Post*, 27 August 1818.
23 O'Meara, *Napoleon in Exile*, Vol. II, 236.
24 Young, *Napoleon in Exile*, Vol. II, 104; Young noted that the articles described were mentioned in O'Meara's will.
25 O'Meara to Finlaison, 10 August 1818, quoted in Benhamou, *Inside Longwood*, 169–74.

CHAPTER 22

1. Lowe to Bathurst, 29 September 1818, Bathurst Private Papers, BL 57/43 f.407.
2. W.J. Burchell, *Travels in the Interior of Southern Africa*, 2 vols, London, Longman, Hurst, Rees, Orme & Brown, 1822; Burchell, 'St Helena Journal', St Helena Archives.
3. Sir George Cockburn was Conservative MP for Plymouth in 1818 and appointed a Junior Lord of the Admiralty from April 1818 to 1827. That Balcombe assisted in his electoral campaign is confirmed in a letter from Lowe to Bathurst of 25 September 1818, BL Add. 20123 f.382: 'Captain Brash went to Mr. Holmes' office who told him that Mr. Balcombe was at the time attending an election.'
4. Balcombe from Hythe to William Fowler, 21 August 1818, Lowe Papers, BL MS Add. 20123 f.320.
5. Kemble (ed.), *St Helena: Gorrequer's diary*, 102, entry for 10 December 1818.
6. Holmes to Stokoe, 26 August 1818, Lowe Papers, BL MS Add 20123 f.329.
7. Chaplin, *Napoleon's Captivity on St Helena*, 233–4; St Helena Council Minutes for 24 August 1818, St Helena Archives.
8. EIC Court of Directors to Lowe, 21 April 1819, quoted in Forsyth, *History of the Captivity of Napoleon at St Helena*, Vol. III, 55.
9. *Morning Post*, *The Times*, (both with headline 'Slave Abolition on St Helena'), 12 November 1818.
10. *Morning Chronicle*, 5 September 1818. Las Cases' *Memoirs* were only a precursor to his massive eight-volume *Mémorial de Saint-Hélène*, not written until after his papers were returned by the Colonial Office after Napoleon's death in 1821.
11. *The Times*, 15 September 1818.
12. *Edinburgh Review*, Vol. 30, September 1818, 444–62.
13. Lowe to Bathurst, 15 May 1819, Bathurst Private Papers, BL 57/44 f.286.
14. William Holmes from Lyons Inn to 'James Forbes', St Helena, 30 August 1818, BL Add. 20123 f.331.
15. Lowe despatch to Bathurst, 29 September 1818, BL Add. 20123 ff.399–406, containing letter from 'James' [William] Balcombe to O'Meara, 24 June 1818.

CHAPTER 23

1. O'Meara to John Wilson Croker, 28 October 1818, quoted in Forsyth, *History of the Captivity of Napoleon at St Helena*, Vol. III, Appendix No. 150, 432–3.
2. John Wilson Croker to O'Meara, 2 November 1818, quoted in Benhamou, *Inside Longwood*, 201.
3. *The Times*, 10 November 1818.
4. *The Times*, 10 November 1818.
5. 'Minute of what passed at the Colonial Office, Sunday 8 November 1818, Earl Bathurst, Viscount Sidmouth and Viscount Melville present. Mr. Balcombe attending', BL MS Add. 20201 f. 193–4.
6. William Balcombe to Earl Bathurst, 9 November 1818, BL MS Add. 20201 ff.195–6.
7. William Fowler on St Helena to William Balcombe c/- Messrs W&J Burnie, 29 September 1818, BL MS Add. 20201 f.191.
8. William Balcombe to Earl Bathurst, 10 November 1818, BL MS Add. 20201 ff.197–8.
9. *Morning Post*, 17 November 1818.
10. *The Times*, 10 November 1818.
11. Sir Thomas Tyrwhitt proposal for horse-drawn railroad presented to the Plymouth Chamber of Commerce, 3 November 1818
12. William Balcombe from Chester Place, Kennington, to cousin Miss Cheal, 14 November 1818. Letter transcribed by author, courtesy of the late Richard a'Beckett and family from their collection of Balcombe family letters. Copies at The Briars, Mt Martha.
13. Gourgaud to Madame Mère and Prince Eugene, October 1818; to Emperor of Russia, 2 October 1818; to Emperor of Austria, 25 October 1818; to Marie Louise, 25 August 1818, in *St Helena Journal of General Baron Gourgaud*, Vol. II, Appendix II, 348–53.
14. *Courier*, 25 November 1818, reprinted in *Aberdeen Journal*, 25 November 1818; also *The Asiatic Journal*, 14 November 1818.

15 Henry Goulburn to Lowe, 16 November 1818, BL MS 20201 f.187.
16 Henry Goulburn to Lowe, 16 November 1818, BL MS 20201 f.187.
17 Bathurst to Lowe, 16 November 1818, BL MS 20201 f. 183.
18 *Bury & Norwich Post*, 18 November 1818. Queen Charlotte died on 17 November 1818.
19 *Morning Chronicle, Bury & Norwich Post*, 18 November 1818.
20 Bathurst to Lowe, 20 November 1818, BL MS Add. 2021 ff. 201–2.
21 *Morning Post*, 25 November 1818.
22 Cardinal Fesch in Rome was Madame Mère's brother and uncle to Napoleon.
23 *Morning Chronicle*, 2 December 1818.
24 *Morning Post*, 2 December 1818.
25 Lowe to Goulburn, 10 October 1818, BL MS 20137 f. 23, letter which arrived in London around late November to early December.
26 Lowe to Bathurst, 23 December 1818, BL MS 20124, ff. 473–6.
27 George Gordon Lord Byron, *The Age of Bronze*, London, John Murray, 1823.

CHAPTER 24

1 Reported in the *Salisbury & Winchester Journal* of 20 December 1819: 'At a meeting of the Bath and West of England Society for the Encouragement of Agriculture, Arts, Manufactures and Commerce, in the presence of Lord Arundel, the Marquis of Lansdowne and various admirals, a paper by Sir Thomas Tyrwhitt was read, who had successfully grown nine acres of flax on Dartmoor and believed much of the moor could be brought into cultivation for flax. It caused "great excitement".'
2 Les Landon, 'Sir Thomas Tyrwhitt: His life and times', *Dartmoor Magazine*, No. 15, n.d.
3 Elaine Sylvester, 'Sir Thomas Tyrwhitt of Princetown', *Margins Literary Magazine*, No. 3, 'Dartmoor', 2008, 44; Landon, 'Sir Thomas Tyrwhitt', 5.
4 See Abell, *Prisoners of War in Britain 1756 to 1815*, 238: 'By the foreign prisoners of war Dartmoor was regarded, and not without reason, as the most hateful of all the British prisons.'
5 John Hirst, *Freedom on the Fatal Shore: Australia's first colony*, Melbourne, Black Inc., 2008, 80: 'The large influx of convicts after 1816 with 2000 arriving each year.'
6 Sir Thomas Tyrwhitt met with Plymouth Chamber of Commerce, 3 November 1818, *Trewman's Exeter Flying Post or Plymouth and Cornish Advertiser*, 5 November 1818.
7 Landon, 'Sir Thomas Tyrwhitt', 5.
8 'Prospectus of the Plymouth & Dartmoor Rail-Road', *Trewman's Exeter Flying Post or Plymouth and Cornish Advertiser*, 11 February 1819.
9 Sir George Magrath MD, quoted in S. Baring-Gould, *A Book of Dartmoor*, London, Wildwood House, (1900) 1982, 259–60.
10 St Helena Archives, 1819–1820 Index of Court of Directors' Minutes: 762, 24 February 1819, 'Mr William Balcombe requests permission to return to St Helena'.
11 Hubert O'Connor, *The Emperor and the Irishman: Napoleon and Dr Barry O'Meara on St Helena*, Dublin, A.A. Farmar, 2008.
12 Barry E. O'Meara, *An Exposition of some of the Transactions at St Helena since the Appointment of Sir Hudson Lowe as Governor of the Island; with an authentic account of the past and present Treatment of Napoleon, corroborated by various Official Documents*, printed for James Ridgway, Piccadilly, price 8s in Boards. The book was advertised as 'Published this day' in the *Morning Chronicle*, 26 May 1819. It had been advertised as 'forthcoming' on 11 March 1819.
13 *The Times*, 5 April 1819.
14 *The Times*, 8 April 1819.
15 Lowe to Bathurst, 16 May 1819, Bathurst Private Papers, BL 57/44 f.292.
16 Lowe to Goulburn, 29 June 1819, Bathurst Private Papers, BL 57/44 f.304.
17 Françoise de Candé-Montholon (ed.), *Journal Secret d'Albine de Montholon, maîtresse de Napoléon à Sainte-Hélène* (*The Secret Journal of Albine de Montholon, mistress of Napoleon on St Helena*), Paris, Albin Michel, 2002. The journal is generally considered unreliable and gives Albine too central a role, but certainly declares her role as Napoleon's mistress.
18 Forsyth, *History of the Captivity of Napoleon at St Helena*, Vol. III, 168.

19   Bathurst to Lowe, Despatch No. 162, 12 July 1819, quoted in Forsyth, *History of the Captivity of Napoleon at St Helena*, Vol. III, 484.
20   Lowe to Bathurst, 26 July 1819, Bathurst Private Papers, BL 57/44 f.320.
21   G. and J. Hearder, 'Sir Thomas Tyrwhitt', *The South Devon Monthly Museum*, Plymouth, March 1836, Vol. VII, 97–9; 'Sir Thomas Tyrwhitt', *Encyclopaedia of Plymouth History*, Plymouth, n.d.: 'The iron rails were on granite sleepers, with an unusual gauge of 4 feet, 6 inches, soon known as the "Dartmoor gauge".'
22   Exeter Museum, *The Regency in Devon*, Exeter, Exeter Museum Publication No. 94, 1978, 4; David R. Fisher, *The History of Parliament Online, 1790–1820*, 'Masseh or Manasseh Lopes (1755–1831)'. See <www.historyofparliamentonline.org>.
23   E.P. Thompson, *The Making of the English Working Class*, Harmondsworth, Penguin Books, [1963] 1984, 752.
24   R.J. White, *Waterloo to Peterloo*, Harmondsworth, Penguin, 1957, 192–3.
25   Samuel Bamford, quoted in Thompson, *The Making of the English Working Class*, 754. (The number killed and wounded was not established with certainty—it may have been many more.)

CHAPTER 25

1   *Morning Post*, 14 August 1819.
2   *The Times*, 3 November 1819, reprinted from the *Morning Chronicle*.
3   *The Times*, 29 November and 6 December 1819.
4   St Helena Archives, 1819–1820 Index of Court of Directors' Minutes: 762, 10 November 1819, Balcombe's request noted.
5   St Helena Archives, 1819–1820 Index of Court of Directors' Minutes: 897, 17 December 1819, 'Request of Mr William Balcombe to return to St Helena discussed in relation to letter from Henry Goulburn.'
6   See Lowe to Bathurst, 16 May 1819, Bathurst Private Papers, BL 57/44 f.292,.
7   Priestley, *The Prince of Pleasure*, 14.
8   The future Queen Victoria was born on 24 May 1819.
9   Wellington quoted in Priestley, *The Prince of Pleasure*, 15.
10   Lowe to Bathurst, 1 December 1819, Bathurst Private Papers, BL 57/44 f.351.
11   St Helena Archives, Longwood Orderly officer noted: 'Napoleon sighted in garden in a dressing-gown, 26 December 1819'. Napoleon's gardening attire also reported in *Caledonian Mercury*, 17 April 1820.
12   John Stanhope, *The Cato Street Conspiracy*, London, Jonathan Cape, 1962; Malcolm Chase, 'Arthur Thistlewood (1774–1820)', *Oxford Dictionary of National Biography*, 2004.
13   The story was thought to be apocryphal until the death of George IV. Then that respectable medical journal *The Lancet* reported that the physicians attending the late king had found 10,000 labelled envelopes in the former monarch's bedside cupboard, each containing a few strands of hair.
14   See Steven Parissien, *George IV: Inspiration of the Regency*, London, John Murray, 2001, 219.
15   The coronation was postponed until 19 July 1821.
16   *The Times*, *Bristol Mercury*, *Glasgow Herald*, 10 July 1820; *Trewman's Exeter Flying Post*, 13 July 1820.
17   *Morning Chronicle*, 14 August 1820; *Newcastle Courant*, 19 August 1820.
18   *Bristol Mercury*, 19 July 1820.
19   Lady Granville to Lady Morpeth, 18 August 1820, quoted in E.A. Smith, *A Queen on Trial: The affair of Queen Caroline*, Phoenix Mill, Sutton Publishing, (1993) 2005, 102.
20   Jane Robins, *Rebel Queen: The trial of Queen Caroline*, London, Simon & Schuster, 2006, 223–7.
21   Robins, *Rebel Queen*, 237, 242.
22   See Smith, *A Queen on Trial*, viii.
23   Parissien, *George IV*, 222.
24   Robins, *Rebel Queen*, 289.

25 R.K. Webb, *Modern England: From the 18th century to the present*, London, George Allen & Unwin, 1969, 163, quoting *Crabb Robinson's Diary*, 1 December 1820, London, Dr William's Library.
26 P.L. O'Reilly to Denzil Ibettson, 11 July 1820, BL Add. 20220 ff. 144–5; Denzil Ibbetson to Major Gorrequer, n.d., BL 20220 ff. 146.
27 Brookes, *St Helena Story*, 239.
28 Broadside by London pamphleteer James Catnach, 1820, BL Add. 38565, intended as satire but taken seriously by some.
29 Bathurst to Lowe, 30 September 1820, quoted in Forsyth, *History of the Captivity of Napoleon at St Helena*, Vol. III, 250–1.
30 Quoted in Frank McLynn, *Napoleon*, London, Jonathan Cape, 1997, 653.
31 Sir William Doveton to Sir Hudson Lowe, 18 January 1820, Lowe Papers, BL Add. 20233, f.109.
32 Forsyth, *History of the Captivity of Napoleon at St Helena*, Vol. III, 242–5.
33 Forsyth, *History of the Captivity of Napoleon at St Helena*, Vol. III, 247.
34 Forsyth, *History of the Captivity of Napoleon at St Helena*, Vol. III, 248.
35 Despatch No. 170, Bathurst to Lowe, 16 February 1821, quoted in Forsyth, *History of the Captivity of Napoleon at St Helena*, Vol. III, 493.
36 Dr Arnott report of 1 April enclosed with letter from Lowe to Bathurst, 10 April 1821, Bathurst Private Papers, BL 57/46, f.467.
37 Lowe to Bathurst, 24 April 1821, Bathurst Private Papers, BL 57/46, f.479.
38 Napoleon I, 'Napoleon's Last Will and Testament', *The Fondation Napoléon*, <www.napoleon.org>.
39 Despatch No. 174, Lowe to Bathurst, 6 May 1821, quoted in Forsyth, *History of the Captivity of Napoleon at St Helena*, Vol. III, 498.
40 Philip Henry Stanhope, *Notes of Conversations with the Duke of Wellington 1831–1851*, Oxford University Press, 1947, quoted in Elizabeth Longford, *Wellington: Pillar of State*, London, Weidenfeld & Nicolson, 1972, 77.
41 Sir William Fraser, *Words on Wellington*, London, John C. Nimmo, 1889, 228.

CHAPTER 26

1 Edwin Emerson, *Comet Lore: Halley's comet in history and astronomy*, New York, Schilling Press, 1910.
2 *John Bull*, 9 July 1821, 53–6; Maik Meyer, 'Charles Messier, Napoleon and Comet C/1769', *International Comet Quarterly*, January 2007, 3–6.
3 Lowe to Bathurst, 20 July 1822, Bathurst Private Papers, BL 57/47 f.545, in which Lowe himself confirmed the argument over the wording of the inscription for the coffin.
4 Wellington at his club, quoted in Gilbert Martineau, *Napoleon's Last Journey*, translated from the French by Frances Partridge, London, John Murray, 1976, 3; Elizabeth Longford, *Wellington*, 78, quoting *The Journal of Mrs Arbuthnot*, Francis Bamford and Duke of Wellington (ed.), London, Macmillan & Co., 1950, Vol. I, 105.
5 See Jill Hamilton, *Marengo: The myth of Napoleon's horse*, London, Fourth Estate, 2000, 201.
6 The French companions departed on the *Camel* on 27 May 1821.
7 Lowe to Bathurst, 26 May 1821, Bathurst Private Papers, BL 57/46 f.492.
8 Lowe to Bathurst, 25 March 1820, Bathurst Private Papers, BL 57/46 f.367; Lowe to Bathurst, 30 April 1820, Bathurst Private Papers, BL 57/46 f.375.
9 Kemble (ed.), *St Helena: Gorrequer's diary*, 154, entry for '1819 end of year'.
10 Lowe to Bathurst, 14 July 1821, Bathurst Private Papers, BL 57/46 f.500.
11 'Secret and Confidential' from EIC Court of Directors to Sir Hudson Lowe, 2 May 1821, BL Add. 20,237, ff.288–301.
12 Address by British residents of St Helena to Sir Hudson Lowe, 25 July 1821, quoted in Forsyth, *History of the Captivity of Napoleon at St Helena*, Vol. III, 313–14.
13 'Plymouth and Dartmoor Railway', Brian Moseley, *Encyclopaedia of Plymouth History*, Plymouth, Devon Record Office publication, 2002.
14 Sidmouth is 22.4 miles from Chudleigh.
15 'The Knowle, Sidmouth, England, Record Id: 4362', Devon Record Office.

16 R.N. Worth, *A History of Devonshire with Sketches of its Leading Worthies*, London, Elliot Stock, 1886, 74–5: 'The west window of the church is a memorial to the Duke of Kent, father of Queen Victoria, who died at Sidmouth in 1820.'
17 Sidmouth's population had risen to 2747 in 1821: D.M. Stirling, *The Beauties of the Shore; Or, a Guide to the Watering-places on the South Devon Coast*, Exeter, Roberts, 1838, 111.
18 Auction listing: *Morning Post*, 15 August 1820; *Salisbury & Winchester Journal*, 19 March 1821. T.L. Fish bought Knowle Cottage, the property of the late Mrs Drax.
19 John Mockett, *Mockett's Journal: A collection of interesting matters relating to Devonshire*, Canterbury, Kentish Observer Printing Office, 1836, 262; Stirling, *The Beauties of the Shore*, 120.
20 Mockett, *Mockett's Journal*, 262.
21 *The Western Times*, 13 October 1828.
22 Anon., *Guide to Illustrations and Views of Knowle Cottage, Sidmouth; the Elegant Marine Villa Ornée of Thos. Fish Esq.*, Sidmouth, J. Harvey, 1834, 11–19; republished by Devon County Council, 2004.
23 *Woolmer's Exeter & Plymouth Gazette*, 11 July 1846, notes of The Knowle: 'Great additions have been made to the numerous objects of interest. A few days since, a large number of valuable animals were received, and also several waggon-loads of curiosities'; on 19 July 1851, announced 'a valuable acquisition of articles . . . many of which were intended for the Crystal Palace'.
24 *Morning Chronicle*, 25 March 1861.

CHAPTER 27

1 Parissien, *George IV*, 304.
2 Robins, *Rebel Queen*, 309.
3 Longford, *Wellington*, 70.
4 Henry Brougham, quoted in *Thomas Creevey Papers*, Harmondsworth, Penguin Books, 1985, 205.
5 Parissien, *George IV*, 311.
6 Quoted in E.A. Smith, *George IV*, New Haven & London, Yale University Press, 1999, 190.
7 Smith, *George IV*, 193.
8 *John Bull*, 6 August 1821.
9 Quoted in Smith, *George IV*, 194.
10 Martineau, *Napoleon's Last Journey*, 3.
11 Lowe (on board the *Dunira* East Indiaman) to Goulburn, 8 September 1821, Bathurst Private Papers, BL 57/46 f.501, re furniture from Longwood; Martineau, *Napoleon's Last Journey*, 23.
12 Forsyth, *History of the Captivity of Napoleon at St Helena*, Vol. III, 315.
13 Forsyth, *History of the Captivity of Napoleon at St Helena*, Vol. III, 316.
14 Lowe from 1 Edgware Road to Bathurst, 1 January 1822, Bathurst Private Papers, BL 57/47.
15 Brookes, *St Helena Story*, 245.
16 Nevill, Earls of Abergavenny research from *The Complete Peerage of England, Scotland, Ireland, Great Britain and the United Kingdom, Extant, Extinct or Dormant*, 13 vols, 1910–1959; reprinted in 6 vols, Gloucester, Alan Sutton Publishing, 2000, Vol. I, 43.
17 No record of Edward Abell's birth has been found except International Genealogical Index suggested birth date of 1801, which must be incorrect. (The handwriting in the 1810 application to the EIC is not that of a nine-year-old, his education would not by then have been 'Classical and Mathematical' and he would not have joined the EIC army and gone into battle at the age of ten.) Keith and Shirley Murley of The Briars, Mt Martha, found records through the Essex Historical Society of the births of Edward's six full brothers and sisters, by their mother Mary née Stock, their father's third wife: Mary-Ann (1784), James (1785), William (1787), Sophia (1788), and twins Charles and Robert (1789). (Only two of these siblings, William and Charles, survived to adulthood.) Given the pattern of birth spacing and the mother's likely exhaustion after the family's move to Alphington, it would be reasonable to speculate on a gap of two years before the birth of the youngest, Edward, therefore positing 1791. It is unfortunate that most of the records of St Gregory's parish—where Abell's details might have been registered—were destroyed in the London Blitz.

18 Francis Abell, Edward's father, was baptised 17 December 1738. Abell family research courtesy of Keith and Shirley Murley of The Briars, Mt Martha.
19 Information on the Abell family background courtesy of Keith and Shirley Murley of The Briars, Mt Martha.
20 Francis Tillett Abell was born c.1764 (and was later a mayor of Colchester). Edward's other half-siblings were Charlotte, born c.1770, and Sarah. Research from Keith and Shirley Murley of The Briars, Mt Martha.
21 Messrs. Dodwell & Miles, *Army of India, Alphabetical List of the Officer of the Indian Army for the Year 1760 to the Year 1837*, London, Longman, Orme & Co., 1811; *Madras Almanac and Compendium*, Madras, 1820.
22 'Major General Sir Henry Torrens' from *Entries for Queen's Royal Surrey Regimental Association*. (Given the disparity in their ages, Francis and Henry Torrens may have been half-brothers.)
23 William Dalrymple, *City of Djinns: A year in Delhi*, London, HarperCollins, 1993, 105–9, 126–30.
24 See Mildred Archer and Toby Falk, *India Revealed: The art and adventures of James and William Fraser*, London, Cassell, 1989, 15; William Dalrymple, *City of Djinns: A year in Delhi*, London, HarperCollins, 1993, 98–9; William Dalrymple, *White Mughals: Love and betrayal in eighteenth-century India*, HarperCollins, 2002, 53–4.
25 Dalrymple, *City of Djinns*, 98–9, 105–7.
26 Dalrymple, *City of Djinns*, 127–30.
27 Kalanga Fort was also known as Nalapani Fort; 'List of Inscriptions on Christian Tombs and Tablets of historical interest in the United provinces of Agra and Oudh'.
28 Sir Charles Metcalfe (1785–1846) was between 1822 and 1845 a British colonial administrator, acting governor-general of India in 1835, and lieutenant-governor of the North-Western Provinces from June 1836 to June 1838; Metcalfe, quoted in G.L. Rai-Zimmdar, *Anglo-Gorkha Friendship*, Lulu.com, 2008, 20.
29 John Pemble, *Britain's Gurkha War: The invasion of Nepal, 1814–16*, Barnsley, UK, Frontline Books, 2009.
30 See Archer and Falk, *India Revealed*, 27–35; James Baillie Fraser, *Journal of a Tour through part of the snowy range of the Himala mountains, and to the sources of the rivers Jumna and Ganges*, London, Rodwell & Martin, 1820.
31 On 22 May 1817, Edward Abell left Madras on the *Benson* for Mauritius. There he joined the *Woodford*, Captain Brady, for his passage to England, calling at St Helena between 9 and 13 October, arriving at Deal on 29 November. The *Morning Chronicle* of 4 December 1817 noted the arrival of 'Edward Abell Esq', a private passenger, not an officer.
32 East India Company Court Book April 1818 to September 1818, 178, 22 May 1818, BL India Office 126-B/167.
33 Abell was approved by Henry Goulburn in May 1818 as the civil agent for Ceylon to the Madras Presidency. BL India Office 126-B/167; the Madras Year Book lists him as a Madras British resident, with 'Occupation: None' until 1820. He does not appear in the Madras Year Book for 1821.
34 *The Asiatic Journal and Monthly Register for British India and its Dependencies*, 1821, gives 19 October 1820 as the date of Francis Torrens' death and lists numerous cases of cholera. FIBIS (Families in British India) notes that Lieutenant-General Francis Torrens, born 1748, died 5 August 1820, 'after uninterrupted residence in this country of 51 years'. He was buried at St Mary's 'New cemetery', Madras.
35 *Asiatic Journal and Monthly Register for British India*, 1822, 286, 491–3, quoting *Madras Courier*, 30 October 1821.
36 Colonel Torrens in India to General Sir Henry Torrens in London, 19 and 24 February 1822, Sir Henry Torrens Papers, BL Add 620967, f.146.
37 John R. Gillis, *For Better, For Worse: British marriages, 1600 to the present*, Oxford University Press, 1985, 141. For this reference and for Lawrence Stone's *Road to Divorce*, I am indebted to Stephen Scheding and his research for his book-in-progress, 'My Friend's Masterpiece: An object lesson in art (& love)'.

38 Balcombe from 28 Essex Street, Strand, to Lowe, 4 April 1822, Lowe Papers, BL Add. 20133, f.304.
39 Lowe, 1 Edgware Road to Wilmot, 7 April 1822, Bathurst Private Papers, BL 57/47, f.519. (NB: In that year Under-Secretary Robert Wilmot changed his name to 'Wilmot Horton', too short a time afterwards to be worth adding this confusion.)
40 Gillis, *For Better, For Worse*, 136–8.
41 Gillis, *For Better, For Worse*, 140.
42 Gillis, *For Better, For Worse*, 129, 194.
43 Edward Abell and Lucia Elizabeth Balcombe marriage certificate, Exminster, 28 May 1822, UK National Archives.
44 *ADB* now gives the correct date, 28 May 1822, but early encyclopaedias and Wikipedia still follow Dame Mabel's line of exactly one year earlier.
45 Sir Hudson Lowe to Lord Bathurst, 18 March 1818, Bathurst Private Papers, BL 57/43 f.189–59.

CHAPTER 28

1 J. Pike, 'Cholera—Biological Weapons', in *Weapons of Mass Destruction*, 2007, <Global Security.com>: 'Hundreds of thousands of Indians and tens of thousands of British troops died during the first cholera pandemic in India 1816–26.'
2 Dalrymple, *City of Djinns*, 145–6.
3 Aleck Fraser letter from St Helena to his brothers William and James in India, 26 March 1813; after Edward's death on 25 April this letter would surely have been sent on to their mother. Fraser Collection, National Register of Archives of Scotland (hereafter NRAS) 2696.
4 Richard Mullen and James Munson, *The Smell of the Continent: The British discover Europe*, London, Macmillan, 2009, xii–xiii.
5 Lowe from 1 Edgware Road to Bathurst, 6 June 1822, Bathurst Private Papers, BL 57/47 f.537.
6 O'Meara's book, *Napoleon in Exile*, was in its fifth edition by 1823.
7 Martineau, *Napoleon's Last Journey*, 22–3.
8 The tower of the Abbaye Saint-Bertin, 'which could be seen for miles around', collapsed in 1946.
9 Edward Satchwell Fraser junior, born 26 April 1786, died 25 April 1813 at St Helena; Alexander (Aleck) Fraser, born 10 April 1789, died 4 June 1816 in India. Information courtesy of Malcolm and Kathy Fraser.
10 Jane Fraser diary, 5 September 1822, Fraser Collection, NRAS 2696.
11 Jane Fraser from Saint-Omer to William Fraser in India, 6 September 1822, Fraser Collection, Bundle 440, NRAS 2696.
12 Jane Fraser diary, 5 September 1822, Fraser Collection, NRAS 2696.
13 In 1832, Betsy's friend, Edward John Eyre assessed her daughter's age as 'about ten'.
14 Jane Fraser diary, 7 September 1822, Fraser Collection, NRAS 2696.
15 In fact, for the period of exactly five months—28 August 1822 to 28 January 1823—when the Frasers' stay coincided with the Balcombes and we have the assistance of Jane's diary, Mrs Balcombe was recorded as either 'unwell' or 'distressed' for 37 days, while Balcombe with his chronic gout was unwell for eight days of the same period.
16 Martineau, *Napoleon's Last Journey*, 5–9.
17 The wedding gift from the Montholons (incorrectly labelled 1832 not 1822) was on display at 'The Briars', Mt Martha, but since the 2014 theft of other Napoleonic relics it was removed from exhibition. It is in storage but will be returned to display. (Information courtesy of Ilma Hackett of 'The Briars'.)
18 Jane Fraser diary, 13 September 1822, Fraser Collection, NRAS 2696.
19 Lowe to Bathurst, 14 September 1822, Bathurst Private Papers, BL 57/47 f.551.
20 William Balcombe to Sir Hudson Lowe from Saint-Omer, 11 October 1822, BL Add. 20233, f.180.
21 Lowe to Bathurst, 23 October 1822, Bathurst Private Papers, BL 57/47 f.559.
22 *The Examiner*, 27 October 1822.
23 *Morning Chronicle*, 26 October 1822.
24 Lowe to Bathurst, 5 November 1822, marked 'Never sent', Bathurst Private Papers, BL 57/47 f.561.

25 Lowe to Bathurst or Wilmot (recipient's name not clear), 5 November 1822, Bathurst Private Papers, BL 57/47 f.563.

CHAPTER 29

1. Jane Fraser diary, 25 October 1822, Fraser Collection, NRAS 2696.
2. Jane Balcombe *née* Green had two brothers—George and Francis Green—but which one was not specified.
3. Lowe to Bathurst, 3 January 1823, Bathurst Private Papers, BL 57/48 f.590.
4. Betsy's daughter, Mrs Charles Johnstone, in an appendix to the third edition (1873) of her mother's *Recollections*, claimed that George IV intervened in favour of Balcombe's appointment: 'George IV ... being convinced by Sir George Cockburn that my grandfather's loyalty was as strong as ever, sent him out to Australia as Colonial Treasurer of New South Wales and all its dependencies', *Recollections of the Emperor Napoleon*, London, Sampson Low, Marston, Low & Searle, 3rd edition, 1873, 312–13. Mrs Johnstone may have come to this probably erroneous conclusion from the fact that the colonial treasurer was designated as a 'Court appointment'.
5. Bathurst to Sir Thomas Brisbane, 2 October 1823, advising of appointment of William Balcombe as NSW Colonial Treasurer, *HRA*, I, Vol. XI, 138, Despatch No. 37 per *Hibernia*; Bathurst to Brisbane, 2 October 1823, advising appointment of Saxe Bannister as NSW Attorney General, *HRA*, I, Vol. XI, 140, Despatch No. 39 per *Hibernia*.
6. Betsy (Mrs L.E. Abell) described Abell's admission in a letter from Sydney to Major-General Sir Henry Torrens, 10 August 1824, NLA MS 7022.
7. Lawrence Stone, *Road to Divorce: England 1530–1987*, Oxford University Press, 1990, 143: without a written deed of separation, 'how could a separated wife prevent her husband from intermittently raiding her home and seizing all her goods and earnings, which by law were still his?' (With gratitude to Stephen Scheding for his introduction to me of the complexities of nineteenth-century marriage and divorce laws and to the Stone and Gillis reference books.)
8. See Hamilton, *Marengo: The myth of Napoleon's horse*, 205.
9. Jane Fraser diary, 22 August 1823, Fraser Collection, NRAS 2696.
10. Christopher Hibbert et al., in *The London Encyclopaedia*, London, Macmillan, 1983, notes that Blackfriars Road was known as Great Surrey Street until 1829.
11. Jane Fraser diary, 22 August 1823, Fraser Collection, NRAS 2696.
12. Gillis, *For Better, For Worse*, 231.
13. Stone, *Road to Divorce*, 187–90.
14. Stone, *Road to Divorce*, 143.
15. Stone, *Road to Divorce*, 141, 149–82.
16. Information on death of Charles courtesy of Abell family research by Keith and Shirley Murley of The Briars, Mt Martha.
17. General Sir Henry Torrens to Mrs Abell, 8 October 1823, Sir Henry Torrens Papers, BL Add. 62096 f.174.
18. The three Bigge reports were published in Parliament in 1822 and 1823, advising the abolition of most features of the old convict system and the separation, as far as possible, of convicts from the mass of the population. 'A pardon by the governor was to restore a man to full legal rights', C.M.H. Clark, Melbourne, Penguin, 1995, *A Short History of Australia*, 50.
19. 'Elizabeth Jane Balcombe Abell', baptised in London on 23 October 1823, IGI Batch C062361 Source No. 0918607. (IGI actually gives this as a birth date, which, as demonstrated, *has* to be incorrect, for on 22 August 1823 the Frasers visited Betsy at Blackfriars and spoke of seeing 'her little infant, a lovely little girl'. The date would be for her baptism.)
20. *The Times*, 21 November 1823, gave an effusive description of the 'stupendous work'. The line was ready for use only to King Tor quarry and would take another four years to extend to Princetown.
21. Balcombe repaid the loan on 15 August 1824, writing to Wilmot Horton, 15 August 1824, 'Sir, I have the honor to enclose your fifty pounds you were so kind as to advance me ... and I beg to assure you it will never be erased from my memory.' Received by Horton on 3 January 1825, (NSW Colonial Treasurer Correspondence, NSW State Records Office.)
22. A.J. Hill, 'Macarthur, Sir Edward (1789–1872)', *ADB*.

CHAPTER 30

1. By 1824, Governor Phillip's government vegetable beds, which gave the name to 'Farm Cove', had been replaced by rolling lawns, although soon enough they were replaced by the streets and buildings of commerce.
2. Many freed convicts, those on tickets-of-leave, and those assigned to employers or to their own spouses lived in The Rocks.
3. Margaret Maynard, in *Fashioned from Penury: Dress as cultural practice in Colonial Australia*, Cambridge University Press, 1994, 18–21, notes that attempts to standardise convict dress in colonial New South Wales had not been successful, but after a quantity of clothing of a coarse yellow cloth (probably kersey) was sent to the eastern colonies by chance in 1817, 'its use became synonymous with Australian convicts in the 1820s and 1830s'.
4. Dame Mabel Brookes, *St Helena Story*, 245, suggested tuberculosis as the probable cause of Jane's death. The captain's log was sought in the NSW State Records Office, but was found to no longer exist.
5. Joseph Tice Gellibrand, the new attorney-general for Van Diemen's Land, wrote from the Cape on 30 January 1824 to his friend Wilkinson in Hobart, 'We have had a fine passage & very good weather': State Library of Tasmania, 'Tasmanian Historical Research Association Papers and Proceedings', N.S. 187/19.
6. Alan Atkinson, *The Europeans in Australia: A history*, Vol. II, Melbourne, Oxford University Press, 2004, 39.
7. E.W. Dunlop, 'Macqueen, Thomas Potter (1791–1854), *ADB*; *HRA*, I, Vol. 12, 141–3, Horton to Brisbane, 20 October 1823; Macqueen to Horton, 21 July 1823; Horton to Macqueen, 18 August 1823.
8. Vivienne Parsons, 'Frederick Goulburn, (1788–1837)', *ADB*.
9. The *Clarence River Advocate*, 24 November 1903, 4, noted that in 1903 'the old oak tree was computed to be 115 years of age at the time it made its disappearance'.
10. Boyes to his wife Mary in England, 12 April 1824: Peter Chapman (ed.), *The Diaries and Letters of G.T.W.B. Boyes*, Vol. 1, 1820–32, Melbourne, Oxford University Press, 1985, 174.
11. Boyes to Mary, 12 April 1824: Chapman (ed.), *The Diaries and Letters of G.T.W.B. Boyes*, Vol. 1, 173.
12. *Sydney Gazette*, 8 April 1824.
13. Earl Bathurst to NSW Governor Sir Thomas Brisbane, 2 October 1823, *HRA*, I, Vol. XI, 138, Despatch No. 37 per ship *Hibernia*; acknowledged by Brisbane on 8 June 1824.
14. R.L. Murray, letter from Hobart to D'Arcy Wentworth in Sydney, 27 March 1824, MLA 754.
15. Brisbane to Bathurst, 8 June 1824, advising that he has fixed Balcombe's salary at £1200 annually, *HRA*, I, Vol. XI, Despatch No. 1, 138.
16. *The Bulletin*, 29 June 1905: 'Soon known as the "Balcombe House", ownership passed in 1837 when William Cox died to his son in England, the Reverend James Cox. It was occupied in 1838 by Sir Maurice O'Connell. CSR bought the site in 1902 and demolished the house to make room for the Colonial Sugar Refineries' big building on the corner of O'Connell Street.'
17. John Hirst, *Freedom on the Fatal Shore: Australia's first colony*, Melbourne, Black Inc., 2008, 13.
18. Michael Cannon, *Who's Master? Who's Man?: Australia in the Victorian Age*, Melbourne, Viking O'Neil, [1971], 1988, 19.
19. Margaret Steven, 'Macarthur, John (1767–1834)', *ADB*; Macarthur had a tenuous connection with George IV in this way: Macarthur met Sir Robert Farquhar in India in 1801 and they became close friends. This friendship became important in giving Macarthur access to 'influential circles' in England. Farquhar's father was physician to the Prince of Wales (afterwards George IV). See Brian Fitzpatrick, *British Imperialism and Australia, 1783–1833*, Sydney University Press, [1939], 1971, 193.
20. Earl Bathurst to NSW Governor Sir Thomas Brisbane, 2 October 1823, plus note 36, 913, re then administration of the finances of the colony, *HRA*, I, Vol. XI, 138, Despatch No. 37 per ship *Hibernia*.
21. Andrew McMartin, *Public Servants and Patronage: The foundation and rise of the New South Wales public service, 1786–1859*, Griffin Press, Adelaide, 1983, 132–3.

22 J.F. Harrison to Under-Secretary Robert William Hay, 14 September 1826, *HRA*, I, Vol. XII, 563–4. (This letter recommending his son was written after the Sydney appointment, seeking another position for James.)
23 The Blue Book of 1827, giving the formal establishment status of the Treasury, notes the appointment of James Stirling Harrison by the governor on 7 April 1825, at the recommendation of the Colonial Secretary Wilmot Horton.
24 George Forbes (ed.), *Sydney Society in Crown Colony Days, being the personal reminiscences of the late Lady Forbes*, ML typescript, 1914, 19–21.
25 Roger Therry, *Reminiscences of Thirty Years' Residence in New South Wales and Victoria*, 1863, facsimile edition, Sydney, Royal Australian Historical Society & Sydney University Press, 1974, 39.
26 Atkinson, *The Europeans in Australia*, Vol. II, 13.
27 Therry, *Reminiscences*, 40.
28 Therry, *Reminiscences*, 41–2.
29 Helen Heney, *Australia's Founding Mothers*, Melbourne, Thomas Nelson Australia, 1978, 4.

CHAPTER 31

1 Forbes (ed.), *Sydney Society in Crown Colony Days*, 19–21.
2 Forbes (ed.), *Sydney Society in Crown Colony Days*, 21.
3 Forbes (ed.), *Sydney Society in Crown Colony Days*, 22.
4 Arthur McMartin, *Public Servants and Patronage: The foundation and rise of the NSW Public Service, 1786–1859*, Sydney University Press, 1983, 187.
5 *Sydney Gazette*, 20 May 1824.
6 Vivienne Parsons, 'Goulburn, Frederick (1788–1837)', *ADB*, indicates that Goulburn's officious manner made a dangerous enemy in Macarthur.
7 Chapman (ed.), *The Diaries and Letters of G.T.W.B. Boyes*, 198 (Wemyss's dinner party was on 27 May 1824).
8 G.P. Walsh, 'Sir John Jamison (1776–1844)', *ADB*.
9 Chapman (ed.), *The Diaries and Letters of G.T.W.B. Boyes*, 198.
10 Chapman (ed.), *The Diaries and Letters of G.T.W.B. Boyes*, 198.
11 'The Fashionable World', *Sydney Gazette*, 1 July 1824.
12 Jamison's 'invisible lady' mentioned in M. le baron de Bougainville, *Journal de la navigation autour du globe*, Paris, Arthus Bertrand, 1837, Vol. I, edited and translated by Marc Serge Rivière as *The Governor's Noble Guest: Hyacinthe de Bougainville's account of Port Jackson, 1825*, Miegunyah Press, Melbourne University Press, 1999, 141–3.
13 'The Fashionable World', *Sydney Gazette*, 1 July 1824.
14 Mary Reibey to her cousin in England, 10 February 1825, in Nance Irvine (ed.), *Dear Cousin: The Reibey Letters*, Sydney, Hale & Iremonger, 1992, 87–8.
15 Christine Wright, *Wellington's Men in Australia: Peninsular war veterans and the making of the empire c.1820–40*, Sydney, Palgrave Macmillan, 2011.
16 J.D. Heydon, 'Sir Thomas Makdougall Brisbane (1773–1860)', *ADB*.
17 *Sydney Gazette*, 1 July 1824.
18 Courtesy Keith and Shirley Murley of 'The Briars', Mt Martha, for land grant research.
19 Charles Bateson, 'David Reid (1777–1840)', *ADB*. Reid's 1829 report on the activity of bushrangers in the Bungonia area led to the stationing of two military detachments there.
20 Brisbane to Bathurst, 18 June 1824, *HRA*, I, Vol. XI, Despatch No. 13.
21 Brisbane's Proclamation of Martial Law, 19 August 1824.
22 *Sydney Gazette*, 22 July 1824.
23 John Macarthur, to his second eldest son John in London, from *Some Early Records of the Macarthurs of Camden*, 337, quoted in C.H. Currey, *Sir Francis Forbes: The first chief justice of the Supreme Court of New South Wales*, Sydney, Angus & Robertson, 1968, 40.
24 Michael Persse, 'William Charles Wentworth (1790–1872)', *ADB*.
25 C.H. Currey, 'Robert Wardell (1793–1834)', *ADB*.
26 Mrs L.E. Abell, letter from Sydney to Major-General Sir Henry Torrens, Horse Guards, London, 10 August 1824, NLA MS 7022.

27 Stone, *Road to Divorce*, 161.
28 Stone, *Road to Divorce*, 187–90.
29 Stone, *Road to Divorce*, 141, 149–82.
30 Stone, *Road to Divorce*, 160.
31 *Asiatic Journal and Monthly Register for British India*, 1822, 286, 491–3, quoting *Madras Courier*, 30 October 1821.
32 See Australian National Gallery NGA 73 661, Richard Browne, 'The Mountain Pheasant', 1819. With thanks to art historian and collector Stephen Scheding for locating this illustration.
33 Lieut. Col. Williams, Bombay, to Torrens, 1 July 1825 and 27 August 1825, Sir Henry Torrens Papers, BL Add. 62096 f.58 and Add. 62096, f. 87.
34 *Sydney Gazette*, 23 September 1824. The shipping lists take some sorting out as there were two *Prince Regent* ships in port in Sydney at the same time, one commanded by Captain W.B. Lambe, the other by Captain Wales. The latter, with E. Abell Esq. on board, left Hobart Town for Mauritius on 24 October 1824. See *Hobart Town Gazette*, 8 October 1824: 'The *Prince Regent* will, we understand, proceed with all possible expedition to England, via the Mauritius, where she will take in a cargo of sugar for the London market.'

CHAPTER 32

1 Forbes (ed.), *Sydney Society in Crown Colony Days*, Ch. III, 'The Beneficent Rule of Sir Thomas Brisbane', 25.
2 Quoted in Dyer, *The French Explorers and Sydney 1788–1831*, 76.
3 Brisbane to Bathurst, 8 February 1825, *HRA*, I, Vol. XI, 514, Despatch No. 34, plus note 131.
4 *Sydney Gazette*, 30 September 1824.
5 Brisbane to Bathurst, 14 August 1824, *HRA*, I, Vol. IX, Despatch No. 14; *Sydney Gazette*, 17 February 1825.
6 *Sydney Gazette*, 11 October 1824.
7 D'Arcy Wentworth to Brisbane, 4 August 1824, Forbes Papers, ML A741; Magistrates to Brisbane, 23 September 1824, Forbes Papers, ML A1381; Currey, *Sir Francis Forbes*, 116.
8 C.A. Liston, Doctoral Thesis, 'N.S.W. Under Brisbane 1821–1825', Department of History, University of Sydney, 1980, 432–3, citing Colonial Returns 1825; *HRA*, I, Vol. XI, 894, Brisbane to Bathurst, 25 October 1825.
9 *Sydney Gazette*, 13 January 1825.
10 'Biography No. XI Barry Edward O'Meara Esq.', *Sydney Gazette*, 7 April 1825.
11 Therry, *Reminiscences*, 47.
12 Bathurst to Brisbane, 6 February 1825, *HRA*, I, XI, Despatch No. 19, 493–4.
13 Brisbane to Bathurst, 8 February 1825, *HRA*, I, XI, No. 34, 514–15; James Stirling Harrison had a family connection to Lieutenant Robert Stirling and his elder brother James Stirling, founder of the Swan River settlement and later governor of Western Australia.
14 *Australian*, 3 March 1825; *Sydney Gazette*, 3 March 1825.
15 Rivière, *The Governor's Noble Guest*, 60: 'He [Governor Brisbane] goes twice a week to Sydney but Lady Brisbane never does so.'
16 'Austral-Asiaticus' letter of 19 March 1825 to London *Morning Chronicle*, published 19 February 1826, in Chapman (ed.), *The Diaries and Letters of G.T.W.B. Boyes*, Vol. I, 618–21; Chapman concedes that Austral-Asiaticus was almost certainly Boyes.
17 *Sydney Gazette*, 15 December 1825; Dr O'Meara's *Napoleon in Exile* was advertised for sale as part of a household auction.
18 The celebrations were remote from George IV's actual birthday, which was 12 August.
19 *Sydney Gazette*, 28 April 1825.
20 Boyes' letter to his wife on 8 May 1825, in Chapman (ed.), *The Diaries and Letters of G.T.W.B. Boyes*, Vol. I, 229. Chapman notes: 'Thomas Hobbes Scott (1783–1860) Archdeacon of NSW. The brother-in-law of Commissioner JT Bigge, he had accompanied him on his tour of inspection of NSW in 1819–21.'
21 *Sydney Gazette*, 19 May 1825, quoting *Hobart Town Gazette*.
22 Forbes (ed.), *Sydney Society in Crown Colony Days*, 17–18 and 127–8.

23 Brisbane to Magistrates of Sydney, 21 May 1825, *HRA*, I, XI, 894–5.
24 Sydney Magistrates to Governor Brisbane, 29 September 1825.

CHAPTER 33

1 G.R. Tipping (ed.), *The Official Account through Governor Phillip's Letters to Lord Sydney*, Sydney, 1988, 42.
2 Colin Dyer, *The French Explorers and Sydney 1788–1831*, St Lucia, University of Queensland Press, 2009, 2, citing *Voyage de Lapérouse*, 362–3.
3 The La Pérouse mystery was to remain unsolved until 1828, when some of the ships' wreckage and monogrammed silver were found at Vanikoro in the Santa Cruz Islands.
4 Dyer, *The French Explorers and Sydney*, 99.
5 Rivière, *The Governor's Noble Guest*, 61–2.
6 Dyer, *The French Explorers and Sydney*, 104.
7 Rivière, *The Governor's Noble Guest*, 62–3.
8 See Dyer, *The French Explorers and Sydney*, 116, on the ratio of the sexes.
9 Rivière, *The Governor's Noble Guest*, 5 July 1825, 62.
10 *Sydney Gazette*, 15 September 1825.
11 Dyer, *The French Explorers and Sydney*, 106.
12 Rivière, *The Governor's Noble Guest*, 79, 179–80, and *Journal de la navigation*, I, 492–3, quoted in Dyer, *The French Explorers and Sydney*, 129–30.
13 Rivière, *The Governor's Noble Guest*, 83–4.
14 Dyer, *The French Explorers and Sydney*, 110.
15 Dyer, *The French Explorers and Sydney*, 120.
16 Rivière, *The Governor's Noble Guest*, 10 September 1825, 126.
17 Dyer, *The French Explorers and Sydney*, 122, notes: 'Although Harriott's date of birth is unknown, she must have been in her late twenties or early thirties when she met the 43-year-old Frenchman.'
18 Dyer, *The French Explorers and Sydney*, 125.
19 Dyer, *The French Explorers and Sydney*, 125.
20 Dyer, *The French Explorers and Sydney*, 125.
21 Louis Claude de Saulces de Freycinet took his wife Rose, disguised as a boy, around the Pacific on the *Uranie*. See Danielle Clode, *Voyages to the South Seas: In search of Terres Australes*, Miegunyah Press, Melbourne University Publishing, 2007, 160–75.
22 Dyer, *The French Explorers and Sydney*, 125.
23 Rivière, *The Governor's Noble Guest*, quoted in Dyer, *The French Explorers and Sydney*, 139.
24 Rivière, *The Governor's Noble Guest*, 35. In 1835, Harriott had become the second wife of Chief Justice Sir James Dowling, who died in 1844.
25 Dyer, *The French Explorers and Sydney*, x–xi.
26 Rivière, *The Governor's Noble Guest*, 217–18, 241–2, Bougainville, *Reports to Minister of the Navy*, I, 536, quoted in introduction to Dyer, *The French Explorers and Sydney*, x–xi, 136–8.

CHAPTER 34

1 Harrison senior to Under-Secretary R.W. Hay, 14 September 1826, *HRA*, I, Vol. XII, 563–4.
2 Courtesy Keith and Shirley Murley for research on Balcombe land.
3 Atkinson, *The Europeans in Australia*, 44; *Sydney Gazette*, 20 October 1825.
4 Balcombe joined the Sydney Masonic Lodge in November or December 1825: *Sydney Gazette*, 28 November 1825.
5 Sudhir Hazareesingh, *The Legend of Napoleon*, London, Granta Books, 2004, 101–3, re 'Napoleonic supporters all over France since 1816, notably among members of the military . . . as well as the Freemasons'. Loyalty to 'Napoleon the Great' became part of the Masonic oath.
6 Summerville (ed.), *Regency Recollections*, 131.
7 *Sydney Gazette*, 8 December 1825.
8 Fitzpatrick, *British Imperialism and Australia, 1783–1833*, 299.
9 John Wallace, a trustworthy and competent member of staff, would stay at the Treasury until 1837, be a valued support for Balcombe's successor and become a respected public figure.

10 Bathurst to Governor Darling, 14 August 1826, *HRA*, I, Vol XII: 'I do myself the Honour to acquaint you that I have been induced, in consequence of Sir Thos. Brisbane's representation that the Colonial Treasurer could not carry on the Business of his Department (in the manner in which it ought to be conducted) without assistance...'
11 J.M. Bennett (ed.), *Some Papers of Sir Francis Forbes*, Sydney, NSW Parliament, 1998, 136.
12 Brian H. Fletcher, *Ralph Darling: A governor maligned*, Melbourne, Oxford University Press, 1984, 29–72.
13 'Darling, Sir Ralph (1772–1858)', *ADB*.
14 *Sydney Gazette*, 25 December 1825.
15 *Monitor*, 19 April 1826; Female Orphan School Minutes, 27 May 1829, 585; Female Orphan School Correspondence 1825–9, AONSW 4/325; Minutes of the Executive Council, 28 December 1829, AONSW 4/1516; on Eliza Darling, see Brian Fletcher, 'Elizabeth Darling: Colonial benefactress and governor's lady', *Journal of the Royal Australian Historical Society*, Vol. 67, Part 4, March 1982.
16 Atkinson, *The Europeans in Australia*, Vol. II, 123, citing Fletcher, 'Elizabeth Darling', 309–10, 312–13.
17 M.H. Ellis, *John Macarthur*, London and Sydney, Angus & Robertson, (1955), 1978, 492–3.
18 NSW Census 1828—'Thomas Tyrwhitt Balcombe—superintendent with the Australian Agricultural Company'.
19 Roger Milliss, *Waterloo Creek: The Australia Day Massacre of 1838*, Melbourne, McPhee Gribble/Penguin, 1992, 54.
20 *Australian*, 29 April 1826.
21 Courtesy Keith and Shirley Murley for research on Balcombe land.
22 S.J. Butlin, *Foundations of the Australian Monetary System 1788–1851*, Sydney, Sydney University Press, 1968, 199.
23 Colonial Secretary Macleay, report to Governor Darling on Bank of NSW investigation, *HRA*, I, Vol. XII, 307.
24 Cheques amounting to $27,200.
25 Darling to Bathurst, 22 May 1826, report on the transactions of Mr. Balcombe, the treasurer, *HRA*, I, Vol. XII, 322.
26 Colonial Secretary Macleay (representing Darling) to Balcombe, 2 June 1826, NSW State Records Office, Vol. 4/235, 70.
27 Darling to Bathurst, Despatch No. 32, 20 May 1826, *HRA*, I, Vol. XII.
28 *HRA*, I, Vol. XII, 337–8; NSW State Records Office, Colonial Treasurer's 'Out Letters', 26 May 1826.
29 Balcombe to Colonial Secretary Macleay, 26 May 1826, *HRA*, I, Vol. XII, 337–8.
30 Macleay to Balcombe, NSW State Records Office, Vol. 4/235, 70.
31 Presumably Darling wrote that Balcombe 'possesses no property' in that it would be claimed by creditors.
32 Darling to Bathurst, 22 May 1826, *HRA*, I, Vol. XII, 321–2.
33 *HRA*, I, Vol. XII, 590.
34 *HRA*, I, Vol. XII, 590.
35 Butlin, *Foundations of the Australian Monetary System*, 527–30.
36 Marjorie Barnard, *The Life and Times of Captain John Piper*, Sydney, Ure Smith, 1973, 138.
37 Barnard, *The Life and Times of Captain John Piper*, 138–40.
38 Butlin, *Foundations of the Australian Monetary System*, 527n.
39 Butlin, *Foundations of the Australian Monetary System*, 527.

CHAPTER 35

1 A.H. Chisholm, 'Wilson, John (?–1800)', *Australian Dictionary of Biography*, Vol. 2, Melbourne, MUP, 1967.
2 J. Jervis, 'Settlement in Marulan–Bungonia District', *Journal and Proceedings, Royal Australian Historical Society*, Vol. 32, Part 2, 1946, 107–42, re Dr David Reid.
3 Government Notice of 5 May 1826, signed 'Alexander Macleay, Colonial Secretary'.

NOTES

4   *HRA*, I, Vol. XII, 1 July 1826, re Australia Bank.
5   Darling to Bathurst, 20 July 1826, *HRA*, I, Vol. XII, 371–3, re Treasurer Balcombe requests allowance for office rent for use of his house.
6   *Sydney Gazette*, 17 October 1825.
7   *Australian*, 15 July 1826.
8   *Australian*, 29 November and 2 December 1826; *Monitor*, 1, 22 and 29 December 1826; Marcus Clarke, 'Governor Ralph Darling's Iron Collar', in *Old Tales of a Young Country*, Melbourne, Mason, Firth & McCutcheon, 1871.
9   *Monitor*, 19 June 1827.
10 Currey, *Sir Francis Forbes*, 192–9; Fletcher, *Ralph Darling*, 245–9.
11 Forbes (ed.), *Sydney in Crown Colony Days*, 51.
12 *Sydney Gazette*, 10 February 1827.
13 Bathurst to Darling, 14 August 1826, *HRA*, I, Vol. XII, 497.
14 List of NSW magistrates, 31 January 1827, *HRA*, I, Vol. XIII, 59.
15 Elizabeth Macarthur on Betsy Abell, quoted in Helen Heney (ed.), *Dear Fanny: Women's letters to and from New South Wales, 1788–1857*, Pergamon Press, Sydney, 1985, 106–7.
16 Captain Chestakoff to Captain John Piper, 30 April 182? (year unclear), MLA, Piper Papers, V2 A255, 447.
17 'Baxter, Alexander Macduff (1798–1836)', *ADB*; *HRA*, I, XIII, October 1827, Governor Darling noted 'Mr Baxter's total incapacity and his total inexperience as a lawyer'.
18 *Australian*, 10 August 1827.
19 *Australian*, 29 August 1827.
20 *Sydney Gazette*, 24 September 1827.
21 Brian H. Fletcher, *Ralph Darling*, 263–4; Clark, *A Short History of Australia*, 64.
22 Darling to Viscount Goderich, Prime Minister, 14 December 1827, with enclosures to and from Sheriff Mackaness, *HRA*, I, Vol. XIII, 638–42, Despatch No. 122.
23 *Sydney Gazette*, 9 January 1828.
24 John Gibson Lockhart (ed.), *Memoirs of the Life of Sir Walter Scott*, 10 vols, 2nd edn, Edinburgh, Robert Cadell, 1839, Vol. 9, 143–4. (Scott was made a baronet by George IV after Scott's lavish welcome for him in Edinburgh in 1820.)
25 Mrs Abell to Captain John Piper, 26 June (the year is unclear but could be 1828), MLA, Piper Papers, V2 A255, 595–6.
26 *Sydney Gazette*, 26 March 1829.
27 Although some biographical records give Balcombe's age at death as 52, he was born on 25 December 1777, so was still 51 at the time of his death.
28 William Balcombe to surveyor Robert Hoddle in 1827.
29 Darling to Sir George Murray, 20 March 1829, *HRA* I, Vol. XIV, 688.

CHAPTER 36

1   Governor Bourke to Secretary of State, 1 May 1833, *HRA*, I, Vol. XVII, 99, confirmed Alexander Balcombe 'dismissed by my predecessor in April 1831, from the situation he held as Clerk in the Commissariat on account of negligence'.
2   *HRA*, I, Vol. XV, 67.
3   *HRA*, I, Vol. XV, 309. Admiral Cockburn wrote to the former prime minister, Viscount Goderich, in July 1829, supporting Mrs Abell's request. Reply came to Darling from Sir George Murray via Under-Secretary Twiss.
4   *Monitor*, 3 April 1830.
5   Alexander M. Baxter to Governor Darling, 8 February 1831, included with Governor Darling's despatch to Sir George Murray, ML A1209, NSW Governors' Despatches to the Secretary of State for Colonies, Vol 20, 1015–18.
6   Darling to Under-Secretary Hay, 28 March 1831, HRA, I, Vol. XVI, 219–21.
7   Colonial Secretary Alexander Macleay to Alexander Baxter, 7 February 1831, ML A1209, NSW Governors' Despatches to the Secretary of State for Colonies, Vol. 20, 1026–7.
8   Fletcher, *Ralph Darling*, 287–8.
9   *Sydney Gazette*, 15 December 1831.

10 *Extracts from the St Helena Records*, compiled by H.R. Janisch, St Helena, 1885.
11 See *Sydney Gazette*, 6 March 1832, for an account of a Sydney resident visiting Napoleon's Tomb.
12 Mrs Abell, *Recollections*, Appendix to the 3rd [4th] edition by Mrs Charles Johnstone, 327.
13 Mrs Jane Balcombe to Viscount Goderich, Earl of Ripon, Secretary of State for the Colonies, 18 July 1832, UK National Archives, CO/201/229-(2).
14 Lucia E. Abell to Lord Marcus Hill, 24 July 1832, BL Add. 40878 f.33 (Ripon Papers Vols. XVII–XIX 'Applications for Colonial Appointments 1832. At that time Lord Ripon, as Lord Goderich, was Secretary of State for War and Colonies.)
15 Martineau, *Napoleon's Last Journey*, 59–65.
16 Mrs Abell, *Recollections*, 315–17 (Appendix, Mrs C. Johnstone, 1873).
17 Viscount Goderich to Governor Bourke, 1 May 1833, with attached Memorandum, *HRA*, I, XVI, 714–15.
18 Ian Hawkins Nicholson, *Shipping Arrivals & Departures Sydney, 1826–1840*, Canberra, A Roebuck Book, 1981.
19 Edward John Eyre, *Autobiographical Narrative of Residence and Exploration in Australia, 1832–1839*, edited and annotated by Jill Waterhouse, London, Caliban Books, 1984, xiv.
20 Eyre, *Autobiographical Narrative*, 5.
21 Eyre, *Autobiographical Narrative*, 20, 29.
22 See Alan Atkinson and Marian Aveling (eds), *Australians 1838*, Sydney, Fairfax, Syme & Weldon, 1987, 142–3.
23 *Sydney Herald*, 30 May 1833; *Monitor*, 1 June 1833.
24 Heney, *Australia's Founding Mothers*, 1.

CHAPTER 37

1 *Hampshire Telegraph*, 1 September 1834; *The Times*, 2 September 1834.
2 Courtesy Keith and Shirley Murley for Kensal Green research.
3 Courtesy Keith and Shirley Murley and the Essex Historical Society for Abell family research.
4 See Theo Aronson, *Queen Victoria and the Bonapartes*, London, Cassell, 1972.
5 A.J.P. Taylor, review of Jasper Ridley, *Napoleon III and Eugénie*, Viking, 1980, in *The New York Review of Books*, Vol. 27, No. 14, 25 September 1980.
6 Philippe Séguin, *Louis Napoléon Le Grand*, Paris, Bernard Grasset, 1990, 68.
7 John Bierman, *Napoleon III and His Carnival Empire*, London, John Murray, 1989, xiii.
8 Mrs Abell, *Recollections*, Appendix to the 3rd [4th] edition by Mrs Charles Johnstone, 315–20.
9 Information courtesy of Keith and Shirley Murley.
10 *Sydney Herald*, 1 April 1840.
11 1841 Census for England and Wales.
12 *Morning Post*, 19 January 1842.
13 *Morning Post*, 22 February 1842.
14 Mrs Abell, series of articles, 'Recollections of the Emperor Napoleon', *New Monthly Magazine*, 1843.
15 Mrs Abell, *Recollections*, Appendix listing subscribers.
16 A.J.P. Taylor, 'His Uncle's Nephew', *The New York Review of Books*, Vol. 27, No. 14, 25 September 1980.
17 *Trewman's Exeter Flying Post*, 28 November 1848. The original notice wrote of 'Broncroft Castle, Salop' and has been changed to 'Shropshire' for the general reader.
18 Mrs Abell, *Recollections*, Appendix to the 3rd [4th] edition by Mrs Charles Johnstone, 128.
19 *Bell's Life in Sydney and Sporting Chronicle*, 19 October 1861.
20 Story told by two Thomas T. Balcombe descendants to The Briars, Mt Martha.
21 Mrs Betsy Abell to Emma Balcombe at The Briars, Mt Martha, 10 June 1869 (Balcombe family letters courtesy of the late Richard a'Beckett and his family).
22 Mrs Abell, *Recollections*, Appendix to the 3rd [4th] edition by Mrs Charles Johnstone, 322–4.

INDEX

1st Battalion of 7th Regiment, Madras Native Infantry 275–7
2nd Battalion of 66th Regiment of Foot 107, 128, 166–9, 179
53rd Regiment of Foot 23, 54, 58, 82, 86, 110, 149

Abell, Charles 274, 303
Abell, Edward 178–9, 216; in India and Nepal 274–80; marries Betsy 284–5, 288–9, 290–1, 293, 297–8, 300–4, 310, 314; arrives in Sydney 330–4, 349–50, 385; inherits bequest 395
Abell, Elizabeth Jane (Bessie): birth and baptism 292, 299–300, 303–5; in NSW 309–10, 319, 334, 382–5, 387–93; return to England 390, 394–7, 400–3, 405–6; Appendix to her mother's *Recollections* 201, 389–90, 396–7, 405–6
Abell, Francis 274
Abell, Frank 274
Abell, Mary 395
Abell, William 274
Aboriginal people 310, 319, 327–8, 346, 363, 372–3
Admiralty 26–7, 45–6, 109, 112, 136–7, 165, 174, 206, 219, 224, 231–3, 247, 253–4
Agricultural Society of NSW 337, 341, 360–1
Alfred (ship) 328–30
Almack's Assembly Rooms 6, 216
Alphington, Devon 273–4
Anglo-Nepalese War 276–8
Apsley, Lord (later Lord Bathurst) 209
Arbuthnot, Mrs 264, 271
Archambault, Achille 114, 147–8, 172
Archambault, Joseph 136, 138, 160–1, 399

Ascension Island 20, 21, 60, 232, 234
Austen, Jane 120, 130, 349, 402
Austral-Asiaticus (Sydney resident) 342
Australia Bank 373
Australian (newspaper) 337, 339, 340, 345, 359
Australian Agricultural Company 362–3, 376, 384

Balcombe, Alexander Beatson: at The Briars 3, 23, 49, 55, 114, 179, 192, 201, 208–9, 231; at Dartmoor 245; at Plymouth 246–51, 254; at Chudleigh 265; at Saint-Omer, France 289, 292, 294, 298–9; in England 304–5; in NSW 309–10, 313, 316, 326–7, 376, 381–4, 386, 391–2, 394; in Port Phillip district 397–8, 403–4
Balcombe, Betsy: at The Briars 3, 4, 8–11, 34–7, 39, 40–1, 47–9, 55, 60–2; sword episode 73, 76; attends admiral's ball 78–9, 85; visits Longwood 90, 99, 103, 110, 113–14, 120, 127, 128–31, 139, 145, 148–50, 152–5, 166–7, 169, 171–2, 176–82, 187, 189, 192, 195–7, 201; in London 208–9, 214–16, 231, 235; at Dartmoor 245; at Plymouth 246–53, 264; at Chudleigh 265–9, 272–3, 280–5; marriage and France 284–5, 288–9, 291–4, 297–8, 300–3; in England 304–5; in NSW 309–10, 313–21, 323–7, 330–5, 341, 348–56, 362–3, 372, 374, 376–8, 380–93; returns to England 394–7, 400–3, 405–6
Balcombe, Cole & Company 5, 208, 228, 236, 259
Balcombe, Emma (née Reid) 397–8, 404–5
Balcombe, Jane: at The Briars 3, 10, 11, 34, 40–1, 47, 49, 76, 85, 89; visits Longwood

90, 99, 103, 110, 113, 120, 127, 131, 145, 148–9, 154–5, 166–7, 176–80, 182, 187, 192, 195–7, 201–2; in London 208–9, 214–16, 231, 235; at Dartmoor 245; at Plymouth 247, 251, 253–4; at Chudleigh 265–7, 272; at Saint-Omer, France 289, 292–3, 297–9; in England 304–5; death 310

Balcombe, Jane (née Green): at The Briars 34, 36–64, 74, 78, 82, 87, 89; visits Longwood 90, 99, 110, 113, 120, 130, 148–9, 150–1, 154–5, 166–7, 176–80, 192–3, 195, 201, 401–2; in England 203–5, 207–9, 221, 229, 231, 235; at Dartmoor 245; at Plymouth 246–51, 253–4, 260; at Chudleigh 265–7, 272, 282; at Saint-Omer, France 289, 291–4, 297–9, 300–1; in England 304–5; in NSW 309–10, 313, 316, 320, 323–7, 335, 341–2, 352–3, 356, 362–3, 378, 381–93; returns to England 394–5

Balcombe, Lydia (née Stuckey) 398, 404–5

Balcombe, Stephen (brother of William) 207–8, 215

Balcombe, Stephen Sr (father of William) 91–3

Balcombe, Thomas Tyrwhitt: at The Briars 3, 49, 179, 201; at Dartmoor 245; at Plymouth 246–51, 254; at Chudleigh 265; at Saint-Omer, France 289, 292, 294, 298–9; in England 304–5; in NSW 309–10, 313, 316, 326–7, 363, 377, 381–4, 386, 391, 394, 398–9; suicide 404–5

Balcombe, William: birth and paternity of 91–4; at The Briars 3, 5, 10, 21–3, 33–5, 37–8, 40, 42–3, 45–6, 49–51, 89, 248–50, 254, 287; purveyor to Longwood 90, 109–10, 112–13, 120–3, 127–8, 131, 133–6, 138–9, 143–4, 147–8, 150–2, 154–7, 160, 166–7, 169, 171–4, 176–9, 180, 183, 187, 190–7, 201–2; in London 203–13, 215, 221, 223–4, 227–37, 239–40; at Dartmoor 245; at Plymouth 246–51, 253–4, 256, 259–60; at Chudleigh 265–7, 272, 280–2, 284–5, 288; at Saint-Omer, France 289, 291–4, 298–9; in England 299–301, 304–5; in NSW 309–21, 323–4, 325–7, 330–45, 348–9, 352–3, 356, 358, 360–1, 363–70, 372–3, 375–84, 389, 391, 393

Balcombe, William Jr 33, 193, 203, 208–9; at Dartmoor 245; at Plymouth 246–51, 254; at Chudleigh 265; at Saint-Omer, France 289, 292–4, 297, 299–300; in England 304–5; in NSW 309–10, 313, 316, 326–7, 337, 376, 381–6, 391, 393–4, 397–8, 404

Balmain, Alexandre Antonovich, Comte de 115, 117, 122, 138, 182–6, 188, 194, 250, 265
Bank of New South Wales 316, 357, 364–9, 375
Bannister, Saxe (NSW attorney-general) 306, 310, 321, 324, 329, 350, 377
Bathurst, 3rd Earl Henry (Secretary of State for War and the Colonies) 15, 92, 109–10, 116–18, 126, 135–7, 145–6, 158–9, 170, 174, 178–9, 183, 190, 202; meetings with William Balcombe 209–12, 219–21; box of letters scandal 223–4, 227–37, 239–40, 248–50, 254–7, 259, 261–2, 265, 273, 282–3, 285, 288, 293, 295–6, 299, 358–9, 365–8; administration of NSW 311–14, 322, 328, 336, 339–40, 373–6, 379, 391
Bathurst, NSW 312, 328, 372, 404
Baxter, Alexander Macduff (NSW attorney-general) 377–8, 385–7, 395
Baxter, Maria del Rosaria Anna Uthair 377–8, 386–7
Beatson, General Alexander 22, 23, 46, 192
Beauharnais, Prince Eugene de (Napoleon's stepson) 49, 196, 188, 238
Bellerophon, HMS 17, 18, 19, 25, 27–8, 98, 114, 327
Bertrand, Countess Françoise-Elisabeth 13–15, 21, 28, 38–9, 64–7, 74–5, 78, 86; at Hutt's Gate 95, 99, 100–1, 110, 114, 119–20, 124, 127, 132; at Longwood Farmhouse 139–40, 143, 145–8, 150, 156, 160, 168, 172, 176–7, 180–5, 189, 192, 202, 249, 254, 260–2, 265, 272, 293, 338, 395
Bertrand, Marshal Count Gatien Bertrand 13, 17, 21, 25–6, 35–9, 41, 64–6, 74–5, 87–9, 103; at Hutt's Gate 95, 108–10, 112, 119, 121–2, 128, 131–3, 136; at Longwood Farmhouse 139, 143, 147–8, 150–1, 156, 160–1, 164, 166, 169, 173–4, 176–7, 180–3, 185–7, 189, 194–5, 218, 225, 229, 254, 260, 265, 272, 293, 338–9, 399
Bigge, Commissioner John Thomas 273, 300, 304, 311, 317, 368
Bingham, Colonel (later General) Sir George Ridout 14, 29, 60, 78, 86–7, 102, 149, 154, 158, 166, 222, 226, 228, 252–3
Bingham, Lady Emma 86, 154, 158, 166, 252
Black Rod, Gentleman Usher of the 21, 25, 97, 208–9, 389
Blackfriars, London 300, 302
Blaxland, Gregory 316, 324, 328, 337
Blaxland, John 316, 324, 337, 351–2
Blessington, Lady 397, 402
Bligh, Governor William 311, 316, 323, 362
Blindman's Buff 103, 153
Blücher, General 7, 16, 17, 97, 132
Blue Mountains (NSW) 6, 312, 328

INDEX

Bonaparte, Jerome (Napoleon's brother) 105
Bonaparte, Joseph (Napoleon's brother, 'Comte de Survilliers') 16, 17, 99, 105, 138, 158, 161, 168–70, 390, 396, 401
Bonaparte, Letizia (Madame Mère) 17, 59, 60, 114, 133, 169, 196, 238, 259, 387
Bonaparte, Louis (Napoleon's brother, former King of Holland) 16, 119
Bonaparte, Louis Napoleon 121, 390, 396–7, 399, 401; President of France 403, 405; Emperor Napoleon III 405–6
Bonaparte, Lucien (Napoleon's brother) 140
Bonaparte, Napoleon 6–11, 15–19, 25–30, 37–101, 150–5; arrival on St Helena 4, 13–15, 24; tour of St Helena 34–9; meets Betsy 36–7; at Longwood 90–101, 104; first meeting with Lowe 108–10; second meeting 111; third meeting 116, 118–21, 123; fourth meeting 124–5; escape plan 126–7, 130; fifth meeting with Lowe 131–2; writes 'The Remonstrance' 133; breaking household silver strategy 134, 136–7; loss of Las Cases 141–6; episode of the cow 147–9; another escape plan 168–70; 48th birthday 170, 171–3; demands Balcombe write to 'secretary of the Prince Regent' 174; health 143, 179–82, 189–90, 195–6, 222, 229, 242, 249, 253, 261–2; farewells Balcombe family 195–7, 202; Gourgaud's 'confessions' about Napoleon 205–7, 212–13, 219, 238–9, 379–80; escape suspected 220–1; farewells O'Meara 221–2; relationship with Albine de Montholon 249; fear of assassination 260; death 262, 263, 264; burial 263–4; inscription on tomb 175–6, 264; legend 263–4; body returned to France 399–400, 403, 405–6
Bonaparte, Napoleon II ('King of Rome', Duke of Parma, Duke of Reichstadt) 15, 48, 99, 116, 130, 162, 262, 338–9, 387, 390
Bonaparte, Pauline (favourite sister of Napoleon) 7, 114
Botanical Gardens, Sydney 319, 334, 350–1, 378
Botany Bay 26, 34, 132, 192, 254, 280, 315, 346
Bougainville, Commodore Baron Hyacinthe Yves de 347–8, 350–6
Bougainville, Louis Antoine, Comte de 347
Boulogne, France 294, 298, 300, 399
Bourbon dynasty 7, 15, 16–17, 88, 127, 162, 181, 212
Bourke, Governor Richard 391
Boyes, George (NSW deputy assistant-commissary-general) 312, 315, 323–4, 342–3

Boys, Reverend Mr Richard 166–8, 217, 275
Brash, Captain 228–9, 236
Briars, The (Bungonia) 357, 371, 376, 380, 382, 384–5
Briars, The (Mt Martha, Victoria) 404
Briars, The (St Helena) 10, 33, 36, 38, 43, 51–2, 60
Brighton, Sussex 90–2, 214, 400–1
Brisbane, Governor Sir Thomas 273, 311, 313–15, 317–18, 322, 325–8, 331, 335–42, 344, 348–9, 351, 358–61, 373, 378
Brisbane, Lady Anna Maria 335, 341, 359
Broncroft Castle 402, 403, 405
Brooke, Thomas 24, 53, 110, 138, 228
Brookes, Dame Mabel 52, 92, 128, 130, 260, 274, 285
Browne, Richard (convict artist) 333
Bunbury, Sir Henry (British Under-Secretary of State) 118
Bungonia, NSW 326–8, 336, 357, 364, 371–2, 376, 380, 384–6, 392, 397–8; gorge 371
Burchell, William John 90–1, 224
Burnie, William and James 213, 235, 255–6
bushrangers 327, 337, 385–6, 393
Byron, Lord 6, 97, 120, 242, 402

Calcutta 159, 192, 275, 280, 395
Camel storeship 265, 271
Campbell, Colonel Sir Neil 7, 107
Campbell, John (Sydney merchant) 321
Cantillon (Subaltern Officer) 262, 339
Cape of Good Hope 10, 115, 117, 138, 144, 149, 157, 165, 185–6, 300, 310
Cape Town 12, 144, 158, 181, 192
Carlton House 22, 30, 208
Caroline, Princess of Brunswick 105, 185, 255–9, 270–2
Carstairs, Honourable George (midshipman) 128–9, 130, 149
Castella, Joao de Nova 68
Castlereagh, Robert Stewart, Lord (Foreign Secretary) 210, 241
Cato Street Conspiracy 257, 259
Cavendish, William, fifth Duke of Devonshire 120
Census 1828, NSW 380
Ceylon 216, 274, 279, 357
Charlotte, Princess (daughter of Prince Regent) 94, 105, 120, 121, 159, 161, 181; death 184–5
Charlotte, Queen (wife of George III) 185; death 241
Cheal, Miss (Balcombe's cousin) 237
Chudleigh, Devon 266, 273, 284
Clarke's, Mrs (boarding school) 33

Clavering, Lady 44, 140
Cochrane, Admiral Lord 212
Cockburn, Rear-Admiral Sir George 9, 14, 15, 21–2, 24, 28–9, 32–8, 45–6, 54, 60, 75, 78–9, 86–9, 96, 98, 100–2, 107–9, 113, 115–16, 118, 121, 132, 169, 196, 204, 215, 224–5, 227–31, 238, 240, 242, 299, 385
Cole, Joseph 42, 187, 192–3, 204, 235, 246, 248, 305
Coleridge, Samuel Taylor 259
Colonial Office 123, 206–7, 209–210, 232–3, 236, 240, 283, 297, 300, 305, 313, 317, 326, 344, 358, 377, 379, 387, 389, 391
Colonial Treasurer NSW 313–14, 317–18, 336, 339–40, 342, 357, 389, 391
Colonial Treasury 357–8, 364–6, 370, 372–3, 376–7
Commissariat stores, NSW 366, 376, 384
Conqueror, HMS 164, 166, 171, 176, 217
Consulate Hotel, St Helena 31, 32, 42
Corsica 27, 49, 97, 108, 175, 217, 263
Cox, William 312–13, 315, 324
Croker, John Wilson, Admiralty Secretary 30, 45, 60, 231–4
Czar Alexander 6, 111, 117, 122, 194, 238

Dalrymple, William 277, 287
Darling, Mrs Eliza 359, 361–2, 378
Darling, Governor Ralph 344, 359–61, 363, 365–9, 373–8, 381–2, 385, 387–8
Dartmoor 237, 243–4, 266; prison 25, 237, 243–4
Darwin, Charles 71, 176
Dawes Point and Battery 322, 343
Deadwood Camp 101, 129, 134, 169, 171–2, 182
Delhi 276, 278, 287, 290
Devil's Punchbowl 114, 129
Devon 237, 250, 273, 280, 375
Devonshire, Duke of 120, 215
Dillon, General Sir Arthur 13, 64, 146
Disraeli, Benjamin 397
Dodds, Luke and Lucia 224
Doveton, Sir William 260–1
Du Camper, Captain Paul-Anne de Nourquer 347–8, 351–5
Dumaresq, Henry 359–60, 380
Dumaresq, William 359–60

East India Company 5–10, 23, 31, 33, 35, 40, 42, 51, 63, 69, 84, 112, 116, 119, 178, 192, 216, 224–8, 246–7, 250, 254, 266, 273–7, 279–80, 388
Egypt 15, 27, 40, 52, 97, 131, 263, 342, 373
Elba, island of 6–10, 14, 16, 26, 34, 49, 61, 83, 98, 100, 107, 160, 187

Elphinstone, Honourable William Fullarton 116, 119, 226
Elphinstone, Margaret Mercer 25, 119–21, 163–4, 180
Eyre, Edward John 391–2, 401

Fehrzen, Major Oliver 149–50, 154, 162, 166–9, 179, 280
Female Factory, Parramatta 361
Female Friendly Society, Sydney 362
Female Orphan School, Sydney 361
Female School for Servants (later School of Industry) 362
Fesch, Cardinal (Napoleon's uncle) 61, 169
Finlaison, John 27, 30, 45, 136–7, 141–2, 144, 157, 217, 219
Fish, Thomas Leversidge 266–9
Flahaut, Auguste Charles Joseph Comte de 16, 119–21, 163, 180, 215
Forbes, Amelia (later Lady) 320–1, 324, 335, 344, 362, 375, 377
Forbes, Francis (chief justice of NSW) 311, 320–2, 324, 337–9, 341, 344, 360, 375, 377, 381, 384, 386
Forsyth, William 222, 273
Fountain, Charles De and Madame de 79, 226
Fowler, William 193, 225, 228, 235–6, 240, 248, 255, 305
Fox, Henry (Lord Holland) 281
Franceschi, Cipriani 30, 53, 217, 260; at The Briars pavilion 60–89; at Longwood 95, 160; death 186–7
Francis I, Emperor of Austria 48, 111, 238, 242
Fraser, Alexander (Aleck) 287, 290
Fraser, Edward Jr 287, 290
Fraser, Edward Satchwell 277, 286–94, 298–9, 301–2
Fraser, James Baillie 278, 286, 293, 298–9, 301
Fraser, Jane 286–7, 290–4, 297–9, 301–2
Fraser, William 276–7, 287, 290
Frazer, Charles (Sydney botanist) 351
French prisoners-of-war 25, 237, 243–4

Galaup, Captain Jean-Francois de, Comte de La Pérouse 346–7
George III, King 6, 22, 26, 91, 208, 210, 214, 241, 255
George Augustus (Prince of Wales, Prince Regent 1811–20, George IV 1820–30) 6, 15, 17, 22, 26, 30, 49, 90–4, 105, 110, 120–1, 128–30, 157, 161, 166, 174, 184, 191, 193, 208–12, 214, 220, 241, 255–9, 262, 323; as George IV 270–6, 281, 299, 343–4, 363, 367–8, 400
Gillespie, Major-General Sir Rollo 276–8

Gillies, Captain Robert 305, 310
Glebe Farm, Sydney 357, 380, 385–6
Glover, John 29, 101, 224
Goderich, Lord 378, 385, 387, 391
Gorrequer, Major Gideon 110, 116, 129, 131–4, 140, 172, 186–90, 193, 225, 265
Goulburn, Henry (under-secretary to Lord Bathurst) 205, 210, 239–40, 249, 272, 279, 312, 358
Goulburn, Major Frederick (NSW colonial secretary) 311, 313, 321–3, 325, 335
Gourgaud, General Baron Gaspard 15, 18, 21, 27, 30, 34–5, 38, 41, 47–8, 64, 71, 75, 78–9, 82, 87; at Longwood 95, 99, 100–2, 105, 109, 112–13, 130, 147–9, 150–1, 158, 160–2, 167–74, 178–80, 182–9, 191, 194–5; in London 202–3, 205–6, 212, 219, 224, 229, 238–9, 242; in France 379–80, 399
Government House, Parramatta 311–12, 335, 378
Government House, Sydney 309, 313, 316, 319, 322, 359–60
Great Surrey Street, Blackfriars 301–2
Griffon, HMS 144, 222, 227
Gurkhas 276–8

Harrison, James Stirling 305, 313, 317–18, 340, 356, 358, 367, 380
Hastings 203–4, 229, 231
Hay, Under-Secretary Robert 389, 391
Heathcote, Ensign George 176–7, 179
Henrietta Villa 348, 351–2, 369
Hibernia (ship) 305–6, 309, 314
Hobart Town 306, 310, 328, 334, 392
Hoddle, Robert 386, 398
Holland, Lady 97, 119, 130, 175
Holland, Lord 97, 119, 138, 159, 181, 191, 299
Holmes, William (naval agent) 204, 213, 225–32, 236–7, 239, 244, 248, 259
Hornsby, Lucia Elizabeth (Betsy's aunt) 207
Hornsby, Thomas 207, 215, 282
Hortense (née de Beauharnais), former Queen of Holland 15, 16, 18, 49, 56, 100, 119, 121, 142–3, 396
House of Lords 159, 193, 258–9, 389
Howe, Robert (editor *Sydney Gazette*) 328, 343, 360
Huff, Mr (tutor) 71–2
Hunter River Valley 362–3, 398
Hutt's Gate 114, 121, 131, 175, 222

Ibbetson, Denzil (new purveyor for Longwood) 195, 259
India 4, 40, 178–9, 216, 274, 276–7, 279, 286–7, 303, 315, 332, 334, 375

Invalides, Les 175, 399–400
Inverary Park, Bungonia 327–8, 371, 373, 392, 397–8

Jackson, Lieutenant Basil 194–5, 249
James Bay 3, 78, 105, 115, 178
Jamestown 5–8, 46, 310
Jamison, Sir John (NSW landowner) 323–4, 340–1, 351, 377
John Murray (publisher) 402
Johnson, Charlotte (Lowe's stepdaughter) 194, 250, 265
Johnstone Esquire, Charles 402–3, 405
Johnstone, Mrs Jane Elizabeth (Bessie) 390, 403
Jones, the Reverend Mr Samuel 72–3
Josephine (de Beauharnais), former Empress 15, 16, 40, 49, 56, 65–7, 112, 268
Josephine (Montholon's maid) 96, 172, 180

Kauffmann, Jean-Paul 151
Keith, Admiral Lord 25–7, 116, 118–20, 163, 218
Kennington 231–2, 238, 248–9
Kent, Edward Duke of 191, 267, 255
Knipe, Miss 'Rosebud' 79, 112, 189, 202
Knowle Cottage 266–9

L'Ouverture, Toussaint 83, 122
La Perouse, Sydney 346–7
Ladder Hill, St Helena 24, 31, 115
Lafitte's Bank 196, 213, 228–9, 297
Las Cases, Marie-Joseph Emmanuel, Count de 15, 18, 26–9, 38–9, 43–4, 399; at The Briars pavilion 52, 77, 82–3, 88–9; at Longwood 95, 100, 104, 112–13, 124, 131–3; arrest 140–3; departs island 144–5, 147, 153; at Cape 157, 160, 186, 189; *Memoirs* 217, 226, 228, 260, 265; *Le Mémorial* 103, 299
Las Cases, Emmanuel de (son of the Count) 26, 38, 43–4, 399; at The Briars pavilion 52, 89; at Longwood 95, 102, 109; under house arrest with his father 141–3; departs island 144; cured at Cape 157–8, 289; horsewhips Lowe 294–6
Latapie, Colonel Paul de 183
Le Page, chef 103, 217
Leopold of Saxe-Coburg-Gotha, Prince 121
L'Espérance 347, 354–5
Letters from the Cape of Good Hope in reply to Mr Warden 181
Lithgow, William (NSW Commissariat) 312–13
Liverpool, NSW 340, 385, 393

Liverpool, Lord, British Prime Minister 26, 157, 195, 210, 219–22, 257, 375, 378
Longwood House 9, 32–3, 86, 87–8, 94–6, 111, 123, 127–9, 132–5, 159–60, 183, 388
Lopez, Dom Fernando 68–9, 70
Louis Philippe, King of France 387, 390, 399
Lowe, Lady (née Susan Johnson) 97, 106, 118, 129, 138, 151, 166–7, 191, 194, 252, 265
Lowe, Lieutenant-General Sir Hudson x, 9, 85, 92, 96–8, 103; arrives at St Helena 106–7; first meeting with Napoleon 108–10; second meeting 111–13; third meeting 116, 118, 120, 122–3; fourth meeting 124–5; final meeting 131–3; relationship with Balcombe 113, 179, 191–4, 248–50, 282–4, 358; warned about a traitor 135–6; arrests Las Cases 140–4; suspicions 157, 168–9, 172, 180, 183, 189–90, 191–4, 223–4, 228–30, 240; attacked by O'Meara 218–22, 241, 246, 289; frees slaves 225–6; dismissal of Stokoe 253–4; leaves St Helena 266, 272–3; attacked by Emmanuel Las Cases 294–6; death 402
Lusitania (storeship) 228–9, 232, 236, 240

Macarthur, Captain Edward 306, 310–11, 326, 376–7
Macarthur, Elizabeth 319, 348, 362, 376–7
Macarthur, John 311, 316, 322–3, 328, 337–8, 348, 351, 357, 362
Mackaness, John (sheriff for NSW) 329, 341, 343–4, 377–9
Mackay, Captain James 46–8, 68, 72, 82
Macleay, Alexander 362, 366–7, 381, 387
Macquarie, Governor Lachlan 273, 316, 320–1
Macqueen, Thomas Potter 311, 326
Madras, India 40, 178, 216, 273, 275, 279–80, 303, 332, 334
Maitland, Captain Frederick 18, 19, 25
Malcolm, Lady Clementina (née Elphinstone) 115–16, 118–21, 123, 128–9, 134, 146–7, 154, 156, 158–9, 162–3, 166–7, 204, 215
Malcolm, Rear-Admiral Sir Pulteney 115–16, 118–21, 123, 126–8, 130, 131–3, 136–7, 139, 143–4, 146–7, 154, 158–9, 162–4, 166–7, 174, 190, 196, 204, 215, 219, 227–30, 242
Malmaison, Chateau de la 16, 18, 24, 49, 52, 98, 112, 175
Marchand, Louis-Joseph, valet to Napoleon 14, 17–18, 25; at The Briars pavilion 35, 37–9, 43, 52, 87–9; at Longwood 95, 103, 107, 135, 143–4, 156, 161–2, 168, 181, 196–7, 260; departs St Helena 265, 272, 339, 399; author of *Mémoires* 143

Marie Louise, former Empress (Bonaparte's wife) 9, 48, 56, 99, 155, 162–3, 169, 171, 238, 242, 262, 338
Marquis of Camden (EIC ship) 194, 205
Marriage Act, English 281, 284–5
Marsden, the Reverend Samuel 316, 337, 351
Martineau, Gilbert 113, 165, 289, 293
Martineau, Michel Dancoisne 42, 151, 175
Mauritius (Île de France) 178, 334, 344, 360
Melville, Lord 27, 30, 157, 219, 233–4
Metternich, Prince, Austrian statesman 9, 74, 93, 117, 161, 185, 188
Molonglo Plains 337, 364, 376, 380, 384–6, 392, 393, 397, 404
Montchenu, Claude Marin Henri, Marquis de, French commissioner 115, 117–18, 122, 152–4, 186, 194
Montholon, Countess Albine de 13, 21, 28, 38, 64, 66–7, 74–5, 78, 103; at Longwood 95, 100, 113, 116, 127, 131–2, 150–1, 160–2, 170, 177, 182, 184, 189; departs St Helena 249, 260, 293, 338
Montholon, General Count de 13, 21, 26, 27, 28, 38, 64, 66, 75, 85, 87, 90, 103; at Longwood 95–6, 109–11, 113, 122–3, 126–7, 133–4, 138, 145, 147, 160, 162, 173, 183–4, 189, 196, 249, 260, 262; departs St Helena 265, 272, 293, 338–9, 350, 396–7, 399
Montholon, Tristan de 99, 103
Morning Chronicle 114, 150, 181, 217–20, 225, 228–9, 241–2, 249, 295, 342
Morning Post 218–19, 221, 226, 237, 241–2, 252, 400
Moscow 10, 39, 47, 114, 148, 171, 188, 263
Mosquito, HMS 232, 237
Murray, Robert Lathrop 314
Murray, Sir George (Secretary of State after Bathurst) 382, 385

Nancy (ship) 387, 388, 389
Napoleon Cottage, Paddington, NSW 398, 405
Napoleonic Wars 5, 34, 207, 267, 288, 314, 325
Neipperg, Count von 9, 48, 171
Nepal, invasion of 276–8
Nesselrode, Count 117
Neuville, Hyde de 160, 169–70
Nevill, Lord William 274
New South Wales Corps 311, 321
New South Wales, colony of 6, 273, 280, 299–300, 303–4, 329, 346
Newcastle, HMS (frigate) 115–16, 118, 128, 154, 166–7

INDEX

Newington (John Blaxland home) 353, 356
Nile, Battle of 18
Northumberland, HMS 3–4, 8, 13, 22, 28, 78, 95, 98, 114, 155, 212, 224, 259
Noverraz (Swiss footman) 43, 96, 148, 399

O'Connell Street, Sydney 311, 341, 352, 373, 380–4
O'Meara, Dr Barry 14, 27, 30, 45, 53, 82, 85; at Longwood 95–6, 102, 107–9, 111–12, 114, 116–18, 121–3, 126–7, 131–2, 135–9, 141–2, 144, 149, 151–7, 167, 169, 171–4, 176–9, 180–2, 184–9, 190, 192, 204, 206, 210, 213, 217–20, 221–2; in England 225, 227, 228–9, 231–2, 234–7, 240–2, 244, 246, 248, 257, 259–60, 282, 288; *Napoleon in Exile* 288–9, 294–6, 298–9, 342–3, 399
Ovens, Major John (NSW governor's ADC) 321
Oxley, John (NSW surveyor-general) 321, 324, 351

Page, Le (Napoleon's chef) 53, 260
'Parramatta party' 316, 321, 359
Patterson, James 276, 279–80, 304, 330, 333
Peninsular War 60, 149, 306, 313, 325, 398
Pergami (Queen Caroline's Italian chamberlain) 258
Peterloo 251, 257
Phaeton, HMS (frigate) 106, 157
Pierron, Napoleon's pantry-head 53, 71, 99, 399
Piontkowski, Captain Charles Frédéric 98–102, 134, 136, 138
Piper, Captain John 317, 321–2, 324–5, 340–1, 347–8, 350–3, 357, 364, 368–70, 372, 377, 380
Piper, Mrs Mary Ann (née Shears) 321–2, 324, 350–3
Plampin, Rear-Admiral Robert 164–8, 176, 178–9, 183, 193, 213, 217, 219, 225, 227, 229, 247, 252–5, 260; mistress 167, 176, 179, 349
Plantation House 32, 35, 38, 106, 123, 129, 147, 151, 154, 165–6, 169, 173, 178, 181, 187
Plymouth 22, 25–7, 118, 237, 244–6, 252, 265, 305–6, 393
Poppleton, Captain Thomas (British orderly officer at Longwood) 96, 101–2, 110–11, 131–2, 134, 162, 174, 188
Port Phillip 397–8
Port Stephens 363, 376, 384
Porteous, Henry 21, 138
Porteous boarding house 21, 24, 38, 41, 75, 118

Portsmouth 135, 165, 224–5, 227, 232, 237, 250, 271–2, 394
Prince Regent (ship) 159, 334
Princess Amelia (ship) 275
Princetown, Dartmoor 237, 243–6, 265

Reade, Lieutenant-Colonel Sir Thomas 113, 122, 127, 131–5, 140, 147, 149–54, 158, 163, 188, 193, 201, 220–1, 228, 252
Receveur, Father 347
Recollections of the Emperor Napoleon by Mrs Abell 8, 36–7, 47, 67, 72, 149, 153, 195, 201, 389, 392, 396, 402, 405–6
Redfern, Dr William 316, 329
Regency period 120, 214, 255, 274
Regentville (Sir John Jamison's Nepean mansion) 323, 351
Reibey, Mary 316, 324–5
Reid, Captain David 404
Reid, Dr David and wife Agnes 327–8, 357, 371–3, 385, 392, 397–8
Reid, Emma Juanna (Mrs Alexander Balcombe) 392, 397–8
'Remonstrance, The' 133, 138, 159
Ritchie, Mrs Harriott 351–4
Robinson, Marianne 'The Nymph' 112, 189, 202
Roche, Lady 58, 117, 124,
Rocks, The, Sydney 309, 334
Rosebud of St Helena 348, 350, 352
Ross Cottage 54, 72, 140–1, 176–7
Ross, Captain Charles 28, 224
Rossi, Francis (Sydney police chief) 344, 350, 353, 386
Rottingdean, Sussex 22, 91–2, 205, 375
Rousseau, Theodore (Bonaparte servant) 136, 138, 160–1
Royal Pavilion, Brighton 214, 400
Rue de Dunkerque (Saint-Omer) 294, 298

Saint-Denis, Louis-Étienne 'Ali' (second valet) 96, 148, 151, 164, 180, 265, 399
St Gregory's parish, London 216, 273, 285, 288
St Helena 3, 5–8, 287, 291–2, 299, 313–14, 340, 348, 352, 368, 373–4, 381, 383, 388, 396, 399
St Helena Archives 105, 178, 202, 254
St Helena Plot 237, 239–41, 265, 340, 342
St Helena Regiment 5, 8
St Helena, RMS 12, 20, 21, 42
St Helenians (Saints) 5, 7, 12, 20
St James church, St Helena 31, 389
St Martin's Church, Exminster 284–5
Saint-Omer, France 285, 287, 292–4, 297–9, 302, 304, 341, 375, 389

St Paul's cathedral, St Helena 5, 186
St Petersburg 39, 182, 188, 194
Santini (servant) 136, 138, 159–60, 260
Schnapper Point, Mornington Peninsula 404
Scott, Archdeacon 344, 351, 381
Scott, James (Las Cases' mulatto servant) 140–1
Scott, Sir Walter 32, 379, 402
Sidmouth, Devon 266–9
Sidmouth, Viscount (Secretary of State for Home Office) 233–4, 238, 257
Skinner, James 276, 277
Smith Hall, Edward 375
Solomon, Saul (merchant) 5, 10, 42, 74, 76, 139, 154, 187, 388
South Atlantic naval station 115, 165, 252
Staël, Germaine de 57, 94
Stanfell, Captain Francis 157, 285
Stirling, Lieutenant Robert 340, 359, 377
Stock, Martha 395
Stock, Mary (Edward Abell's mother) 274
Stokoe, Dr John (surgeon) 165–6, 171, 176–8, 217, 225, 227–9, 240, 247–8, 250, 253–4
Stonyhurst College, Lancashire 288
Sturmer, Baron Barthelemy von (Austrian commissioner) 93, 115, 117, 158, 185, 187–8, 194, 202
Sturmer, Baroness von 115, 117, 140, 145, 158, 171, 173, 188, 194
Sudds and Thompson affair 374–5
Supreme Court of NSW 322, 357
Sweetman, Thomas (convict burglar) 377
Sydney Cove 309, 311, 322, 346
Sydney Gazette 324, 328, 330, 338–9, 343–4, 358, 360, 364–5, 373, 379, 381, 388
Sydney Town 304, 315–16, 318, 321, 326, 332, 334–5, 337, 374
Sydney Turf Club 341, 378–9

Talleyrand Périgord, Count Charles Maurice de 7, 118–19, 163, 262–3
Terry, Charles (William Balcombe's stepfather) 93, 193, 205
Terry, Mary (William Balcombe's mother) 205, 207
Terry, Samuel 316
Thackeray, William Makepeace 31, 159
Therry, Roger 318, 339, 386
Thorpe & Sons, St Helena 20, 32
Tidey, Alfred (Victorian artist) 60, 402
Times, The 25, 62, 124, 152, 159–60, 203, 212, 218–19, 221, 227, 231–2, 237, 247–8, 253–4, 259

Timms, Sarah (the Balcombe sisters' African nanny) 34, 203, 207, 245, 247, 249
Toby (Balcombes' Malay slave) 33, 82–5, 88, 121–2, 226, 294
Tor Royal, Dartmoor 237–8, 244
Torrens, Lieutenant-General (formerly Colonel) Francis 276, 279–80, 303
Torrens, Major-General Henry 276, 280–1, 303–4, 330–1, 333–4, 349, 360
Trafalgar, Battle of 18, 327
Tuileries palace 7, 13, 54, 64, 132–4, 357
Tunbridge Wells 296, 298, 394–5
Tyrwhitt, Sir Thomas 21–3, 25, 33, 45, 49, 50, 90–1, 93, 97, 174, 179, 190–1, 193, 195, 202–4, 207–11, 215, 230, 234–7, 242–4, 249–50, 255–6, 266–8, 270–1, 273–4, 281–5, 288, 293, 299–300, 304–5, 314, 367–8, 389, 393; Dartmoor prison 243–4, 256, 265; Plymouth and Dartmoor Railroad 244–5, 250, 255–6, 266, 273, 282, 304, 389; Queen's Trial 257–9; death 393

Union brewery, St Helena 10, 23, 194, 255–6

Vandyke, Mary (Balcombe by marriage, then Terry) 91, 93
Vesey, Esther (Marchand's mistress) 161–2, 168, 171

Wallace, John 359, 367, 380
Wardell, Robert 328–9, 337, 375, 377
Warden, Dr William 13, 14, 15, 29, 155–6, 181
Waterloo, Battle of 7, 15–16, 25, 53, 71, 87, 97–8, 115–16, 119, 161, 186, 210, 264, 313, 325
Wellington, Duke of 7, 15, 26, 60, 97, 116, 149, 181, 212, 216, 241, 255, 262, 264, 270–1, 313, 325, 336, 339, 359
Wemyss, William (NSW deputy commissary-general) 323, 335
Wentworth, D'Arcy (Superintendent of Police in Sydney) 314, 317, 323, 329, 369, 377
Wentworth, William Charles 328–9, 337–8, 341, 345, 359, 375, 378
Wilks, Governor Mark 4–9, 21, 46, 79, 86, 107, 109–10, 113
Wilks, Laura 75–6, 79, 109–10
Wilmot Horton, Robert (Colonial under-secretary) 283, 305, 314, 331, 358
Wm Burnie & Co. 213, 255–6
Woodford (EIC ship) 178, 279

Younghusband, Catherine 58, 60, 74, 78, 86, 117, 124